Transfer of Undertaking in the European Union

Studies in Employment and Social Policy

VOLUME 60

Editors

Objective

Studies in Employment and Social Policy series seeks to provide a forum for highlighting international and comparative research on contemporary areas of significance for evaluation and regulation of the world of work.

Introduction

Launched in 1997, the Studies in Employment and Social Policy Series now boasts over fifty titles, addressing key policy and development issues in the fields of industrial relations, labour law, social security, and international labour regulation.

Content

With contributions from leading figures in the field, the series brings together key policymakers, academics, and regulators, providing a unique context in which to analyse and evaluate the rapid and dramatic work and social policy developments taking place around the globe.

The titles published in this series are listed at the end of this volume.

Transfer of Undertaking in the European Union

A Comparative Analysis

Edited by

Roberto Cosio
Filippo Curcuruto
Vincenzo Di Cerbo
Giovanni Mammone

Wolters Kluwer

Published by:
Kluwer Law International B.V.
PO Box 316
2400 AH Alphen aan den Rijn
The Netherlands
E-mail: lrs-sales@wolterskluwer.com
Website: www.wolterskluwer.com/en/solutions/kluwerlawinternational

Sold and distributed by:
Wolters Kluwer Legal & Regulatory U.S.
920 Links Avenue
Landisville, PA 17538
United States of America
E-mail: customer.service@wolterskluwer.com

ISBN 978-94-035-4471-7

e-Book: ISBN 978-94-035-4481-6
web-PDF: ISBN 978-94-035-4491-5

Editors

Roberto Cosio, President of the Labour Commission of the UAE (Union of European Lawyers), Vice President of ASFEUR (Forensic Association for Europe), member of the national executive board of the CSDN (Domenico Napoletano Study Center), and former President of AGI Sicily, is a lawyer specialized in Labor Law, with particular focus on the jurisdiction of the High European Courts. He is the author of around 250 publications, in addition to 13 volumes as either author or editor. He has participated as a speaker or contributor in approximately 400 national or international conferences.

Filippo Curcuruto became a judge in 1974, and he was first appointed as Labour Judge to a Court of First Instance. In 1980, he was assigned to a special office within the Italian Ministry of Justice that drafts legislation dealing with issues, among others, related to European law. Here he worked for several years.

From 1993 to 1999, he served at the Research Division of the Italian Supreme Court (*the Ufficio del Massimario della Corte di Cassazione*). Afterwards, the Ministry of Justice appointed him the Head of the office dealing with claims brought before the labour Courts by the Ministry employees.

In 2002, he was appointed as Member Judge of the Supreme Court assigned to the Labour Chamber and was also nominated as Member of the Supreme Court's Joint Chambers in civil-law matters, where he worked until 2011.

From 2011 to 2015, he served as the President of the Labour Court of Appeal of Rome.

From 2005 to 2009, he was a Senior Lecturer of Labour Law at the Postgraduate School of Law at the University of Rome 'La Sapienza.' He is the author of several publications in the fields of civil law, civil procedure, labour law and European law.

He has also been involved in the initiatives carried out by the Associations of the European labour-law judges (*European Association of Labour Court Judges – EALCJ*) within the European Union (EU) and the European and International Labour Office. He retired in 2015; however, he continues to work in the field of law, particularly labour law, in the capacity of a lawyer.

Vincenzo Di Cerbo, Italian judge since 1976, was appointed as a first instance judge in 1977. From 1993 to 1997, he served in the 'Ufficio del Massimario della Italian Corte di Cassazione' (The Research Division of the Court). From 1997 to 2004, he served as 'legally qualified Member of the Boards of Appeal at the European Patent Office (EPO) in Münich. During this period, for three years, he was also appointed Chairman of the 'Disciplinary Committee' of the Office. At the end of 2004, he was appointed member of the Italian Supreme Court. In April 2008, he was elected member of the Supreme Court Judges Council (Consiglio Direttivo). From 2010 to 2016, he also served as Member of the Supreme Court Joint Chambers in civil Law matters (Sezioni Unite Civili). Moreover, since 2012, he has been appointed Director of the CED (i.e., IT Documentation Department of the Supreme Court). Finally, he served as Chairman of the Supreme Court Board with jurisdiction on Labour and Social Welfare. Lecturer at Rom 'Università la Sapienza' (Post-Graduate school for lawyers), and LUISS University of Rome. Author of several books and essays in the field of Labor law, Process law and IT law.

Giovanni Mammone served as a judge from 1977 to 2020. In 1998, he was appointed to the Court of Cassation, where he was permanently attached to the Labour Section, first as a research magistrate, then as a counsellor, and subsequently as Section President. From 2018 to 2020, he served as First President of the Court and President of the United Sections (*Sezioni unite*), the highest body of national ordinary jurisdiction, and resigned upon reaching the maximum age for service. During his career, he also served as an elected member of the Superior Council of the Judiciary (from 2002 to 2006) and as Secretary General of the Court of Cassation (in 2016 and 2017).

He has carried out intense scientific activity, publishing a volume on the history and the jurisdictional asset of the Court of Cassation (*Corte di cassazione e giurisdizione*, 2023), as well as numerous studies on labour and social security law, civil procedural law, and judicial organization.

He was a teacher at the University of Rome 'La Sapienza' and at the Training School of Judiciary (*Scuola Superiore della Magistratura*) in Florence. He actually follows to be a contributor of important law journals, primarily on labour and social security matters.

He is actively involved in the initiatives carried out by the Associations of the European labour law judges (*EALCJ*, within the EU, *ELCJ*, within the *International Labour Office*).

Contributors

Jan Augustin is an attorney at PRK Partners, where he specializes in employment law, foreign investments, competition law, corporate law, and litigation. He advises both domestic and international clients across a broad range of industries, including retail, food and beverage, tobacco, construction, energy, and finance.

Jan earned his Master's degree (Mgr.) and Doctor of Laws degree (JUDr.) from the Faculty of Law at Pan-European University in Bratislava. As part of his legal education, he participated in the Erasmus Programme, completing a semester at the University of Copenhagen, Faculty of Law.

Since joining PRK Partners in 2011, Jan has built a reputation for his comprehensive and practical legal advice, with a strong focus on cross-border matters and regulatory compliance.

He is fluent in Slovak and English.

Nina Bakovnik joined the law firm in August 2018 and has since then primarily focused on labour law. After completing her studies in the UK, she specialized in European and international labour law, anti-discrimination law and private international law at the LL.M. program at the Universiteit van Amsterdam. She previously worked as a legal advisor in Slovenia in the areas of employment relations, discrimination and workers' co-management. Her work mainly involves advising domestic and foreign clients on individual and collective labour relations, managing complex employment restructurings and representing clients in administrative and judicial proceedings.

Michel Blatman After a career as a trial judge in various courts and then at the Court of Appeal of Riom (Auvergne), Michel Blatman became a Counsellor at the Labor Chamber of the Court of Cassation from 2003 to 2014. In addition to his judicial activities, he has participated in numerous training activities with master's students in employment law, and occupational training with industrial tribunals, workers' and employers' unions, various institutions such as the National School of the Judiciary (Ecole Nationale de la Magistrature, 1999-2011), in particular with foreign judges. He has also spoken at numerous conferences in France and Thessaloniki (Greece). At the international level, he has participated in the work of the European Association of Labour Court Judges (EALCJ), of which he was elected president for one year (2011), and in the work of the European Labour Court Judges Meetings (ELCJM) organized under the aegis of the International Labour Organization (ILO). Mr. Blatman is also the author, after he retired in 2014, of a report to the French Défenseur des Droits (Defender of Rights) on 'the direct effect of the provisions of the United Nations Convention on the Rights of Persons with Disabilities' (2016). He is also the co-author of various books in labour law, some of them written In French: 'The notion of worker' (Dalloz International Law Directory); 'The state of health of the employee: from the preservation of health to the protection of employment' (Liaisons, 2005, 2009 and 2014); 'The right of withdrawal at the double risk of subjectivity and uncertainty', in Mélanges en l'honneur de Michel Morand, études de droit social, Collection Axe Droit Lamy, Wolters Kluwer, 2016) ; 'Working Conditions' (Dalloz, References collection, 2021-2022, 2024-2026); 'Health and safety at work – acting for health at work' (Groupe Revue fiduciaire de France, 2024); 'Collective Dismissal in The European Union – A comparative Analysis', Wolters Kluwer, 2017.

Mihaela Braut Filipović is an Associate Professor at the Department of Commercial Law and Company Law at the Faculty of Law, University of Rijeka. She obtained her PhD in 2014 from the Faculty of Law in Zagreb. She is a member of the European Law Institute, the European Academy of Management, the Croatian Comparative Law Association, the Institute of Corporate and Financial Law of the Faculty of Law in Rijeka. She teaches several courses at various levels of study at the Faculty of Law in Rijeka. She is the author of numerous scientific articles in the fields of commercial law, company law, family business and capital market law, and has participated in international and domestic conferences.

Prof. Merle Erikson graduated from the University of Tartu in 1994, and the doctor iuris degree was conferred on her in 2001. From 1994 to 2011, Merle Erikson was a lecturer and associate professor of labour and social security law at the School of Law of the University of Tartu. Since 2011, she has been a labour law professor at the University of Tartu. Her main areas of research and teaching are international labour law, the European Union social policy and labour law, comparative labour law, and Estonian labour and social security law. Prof. Erikson has carried out research at various universities in Europe and Asia. In 2024, she was a visiting researcher at Meiji University. Prof. Erikson has published over 110 publications and participated in dozens of international and Estonian research projects. Recently, she has focused on studying the impact of technological developments on employment relationships. Prof. Erikson has been involved in drafting the Estonian labour law Acts.

Fritzsche Friederike studied law at the University of Hamburg and completed her legal clerkship at the Regional Court of Cologne. She has been admitted to the bar as an attorney since 2020. From 2021 to 2025, she worked at the Cologne office of an international law firm, advising national and international companies on all aspects of individual and collective employment law. Since 2025, Ms Fritzsche has been serving as an in-house Senior Employment Legal Counsel in Germany.

Agnieszka Godusławska Lawyer, author of studies and publications on labour and commercial subjects.

Júlio Gomes, LLM (Columbia University, New York), DPhil (Oxford). Since 2014 Judge at the Portuguese Supreme Court (2014-2017, Civil Section; 2017-2025, Social Section).

Invited Professor at the Portuguese Catholic University (Law School in Oporto, and Global Law School in Lisbon). Before 2014, Professor at the Portuguese Catholic University (Law School in Oporto), Visiting Professor in Summer Courses at the University of Toulouse, São Paulo and Vigo.

Member of the Advisory Board on Unjust Enrichment and *negotiorum gestio* of the Study Group on an European Civil Code presided by Professor Christian von Bar. Member of the Trento Project ('the common core of European Private Law').

Has published in the areas of Labour Law, Law of Obligations and Insurance law.

Anthony Kerr is a graduate of the Universities of Dublin (TCD) and London (LSE) and is now a Senior Counsel at the Bar of Ireland and an Adjunct Associate Professor at the Sutherland School of Law in University College Dublin. He is the Ireland representative on the European Centre of Expertise in the field of labour law, employment and labour market policies, a member of the European Labour Law Network, a National Reporter for the International Labour Law Reports, and a member of the Executive Committee of the Institute of Employment Rights.

Mette Klingsten is a Supreme Court Attorney with extensive expertise in labour and employment law, litigation, and board advisory work.

Mette Klingsten advises both Danish and international companies on the full range of employment law, from individual contracts to collective agreements. Her practice covers company transfers, workforce restructuring, and the planning and execution of both individual and collective dismissals. With extensive experience in cross-border employment, she regularly helps businesses address complex international employment issues, drawing on her global professional network to ensure comprehensive solutions.

Mette Klingsten also advises boards and executives on hiring and termination processes, remuneration structures, duties and rights, and competitive conditions. She has distinct expertise in designing incentive schemes and compensation structures, including warrant programs, bonus agreements, and remuneration policies. In addition, she represents clients in litigation and arbitration within her field of expertise, combining practical business insight with legal precision.

Diana Labokaitė Born in 1966 in Kaunas district, Lithuania. Studied journalism at Vilnius University (received a master's degree in 1989), later studied law at Vilnius University (received a master's degree in 1996). Practiced as a lawyer in 1996-2003, since 2003 appointed as a judge of Kaunas District Court, since 2016 works as a judge of the Civil Cases Division of Kaunas Regional Court. She examines civil, labor and bankruptcy cases. In 2011-2016 she additionally worked as an expert in the European Union TAIEX (Technical Assistance and Information Exchange) program in the Northern Cyprus Community, providing consultations to specialists of this community in the development of labor dispute resolution, anti-discrimination, and equal opportunities laws.

She has written a review of Lithuanian court practice in the application of the European Union Directive on collective dismissals for the publication 'Collective dismissal in the European Union', which was published in 2017 by Wolters Kluwer Publishing House.

Agnieszka Lisiecka is an advocate, mediator, executive MBA (SGH) and has specialized in individual and collective labor law for 25 years, and has a litigation practice in this area. She advises domestic and foreign entrepreneurs in employment law matters at every stage of their operations activity – at the stage of hiring, continuation and termination of the employment relationship. She conducts restructurings, investigations, audits, advises on the industrial relations as well as represents employers before administrative authorities. Her area of particular interest is the broadly defined area of ESG and D&I including protection of employees' personal rights, countering mobbing and discrimination, inclusion and diversity policies, as well as internal investigations.

Dr. Benjamin Münnich works as a lawyer specializing in labor law at CMS Hasche Sigle in Cologne and is a former athlete of the German national judo team. Benjamin Münnich advises on all areas of individual and collective labor law. His focus is on supporting medium-sized and international corporations in restructuring, personnel adjustments, transfers of operations, and transaction projects. In 2024 he received his doctorate from the University of Düsseldorf with a topic in medical law.

Iris Pensa is a partner and mediator specializing in labor law and human rights law. She leads the labor and immigration department in the office and manages a team that advises companies on establishing and improving sustainable policies from an ESG perspective.

Iris ensures compliance with the ten principles of the UN Global Compact, covering human rights, labor standards, environmental responsibility, transparency, and anti-corruption. She meticulously integrates these principles into all her services and client advice, ensuring a comprehensive and ethical approach in her practice. She is also the main contact person for all matters that the firm may undertake on a pro bono basis, considering the specific circumstances of each individual case.

In addition to her primary responsibilities, Iris is the head of the Mediation Center at the Slovenian Bar Association.

Iris is dedicated to promoting a sustainable and fair working environment, providing clients with expert guidance and integrity in all legal matters.

Lubomír Ptáček graduated from the Faculty of Law of Charles University in Prague. He is a judge since 1999 and since 2011 is a judge of the Supreme Court (Nejvyšší soud). Actually is President of the Panel, member of the Grand Panel and the Records Panel of the Civil and Commercial Division of the Supreme Court. He is a lecturer at the Judicial Academy of the Czech Republic and the Judicial Academy of the Slovak Republic. He is the co-author of significant commentaries (on the Labour Code; on the Act on Private International Law; on the Act on Family; and on the Civil Code), as well as professional publications and proceedings. He was named 'Lawyer of the Year 2019' in the field of family law. He also held the position of President of the European Association of Labour Court Judges (EALCJ) for several terms.

Alejandro Rausell is a Prosecutor of the Valencia Provincial Prosecutor's Office and Attorney of the Technical Office of the Supreme Court (Social Department).

Kassimira Sredkova is professor in Labour Law and Social Security, PhD in Law. Educated at Sofia University 'St. Kliment Ochridski' (Bulgaria). Specializations in Belgium, Austria, Germany, Hungary, Russia. President of Bulgarian Association for Labour Law and Social Security and member of the International Association for Legislation. Member of the European Committee of Social Rights in the Council of Europe (2015-2020). Member of the Committee for Freedom of Association of the LO (2002-2003). Member and President of the Consultative Council for Legislation at the Parliament (2001-2009). Legal adviser to the President of the Republic of Bulgaria (2003-2012). She has more than 250 monographies, School books, Articles and other publications in Bulgaria and abroad in the fields of Labour Law, Social Security, International Labour Law and the EC-Law.

Nicos Trimikliniotis is a Professor of Sociology, Social Sciences and Law and heads the Centre for Fundamental Rights at the University of Nicosia. He leads *Digital Transitions & Society (DIGITS)*, an interdisciplinary research initiative critically examining the implications of emerging technologies on cultural and political systems. He is also a Barrister, associate member of Garden Court Chambers. He is the national expert for Independent Network of Labour Migration, *expert for the Odysseus Network* on immigration and asylum, and for the Global Citizenship Observatory (*GLOBALCIT*). He has researched subjects such as labour law, social transformation, migration and asylum law, border regimes, conflict, state theory, citizenship, and discrimination, and numerous expert reports on fundamental rights in Cyprus.

Cristina Tudoran is a Partner in the Employment Law practice at Filip & Company, combining substantial experience in legal advisory work with a strong background in litigation. A PhD candidate at the University of Bucharest, Faculty of Law, Cristina's research examines in depth the impact of business transfers on employment relations, with a particular focus on the interplay between national and EU legislation. In addition to her professional work, she teaches Employment Law seminars to final-year law students and actively contributes to scholarly discourse in her field. Cristina has built a distinguished career at the forefront of complex legal disputes, guiding clients through high-profile and precedent-setting cases in employment law, administrative matters, and management conflicts. Drawing on her deep expertise, she is advising leading companies in sectors as varied as FMCG, energy, IT, banking, retail, and pharmaceuticals. Her work spans internal restructuring processes, business transfers and post transfer integrations, employment aspects of M&A, as well as navigating the delicate art of high-stakes negotiation, both individual and collective.

Yvett Varga is an attorney-at-law, working as an associate at Oppenheim Law Firm in Budapest, Hungary. She focuses on complex cross-border litigation and arbitration cases in civil, commercial, labour and administrative matters. She has a master's degree in law from Eötvös Loránd University (ELTE) and has been admitted to the Budapest Bar Association since 2022. Besides practicing as an attorney, she has worked as a lecturer at the Civil Law Department of ELTE since 2020 and authored several publications in the field of dispute resolution. She is the winner of multiple reputable Hungarian legal awards (including Pro Scientia Golden Award and Hajnóczy Award). In addition to her native language, she speaks English, German and French.

Antonija Zubović is an Associate Professor at the Department of Commercial and Company Law at the Faculty of Law in Rijeka. She received her PhD from the Faculty of Law in Zagreb in 2012. She was a member of the Working Group of the Negotiating Team of the Republic of Croatia for Accession to the European Union in the field of company law. She is a registered arbitrator with the Permanent Arbitration Court of the Chamber of Commerce, Croatia. In 2014, she was granted international scholarship for research at the Max Planck Institute for Comparative and International Private Law, Hamburg, Germany. In 2018, she received the Award for Teaching Excellence of the University of Rijeka. She participated as a member of the research team in scientific research projects of the Ministry of Science, Education and Youth of the Republic of Croatia, the Croatian Science Foundation and the University of Rijeka. She is a member of the European Law Institute, the Commission for Commercial Law and Practice of the Croatian National Committee of the International Chamber of Commerce – ICC Croatia, the Croatian Academy of Legal Sciences, the Croatian Comparative Law Association, the Institute of Corporate and Financial Law of the Faculty of Law in Rijeka. She actively participates in international and national seminars and conferences and has published scientific papers and articles in the field of commercial law, company law and capital market law.

Summary of Contents

Table of Contents

Introduction

Roberto Cosio, Vincenzo Di Cerbo, Filippo Curcuruto & Giovanni Mammone

With an extraordinarily concise text of only 10 articles, Directive 77/187/EEC of the Council of the European Economic Community was published on 14 February 1977. It was aimed at 'safeguarding workers' rights in the event of transfers of undertakings, businesses or parts of businesses'. The directive came into force twenty years after the signature of the Treaties of Rome, at a time when the territorial expansion of the Community and the evolution of entrepreneurship were modifying the economic framework of Europe and requiring social policy choices suited to the new reality.

On the basis of these assumptions, the Community deemed it appropriate to carry out a balancing intervention within the European labour market aimed at regulating the phenomenon of transfers of undertakings by adopting the provisions 'necessary to provide for the protection of employees in the event of a change of employer, in particular, to ensure that their rights are safeguarded'. Such regulation necessarily had to be conceived in a community perspective, due to the diversity of legislation and the need to harmonize 'the extent of protection of workers in this respect', given that 'such differences could have had a direct impact on the functioning of the common market'.[1]

By defining these objectives, the 1977 directive aimed at bringing order to the internal market, by directing the Member States towards a common discipline of the new economic model that was emerging and that, in the context of the crisis of large industrial enterprises, suggested the adoption of restructuring measures of a productive and reorganizational nature. These upheavals were not only a harbinger of potential alterations to the Community common market, but at the same time required interventions to protect the workforce affected by the restructuring phenomena, in compliance with the social policy objectives that were the basis of the Economic Community.

The immediate purpose of the directive was therefore to protect workers in the event of a change of employer-entrepreneur, to ensure the maintenance of their rights. And to pursue this objective, in addition to defining the obligations of the active subjects of the transfer (transferor and transferee), it also defined the prerogatives of

1. *See* the preamble to the directive.

the third category of interested subjects: the workers, who, in the context of a transfer procedures, were guaranteed information and consultation through their 'representatives'.

Subsequently, with Council Directive 98/50/EC of 29 June 1998, the Community took note of the changes that had occurred in the internal market over time and adapted the first directive accordingly. The new interpretation of the 'internal market' was broader: it considered the already made entrepreneurial choices and their impact on the social structure of the Community. In particular, the policies adopted by the Member States for the rescue of companies in economic difficulty and the need to adapt the legislation of the States to the principles of the 'Social Charter', adopted in 1989,[2] to allow that 'the completion of the internal market must lead to an improvement in the living and working conditions of workers in the European Community'.

Among the innovations introduced by the new directive, it is worth remembering the definition of the concept of 'transfer of undertaking': 'there is a transfer within the meaning of this Directive where there is a transfer of an economic entity which retains its identity, meaning an organized grouping of resources which has the objective of pursuing an economic activity, whether or not that activity is central or ancillary'.

It should also be noted that the Member States were allowed to make agreements with the trade union on different working conditions for workers if the transferred company is in a crisis situation, with the aim 'to safeguard employment opportunities by ensuring the survival of the undertaking, business or part of the undertaking or business'.

Given the importance of the matter and considering the succession of regulations that had occurred (for which the 1977 directive was still in force, but with the content established by the 1998 directive), in 2001, the Council of the European Union deemed it appropriate to submit Directive 77/187/EEC to the codification process in order to to coordinate in a single text the combined provisions of the original 1977 text as amended by the subsequent integrations provided for by the 1998 directive.[3] This led to Council Directive 2001/23/EC of 12 March 2001 'on the approximation of the laws of the Member States relating to the safeguarding of employees' rights in the event of transfers of undertakings, businesses or parts of undertakings or businesses' which (at present) represents a sort of European statute of the rights of employees of companies affected by the transfer of a business or similar economic situations.[4]

2. The preamble of the directive 1998/98/EEC said that the Charter disposed that 'The completion of the internal market must lead to an improvement in the living and working conditions of workers in the European Community. The improvement must cover, where necessary, the development of certain aspects of employment regulations such as procedures for collective redundancies and those regarding bankruptcies. Information, consultation and participation for workers must be developed along appropriate lines, taking account of the practices in force in the various Member States. Such information, consultation and participation must be implemented in due time, particularly in connection with restructuring operations in undertakings or in cases of mergers having an impact on the employment of workers'.
3. The procedure of official codification, consolidation and recasting involves the codification of a specific discipline as formalized in a legal act already in force and in subsequent acts which have specifically modified or integrated it.
4. The directive 77/187/EEC is repealed. References to the repealed Directive shall be construed as references to Directive 2001/23/CE.

The heading of the 2001 Directive continues to refer to 'approximation of the laws of the Member States' and, undoubtedly, this is its essential purpose in the logic of European legislation, which has, as its primary objective, that of implementation of similar social and legal conditions in all Member States to promote the development of the single market. However, the directive has also fulfilled the function of contributing to the social governance of important phenomena that have characterized the economic structures of the States and of Europe as a whole between the end of the last century and the beginning of the new one.

After the industrial reconversions of the 1980s, the European economy has experienced phenomena such as production decentralization, outsourcing, company relocation and the spread of service contracts. This new production horizon – according to which the use of company transfers, splits and recompositions have been widespread – has allowed for the reduction of costs and the optimization of resources, but has also caused significant social costs and job losses.

These phenomena on the legal level are usually implemented through civil contractual relationships which, however, inevitably have significant impacts on the working conditions of employees and on the employment levels and therefore require a contextual regulation of their effects in the field of employment law.

Member States have therefore been faced with the need to adapt their national legal system to the European directives, whose function has proven to be not only that of allowing the requested process of legal integration but also that of regulating the phenomenon of outsourcing in a coherent manner, on an economic and social level. A clear symptom of the complexity of the legal definition of the single cases of transfer is the frequency of disputes that are brought before Labour Courts and the European Court of Justice regarding the protection of the rights of workers of the transferred company in the event of a sale, transfer of a branch of the company as well as public and private procurement contracts, which, in practical terms, are the most functional legal means for outsourcing techniques.

Having illustrated the meaning of Directive 2001/23/EC and after the appropriate framing premises, the time has come to illustrate to readers the objectives that this book aims to achieve.

The research has been carried out in a political and economic situation which is quite different from that in which the European discipline above described was defined. The birth of the European Union at the beginning of the millennium, with the consequent expansion of the field of application of the 2001 Directive to 28 States (now 27) and the changed economic framework in the Union area, raises new problems. Delocalization techniques remain, but there are also growing phenomena of social dumping, especially in the field of service delivery. In order to face said phenomena,

---

It should also be noted that Directive 2015/1794/EU of the European Parliament and of the Council of 6 October 2015 subsequently intervened and took into consideration the position of maritime workers, excluded from the Directive 2001/23/EC, specifying that the latter also applies 'to a transfer of a seagoing vessel that is part of a transfer of an undertaking, business or part of an undertaking or business within the meaning of paragraphs 1 and 2, provided that the transferee is situated, or the transferred undertaking, business, or part of an undertaking or business remains, within the territorial scope of the Treaty'.

the Union is seeking further effective forms of legal protection for the workers concerned.

Directive 2001/23 was written before the Lisbon Treaty, at a time when the European economy was experiencing different events and did not have to deal with globalization, financial crises and resilience after the pandemic. We therefore asked the Authors to highlight whether European legislation and the national laws that apply it are sufficient to manage, at the labour level, the corporate and entrepreneurial movements that will reposition the economy in the Union in the coming years. We also urged our collaborators to proceed with a critical analysis of national legislation, paying special attention to judicial disputes, illustrating their content if possible, and considering the solutions offered by the judges.

This book is therefore an opportunity both to analyse national systems and verify how the jurisprudence of the Court of Luxembourg has been implemented and to carry out an overall critical analysis of the existing legal situation. The aim is to provide readers with innovative ideas to address the many practical problems that arise today, and will arise in the future, when dealing with labour issues in the matter of transfer of business.

In conclusion to this introduction, as editors and coordinators of the work, we believe it is our duty to thank and compliment the Authors of all the essays in publication. Their contribution, for the completeness of the exposition of national legislation and the validity of the observations reported, constitutes a high-level contribution for the understanding of the proposed subject and, ultimately, for the increase of the protection of workers, or of the weakest category of subjects involved in business transfers.

All that remains is to wish you a good read!

CHAPTER 1

Bulgaria: Change of Employer in Bulgaria

Krassimira Sredkova

§1.01 INTRODUCTION

According to Bulgarian legislation, the employment relationship is a relationship regulated by law which concerns the provision of workforce and the related legal relationships (Article 1, paragraphs 1-2 of the Labour Code (LC)). It develops between a natural person (worker or employee) and another natural person, legal entity or its subdivision (employer). The worker or employee enters into an employment relationship with a specific employer that bears the rights and obligations towards him/her. Therefore, the employment relationship exists with the employer with whom it was created, either until the death of the worker or employee (Article 325, item 11 LC) or until the closure of the undertaking (Article 328, paragraph 1, item 1 LC), unless it is terminated earlier on any of the grounds provided for in law.

By way of exception, the employer's party can be taken up by a legal entity other than the one with which the employment relationship was created. These cases are governed by Article 123-123a and Article 130b LC. Similar regulation has existed in Bulgarian law since the year 1936. It was first laid down in Article 59 of the 1936 Ordinance-Law on Employment Contract; and, later on, in Article 37 LC of 1951 and Article 123 LC of 1986 and their subsequent amendments and supplements, which will be considered below. This regulation has been the subject of scientific research by established labour law jurists such as Prof. Kruger Milovanov, Prof. Vassil Mrachkov, Prof. Atanas Vassilev, Prof. Emil Mingov, etc., and also by newly occurred names in labour law science, such as Andrey Aleksandrov, whose doctoral thesis was focused on issues of this topic.

§1.02 LEGAL REGULATION

[A] Sources

As it was pointed out, the regulation of a change of employer in Bulgaria has existed since the year 1936. It is currently contained in *Article 123-123a and Article 130b LC*. In recent years, it has also complied with the EU requirements reflected in Directive 2001/23/EC of 2001 on the approximation of the laws of the Member States relating to the safeguarding of employees' rights in the event of transfers of undertakings, businesses or parts of undertakings or businesses.

In legal theory, as well as in judicial and administrative practice, it is generally accepted that the current legal framework in Bulgaria that is set out in Article 123 and Article 123a LC after its separation in a stand-alone text is a manifestation of the approximation of those laws of the EU Member States which relate to the safeguarding of employees' rights in the event of transfers of undertakings, businesses or parts of undertakings or businesses. The specific parameters of Article 123 LC are found in Council Directive 2001/23/EC of 2001. According to Article 1, paragraph 1(a), it applies to all transfers of undertakings, businesses or parts of undertakings or businesses to another employer as a result of a legal transfer or merger and, pursuant to Article 1(b), a transfer is present where there is a transfer of an economic entity which retains its identity. A Directive is an act which is binding as regards the achievement of a certain result by the Member States to which it is addressed, giving the national authorities the freedom of choosing the form and means of achieving that result. The achievement of the objectives of the Directive has been fully reflected in the Bulgarian labour legislation, namely, in Article 123 LC, which gives a detailed and exhaustive regulation of the cases of maintaining the employment relationship in the event of a change of the employer due to a change of the owner of the undertaking or a separate part thereof, assignment or transfer of activity from one undertaking to another, including the transfer of tangible assets, various forms of reorganization of the undertaking (merger, takeover, distribution of activity, transition of a separate part of one undertaking to another) and a change of the legal and organizational form of the undertaking. Beyond its regulation are the close hypotheses of Article 123a LC, which the Bulgarian legislator has found it appropriate to include under Article 8 of the Final Provisions of the Directive. The Member States are given the right to apply or introduce statutory, regulatory or administrative provisions which are more favourable to workers, as well as to promote or permit collective bargaining agreements or agreements between the social partners which are more favourable to workers. In this respect, Bulgarian labour legislation provides a more comprehensive protection of workers' and employees' rights in the event of a change of employer than that provided for in the Directive. Bulgarian labour legislation regulates cases of maintaining an employment relationship with the new employer not only in the event of a legal transfer or merger of an undertaking and business, or a separate part thereof, but also in case of a temporary change in the use of property through letting out an undertaking or a separate part thereof for rent, lease or concession. Protection is established imperatively and can neither be extended nor narrowed. These matters have been analysed in detail and proven by the SCC in ID No. 2-2011-GACD on c.c. No. 558/2009. They are also explicitly noted in ID No. 10-2014-GACD on c.c. No. 10/2014 - 'in Bulgarian legislation, the norms of Art. 123 LC and Art. 123a LC create a more comprehensive protection of workers' and employees' rights in case of a change of employer than that provided for by Council Directive 2001/23/EC of 12.03.2001, the regulation being imperative and exhaustive'.

[B] Purpose

The purpose of the legal framework for a change of employer is *the protection of workers and employees*. In case of a change, the employment relationships are preserved, guaranteeing the workers' and employees' constitutional right to employment. This regulation is particularly relevant and significant at the current stage of major structural changes in the economy and a high level of unemployment. It is an expression of the practical application of the principle of labour protection, which is formulated in Article 1, paragraph 3 LC. The preservation of an employment relationship with the new employer takes place by virtue of law (Article 123-123a LC). It is not necessary to prepare a special written act (a new employment contract or an additional agreement) in which the parties express their consent for the effected change. 'In the conditions of Art. 123 LC, the employment relationship between the worker or employee and the new employer is maintained as it previously existed in respect of all its essential elements - nature of work, place of work, duration of the contract, labour remuneration, etc.' (Decision No. 808-2000-III C.D., SCC).

§1.03 GROUNDS

[A] General Characteristic

The Labour Code explicitly and comprehensively regulates the grounds for preserving an employment relationship in case of changes in the employer. These changes can be divided into three groups depending on their content:

(a) restructuring (reorganization) of the undertaking;
(b) change of the owner of the undertaking;
(c) change in the use and management of the undertaking.

What all grounds have in common is that the activity of the undertaking in which the employment relationship takes place is preserved.[1]

1. According to Bulgarian legislation, an undertaking is any place - an undertaking, an institution, an organization, a cooperative, an establishment, a site and the like, where employed labour is performed (§ 1, item 2 SP LC).

[B] Categories of Grounds

Restructuring (reorganization) of an undertaking

[1] General Characteristic

The employment relationship is preserved in the event of a restructuring (reorganization) of the undertaking (Article 123, paragraph 1, items 1-4 LC). In these cases, we are talking about structural changes in the organization of production and activity and in the related work process, which changes do not affect the essence of the employer's subject of activity. For this reason, the employment relationships in the reorganized undertakings are preserved. In its Decision No. 183–2013–IV C.D. on c.c. No. 705/2012, the SCC emphasizes that 'pursuant to Art. 123, para. 1 LC, in case of a change of an employer as a result of merger of undertakings; takeover of an undertaking by another one; allocating the activity of an undertaking between two others or more; transfer of a separate part or changing the legal organizational form; change of the owner or transfer of activity or tangible assets, the employment relationship with workers and employees is not terminated. It continues existing with the new employer in the same form and with the same basic characteristics, the rights and obligations of the transferor under the employment relationship being transferred to the transferee – Art. 123, para. 2 LC'.

The restructuring must be distinguished from the closure of an undertaking or a part thereof as grounds for termination of employment relationships. In the event of closure of the entire undertaking under Article 328, paragraph 1, item 1 LC, both the legal entity and the activity it carries out disappear. Therefore, the workforce performing this activity is no longer necessary and the employment relationships with the workers and employees that are the holders of this force are terminated. Upon closure of a part of an undertaking under Article 328, paragraph 1, item 2, hypothesis 1 LC, the activity of the separate structural part of the undertaking is also suspended and, along with the cessation of activity, the existence of the relevant part as a structural element of the undertaking is also suspended.[2] In reconstruction, the activity is preserved. That is why the employment relationships are also preserved and not terminated.

2. *See* **Мръчков, В. Прекратяване на трудовия договор поради преустановяване дейността на предприятието. – В:** ***Мръчков, В., Кр. Средкова, Ат. Василев, Ем. Мингов.*** **Коментар на Кодекса на труда. 13. изд. София: Сиби**, 2021, 976-982 (Mrachkov, V. Termination of the Employment Contract due to Cessation of the Activity of the Undertaking. – In: *Mrachkov, V., Kr. Sredkova, At. Vassilev, Em. Mingov.* Commentary on Labour Code. 13th ed. Sofia: Sibi, 2021, 976-982); **Средкова, Кр. Трудово право. Специална част. Дял I. Индивидуално трудово право. София: Университетско издателство 'Св. Климент Охридски'**, 2011, 439-440 (Sredkova, Kr. Labour Law. Special Part. Section I. Individual Labour Law. Sofia: University Publishing House 'St. Kliment Ohridski', 2011, 439-440).

[2] Restructuring Hypotheses

Article 123, paragraph 1, item 1 LC lays down *the merger* of undertakings as grounds for a change of the employer. A merger consists in the disappearance of two or more different and separate entities from legal reality and the creation of a new legal entity in lieu thereof. In the event of a merger, the scope of activity of the former independent undertakings that has been carried out separately by them is preserved and starts being carried out by one entity, namely, the newly established undertaking. The latter becomes the employer of the workers and employees of the former undertakings.

Similar to the hypothesis of merger is the one set out in Article 123, paragraph 1, item 2 LC, i.e., *the takeover of one undertaking by another*. Here, one independent undertaking joins another one that takes over its activities and continues existing as an independent legal entity.

Article 123, paragraph 1, item 3, LC lays down *the allocation of activities* as grounds for change of the employer. It is present when new legal entities are created in place of the legal entity that existed prior to the change. The previous legal entity is preserved along with a part of its activity and, in addition, a new legal entity is created, namely, the separated part of the undertaking, with the specific part of the activity that used to be performed by the whole undertaking prior to the change. In this case, the newly established legal entities are the employers.

Article 123 paragraph 1, item 4 LC provides for *the transfer of a separate part of one undertaking to another* as grounds for a change of the employer. In these cases, part of the activity of the undertaking, either together with the tangible assets or the tangible assets only, is transferred or assigned to another undertaking. In order for it to serve as grounds for preserving the employment relationships, such an action must relate to an activity carried out prior to the transfer or assignment. These grounds will not be present if machines are transferred without their productive use being continued by the respective workers and employees (*see also* Decision No. 1367-2001-III C.D., No. 923-2004-III C.D., No. 157-2008-IV C.D. SCC). In this case, the employment relationships are preserved with the current employer.

[C] Change of the Legal and Organizational Form of the Undertaking

In case of a change of the legal and organizational form of the undertaking, the employment relationships are preserved, yet with another employer. These grounds are provided for in Article 123, paragraph 1, item 5 LC. In such cases, the activity is preserved; however, the legal form in which it is carried out is changed, for example, a limited liability company is transformed into a joint-stock company. This rule has been affirmed in numerous cases of the SCC practice (e.g., Decision No. 21-2008-IV C.D., No. 726-2010-IV C.D., No. 412-2011-IV C.D.).

[D] Change of the Owner of the Undertaking

The change of the owner of an undertaking or a separate part thereof also forms grounds for change of the employer while preserving the employment relationship (Article 123, paragraph 1, item 6 LC). These grounds have been traditional of Bulgarian legislation - they were provided for in Article 59 of the Ordinance-Law on Employment Contract of the year 1936 and were restated in the new labour legislation through the 1992 amendment to the operative Labour Code. These grounds are applicable in all cases of a change of ownership of the means of production that the work process is carried out with - privatization of public undertakings,[3] classical sale, etc. The new owner of the undertaking is the employer. Such is the constant practice of the SCC reflected in Decision No. 1030-2001-III C.D., No. 1301-2004-III C.D., No. 15-2005-III C.D., No. 831-2006-III C.D., No. 384-2007-III C.D., No. 157-2008-III C.D. and others.

The change of ownership may relate to:

(a) *the whole undertaking*. In these cases, the change of employer concerns all individual employment relationships with the undertaking;
(b) *part of the undertaking*. The law requires that this part should be a separate one. In this case, the change only concerns the individual employment relationships in the respective separate part.

The employer is also changed in the event of *assignment* or *transfer of activity and tangible assets* from one undertaking to another (Article 23, paragraph 1, item 7 LC). In such cases, part of the entity's activities, along with tangible assets or tangible assets only, are transferred or assigned to another undertaking. The sale of shares from one joint-stock company to another is not a change of employer within the meaning of the provision of Article 123 LC. Such a change would be the sale of an undertaking to the company-employer within the meaning of Article 15 of the Commercial Law as it concerns a whole set of rights, obligations and factual relationships. If the opposite is assumed, this would mean to arrive at the absurdity that any transfer of stock or shares, or a change in the stockholders of the company, respectively, constitutes a change of

3. In its Decision No. 153 of 2001 on c.c. No. 1132/2000, the SCC points out that 'the privatization of a state-owned undertaking carried out under Art. 3, para. 1, item 1 of the Law on Transformation and Privatization of State-Owned and Municipal Undertakings ..., regardless of whether it concerns the sale of stocks and shares owned by entire undertakings, or separate parts thereof, or property of liquidated undertakings, or unfinished construction sites, or non-residential properties that are used for business purposes (shops, studios, warehouses, service centres, workshops, etc.), constitutes a transfer of an undertaking .... In this case, it is impossible to think about a private transaction between legal entities, by virtue of which the latter transfer rights *in rem* over real estates under the general civil law procedure. It is beyond doubt that, as far as the new owner of the privatized object is concerned, it is the provision of Art. 123, para. 3 LC that shall apply, this being the provision which generally regulates the employment status of the workers and employees working at the undertaking at the time of privatization. Their employment relationships are not terminated and continue existing in accordance with the individual employment contracts signed with the previous employer. This takes place by virtue of the law, without a need for an explicit clause in the privatization contract or reframing the employment contracts with the acquirer of the entity'.

employer within the meaning of the provision of Article 123 LC. Such is the opinion of the SCC, which is reflected in Decision No. 2170–2006–III C.D. In judicial practice, it is also assumed that in cases where one state institution is closed and its functions and activities, assets and liabilities, and rights and obligations pass to another - either an existing or a newly established state institution - there is legal succession on the part of the employer under the imperative provision of Article 123, paragraph 1, item 7 of LC, by virtue of which the existing or the newly established state institution-legal successor becomes party-employer under the existing employment relationships with the closed state institution in lieu of the latter (Decision No. 99–2013–III C.D., SCC).

[E] Change in the Way of Using the Property of an Undertaking

[1] General characteristic

There are also cases of change of the employer where the undertaking in which the employment relationships take place, and the activity and the legal and organizational form of the undertaking are preserved; however, the way of using the property is changed. These cases are provided for in Article 123a LC and consist in letting out the undertaking for rent, lease or concession.

The provision of Article 123a LC gradually extends the scope of application of workers and employees protection to include lease, rent and concession contracts. The changes follow the economic realities and take into account the development of law in other areas, yet, they are based on the legislative concept of preservation of the employment relationship when letting out an undertaking or a part thereof to another employer under the *locatio-conductio* (rental contract), which is well known from Roman law, and its derivative contracts of lease and concession. They have their projection on employment relationships because of the need to protect a significant public interest. The regulation guarantees the rights of workers and employees as the weaker party to the labour relationship and aims at freedom and protection of labour (Article 1, paragraph 3 LC). Therefore, the Bulgarian legislator has pointed out exhaustively the hypotheses in which the employment relationships with workers and employees are not terminated. As the SCC states, 'the provision of Aer. 123a LC is a manifestation of the enhanced labour protection that the Bulgarian state provides in the cases of letting out an undertaking or a separate part thereof for rent, lease or concession. It is in line with the objectives of Council Directive 2001/23/EC of 12 March 2001 and is a positive expression thereof in our domestic law'. (ID No. 2–2011–GACD on c.c. No. 558/2009, SCC).

[2] Hypotheses

In the hypothesis of *letting out for rent*, the owner of the undertaking grants the right of its use for a certain period of time for a certain price (Article 228 of the Law on Obligations and Contracts). The term of renting is of no importance. As the tenant receives the undertaking along with its means of production and draws benefits from it, the tenant becomes the employer of the workers and employees concerned.

The letting out on lease of the undertaking also brings about the preservation of employment relationships with its workers and employees. The lease contract is one by which the lessor undertakes to grant the lessee the right of temporary use of the object of the contract, while the lessee undertakes to make certain lease payments, and the yields from the leased object become the property of the lessee from the moment of their separation (Article 2 of the Law on Lease in Agriculture). The lessee becomes the employer of the workers and employees of the leased undertaking (Article 123a, paragraph 2 LC).

Employment relationships are also preserved where *the undertaking is let out on concession*. A concession contract is one by which the grantor gives to a trader-concessionaire the right to exploit an object or service of public interest, in return for the concessionaire's obligation to build, manage and maintain the object of concession or to manage the service at the concessionaire's own risk (argument based on Article 2 of the Concessions Law). In this case, the concessionaire becomes the employer of workers and employees of the undertaking that is let out on concession (Article 123a, paragraph 2 LC).

§1.04 PROCEDURE FOR IMPLEMENTING THE CHANGE

[A] Time of Change

The change of employer in the cases considered above takes place *ex lege*. It occurs at the time of occurrence of the grounds provided for by law, without any actions being necessary on the part of the workers and employees or the employer.

In this respect, one major shortcoming of the 2006 changes in Article 123 LC must be pointed out. In paragraph 2 of Article 123 LC, the two employers – the one before and the one after the change – are characterized as 'employer-transferor' and 'employer-transferee'. This is both linguistically and legally incorrect. In these cases, there is neither a transfer nor an acquisition, respectively, of workers and employees, because they have not been a commodity ever since the time of slavery. The change of employer takes place immediately by operation of law. The legislative body has made an incorrect transfer of terminology used in Directive 2001/70/EC. Indeed, the Directive uses the terms 'transferor' and 'transferee', but they relate to the transaction of transfer of ownership (the Directive concerns these cases only!). The Bulgarian legislator has failed to take into account that the Directive does not refer to an 'employer-transferor' and an 'employer-transferee'. The correct Bulgarian terms in this case are 'current' or 'previous', and 'new' employer, respectively.

[B] Obligations of Employers

The 2006 supplements to the Labour Code, namely, the creation of the new Article 130b, have laid down certain employer obligations to be met before the changes under Article 123 or Article 123a LC take place. These obligations are:

(a) *provision of information* (Article 130b, paragraphs 1-3 and 5-7 LC);

The required content of the information is defined in Article 130b, paragraph 1 LC: the envisaged change and the date of its implementation, the reasons for the change, etc. The information is owed to the workers' and employees' representatives under Article 7, paragraph 2 LC[4] and the trade union organizations. Each of the two employers – the previous and the new one – owes information to the respective representatives of its undertaking. If there are no workers' or employees' or trade unions' representatives in the undertaking, the information is provided to the workers and employees themselves (Article 130b, paragraph 5 LC). The information must be provided within a specified period, namely, not later than two months before the change is implemented (Article 130b, paragraph 2 LC);

(b) *conduct of consultations* (Article 130b, paragraph 4 LC);

Consultations must take place where any of the employers envisages some special measures in respect of the workers and employees. Consultations are held with the workers' and employees' representatives under Article 7, paragraph 2 LC and the representatives of trade unions. The aim must be to reach an agreement; however, the conclusion of such is not mandatory.

[C] Employment Relationship Content after the Change

In the event of change of the employer, the employment relationships with the workers and employees are preserved as they were at the time of the change, i.e., they have the same content (argument based on Article 123, paragraph 2 and Article 123a, paragraph 2 LC; Decision No. 178–2000–III C.D., SCC). This takes place immediately by operation of law. It is not necessary for the new employer to conclude new employment contracts or additional agreements (Decisions No. 153–2001–III C.D. and No. 1037–2001–III C.D., SCC). The new employer's rights and obligations under these legal relationships arise *ex lege*.

4. According to Article 7, para. 2 LC, it is at a general meeting that the workers and employees are entitled to elect their representatives who will represent their common interests in matters regarding labour and social insurance matters before their employer or before the state authorities.

[D] Responsibility for Those Obligations to Workers and Employees Which Have Arisen Prior to the Change of Employer

Article 123, paragraph 4 and Article 123a, paragraph 3 LC explicitly regulate the legal succession in those financial obligations to workers and employees which have arisen prior to the change of the employer. These might be obligations to pay labour remuneration or benefits under the employment relationship, and the like. As a rule, the responsibility lies with *both employers* (Article 123, paragraph 4, item 2 and Article 123a, paragraph 3 LC). The responsibility lies with *the new employer* in the cases of merger of undertakings, takeover of an undertaking and change of the legal and organizational form (Article 123, paragraph 4, item 1 LC).

§1.05 GUARANTEES FOR WORKERS' AND EMPLOYEES' RIGHTS

In the event of change of employer, the law provides for some guarantees for the rights of workers and employees. These are:

(a) the right of workers and employees *to inform the labour inspectorate* of the employer's failure to fulfil the employer's obligations to provide information and to conduct consultations in connection with the change (Article 130, paragraph 6 LC). The aim is to oblige the employer to provide the necessary information and, possibly, to be sanctioned for non-compliance with labour legislation;

(b) the right of the worker or employee *to unilaterally terminate his/her employment relationship with the new employer without giving a prior notice* (Article 327, paragraph 1, item 3a LC). In order for these grounds for termination of the employment relationship to be present, the cumulative presence of the following elements is necessary:

> First, *a change of employer*. As stated above (*see* §1.03[B]-[E]), this is possible in the hypotheses of Article 123, paragraph 1 and Article 123a, paragraph 1 LC. In such cases, the employment relationship is preserved and its content remains the same as the content it had as of the date of the change.
> Second, *a significant deterioration in the working conditions at the new employer*. The working conditions include both material conditions (working environment) and the rights of the worker or employee – labour remuneration, leave, etc. A significant deterioration occurs if there is a considerable change towards a less favourable, i.e., a worse state of safety at work, a decrease in labour remuneration, etc. The comparison is made against the working conditions that existed prior to the change. The comparison is drawn specifically in each separate case.
> Third, *a causal link between the change of employer and the deterioration of working conditions*. The deterioration of working conditions must be due to the very change of employer, and not to other reasons, e.g., reduction of the worker's or employee's dexterity, impact of the current market situation, etc.

The termination of the employment relationship on these grounds must be motivated by a specific indication of the significantly deteriorated working conditions and the extent of their deterioration;

(c) *the restoration of employment relationships with the previous employer after the expiry of the period of change* (Article 123a, paragraph 4 LC). This right is present in the event that the change of the employer is due to a change in the way in which the undertaking is used – its being let out for rent, lease or concession. Inasmuch as these contracts are always fixed-term ones, these grounds for a change of the employer exist during the period for which the contract concerned is concluded. After its expiry, it is again the previous employer, i.e., the employer prior to the change – the landlord, the lessor or the grantor – that becomes an employer. This takes place immediately by operation of law.

CHAPTER 2

Croatia: Employees' Rights in the Event of Transfers of Undertakings, Businesses or Parts of Undertakings or Businesses in Croatia*

Antonija Zubović & Mihaela Braut Filipović

§2.01 INTRODUCTION

The protection of employees in the transfer of undertakings, businesses or parts of undertakings or businesses was first regulated in Croatia by the provisions of the 1995 Labour Act.[1] Significant legislative changes in this area of labour law occurred in 2001,[2] while subsequent changes and new Labour Acts from 2009,[3] 2014[4] and the latest from 2022[5] maintained the same provisions. The Croatian Labour Act directly transposes the Council Directive 2001/23/EC[6] into the Croatian legal order.[7] However, the application

* This paper is written under the support of the University of Rijeka project (uniri-drustv-18-43) 'Legal Aspects of Companies Restructuring and Transition Towards New Corporate Governance Culture.'

1. Labour Act, Official Gazette of the Republic of Croatia (further: OG) No. 38/1995, Articles 129 and 197.

   Croatian Labour Act since 1995 has been subject to several revisions. Labour Act (1996), OG Nos 38/1995, 54/1995, 65/1995, 102/1998, 17/2001, 82/2001, 114/2003, 123/2003, 142/2003, 30/2004, 68/2005, 94/2009; Labour Act (2010) OG No. 149/2009, 61/2011, 82/2012, 73/2013; Labour Act (2014), OG No. 93/2014, 127/2017, 98/2019, 151/2022.
2. Labour Act, OG No. 17/2001, Article 44.
3. Labour Act, OG No. 149/2009, Article 133 and Article 149 paras 3 and 11.
4. Labour Act (2014), Article 137 and Article 150 para. 3.
5. Labour Act, OG No. 151/22.
6. Council Directive 2001/23/EC of 12 March 2001 on the approximation of the laws of the Member States relating to the safeguarding of employees' rights in the event of transfers of undertakings, businesses or parts of undertakings or businesses, OJ L 82 of 22/3/2001, 16.

of Directive 2001/23/EC leads to controversies and ambiguities, e.g., concerning the lack of definition of the terms 'undertaking' and 'business' and the problematic definition of transfer in practice, especially in the case of involuntary and indirect transfer between transferor and transferee.[8] Therefore, the Court of Justice of the European Union (hereinafter 'CJEU') has an important role in removing doubts regarding the employees' right to protection.

According to Article 137(2) of the Labour Act, an employee whose employment contract has been transferred shall retain all the rights arising from the employment relationship he has acquired up to the date of transfer of the employment contract. However, the employer to whom the employment contracts are transferred shall assume all rights and obligations under the transferred employment contract from the moment of transfer in an unchanged form and scope.[9] This provision aims to preserve the continuity of the employment relationship by maintaining all the employee's rights under the transferred contract and by prohibiting termination of the contract solely on the grounds of the transfer.

It should be noted that the provisions of the Labour Act on the transfer of employment contracts also apply to institutions and other legal entities.[10]

Although the Croatian legislator has tried to regulate the issue of business transfers within a legal framework, many questions have arisen in practice. Therefore, for the correct application and interpretation of the legal framework applicable to business transfers, it is necessary to refer to the case law and the opinions of the relevant ministries. Thus, the authors shall analyse relevant legal frameworks, Croatian case law and opinions of the Ministry of Economy, Labour and Entrepreneurship to point out open issues in practice and *de lege ferenda* possible solutions.

§2.02 CONDITIONS FOR APPLICATION OF SAFEGUARDING MEASURES OF EMPLOYEES' RIGHTS IN THE TRANSFER OF UNDERTAKINGS OR BUSINESSES

Directive 2001/23/EC applies to any transfer of an undertaking, business or part of an undertaking or business to another employer as a result of a 'legal transfer' or 'merger'.[11] Defining element of what should be considered a transfer has been implemented in Article 137(1) of the Labour Act, which provides that a transfer can occur by status change (statusna promjena) of the company or by a legal transaction (pravni posao). Thus, while the Labour Act uses the term 'legal transaction', the Directive uses the term 'legal transfer', which prima facie seems to be broader. The applicability of Directive 2001/23/EC was discussed before the CJEU in many cases,

7. Labour Act, Article 2.
8. Ivana Vukorepa, *Faktičan (neizravan) prijenos gospodarske cjeline i utjecaj na radnopravni položaj radnika*, 72 Zbornik Pravnog fakulteta u Zagrebu 1-2, 621 (2022). Iris Gović, *Prenošenje ugovora o radu na novog poslodavca* (Željko Potočnjak (ed.), Radni Odnosi u Republici Hrvatskoj, Organizator, Pravni fakultet, 2007).
9. Labour Act, Article 137, para. 3.
10. Labour Act, Article 137, para. 14.
11. Directive 2001/23/EC, Article 1, para. 1.

such as, e.g., the *Schmidt* case.[12] The reasoning and conditions for the applicability of the Directive have gradually developed to include not only the direct contractual relations between transferor and transferee (e.g., sale or lease of an undertaking, etc.) but also to apply to indirect transfers. The latter may occur primarily at the will of a third party (e.g., one company loses the right to provide a specific financial service and the other gains it), provided that the transfer concerns an 'economic activity that retains its identity'.[13] According to the case law of the CJEU, the concept of legal transfer must be interpreted with sufficient flexibility to meet the objective of the Directive to protect employees in the event of a transfer of an undertaking. The legal practice of the Croatian courts is also developing in this direction.

The following condition for the applicability of Directive 2001/23/EC is that there is a transfer of an economic entity which retains its 'identity', meaning an organized grouping of resources which has the objective of pursuing an economic activity, whether or not that activity is central or ancillary. The Labour Act in Article 137(1) uses the term 'economic integrity' instead of 'economic identity'.[14] However, there is no analysis or comment on the potentially differing meaning of 'economic integrity' compared to the Directive's 'economic identity' in Croatian court practice.[15] The standpoint taken in Croatian court practice is that in interpreting the elements of Article 137(1) of the Labour Act, the courts should always have in mind the goals of the said provision. The Croatian courts consider that the primary goal of Article 137(1) of the Labour Act is to retain employees' rights.[16] Thus, we argue that the notion behind different terminology remains the same. The question of retaining the economic identity of the transferred undertaking under the Directive or the economic integrity of the Labour Act must be answered in each case, depending on the overall circumstances, taking into account all of the conditions for the application of the respective provisions.

Further, Directive 2001/23/EC does not define 'undertaking' and 'business'. The Croatian legislator has not defined these terms either, which raises the question of the interpretation of these provisions of the Labour Act. A definition of the term 'undertaking' has been given in the doctrine, which states that an undertaking is an organized economic and legal entity through which the owner of the undertaking acts on the market.[17] However, it should be noted that an undertaking itself is not a legal entity and it has no legal capacity. What is considered a legal entity in Croatia is a legal or natural person to whom the undertaking belongs. Thus, an owner of an undertaking has legal capacity while the undertaking has no legal implications in the statutory company law.

12. CJEU, C-392/92, *Schmidt v. Spar- und Leihkasse der früheren Ämter Bordesholm, Kiel und Cronshagen* [1994] ECR I-01311. *See also* Nada Bodiroga-Vukobrat and Hana Horak, *Radni odnosi kod statusnih promjena u europskom pravu*, 24 Zbornik Pravnog fakulteta Sveučilišta u Rijeci 1, 393 (2003), at 400.
13. Vukorepa, *supra* n. 8, at 622.
14. Iris Gović Penić, *Prenošenje ugovora o radu na novog poslodavca*, https://www.iusinfo.hr/strucni-clanci/prenosenje-ugovora-o-radu-na-novog-poslodavca (accessed 12 February 2023), at 2.
15. *Ibid.*, at 3.
16. County Court in Bjelovar Decision No. Gž-429/16 of 17 November 2016.
17. Jakša Barbić, *Pravo društava, Knjiga prva, Opći dio*, Organizator, 2008, at 223.

The undertaking is an economic term, designating a community of property and persons, a combination of capital and labour under a single management aimed at achieving economic goals and a unique appearance in the market. The property of the undertaking belongs to the owner, and the employees also have an employment relationship with him. If the owner of the undertaking changes, then all employment contracts are transferred to the new owner. Undertaking owners can be any legal entities and natural persons. The Labour Act regulates not only the transfer of an undertaking or part of an undertaking but also the transfer of businesses or parts of businesses. Case law has attempted to provide answers to these questions by linking them to the condition of retaining economic integrity. Importantly, when considering whether the conditions for applying Article 137(1) of the Labour Act are fulfilled, the Croatian courts consider the criteria elaborated in the case law of the CJEU.

Article 137(1) of the Labour Act expressly provides that all employment contracts of the employees employed in the transferred undertaking or its part, or those connected with the business or part of the business being transferred, shall be transferred to the new employer. Thus, according to Croatian labour law, the following conditions must be met for the transfer of an employment contract: status change or legal transaction; status change or legal transaction must result in the transfer of an undertaking, business or part of an undertaking or business to a new employer; the transferred undertaking, business or part of an undertaking or business retains its economic integrity; the employees whose contracts are transferred must work in the undertaking or part of the undertaking that is the subject of the transfer, i.e., they must be connected with the performance of the business or part of the business that is the subject of the transfer. The authors shall further analyse Croatian court practice to demonstrate how these elements are understood before Croatian courts.

For example, the Supreme Court of the Republic of Croatia explicitly states that the provision of Article 137 of the Labour Act does not apply when the transferor transfers only a part of its business to the transferee (regardless of whether it sells only assets or transfers the entire business of a division of a company) if the latter does not represent independent economic integrity.[18] The fact that the employer has decided to use the services of a third legal entity for part of the business activities, instead of carrying out these activities itself, is not a situation covered by Article 137(1) of the Labour Act, since it is not a transfer of a business that retains its independent economic integrity.[19] Croatian scholars argue that Article 137(1) of the Labour Act should be interpreted to encompass both the case of a transfer of the central activity and the case of a transfer of the ancillary activity of the business.[20] This is accepted in the court practice and again connected with the requirement to transfer an economic entity that retains its economic integrity. For example, the Supreme Court of the Republic of Croatia stated that the transfer of a part of the business that the employer had exercised until then (physical and technical protection work in its facilities) resulted in the

18. Supreme Court of the Republic of Croatia Judgment No. Revr-189/2017-2 of 17 April 2019.
19. Supreme Court of the Republic of Croatia Judgment No. Rev 2881/2018-3 of 11 November 2020.
20. Iris Gović Penić, *Prijenos ugovora o radu na novog poslodavca prema praksi Suda Europske unije i domaćih sudova*, Financije, pravo i porezi 5, 102 (2016).

transfer of the employment contracts of the employees connected with this part of the business.[21] However, if the transferor has transferred only some activities of the business, but not all or part of the undertaking or business, the conditions for the transfer of the employment contract of those employees who will no longer perform all but only a part of former job activities are not met.[22]

Croatian courts specially discussed the legal consequences of the lease for the employees' rights. If the lease has resulted in the transfer of part of the business, the employment contracts of the employees covered by that business shall also be transferred.[23] On the other hand, a transfer of the employment contract shall not be triggered if the employer decides not to perform only an insignificant part of his work, e.g., if he/she decides to rent only a part of his office space and equipment to a third party.[24]

Furthermore, the Supreme Court of the Republic of Croatia has expressly stated that not every property transfer results in an employment contract transfer.[25] If the employer transfers only the real estate ownership without transferring the undertaking or part of it,[26] the employment contract is not transferred.[27] On this issue, Croatian case law is aligned with the practice of the CJEU.[28]

In national case law, numerous court decisions exist on when an employment contract is deemed to have been transferred to a new employer. For example, the Constitutional Court and the Supreme Court of the Republic of Croatia have ruled that an employer may freely assume the obligations that generally apply when an employment contract is transferred to a new employer. In other words, it is not prohibited to take over the rights and obligations under the employee's employment contract (rights acquired under the employment contract with the previous employer and exercised with the new employer).[29] With this position, the Croatian courts have adopted the

21. Supreme Court of the Republic of Croatia Judgment No. Revr-1149/13 of 9 September 2014.
22. Supreme Court of the Republic of Croatia Judgment No. Revr-333/07 of 24 October 2007.
23. County Court in Dubrovnik Judgment No. Gž-4986/14 of 2 April 2014.
24. County Court in Zadar Judgment No. Gž-46/12 of 24 January 2012.
25. Supreme Court of the Republic of Croatia Judgment No. Revr-592/07 of 12 September 2007 takes the position that the transfer of property is not in itself the basis for transfer of employment contracts.
26. Supreme Court of the Republic of Croatia Judgment No. Revr- 963/2015-3 of 13 July 2016 points out 'The transfer of an undertaking or part of an undertaking to a new employer implies that the person to whom the property is transferred is engaged in economic activity and that the purpose of this transfer is the continuation of that activity. The mere transfer of the employer's property, without the will of the contracting parties to transfer the property with economic integrity to the acquirer as a new employer, does not represent a legal transaction from Article 129 of Labour Act (1996). This is because when assessing whether there has been a transfer under the Article 129 of Labour Act (1996), one should take into account all the facts that characterize the transaction, i.e. should the economic activity be actually continued or taken over by the new employer with these or similar activities.' Gović Penić, *supra* n. 14, at 15. Authors emphasize that the former Article 129 of Labour Act (1996) corresponds to current Article 137 of Labour Act.
27. Supreme Court of the Republic of Croatia Judgment No. Revr-8/09 of 21 October 2009.
28. CJEU, C-340/01, *Carlito Abler and Others v. Sodexho MM Catering Gesellschaft mbH.* [2003] ECR I-14023. CJEU, C-172/99, *Oy Liikenne Ab v. Pekka Liskojärvi and Pentti Juntunen* [2001] ECR I-00745.
29. Constitutional Court of the Republic of Croatia Judgment No. U III/1415/03 of 30 March 2006, Supreme Court of the Republic of Croatia Judgment No. Revr-8/09 of 21 October 2009.

same position as CJEU, which interpreted that it is permissible to allow the transferee to take over the employment relationship from the transferor if the part of the undertaking that is the subject of the transfer does not constitute a functionally autonomous economic entity already existed before the transfer. For such understating, it is irrelevant if the transferor exercises extensive, overriding powers over the transferee after the transfer of part of the undertaking concerned.[30]

At the same time, the case law assumes that even if an employee enters into a new employment contract with a new employer, it shall be qualified not as a new employment contract but as a transferred employment contract if conditions for the application of Article 137 of the Labour Act are met.[31] It is expressly stated that it is legally irrelevant for the exercise of employee rights that the employees concluded new employment contracts with the new employer, as the transfer of employees would occur even without the agreement concluded by the employers on the day after the transfer/takeover of the part of the undertaking and the employees.

In judicial practice, the case of a break in the continuity of the employee's employment relationship for several months has also been discussed. Namely, the employee's employment relationship with the employer ended on 5 December 2014, and with the company P. L.L.C. it began on 17 June 2015. The court took the position that the transfer of an employment contract to a new employer within the meaning of the legal provisions of the Labour Act implies the simultaneous termination of the employee's work (and employment relationship in general) with the employer transferring part of the business or the entire business, and the beginning of the performance of the same duties of that employee (and the beginning of the employment relationship) with the employer taking over part of the business or the entire business. Thus, the court concludes that the fact that the plaintiff (employee) agreed with the new employer that the time he worked for the previous employer would be included in the continuity of his employment relationship with the new employer has no effect,[32] and it ruled that there was no continuity of employment in this particular case.

However, while examining the legal practice of the Croatian courts, we came across a decision that differs from the position of the CJEU. The Supreme Court of the Republic of Croatia has ruled that if a company (founder) establishes another (newly established) company and the employee was employed first by the founder and then by the newly established company, there is no legal succession between these employers of the employee, nor is the responsibility of the last employer for the obligations entered into with the previous employer based solely on the fact that one company is the founder of another company.[33] Comparing this position of the case law of the Supreme Court of the Republic of Croatia with the decisions of the CJEU, in particular in the cases C-234/98[34] and C-242/09,[35] in which the concept of an employment

30. CJEU, C-458/12, *Lorenzo Amatori and Others v. Telecom Italia SpA and Telecom Italia Information Technology Srl* [2014].
31. Supreme Court of the Republic of Croatia Judgment No. Revr-445/05 of 6 July 2005.
32. Supreme Court of the Republic of Croatia Judgment No. Rev 1610/2019-2 of 7 May 2019.
33. Supreme Court of the Republic of Croatia Judgment No. Revr-260/11 of 1 December 2011.
34. CJEU, C-234/98, *G. C. Allen and Others v. Amalgamated Construction Co. Ltd.* [1999] ECR I-08643.

contract or employment relationship, as well as the concept of an undertaking and its transfer, are interpreted broadly, one comes to the conclusion that the Croatian court takes a different position.[36] Namely, the Croatian court considered that such a request or claim is unfounded if, at the same time, there has been no transfer of an undertaking within the meaning of the legal definition of transfer, or if the employee does not prove that this new establishment is aimed at fraudulently avoiding the fulfilment of obligations to the employee.[37]

To conclude, under the Labour Act, there must be a status change or a legal transaction by which an undertaking, business or part of an undertaking or business is transferred to the new employer while retaining its economic integrity. Then, all employment contracts of employees working in that undertaking or part of an undertaking which is the subject of the transfer, or which are connected with the business or part of business which is the subject of the transfer, are transferred to the new employer, regardless of whether they are fixed-term or indefinite duration employment contract, full-time or part-time employment contracts. Analysis of Croatian case law leads to the conclusion that the courts, when interpreting the question of whether the conditions for the transfer of an employment contract have been met, proceed from the objective of the legal provision, which is the protection of employees' rights. In particular, the goal is that the employee retains the acquired rights under the employment contract after the transfer, where the new employer must fulfil obligations imposed by the previous employer.[38] Croatian case law provides a further understanding of which conditions must be fulfilled to apply safeguarding measures of employees' rights in the transfer of undertakings or businesses under Article 137(1) of the Labour Act.

§2.03 THE POSSIBILITY OF THE EMPLOYEE TO OBJECT TO THE TRANSFER OF THE EMPLOYMENT CONTRACT

The decision on the transfer of the business is an autonomous decision of the employer, which is explicitly stated in the case law of the Croatian courts.[39] Because the employee cannot influence the transfer of the undertaking or the business or its parts, the question arises of whether the employee can object to the transfer of the employment contract if he/she does not want the transfer.

Here we must distinguish between two scenarios. In the first, the former employer ceases to exist, while in the second, the former employer still exists and continues to operate. In a situation where the former employer ceases to exist due to the business transfer, the employee has no legal interest and no possibility to object to

35. CJEU, C-242/09, *Albron Catering BV v. FNV Bondgenoten and John Roest* [2010] ECR I-10309.
36. Gović Penić, *supra* n. 14, at 4. Gović Penić, *supra* n. 20, at 108.
37. Confirmed by Supreme Court of the Republic of Croatia in Judgment No. Revr-260/11 of 1 December 2011.
38. County Court in Bjelovar Judgment No. Gž-429/16 of 17 November 2016. Antonija Zubović, *Položaj radnika u postupku preuzimanja dioničkih društava*, 38 Pravni vjesnik 3-4, 37 (2022).
39. Supreme Court of the Republic of Croatia Judgment No. Revr-485/12 of 12 February 2013, Supreme Court of the Republic of Croatia Judgment No. Revr-849/12 of 29 January 2013.

the transfer of the employment contract. The employer may terminate the employee's employment contract before the actual transfer of the business. In this case, both employers may be held jointly and severally liable for the obligations to the employees that arose before the transfer.[40]

However, the situation is somewhat more complicated if the former employer still exists and continues to operate after the business transfer. Neither the Labour Act nor Directive 2001/23/EC explicitly mention the issue of the employee's consent to the transfer of his employment contract to a new employer, so the answer to this question must be sought following the objective that the Labour Act and Directive 2001/23/EC are trying to achieve, namely the protection of employees in such a way that they retain the rights they had prior to the transfer of their employment contract, as well as protection against dismissal solely due to the fact of the transfer of the undertaking. In answering this question, the Croatian courts have taken different positions. For example, the first-instance court concluded that the employee does not have to consent to transfer the employment contract. In contrast, the second-instance court in the same case concluded that an employee who does not want his employment contract to be transferred to a new employer has the right to object to the transfer if the employer continues to operate after the transfer of the business.[41] In its decision, the second-instance court refers to the case law of the CJEU.[42] Another argument of the court in favour of this understanding is the violation of the employee's fundamental right arising from the employment relationship to choose the employer for whom he/she will work if the employee were forced to work for an employer whom he did not freely choose.

However, it should be noted that the case law[43] explicitly takes the position that an employee who objects to the transfer of an employment contract to a new employer no longer enjoys the protection of Article 137 of the Labour Act as well as the protection of Article 3(1) of the Directive. The consequence is that the employee's employment relationship will continue to be assessed based on the relevant provisions of the Labour Act. Thus, if the employee has objected to transferring the employment contract to the new employer, his/her contract shall not transfer to the new employer. His/her employment relationship shall depend on whether the former employer needs the employee's work. Suppose the employer no longer needs the work of a particular employee. In that case, it may decide to terminate the employment contract (business-related termination of the employment contract),[44] which includes the right to a notice period and severance pay. It should be noted that the decision to terminate the

40. Labour Act, Article 137, para. 13.
41. County Court in Zagreb Judgment No. Gž R-338/2019-2 of 19 March 2019.
42. In particular, it refers to the following judgments: CJEU, C-171/94, *Albert Merckx and Patrick Neuhuys v. Ford Motors Company Belgium SA.* [1996] ECR I-01253. CJEU, C-105/84, *Foreningen af Arbejdsledere i Danmark v. A/S Danmols Inventar, in liquidation* [1985] ECR 02639; CJEU, C-51/00, *Temco Service Industries SA v. Samir Imzilyen and Others* [2002] ECR I-00969.
43. County Court in Zagreb Judgment No. 16 Gž R-338/2019-2 of 19 March 2019, which refers to the ECJU, C-105/84, *Foreningen af Arbejdsledere i Danmark v. A/S Danmols Inventar, in liquidation* [1985] ECR 02639.
44. Željko Potočnjak, *Zaštita stečenih prava radnika u slučaju prijenosa poduzeća, pogona ili njegovih dijelova na drugog poslodavca prema pravu Europske unije*, 381 (Petar Miladin and

employment contract may not be based on the fact that the employee's employment contract was not transferred by his will, but on the fact that the employer no longer needs the employee's work after the transfer of the business. A prerequisite for the termination's admissibility is that the reason for termination (the lack of need for the employee's work) actually exists. If the employer still needs a particular employee's work after the business transfer, he cannot terminate the employment contract due to business-related reasons. In this procedure of termination of the employment contract, the employer must comply with all other legal obligations provided for termination of the employment contract by this type of termination.

Directive 2001/23/EC explicitly states that a transfer is not grounds for termination of the employment contract. It means that a dismissal of the employee based only on the fact of the transfer would be inadmissible, regardless of who made this decision, the former or the new employer. Croatian employers and courts accept this legal solution, although the Labour Act does not contain a similar provision.[45] According to the case law of the CJEU, after a transfer of an undertaking, the employee can sue the new employer for exercising the rights arising from the employment relationship.[46] It is a legal consequence of Directive 2001/23/EC, under which the employment contract automatically transfers to the new employer even without special consent from the employer.[47] However, according to the Directive, dismissals for business-related reasons are permitted if changes in the workforce are necessary for economic, technical or organizational reasons. In the same line of reasoning, Croatian law takes the position that if, after the transfer, there is a surplus of labour with the new employer, termination for business-related reasons is possible, but with the recognition of the continuity of the employment relationship and with the application of all provisions of the Labour Act and other regulations governing this type of termination of the employment contract. Croatian courts consider that dismissal with the offer of an alternative employment contract is also permissible.[48]

A special case for consideration is if the transfer entails a substantial change in the working conditions to the employee's detriment. For example, if an employee terminates his/her employment contract because his/her working conditions have changed significantly to his/her disadvantage after the transfer of the employment relationship, the employer should be deemed to have concealed the termination, and the employee's rights should be recognized if the employer terminates for reasons beyond employee's control.[49]

Miljenko Giunio (eds), Zbornik radova 55. susreta pravnika, Hrvatski savez udruga pravnika u gospodarstvu, 2017).

45. Gović Penić, *supra* n. 14, at 6.
46. CJEU, C-396/07, *Mirja Juuri v. Fazer Amica Oy* [2008] ECR I-1883.
47. CJEU, C-51/00, *Temco Service Industries SA v. Samir Imzilyen and Others* [2002] ECR I-00969.
48. Supreme Court of the Republic of Croatia Judgment No. Revr-749/07 of 22 November 2007.
49. First of all, this would include the right to severance pay, notice period, etc. This point of view is also confirmed by the EU Court in its decisions. CJEU, C-396/07, *Mirja Juuri v. Fazer Amica Oy* [2008] ECR I-1883. Iris Gović Penić, *Primjena prakse Europskog suda za ljudska prava (Strasbourg) i suda Europske unije (Luxembourg) u suđenju u radnopravnim sporovima u Republici Hrvatskoj* (2019), 57, https://www.pak.hr/cke/obrazovni%20materijali/primjena prakseESLJPisudaEU.pdf (accessed 1 March 2023.). About termination of employment contract

Employees' monetary claims towards the former employer are protected as well. Croatian Ministry of Economy, Labour and Entrepreneurship issued an Opinion in this regard, according to which, in case of termination of the employment relationship (e.g., by an agreement between the employee and the former employer), monetary claims of the employee against the former employer remain. However, the possibility of recovery depends on several facts, especially if the employer is a company. Thus, it shall depend on whether the same legal entity still exists. Further, relevant is the amount of a shareholder's personal assets when the company's assets are insufficient to cover the employee's demand. If the shareholder abuses the fact that, as a shareholder, he or she is not liable for the company's obligations, he might be liable with his/her personal assets for the company's liabilities, which would certainly include employee's demands.[50]

§2.04 OBLIGATION TO INFORM THE NEW EMPLOYER ABOUT THE RIGHTS OF EMPLOYEES AND THE TRANSFER OF EMPLOYMENT CONTRACTS

The Labour Act expressly requires that an employer who transfers an undertaking, part of an undertaking, a business or part of a business to a new employer must fully and truthfully inform the new employer in writing of the rights of the employees whose employment contracts are being transferred.[51] This provision has a dual function. On the one hand, it creates clearer and more reliable relations between the transferor and the transferee. On the other hand, it makes the legal position of the employee clearer and more reliable both vis-à-vis the transferor and the transferee.[52]

The employment contract shall be transferred without notification to either the new employer or the employee. Under Article 137(5) of the Labour Act, the failure of the employer to inform the new employer in writing of the employees' rights shall not affect the rights of employees whose employment contracts have been transferred to the new employer. Equally, a failure to notify the employee of the transfer shall not have a constitutive effect on the transfer of the employment contract.

§2.05 THE OBLIGATION OF THE TRANSFEROR TO INFORM AND CONSULT EMPLOYEES' REPRESENTATIVES REGARDING THE PLANNED TRANSFER OF UNDERTAKING

The Labour Act expressly obliges the employer to inform the works council and all employees affected by the transfer in writing of the transfer of the undertaking, part of

generally *see* in Sandra Laleta, *Prestanak ugovora o radu*, PhD thesis, Faculty of Law University of Zagreb, 2011.

50. Companies Act, OG Nos 111/93, 34/99, 121/99, 52/00, 118/03, 107/07, 146/08, 137/09, 125/11, 152/11, 111/12, 68/13, 110/15, 40/19, 34/22, 114/22, 18/23, Article 10. Opinion of the Ministry of Economy, Labour and Entrepreneurship of the Republic of Croatia, of 18 October 2019, https://www.iusinfo.hr/misljenja-i-tumacenja/MMIN201D20191018N658 (accessed 1 March 2023).
51. Labour Act, Article 137, para. 4.
52. Potočnjak, *supra* n. 44, at 427.

the undertaking, business or part of the business to the new employer in due time before the day of the transfer.[53] The notification must contain information on: (1) the date of transfer of the employment contract, (2) the reasons for the transfer of the employment contract, (3) the effects of the transfer of the employment contract on the legal, economic or social position of the employee, (4) the planned measures towards the employers whose contracts are transferred. In addition to the obligation to inform the works council and the employees, the employer must consult the works council on the intended decision before making a decision that is important for the employee and provide it with the information that is important for the decision and the assessment of its effects on the employee's position.[54] The employer shall consult the works council on the anticipated legal, economic and social consequences that may arise for employees.

Croatian courts discussed whether the employer is obliged to submit to the works council a list of employees whose employment contracts shall be transferred to the new employer. However, the courts took differing opinions on this matter. In particular, the Court of First Instance held that the employer is not obliged to do so. But the court of second instance took the opposite view, pointing out that all information, including the list of employees whose employment contracts are being transferred, must be submitted to the works council in full and in good time so that the works council is (actually) able to make comments and suggestions on the employer's decision. In that way, the results of the discussion could actually be incorporated into the decision-making process.[55]

Further, the employer shall be obliged to give the works council the opportunity to hold a meeting before issuing a final statement on the employer's intended decision. Following that, the employer may provide additional answers and explanations to the statement issued by the works council. More precisely, the works council is obliged to inform the employer of its opinion on the intended decision within eight days; if this obligation is not fulfilled, it is presumed (*praesumptio juris et de jure*) that there are no objections and proposals against the decision.[56] If the works council objects to the transfer of the business or part of the business to a new employer, it must give written reasons for its objection to the employer's decision.

Suppose the employer does not have a works council. In that case, it should hold a consultation procedure with the trade union representative (sindikalni povjerenik). If there is no trade union representative, the employer has no obligation to consult regarding this decision, as there is in fact no one to consult with.

Although the opinion of the works council is only advisory in nature, the employer's failure to consult the works council prior to the decision on the transfer of the undertaking or part thereof results in the nullity of such decision, which has been

53. Labour Act, Article137, para. 6.
54. Labour Act, Article 150, para. 3.
55. County Court in Zagreb Judgment No. Gž R-338/2019-2 of 19 March 2019.
56. Labour Act, Article 150, para. 6.

confirmed by the Croatian Constitutional Court.[57] In court practice, the question arose as to the possibility of an oral consultation of the trade union representative, with the court taking the position that such a consultation is permissible and sufficient to comply with the procedure prescribed in Article 150 of the Labour Act,[58] even if it must be proven in court proceedings that it actually took place.[59]

Also, the employer commits a serious offence if he fails to inform or consult the works council on matters and in the manner prescribed by the Labour Act. A fine of EUR 4,110.00 to EUR 7,960.00 can be imposed for this violation.

Pursuant to the provisions of Article 137(10) of the Labour Act, a works council established in a transferred undertaking or part of a transferred undertaking, business or part of a business that has preserved its autonomy shall continue its work at the latest until the end of the mandate for which it was elected.[60]

If the undertaking, part of the undertaking, business or part of the business that has been transferred does not preserve its autonomy and the work of the works council cannot continue, the employees whose contracts have been transferred shall retain their right of representation until the conditions for the election of a new works council have been created, i.e., until the expiry of the mandate of their previous representative.[61] In this line of reasoning, the Ministry of Labour and Pension System elaborated on the status of the works council in the case of a merger of two joint stock companies. The Ministry of Labour and Pension System has considered that the trade union representative of the merged company, which ceased to exist after the merger, retains the right to represent the employees whose employment contracts were transferred and whom he represented before the merger until the end of the mandate or until the election of a new works council.[62]

In judicial practice, no significant court decisions are related to the continuation of the works council.[63] Nevertheless, it can be seen from some decisions that the clarifying dilemmas concerning the continuation of the works council are handled flexibly. For example, the court held that the consultation procedure before the termination of the employment contract was lawfully conducted[64] in a situation where the new employer, after the merger, consulted the trade union representative of the acquiring company rather than the trade union representative of the merging company, which no longer exists, i.e., the employee's previous employer.

57. Labour Act, Article 150, para. 12. Constitutional Court of the Republic of Croatia Judgment No. U-I-3763/2004 of 18 October 2006.
58. Supreme Court of the Republic of Croatia Judgment No. Rev-477/08 of 14 October 2008.
59. High Administrative Court of the Republic of Croatia Judgment No. Usoz-126/15-8 of 26 February 2016.
60. The mandate of the works council is four years. Labour Act, Article 144.
61. Labour Act, Article 137, para. 11.
62. Ministry of Labour and Pension System (Klasa: 110-01/12-01/399, Ur.br.524-03-01-01/3-12-2) of 17 December 2012.
63. Gović Penić, *supra* n. 14, at 8.
64. Supreme Court of the Republic of Croatia Judgment No. Revr-298/2007 of 4 July 2007.

§2.06 THE MOMENT OF THE TRANSFER OF THE EMPLOYMENT CONTRACT

The Labour Act expressly provides that employment contracts shall be transferred to the new employer when the transfer becomes legally effective in accordance with the laws and regulations under the legal transaction leading to the transfer of the undertaking, business or part of the undertaking or business.[65] Thus, the transfer can take place through status changes such as merger, acquisition or division or by legal transaction such as a contract of sale, contract of donation, etc.

In the case of the acquisition of the company, the employment contracts are transferred by entering the status change of acquisition in the court register of the acquiring company.[66] In the case of a merger, the employment contracts are transferred by entering the new company in the court register.[67] In the case of a division of the company, it is necessary to distinguish between two scenarios. In the first, the divided company's rights, obligations and legal relations are transferred to newly established companies (division with incorporation). In the second, the divided company's rights, obligations and legal relations are transferred to already existing recipient companies (division with takeover). In the first case, the employment contract transfer occurs at the moment when the newly established company acquires legal personality, i.e., when it is registered in the court register.[68] In the second case, the employment contract transfer occurs when the division is entered in the court register.[69] If it is a contract of sale, the transfer shall occur at the time of the conclusion of the contract under the provisions applicable to the sale. If it is a contract of donation, then when the contract of the donation was concluded.

According to the Ministry of Economy, Labour and Entrepreneurship, even if the name of the company after the transfer changes, the company is considered a legal successor, provided that the conditions for the transfer under the Labour Act are met.[70]

All employment contracts in the undertaking or part of the undertaking or who are connected with the business or part of the business that is the subject of the transfer shall also be transferred *ex lege* to the new employer at the time of the transfer. The employment contracts of foreign employees shall also be transferred without the need to obtain a new work permit since no new employment relationship is established, but only the existing contract is transferred.[71] Since employment contracts are transferred *ex lege*, no new employment contracts should be concluded with employees whose

65. Labour Act, Article 137, para. 8.
66. Companies Act, Article 522, paras 3 and 4.
67. Companies Act, Article 533, paras 5 and 6.
68. Companies Act, Article 550.n.
69. Companies Act, Article 550.r.
70. *See* Opinion of the Ministry of Economy, Labour and Entrepreneurship of the Republic of Croatia, of 18 October 2019.
71. Opinion of the Ministry of Economy, Labour and Entrepreneurship of the Republic of Croatia, Directorate for Labour Market and Employment (Klasa 110-01/04-01/341, Ur.br.526-08-04-2), of 4 October 2004.

employment contracts have been transferred. The previously concluded contracts remain in force.[72]

§2.07 TRANSFER OF EMPLOYMENT CONTRACTS IN THE CASE OF BANKRUPTCY AND RESTRUCTURING PROCEEDINGS

If the transfer of the undertaking, business or part of the undertaking or business takes place in the course of bankruptcy proceedings or restructuring, the rights transferred to the new employer may be restricted in accordance with special provisions, a collective agreement or an agreement between the work council and the employer.[73]

The most frequent court decisions related to the bankruptcy of the employer based on the Labour Act are the decisions in which the opening of bankruptcy proceedings is a special reason for the termination of the employment contract,[74] while the transfer of employment contract is possible but is rare in practice. The legal basis for the termination of the employment contract would be the provision of Article 191 of the Bankruptcy Act,[75] which in paragraph 1 provides that opening bankruptcy proceedings shall not result in the termination of employment or service contracts concluded with the debtor as an employer. However, paragraph 2 of the same article explicitly states that opening bankruptcy proceedings is a special justified reason for terminating the employment contract.[76]

After opening bankruptcy proceedings, the bankruptcy trustee, on behalf of the employer's debtor and the employee, can cancel the employment contract, regardless of the agreed duration of the contract and the legal or contractual provisions on employee protection. The notice period is one month unless the law provides a shorter period.[77] If the employee considers that the termination of his employment is not in accordance with the law, he may request the protection of his rights under the provisions of the Labour Act. In this case, the bankruptcy trustee may conclude new

---

72. According to the Opinion, the 'old' employer is not obliged to provide the worker with the right to annual leave, neither in proportion nor in full, but this obligation is transferred to the new employer to whom the employment contracts were transferred. *See* Opinion of the Ministry of Economy, Labour and Entrepreneurship of the Republic of Croatia, of 18 October 2019.
73. Labour Act, Article 137, para. 9. The reduction of the rights of workers within the bankruptcy procedure only applies to the transfer of the undertaking or its part within the bankruptcy procedure, and not when the property of the bankrupt debtor is sold, or even when it is done as a whole. *See* Jakša Barbić, *Prijenos ugovora o radu prijenosom poduzeća i pogona poduzeća*, Hrvatska pravna revija 7, 1 (2002), at 13.
74. Supreme Court of the Republic of Croatia Judgment No. Revr-1799/09 of 15 September 2011.
75. Bankruptcy Act, OG Nos 71/15, 104/17, 36/22.
76. The amendment to the Bankruptcy Act from 2022 stipulates that the decision on the opening and closing of bankruptcy proceedings (cases in which the open bankruptcy proceedings are not carried out) will be delivered to the debtor's employees in order to avoid situations where the debtor's employees are not notified of the termination of employment (Bankruptcy Act, Article 132). Moreover, the novelty is that the court will also deliver the decision on the conclusion of bankruptcy proceedings to the debtor's employees (Bankruptcy Act, Article 286). This is important from the perspective of the rights that the worker realizes based on the Act on the Insurance of Workers' Claims (OG No. 70/17, 18/23). *See* Dejan Bodul, *Dodatna zaštita za radnike (ali stari problemi) u noveli Stečajnog zakona iz 2022*, Radno pravo 6, 21 (2022).
77. Bankruptcy Act, Article 191, para. 3.

fixed-term employment contracts to complete the work started and repair any damage with the court's consent. Wages and other income from employment shall be determined by the bankruptcy trustee, with the approval of the court, in accordance with the law and the collective agreement. Wages and other income from employment to which a claim has arisen after the opening of bankruptcy proceedings shall be settled as liabilities of the bankruptcy estate.

From the above, it is clear that the Bankruptcy Act gives the bankruptcy trustee the possibility to terminate the employment contract and conclude new employment contracts for a fixed period of time in order to complete the work started. In our opinion, the application of the institute of transfer of employment contracts in practice could be made in the case of the continuation of the company when a bankruptcy plan is drawn up under Article 303 of the Bankruptcy Act. According to this provision, a bankruptcy plan may be drawn up after the opening of bankruptcy proceedings, in which it is possible to deviate from the legal provisions on the payment and distribution of the bankruptcy estate. The bankruptcy trustee is obliged only to consult the works council, as the powers of the works council are limited under Article 192 of the Bankruptcy Act, which provides that employees' right to participate in the decision-making process expires with the opening of the bankruptcy proceedings.

At the same time, it should be noted that Article 137(9) of the Labour Act also covers the transfer of employment contracts in restructuring procedures. Significant changes to the Croatian legal framework regulating the position of employees in pre-bankruptcy proceedings, in which the restructuring plan is drawn up, were made by the latest amendment to the Bankruptcy Act, which entered into force on 31 March 2022. The tendency of the changes is, among other things, to preserve the continuity of business operations and the jobs of employees through various measures. Thus, the proposal for a restructuring plan has been expanded to include a description of the debtor's economic situation and the situation of the employees, as well as a description of the reasons for and the extent of the debtor's difficulties and the manner of informing and consulting the employees.[78] If the restructuring plan provides for measures that result in changes in the organization of work or the employment contracts with employees, these measures must be approved by the employees.[79] It should be emphasized that the individual and collective rights of the employees arising from national labour law and the labour law of the European Union are not affected by the pre-bankruptcy proceedings.[80]

§2.08 PROTECTION OF EMPLOYEE'S RIGHTS PROVIDED BY THE COLLECTIVE AGREEMENT

According to Directive 2001/23/EC, the new employer (transferee) is obliged to continue to observe the terms and conditions agreed in the collective agreement that

78. Bankruptcy Act, Article 27.
79. Bankruptcy Act, Article 66, para. 7.
80. Bankruptcy Act, Article 66, para. 6.

applied to the previous employer (transferor) until the date of termination or expiry of the collective agreement or the entry into force or application of another collective agreement. However, Member States are authorized to limit the period of compliance with these terms and conditions, which should not be less than one year. The Croatian legislator opted for the shortest possible period (one year).

According to Article 137(12) of the Labour Act, if a collective agreement has been concluded in the undertaking or part of the undertaking or is connected to the business or part of the business to be transferred, it shall continue to apply to the employees until the new collective agreement is concluded, but for no longer than one year.[81] Several questions arise in the application of this provision. Namely, since it is *ius cogens* provision, the application of this provision may result in discrimination against employees.[82] For example, there may be unequal treatment in terms of income and other rights between 'old' and 'new' employees of the new employer, i.e., between those who have worked for the new employer and those whose employment contract has been transferred to the new employer.

Let us take an example where two companies merged with the acquiring company. When the status changes were implemented, the employment contracts of employees working in the merged companies were transferred to the new employer. The collective agreements of merged companies, which were applicable until the merger, continued to apply to employees after the status changes. As a result, three collective agreements would simultaneously be applicable in the company. Consequently, employees would have different rights and wages for performing the same tasks under the same conditions within the same company/employer.[83]

One solution could be to specify that Article 137(12) of the Labour Act does not apply if the new employer already has a collective agreement, which would avoid competition between two collective agreements or possible anti-discrimination disputes.[84] Or it could be stipulated that if the collective agreement of the new employer is more favourable to employees than the collective agreement of the previous employer, the more favourable collective agreement shall apply. Such a solution would be in favour of employees whose employment contracts are transferred.

The question arises whether the content of the transferred employment contract changes with each amendment of the collective agreement that was in force at the time of the transfer of the employment contract. In light of the CJEU case law,[85] there is no

81. In the case law of the Croatian courts, there are decisions in which, in the case of a transfer of an undertaking, particular weight is given to the fact that the employers have agreed on the application of a collective agreement, i.e., that the collective agreement concluded with the previous employer applies to the rights of the employees. Supreme Court of the Republic of Croatia Judgment No. Revr-114/13 of 6 April 2016. Gović Penić, *supra* n. 49, at 61-62.
82. Ivana Grgurev, *Produžena primjena pravnih pravila sadržanih u kolektivnom ugovoru: (ne) potreban institut?*, 60 Zbornik Pravnog fakulteta u Zagrebu 5, 1081 (2010).
83. *See* more in *Nastavak primjene kolektivnog ugovora nakon prenošenja ugovora o radu na novog poslodavca*, https://www.iusinfo.hr/aktualno/u-sredistu/25989 (accessed 11 March 2023).
84. Grgurev, *supra* n. 82.
85. CJEU, C-108/10, *Ivana Scattolon contro Ministero dell'Istruzione, dell'Università e della Ricerca* [2011] ECR I-07491; CJEU, C-426/11, *Mark Alemo-Herron and Others v. Parkwood Leisure Ltd.* [2013].; CJEU, Joined Cases C-680/15 and C-681/15., *Asklepios Kliniken Langen-Seligenstadt*

obligation that subsequent changes or amendments automatically lead to changes in the terms and conditions of employment from the transferred employment contracts. It should be noted that the Labour Act does not provide for the direct application to transferred employment contracts of all amendments to the collective agreement in force at the time of the transfer. Therefore, there is no obligation that subsequent amendments, i.e., the conclusion of a new collective agreement, automatically lead to changes in the terms and conditions of employment in the transferred employment contracts.[86]

However, a different conclusion can be reached if, for example, the application of the collective agreement has been extended to both the previous employer and the new employer by a decision of the Minister or if the new employer has also signed the same collective agreement. If the collective agreement expires after one year, in order to determine whether or not the employees are entitled to certain rights at the time of termination, it is necessary to determine the time when the employees acquire those rights, i.e., whether they acquired a certain right before the expiration of the year following the transfer or after. For example, if the collective agreement gives employees a particular right and that right is acquired in August, while the collective agreement expires in June, then the employees are not entitled to that particular right for that year. However, if this right is acquired in May, then the employees have this right for this year.

In connection with the provision of Directive 2001/23/EC on the application of the collective agreement, the CJEU also took the position that the national legislation does not have to oblige the new employer that after the expiry of one year, i.e., after the expiry of the collective agreement of the previous employer, the new employer should recognize the working conditions the transferred employees had with the previous employer.[87]

If the salary issue is regulated only by the collective agreement, the collective agreement should continue to be applied after the expiration of one year from the date of transfer. Any other interpretation would easily result in the employee not retaining his rights under the transferred employment contract, which would be contrary to the objectives of Directive 2001/23/EC. This position is in line with the case law of the CJEU.[88]

§2.09 THE LIABILITY OF THE TRANSFEROR AND THE TRANSFEREE IN CASE OF TRANSFER OF THE EMPLOYMENT CONTRACT

According to Article 137(13) of the Labour Act, if the undertaking, business or part of the undertaking or business is transferred to the new employer, the transferee and the

GmbH v. Ivan Felja and Asklepios Dienstleistungsgesellschaft mbH v. Vittoria Graf [2017]; CJEU, C-328/13, *Österreichischer Gewerkschaftsbund protiv Wirtschaftskammer Österreich – Fachverband Autobus-, Luftfahrt- und Schifffahrtsunternehmungen* [2014].

86. Gović Penić, *supra* n. 14, at 9.
87. CJEU, C-396/07, *Mirja Juuri v. Fazer Amica Oy* [2008] ECR I-1883.
88. CJEU, C-328/13, *Österreichischer Gewerkschaftsbund protiv Wirtschaftskammer Österreich – Fachverband Autobus-, Luftfahrt- und Schifffahrtsunternehmungen* [2014].

transferor shall be jointly and severally liable for the obligations arising prior to the date of transfer from an employment contract or employment relationship existing at the date of transfer.

Joint and several liability means that the employee may demand the realization of his rights either from the former employer, the new employer, or both. The decision as to who should demand the realization of his rights depends entirely on the will of the employee. However, the obligations arising after the transfer must be fulfilled by the new employer unless the conditions for the obligation of a person with whom no employment contract has been concluded but who, by the transfer of the business or otherwise, fraudulently evades the fulfilment of his obligations to the employee, are met. Authors shall discuss this particular solution of Croatian law in the following chapter.

In practice, there is also the question of the responsibility to deal with the documents on the employees collected by the old employer before the transfer and relating to the personal data of the employees whose employment contract is transferred to the new employer. The Ministry of Economy, Labour and Entrepreneurship points out in its opinion[89] that there is joint and several liability of the old and the new employer for this matter as well. Therefore, regardless of the employer with whom the documents mentioned before were kept, they are both obliged to comply with the legal framework applicable to the protection of personal data.

§2.10 FRAUDULENT AVOIDANCE OF OBLIGATIONS TOWARDS EMPLOYEES

By the provision of Article 137(15) of the Labour Act, Croatian law expands the circle of persons who may be responsible for fulfilling obligations to the employee in the event of a transfer of an undertaking. It is expressly provided that a person who, by transferring the undertaking, business, or part of the undertaking or business, or otherwise fraudulently avoids his obligations to the employees, shall, at the request of the employees, be ordered by the competent court to fulfil his obligations, even if the employment contract was not concluded with such person. Thus, even a person with whom no employment contract has been concluded may be liable for fulfilling obligations towards the employee. An important presumption of liability is the fraudulent avoidance of obligations towards employees.

It should be noted that Directive 2001/23/EC does not contain such a provision. However, this provision of the Labour Act represents the fulfilment of the obligations of the EU Member States to introduce into their national legal systems such measures as are necessary to give all employees and their representatives who believe that they have been harmed due to the failure to fulfil obligations under Directive 2001/23/EC, the possibility of claiming their right in judicial proceedings after having exhausted all

89. Opinion of the Ministry of Economy, Labour and Entrepreneurship of the Republic of Croatia, of 12 July 2020, https://www.iusinfo.hr/misljenja-i-tumacenja/MMIN201D20200612N670 (accessed 1 March 2023).

other legal remedies. Also, it enhances the prevention of the abuse of proceedings in the event of insolvency, which could deprive employees of their rights under the Directive.

Its application can be in a typical case in practice when a new company is established, in which the undertaking or part of it is being invested. Transfer of the employment contract could occur without fulfilling obligations to the employees whose contracts have been transferred, while, however, investors/shareholders draw benefits from the newly established company. According to Article 137(15) of the Labour Act, the employee may bring an action not only against the person to whom the undertaking has been transferred but also against the person to whom the undertaking has not been formally transferred if that person has performed acts aimed at fraudulently avoiding the fulfilment of the obligations to the employee. Case law confirmed that in the following situation. The employee's employment with the former employer had been terminated by mutual consent following the decision to restructure the former employer. After that, a new employment contract was concluded with the new employer. However, the new employer terminated this contract without recognizing the continuity of the employment relationship. The crucial fact was that the former employer was the sole shareholder/founder of the new company, which then became the new employer. The court found that due to these specific circumstances, a fraudulent violation of the employee's rights has been committed.[90] Thus, the new employer was obliged to pay the employee a severance payment, taking into account the number of years of service with the former employer.

The person who committed the abuse shall be liable for the obligations to the employee with all his assets, regardless of the value of the transferred undertaking or its part. Any other agreement between the former and the new employer would be null and void. Thus, the employee may demand salary, wage compensation, severance pay, holiday pay, anniversary pay, damages, and all other rights arising from the employment relationship from that person.

§2.11 CONCLUDING REMARKS

The aim of Directive 2001/23/EC is to ensure the protection of employees' rights in the event of transfers of undertakings, businesses or parts of undertakings or businesses. However, immediately after the adoption of Directive 2001/23/EC, it was pointed out that the Directive has certain gaps and that some solutions need further clarification. The CJEU has attempted to address these gaps and ambiguities, which largely focus on clarifying doubts in cases where employees are entitled to protection. Opinions of the CJEU are followed by the Croatian courts when making decisions related to the transfer of undertakings. Directive 2001/23/EC has been transposed into Croatian law. However, given that a Directive was adopted 22 years ago and that events in the corporate sector have changed concerning the labour law implications of certain corporate

90. County Court in Zagreb Judgment No. Gžr-1504/02 of 17 September 2002. Gović Penić, *supra* n. 49, at 66.

decisions, many issues regarding its application occur. The same conclusion stands for the Labour Act, which transposed the provisions of the Directive into Croatian law.

One of the open issues is the position and protection of employees in bankruptcy proceedings. It appears that the Croatian Bankruptcy Act allows the bankruptcy trustee to terminate the employment contract, which is a solution in line with both the provision of Article 137(9) of the Labour Act and the practice of the Croatian courts. The analysis of bankruptcy law shows that the frequent amendments to the Bankruptcy Act have improved the position of employees in bankruptcy proceedings in the Republic of Croatia. The frequent changes in the position of employees in bankruptcy proceedings are also related to the attempt to ensure social peace, especially after a large number of employees were dismissed by the opening of bankruptcy proceedings against their former employer.[91] Importantly, it is established that the claims of the first higher order of payment include the claims of the employees and former employees of the debtor that arose from the employment relationship before the opening of the bankruptcy proceedings. The settlement of these claims must be in accordance with the special provisions on the payment of wages, contributions to compulsory insurance from wages and related taxes and surtaxes.[92] However, the amendment to the Bankruptcy Act in 2022 sought to facilitate access to preventive restructuring measures for viable companies in financial difficulties by allowing early structural adjustments to avoid redundancies.[93] In authors' opinion, the application of the institute of transfer of employment contract is possible in practice if the company continues to exist, for example, in restructuring procedures and the implementation of a bankruptcy plan in bankruptcy proceedings. Therefore, the protection of employees should be ensured by the legal framework applicable to these procedures.

Another issue that gives rise to doubts in practice is the question of the extended validity of the collective agreement. Under Croatian law, in the event of a transfer of an undertaking, the collective agreement continues to apply to the employees until the new collective agreement is concluded, but for no longer than one year. The application of this provision may lead to discrimination against employees. Authors consider that this could be avoided by specifying that this provision does not apply if the new employer already has a collective agreement, in which case the same collective agreement of the new employer would apply to 'old' and 'new' employees. However, this solution is in the interest of the employees whose employment contracts are transferred only if the new collective agreement is more favourable than the former. On the contrary, if it is less favourable, the question arises regarding the protection of acquired rights when an employment contract is transferred. The solution could be that if the collective agreement of the new employer is more favourable to the employees,

91. Vanja Smokvina, Dejan Bodul and Ante Vuković, *O načelu socijalnog postupanja u stečajnom postupku s naglaskom na prava radnika*, 34 Zbornik Pravnog fakulteta Sveučilišta u Rijeci 1, 525 (2013).
92. Bodul, *supra* n. 76, at 17.
93. About restructuring models *see* more in Edita Čulinović-Herc, Antonija Zubović and Mihaela Braut Filipović, *The Preventive Restructuring of Companies in Difficulties: One-Size-Fits-All or Tailor Made Solutions?*, 39 Zbornik Pravnog fakulteta Sveučilišta u Rijeci 4 (2018) at 1447 https://doi.org/10.30925/zpfsr.39.4.1 (accessed 22 August 2025).

then that collective agreement should apply. Such a solution would benefit the employees whose employment contracts are transferred. Moreover, there would be no discrimination, as the same (more favourable) collective agreement would apply to all employees.

It should also be noted that Croatian law provides additional protection for employees beyond the provisions of Directive 2001/23/EC. It concerns the protection of employees against economic fraud and fraudulent avoidance of their rights towards a person who fraudulently evades his obligations to employees by transferring the undertaking, business or part of the undertaking or business, or in any other way. If such a case occurs, the competent court shall order that person to fulfil his obligations at the request of the employees, even if the employment contract was not concluded with that person. The purpose of this provision is to protect employees in cases where the employer establishes new commercial companies in which the undertaking or part of the undertaking invests, so that the employees are transferred to the newly established companies. In practice, the problem arises that these newly established companies do not have any assets from which the employees' claims can be settled, while however, the employer (founder of the company) benefits from these companies.[94]

To conclude, Croatian labour law provides protection to employees in cases of transfer of undertakings or businesses in line with Directive 2001/23/EC. Croatian courts have a significant role in applying and interpreting relevant provisions, which they diligently do by following the rulings of the CJEU on various issues concerning employees' protection. Still, one must conclude that open issues deserve further consideration. The goal of this article was to present current standpoints and challenges in Croatian practice so that it serves as a good incentive for further development of employees' protection in this domain.

94. Barbić, *supra* n. 73, at 13.

CHAPTER 3

Cyprus: Employees' Rights in the Event of Transfers of Undertakings, Businesses or Parts of Undertakings or Businesses in Cyprus

Nicos Trimikliniotis

§3.01 INTRODUCTION

This chapter aims to present the challenges pertaining to transfers of undertaking in the context of Cyprus in the hope of pinpointing the sufficiency or otherwise and emerging issues, gaps and problems in European legislation and the national laws. Managing corporate and entrepreneurial movements in a changing economic environment in the Union in the coming years promises to be even more challenging. This chapter outlines the national legislation on business transfers in the Republic of Cyprus (RoC)[1] when implementing the EU acquis. It scrutinizes the transposition of Directive 2001/23/EC (herein referred to as 'the Directive') and the level of compliance with the EU acquis, as laid out in jurisprudence of the Court of Justice. After critically engaging various

1. This chapter covers the RoC. It does not cover the 'Turkish Republic of Northern Cyprus' only recognized by Turkey, which since 1974 occupies the northern part of the country. The ECtHR has ruled that the TRNC is a subordinate local administration as Turkey's army 'exercises effective overall control over that part of the island' and that 'such control [...] entails her responsibility for the policies and actions of the "TRNC"' (*Loizidou v. Turkey*, ECHR 18 December 1996, 108 ILR 443, 466-467, para. 56). Also, it does not cover Sovereign British Base Areas which covers a total of 98 square miles and around 3 % of the territory. The status of the British bases is governed by Protocol No. 3 on the sovereign base areas of the United Kingdom of Great Britain and Northern Ireland in Cyprus following BREXIT. In the Preamble, it is reaffirmed that 'the withdrawal of the United Kingdom from the Union should not affect the rights and obligations of the Republic of Cyprus under Union law or the rights and obligations of the parties to the Treaty of Establishment'.

issues on the operation of the transfer of undertakings, some ideas about the way forward are offered.

§3.02 THE LAW ON TRANSFERS OF UNDERTAKINGS IN CYPRUS IN VIEW OF EU ACCESSION

The regulation protecting worker rights in the context of transfer of undertaking in Cyprus was shaped during the process of harmonization to EC acquis. EU law on the subject developed in response to global transformations in a world of turbulences and crises. Cyprus with an internationally exposed economy has been heavily affected by financial, economic and political turbulences in the world and its own region in the Eastern Mediterranean. The economy is heavily dependent on tourism and services; globalization and financialization have been a key force in shaping this small economy, characterized by SMEs which make up 98% of the firms in the country. Labour law in Cyprus, despite an established tradition of strong tripartism and collective bargaining, has been under pressure, particularly after the financial crisis, the pandemic and the post-pandemic crises. Post-accession Cyprus has faced a series of crises, which have placed immense pressures on collective bargaining and safeguarding rights of workers.[2] In this context, a robust system for protecting workers' rights in transfer of undertakings is therefore of particular importance.

Cypriot lawmakers were concerned about protecting rights of employees in case of transfer of undertakings before accession to the harmonization of legislation with the EU acquis. The Termination of Employment Act[3] provides that where the business or part of the business of an employer is transferred as such to another employer or where an employee is transferred from one company to another where the employee is not entitled to payment due to redundancy,[4] then all weeks of employment with the first employer are considered employment with the second employer when calculating the period of employment.

The Cypriot Law purporting to transpose Directive 2001/23/EC[5] is the Act safeguarding and securing the rights of employees in the event of transfers of undertakings, businesses, or part of businesses (hereinafter 'the Cypriot Act on Transfers of Undertakings', or CATU).[6] Minor amendments introduced in 2003[7] defined the term 'economic, technical and organisational reasons'; the determination

---

2. *See* Trimikliniotis, N. (2023) 'Recent Trends of Collective Bargaining in Cyprus', Papademetriou, C. (ed.) *Recent Trends of Collective Bargaining in Balkan and Southeastern European States*, Athens: Sakkoulas, pp. 21-34.
3. Part 1, Second Table, Ο περί τερματισμού της απασχόλησης Νόμος 24/67, http://www.cylaw.org/nomoi/enop/non-ind/1967_1_24/full.html (accessed 22 August 2025).
4. In accordance with para. (c) of section 20 of this Act.
5. The basic law of 2000 was based on the two previous directives, 77/187/EEC and 98/50/EC, consolidated under Directive 2001/23/EC.
6. *Ο Περί της Διατήρησης και Διασφάλισης των Δικαιωμάτων των Εργοδοτουμένων κατά τη Μεταβίβαση Επιχειρήσεων, Εγκαταστάσεων ή Τμημάτων Επιχειρήσεων ή Εγκαταστάσεων*, 104(I)/2000, as amended by Laws 39(I)/2003 and 162(I)/2018, available at https://www.cylaw.org/nomoi/enop/non-ind/2000_1_104/full.html (accessed 22 August 2025).
7. Law 39(I)/2003.

of the competent court as the Labour Disputes Court, as per section 8A CATU; and the manner of calculation of compensation due to the employee.

When the initial Act of CATU was enacted in 2000, it was silent as to its territorial application, as Directive Article 1.2 had not been transposed.[8] This could be interpreted as having no territorial restrictions and thus extends to transfers from outside the EU.[9] Prior to the 2018 amendment, section 3(4) provided that this law shall not apply to maritime vessels.[10] The law then was amended in line with Directive 2015/1794[11] as regards seafarers and also amended the scope of application providing that the Act shall apply to a transfer of a Cypriot sea-going vessel which is part of a transfer, business, establishment or a part of an undertaking or part of an undertaking or establishment within the meaning of the provisions, provided that the transferee is domiciled or the transferred the undertaking, establishment or part of an undertaking or establishment remains within the territorial scope of the Treaty on the Functioning of the European Union (section 3(4)). Also, it reduced the scope of application as the Act does not apply where the object of the transfer consists exclusively of one or more sea-going vessels when the object of the transfer consists exclusively of one or more sea-going vessels (section 3(5)).[12]

The CATU applies to transfers of undertakings, businesses or parts of businesses to another employer as a result of a legal transfer or merger,[13] including public and private enterprises engaged in economic activities, irrespective of whether they are profit-making or not. An administrative reorganization of public authorities or the transfer of administrative functions between public administration authorities shall not be deemed as a 'transfer' within the meaning of this law.[14] The scope of application covers public and private enterprises engaged in economic activities, whether or not they are for profit; however, the administrative reorganization of public administrative authorities or the transfer of administrative functions between public administrative authorities shall not be considered a transfer falling within the scope of this Law as per CATU section 3(3), whether or not that activity is central or ancillary.

§3.03 MEANING AND TYPES OF TRANSFER: CONDITIONS FOR A 'TRANSFER' OF UNDERTAKING

Business practices have developed different ways and types of transfer of undertaking, in part of all business operations for different reasons (ownership, sharing profits,

8. This restricts the scope of the Directive to transfers 'within the territorial scope of the Treaty'.
9. Such case was decided by British courts in *Holis Meal Industries v. GMB* [2008] IRLR 187, involving a transfer of a UK business to an Israeli company operating in Israel.
10. The Greek text reads: '3(4) Ο παρών Νόμος δεν εφαρμόζεται επί θαλάσσιων σκαφών.'
11. Directive (EU) 2015/1794 of the European Parliament and of the Council of 6 October 2015 amending Directive 2008/94/EC of the European Parliament and of the Council, 2009/38/EC and 2002/14/EC and Council Directives 98/59/EC and 2001/23/EC.
12. The Greek text reads: 3(5) Ο παρών Νομός δεν εφαρμόζεται όταν το αντικείμενο της μεταβίβασης αποτελείται αποκλειστικά από ένα ή περισσότερα ποντοπόρα σκάφη.
13. Section 3(1) of the Cypriot Law.
14. Article 3(3) of the Cypriot Law.

costs, convenience, tax, etc.). Cypriot Labour Law has drawn on the trends and approaches of the Luxembourg jurisprudence, which has not been consistent in the case law produced. There has been no public debate on the subject, but a couple of texts on Cypriot Labour Law have been critical of the uncertainty resulting from the different approaches taken by the CJEU, in many ways reflecting the more robust scholarly criticism of jurisprudence of the CJEU.[15]

The uncertainty derives from the different approaches taken by the Luxembourg Court, after the court has changed its approach, putting in doubt the *Spijkers* criteria,[16] which set out the key factors that national courts must take into account when deciding whether the entity has retained its identity. This is an approach that requires that the court takes *the totality of factors into account* and subsequent cases ruled that this means that no single factor can be deemed as decisive.[17] The Luxembourg Court then left matters to be decided by the national courts, but provided no means of determining the relative weight of the various factors. The oscillation between the 'activity' and 'economic activity' eventually led to two contrasting approaches, the 'labour approach' (French *entreprise-activité*) versus the commercial law approach (*entreprise-organization*). With *Süzen,*[18] there has been doubt as to the approach national courts should take.

The Cypriot Supreme Court (SC) regularly cites the Luxembourg jurisprudence on transfers of undertaking when it comes to examining whether the entity can maintain its identity after it has been transferred to the new employer. The wording of the CATU is that of Article 1 of the Directive.[19] The CJEU (paragraph 39)[20] ruled that that, since a group of workers engaged in a joint activity on a permanent basis may constitute an economic entity, such an entity is capable of maintaining its identity after it has been transferred where the new employer does not merely pursue the activity in question but also takes over a major part, in terms of their numbers and skills, of the employees specially assigned by his predecessor to that task. In those circumstances, the new employer takes over a body of assets, enabling him to carry on the activities or certain activities of the transferor undertaking on a regular basis.[21] Thus, the fact that the operating resources necessary for the pursuit of the economic activity were not transferred does not necessarily preclude the entity at issue in the main proceedings from retaining its identity, the taking-over of the majority of the drivers must be

15. For instance, Yiannakourou, S. (2022) ***Κυπριακό Εργατικό Δίκαιο***, 2nd ed. Athens: Nomiki Bibliothiki, p. 286, criticisms of reflect the critical analysis provided by Barnard, C. (2012) *EU Employment Law*, 4th ed., Oxford University Press, pp. 591-597; Emilianides, A. and Ioannou, C. (2024) *Labour Law in Cyprus*, The Netherlands: Wolters Kluwer, do not criticize or point any contradictions in the CJEU judgments; Polyviou (2018) ***Το Κυπριακό Εργατικό Δίκαιο Κύπρου. Θεωρία και Πράξη***. Nicosia: Chryssafinis & Polyviou, also does not criticize the CJEU but points to the importance of a broad interpretation properly embedding and understanding the principles in the national context.
16. Case 24/85 [1986] ECR 1119. *See* Barnard, *supra* n. 15, pp. 591-600.
17. Case C-392/92 *Schmidt* [1994] ECR 1-3111, para. 16; Case C-13/95 *Süzen*.
18. Case C-13/95, *Süzen v. Zehnacker Gebäudereinigung GmbH Krankenhausservice*, Judgment of the Court of 11 March 1997, ECLI:EU:C:1997:141.
19. Articles 1.1(a), 1.1(c), and 1.3.
20. Case C–298/18, 27 February 2020, *Grafe*.
21. The court cited the judgment of *CLECE*, C-463/09, EU:C:2011:24, para. 36.

regarded as a factual circumstance to be taken into account in order to classify the transaction concerned as a transfer of an undertaking. In this respect, it is apparent from the facts at issue in the main proceedings that the members of staff taken on by the new operator are assigned to the same or similar tasks and hold specific qualifications and skills which are essential to the pursuit, without interruption, of the economic activity concerned. Hence, the CJEU (paragraph 41) ruled that the answer to the questions referred is that Article 1(1) of Directive 2001/23 must be interpreted as meaning that, in the context of the takeover by an economic entity of an activity the pursuit of which requires substantial operating resources, under a procedure for the award of a public contract, the fact that that entity does not take over those resources, which are the property of the economic entity previously engaged in that activity, on account of legal, environmental and technical constraints imposed by the contracting authority, cannot necessarily preclude the classification of that takeover of activity as a transfer of an undertaking, since other factual circumstances, such as the taking-over of the majority of the employees and the pursuit, without interruption, of that activity, make it possible to establish that the identity of the economic entity concerned has been retained, this being a matter for the referring court to assess.

The Supreme Court has CJEU jurisprudence when ruling on the leading cases. In *Savvides*,[22] the appellant was an employee of SSP Catering (respondent No. 1) who was managing the shops of Larnaca Airport on the basis of a contract. In 2006, respondent No. 1 informed the appellant that the management of the airport was taken over by an investor and they would no longer manage the airport shops; therefore, his services were being terminated on the ground of redundancy. At the same time, respondent No. 1 also dismissed 22 more employees and informed the competent ministry accordingly. Respondent No. 3, who took over the airport shops from the investor, proposed to hire the appellant, but he declined. The appellant then sued respondent No. 1 at the Labour Tribunal for compensation for unlawful termination of his employment. The respondents 1 and 3 claimed that this was not a case of transfer of an undertaking and therefore the provisions of Directive 2001/23/EC and the transposing legislation, CATU, did not apply. The Redundancy Fund disputed this argument, claiming that this was a transfer of an undertaking and the relevant Directive applied. The trial court rejected the claims against all three respondents. It ruled that there was a transfer of an undertaking from respondent 1 to respondent 3 within the meaning of the Directive, as respondent 3 continued with the operations of respondent 1 and proposed employment to the appellant on the same conditions as previously and with more favourable terms on the basis of a new collective agreement. The trial court concluded that the appellant was not entitled to compensation for redundancy either because he rejected the offer for employment from respondent 3. The appellant appealed against the trial decision, arguing that there was no transfer of undertaking within the meaning of the Directive because respondent 1 transferred to respondent 3 only vacant possession of the shops; and the identity of the undertaking was not retained, so there was no information as to what type of enterprise the investor would set up. The Appeal Court agreed with this

22. Civil Appeal No. 179/2009, 20 September 2012.

argument and allowed the appeal. The Appeal Court pointed out that the trial court appears to have been influenced by the appellant's refusal to accept the employment offer of respondent 3, which was not the operative factor in this case.

In *CTC-ARI Airport Ltd v. Charalambos Andreou, SSP Catering Cyprus Ltd. Redundancy Fund*[23] is factual along the same lines but different in outcome. Along the same facts as *Savvides* (above), respondent No. 2 was managing the Larnaca airport shops until 2006 when the government assigned the management of the airport to an investor, namely Hermes Airport Ltd (Hermes). Hermes informed respondent 2 that its contract for management of the airport shops would be terminated and the management would be taken over by CTC-ARI Airports Ltd (the appellant). Respondent 1, who was at the time employed by respondent 2, was informed that his services would, in turn, be terminated due to redundancy. Respondent 1 applied to the Redundancy Fund for compensation, but his application was rejected on the ground that he had refused to continue working at the airport, as an employee of the appellant. The trial court found that termination of the employment of respondent 1 was unlawful, as the obligations of the transferor of an enterprise are assigned to the transferee to ensure the continuation of the employment of the workers by the new employer. The Appeal Court affirmed the findings of the trial court, clarifying that the obligations of respondent 2 were, by operation of the law, assigned to the appellant and that the obligation towards the dismissed employee amounted to a duty to pay compensation and not the offer of continuation of his employment. The court rejected the argument of the appellant that they had no obligation to compensate respondent 1 because he had rejected their offer of employment. On appeal, the Supreme Court endorsed the finding of the trial court that the law transposing the Directive does not compel an employee to remain in the service of the transferee and that each employee has the freedom to decide whether he will continue working for the new employer or not. However, the Appeal Court found that the trial court had erred in that it assumed that the appellant did not make a firm and specific offer of employment to respondent 1. Through testimony delivered at the hearing, it became clear that respondent 1 had unequivocally informed the appellant that he was not interested in continuing to work at the airport shops because he was tired and wanted to rest, which was the reason why the appellant did not proceed to make a firm offer to him, as it had done with the other employees. The unequivocal position of respondent 1 that he did not want to continue working was also the reason why the appellant proceeded to restructure the enterprise, as a result of which the position previously held by appellant 1 was cancelled. As a consequence of the refusal of respondent 1 to work for the appellant, there was no right to compensation either from the appellant or from the Redundancy Fund. The court differentiated this case from the facts of *Savvides* (above), were the court found that there was an entitlement to compensation from the Redundancy Fund, in that the respondent in this case is seen as unreasonably refusing the offer of another suitable employment, which according to Article 20(a) of Law 24/1967 causes him to lose his

23. *CTC – ARI Airport Ltd N. (1)* ***Χαραλαμπου Ανδρεου****, (2) SSSP Catering Cyprus Ltd, (3)* ***Ταμείο Πλεονάζοντος Προσωπικού****,* Civil Appeal No. 359/2009, 26 November 2014.

right to redundancy compensation. The Appeal Court therefore allowed the appeal and set aside the trial court decision.

The notion of 'transfer' of undertaking does not mercenarily require transfer of ownership, as decided by *Ny Molle Kro*[24] which was also adopted in case of *Hadjinichola*, which applies to both voluntary transfer of business, as well as in involuntary situations in what the court referred to as 'irregular evolution of a contract'.[25]

In the case of *Kontou*,[26] the SC construed that section 5 of CATU expressly provides that the transfer of an undertaking, an establishment or part of an undertaking or establishment does not in itself constitute grounds for dismissal for the transferor or transferee. These are terms used in the Directive. However, the case law of the ECJ, bearing in mind that the above terms may be rendered differently in the language of each Member State, avoids the use of these terms and uses the term 'economic entity', since the purpose of the Directive is to ensure the continuity of the employment relationships existing within an economic entity, irrespective of the change of employer. CATU refers to 'economic entity' and section 3(2) of CATU expressly provides that a transfer within the meaning of the Law 'is considered a transfer of an economic entity that retains its identity, understood as a set of organised resources for the purpose of carrying out an economic activity, regardless of whether this activity is primary or secondary'. The SC approved the decision of the Court of First Instance, citing Luxembourg Court case law,[27] to reject the submission of the appellant that the non-transfer of ownership of the motor vehicles to transferee (Logistic) was decisive for the non-application of the protective provisions of the Directive. The SC reiterated that the motor vehicles were not transferred to the transferee but were provided to the transferee by the appellant to be used exactly as before, i.e., for the transportation/ delivery of envelopes and other items. Citing numerous CJEU rulings,[28] the Supreme Court suggested that the Luxenberg court has established certain crucial elements that national courts must take into account. These include: (a) the transfer or not of tangible assets such as buildings, machinery, equipment, etc., (b) the transfer or not of intangible assets such as trademarks, patents, etc., (c) whether or not the transferee hires a significant number of staff, (d) whether or not there is a transfer of customers, and (e) the degree of similarity between the activities carried out before and after the transfer, etc, the SC stated:

> We reiterate that the weight to be given to each of these in the overall assessment and evaluation will depend on the particular facts of each case, not excluding the nature of the business or establishment and the methods of production and work applied in it.

24. *C-287/86 – Landsorganisationen i Danmark for Tjenerforbundet i Danmark v. Ny Mølle Kro.*
25. ***Σοφοκλή Χατζηνικόλα v. Α. Δαμιανού & Σία και Ορφανίδης Δημόσια Εταιρεία Λτδ***, 590/2011, p. 11. *See* Polyviou, *supra* n. 15, p. 523.
26. ***Σ. Κοντού και Α. Κώστα v. G.A.P. AKIS EXPRESS LTD ΚΑΙ ΤΑΜΕΙΟ ΠΛΕΟΝΑΖΟΝΤΟΣ ΠΡΟΣΩΠΙΚΟΥ,*** (Πολιτική Έφεση Αρ. 51/2015) 18 July 2023.
27. C-340/01 *Alber* [2003] ECR 1-14046, C-287/86 *Ny Moole Kro* [1987] ECR 1-5465, C-209 *Watson Rask* [1992] 1-5755.
28. C-287/86 *Ny Molle Kro* (1987), 5479, C-13/95 *Suzen* (1997), 1275 *Oy LiiKenne* (25.1.2001), C-51/00 *Temco Service Industries* (2002), 969.

The SC distinguished case of *Kontou* as materially different from the facts of *Savvidis*, where it was held that the provisions of the Directive and by extension our harmonizing law did not apply. In the case *Savvidis*:

(a) There was no contractual tie or relationship of any kind between the transferor and transferee. It is recorded in the judgment of the Court of Appeal that this element may not have been decisive, but it provided a serious indication that no transfer had taken place.
(b) The transferee received from the transferor empty premises of shops where the latter had previously employed the employee. It is recorded in the judgment of the Court of Appeal that this element should not have been assessed by the Court of First Instance in isolation in order to satisfy itself that this element 'does not constitute in itself a material element which could alter the identity of the transferred establishment', but should have been assessed by the Court of First Instance together with the other elements before it.
(c) Possession of the shops did not pass to the transferee while a contract was in force under which the transferor held the shops, but It is recorded in the judgment of the Court of Appeal that the contract was terminated not as a result of termination, as was the case in *Suzen*, but in circumstances more favourable to the Applicant, namely the expiry of the agreed period of validity.

In the early case, case *Giannoula Tomazou*[29] which dates from 2003, the Supreme Court ruled that the Labour Court correctly rejected the applications of the appellants[30] on the ground that, *inter alia*, that the new company was established to ensure the continuity of the supply of services from the appellants given that none of them had registered as unemployed during the substantive time and the appellants had been paid for the full amount of their monthly pay for without any break. The SC also approved the Labour Court's ruling that the new company took over the reputation, the clientele, the volume of work and the whole of the equipment of the employer/transferee company.[31]

Another early case, *Kyprianides*,[32] the Labour Disputes Court decided on unlawful termination of employment of the Managing Director of a company involved in sweet production and confectioneries. The employer dismissed him on the ground of redundancy, 'which resulted from the reduction of activities of the respondents following the sale of the confectionary and the sweet producing factory ... and the termination of the operation of the restaurant "XO"'. A crucial issue in the case

29. Civil appeal case No. 11418, 16 July, 2003, 1 A.A.D. 1078.
30. Under para. 7, Part II of the Second Table of law on Termination of Employment 24/67.
31. The relevant text of the court decision (in Greek) reads as follows: 'Το δικαστήριο ορθά θεώρησε ότι περαιτέρω, η νέα εταιρεία είχε αναλάβει τη φήμη, την πελατεία, τον κύκλο εργασιών και όλο τον εξοπλισμό της εργοδότριας εταιρείας'.
32. *Theodoros Kyprianides v. R. Rousounides Enterprises Ltd*, Case No. 4/05, issued 31 January 2006 by the President of the court, K.D. Kamenos. This is a first instance case, therefore not binding on other judges.

involved whether, under the circumstances described, there were real conditions of redundancy during the essential time of termination of employment. The court decided that it was apparent from the facts that the redundancy occurred due to the reduction of activities of the respondent company *after* the sale of the confectionery and the sale of the restaurant. The judge distinguished between the legal situation that resulted from the changing of the ownership of the confectionary and the laboratory, which he referred to as 'transfer' for the purposes of the Cypriot Law on transfers and the termination of operations of the restaurant, which ceased to operate altogether. The judgment contains some confusing *obiter* remarks as to the obligations of employees to transfer to the new company. The interpretation of the provision contained in Article 4(1) of the Cypriot Law that purports that 'the transferor's rights and obligations arising from a contract of employment or from an employment relationship existing on the date of a transfer shall, by reason of such transfer, be transferred to the transferee', as set out in the verbatim reproduction of the wording of the Directive, does not create an obligatory regime in 'transferring employees with the transfer of the company'. Although this remark may appear to be stating the obvious, it fails to engage with the complex issues as regards the right of employees who do not wish to continue under the new ownership, management, or structure, even if the terms and conditions of employment are unchanged. Only slave labour is literally and absolutely of 'compulsory nature'; thus, employees may naturally resign, if they wish to terminate their contract of employment. The question is whose fault. There is therefore an element of 'compulsion' in the sense that employees are *not* entitled to claim redundancy, if they choose not to work for the new ownership, management or structure, in cases where their employment relationship and the terms of employment remain the same. Should there be a change of the terms of employment at the expense of the employee resulting in termination of the contract of employment, then the fault will lie with employer. The court did not refer to any ECJ court cases, such as *Katsikas,*[33] *Merckx, Neuhuys*[34] and other cases. In this case, the central issue was the dismissal of the Managing Director. The court considered the provision of the Cypriot Law on the reason for dismissal, which expressly states that 'the transfer of the undertaking, business or part of the undertaking or business shall not in itself constitute grounds for dismissal by the transferor or the transferee'. However, it is further stated that the law 'shall not stand in the way of dismissals that may take place for economic, technical or organisational reasons entailing changes in the workforce'. Such changes are defined by section 18 of the Termination of Employment Laws of 1967-2001 (see above). The court decided that, in the particular case, the alleged ceasing of certain departments was the result of the sale, hence the dismissal is caused by the actual transfer contrary to Article 5(1) of the Cypriot Law. Also, the two confectionaries and the machinery of the factory were actually transferred as 'economic entities' to another company. Moreover, even if these departments were cancelled in accordance with the law, the position of the Managing Director could have not been redundant as such, given that the company is still be

33. Joined cases C-132/91, C-138/91 & C-139/91 [1992] ECR I-6577.
34. [1996] ECR I-1253.

operating. The court affirmed the principle that mere economic problems of the company will not suffice to create an 'automatic' reason for dismissal; only the difficulty or inability in locating funders or loans shall satisfy as reasons for redundancy. The court also ruled on the violation of section 8.1 of CATU, which transposes Article 7.1 of the Directive, which provides that the transferor and transferee shall be required to inform the representatives of their respective employees affected by the transfer the date or proposed date of the transfer, the reasons for the transfer, the legal, economic and social implications of the transfer for the employees and any measures envisaged in relation to the employees.

§3.04 DEBATES AND COMMENTS ON EU AND CYPRIOT LAW ON TU

Over the last quarter of century that the CATU has operated, there has been little public debate on the subject – neither the Labour Advisory Committee, nor the Parliamentary Committee on Labour has discussed the operation of safeguarding the rights of workers in transfer of undertakings situations. The few commentaries on EU and Cypriot case law on the subject are from the legal texts on Labour law, but these have not provided any uniform position or criticism. The three texts that refer to EU and Cypriot jurisprudence of the subject adopt very different approaches. Emilianides and Ioannou (2024) describe with the aim of briefly summarizing ECJ/CJEU and SC decisions without commenting or pointing to inconsistencies or problems in the implementation of the Directive and CATU. Yiannakourou (2022, 280-291)[35] offers a critique of the Luxembourg case law, suggesting that the jurisprudence creates legal uncertainty and does not offer sufficient guidance to national courts. Citing the changes in the trends CJEU decision in *Suzen*, *Piscarreta Picardo*[36] and *CLECE,*[37] she speaks of backtracking and a case-to-case approach that is deficient in a holistic approach that lays down the conceptual elements of what constitutes a 'transfer'.

The text by Polyviou[38] (2018, 517) takes a rather different approach, even though he does not embark on direct criticism of EU case law. He instead considers that the EUCJ principles jurisprudence must be read as a lying out broad principles to be interpreted in context, suggesting that in Cyprus, this is how EU law is understood and applied. He favours a kind of *broad-reading of principles approach,* suggesting three basic principles to understand the protection of the rights of employees in cases involving transfer of undertakings. First, that whole point of the Directive is to safeguard the rights of workers as a matter of public and social policy of the EU, in the way the British court decided in the case of *Lister.*[39] Second, the approach must be one of broad interpretation suggesting that the court must take not a literal approach but a *purposive interpretive approach* in construing legislation, including EU law. Third, all the basic terms used by the EU Directive acquire their meaning within national law, not

35. Yiannakourou's text is EU-centred. Her legal training in Greece, in the continental legal tradition.
36. C-416/16 *Luís Manuel Piscarreta Ricardo v. Portimão Urbis EM SA and Others.*
37. Case C-463/09, *CLECE SA v. María Socorro Martín Valor and Ayuntamiento de Cobisa.*
38. A veteran legal practitioner, trained in the Btitish common law tradition.
39. *Lister v. Forth Dry Dock & Engineering Co Ltd* [1988] UKHL 10.

within some unified Labour Law or contract law at the EU level. As such, EU law must co-exist with national law, which, if in conflict, then EU Law prevails. Quoting Advocate General at the time in *Wendelboe,*[40] Polyviou (2018, 519) aptly suggests that the correct approach is that EU acquis principles demand that national law must be guided by the necessity of effective protection of the employees during the transfer of undertakings, 'providing for a remedy which is effective and not merely symbolic.'

It is noteworthy that in transfer of undertakings case law, the trend has been for Cypriot courts to safeguard the rights of employees, whether they found that a transfer has or has not taken place.

§3.05 SAFEGUARDING EMPLOYEES' RIGHTS IN TRANSFER CASES

Employees are protected from dismissal in cases of transfer of undertakings. The principal rights and obligations to be transferred onto the transferee, as per Article 3 of the Directive, are transposed via section 4 of the CATU. Section 4(1) of CATU copies verbatim the text of the first paragraph of Directive Article 3.1. If the employee refuses to transfer,[41] the general employment law and common law rules apply as regards 'whether there has been a substantive change in the employees' working conditions'. British court cases are in any case persuasive authority, in the absence of Cypriot case law to the extent the British court cases interpret common law.

The definitions contained in Article 2.1 of the Directive are inserted verbatim into Article 2 of the Cypriot Law. As for the term 'employee',[42] this is described in Cypriot Law as a person working for another person either under a contract of employment or apprenticeship or under such circumstances that the existence of an employment relationship may be inferred. 'Employee' representatives are defined in Article 2 of the Cypriot Law as 'representatives of employees provided for in legislation or by practice'. This in practice means the recognized trade unions. The Cypriot Law makes no mention of the excluded limitations set out in Article 2.2 of the Directive. It may therefore be inferred that the Cypriot Law does not exclude from its scope any of the employment contracts or the employment relationships described in Directive Article 2.2.

Article 4(1) of CATU also states that transferor and transferee may agree to remain jointly and severally liable for obligations arising before the transfer, following again the text of the Directive as this appears in the second paragraph of Directive Article 3.1. In other words, the Cypriot Law does not render the transferee and the transferor jointly and severally liable; it merely provides that it is not unlawful for them to agree to be jointly and severally liable, which is however an optional arrangement for them.

Directive Article 3.2 has not been transposed into national legislation in Cyprus. In effect, there are no measures in place to ensure that the transferor notified the

40. Sir Gordon Slynn, (opinion, ECLI:EU:C:1984:337) in case *C-19/83 – Wendelboe v. L.J. Music* (judgment ECLI:EU:C:1985:54).
41. As was the situation with the UK case of *Katsikas* joined cases C-132/91, C-138/91 and C-139/91.
42. In this text, the terms 'employee' and 'worker' are used interchangeably.

transferee of all rights and obligations transferred at the time of transfer of an undertaking. Practice in Cyprus, however, commands detailed accounting and administrative procedures in place whenever there is a transfer of an undertaking, particularly when there are large corporations involved, and it is often the case that a full declaration of assets and liabilities towards third parties (which in this case would include employees) is required of the transferor. It is more likely than not that the contract between transferor and transferee *will* provide that the transferor remains liable for debts and other liabilities it has not declared to the transferee, although this does not affect employees who are regarded by the law of contract as third parties to the legal relationship between transferee and transferor.

Section 4(2) of the CATU provides, in exactly the same terms as Directive Article 3.3, that the transferee must observe the terms of the collective agreement until its termination or expiration with a minimum term of one year. In case the transferee is bound by another collective agreement, then the provisions that are more beneficial to the employees apply. In addition, the transferee is required to observe the terms of the collective agreement applicable to the transferor in accordance not only with the collective agreement itself but also with practice. The minimum term of one year presumably starts from running date of the transfer and is defined as 'a minimum period of retaining the terms of employment of one year'. It is not explicitly stated in the law, but on the basis of general labour law principles, we may perhaps presume that should there be a new collective agreement containing rights more beneficial to the employees that comes into force *before* the expiry of the minimum one-year period, then the new collective agreement applies.

As a matter of practice, there have been various transfers of undertakings which were regulated without the cases ending in court. Prior to transposition the merger of the companies Pepsi with 7up in which it was decided by an agreement of the trade unions with the employers of the transferor and the transferee that a number of employees would be made redundant and were to be given additional damages, while others, who would continue their employment under the transferee would continue under the same terms of employment as in the collective agreement. It was also agreed, following a letter by the Redundancy Fund for the purposes of redundancy, that there would be 'continuous employment' for the employees transferred. Due to the strong tripartite tradition in Cyprus, whenever there was a strong and large undertaking, the above practice was followed (i.e., collective bargaining that by and large safeguarded the implementation of transfer of the rights). However, in smaller businesses, particularly in industries where there are no strong trade unions, this was not the practice.[43] As regards the banking sector, prior to the transposition of the Directive, there were three cases of transfers which were resolved amicably with the full transfer of the rights of all employees. There has been no case since the law that transposes the Directive in this sector.[44] Following the enactment of the law, soon after it came into effect, the large soft drink Limassol-based producer KEAN decided to transfer its distribution

43. Interviews with trade unionists from SEGDAMELIN PEO and SEK.
44. This involved the take over of Charter Bank by Bank of Cyprus in 1981, Gredleys by Laiki Bank in 1982 and Barcleys by Elliniki Bank in 1996.

branch in Nicosia to beer producer Carlsberg. KEAN issued letters of redundancy to several employees, such as cleaners, proposing transfer to the new management, but with conditions of employment adverse for the workers. The case went to court, but an out-of-court settlement was reached. According to trade unionists, the settlement was evidence of acceptance of the fact that the employees were adversely affected by the transfer. In any case, the issue was resolved amicably.[45] From the employers' point of view, a minimum of one year's period (or longer if the collective agreement is valid for a longer period) is adequate, although in practice, the full harmonization of benefits may take many years.[46] The Ministry of Labour similarly sees no issue on the subject.[47] Trade unionists have expressed the concern that in practice the new employer may merely wait for one year before adopting a harsher regime and there is little the employees can do,[48] other than take action. The provision that requires the employer-transferee to observe collective agreements, for a minimum term of one year under Article 4(3)(a) of the Cypriot Law, is considered by trade unions to be inadequate.

Article 4(3)(a) of the Cypriot Law, following the wording of Directive Article 3.4(a), excludes from the scope of Article 4(1)[49] and 4(2)[50] the rights of employees to benefits connected with old age or disability or survivor's benefits under supplementary company or intercompany pension schemes which are outside the state social security system. In effect, this category of employees' rights is not to be transferred from transferor to transferee and the latter is under no obligation to secure these rights even if they are safeguarded by the collective agreement, which the transferee is otherwise obliged to observe.

According to CATU 4(3)(b), which purports to transpose Directive Article 3.4.(b), the rights of the employees who had, by the time of the transfer, left the business of the transferor will maintain the rights, acquired or to be acquired, for benefits connected with old age or disability or survivor's benefits under supplementary company or intercompany pension schemes. Other than the aforesaid provision, no measures are foreseen by the CATU in order to protect the interests of this group of employees and no enforcement mechanism is provided.[51] No secondary legislation in the form of regulations has been enacted to establish an effective enforcement mechanism.[52]

45. Trade unionists from PEO and SEK were advised by their lawyers at the time that there was a gap in the Cyprus legislation which would have prevented them from obtaining court judgment in their favour. However, no details were given. In the case of *Roussounides*, which did go to court, no such gap was located.
46. Interview with Employers and Industrialists Federation OEB.
47. Interview with Industrial Relations Unit, Ministry of Labour and Social Insurance.
48. Interview with tradeunioist, SEK.
49. Purporting to transpose Directive Article 3.1.
50. Purporting to transpose Directive Article 3.3.
51. The Equal Treatment in Employment and Occupation Law of 2004 No. 58 (1)/2004. There may be an issue of discrimination on the ground of age that ought to be considered, as the transposition of Directive 78/2000 came into effect with laws 42(I)/2004 and 58(I)/2004. *See* Demetriou, C. (2023) *Country Report Non-discrimination Transposition and Implementation at National Level of Council Directives 2000/43 and 2000/78*, Cyprus, Reporting Period 1 January 2022-1 January 2023, Directorate-General for Justice and Consumers, https://www.equalitylaw.eu/downloads/5973-cyprus-country-report-non-discrimination-2023 (accessed 22 August 2025).
52. This was a possilbility anticipated after accession to the EU (Trimikliniotis, N. (2006) Directive 2001/23/EC on the Approximation of Laws of the Member States Relating to the Safeguarding of

§3.06 PROHIBITION OF DISMISSAL SOLELY ON THE GROUND TRANSFER

Section 5(1) CATU replicates Article 4.1 of the Directive to the effect that dismissals made because of a transfer are unlawful, unless they take place as a result of economic, technical or organizational reasons which result in changes in the workforce. The CJEU[53] (paragraph 36) noted that under Article 4(1) of that Directive, while the transfer of an undertaking or part of an undertaking cannot constitute in itself a ground for dismissal for the transferor or the transferee, other than in the situations mentioned in Article 4(1) of that Directive, that provision does not however preclude the possibility of dismissals occurring for economic, technical or organizational reasons entailing changes in the workforce. Further, Article 4(2) states that if the contract of employment is terminated because the transfer involves a substantial change in working conditions to the detriment of the employee, the employer is to be regarded as having been responsible for termination. The CJEU noted that if the division of the contract of employment proves to be impossible or entails a deterioration in the working conditions and rights of the worker guaranteed by Directive 2001/23, that contract may be terminated, and the termination must be regarded, under Article 4(2) of Directive 2001/23, as the responsibility of the transferee(s), even when that termination has been initiated by the worker. Hence, the CJEU (paragraph 38) ruled that where a transfer of undertaking involves a number of transferees, Article 3(1) of Directive 2001/23 must be interpreted as meaning that the rights and obligations arising from a contract of employment are transferred to each of the transferees, in proportion to the tasks performed by the worker concerned, provided that the division of the contract of employment as a result of the transfer is possible and neither causes a worsening of working conditions nor adversely affects the safeguarding of the rights of workers guaranteed by that Directive, which it is for the referring court to determine. If such a division were impossible to carry out or would adversely affect the rights of that worker, the transferee(s) would be regarded as being responsible for any consequent termination of the employment relationship, under Article 4 of that Directive, even if that termination were to be initiated by the worker.

CATU section 2 defines 'economic, technical or organisational reasons' as those specified in Article 18(c) of the Termination of Employment Laws of 1967-2001, which lists[54] the following:

(i) modernization, mechanization or any other change in the methods of production or organization which reduces the number of necessary employees;

Employees' Rights in the Event of Transfers of Undertakings, Businesses or Parts of Businesses, Report on Cyprus, Report of the EU Commission, Human European Consultancy in partnership with Middlesex University Business School), but was never realized.

53. In Case C-344/18, 26 March 2020, *ISS Facility Services NV*.

54. The Termination of Employment Act 1967-2001 set out these and other factors as reasons giving rise to compensation on the ground of redundancy.

(ii) change in the products or in the methods of production or in the necessary specializations of the employees;
(iii) abolition of departments;
(iv) difficulties in the placement of products in the market or credit difficulties;
(v) shortage of orders or of raw materials;
(vi) rarity of means of production;
(vii) Reduction in the volume of the work or of the undertaking.[55]

There are *no exceptions* in the CATU limiting the scope of application of the protection against dismissal. According to the law, this protection is afforded to *all* employees without exception, as the RoC did not take the option of excluding certain specific categories of employees in respect of protection against dismissal, as allowed by Article 4.1 of the Directive. Therefore, the general provisions of Cypriot employment apply, i.e., the law on Termination of Employment applies, which affords protection to those who have worked of the minimum continuous employment with a minimum of 26 weeks until age of retirement. Those who work less than 26 weeks are not protected. According to CATU section 5(2) (Directive Article 4.2), a transfer resulting in substantial changes in the terms of employment to the detriment of the employee will render the employer responsible for termination and liable to pay compensation to employee.[56]

When dismissals are deemed to be unlawful, then the provisions of law on unfair dismissal apply as with all other unlawful terminations of employment. If the transfer results in substantial changes in the terms of employment to the detriment of the employee, the employer shall be considered responsible for terminating the employment contract or the employment relationship.[57] The general provisions relating to termination of employment[58] require that the employee must have twenty-six weeks of 'continuous employment' to be entitled to compensation for unfair dismissal. Employees having less than 26 weeks' employment are not protected at all against dismissal.[59]

§3.07 PROTECTION FROM DISMISSAL

The provision in the first paragraph of Directive Article 4.1 is used verbatim in CATU section 5(1) to the effect that dismissals made as a result of a transfer are unlawful unless they take place as a result of economic, technical or organizational reasons which result in changes in the workforce. To the extent that dismissals are deemed to be unlawful, the provisions of law on termination of employment apply. If the transfer

55. This covers situation where the business is reduced, or if the undertaking ceases to offer certain service or product or one of its departmentis closed.
56. *Theodoros Kyprianides v. R. Rousounides Enterprises Ltd*, Case No. 4/05.
57. CATU section 5(2) transposing Directive Article 4.2.
58. Section 3(1) of the Termination of Employment Act.
59. The only provisions in Cypriot Law for protection of employees working less than 26 weeks from dismissal are the laws transposing the anti-discrimination directives 2000/43/EC and 2000/78/EC, the Gender Equality Directives and the laws on protection of maternity, which prohibit dismissing the employee from dismissal from the moment the employee announces to the employer that she is pregnant.

results in substantial changes in the terms of employment to the detriment of the employee, the employer shall be considered responsible for terminating the employment contract or the employment relationship.[60] The general provisions relating to unfair dismissal as regulated by section 3(1) of the Termination of Employment Act require that the employee must have 26 weeks of 'continuous employment' in order to be entitled to compensation for unfair dismissal. The only provisions in Cypriot Law for protection of employees working less than 26 weeks from dismissal are the laws transposing the anti-discrimination directives 2000/43/EC and 2000/78/EC, the Gender Equality Directives and the laws on protection of maternity, which prohibit dismissing the employee from dismissal from the moment the employee announces to the employer that she is pregnant.

According to the employers' association, the interpretation of the terms 'economic, technical or organisational reasons' was considered to be 'too ambiguous' and thus warranted an amendment of the Termination of Employment Act.[61] After an agreement of the tripartite Labour Advisory Body, the above-mentioned amendment was introduced for redundancy situations.

§3.08 OBLIGATION TO INFORM AND CONSULT EMPLOYEES' REPRESENTATIVES

Purporting to transpose paragraph 1 of Directive Article 7.1, CATU requires both the transferee and the transferor to inform the representatives of the employees: the date or the proposed date of the transfer; the reasons for the transfer; the legal, economic and social consequences for the employees; and the measures to be taken in relation to the employees.[62] However, CATU allows the option to the transferee and the transferor to inform the employees themselves, instead of the representatives of the employees, which is not in conformity with the directive. The transferor must communicate the aforesaid information to the employees or their representatives 'promptly' before the transfer takes place.[63] Moreover, the transferee must communicate the aforesaid information to his employees or their representatives also 'promptly' and before his employees' working conditions are affected directly by the transfer.[64]

CATU 8(3) (verbatim copy of Directive Article 7.2) creates an obligation for both the transferor and the transferee to consult the employees with the intent to reach a consensus, before taking any measures changing their working regime. There is a difference in the wording between the Directive and CATU in that the Cyprus Law, as in the previous sections, creates an obligation to inform or consult either the employees' representatives or the employees themselves, while the Directive requires interaction with only the representatives. This is not in conformity with the directive. The first paragraph of Directive Article 7.3 was not transposed into Cypriot Law.

60. CATU section 5(2), transposing Directive Article 4.2.
61. Interview with OEB officer.
62. Section 8(1)(a) CATU.
63. Section 8(1)(b) CATU, transposing para. 2 of Directive Article 7.1.
64. Section 8(1)(c) CATU, transposing para. 3 of Directive Article 7.1.

The is a general Arbitration Law in Cyprus setting up the procedures to be followed when the parties involved have agreed to submit to arbitration or make such agreement subsequently when the dispute arises. However, there is no procedure entitling representatives of employees to appear in arbitration proceedings on their behalf. The vast majority of industrial disputes are regulated on the basis of a non-binding mediation procedure provided for by the 'Industrial relations Code', which is a trilateral agreement as to the procedures in cases of industrial relations disputes and the renegotiation of collective agreements.[65]

The second and third paragraphs of Directive Article 7.3 are transposed into section 8(4) CATU, which provides that information and consultation must cover at least the measures affecting the employees and must take place 'promptly before the transfer occurs. It is noted that the Cypriot Law uses the term "transfer" rather than "change of business"' which is used in the Directive, presumably because the Directive uses that term in reference to the provisions of the first paragraph of Article 7.3, which was not transposed into the Cypriot Law.

As for the rules on controlling employers per Article 7 of the Directive, section 8(1)(d) of CATU carries verbatim the provisions of the first paragraph of Directive Article 7.4, while Article 8(2) of CATU carries verbatim the provisions of the second paragraph of Directive Article 7.4.

Provisions are made in the situation where there are no employee representatives (Article 7.6 Directive). Article 8(5) of the Cypriot Law provides that where there are no representatives of the employees for reasons outside their power, then the information set out in section 8(1) of CATU (Directive Article 7), being the date or proposed date of the transfer, the reason, the legal, economic and social implications of the transfer for the employees and the measures envisaged, must be communicated to the employees 'promptly'. The right (or duty) of the employer to inform the employees directly, whether there are representatives appointed or not, was already provided for in previous sections, in contrast to the Directive, which provides for communication to the representatives when these are available. It is noted that the Cypriot Law uses the term 'promptly' to describe the timing of the communication, whilst the Directive uses the term 'in advance'.

None of these matters have arisen in practice. Social partners have not provided any comments on the subject.

§3.09 LIQUIDATION AND BANKRUPTCY

Section 6 of CATU carried verbatim the text of Directive Article 5.1, with only a minor difference in the description of the competent public authority supervising the liquidation.[66] In effect, this provision seeks to exclude the operation of sections 4 and 5

65. *See* Slocum, J.H (1972) *The Development of Labor Relations in Cyprus*, Nicosia: Government Printing Office, Republic of Cyprus, Sparsis, M. (1998) *Tripartism & Industrial Relations, The Cypriot Experience*, Nicosia, Trimikliniotis, *supra* n. 2.
66. The Cypriot Law uses the term 'the competent body in accordance with the law' to define the competent authority supervising the liquidation.

CATU (transposing Directive Articles 3 and 4, respectively) for cases where the transferor is subject to liquidation proceedings. CATU section 6 stipulates that the provisions relating to the safeguarding of the employees' rights (Directive Article 3; CATU section 4) and to dismissals of employees as a result of transfers (Directive Article 4; CATU section 5) shall not apply to transfers where the transferor is subject to bankruptcy or insolvency proceedings, or any other analogous insolvency proceedings instituted with a view to liquidate the transferor's assets and which is carried out under the supervision of the competent authority appointed by the law.[67] It is not possible to assess at this stage what the answer will be in insolvency proceedings that would lead to a rescue of part of the undertaking.

Directive Article 5.2 has not been transposed into the Cypriot Law. CATU is silent on the issue of transfer of debts and on the possibility of an agreement between employees, transferees and transferors to change the terms of employment.

CATU section 9(1) provides that any employer who deliberately resorts to insolvency proceedings in order to deprive employees of their rights under the Cypriot Law is guilty of an offence and liable to a penalty not exceeding CYP 1,000 (approximate Euro equivalent: 1,724). This amount is clearly inadequate as a deterrent. Moreover, in practice, proving that the employer acted deliberately in a way to deprive employees of their rights is extremely hard to meet. At the same time, the employee becomes entitled to compensation under, *inter alia*, the Termination of Employment Act. Another law[68] provides for the compensation of employees of insolvent employers from a special fund, set up and managed by the state social insurance office.

From the perspective of the Ministry of Labour, the view was that no abuse was known to have taken place and such a case had never been dealt with.

§3.10 EMPLOYEE REPRESENTATIVES

CATU section 7(1)(a) provides that where the undertaking preserves its autonomy, the status, representation, and exercise of the function of the employees' representatives shall be preserved on the same terms and shall be subject to the same conditions applicable before the transfer, in accordance with the applicable legal, regulatory, administrative provisions or collective agreements or practice. The law does not define 'Employee representatives' as 'representatives of employees provided for in legislation or by practice', which in practice means the recognized trade unions. The above provision however does not apply where the preconditions for a fresh appointment of representatives (or for the reappointment of the representation) are in place, in accordance with the applicable legal, regulatory, administrative provisions or

67. This is the Social Insurance fund according to the Regulating the Protection of the Rights of Employees in the event of the Employer's Insolvency Act No. 25(I)2001. This the purpose of harmonizing Cypriot legislation with Directive 80/987/EEC.
68. Law 25(I)2001. However, this is a measure intended to protect the employees' rights; it does not serve the purpose of dissuading potential employers from misusing the insolvency proceedings.

collective agreements or practice, or following an agreement with the representatives of the employees.[69]

If the undertaking does not preserve its autonomy, the transferor and the transferee must take measures to ensure that the employees who were represented before the transfer will continue to be represented during the period necessary for the reconstitution or reappointment of the representation of employees in accordance with the law or the practice.[70] In effect, the law transfers the obligation of the Member State to take measures to safeguard the rights of the employees onto the transferor and the transferor and does not specify what these measures will be, nor does it introduce an enforcement mechanism. It is questionable whether the 'measure' of obliging the employer to take measures to safeguard the rights of employees in such a general manner is in conformity with the Directive.

ACTU section 7(2) (verbatim the wording of Directive Article 6.2) secures the protection of the representatives whose term has expired as a result of the transfer, adding an extra proviso to preserve the protection afforded to them by collective agreements.

The provisions of paragraph 3 of Directive Article 6.1 have not been transposed into the Cypriot Law. The issue is only of academic value at present, as Cyprus has no work councils.

§3.11 SANCTIONS

The Labour Disputes Court is appointed as the competent court to resolve civil law disputes arising out of the implementation of the Cypriot Law.[71] The sanctions provided are the following:-

- An employer who deliberately resorts to insolvency procedures for the purpose of depriving the employees of their rights is subject to a penalty not exceeding CYP 1,000 (approximate Euro equivalent: 1,724) without prejudice to the employees' right to compensation.
- An employer in breach of his obligations regarding information and consultation, as these are set out in CATU section 8 of (Article 7 of the Directive), is subject to a penalty not exceeding CYP 500 (approximate Euro equivalent: 862)[72]
- Where, as a result of a transfer, an employment relationship is terminated either by the transferor or the transferee and such dismissal is not due to economic, technical or organizational reasons which presuppose changes on the level of employment, the dismissal is illegal and the employee is entitled to compensation calculated in accordance with his/her years of service and

69. CATU, section 7(1)(b).
70. CATU, section7(1)(c).
71. CATU 8A.
72. CATU 9(2).

conditions of work applicable at the business of the transferor, applying in all other respects the provisions of the Termination of Employment Act.

The Termination of Employment Act provides a comprehensive formula to determine whether any particular dismissal is lawful. These laws also provide guidelines to be taken into consideration when calculating the compensation payable in the event that the dismissal is deemed unlawful. The final determination of the damages due to the wrongfully dismissed employee is largely left to the Court's discretion. Section 3(1) of this law secures the right of an employee to compensation, provided that had been employed for a continuous period of at least 26 weeks by the same employer prior to dismissal. Section 5 of the same law lists the circumstances under which a dismissal does not give rise to the right to compensation, which include failure by the employee to perform his/her work in a reasonably satisfactory manner; redundancy, force majeure, expiration of fixed term contract, attaining of retirement age, serious misconduct, commission of a criminal offence, etc.

The Cypriot Law further provides that a dismissal made due to the transfer is still considered to be a dismissal due to the transfer (and is thus unlawful) even if it takes place prior to the transfer.[73]

The sanctions provided in CATU are probably not dissuasive or effective enough. The amounts of CYP 1,000 and CYP 500 provided by the law as damages to be paid in case the employer resorts to insolvency procedures and in case the employer is in breach of his obligation for information and consultation, respectively, are clearly too small to have any dissuasive effect. The only possibility for any employer to be called to pay substantial amounts of money for violating this law is where a highly paid employee, working for the same employer for several years, is dismissed as a result of the transfer, under circumstances that do not justify payment from the redundancy fund. This is a very specific scenario and is not a frequent occurrence. Trade unionists interviewed for the purposes of this report stated that violations of the law are very common in small enterprises and in sectors of the economy which are not trade union strongholds. One may be led to the conclusion that the impact of the law may be better assessed by the tools it has offered to the trade unionists rather than by the implementation of the law on its own right and by the fear of sanctions.

§3.12 LITIGATION

As for sanctions, CATU section 9(2) stipulates that employers who violate the provisions for information and consultation shall be guilty of an offence and subject to a fine of up to 500 Cyprus pounds. The transferor must give such information to the representatives of his employees in good time, before the transfer is carried out. In this context, the court decided that there was no case of redundancy; the dismissal was unfair and the company was obliged to pay damages under Article 3(1) of the Termination of Employment Law.

73. CATU 10(2).

§3.13 CONCLUSIONS: CRITICAL REMARKS ON THE LEGAL FRAMEWORK ON PROTECTING WORKER RIGHTS IN TRANSFERS OF UNDERTAKING

The Directive 2001/23 was conceived and passed before the Lisbon Treaty, in a different economic and business era from the current crisis-ridden world of today, since the financial crisis, the pandemic, the inflation-plagued and refugee-and-war-ridden realities of the world before us. It is difficult to give a simple answer to the question of whether European legislation and the national laws that apply it are, and will be in the future, sufficient in managing the complex and ever-changing corporate and entrepreneurial movements that will reposition the economy in the Union in the coming years.

Like other harmonization legislation, the harmonizing legislation, CATU, went through Parliament, without a proper scrutiny and without embarking on a proper critical analysis to find the most suitable solutions that are best-suited for the Cypriot context. Nonetheless, a critical analysis of the Cypriot legislation, the jurisprudence and implementation in the disputes over the last quarter of century demonstrates that the EU framework, as implemented and understood in Cyprus, has overall been *positive*. The weakness and contradictions in the case law of the Court of Luxembourg, at least so far, have had minimum effects, in that the Cypriot courts have taken a broader reading of the purpose of the directive, which is to protect the rights of workers in transfer situations. The Cypriot Law has transposed the Directive in a manner that contains the most important provisions and the primary objectives of the Directive have largely been achieved. However, there are some issues that remain unclear as to the interpretation and implementation. Despite a long tradition of tripartism with the regular and generally good functioning of the Labour Advisory Council, there has been minimal legislative intervention to address safeguarding of the rights of employees in cases of transfer of undertakings. Overall, employers' representatives and the Ministry of Labour see few, if any, undesired effects in the implementation of the Directive; neither have there been, they claim, any contractual arrangements developed for the purpose of avoiding the Directive. On the contrary, they claim that the Directive had a positive effect in maintaining the rights of workers. Only three minor amendments to the basic law have been made and these did not touch upon any of the controversial issues pertaining to such matters.

There is now a 25-year long experience of the practice of the framework, but there has been little public debate as occasional in the popular media on the subject by trade unionists in the context of negotiations or disagreements over particular disputes at the time of controversial transfers. The only critical commentary, albeit limited, as the approach taken is rather descriptive, rather than analytically critical, comes from legal commentary that has appeared in a couple of Labour Law texts.

There are certain points of the law, which are of questionable conformity with the Directive or which render its practical implementation difficult, either because no enforcement mechanism is provided, or because the test imposed is difficult to meet. Section 9.1 of the CATU renders the employer guilty of an offence *only* if it can be proved that the reason he resorted to insolvency was *to deprive the employees of their rights*. In this case, even if this stringent test is met, the penalty provided is inadequate as a deterrent (CYP 1,000 = EUR 1,724). Another issue is found in section 7(1)(a) of CATU (Article 6 of the Directive), where the measure taken by the Cypriot authorities is to oblige employers to take measures, without setting up an enforcement mechanism or specifying what such 'measures' shall be. Another contentious point is section 8.1 and 8.3 of CATU (Directive Article 7.1 and 7.2), although the Directive requires that the employers inform and consult the employee's representatives, the Cypriot Law allows the employers the alternative to discharge this obligation by merely informing and consulting the employees themselves.

Employers and the Ministry of Labour claim that the Directive had a positive effect in safeguarding the rights of workers. However, trade unions stress that the Directive has strengthened the rights of workers in certain cases, but there are ambiguities that prevent the full implementation of the transfer of employees' rights. In some transfer occasions, however, trade unionists claim, workers were forced to accept inferior employment terms in an effort to safeguard their employment.[74] Cases of misuse of employment status to avoid the responsibilities imposed by the law have been pointed out by trade unions.

There is a question mark as to whether employees who are third country nationals are properly covered by the transfer laws, as the work permit for this group of workers is issued to the particular employer by the Labour Office. It is possible that third country migrant workers may be excepted from enjoying such rights, which is not acceptable under the directive. No case has gone to court to know for certain.

Also, Article 1.2 of the Directive does not appear in CATU which defines the territorial confines of the application of the Directive as within the territorial scope of the Treaty. We may thus presume that the Cypriot Law extends beyond the confines of the EU.

In spite of the protection afforded to them by the law: a new management arrangement, ownership, codes of practice and generally the culture/ form of operation under a new employer, even if there is a continued going concern and despite what the letter of the law says, in practice are factors that exert a great deal of pressure on workers and the general employment relations are necessarily affected.[75] Unless there are further safeguards, closer monitoring well after the period of the transfer and a system of dealing swiftly and effectively with any practices of abuse, beyond the slow and reactive court system the measures adopted as a result of transposition of the Directive will be inadequate. Moreover, there ought to be measures encouraging and supporting trade unions, interested parties and other observatories to closely monitor and interfere using their strength and influence. Finally, there is a need to support and encourage workers and trade unions, where it is appropriate, to take complaints to court: it seems unlikely that cases of abuse or violation of the law are generally 'resolved' by other means prior to going to court, but many cases are simply not taken up.

74. Interview with trade uionist SEK.
75. Interview with trade inionist, PEO.

The theoretical benefits are not always translated into practical and tangible benefits and rights for employees, no matter how well-intended or well-drafted the law is. Employers are happy with the progress of implementation and the awareness of the rights that the Directive (and hence the Cypriot Law) provides for employees during transfers, although it is recognized by the Employers Federation that there is still some confusion among many firms as to the distinction between redundancy and transfer.[76] Trade unionists claim that the Directive has made an overall positive difference and these rights are invoked and referred to during the bargaining process. However, there are problems in the implementation and interpretation of who exactly is entitled to certain rights. Moreover, there are many instances of disguising employment as subcontracting, etc. The rights provided in the Transfers Directive are limited: the only practical implication of complying with the Directive, in terms of 'hard law', is the provision for one year for which the transferee is obliged to observe the rights of employees. The rest is essentially a set of 'soft law' provisions on consultation and information, which refer to procedural aspects and are easily bypassed.[77]

As for practical implementation, there is certainly increasing awareness of the employee rights that are transferred, while there are still some practices, in many cases by publicly owned companies and institutions, attempting to avoid the implementation of the Directive via *concealed employment*, *contracting out* and successive tendering remain difficult to deal with and generally undermine workers' rights. Moreover, a great deal more can be done on the subject of information and consultation. The role of trade unions and employers is crucial, while a more active role by the Ministry of Labour can strengthen the tripartite monitoring, which will in turn ensure a more effective implementation of the Directive.

76. Interview with officer of Employers and Industrialists Federation OEB.
77. Interview with SEK trade unionist.

Chapter 4
Czechia

Lubomír Ptáček

§4.01 RIGHTS OF EMPLOYEES IN THE EVENT OF TRANSFERS OF UNDERTAKINGS, ESTABLISHMENTS OR PARTS OF UNDERTAKINGS OR ESTABLISHMENTS IN THE CZECH REPUBLIC

The Czech legislation on the transfer of rights and obligations under employment relationships, as regulated in the provisions of section 338 of the Labour Code, is an implementation of Council Directive 2001/23/EC of 12 March 2001 on the approximation of the laws of the Member States relating to the safeguarding of employees' rights in the event of transfers of undertakings, businesses or parts of undertakings or businesses into the Czech legal order, the purpose of which is to 'provide for measures to protect employees in the event of a change of employer, in particular to ensure that their rights are safeguarded', and which replaced the previously effective Council Directive 77/187/EEC of 14 February 1977 on the approximation of the laws of the Member States relating to the safeguarding of employees' rights in the event of transfers of undertakings, businesses or parts of businesses. A transfer under Council Directive 2001/23/EC means, as is clear from Article 1(1)(b) of that Directive, the transfer of an economic unit which retains its identity, regarded as an organised grouping of resources, the purpose of which is to carry on an economic activity as a main or ancillary activity.

A peculiarity of Czech private law is that, with effect from 1 January 2014, private law was recodified and previously separate legal provisions (e.g., the Family Law Act) were incorporated into the Civil Code or abolished (the Commercial Code). Even after the recodification of private law, the Labour Code retained its status as a separate legal regulation. Application of the Labour Code to the Civil Code is based on the principle of subsidiarity. Labour relations are governed by the Labour Code. Where the Labour Code cannot be applied, the Civil Code governs. At the same time, it has been legislatively established that the subsidiary application of civil law is only possible in accordance with the fundamental principles of labour law relations. In other words, it is not possible to apply those provisions of the Civil Code which would conflict with those principles. Naturally, the provisions of the Civil Code can only be applied to employment relations if the Labour Code does not regulate the issue differently.[1]

The legal regulation of the transfer of rights and obligations under employment relationships was changed by an amendment to the Labour Code, introduced by Act No. 285/2020 Coll. with effect from 30 July 2020. The legislator described the previous legal regulation as considerably unbounded in comparison with the European regulation, as the transfer already took place when the employer's activities or tasks, or part of them, were merely transferred to another eligible employer. Consequently, the transfer was not conditional on the identity of the transferred economic unit being preserved. As a result of such a broad regulation of the transfer, most cases of insourcing, outsourcing or even a mere change of supplier involved the transfer of rights and obligations under employment law, which in practice created considerable problems. This is particularly true in the case of a change of supplier, where the legal relationship between the existing employer and the transferee employer (supplier) is completely absent. The legislation effective from 30 July 2020 thus clarifies the existing wording and, in accordance with the case law of the CJEU, newly establishes the conditions that must be cumulatively fulfilled for the transfer of activities in the above-mentioned cases to result in the transfer of rights and obligations under employment law. However, these conditions do not apply to cases where a specific legal provision provides that a particular business transaction is to be considered as a transfer of the employer's activity. This is not the case, for example, in the case of the purchase of a factory or a merger by amalgamation, cases in which the Civil Code expressly provides that they are to be considered a transfer of the employer's activity. In these cases, therefore, the rights and obligations arising from the employment relationship are transferred regardless of whether the conditions set out in section 338(3) are met.[2] Despite the above criticism of the legislator, it should be noted that the Supreme Court, even in the context of the legislation in force until 29 July 2020, has explicitly adhered to the European concept of an economic unit that retains its identity.[3]

In its judgment of 14 November 2017, Case No. 21 Cdo 2746/2017,[4] the Supreme Court concluded that the transfer of rights and obligations under employment law may occur even when the client terminates the contract for the provision of services with the existing supplier and concludes a contract for the provision of the same or similar services with a new supplier [cf. also the judgment of the Court of Justice of the

1. Bělina, Miroslav. § 4 [Application of the Civil Code]. In: Bělina, Miroslavet al. 3rd ed. Prague: C.H. Beck, 2019, p. 44, marg. no. 18.
2. Explanatory Report to Act No. 285/2020 Coll., amending the Labour Code and certain related acts.
3. Janšová, Marie. § 338 [Transfer of Rights and Obligations under Labour Law]. In: Valentová, Klára et al. 2nd ed., C.H. Beck, 2022, p. 1086.
4. All Supreme Court decisions are traceable at www.nsoud.cz (accessed 22 August 2025).

European Union of 11 March 1997 in Case C-13/95, *A.S. v. Zehnacker Gebäudereinigung GmbH Krankenhausservice*, from which it follows that Article 1(1) of Directive 77/187 (now cf. Article 1 of Council Directive 2001/23/EC) must be interpreted as meaning that the directive also applies where a person terminates his contractual relationship with an undertaking which provides cleaning services for him and subsequently concludes a contract with another undertaking in order to cover the performance of a similar activity, where at the same time there is a transfer of the relevant tangible or intangible elements of the undertaking or the taking over of a substantial part of the staff, in terms of the number and expertise of the employees assigned by the predecessor to the performance of the obligation arising from the contract in question; cf. the judgment of the Court of Justice of the European Union of 20 November 2003 in Case C-340/01 C.A. and *Others v. Sodexho MM Catering Gesellschaft mbH*, according to which Article 1 of Directive 77/187 (now Article 1 of Council Directive 77/187/EEC) does not apply to a contract of employment. Section 338(2) and 338(3) of the Act. Article 338(2) and (3) of the Labour Law do not make the transfer of rights and obligations, which is a consequence of the transfer of an activity or tasks (part of an activity or tasks) of an employer to another employer, conditional upon the simultaneous takeover of material components used to ensure the performance of the transferred activity. Nor is the transfer of material components a necessary condition for the transfer of an 'economic unit' within the meaning of Article 1(1)(b) of Council Directive 2001/23/EC. According to the case law of the Court of Justice of the European Union concerning that directive, which must be considered when interpreting the provisions of Article 338(2) and (3) of the Law on the Internal Market of the Labour Code, which implements it, it is necessary to take into account all the circumstances of the case, including the type of undertaking or business, the existence of the transfer of tangible assets (such as buildings and movable property) at the time of the transfer, the takeover of the core employees, the takeover of customers, the degree of similarity between the activities carried out before and after the transfer, and the period of any interruption in the exercise of the activity, when deciding whether a transfer has taken place. These factors must not be considered in isolation but in relation to each other. Account must also be taken of the specificities of the various sectors, since there are activities for which working capital is necessary and the identity of the economic unit is preserved when that capital is transferred to the acquirer (the new employer), but there are also sectors where the activity relies to a significant extent on labour (e.g., cleaning, caretaking); in such cases, the economic unit is a group of employees carrying on a common activity. The identity of such a unit would then be preserved in the transfer if the acquirer not only took over the activity in question, which it would also continue to carry out, but would also have to take over a substantial part of the employees (in terms of number and expertise) used by the previous employer in that activity; if the new operator of the activity takes on new employees to carry it out, there is no transfer of the economic unit (cf. judgment of the Court of Justice of the European Union of 18 March 1986 in Case 24/85 *J.M.A.S. v. G.B.A.CV and A.B.e.Z.* BV, and the judgment of the Court of Justice of the European Union of 20 January 2011 in Case C-463/09 CLECE, *S.A. v. M.S.M.V, A.d.C.*). The fact that the transfer is not accompanied by a transfer of movable assets, nor the number of employees affected by the transfer, are not sufficient grounds for not applying Council Directive 2001/23/EC; whether there is a transfer within the meaning of that directive may be inferred from the activities of the new employer, who actually continues to carry out the same or similar activities or resumes such activities (cf. judgment of the Court of Justice of the European Union of 14 April 1994 in Case C-392/92 *Ch. S. v. Spar- und Leihkasse der früheren Ämter Bordesholm, Kiel und Cronshagen*). Therefore, the Supreme Court concluded that the transfer of rights and obligations under the provisions of section 338(2) and (3) of the Labour Law Act to the employee's rights and obligations under the Labour Law Act was not a violation of the provisions of section 338(2) and (3) of the Labour Law Act. According to Labour Law, the taking over of the employer's contract by another contractor may occur on the basis of the termination of the contract for the provision of services concluded with the employer by the client and the conclusion of a contract for the provision of the same or similar services with the new contractor, even without taking over the tangible and intangible components used to ensure the performance of the agreed activity, if the performance of this activity relies to a substantial extent on the workforce and if the new contractor takes over a substantial part of the employees (in terms of their number and expertise) used by the employer in this activity.

§4.02 CONDITIONS OF TRANSFER

The transfer of rights and obligations under employment law requires two conditions. First, there must be a legal reason for the transfer, and second, the condition of an eligible employer must be met. Specific laws may then add additional conditions for the employer (obligation to notify or make a qualified request), including for the transferring employee (e.g., negative lustration certificate).[5]

The Labour Code stipulates that the transfer of rights and obligations under employment relationships may occur only in cases provided for by this Act or a special legal regulation. Other legal provisions are, for example, the Civil Code, Act No. 125/2008 Coll., on the transformation of commercial companies, the Insolvency Act or the Act on State Enterprise. Administrative reorganisation of public administration bodies or the transfer of administrative functions between public administration bodies is not covered by Directive 2001/23/EC. Nevertheless, the Czech legislator has included these activities in the Labour Code. In these cases, it is not the transfer of rights and obligations under employment law between employers, but the transfer of the exercise of rights and obligations under employment law. Since the Labour Code, within its EU-Conformist interpretation, covers most of the factual events for which the transfer of rights and obligations under employment law is relevant (see next point), the question arises as to how to proceed in the event that a special legal regulation has an explicit provision also regulating the transfer of rights and obligations under employment law (positive conflict of scope) or, on the contrary, does not have an

5. Štefko, Martin. Labour Code, Practical Commentary, Wolters Kluwer, 2022.

explicit regulation in this respect.[6] Doctrinal opinions are inclined to the view that the labour law regulation of the transfer of rights and obligations under labour law is to be applied to the transfer of rights and obligations under a special private law based on the principle of subsidiarity, and in the case of public law regulations (such as the service relationship) should be based on analogy.[7]

§4.03 LEGAL REASON FOR THE TRANSFER AND ELIGIBLE EMPLOYER

The Labour Code defines legal grounds for transfer as cases of transfer of the employer's activity or part of it. If the activity of the employer or part of it is transferred, the rights and obligations under the employment relationship are transferred in full to the transferee employer; the rights and obligations under the collective agreement are transferred to the transferee employer for the duration of the collective agreement, but no longer than until the end of the following calendar year. Part of an employer means a unit of the employer which has dedicated resources (buildings, machinery, tools, etc.) and premises for carrying out that activity,[8] or such a unit for which separate accounts are kept in respect of that unit.[9]

According to the case law of the CJEU, these may be core activities or also ancillary activities which are not the employer's core business, and which may be carried out by only one employee.[10] As the case law of the CJEU and the above-mentioned decision of the Supreme Court have already established, the transfer of rights and obligations under employment relationships is not conditional on the simultaneous takeover of the material components used to ensure the performance of that activity.

Court case law[11] before the amendment to the Labour Code effective from 30 July 2020 held that the transfer of rights and obligations under employment relationships always occurs when a legal act (contract) has been made or another legal event has occurred, which (according to the law) involves the transfer of an activity or part of an activity or tasks or part of tasks to another employer, all provided, that the transferee natural or legal person is capable of continuing as an employer to perform the tasks or activities of the former employer or to engage in activities of a similar kind, irrespective of the legal reason for the transfer, whether it also involves the transfer of ownership

6. Štefko, Martin. § 338 [Transfer of Rights and Obligations under Labour Law Relations]. In: Bělina, Miroslav et al. 3rd ed. Prague: C.H. Beck, 2019, p. 1386, marg. No. 10.
7. Štefko, Martin. Labour Code, Practical Commentary, Wolters Kluwer, 2022.
8. Supreme Court judgment of 6 May 1997, Case No. 2 Cdon 1053/96.
9. Judgment of the Supreme Court of 7 September 1999, Case No. 33 Cdo 1199/98.
10. CJEU Schmidt C-392/92. Neither the fact that the transfer relates only to an ancillary activity of the transferor which is not necessarily linked to the objectives pursued by the transferor, nor the fact that the transfer is not linked to the transfer of movable assets, nor the number of employees affected by the transfer are sufficient grounds for not applying the Directive. Since the decisive criterion for determining whether there has been a transfer within the meaning of the directive is whether the undertaking in question retains its identity, which may be inferred from the activities of the new employer, which in fact continues to carry on the same or similar activities or begins to do so again.
11. Judgment of the Supreme Court of 14 November 2017, Case No. 21 Cdo 2746/2017.

rights and whether the former employer has lost the capacity to be an employer. Section 338(3) of the Labour Code then sets out what is to be regarded as the employer's 'tasks' or 'activities' in connection with the transfer of rights and obligations under employment law. If all the prerequisites required by the Labour Code or special legislation are met, the consent of the employees of the former (current) employer concerned is not required and the rights and obligations under the employment relationship are transferred to the transferee employer, even if the employees do not consent.[12] Therefore, the transfer of rights and obligations under the employment relationship occurs by law, without the employee's consent and without the need to terminate the employee's employment relationship with the former employer and conclude a new employment contract with the transferee employer.[13] The legal act involving the transfer of the employer's activities or part of the employer's activities or tasks to another employer need not be merely a contract concluded between the former employer and the transferee employer. Such a transfer is based on any legal act as a result of which the employer ceases to carry out the existing activity (performance of the existing tasks) in whole or in part and another legal or natural person capable of doing so continues that activity (performance of the tasks) or an activity of a similar kind in its place. Therefore, the case law of the courts has previously held that the transfer of an activity or tasks (part thereof) to another employer may take place – without the former employer and the transferee employer being in a contractual relationship – through the legal actions of a third party.[14]

The amendment to the Labour Code effective as of 30 July 2020 requires that the transfer of rights and obligations under employment relationships should only take place if both the transferee and the transferor have jointly and purposefully prepared for the change. Subject to the exceptions provided for by the Labour Code,[15] the transfer of rights and obligations under employment law in the event of a transfer of the employer's activity or part thereof to another employer is now subject to the cumulative fulfilment of the following conditions:

(a) the activity is carried on in the same or similar manner and extent after the transfer;
(b) the activity does not consist wholly or mainly in the supply of goods;
(c) immediately before the transfer, there is a group of employees which has been deliberately created by the employer for the exclusive or predominant purpose of carrying on the activity;

---

12. Judgment of the Supreme Court of 9 September 2010, Case No. 21 Cdo 4030/2009.
13. Judgment of the Supreme Court of 14 January 2010 Case No. 21 Cdo 3945/2008.
14. Supreme Court judgment of 14 July 2016, Case No. 21 Cdo 3712/2015.
15. For example, in a merger pursuant to section 178(1) of the Civil Code. In the case of a merger of at least two participating legal entities. A merger shall be deemed to be a transfer of the employer's business. Another exception is, e.g., the purchase of a factory pursuant to section 2175(2) of the Civil Code. By purchasing a plant, the purchaser acquires everything that belongs to the plant as a whole. The purchase of a plant is also considered to be a purchase of a plant if the parties exclude an individual item from the purchase without the whole losing its characteristic of a plant. The purchase of a factory shall be deemed to be a transfer of the employer's business.

(d) the activity is not intended to be of short duration or to consist of a single task; and
(e) property, or the right to use or enjoy it, is transferred if the property is essential to the activity in view of the nature of the activity, or a substantial part of the employees used by the former employer in the performance of the activity is taken over if the activity depends to a substantial extent on the employees and not on the property.

If all the above conditions are not met at the same time, the transition will not take place.

The Labour Code provides for an eligible employer as an additional condition. In addition to legal personality, the successor employer must also be able to lawfully continue to perform the tasks or activities of the former employer or to engage in activities of a similar nature.[16] It must have the relevant authorisations (rights, licences, or concessions) to operate and must also be sufficiently well endowed to be able to continue the activities taken over without major interruption of work. These conditions must be met regardless of the legal basis for the transfer and whether there is a transfer of ownership.

The rights and obligations of the former employer towards employees whose employment relationships have terminated before the effective date of the transfer of rights and obligations under employment relationships remain unaffected unless the Insolvency Act provides otherwise. Employees who have pecuniary claims against the employer (the bankrupt) are its creditors; these claims, as well as the claims of other creditors, can only be satisfied in the insolvency proceedings (principle of proportional satisfaction of all creditors from the bankrupt's assets).

Martin Štefko[17] reminds that the reason for the transfer of rights and obligations under employment law is the law, not a contract. Thus, in contrast to the more restrictive EU legislation (cf. CJEU C-186/83, *Botzen*), the transfer under the Czech legislation occurs in a broad sense, i.e., also in the case of employment relationships of employees who work for the transferred part of the employer or participate only partially in the performance of the transferred tasks. Thus, employees performing support and auxiliary activities must also be included in the transfer. However, the transfer will only take place in the relevant part of the working time of the employees affected by the transfer. If part of the existing employer or part of the tasks or activities of the existing employer is transferred to the transferee employer, the rights and

16. Cf. CJEU Albron Catering, C-242/09. In the case of a transfer within the meaning of Directive 2001/23/EC of 12 March 2001 on the approximation of the laws of the Member States relating to the safeguarding of employees' rights in the event of transfers of undertakings, businesses or parts of undertakings or businesses belonging to a group to an undertaking outside that group, the 'transferor' within the meaning of Article 2(1)(a) of that Directive, an undertaking of the group to which the employees are permanently assigned without having concluded an employment contract with it, even though the undertaking with which the employees concerned have concluded such an employment contract is part of that group, may also be regarded as a transferor.
17. Štefko, Martin. Labour Code, Practical Commentary, Wolters Kluwer, 2022.

obligations of the transferee employer shall be transferred only in respect of employees who had a permanent workplace in the transferred part on the date of the transfer (i.e., not in respect of employees who were only temporarily transferred or sent there on a business trip) or who performed work tasks there on the basis of a work activity agreement or a work performance agreement. If the employee performed secondary activities in the transferred part and if the employment relationship had a permanent workplace in another part of the former employer, only the rights and obligations arising from his secondary activities are transferred to the transferee employer (this employment relationship, however, loses the nature of secondary activities).

§4.04 THE POSITION OF EMPLOYEES AND TRADE UNIONS IN THE TRANSITION OF THE EMPLOYER

The employment relationship is transferred regardless of the employee's will. Thus, even someone with whom the employee has not previously agreed on the performance of work, or even necessarily disagreed with it, becomes an employer if the legal conditions are met.[18] Even if, when the conditions of the Labour Code are met, the rights and obligations under the employment relationship are transferred to the transferee employer by operation of law, without the employee's consent and without the need to terminate the employee's employment relationship with the former employer and to conclude a new employment contract with the transferee employer, in practice it often happens that the parties conclude the relevant agreements on termination of employment and the subsequent employment contract for reasons of legal certainty. In principle, the case law considers a procedure whereby the existing employment relationship is terminated on an agreed date and a new one is established without any transfer of rights and obligations to be permissible.[19] If an employee enters into an agreement to terminate the employment relationship with the former employer due to the transfer of the employer's business or part of the employer's business or the transfer of the employer's tasks or part of the employer's tasks to another employer, and at the same time enters an employment contract with the transferee employer, a probationary period may be agreed in the employment contract. However, if the purpose of such a procedure on the part of the transferee employer would be to avoid the transfer of the rights and obligations of the employment relationship between the employee and the former employer to the transferee employer in order to enable the transferee employer to terminate the employment relationship with the employee during a probationary period, which cannot be agreed upon in the case of a transfer of rights and obligations under employment law, the probationary period arrangement would be invalid for breach of good morals.[20]

18. Resolution of the Supreme Court of 22 January 2014, Case No. 21 Cdo 753/2013 or judgment of 14 July 2010, Case No. 21 Cdo 2520/2009.
19. Judgment of the Regional Court in Ostrava of 10 April 2018, Case No. 16 Co 16/2018.
20. Judgment of the Supreme Court of 24 September 2014, Case No. 21 Cdo 3046/2013.

The transfer cannot take place for employees whose employment relationship with the transferor did not commence until after the date of transfer.[21]

The rights and obligations of the former employer towards employees whose employment relationships have ceased by the date of the transition remain unaffected by the transition, i.e., the original employer remains the subject of those rights.[22] If the rights and obligations under the employment relationship are not transferred to another employer on the termination of the employer, the injured party (survivor) has the right to claim compensation directly from the insurance company to the same extent as the insured employer would have been obliged to compensate him. In the event of the dissolution of an employer without legal representation, claims for compensation for occupational injuries or diseases arising before 1 January 1993 are transferred to the State.[23] Claims for compensation for occupational injuries or diseases arising after 1 January 1993 and covered by statutory employers' liability insurance are transferred to the relevant (accident) insurance company (i.e., Česká pojišt'ovna, a.s. or Kooperativa, a.s.).

The rights and obligations under the collective agreement are transferred to the successor employer for the duration of the collective agreement, but no later than the end of the following calendar year. Representatives of employees whose employment relationships have been transferred to the transferee should continue to represent the interests of those employees.[24] If the transferee (acquiring employer) does not cooperate with the employee representatives and inform them in advance, they are entitled to compensation.[25]

21. CJEU C-287/86, *Ny Molle Kro*.
22. Judgment of the Supreme Court of 4 November 2013, Case No. 21 Cdo 2911/2012.
23. Supreme Court judgment of 23 September 2010, Case No. 32 Cdo 2637/2009.
24. CJEU in Case C-151/09, *UGT-FSP*. The transferred economic unit will retain its autonomy within the meaning of Article 6(1) of Directive 2001/23/EC of 12 March 2001 on the approximation of the laws of the Member States relating to the safeguarding of employees' rights in the event of transfers of undertakings, businesses or parts of undertakings or businesses, in so far as the powers conferred on the managers of that unit within the transferor's organisational structures, namely the power to organise work within that unit relatively freely and independently in the pursuit of economic activity, are retained, and, more specifically, the powers to issue orders and instructions, to allocate tasks to subordinate employees of the unit concerned and to decide on the use of the material resources at its disposal, without direct intervention by other organisational structures of the employer, have not changed substantially within the organisational structures of the transferee. A mere change in the most senior managers cannot, in itself, undermine the autonomy of the unit being transferred, unless the new most senior managers have powers which enable them to organise directly the activities of the employees in that unit and thus to replace the direct supervisors of those employees in taking decisions within that unit 1(a) and (b) of Directive 2001/23/EC on the approximation of the laws of the Member States relating to the safeguarding of employees' rights in the event of transfers of undertakings, businesses or parts of undertakings or businesses must be interpreted as meaning that that directive may also be applied in a situation in which the transferred part of the undertaking or business does not retain its organisational autonomy, provided that the functional link between the various factors of production transferred is maintained and that that link enables the transferee to use those factors for the purpose of carrying on the same or similar economic activity, which is a matter for the referring court to ascertain. A conception of the identity of the economic unit which rests solely on the factor of organisational autonomy cannot be accepted, particularly in the light of the objective pursued by Directive 2001/23, which is to ensure effective protection of employees' rights in the event of a transfer. That would mean that the

The information obligation must be fulfilled well in advance, no later than 30 days before the transfer of rights and obligations to another employer. The incumbent employer and the transferee employer are obliged to inform the trade union and the works council of the transfer and to discuss with them in order to reach an agreement:

(a) the fixed or proposed date of transfer;
(b) the reasons for the transfer;
(c) the legal, economic and social consequences of the transfer for the employees;
(d) measures in preparation in relation to staff.

If the employer does not have a trade union organisation or a works council, the former employer and the transferee employer must inform the employees who will be directly affected by the transfer of the facts referred to in paragraph 1 at least 30 days before the effective date of the transfer of rights and obligations to another employer.

After the merger has taken effect (and after the dissolution of the previous employer), the employer's information and consultation obligation towards the trade union on the transfer of the employer's activities (part thereof) or tasks (part thereof) to another employer, which results in the transfer of rights and obligations under employment law to the acquiring employer, no longer exists, even if none of the employers has complied with it by then. The fact that the employer (either the existing or the transferee employer) has not fulfilled this obligation does not prevent the conversion of the existing employer from taking place and cannot prevent the transfer

application of that directive would be precluded in relation to the acquired part of the undertaking or establishment simply because the acquirer decides to dissolve that acquired part of the undertaking or establishment and incorporate it into its own structure, thereby depriving the employees concerned of the protection afforded by that directive.

25. Judgment of the Supreme Court of 21 October 2015, Case No. 21 Cdo 4952/2014: after the effective date of a transformation of an employer consisting in a merger by merger, in which the activities or tasks of the employer or part thereof are transferred to another employer, resulting in the transfer of rights and obligations under employment law, a trade union operating at the employer cannot successfully demand that the acquiring employer inform it of this transformation and discuss this measure with it. However, if the trade union suffers damage as a result of the employer's breach of the obligation to inform it of the conversion and to discuss the conversion with it before it takes effect, the trade union may claim compensation. The Supreme Court judgment of 26 March 2013, Case No. 21 Cdo 268/2012: If the employer's termination of the employment relationship has not been finally determined to be null and void with respect to the person to whom the rights and obligations under the employment relationship had been transferred before the court's decision, an employee who has not been assigned work after the final determination of the nullity of the termination of the employment relationship, although he or she has announced that he or she insists on continued employment, is not entitled to wage compensation either with respect to that person (the transferee employer) or with respect to his or her former employer. In the event that the former or the successor employer has not fulfilled the information obligations or otherwise ensured that the relevant trade union body, the works council or the individual employees have been duly and timely informed of the transfer of rights and obligations under employment law, the employee shall be liable for the damage suffered by him as a result of the breach of these legal obligations; several parties shall be jointly liable for the damage, provided that the performance of one of them for compensation shall extinguish the obligation of the other to the extent of such performance.

of the rights and obligations under employment law to the transferee employer that relates to it. However, a breach of that legal obligation is an administrative offence and may give rise to liability of the employer for damage caused to the trade union.[26]

Employees whose employment relationship was terminated before the time of the transfer in violation of the Labour Code are[27] viewed as if they were still employed by the employer, although the new employer did not take them over. An employee who has been unfairly dismissed by the transferring employer shortly before the transfer of employment rights and obligations and has not been taken over by the new employer may, according to the CJEU's decision in Dethier Equipement, invoke his claims against the transferring employer.[28]

§4.05 LEGAL EFFECTS OF THE TRANSFER

The transferee employer assumes the rights and obligations of the transferring employer. The transferee employer therefore assumes all rights and obligations arising from the employment relationship existing on the date of the transfer, including individual claims for compensation for occupational injury or disease.[29] Also assumed are the arrangements relating to all social benefits provided by the collective agreement to the assumed employees.[30] If the rights and obligations under the employment relationship are transferred, the transferee employer always assumes the obligations of the former employer under the collective agreement governing the individual or collective relationship between the employer and the employees, if these give rise to claims of an unspecified number of individual employees (so-called normative obligations). The basic obligations in the relationship between the employee and the employer are the employer's obligation to assign the employee to work in accordance with the employment contract, to pay him/her a wage (salary) for the work performed, to create conditions for the successful performance of his/her work tasks and to observe other working conditions laid down by law or by a collective or employment contract, and the corresponding obligation of the employee to perform the work under the employment contract personally at the specified working hours and to observe

26. Judgment of the Supreme Court of 21 October 2015, Case No. 21 Cdo 4952/2014.
27. CJEU decision in Bork, C-101/87.
28. Štefko, Martin. Labour Code, Practical Commentary, Wolters Kluwer, 2022; CJEU, C-319/94, *Dethier Équipement*: the purpose of Article 4(1) of Directive 77/187 [ed.: now Article 4(1) of Directive 2001/23/EC] is to protect the employee against dismissal on the sole ground of the transfer of rights and obligations under the employment relationship. Both the transferee and the transferor are entitled to give notice to the employee for economic, technical or organisational reasons. An employee who has been unfairly dismissed by the transferor shortly before the transfer within the meaning of Directive 77/187 and whose rights and obligations under the employment relationship have not been taken over by the new employer may claim the invalidity of the dismissal against the transferee (i.e., the new employer), since the employment relationship must still be regarded as existing. (...) The provisions of Directive 77/187 governing the protection of employees must be regarded as mandatory, i.e., they cannot be derogated from to the detriment of employees.
29. CJEU in Beckmann, C-164/00, para. 40; CJEU C-19/83 Wendelboe or the judgment of the Supreme Court of 4 November 2013, Case No. 21 Cdo 2911/2012.
30. Judgment of the Supreme Court of 18 September 2007, Case No. 21 Cdo 2843/2006.

work discipline in accordance with the employer's instructions. Where there is a transfer of rights and obligations arising from employment relationships, it follows from the nature of the case that those rights and obligations are assumed by the transferee employer in the same quality and with the same characteristics as they were with the former employer. The scope of the rights and obligations under the employment relationship being transferred is determined by the rights and obligations which the former employer had under the employment relationship with the employees affected by the transfer. At the moment of the transfer of rights and obligations under the employment relationship, from the point of view of the employee, only a change in the person of the employer occurs, while the content of the employment relationship itself remains unaffected. From the point of view of the content of the employment relationship, therefore, the same legal situation applies as if there had been no change in the person of the employer at all. However, the content of the employment relationship also includes the entitlements that accrue to individual employees under the collective agreement (normative obligations). The transferee employer (an organisational unit of the State) assumes the normative obligations under the collective agreement in the same form (under the same conditions) as they would have arisen under the collective agreement if the transfer (exercise) of rights and obligations under the employment relationship had not taken place at all, until the period for which the collective agreement was concluded expires or otherwise ceases to have effect. While the transferee employer is obliged to assign work to the employees (whose employment relationship has been transferred) or to compensate them for wages or salary until the employment relationship with them is terminated, if no work can be assigned, it is not obliged to continue the activities of the former employer without interruption. The transferee employer shall be entitled to all legal and factual actions to which it has been entitled under the Act. The transferee employer is also entitled to manage and organise the work of its employees.[31]

One of the cases in which the rights and obligations arising from employment relationships are transferred is also the monetisation of the debtor's business by the insolvency administrator by a single contract under the Insolvency Act. According to the Insolvency Act, the monetisation of the debtor's business by a single contract transfers to the purchaser the rights and obligations arising from the employment relationships with the employees of the debtor's business, except for employment claims of the debtor's employees arising before the contract takes effect; no other obligations are transferred to the purchaser. Not all rights and obligations arising out of employment relationships that ever arose for the debtor in the course of the operation of the business shall pass to the acquirer, but only rights and obligations (with the exception of employment claims of the debtor's employees arising before the effectiveness of the agreement) towards those employees whose employment relationship with the debtor continued at least on the date on which the agreement for the realisation of the debtor's business became effective. If the employment relationship ended before that date, the rights and obligations of the debtor towards the former employees remain

31. Judgment of the Supreme Court of 11 April 2002, Case No. 21 Cdo 1105/2001.

unaffected by the agreement pursuant to section 290 of the Insolvency Act. This conclusion is also in line with the purpose of the Insolvency Act, which is to ensure that the operation of the debtor's business is not interrupted, since the continuation of the debtor's business requires that the acquirer only takes over the rights and obligations towards the employees whose employment relationship continues and who are thus to continue to work in the transferred business.[32]

§4.06 LEGAL PROTECTION OF EMPLOYEES: ACTION FOR SUBSTANTIAL DETERIORATION OF WORKING CONDITIONS

An employee whose employment relationship has been transferred to a new employer cannot be forced to remain in that employment relationship. Therefore, he/she may terminate the employment relationship himself/herself by notice or by agreement. The Labour Code provides that if the employee's notice of termination is given within two months of the effective date of the transfer of rights and obligations under the employment relationship or the effective date of the transfer of the exercise of rights and obligations under the employment relationship, or if the employee's employment relationship is terminated by agreement within the same period, the employee may apply to the court for a declaration that the termination of the employment relationship was due to a substantial deterioration in working conditions in connection with the transfer of rights and obligations under employment law or the transfer of the exercise of rights and obligations under employment law. In such a case, the employee is entitled to severance pay.

A severance payment is a one-off financial contribution to help an employee to overcome the (often difficult) social situation in which he or she finds himself or herself because, through no fault of his or her own (for reasons on the employer's side or because of an adverse health condition due to an occupational accident, occupational disease or occupational disease risk, or because he or she has reached the maximum permissible exposure), he or she has lost his or her previous job. Severance pay is intended to compensate (mitigate) at least partly the consequences for the employee of the termination of his/her previous employment and the need to find a new job or to engage in other gainful employment by means of a lump sum payment by the employer. The legal regulation of severance pay is based on the International Labour Organisation Convention No. 158 of 22 June 1982 concerning the termination of employment at the initiative of the employer, although the Czech Republic is not bound by it, as it has not yet ratified it. This Convention provides that a dismissed employee

32. Judgment of the Supreme Court of 30 October 2019. Case No. 21 Cdo 1443/2019: Monetisation of the debtor's business by a single contract pursuant to § 291 para. 291 (1) of the Insolvency Act, the rights and obligations arising from employment relationships (with the exception of employment claims of the debtor's employees arising prior to the effective date of the agreement) are transferred to the purchaser only in respect of those employees of the debtor's business whose employment relationship with the debtor continued at least on the date on which the agreement on the monetisation of the debtor's business became effective.

should be 'entitled to severance pay or other similar benefits' paid directly by the employer or from funds generated by employers' contributions.[33]

The pilot decision in the case of substantial deterioration of working conditions was the Supreme Court's judgment of 28 January 2020, Case No. 21 Cdo 1148/2019. In this case, the employee sought a determination that the termination of employment was due to a substantial deterioration of working conditions in connection with the transfer of rights and obligations under the employment relationship to the defendant. In particular, the applicant pleaded that, under an employment contract of 4 February 2002, amended on 1 January 2007, he was employed by B. as manager of a shop in XY. By means of the contract for the purchase of part of the sales plant concluded on 15 December 2015 between B. and the defendant, the rights and obligations arising from the employment relationship of the employees were transferred to the defendant. Immediately after the transfer of the rights and obligations under the employment relationship to the defendant, however, there began to be fundamental changes in the working conditions compared with the previous situation. The original organisational structure was completely changed, not only in the shop, of which the applicant was the manager at the time, but also in the supervisory units, and the change in organisational structure was accompanied by a change in competences and powers. The applicant's job description was changed, which was also not discussed with him in any way and did not correspond to the job description included in the applicant's employment contract. The introduction of new duties was not only never discussed with the applicant, but was only ever brought to his attention in the form of so-called regulations sent to him by e-mail. Thus, in a period of only the first two months after taking over the employment relationship from its predecessor, the defendant issued 61 orders of approximately 300 pages of text defining new managerial duties and shop processes. At the same time, various Polish-speaking persons began to arrive at the shop of which the applicant was the manager, in particular a Polish-speaking 'consultant' or 'resident' sent by the new owner to carry out his instructions. This 'consultant' interfered in a very substantial way in the decision-making and organisational processes of the shop, bypassing the applicant as shop manager by himself assigning tasks to subordinate shop employees and changing the instructions issued by the applicant as shop manager. There were also quite substantial changes in the previously established work processes and the equipment used. The defendant abolished the positions of the three administrative staff and placed all that work on the plaintiff alone. Most of the e-mail communication and all telephone conversations with the applicant were conducted by the defendant in Polish, which made it very difficult for the applicant to communicate and understand properly. The new owner severely limited the means of communication. In particular, out of five personal computers with independent access to e-mail, only two computers with such access remained in the shop, and out of six telephones with off-site calling privileges, only two telephones with off-site calling privileges were available to the manager and his deputy. In the

33. Doležílek, Jiří. § 67 [Amount; Average Earnings; Date of Payment]. In: Bělina, Miroslav et al. 3rd ed. Prague: C.H. Beck, 2019, p. 394, marg. Nos 1-2.

shop manager's office area, a security camera was positioned to occupy a substantial part of the office, in particular his desk area, so that his activities could be monitored by the camera. The applicant's working conditions thus deteriorated substantially compared to the situation before the transfer of the rights and obligations arising from the employment relationship to the defendant, and it was for that reason and for that reason alone that the applicant resigned from his employment with the defendant.

The trial court granted the employee's motion. It took the view that, whereas before the transfer of the rights and obligations arising from the employees' employment relationship to the defendant the applicant was represented by three section managers under clearly defined conditions, after the change two representatives were to represent the applicant, but those persons were not officially appointed to their posts until after the transition had taken effect. Thus, a situation arose where the only responsible person on the shop floor was the applicant, who could not delegate part of his work and responsibility to the two deputy managers, at least not officially and permanently, since he lacked the necessary framework for that, but was still solely responsible himself. The absence of firm rules was also linked to the presence of 'residents' on the shop floor – persons who spoke Polish, who acted as a third representative, *inter alia*, to control the manager and his deputies, monitor them and react to mismanagement of the branch. Although the 'resident' was supposed to be the manager's deputy (and presumably his subordinate), he was also supposed to control him and report to the Polish headquarters on mismanagement of the branch. Moreover, it was not even clear who this third deputy was, as these persons took turns. The applicant was obliged to check the incoming mail regularly (every hour), and the greater part of the mail was in Polish, which was not the case before, and in general more matters were dealt with in Polish at the shop, dealing with suppliers, service companies, etc., and his overtime increased, which was related to the organisational changes made, when the number of staff was reduced (one person in the management and three administrative staff). The installation of cameras aimed directly at the applicant's desk, where he spent at least half of his working time, also worsened the working conditions, particularly in a situation where, as the manager of the shop, he was not communicated with or informed of the reasons for the installation of the cameras in that place, how the output would be handled and whether it was a permanent measure. The Court of First Instance concludes that, in sum, the applicant's working conditions have deteriorated, and substantially so, because of the transfer of his rights and obligations under the employment relationship to the defendant.

On the employer's appeal, the Court of Appeal upheld the judgment. It held that if rights and obligations are transferred to a new employer, the new employer takes over the rights and obligations in the same quality and with the same characteristics as those of the original employer, including the conditions under which the agreed type of work is performed; at the time of the transfer, only one of the subjects of the employment relationship, i.e., the employer, changes, while the actual content of the employment relationship remains unaffected. However, the changes by which the defendant claims to have sought to reorganise the loss-making shops (including the one where the applicant worked) were not merely cosmetic and insubstantial, but 'completely modified' the content of the applicant's employment relationship, contrary to the above-mentioned premise. The organisational structure of the shop was changed in terms of its content and scope (replacing the three departmental managers with two deputy managers), while the two deputy managers' posts were not actually filled until at least 11 February 2016, and their work activities, i.e., their rights, duties and responsibilities, were until then actually exercised by the applicant. At that time, it was not possible to perform work tasks during standard working hours, which indirectly suggests that there was a significant increase in overtime hours. Any compensation by way of a reduction in other work tasks was, therefore, according to the Court of Appeal, essentially unrealistic. On the contrary, the so-called residents, who, according to the defendant, were supposed to be subordinate to the applicant, were, on the contrary, subject only to the Polish management, and, moreover, that position was not held by only one person, whereas, on the contrary, the residents were obliged to supervise the work of the shop manager and his deputies. The lack of transparency of that position, which was not mentioned in the defendant's official organigram but was in fact created, and the lack of clarity of the responsibilities of those persons, as well as the language barrier, all undoubtedly also had a significant negative impact on the performance of the applicant's work and the fulfilment of his duties. Also, the change in the language of communication between the employee and the employer, which in effect implies the necessity of having qualified knowledge of a foreign language (even though it belongs to the Slavic languages), is certainly a change in the characteristics of the original employment relationship, to the worse, if the employee has only a limited knowledge of that language. The further substantial deterioration in the applicant's working conditions was also caused by the fact that the defendant introduced new programmes and procedures without training the management and staff of the shop. The installation of cameras in the manager's office, aimed directly at the applicant's desk, can also be regarded as a substantial deterioration in working conditions. Moreover, the conditions of the Labour Code for surveillance of an employee to become a lawful activity have not been established in the proceedings.

The Supreme Court dismissed the employer's appeal. It recalled that if the rights and obligations are transferred to a new employer, then the new employer takes over those rights and obligations in the same quality and with the same characteristics as those of the original employer, including the conditions under which the agreed type of work is performed, and that the moment of the transfer only changes one of the subjects of the employment relationship, i.e., the employer, while the actual content of the employment relationship remains unaffected.

It is characteristic of the transfer of rights and obligations under employment relationships and of the transfer of the exercise of rights and obligations under employment relationships that the rights and obligations under the employment relationship or the exercise of rights and obligations under the employment relationship of the employee are transferred to the transferee employer or to the transferee organisational unit of the state without the consent of the employees affected thereby being required and that none of the employees affected by such transfer can prevent it (on the part of the employer) by his or her legal action. Thus, an employee in whose relationship the rights and obligations under the employment relationship have been transferred or in whose relationship the exercise of the rights and obligations under the employment relationship have been transferred is obliged to continue to work for the transferee employer or for the transferee organisational unit of the State, even if he does not consent to the change in the subject of the employment relationship.

Since – as the case law of the Court of Justice of the European Union has established – 'an employee is not a commodity but a human being with human dignity' and since an employee 'should have the right to oppose the transfer of his employment relationship by his own legal action in the event of disagreement with the person of the new employer', the law (cf. Act No. 365/2011 Coll., amending Act No. 262/2006 Coll, Labour Code, as amended, and other related laws, Part One, points 56 and 300, which implemented Council Directive No. 2001/23/EC, on the approximation of the laws of the Member States relating to the safeguarding of employees' rights in the event of transfers of undertakings, businesses or parts of undertakings or businesses), that an employee who gives notice of termination of employment in connection with the transfer of rights and obligations under employment relationships or the transfer of the exercise of rights and obligations under employment relationships shall have his employment terminated no later than the day preceding the date on which the transfer of rights and obligations under employment relationships takes effect or the date on which the transfer of the exercise of rights and obligations under employment relationships takes effect (cf. section 51a of the Labour Code). Thus, a notice of termination of employment given by an employee in connection with the transfer of rights and obligations under the employment relationship or the transfer of the exercise of rights and obligations under the employment relationship and, in this context, the shortening of the notice period is a legal means by which he may prevent the transfer of rights and obligations under his employment relationship to the transferee employer.

However, it should be borne in mind that a notice of termination of employment given by an employee 'in connection with' the transfer of rights and obligations under the employment relationship or the transfer of the exercise of rights and obligations under the employment relationship is given if the notice was given before the effective date of the transfer of rights and obligations under the employment relationship or the transfer of the exercise of rights and obligations under the employment relationship, and, at the same time, if, according to the content of the notice, the reason or at least the motive for the termination of the employment relationship was the expected transfer of rights and obligations under employment relationships to the transferee employer or the transfer of the exercise of rights and obligations under employment relationships to the transferee organisational unit of the State.

However, the new circumstances which subsequently arise because of the transfer of rights and obligations under the employment relationship may sometimes only become apparent after the transfer has taken effect and the employee, as in the present case, has become familiar with the new terms and conditions of employment as set out by the transferee employer. In this case, the provisions of Article 339a(1)(a) Labour Code provide that if the employee's notice of termination is given within two months of the date on which the transfer of rights and obligations under the employment relationship became effective or the transfer of the exercise of rights and obligations under the employment relationship became effective, or if the employee's employment relationship was terminated by agreement within the same period, the employee may apply to the court for a declaration that the termination of the employment relationship was due to a substantial deterioration in working conditions in connection with the transfer of rights and obligations arising from labour relations or in connection with exercise of rights and obligations under employment law.

The aim (purpose) of the legal regulation of the transfer of rights and obligations under labour law relationships is – among other things – the special protection of employees, as follows in particular from the provisions of section 1a(1)(a) and (d) of the Labour Code. The protection of employees consists, on the one hand, in the (automatic) transfer of rights and obligations under employment relationships from the transferor (the former employer) to the transferee (the new employer), on the other hand, in the prohibition of termination of the employment relationship for reasons consisting in the preparation for the structural change (transition) and in the actual implementation of the structural change (transition), and, on the other hand, in the extended information and consultation obligations of the employer (cf. section 339a of the Labour Code).

The same category (increased protection of the employee) also includes the employee's option enshrined in section 339a of the Act. The same category (increased protection of the employee) also includes the employee's option enshrined in Section 339a of the Labour Code, to seek a determination that the reason (unjustified or otherwise justified) for the termination of employment or the agreement on termination of employment was a substantial deterioration of working conditions in connection with a change of employer.

The law does not specifically state, nor is it possible to do so for each individual case, 'what all falls under the terms and conditions of employment within the meaning of Section 339a of the Act. Labour', as the appellant puts the question; it only imposes a general obligation on the employer to create conditions for the performance of the employee's work tasks. Undoubtedly, the working conditions must be 'satisfactory' or 'satisfactory and safe', but it does not define the concept of 'deterioration of working conditions', nor does it define under what circumstances a deterioration may be 'substantial'.

Therefore, the concept of working conditions cannot be reduced only to the circumstances regulated by the Labour Code – type of work, place of work, remuneration, etc. Such conditions must be all the conditions (circumstances) perceived by (acting on) the employee in the performance of work under the employment contract. The fact that it is primarily those conditions which are enshrined in the employment contract and its related documents (job description, work rules, etc.) is only the basis for the perception of the whole complex of other conditions (circumstances) which affect the employee in the performance of his/her work. By contrast, those conditions (circumstances) which arise from the legislation cannot be relevant, since they (in themselves) relate to the work performed by the employee, irrespective of the change of employer. However, the methods (means) used to implement the legislation in a particular workplace in relation to particular employees may be relevant, as these may also change with a change of employer. How the new conditions are assessed by the employee or the successor employer is irrelevant to the conclusion as to the extent to which the deterioration in working conditions has reached a substantial level.

It follows from the foregoing that the concept of working conditions will not be a fixed constant, a list of circumstances to be considered whenever it comes to assessing whether there has been a substantial deterioration in working conditions. Section 339a(1) of the Labour Code belongs to the category of legal norms with a relatively vague hypothesis, i.e., norms whose hypothesis is not set out directly in the legislation and which thus leave it to the court's discretion to define the hypothesis of the legal norm itself in each individual case from a wide, unlimited range of circumstances. In assessing whether there has been a substantial deterioration in working conditions within the meaning of section 339a(1) of the Act, the Court of First Instance must determine whether there has been a substantial deterioration in working conditions. The court may thus consider, for example, the following: the circumstances affecting the performance of work in terms of economic, social, technical and technological, psychological, physical and physiological, health, safety, as well as the difficulty of the work (physical or psychological) and its quantity, the quality of the working environment and of the working and interpersonal relations at the workplace (as mentioned by the applicant), the organisational changes made, the possibilities of language communication, the new programmes and management introduced, the degree of control over work and personal (private) activities, the new requirements for work reporting (as the courts have found), etc. At the same time, the aspects (circumstances) outlined may have varying degrees of relevance in each individual case in the light of its other circumstances. If the hypothesis of the legal rule has been correctly defined, the decision in the case cannot be contrary to law on the ground that other circumstances have not been clarified or that other circumstances which cannot be regarded as relevant or important in the case under consideration have not been considered.

The Court of Appeal agrees with the Court of Appeal's conclusion that the applicant's employment conditions had substantially deteriorated as a result of the transfer of rights and obligations under the employment relationship and that the applicant had terminated his employment by giving notice for that reason. In that connection, the Court of Appeal correctly took into account, in particular, the fact that the structure of the applicant's responsibilities had been changed, that communication had shifted to an emphasis on the Polish language, that the amount of overtime had increased, that there had been changes in the technical conditions of work (IT technology and programmes, the number of communication devices), reporting and the introduction of a CCTV system to monitor the applicant as well. Thus, the Court of Appeal defined the Labour Code in accordance with the law.

That decision is relevant to the determination of the circumstances in which a substantial deterioration in working conditions may be considered. However, it does not deal with an aspect that has been criticised in the literature. Although severance pay does provide some satisfaction, it is not fully sufficient. According to Martin

Štefek,[34] the employee is substantially limited in his right, since he can only claim severance pay as compensation for an employment relationship terminated prematurely without his fault, not full compensation. The amount of severance pay is determined in accordance with section 67(1) of the Labour Code,[35] the duration of the employment relationship with the transferring employer must also include the duration of the employment relationship with the former (transferring) employer. Martin Štefko describes the regulation in question as pro-employer from the point of view of the knowledge of practice, and therefore as not sufficiently functional in terms of protection of bullied or discriminated employees in terms of limiting satisfaction.[36]

§4.07 REDUCTION OF THE NOTICE PERIOD

The special protection of the employee in the transfer of rights and obligations under employment law is also reflected in the shortened notice period under section 51a of the Labour Code. In the case of the transfer of rights and obligations under employment law or the transfer of the exercise of rights and obligations under employment law, the employee's consent is not required for the transfer of rights and obligations, nor can the employee prevent it. He is therefore obliged to continue to work for the employer to whom the rights and obligations, or the exercise thereof, have been transferred, even if he does not consent to the change of employer. If the employee does not want to work for the employer who is taking over, he may terminate the employment relationship by

34. Štefko, Martin. Labour Code, Practical Commentary, Wolters Kluwer, 2022.
35. Section 67(1) of the Labour Code. (a) to (c) or by agreement for the same reasons shall be entitled to a severance payment from the employer upon termination of employment in an amount of at least: (a) one times his average earnings if his employment with the employer lasted less than one year, (b) twice his average earnings if his employment with the employer lasted at least one year and less than two years, (c) three times his average earnings if his employment relationship with the employer lasted at least two years 4. The duration of the employment relationship shall be deemed to include the duration of the previous employment relationship with the same employer, provided that the period between the termination of that employment relationship and the beginning of the subsequent employment relationship does not exceed six months.

    Section 67(2) of the Labour Code: an employee whose employment is terminated by notice given by the employer for the reasons specified in section 52(d) or by agreement for the same reasons shall be entitled to a severance payment from the employer at the termination of employment in an amount of at least 12 times the average earnings. If the employment relationship with the employee has been terminated because he or she is no longer able to perform his or her previous work because of an occupational accident or occupational disease, according to a medical report issued by an occupational health service provider or by a decision of the competent administrative authority reviewing the medical report, and the employer has fully discharged his or her obligation under Section 270(1), the employee shall not be entitled to severance pay under the second sentence.

    Section 67(3) of the Labour Code: for the purposes of severance pay, average earnings means average monthly earnings.

    Section 67(4) of the Labour Code: the employer is obliged to pay the severance pay to the employee after the termination of the employment relationship on the next pay date specified by the employer for payment of wages or salary, unless the employer agrees in writing with the employee to pay the severance pay on the date of termination of the employment relationship or on a later date of payment.
36. Štefko, Martin. Labour Code, Practical Commentary, Wolters Kluwer, 2022.

giving notice. In such a case, the notice must be given before the effective date of the transfer of rights and obligations under employment law or the transfer of the exercise of rights and obligations under employment law and the reason for the notice (or at least the motive for the notice) must be the expected transfer of rights and obligations under employment law or the transfer of the exercise of rights and obligations under employment law. Thus, this is a special provision to section 50(3) of the Labour Code, according to which an employee may give notice to the employer for any reason or for no reason at all since notice under section 51a of the Labour Code requires a 'connection' with the transition of rights and obligations under employment law or the transition of the exercise of rights and obligations under employment law.

The provisions of section 51a were amended by Act No. 285/2020 Coll., which entered into force on 30 July 2020. Until the adoption of the amendment, if the employee gave notice in connection with the transfer of rights and obligations under employment law or the transfer of the exercise of rights and obligations under employment law, the employment relationship shall terminate no later than the day preceding the effective date of the transfer of rights and obligations under employment law or the effective date of the transfer of the exercise of rights and obligations under employment law.

According to the explanatory memorandum to the amendment, the legal regulation of section 51a effective as of 1 January 2012 enforced the employee's right to freely choose the employer, thus exposing the existing and especially the transferring employer to considerable uncertainty, since the number of employees to be transferred was not clear until the effective date of the transfer. It was not impossible that the employees would wait until the last possible moment to give notice. This was particularly problematic from the point of view of the successor employer, who might not have had sufficient time to find replacements for those employees who did not eventually transfer, which could ultimately have jeopardised the smooth continuation of the predecessor's activities. Another problematic point of the previous legislation was the fact that notice under section 51a could only be given until the day before the effective date of the transition. Thus, if the employee was not informed of the transition and it subsequently took place, he could only give notice to the transferee employer with the traditional length of notice. The employee was thus ultimately obliged to work for an employer with whom he had not entered an employment relationship of his own free choice for several months in a dependent position.

§4.08 A NOTICE OF TERMINATION OF EMPLOYMENT GIVEN BY AN EMPLOYEE WHO HAS BEEN INFORMED OF THE TRANSFER IN A TIMELY MANNER

With effect from 30 July 2020, the Labour Code consistently distinguishes whether a notice of termination due to the transfer of rights and obligations under employment relationships or due to the transfer of the exercise of rights and obligations under employment relationships was delivered to the employee before the effective date of the transfer or after the effective date of the transfer.

The provisions of section 51a(1) apply to situations where the employee was informed of the transfer of rights and obligations under the employment relationship to another employer within the scope of section 339 in time, i.e., no later than 30 days before the transfer, or before the effective date of the transfer. If the employee does not wish to continue to work for the transferring employer, he or she may resign on the grounds of the transfer and the employment relationship shall end no later than the day preceding the effective date of the transfer. In order to enhance the legal certainty of the incumbent and the transferee employer as to the number of employees who are to be transferred, this option of the employee is limited to a period of 15 days, starting from the date on which the employee is informed directly, pursuant to the provisions of section 339(1) of the Labour Code, of the name and registered office of the transferee employer, if a legal person, or the name and address, if a natural person; of the fixed or proposed date of the transfer; of the reasons for the transfer, the legal, economic and social consequences of the transfer for the employees and of the measures envisaged in relation to the employees (including envisaged structural changes, rationalisation or organisational measures, measures affecting employment, measures in connection with collective redundancies).

Failure by the former employer or the successor employer to comply with the information and consultation obligations pursuant to section 339, or failure to reach agreement in consultation with the relevant trade union body, works council or directly affected employees, shall not render the legal act by which the transfer of rights and obligations under employment law is effected null and void or apparent (section 19(2)). Failure to comply with the information and consultation obligation under section 339(1) (but not (2)) within the time limit is an offence for legal entities and natural persons engaged in business in cooperation between the employer and the body acting on behalf of the employees (sections 10 and 23 of the Labour Inspection Act). Other sanctions may be imposed in accordance with Act No. 250/2016 Coll., on liability for offences and proceedings thereon.

§4.09 A NOTICE OF TERMINATION OF EMPLOYMENT GIVEN BY AN EMPLOYEE WHO HAS NOT BEEN INFORMED OF THE TRANSFER IN TIME OR AT ALL WITHIN THE SCOPE OF SECTION 339 OF THE LABOUR CODE

Section 51a(2) then applies to situations where the employee was not informed of the transfer in time or even at all within the scope of section 339. The second paragraph distinguishes whether the employee's notice in such cases was served on the employer before the effective date of the transition, or afterwards. If the employee's notice was given before the date on which the transition takes effect, then, under the provisions of section 51a(2)(a), the employment relationship ends on the day before the date on which the transition takes effect. If the employee's notice is given subsequently, i.e., within two months of the date on which the transition takes effect, the employment relationship shall, pursuant to section 51a(2)(b), end on the expiry of the notice period, which shall be 15 days and shall commence on the date on which the notice is delivered to the employer. The two situations have in common that the employee is not limited by the 15-day period under paragraph 1, which is set in the event that the employee was informed of the transfer in good time, i.e., not later than 30 days before the transfer.

CHAPTER 5

Denmark

Mette Klingsten

§5.01 HISTORY OF THE RULES AS IMPLEMENTED IN DENMARK

Council Directive 77/187/EEC on the approximation of the laws of the Member States relating to the safeguarding of employees' rights in the event of transfers of undertakings, businesses or parts of businesses was implemented into Danish law by Law No. 111 of 21 March 1979. The rules have therefore been in force in Denmark for 45 years. This Directive was amended by Directive 98/50/EC, which was later repealed and replaced by Directive 2001/23/EC of 12 March 2001. The Directive, as last amended by Directive (EU) 2015/1794, is commonly referred to as the 'Acquired Rights Directive.'

The 1998 Directive was implemented in Denmark by Act No. 441 of 7 June 2001. A consolidated version of the Danish Acts as of 2002 is found in Executive Order No. 710 of 20 August 2002, as last amended by Act No. 385 of 26 April 2017 in connection with the removal of the exemption concerning seagoing vessels. Furthermore, a codification of an already existing practice was incorporated by Act No. 530 of 27 March 2021, adding a new section to the Danish Act concerning transfer in connection with restructuring or bankruptcy proceedings. In these cases, the transferee only assumes rights and obligations towards employees, which relate to the time after the commencement of the restructuring proceedings or the date of the bankruptcy decree.

The social partners play an essential role in the Danish labour market. Collective bargaining agreements are very important for the labour market for employees, not only in the large industry, construction, and retail sectors but also for employees working as engineers or in banking. In the private sector, about 70% of the employees are covered by a collective bargaining agreement (depending on how the calculation is made), and in the public sector (including both the state and the regional and local municipalities), close to 100% of employees are covered by collective bargaining agreements. Thus, collective bargaining agreements form an essential part of the Danish labour market system.

Despite this, collective agreements have not been used to implement the Acquired Rights Directive, which has instead been implemented by separate legislation (The Business Transfer Act). This Act covers all employees with the definition of employee being 'an employee' in an 'employment relationship', meaning an individual working under the instruction of an employer and with the normal characters of being an employee.

Most, but not all, rules of the Danish Business Transfer Act are directly implemented in the directive's provisions; however, with adaptations for Danish-specific rules, for example, on labour market pensions. *See* under §5.07 below.

Furthermore, the Danish Business Transfer Act includes a provision a section 4a, which does not follow from the EU directives cf. below. This provision governs the status of collective bargaining agreements in connection with transfers of undertakings. This section has been further developed by decisions from the industrial arbitration tribunal and the labour court.

The Industrial Arbitration Tribunal has held that a transferee (buyer) of a business did not automatically become a party to a collective agreement, which covered the transferring employees. The buyer was only obliged to ensure that the individual employees' employment terms and conditions as at the time of the takeover, including the conditions that followed from the collective agreement, were transferred. However, in contrast to this, the courts have maintained previous practice, according to which a buyer, by being passive, can be considered to have agreed to the collective agreement. In a ruling in the *Superfos* Case, the court held that the buyer could wait almost six weeks before indicating whether the buyer wished to release itself from the collective agreement applicable to the business, which the buyer had purchased.

The Danish Parliament found that it was inappropriate that the Danish Act on Business Transfers did not comprehensively describe the details of the law in this area. There were no rules on what a reasonable period would be to renounce and thereby not be bound by a CBA, or when there would be deemed to have been an undue delay and thus no longer a right to renounce.

This uncertainty was solved by the introduction of section 4a, subsection 1 of the Act.

The social partners were involved in the implementation of the Directive and the drafting of the Danish Act on Transfer of Undertakings, which was drafted on the basis of the 'Report of the Committee for the Preparation of Implementing Legislation of the EEC Directive on the Legal Position of Employees in the event of a Transfer of Undertakings', consisting of members from the Danish Employers' Confederation (DA), the Confederation of Trade Unions (LO, now FH) and the Ministries of Trade, Justice and Labour.

In connection with the discussion of the bill in the Danish Parliament (in Danish 'Folketinget'), there were several discussions on whether the bill went beyond the directive on individual points, as well as discussion of the position of collective agreements in the event of a transfer of undertakings. This last item was solved with the inclusion of the abovementioned section 4a; however, despite this, a number of issues still arise in this area.

The Danish Act on Transfer of Undertakings does not include a provision governing the situation where an employee is terminated in contravention of the rules of the Act in the absence of economic, technical, or organisational reasons. This is an important topic and is discussed further below.

§5.02 COMMENTS ON THE CONCEPTUAL APPLICATION OF THE ACT

In the Danish text of the Acquired Rights Directive, the term 'workers' (in Danish 'arbejdstagere') is used to refer to persons protected by the Acquired Rights Directive. The Danish Act uses the term 'employees' (in Danish 'lønmodtager') instead. The terminology used in the Act on Transfer of Undertakings is not intended to alter the scope of the Act, i.e., which persons that are protected by the Act in relation to the Directive. The term 'employees' is just more commonly used in Danish labour law terminology than the term 'workers'.

Article 1(1)(a) of the Acquired Rights Directive defines a 'transferor' as 'any natural or legal person who, as a result of a transfer within the meaning of Article 1(1), ceases to be the owner of the undertaking, business or part of the undertaking or business'. Article 1(1)(b) of the Acquired Rights Directive defines the concept of 'transferee' as 'any natural or legal person who, as a result of a transfer within the meaning of Article 1(1), becomes the owner of the undertaking, business or part of the undertaking or business'.

Danish law does not contain similar definitions, and merely uses the terms 'transferor' and 'transferee'. These concepts are however understood in accordance with the definitions laid down in the Acquired Rights Directive.

The Acquired Rights Directive uses the terms '*transfer* of an undertaking, business, or part of an undertaking or business' and 'the date of transfer' of an undertaking.

Previously, the wording on the Act on Transfer of Undertakings didnot distinguish between 'transfer' meaning the date of the agreement between the transferor and the transferee and 'effective date of transfer', but only used the concept of transfer in various forms, not distinguishing between the date of signing of the business transfer agreement and the date of the transfer of the employees (the closing date). The term 'transfer' was understood both as an expression of the agreement on the sale, etc., of the business and as an expression of the subsequent actual transfer of the business on the agreed date of acquisition. The latter was the case, for example, in section 2(1), which referred to the date of transfer and where the term was to be understood as the date of acquisition or transfer. In 2001, section 2(1) was amended to make it clear that the transferee assumes the obligations of the transferor towards the employees employed (and not released, cf. below) at the time of the actual takeover. This will typically be the closing date mentioned in the asset purchase agreement or the supplier agreement entered in connection with a tender. However, if the actual takeover takes place on a date other than the agreed date, for instance, in connection with an anticipated bankruptcy, the actual date of the transfer will apply. This could be relevant and important, for instance, if the buyer starts running the business and has been given the keys to 'the shop' prior to the agreed start date.

By way of example, this could be relevant in the determination of whether the employee's individual notice period expired before or after the closing date or whether an employee was released before or after the closing date and thus whether the employee was transferred or not. Pursuant to Danish law, employees who are actively working, on parental leave, off on holiday, off due to illness, or suspended from the obligation to work will transfer over to the buyer by virtue of the Transfer of Undertakings Act. However, employees who have been released from the obligation to work prior to the transfer date would not transfer pursuant to the rules in the Business Transfer Act.

§5.03 TERRITORIAL SCOPE OF THE ACT

In a transfer situation, the general principle is that Danish law will apply when the company or part of the business being transferred is located in Denmark.

In addition, it follows from section 1(1) of the Act on Transfer of Undertakings that the Act applies to the transfer of a business or part thereof which falls within the area to which the TFEU applies, essentially within the borders of the EU.

As a result of the EEA Agreement, the Directive is extended to the entire EEA territory so that the rules also apply to Norway, Iceland, and Liechtenstein.

However, section 1(1) does not determine which country's legal rules should apply in the event of a cross-border transfer. This is determined in accordance with ordinary rules of private international law. The Danish Act only applies if ordinary Danish rules of private international law result in Danish law being applicable to the case relationship (typically, the location of the workplace).

If a Danish company buys a company located in Sweden where the work is carried out in Sweden, the relationship between the Danish company as acquirer and the Swedish company's employees will typically be regulated by Swedish law, and it will be the Swedish rules implementing the directive that determine the rights and obligations of the Danish buyer. In cases where Swedish employee choose to bring proceedings against the Danish acquirer at the Danish court of residence in Denmark (even though they would be able to bring the action in a court in Sweden), the dispute shall not be settled in accordance with the Danish Act on Transfer of Undertakings, but according to the Swedish rules implementing the Directive. Similarly, if a Danish company acquires a company located in Germany, the transfer will be governed by German law and the German rules of the BGB implementing the Directive. This takes on practical significance to the extent that the Directive has been implemented differently in Denmark and Germany.

If the place of work for the employees is in Denmark, Danish law is applicable regardless of whether the seller or buyer is Danish or not. So, by way of example, if a German company buys the activities of a branch of a Swedish company located in Denmark and with employees working in Denmark, then the Danish Act on Transfer of Undertakings will govern the rights and obligations of the employees in relation to the transfer irrespective of whether the buyer and the seller may have agreed that transfer agreement is governed by German law.

§5.04 SAFEGUARDING EMPLOYEES' RIGHTS IN THE EVENT OF TRANSFERS OF UNDERTAKINGS

The Act on Transfer of Undertakings is intended to safeguard employees' rights in connection with transfers of undertakings in accordance with the Acquired Rights Directive. The provisions of the Act on Transfer of Undertakings are mandatory to the same extent as the directive. This applies regardless of who takes the initiative to derogate from the law and regardless of whether the employee receives other advantageous terms which outweigh the disadvantages by waiving his or her rights under the Act.

At both national and EU level, economic developments are leading to changes in the structure of undertakings, in particular because of transfers of undertakings, businesses or parts of businesses to other owners as a result of transfers, mergers, divisions and other types of transfer. It is necessary to adopt provisions to protect employees in the event of a change of employer, in particular to ensure that the employees' rights are safeguarded.

The ordinary Danish courts, the Labour Court, and industrial arbitration tribunals have made several decisions concerning the interpretation of the rules on employees' rights and obligations in connection with transfers of undertakings. Danish courts have also submitted many cases to the European Court of Justice, including many of the important cases in the early days of the Acquired Rights Directive. According to EU law, the decision whether to submit a preliminary reference to the European Court of Justice rests with the national court concerned. However, if it is a court of last instance and if an answer to a question of interpretation of the directive is necessary to determine a case, the national court must submit a preliminary question. If it refrains from doing so, the Member State concerned may be held liable for a breach of EU law. According to Article 267 of the TFEU, a preliminary reference may be submitted if two premises are jointly met: (i) a question of EU law is raised before a national court; and (ii) a decision on that question is necessary for the national court to give judgment on the case, which the national court is to decide.

The judgment in the case concerning *Daddy's Dance Hall* from 1988 (Case 324/86) was important to the interpretation of the directive, also in many of the later cases concerning mergers. In this case, the Danish Supreme Court posed two questions to the European Court of Justice. In the *Daddy's Dance Hall* case, Mr Tellerup was employed as a restaurant manager by the transferor, Irma Catering A/S. When its lease was terminated, Irma Catering dismissed all its staff, including Mr Tellerup, whose statutory period of notice expired on 30 April 1983. But Irma Catering continued to run the business with the same staff until 25 February 1983, with effect from which date a new lease was concluded between the landlord and Daddy's Dance Hall A/S. Daddy's Dance Hall immediately re-employed the employees of the former lessee, including Mr Tellerup, to do the same jobs as before. The new management contract, which was concluded with Mr. Tellerup, provided that his remuneration, which had previously been in the form of commission, would take the form of a fixed salary. At his request, a trial period of three months was agreed on, during which either side could give 14 days' notice. This was a shorter period of notice than that to which Mr. Tellerup was entitled if his employment with the transferor was taken into account. He was dismissed on 26 April 1983 with 14 days' notice. The Danish Supreme Court asked the European Court of Justice two questions. First, the European Court of Justice was asked to consider whether Article 1(1)of the Acquired Rights Directive was applicable in a situation where a non-transferrable lease of a business is terminated and as a result, without there being any interruption in the running of the business, the owner leases the business to a new lease-taker, who re-employs the staff, who had been given notice but had not left their employment, and buys the former leaseholder's stock, which could be used to run the business? This was the first time this question had been raised, although it was raised in different forms in the subsequent years.

The European Court of Justice emphasised that the purpose of the Acquired Rights Directive is to ensure, so far as possible, that the rights of employees are safeguarded in the event of a change of employer by allowing them to remain in employment with the new employer on the terms and conditions agreed with the previous employer. The directive is therefore applicable where, following a legal transfer or merger, there is a change in the natural or legal person who is responsible for carrying on the business and who by virtue of that fact incurs the obligations of an employer vis-à-vis employees of the undertaking, regardless of whether ownership of the undertaking is transferred.

It follows that where, upon the expiry of the lease, one leaseholder ceases to be the employer and a third party becomes the employer under a new lease concluded with the owner, the resulting operation can fall within the scope of the directive as defined in Article 1(1). The fact that in such a case the transfer is effected in two stages, in that the undertaking is first retransferred from the original leaseholder to the owner and the latter then transfers it to a new leaseholder, does not prevent the Acquired Rights Directive from applying, provided that the economic unit in question retains its identity; that is so in particular when, as in this case, the business is carried on without interruption by the new leaseholder with the same staff as were employed in the business before the transfer. Therefore, the Acquired Rights Directive must be interpreted as meaning that its provisions apply where, upon the termination of a non-transferable lease, the owner of an undertaking leases it to a new leaseholder, who carries on the business without interruption with the same staff who had been given notice on the expiry of the initial lease. In other words – and as decided in many subsequent cases, the directive is applicable even though the two employers had not entered into any agreement concerning the transfer of a business.

The second question was whether an employee may waive rights conferred upon him by the Acquired Rights Directive if the disadvantages resulting from his waiver are offset by such benefits that, taking the matter as a whole, his rights are not altered in such a way as to leave him in a worse position.

The European Court of Justice held that the purpose of the Acquired Rights Directive is to ensure that employees' rights resulting from a contract of employment or employment relationship are safeguarded in a transfer situation. Since this protection was a matter of public policy, and therefore independent of the will of the parties to the contract of employment, the rules of the directive, in particular those concerning the protection of workers against dismissal by reason of the transfer, had to be considered mandatory, so that it is not possible to derogate from them in a manner unfavourable to employees. It follows that the employees are not entitled to waive the rights conferred on them by the directive and that those rights cannot be restricted even with their consent. This interpretation is not affected by the fact that, as in this case, the employee obtains new benefits in compensation for the disadvantages resulting from an amendment to his contract of employment, so that, taking the matter, he is not placed in a worse position than before. However, as the court held in the *Danmols Inventar* case from 1985 (Case C-105/84), the directive is intended to achieve only partial harmonisation, essentially by extending the protection guaranteed to workers independently by the laws of the individual Member States to cover the case where an undertaking is transferred. It is not intended to establish a uniform level of protection throughout the Community on the basis of common criteria. Thus, the directive can be relied on only to ensure that the employee is protected in his relations with the transferee to the same extent as he was in his relations with the transferor pursuant to the rules of the Member State concerned. Consequently, in so far as national law allows the employment relationship to be altered in a manner unfavourable to employees in situations other than the transfer of an undertaking, in particular as regards their protection against dismissal, such an alternative is not precluded merely because the undertaking has been transferred in the meantime and the agreement has therefore been made with the new employer.

Since by virtue of Article 3(1) of the Directive, the transferee is subrogated to the transferor's rights and obligations under the employment relationship, that relationship may be altered with regard to the transferee to the same extent as it could have been with regard to the transferor, provided that the transfer of the undertaking itself may never constitute the reason for the alteration. For the above reasons, the answer to these questions must be that an employee cannot waive the rights conferred on him by the mandatory provisions of the Acquired Rights Directive even if the disadvantages resulting from his waiver are offset by such benefits that, taking the matter as a whole, he is not placed in a worse position. Nevertheless, the directive does not preclude an agreement with the new employer to alter the employment relationship, insofar as such an alteration is permitted by the applicable national law in situations other than the transfer of an undertaking. Under Danish law, it would not be permissible to enter into an agreement whereby an employee was to enter a new trial period - say after two years of uninterrupted employment in connection with a promotion or agreed changes to the employment - even if such agreement was voluntary.

After the European Court of Justice rendered its decision on the preliminary questions asked, the defendant, Daddys Dance Hall A/S accepted as part of the decision of the Danish Supreme Court that the plaintiff was entitled to three months' notice of termination, as his length of service should be counted from his employment with the first leaseholder, thus entitling him to three months' notice of termination and thus that the agreement concerning a new trial period could not be upheld.

Nowadays, it is perhaps fair to say that Danish courts are not always very keen on asking questions to the European Court of Justice when the parties ask for this, and of course, Danish courts should take the 'Acte clair' doctrine into consideration. National courts must refrain from requesting a preliminary ruling under Article 267(3) TFEU from the Court of Justice of the European Union if the interpretation of, for instance, a directive is obvious, cf. the CILFIT judgment (Case C-283/81). In this case, the Court of Justice of the European Union confirmed the existence of the acte clair doctrine and laid down the conditions for its application. Cases are acte clair when the correct application of EU law is so obvious that there is no scope for reasonable doubt. Over the years, the European Court of Justice has answered many questions from various Member States concerning the interpretation of the Acquired Rights Directive, so the need for additional rulings should – all things being even – diminish.

In practice, there have been several key issues of practical relevance. Some of these topics are described below in sections §5.05-§5.08.

§5.05 A TRANSFER OF AN ECONOMIC ENTITY THAT RETAINS ITS IDENTITY

Section 1 of the Danish Transfer of Business Act regulates the scope of the Act. Section 1(2) provides that the rules also apply to public and private undertakings engaged in an economic activity, whether or not they are profit-making. It follows from Article 1(1)(b) of the Directive that the definition of a transfer covered by the Directive is 'a transfer of an economic entity which retains its identity'. In many judgments, the European Court of Justice has ruled on what is required in order for an entity to retain its identity after the transfer.

For a long time, it was widely accepted that in those industries which are characterised by the absence of significant operating assets (e.g., movable property) and where the activity is thus mainly labour-based (e.g., cleaning), the decisive factor in relation to the question of whether identity is preserved is whether the acquirer takes over a significant part of the workforce by number and qualifications who were engaged by the transferee in the activity being transferred (*see*, for example, C-13/95 – *Süzen*, paragraph 21, and C-200/16 – *Securitas*, paragraph 29).

This is different in industries where the existence of operating assets is essential to the conduct of the business. In such a situation, the transfer of the operating assets concerned becomes central to the assessment.

The issues are often considered in an outsourcing situation in which there is a tripartite relationship. Such outsourcing situations do not prevent the application of the Act on Transfer of Undertakings even in the absence of: (i) a direct contractual relationship between the 'transferor' and the 'transferee'. The determination of the applicability of the law also depends on whether: (ii) there is a transfer of the economic unit. However, the termination of a contract between a contracting entity and a contractor, whereafter the contracting entity concludes a new contract with another provider under a similar contractual construct (change of supplier), is not in itself sufficient for the application of the law.

As regards the question of whether or not to take over employees in undertakings characterised by 'man-power' in the context of the transfer of undertakings, *Süzen* must continue to be regarded as the leading case and expression of applicable law. This is also confirmed by the European Court of Justice in the CLECE case, Case C-463/09, where a cleaner was terminated in connection with the cessation of the employer's contract with a public authority. The municipal contracting authority retracted the cleaning task itself and employed five staff members to carry out the task of cleaning its premises, even though the CLECE employee had made his manpower available. In this regard, the European Court of Justice ruled that the Directive should be interpreted as not applying to a situation where a municipality that had entrusted the cleaning of its premises to a private undertaking decided to terminate the contract with that undertaking and to carry out the cleaning of those premises itself recruited new staff for that purpose.

An alternative solution may be to take the view that, if it was natural for the transferee to take over a substantial part of the workforce because he did not have the staff to perform the task himself and the transferee has sought to recruit new employees to perform the task, including, possibly, some of the employees previously employed by the transferor, the Act on Transfer of Undertakings applies. This line was followed by the English Court of Appeal in *ECM (Vehicle Delivery Service) Ltd. v. Cox and Others* (1997 I.R.L.R.) (UK Court of Appeal), where the court took into account elements from the *Süzen* decision, but held that the continuation of the same activity/activities carried out by the acquirer was sufficient to constitute a transfer of an undertaking. The decision states that the transferee cannot prevent the application of the rules on the transfer of undertakings simply by refusing to take over the employees whom he would normally take over if the acquirer had its own employees who could perform the task won in the tender. No employees were transferred and therefore there was no transfer covered by the Directive. In addition, reference may be made to *ADI (UK) Ltd v. Willer* ((Court of Appeal), 22 June 2001), in which the English Court of Appeal held that if no employees were transferred in an otherwise labour-intensive operation, there was no transfer of an undertaking, unless the reason for not transferring employees was a desire to avoid the application of the rules of the Directive.

However, when reading English decisions, it should be noted that the *principles of Süzen* have generally not been applied in English law since 2006, when the English TUPE was amended, so that English law now goes beyond the provisions of the Directive. Under English law, there is now an automatic transfer of an undertaking in various outsourcing and insourcing situations, namely: (1) outsourcing, (2) re-contracting (i.e., where an existing tender contract is outsourced to a new contractor) and (3) insourcing (where a previously outsourced service is withdrawn 'in-house'). However, it is still a condition that the post-transfer activities must be essentially of the same nature as before the transfer.

The question of a business which retains its identity has also been of particular significance in the so-called three-party relations.

It is well know that the European Court of Justice has ruled that an undertaking of a public transport activities such as the operation of local bus routes previously operated by another undertaking, following a procedure for the award of a public service contract, may fall in the material scope of the Directive (*see*, for example C-172/99 – Liikenne, paragraph 25).

In view of the possible application of the Directive, it is necessary to consider the factual circumstances of the particular transaction, including whether operating assets such as vehicles are being transferred, whether its employees are taken over by the new employer, whether its customers are transferred, etc. These are merely an example of single factors to be considered in the overall assessment. In *Liikenne*, the court held that bus transport cannot be regarded as an activity based on manpower, as it requires substantial equipment. The fact that operating assets were not transferred consequently led to the Directive not being applicable. This approach has also been followed by Danish courts, hereunder in a Supreme Court decision from 2016.

However, it should be noted that the new operator of a bus route as a result of new technical and environmental standards required by the contracting authority may not take over the undertaking's operating assets. This situation does not necessarily preclude the taking over of the activity concerned from being classified as a 'transfer of an undertaking' within the meaning of the Directive (*see*, for example, C-298/18 – Grafe und Pohle, paragraph 35).

In conclusion, it must still be presumed that the transferring of operating assets is necessary for an undertaking to conduct its primary functions is still needed in order to fall within the scope of the Directive, but certain circumstances may lead to a different result.

§5.06 REORGANISATION IN THE PUBLIC SECTOR

An exception applies to the reorganisation of public administrative authorities or a transfer of administrative functions between public administrative authorities in accordance with what is laid down in the Acquired Rights Directive. An administrative reorganisation of public administrative authorities or a transfer of administrative functions between public administrative authorities is not a transfer within the meaning of the Directive.

In a recent case, joined cases C-583/21 and C-586/21, the European Court of Justice, has ruled on whether the Directive should be interpreted to apply in a situation where a notary who is a public employee and at the same time a private company manager for his employees takes over the notary office (including the notarial register and the employees who worked for the former notary).

The question involved whether notarial activities fall under the exception for public authorities. In this regard, the European Court of Justice noted that Spanish notaries are public servants appointed by ministerial orders following a selection.

The European Court of Justice found that Spanish notaries did not fall under the exception of reorganisation and transfer within the public sector, citing, among other things, that citizens are free to choose a notary and that notaries carry out their activities under competitive conditions, which is not characteristic of the exercise of powers that are attributed to public authority.

In Denmark, the principles of the Act on Transfer of Undertakings have been applied (on the basis of special legislation) in connection with the transfer of employees of the municipal and regional tax authorities in connection with a reorganisation of the tax service and a transfer of tasks from the municipalities to the state, regardless of the fact that this was not part of the mandatory scope of the Act. In accordance with the Acquired Rights Directive, the Danish Act on Transfer of Undertakings does not apply to the transfer of administrative functions between public authorities, cf. section 1(2) of the Act. Thus, in the event of a transfer of tasks from one public authority to another, the Act on Transfer of Undertakings does not apply to employees engaged in public authority tasks pursuant to current law; however, it will apply to other groups of employees, including employees engaged in operational tasks not involving the exercise of such authority. To ensure a uniform legal basis for all employees and other non-civil servant employees, a law was passed in the Danish Parliament, which meant that the Act on Transfer of Undertakings applied *mutatis mutandis* to those employees, etc., who were otherwise not covered by the Act on Transfer of Undertakings. This extended the scope of application of the Act in these particular situations. This also had the practical consequence that, as a general rule, employees are obliged to accept a change of employer and could not regard the change of employer as a (cause of) termination, provided that no other significant changes were made to the terms of employment of the individual employees in connection with the transfer.

In Denmark, the rules have been implemented so that there is no principle of consent from the individual employee in a transfer situation. The Act on Transfer of Undertakings means that employees generally have the right to continue employment on the previous terms. The assessment was that it was sensible that the employees, etc., who were transferred from municipal employment to employment in the state, were given uniform rights in connection with the transfer, including that the conditions of employment of the persons concerned should continue unchanged. However, it was clarified that the employees were generally obliged to fulfil their employment agreements when employed by the state after their assignment was transferred. Thus, they could not consider themselves made redundant even though they had been transferred to a new employer. This was of course also a good solution for the Danish municipalities and the Danish state, since it would have been very expensive to terminate the tax employees, since many of them had the right to severance pay in the event of termination. Although the transfer of the tax tasks was covered by the definition of 'An administrative or statutory reorganization of public, administrative authorities or a transfer of administrative functions between public, administrative authorities' and as such not a transfer within the meaning of the Transfer of Undertakings Act, the legislator chose to adopt a separate law, applying the principles of the act also in this situation.

§5.07 COLLECTIVE AGREEMENTS IN THE EVENT OF THE TRANSFER OF UNDERTAKINGS

The Danish labour market is highly regulated by collective agreements, which is one of the main reasons why a number of labour law issues are regulated by collective agreement rather than by legislation, such as the normal number of weekly work hours, minimum pay, labour market pensions, additional holidays, etc. The position of collective agreements in connection with transfers of undertakings is therefore very important.

Section 2(1) of the Danish Act on Transfer of Undertakings reads as follows:

> 2. Where all or part of an undertaking is transferred, the transferee shall be directly subrogated to the rights and obligations existing at the time of the acquisition under:
> (1) collective agreement and agreement,
> (2) provisions on pay and working conditions established or approved by public authorities; and
> (3) individual agreement on pay and working conditions.

The provision was clarified in 2001 so that the word 'date of transfer' was changed to 'date of takeover' to clarify that these were rights and obligations at the time when the employees are transferred to employment with the transferee and not at the time when the transferor and transferee concluded the agreement on the transfer of activity.

The Acquired Rights Directive stipulates that it is the individual conditions under the collective agreement that must be respected. According to Article 3(3) of the Directive, 'the transferee shall maintain the pay and working conditions applicable to the transferor under a collective agreement'. The Directive does not, therefore, bind the transferee by the transferor's collective agreement as a whole. This has also been determined by the European Court of Justice on several occasions. The European Court of Justice ruled in case C-105/84 (*Danmols Inventar*) – also one of the first and important decisions involving questions from a Danish court – that a transferee is not bound by the transferor's collective agreement. However, the transferee is obliged to respect the individual conditions of each worker following from the collective agreement. *See also* another important early case involving Danish matters, case C-287/86, *Ny Mølle Kro*.

During the 1990s, there was uncertainty in Denmark in relation to what applied in relation to the collective agreements in connection with business transfers. In February 1996, in the *Superfos* case, it was held that section 2(2)(2) of the Transfer of Undertakings Act does not imply that the transferee automatically becomes a party to the transferor's collective agreement. Thus, it is clear from the Superfos decision that it is the individual employee's rights are maintained, while the collective agreement as a whole is not necessarily transferred.

This must follow from the aim of the Directive, which is to protect employees' rights and to ensure that employees are not placed at a disadvantage as a result of the transfer. However, there is no protection for the employees' union. The important thing about the Superfos decision is also that it was established that the transferee may renounce the collective agreement by means of a simple notification to the union, which is a party to the collective agreement.

In 2001, a new provision was inserted in section 4a of the Act on Transfer of Undertakings to codify case law, as expressed in, for instance, the Superfos decision, where a court had the opportunity to decide on the status of collective agreements in connection with business transfers.

Section 4a reads as follows (in a translated form):

> A transferee must inform the trade union concerned within 5 weeks of the date on which it knew or ought to have known that the employees or part of the employees of the undertaking being transferred have been covered by a collective agreement, but not earlier than 3 weeks after the takeover, if the latter does not wish to accede to the agreement. Otherwise, the transferee shall be deemed to have acceded to the collective agreement.
>
> section 2. ...
>
> section 3. [...]

The purpose of this section 4a is that the transferee may, within the time limits specified in that provision, renounce the collective agreement. There are two different deadlines for the transferee to renounce the agreement. A period of three weeks after the date of takeover and a period of five weeks in relation to the time when the transferee became aware, or ought to have known, that a collective agreement was in force. This means that an acquirer always has three weeks after the actual date of takeover to renounce the collective agreement, regardless of when the transferee became aware of the collective agreement. The three-week rule is thus the practical main rule, since in many situations the transferee will know a long time before the takeover date that a collective agreement is in place at the transferor's business.

If the transferee does not renounce the collective agreement within three weeks of the date of takeover, it becomes relevant to consider whether the five-week deadline can be applied.

In this case, the transferee must renounce the agreement within five weeks of the time when the transferee knew or ought to have known that an agreement existed with the transferor. The five-week period is only relevant if the transferee did not know in advance that the transferee was bound by a collective agreement.

If the transferee renounces the collective agreement, the employees are still entitled to protection of their individual rights following the collective agreement.

The individual terms can be changed with the employees' individual notice periods, but will always apply at least until the normal expiry date of the collective agreement.

If the transferee does not take any action in relation to renouncing the collective agreement, the transferee will be bound by the transferor's collective agreement by acquiescence. This implies that the transferee will be in a position where the transferee has the same legal position as if the transferee had entered into the collective bargaining agreement itself.

Even though collective agreements typically have a duration of two or three years, and would typically end 31 March two or three years after the effective date, it is also normal in Denmark for a collective agreement to remain in force until a new agreement has been negotiated between the parties or industrial action is taken (strike or lock-out). This means that the Act on Transfer of Undertakings is a very special opportunity to renege from the transferor's collective agreement in connection with the transfer of business, which then allows flexibility in connection with terms and conditions going forward. However, the deadline is important if the acquirer does not want to be bound by an agreement and failure to renounce the agreement within the deadlines will mean that the transferee loses the right to renounce.

Even though the rules around renouncing the transferor's collective agreements in connection with business transfers are fairly well established with a number of cases having been solved by arbitration, by the Labour Court and by the ordinary courts during the past 45 years, there are still cases where there the interpretation of the rules on business transfers in specific cases are not clear.

In a recent judgment delivered by the Danish Supreme Court on 30 January 2024, the Supreme Court had to determine the protection of a shop steward in the event of a business transfer, where the collective agreement was renounced.

The case concerned a situation where a regional authority responsible for a number of hospitals (Region Hovedstaden) transferred its so-called respiratory systems for patients who were respirator users to a private supplier.

In connection with the business transfer, a private supplier had taken over nearly 100 employees from Region Hovedstaden.

The employee was before the transfer elected as union representative. However, the company, which took over the tasks from Region Hovedstaden, was not covered by a collective agreement before the transfer and chose to renounce the collective agreement of Region Hovedstaden and thereby also the frame agreement in connection with the business transfer.

The new employer, the private company, notified the employee of changes to the terms of employment, which the employee refused to accept and therefore the employment relationship came to an end. The normal rule under Danish law is that an employee, who cannot accept a material change to its terms and conditions, which is notified by the employer, can decide to consider himself or herself made redundant with the normal notice period (on the part of the employer).

The main dispute to be considered in this case was whether the employee maintained the position of employee-elected union representative after the business transfer, and whether the employee maintained the extended protection in this regard, including the right to extended notice of termination.

The Supreme Court agreed with the High Court, which held that 'the basis for employee representation lapses' in clause 4, pursuant to section 2 in the Act on Transfer of Undertakings, and therefore 'the mandate of the representatives (...) expires'. The Acquired Rights Directive must be understood in the way that it covers such a situation where the collective agreement, from which the right to elect union representatives and the rights of such union representatives follow, is renounced by the transferee pursuant to the Act on Transfer of Undertakings, clause 4 a, section 1. Thus, the consequence of the renouncing of the collective agreement is that the union representatives' protection against termination also lapses; however, with certain modifications

The Supreme Court found that the appellant's function as an employee-elected union representative had ended due to the business transfer, where the current collective agreement was renounced. The protection applying to union representatives therefore also lapsed nine months after the end of her function. It was therefore not contrary to the Act on Transfer of Undertakings to notify the employee of the changed terms of employment with her usual notice period.

§5.08 PROTECTION AGAINST TERMINATION IN THE EVENT OF A BUSINESS TRANSFER

It is a fundamental right deriving from the Acquired Rights Directive that the employees comprised by a business transfer have the right to continue working in the business after the transfer. It follows from Article 4(1) of the directive that: 'The transfer of an undertaking, business or part of an undertaking or business shall not in itself constitute grounds for dismissal by the transferor or transferee', however with the exemption that employees can be made redundant for economical, technical or organisational reasons ('ETO-reasons').

Article 4(1)(1) is implemented in section 3(1) of the Act on Transfer of Undertakings, according to which 'Dismissal due to the transfer of an undertaking or part thereof shall not be considered reasonably justified by the circumstances of the undertaking, unless the dismissal is due to economic, technical or organisational reasons leading to changes in employment.'

The question is therefore whether there is a genuine ban on dismissal or a ban on unfair dismissal, which alone can give rise to compensation (and not necessarily that the individual keeps the job).

The judgment of the Court of Justice of the European Union of 15 June 1988, P. Bork International A/S C-101/87, concerned termination of an employee and subsequent re-employment in connection with closure of the company. The company was sold immediately afterwards, after which the acquirer rehired several of the employees for whom the notice period had not yet expired. The Court held (paragraph 18) that the employees of the undertaking whose contract of employment or employment relationship was terminated with effect from a date prior to that of the transfer, contrary to Article 4(1) of the Directive, had to be regarded as still in the employment of the undertaking on the date of the transfer, with the result, in particular, that the employer's obligations towards them were automatically transferred from the transferor to the transferee in accordance with Article 3(1) of the directive. In order to determine whether the employees were dismissed solely as a result of the transfer, contrary to Article 4(1), it is necessary to take into consideration the objective circumstances in which the dismissal took place and, in particular, the fact that it took effect on a date close to that of the transfer. Consequently, employees employed by the undertaking whose contract of employment or employment relationship has been terminated earlier than the date of the transfer in breach of Article 4(1) of the Directive must be regarded as if they were still employed by the undertaking at the time of the transfer, with the result, *inter alia,* that the employer's obligations towards the employees are automatically transferred from the transferor to the transferee by virtue of the Article 3(1) of the Directive. It follows from the judgment of the European Court of Justice that the employment relationship is to be considered to have been maintained if the termination of the worker is contrary to Article 4(1) of the Directive.

In an article, a former Supreme Court judge named Per Walsøe argues that the court's ruling in the Bork case is an expression of a philosophy of performance in kind and that the legal effect of a violation of Article 4(1) of the Directive is that the employment relationship is maintained and thus an outright prohibition of dismissal.

The judgment of Court of Justice of the European Union of 12 March 1998, *Dethier,* C-319/94, (paragraph 41) also points in the direction of this, as the court mentions that the contract of employment of a person unlawfully dismissed shortly before the transfer must be regarded as still existent as against the transferee even if the dismissed employee was not taken on by him after the undertaking was transferred.

However, the conclusion in Danish theory and case law is that the employee is not entitled to remain in his or her position or to be reinstated by virtue of the rules of the Act on Transfer of Undertakings if the employee is successful and a Danish court finds that the employer is in violation of the rules of the Act. It is also apparent from a decision from the High Court Western Division (U 2009.307 V), which is a case which I have dealt with in court, that a school consultant employed under collective agreements was not entitled to reinstatement, but rather compensation for dismissal in breach of the Act on Transfer of Undertakings. It is evident from the decision of the High Court that there is, in the High Court's view, no basis under administrative law covering employees in the public sector such as the school consultant or in the Act on Transfer of Undertakings and the underlying Directive that the effect of the dismissal must be annulled with the consequence that the employee must continue to be regarded as an employee. In the specific case, the employee, who had been terminated contrary to the rules, was awarded a compensation, but he did not get the job back which he had prior the establishment of a cooperation agreement between a number of municipalities, which was considered to be a transfer of an undertaking (which the municipality, which had terminated him was likely not aware of when it applied a process, whereby all the school consultants were to apply for a job in the new organisation).

A dismissal in connection with a transfer of an undertaking may be objectively justified on economic, technical or organisational grounds, and will in that case not be unlawful. This could be the case if both the transferor and the transferee have two large financial departments and can do with half of the staff for synergy reasons after the transfer of the business. The starting point is that the employer has the burden of proving that the termination is not based on the transfer of business. According to Danish law, the consequences of unfair dismissal will be compensation and not reinstatement as described above. The Act on Transfer of Undertakings does not contain a compensation provision, which means that the compensation provision must be found in other legislation, such as section 2b of the Salaried Employees Act and section 4(3) of the Main Agreement between the Labour Market Partners or other collective bargaining agreements, such as in the case with the school consultant. According to the traditional Danish interpretation, the dismissal will, generally, stand and the employee will only be entitled to compensation where there is a special legal basis for this.

If the employee is not a salaried employee or does not meet the seniority requirement in section 2b (12 months) of the Salaried Employees Act or section 4(3) (9 months) of the main agreement and is not covered by other rules or collective agreements that give him the right to compensation or dismissal in the event of unfair dismissal, the provision of section 3 of the Transfer of Undertakings Act is, according to the traditional Danish interpretation, meaningless as compensation will not be triggered for the employee who has been terminated contrary to the rules, and has no right to be reinstated in the job. This is because there is no right to reinstatement or compensation in any of the provisions of the Act on Transfer of Undertakings. This is hardly in line with Denmark's obligations under EU law, including the obligation to ensure an efficient effect of the Directive. There is a provision in the Act on Transfer of Undertakings according to which a transferor or a transferee, who are not acting in compliance with the Act, can be fined. However, this provision has so far never been used in practice. Under Danish law and as a clear main rule, fines cannot be issued by an administrative body (unless there is a specific legal basis therefore and typically this can also be brought before the courts). This rule is therefore partially without any real teeth.

CHAPTER 6
Estonia

Merle Erikson

§6.01 INTRODUCTION

The employer's prohibition against terminating the employee's employment contract due to the transfer of undertaking was already included in the first Republic of Estonia Employment Contracts Act[1] (*Eesti Vabariigi töölepingu seadus* – EVTLS), adopted after the restoration of Estonia's independence[2] in 1992.

In connection with Estonia becoming a member of the European Union (EU) in 2004, the EVTLS was brought into line with the EU Directive 2001/23/EC on the approximation of the laws of the Member States relating to the safeguarding of employees' rights in the event of transfers of undertakings, businesses or parts of undertakings or businesses[3] (Directive).

Currently, the protection of employee rights in the case of the transfer of undertaking is regulated by the Employment Contracts Act[4] (*töölepingu seadus* – TLS),

1. Republic of Estonia Employment Contracts Act, passed on 15 April 1992 – RT 1992, 15/16; RT I 2009, 11, 67 (available in Estonian at https://www.riigiteataja.ee/akt/13147581; accessed 15 September 2025). Under §6 of this Act, reorganisation of an enterprise, agency or other organisation, change of subordination, owner or form of ownership or the transfer of undertaking does not terminate the employment contract. This Act is no longer in force as of 1 July 2009. A similar principle was stipulated in §34 of the Soviet-era Labour Code, valid before the EVTLS.
2. Estonia regained its independence in 1991.
3. OJ L 82, 22.3.2001, pp. 16-20. *This Directive incorporated Directives* 77/187/EEC on the approximation of the laws of the Member States relating to the safeguarding of employees' rights in the event of transfers of undertakings, businesses or parts of undertakings or businesses (OJ L 61, 5.3.1977, pp. 26-28) and 98/50/EC amending directive 77/187/EEC on the approximation of the laws of the Member States relating to the safeguarding of employees' rights in the event of transfers of undertakings, businesses or parts of businesses (OJ L 201, 17.7.1998, pp. 88-92).
4. Employment Contracts Act, passed on 17 December 2008 – RT I 2009, 5, 35; 23.12.2024, 6 (https://www.riigiteataja.ee/en/eli/ee/520032023012/consolide/current; accessed 15 September 2025).

which must be applied in conjunction with the definition of an undertaking defined in the Act on the General Part of the Civil Code[5] (*tsiviilseadustiku üldosa seadus* – TsÜS) and the regulation on the transfer of an undertaking in the Law of Obligations Act[6] (*võlaõigusseadus* – VÕS).

In the Estonian legal literature, it is pointed out that the purpose of establishing the regulation of the transfer of undertaking is the protection of the rights of both obligees and, more narrowly, employees[7] from the situation when the company wants to get rid of the obligation by raising the undertaking to a new legal person and continuing operations through the new legal person without fulfilling the obligations arising from previous activities.[8] However, when interpreting the Directive, one must not forget the employer's interests – his right to entrepreneurial freedom.[9]

In the article's author's opinion, the Directive has generally been successfully adopted into Estonian law. Employees are guaranteed the transfer of rights and obligations arising from both the employment contract and the collective agreement, termination of the employment contract due to the transfer of the undertaking is prohibited, and the solidary liability of the transferee and transferor has been established. There are a few disputes concerning the transfer of undertaking in Estonian labour dispute bodies.[10]

This chapter aims to find an answer to whether the Estonian regulation and practice concerning the transfer of undertaking are in line with the objectives of the Directive and the possible development directions in this field. More specifically, the focus is on three topics – the concept of a transfer of undertaking, the protection of employees' rights in case of the transfer of undertaking in the event of the transferor's insolvency, and informing and consulting the employees (representatives).

The first topic is discussed because the transfer of undertaking has been assessed in many court cases.[11] The second topic deserves to be addressed because, in the opinion of the article's author, the Directive's provisions have not been correctly

5. An Act on the General Part of the Civil Code, passed on 27 March 2002 – RT I 2002, 35, 216; 31.12.2024, 48 (https://www.riigiteataja.ee/en/eli/ee/503022023002/consolide/current; accessed 15 September 2025).
6. Law of Obligations Act, passed on 26 September 2001 – RT I 2001, 81, 487; 8.7.2025, 26 (https://www.riigiteataja.ee/en/eli/ee/524032023004/consolide/current; accessed 15 September 2025).
7. M. Leppik & M. Lillsaar, Transfer of Undertaking in Tax Law. Analysis of Case Law, Legal Information Department, Supreme Court of the Republic of Estonia, 2013, pp. 4-5 (available in Estonian at https://www.riigikohus.ee/sites/default/files/elfinder/analyysid/2013/ettevotte_yleminek_maksuoiguses_m.lillsaar_m.leppik.pdf; accessed 15 September 2025).
8. M. Tamme, Law of Obligations Act I, General Part (§§ 1-207), Commented Edition, authors P. Varul, et al., Tallinn: Juura, 2016, §180 comm. 4.4.1. (in Estonian).
9. N. Bruun & S. Laulom, Restructuring of Companies, in: T. Jaspers, F. Pennings and S. Peters (eds), European Labour Law, Cambridge, United Kingdom: Intersentia, 2019, p. 332.
10. In Estonia, individual labour disputes are settled by labour dispute committees and courts (whose decisions are available in Estonian online, respectively, at www.ti.ee and www.riigiteataja.ee; accessed 15 September 2025).
11. M. Vutt, Transfer of an Undertaking, Legal Information Department, Supreme Court of the Republic of Estonia, 2010, p. 31 (available in Estonian at https://www.riigikohus.ee/sites/default/files/elfinder/analyysid/2010/ettevotteyleminek_margit_vutt.pdf; accessed 15 September 2025).

transposed into Estonian law in this regard. And the third topic is important because, due to the little-developed collective labour relations, a meaningful discussion between employees and employers usually does not occur.

Estonian law is compared with the Directive, its interpretations,[12] and the corresponding analyses and opinions to achieve the study's goal.

§6.02 THE CONCEPT OF THE TRANSFER OF UNDERTAKING

[A] What Is an Undertaking?

The Directive does not provide for the definition of an undertaking. Still, it can be read from Article 1(b), according to which a transfer means a transfer of an economic entity that retains its identity, meaning an organised grouping of resources that has the objective of pursuing an economic activity.[13] It is also important to note that, under Article 1(c), public and private undertakings engaged in economic activities, whether or not they are operating for gain, have been kept in mind. Thus, the company is characterised by the following keywords: organised grouping of resources (economic entity), economic activity, operating both in the private and public sphere and operating both for-profit and not.[14]

In Estonian law, the concept of an undertaking is construed similarly. The notion of an undertaking is stipulated in TsÜS §66^1, according to which undertaking[15] means the economic unit through which the person operates. Based on the TsÜS, the meaning of undertaking is interpreted broadly – all employers can have an undertaking, i.e., in addition to sole proprietors and companies, for example, a foundation, a non-profit organisation,[16] or a public legal person. The term undertaking is not only related to a company. Thus, it does not matter who owns the undertaking; the main thing is that it is an operating entity.[17]

Under VÕS §180(2), an undertaking comprises the things, rights, and obligations relating to and in the service of the management of the undertaking, including contracts relating to the undertaking. The principle provided in the Directive, according to which the undertaking (economic entity) is an organised grouping of resources, is

12. Although the Court of Justice of the European Union (CJEU) has made more than 60 decisions regarding the transfer of undertaking in connection with the protection of the rights of employees (*see* https://curia.europa.eu/jcms/jcms/j_6/en/; accessed 15 September 2025), this chapter deals only with decisions important in the context of Estonia.
13. Whether or not that activity is central or ancillary.
14. The CJEU has expressed such approach in many cases. *See*, for example C-343/98, 14.9.2000, *Collino and Chiappero*, ECLI:EU:C:2000:441; C-175/99, 26.9.2000, *Mayeur*, ECLI:EU:C:2000:505.
15. The author uses the term undertaking in this chapter. The terms business and enterprise are used in the translations of the TsÜS and the VÕS/TLS, respectively.
16. E. Käärats, et al., Comments on the Employment Contracts Act, Ministry of Economic Affairs and Communications. Tallinn, 2024, §112 comm. 2 (available in Estonian at https://www.mkm.ee/sites/default/files/documents/2024-09/TLS%20selgitused_2024%20august.pdf; accessed 15 September 2025).
17. *Supra* n. 8, §180 comm. 4.2.

well expressed from this provision – both the things, rights, and obligations must be related to and in the service of the management of the undertaking, i.e., it is a whole entity.

Thus, the concept of undertaking used in Estonia is in line with the Directive. The following analysis of the criteria for the transfer of undertaking also helps to better understand the nature of the undertaking (and its transfer).

[B] Criteria for the Transfer of an Undertaking

According to Article 1(b) of the Directive, a transfer is made if an economic entity that retains its identity is transferred. From the author's viewpoint, maintaining identity is the most essential point of reference in evaluating the transfer of undertaking. The retention of the identity of the economic entity is also focused on by the CJEU in dozens of cases, citing criteria based on which the transfer of the undertaking can be evaluated.

The most well-known is the *Spijkers* case[18] settled in 1986, which the court has later repeatedly referred to. The CJEU decided in that case that 'it is necessary to consider whether having regard to all the facts characterising the transaction, the business was disposed of as a going concern, as would be indicated inter alia by the fact that its operation was actually continued or resumed by the new employer, with the same or similar activities'.

Also, the CJEU explains that to assess the transfer of an undertaking, there must be analysed 'all the facts characterising the transaction in question, including the type of undertaking or business, whether or not the business's tangible assets, such as buildings and movable property, are transferred, the value of its intangible assets at the time of the transfer, whether or not the majority of its employees are taken over by the new employer, whether or not its customers are transferred and the degree of similarity between the activities carried on before and after the transfer and the period, if any, for which those activities were suspended. It should be noted, however, that all those circumstances are merely single factors in the overall assessment which must be made and cannot, therefore, be considered in isolation' (paragraph 13). These criteria have different weights for different types of undertakings. It is important to identify what constitutes the core of a particular kind of undertaking.[19]

The previously described circumstances have remained the basis for evaluating the transfer of an undertaking. Since the legal ways of transfer have become more complicated (outsourcing, leasing arrangements, transfer of public services, etc.) over the years, the court has supplemented and clarified its positions in many later decisions. For example, in the *Schmidt* case,[20] which caused more discussion, the court had taken the position that the transfer of an undertaking covers a situation 'in which an undertaking entrusts by contract to another undertaking the responsibility for

18. C-24/85, 18.3.1986, *Spijkers*, ECLI:EU:C:1986:127.
19. *Supra* n. 11, p. 31.
20. C-392/92, 14.4.1994, *Schmidt*, ECLI:EU:C:1994:134.

carrying out cleaning operations which it previously performed itself, even though, before the transfer, such work was carried out by a single employee' (paragraph 20). Thus, one employee can also form an undertaking. Also, when analysing other situations of the transfer of an undertaking, the court generally gives broad protection to the employee.[21]

The Estonian TLS does not stipulate the criteria for evaluating the transfer of an undertaking. However, it can be read from there that retaining the economic entity's identity is also considered necessary in Estonia. TLS §112(1) states that if the undertaking continues the same or similar economic activities, employment contracts transfer to the transferee of an undertaking unamended. Thus, the Estonian legislator has considered the continuation of similar activities of the economic entity as the most important indicator of the transfer of an undertaking. However, this single criterion cannot be used to judge whether an undertaking has transferred, but all aspects of the transfer must be assessed.[22]

As stated in the introduction, the existence of the transfer of an undertaking has caused the most disputes in Estonia. Thus, the court has mainly analysed the criteria for the transfer of the undertaking.[23] If, before Estonia joined the EU, the Estonian Supreme Court also made decisions contrary to the Directive,[24] the latest decisions are entirely in line with it. Thus, if in 2000, the Supreme Court was of the opinion that an undertaking is transferred when it is transferred as a whole, i.e., in a collection and at one time,[25] then in a decision made in 2010, the court expressed a different position.

In this decision, the Supreme Court explains for the first time that the criteria known from the *Spijkers* case must be used as a basis for determining the transfer of an

21. *See* R. Blanpain, European Labour Law, 14th ed, 2014, Alphen aan den Rijn: Kluwer Law International, pp. 844-870. *Supra* n. 9, pp. 333-338.
22. *See also* C-13/95, 11.3.1997, *Süzen*, ECLI:EU:C:1997:141, para. 15; *Supra* n. 8, p. 883.
23. Courts have evaluated the transfer of an undertaking in both administrative (tax law) and civil cases, including the latter more broadly than only in labour disputes (e.g., in the case of a freight transport contract). In both administrative and civil cases, the courts have used the principles derived from the Directive when evaluating the transfer of an undertaking. *See also, supra* n. 7, pp. 8-14.

    For example, the Supreme Court has explained in a dispute concerning the law of obligations that although the Directive and the corresponding case law deal with the transfer of an undertaking primarily from the aspect of protecting the rights of employees, the verification of the elements characterising the transfer of an undertaking presented there is relevant in all cases concerning the transfer of an undertaking. Judgment of the Estonian Supreme Court of 12 June 2019 in case No. 2-18-2908, para. 13.
24. The Supreme Court of Estonia analysed the situation in which the new owner bought the newspaper's trademark acquired the previous owner's property from the bankruptcy estate, and employed most of the newspaper's editorial office employees. Although the editorial board continued to publish the newspaper, the Supreme Court found that it was not a transfer of the undertaking because the transfer of the undertaking as *a whole unit* (transfer on one legal basis) had not occurred. Based on the Directive, however, it is identifiable here that an economic entity that retained its identity was transferred. Judgment of the Estonian Supreme Court of 16 February 2000 in case No. 3-2-1-7-00, Part IV.

    However, the Supreme Court has held that the rules of the transfer of an undertaking apply if a new educational institution is created during the reorganisation of two educational institutions managed by the Ministry of Education and Science. Judgment of the Estonian Supreme Court of 8 November 2006 in case No. 3-2-1-103-06, para. 12.
25. Judgment of the Estonian Supreme Court of 16 February 2000 in case No. 3-2-1-7-00, Part IV.

undertaking.[26] The court gives a clear indication here that although the employer got possession of the undertaking (tennis hall) due to the termination of the lease contract and acquired its furnishings at a public auction, the fact that the employer continued the same economic activity, offered services to the same clients and entered into employment contracts with the same employees also plays an important role. Therefore, according to the Supreme Court, it is necessary to analyse whether the identity of the transferred undertaking (economic entity) has been retained.

In this decision, the court took another important stand on the proof of the transfer of the undertaking. According to procedural law, the employee must prove that the undertaking has been transferred. The Supreme Court considers that in a dispute where the employee wants to prove the continuation of the employment contract due to the transfer of the undertaking, it is difficult for him to do so due to the information asymmetry. The information and evidence are in the employer's possession, who is not interested in publishing it. Thus, in labour disputes, it must be determined whether the transfer actually took place or not.[27] Thus, the court highlights here the need to follow the principle of protection of the employee as the weaker party of the employment relationship in labour disputes.

The Supreme Court emphasised the principle of retaining the identity of the economic entity in the decision made in 2011. According to the circumstances of this case, the company bought the property of another company, took over its software licences, and rented commercial premises used by the former company. Employees and clients also transferred, and economic activity remained the same. In this decision, the court explained the principles of several CJEU rulings[28] and found that, when determining the transfer of an undertaking within the framework of a labour dispute, it must first be controlled whether an independent economic entity that continues its activities has been transferred. If it is impossible to identify a complete economic unit due to the specific nature of the business, the economic unit can be a unit of employees with permanent common tasks.[29] In this decision as well, the reasoning in the Supreme Court clearly indicates that, in the given circumstances, it was a transfer of the undertaking.

Therefore, the Estonian Supreme Court and, based on this, the lower level courts and labour dispute committees,[30] when assessing the transfer of an undertaking, are based precisely on the rules of the Directive[31] and the guidelines of the relevant CJEU practice. In the opinion of the Estonian courts, in the case of the transfer of an

26. Judgment of the Estonian Supreme Court of 20 October 2010 in case No. 3-2-1-82-10, para. 16.
27. *Ibid.*, paras 14 and 15.
28. C-24/85, 18.3.1986, *Spijkers*, ECLI:EU:C:1986:127; Joined cases C-127/96, C-229/96 and C-74-97, 10.12.1998, *Hernández Vidal et al*, ECLI:EU:C:1998:594; C-458/05, 13.9.2007, *Jouini and Others*, ECLI:EU:C:2007:512.
29. Judgment of the Estonian Supreme Court of 15 June 2011 in case No. 3-2-1-41-11, para. 15.
30. The opinions of the Supreme Court are not directly binding on the courts of lower levels or the labour dispute committees, but in practice, both the courts and the labour dispute committees rely on the opinions of the Supreme Court in their decisions.
31. In one administrative case, the Supreme Court has identified four additional criteria by which to evaluate the transfer of a company. These are the takeover of intangible assets and organisation, continuity of customer and contracting authority relations, previous activities of the transferee

undertaking, it is necessary to identify, first of all, the transfer of an entity that retains its identity, no matter on what legal bases the things, rights, and obligations that belong to the undertaking are transferred.

§6.03 TRANSFER OF AN UNDERTAKING IN THE EVENT OF THE TRANSFEROR'S INSOLVENCY

In case of insolvency of the transferor, the legal person is terminated, or the undertaking is rehabilitated according to specific procedural rules, whose primary purpose is to protect the rights of creditors. In the event of the transfer of an undertaking, the interests of employees and other creditors are often in conflict during insolvency proceedings because, for creditors, the transfer of an undertaking without employees is usually more favourable. At the same time, in many cases, the transferee continues the undertaking's previous activities, and the dismissal of employees during insolvency proceedings is unjustified. Therefore, during the transfer of the undertaking, a compromise must be found that considers the interests of both employees and other creditors.[32]

Based on CJEU practice,[33] in 1998, an article was added to the original version of the Directive, which regulates the legal status of employees in case of insolvency of the transferor. This is Article 5 of the current Directive, which establishes the following: unless Member States provide otherwise, employee protection rules[34] do not apply to any transfer of an undertaking where the transferor is the subject of bankruptcy proceedings or any analogous insolvency proceedings which have been instituted with a view to the liquidation of the assets of the transferor and are under the supervision of a competent public authority[35] (Article 5(1)).

Therefore, by assumption,[36] the ban on termination of employment contracts does not apply to the transfer of an undertaking in the event of a procedure meeting the following conditions: (1) if the transferor is the subject of bankruptcy proceedings or similar insolvency proceedings; (2) the purpose of the proceedings mentioned above is to liquidate the assets of the transferor;[37] and (3) the proceedings mentioned above take place under the competent authority's supervision.[38]

---

of the undertaking, place of business of the transferor and the transferee, and overlapping of members of the management bodies. Judgment of the Estonian Supreme Court of 1 June 2011 in case No. 3-3-1-20-11, para. 11.

32. M. Muda, Protection of Employees' Rights in the Event of the Reorganisation of the Employer's Activities, *Dissertationes iuridicae universitatis Tartuensis 5*, Tartu: TÜ Kirjastus, 2001, p. 92 (Summary in English).
33. C-135/83, 7.2.1985, *Abels*, ECLI:EU:C:1985:55; C-362/89, 25.7.1991, *d'Urso*, ECLI:EU:C:1991:326; C-472/93, 7.12.1995, *Spano and Others*, ECLI:EU:C:1995:421, etc.
34. This means Articles 3 and 4 of the Directive.
35. Which may be an insolvency practitioner authorised by a competent public authority.
36. A Member State may grant greater protection to employees than is provided for in Article 5 of the Directive.
37. According to the CJEU, a procedure aimed at ensuring the continuation of the undertaking in question does not satisfy that requirement. *See* C-362/89, 25.7.1991, *d'Urso*, ECLI:EU:C:1991:

There are different approaches in the Member States on how to deal with an entrepreneur in payment difficulties.[39] However, regardless of the procedural packages offered to solve insolvency problems, an insolvent entrepreneur usually has two alternatives: trade himself out of difficulties (usually, this happens after the company's reorganisation) or go into liquidation.[40] In this light, it is important to note that, according to the Directive, employees may be left unprotected in the event of insolvency of the transferor only if the purpose of the proceedings is to liquidate the transferor's assets. If the company is rehabilitated and continues to operate, then the rights of the employees are safeguarded.

When interpreting the Directive, the CJEU has looked very carefully at the requirement that the proceedings must be supervised by a competent public authority and the purpose of the proceedings.[41] However, considering the ever-changing domestic regulations, the court has recently pointed out in the *Federatie Nederlandse Vakbeweging* case[42] an additional requirement to secure legal certainty. The decision concerns the Dutch *pre-pack* procedure,[43] which, in the court's opinion, must be regulated by statutory or regulatory provisions (paragraph 66), although this is not prescribed by Article 5(1) of the Directive.[44] As studies have shown that the Dutch pre-packed bankruptcy better protects an employee's interest in maintaining employment, compared with going-concern sales in conventional bankruptcy,[45] then in the

326, paras 31 and 32; C-472/9, 7.12.1995, *Spano and Others*, ECLI:EU:C:1995:421, para. 25; C-126/16, 22.6.2017, *Federatie Nederlandse Vakvereniging and Others*, ECLI:EU:C:2017:489, para. 47.

38. K. Künnapas, The Rights of Employees upon Transfer of an Insolvent Employer: Has Harmonisation Failed? *Juridica*, 2011/2, p. 123 (in Estonian).
39. *See*, for example, M. Sargeant, Implementation Report Directive 2001/23/EC on the approximation of laws of the Member States relating to the safeguarding of employees' rights in the event of transfers of undertakings, businesses or parts of businesses, All 25 Member States, Human European Consultancy & Middlesex University Business School, 2007, pp. 54 ff.
40. *Supra* n. 38, p. 123.
41. *Supra* n. 9, p. 348.
42. C-237/20, 28.4.2022, *Federatie Nederlandse Vakbeweging*, ECLI:EU:C:2022:321.
43. The *pre-pack* is a national practice derived from case law which makes it possible, in the context of the liquidation of a debtor's assets, to prepare the sale of all or part of an undertaking forming part of its assets in order to increase the chances of creditors being repaid in full. The preparations for sale consist, *inter alia*, in negotiating an agreement with one or more candidates on the basis of which all or part of the undertaking in question will be transferred to them after the debtor has been declared insolvent. The *pre-pack* differs from other sales transactions prior to a declaration of insolvency in the sense that the sales transactions organised in connection with it are prepared by an insolvency administrator, known as a 'prospective insolvency administrator', under the supervision of a supervisory judge, known as the 'prospective supervisory judge'. They are appointed by the competent court and their status and functions are determined by the case law of the Supreme Court of the Netherlands. *Ibid.*, paras 18 and 19.
44. In this case, the CJEU decided that in the case of the *pre-pack* procedure, employees are not guaranteed the protection provided for in Articles 3 and 4 of the Directive. This decision has caused considerable discussion because the court, not following the Advocate General's Opinion, made the contrary conclusion in the previous case concerning the *pre-pack* procedure (i.e., C-126/16, 22.6.2017, *Federatie Nederlandse Vakvereniging and Others*, ECLI:EU:C:2017:489).
45. H. Aalbers, et al., Does Pre-packed Bankruptcy Create Value? An Empirical Study of Postbankruptcy Employment Retention in the Netherlands. *International Insolvency Review*, 2019/28(3), p. 337 (https://doi.org/10.1002/iir.1353; accessed 15 September 2025).

general framework, the CJEU's position is still primarily aimed at protecting employees.

In Estonian law, the approach is different. TLS §112(1) and (3) establish the general rights of employees in the case of the transfer of an undertaking. According to §112(1), employment contracts transfer to the transferee of an undertaking unamended pursuant to the VÕS if the undertaking continues the same or similar economic activities. A transferor and transferee of an undertaking are prohibited from terminating an employment contract due to the transfer of the undertaking (§112(3)). The difference applicable in case of insolvency of the transferor is set out in TLS §112(4), which states that there is no transfer of employment contracts, and they may be terminated due to the transfer of the undertaking in the case of the declaration of bankruptcy of an employer.

Thus, the TLS regulation is general and does not provide the principle stated in Article 5(1) of the Directive, under which the purpose of the insolvency proceedings must be to liquidate the assets of the transferor. In the Explanatory Memorandum to the TLS, it is mentioned that in case of employer bankruptcy, the rights of employees are no longer protected when the undertaking is transferred.[46] Still, the authors of the Act do not specify the reason for this.[47] One must be familiar with the procedure for conducting bankruptcy proceedings in Estonia to analyse whether such an approach is justified.

According to §1(1) of the Bankruptcy Act[48] (*pankrotiseadus* – PankrS), bankruptcy means the insolvency of a debtor[49] declared by a court ruling.[50] A debtor is insolvent if the debtor is unable to satisfy the claim of a creditor that has fallen due and such inability, due to the debtor's financial situation, is not temporary (PankrS §1(2)).[51] If bankruptcy is declared, bankruptcy proceedings commence, and the court decides, *inter alia*, on the time and place of the first general meeting of creditors and

46. The Explanatory Memorandum notes that compared to the current law, in the event of bankruptcy, the employer only has to inform and consult the employees when the company is transferred to another person. Explanatory Memorandum to the Employment Contracts Act 299 SE, 23.10.2008, p. 82 (available in Estonian at https://www.riigikogu.ee/; accessed 15 September 2025). Under the EVTLS, which was in force before the TLS, employees were also protected in the case of a transfer of an undertaking when the transferor was declared bankrupt.
47. According to the article's author, the reason may be that the legislator wanted to protect other creditors' interests more than the employees. If the employment contract is terminated due to bankruptcy, the employees' claims will be satisfied by the Unemployment Insurance Fund.
48. Bankruptcy Act, passed on 22 January 2003 – RT I 2003, 17, 95; 14.3.2025, 17 (https://www.riigiteataja.ee/en/eli/ee/503052023007/consolide/current; accessed 15 September 2025).
49. For the purposes of this article, the debtor is also the employer.
50. In addition to declaring insolvency, the company can also be reorganised. A company's reorganisation means applying a set of measures based on a reorganisation plan to overcome economic difficulties, restore its liquidity, improve its profitability and ensure its sustainable management. *See* §2 of the Reorganisation Act. Reorganisation Act, passed on 4 December 2008 – RT I 2008, 53, 296; 14.3.2025, 5 (https://www.riigiteataja.ee/en/eli/ee/523032023005/consolide/current; accessed 15 September 2025). If the undertaking is transferred during the reorganisation procedure, the rights of the employees are protected.
51. A debtor who is a legal person is insolvent also if the assets of the debtor are insufficient for covering the obligations thereof and, due to the debtor's financial situation, such insufficiency is not temporary (PankrS §1(3)).

appointment of a trustee in bankruptcy (PankrS §31(6)). The debtor's further activities are organised by the trustee, who is also the employer of the employees.

It is important to emphasise that bankruptcy proceedings do not always involve liquidating the employer's assets (or the employer as a legal person). According to PankrS §129(1), if a bankruptcy estate includes an undertaking, the trustee must prepare a plan for continuing the activities of the undertaking (rehabilitation plan)[52] or make a proposal for terminating the activities of the undertaking. The first general meeting of creditors confirms the rehabilitation or termination of activities of an undertaking (PankrS §129(3)-(5)). The court must approve a decision on the termination of the activities of an undertaking (PankrS §129(6)). PankrS §129(8) establishes that if it is more expedient to sell an undertaking as a set of assets in bankruptcy proceedings, the general meeting, on the trustee's proposal, may decide that the activities of the undertaking be continued until the sale of the undertaking.

Thus, in case of bankruptcy of the transferor, the undertaking may cease to operate (resulting in the liquidation of its assets), the undertaking may continue to operate if it is rehabilitated, and the sale of the undertaking as a whole may also be possible (in this case, too, it is a liquidation of the undertaking's assets). Regarding the latter, it has been stated in the legal literature that since the VÕS regulation on the transfer of the undertaking does not apply in case of bankruptcy,[53] the feasibility of selling the undertaking is unclear because the procedures and bases for the transfer of obligations and contracts are not regulated. In practice, undertakings have been transferred in bankruptcy proceedings, but disputes related to these transactions have not reached the courts.[54]

According to the article's author, §112(4) of the TLS, which states that employees do not have protection in case of the transfer of the undertaking if the transferor has been declared bankrupt, is contrary to the Directive.[55] The principles of the transfer of the employment contract and the prohibition of the termination of the employment contract provided for in the Directive (Articles 3 and 4) must be applicable in case of bankruptcy of the transferor if the purpose of the relevant procedure is to bring the debtor out of payment difficulties (rehabilitation).

A Member State is not obligated to apply these rules if the transferor is a debtor in bankruptcy proceedings, resulting in the transferor's assets being liquidated. Consequently, if the undertaking's activities are terminated through bankruptcy proceedings, there is no obligation to ensure the transfer of employment contracts. In this case, other creditors' interests may be protected, i.e., if it is more profitable to sell the debtor's undertaking (assets) without employees, then the employment contracts

52. A rehabilitation plan prescribes the measures required for the rehabilitation of an undertaking.
53. Under VÕS §181, the provisions of the transfer of undertaking do not apply to the transfer of an undertaking in the event of the merger, division or transformation of legal persons or if an undertaking is taken over pursuant to law, in particular in the case of compulsory execution or bankruptcy proceeding.
54. *Supra* n. 8, p. 895.
55. *See also supra* n. 38, pp. 124-125.

with the latter can be terminated before the transfer. It is not important here that the transferee intends to continue the same or similar activities in the undertaking.[56]

Proceeding from the above, the composition provided for in TLS §112(4) should not be related to the declaration of bankruptcy but to the decision to liquidate or rehabilitate the undertaking. In the latter case, the rights of employees must be protected. Making such a change in §112(4) of the TLS would eliminate the contradiction with the EU law.[57]

Also, Article 5(4) of the Directive cannot be ignored, which states that Member States must take appropriate measures to prevent misuse of insolvency proceedings in such a way as to deprive employees of the rights provided for in the Directive. As mentioned above, under PankrS §129(8), selling an undertaking as a set of assets in bankruptcy proceedings is possible. In this case, too, it is a liquidation of the undertaking's assets, and according to the Directive, the rights of employees do not have to be protected.

However, in the opinion of the article's author, it is not in conformity (with the idea) of the Directive if the undertaking going into liquidation is sold as a whole, and the transferee continues the same or similar activities.[58] In such a case, the transfer of employment contracts should be guaranteed, and the termination of (parts of) employment contracts due to the declaration of bankruptcy of the employer[59] should be prohibited.

According to statistics, Estonia's share of bankrupt companies is not large among all Estonian companies.[60] For example, in 2021, 285 companies were found to be insolvent in Estonia, and bankruptcy was declared for 100 of them.[61] Also, mainly micro-firms operate in Estonia, where the number of employees is small.[62] Thus, the undertakings are small, and the possible transfer of the undertaking in the event of bankruptcy proceedings does not affect a significant number of employees. Since small undertakings usually do not have a trade union,[63] employees are less aware of their

56. M. Muda, Transfer of Enterprise in the Case of Employer's Insolvency, *Juridica*, 2001/2, pp. 126-127 (in Estonian).
57. *Supra* n. 38, p. 125.
58. *See also supra* n. 56, p. 127.
59. According to TLS §89(1) and (2), the employer may terminate the employee's employment contract for the following economic reasons: cessation of work; termination of the activities of the employer; and declaration of bankruptcy of employer or termination of bankruptcy proceedings, without declaring bankruptcy, by abatement.
60. Creditinfo, Bankruptcies in Estonia in 2021, 2022, p. 5 (available in Estonian at https://web.creditinfo.ee/Pankrotid_Eestis_2021.pdf; accessed 15 September 2025).
61. In 185 cases, bankruptcy was not declared, and the company went into liquidation because the company's assets were too low to cover the costs of the bankruptcy process. *Ibid.*, p. 4.
62. In 2024, 94.9% of Estonian companies were micro-firms (0-9 persons employed), 4.2% were small (10-49 persons employed), 0.7% were medium-sized (50-249 persons employed), and 0.1% were large (250+ persons employed) firms. European Commission, Internal Market, Industry, Entrepreneurship and SMEs. SME fact sheets, EU countries in 2025, Estonia (https://single-market-economy.ec.europa.eu/smes/sme-strategy/sme-performance-review_en#paragraph_885; accessed 15 September 2025).
63. However, it should be noted that in Estonia, the role of trade unions in shaping labour relations is generally unimportant. In 2019, 6% of employees belonged to trade unions. OECD, Trade Union Dataset, 29.11.2023 (https://stats.oecd.org/Index.aspx?DataSetCode=TUD; accessed 15 September 2025).

rights. This may also be the reason why there are no disputes on the transfer of an undertaking related to the employer's bankruptcy in labour dispute bodies.

Regardless of the absence of disputes, it must be recognised that the transposition of the Directive into Estonian law has failed regarding the bankruptcy of the transferor of the undertaking. In the case of rehabilitation of the undertaking, the rights of employees must be protected in any case, as well as when the undertaking is transferred as a set of assets during the liquidation of the undertaking. Therefore, TLS needs to be amended accordingly.

§6.04 INFORMING AND CONSULTING EMPLOYEES' REPRESENTATIVES

The Directive also ensures the protection of employees in case of the transfer of an undertaking through the involvement of the employees (representatives) in the transfer process. Namely, according to the Directive, employees must be informed and consulted about what is happening. Under Article 7(1), the transferor and transferee must inform the employees (representatives) concerned of the following: the date or proposed date of the transfer; the reasons for the transfer; the legal, economic and social implications of the transfer for the employees; and any measures envisaged for the employees. The transferor and transferee are required to give such information to the employees (representatives) in good time.[64] Article 7(2) establishes that where the transferor or the transferee envisages measures about his employees, he must consult the employees (representatives) in good time on such actions to reach an agreement.[65]

The above shows that the obligation to provide information is more general, and the transferor and transferee must follow it always. In contrast, the consultation obligation is focused on measures that the transferor or transferee envisages taking about the employees. One can assume that this will happen in most cases of transfer.[66] Since the purpose of holding consultations is to conclude an agreement between the employees and the employer, conducting them is more than just a formality.[67]

In connection with the transposition of information and consultation provision of the Directive, the CJEU has found that to ensure the protection of employees, the Directive must be transposed by legal act if (the corresponding obligations arising from) collective agreements do not cover all employees.[68]

Unlike the protection of the rights of employees in the event of the undertaking transfer during the transferor's bankruptcy proceedings, the rules regarding information and consultation have been correctly transposed into Estonian law. According to TLS §113(1), the transferor and transferee of an undertaking must submit, in good time

64. The transferor must give the information before the transfer is carried out. The transferee must provide the information before his employees are directly affected by the transfer regarding their conditions of work and employment.
65. These obligations apply irrespective of whether the employer or an undertaking controlling the employer takes the decision resulting in the transfer (Article 7(4)).
66. *Supra* n. 9, p. 359.
67. *See also supra* n. 32, p. 128.
68. C-235/84, 10.7.1986, *Commission of the European Communities* v. *Italian Republic*, ECLI-:EU:C:1986:303, paras 17 ff.

but not later than one month before the transfer of the enterprise, to the employees' representative or, in their absence, the employees the notice in a form reproducible in writing (e.g., via e-mail, intranet).[69] TLS §113(2) states that if the transferor or the transferee of an enterprise intends, due to the transfer of the enterprise, to make changes affecting the situation of the employees, they must consult the employees' representative or, in their absence, the employees with the goal of reaching an agreement on the measures planned.[70]

Fulfilment of the afore-described obligations is ensured by the fact that, in addition to issuing an injunction, the Labour Inspectorate may initiate misdemeanour proceedings against the employer and apply a fine for failing to inform and consult when the undertaking is transferred.[71]

Thus, as coming from the above, TLS is formally in accordance with the Directive and no legal disputes have arisen either. However, how employees' representatives are informed and consulted in practice raises questions. Before accession to the EU, employee involvement was an unfamiliar phenomenon in the Estonian legal order. Several EU Directives[72] provide for the information and consultation of employee representatives, and the corresponding regulation is based on the traditions of many Member States. However, Estonia has no such practices, primarily for historical reasons.[73] After joining the EU, meaningful involvement of employees in the company's decision-making processes has been one of the most problematic areas.[74]

69. The notice must contain at least the following information: (1) the planned date of transfer of the enterprise; (2) the reasons for the transfer of the enterprise; (3) the legal, economic and social consequences of the transfer of the enterprise for the employees; and (4) the measures planned with regard to the employees.
70. Upon consultation, the employees' representative has or, in their absence, the employees have the right to meet with the representatives of the transferor and transferee of the enterprise and make proposals relating to the measures planned regarding the employees no later than within 15 days as of the submission of the notice. The undertaking's transferor and transferee must justify disregard for the proposals (TLS §113(3)).
71. *Supra* n. 16, §113 comm. 5. Under TLS §129(1) and (2), failure to perform the obligation to inform and consult upon transfer of undertaking, committed by an employer, is punishable by a fine of up to 300 fine units. The same act, if committed by a legal person, is punishable by a fine of up to EUR 32,000. According to §47(1) of the Penal Code, a fine unit is the base amount of a fine and is equal to EUR 8. Penal Code, passed on 6 June 20018 – RT I 2001, 61, 364; 05.7.2025, 9 (https://www.riigiteataja.ee/en/eli/ee/520032023010/consolide/current; accessed 15 September 2025). Hence, the value of 300 fine units is EUR 2,400.
72. For example, Directives 89/391/EEC on the introduction of measures to encourage improvements in the safety and health of workers at work (OJ L 183, 29.6.1989, pp. 1-8), 98/59/EC on the approximation of the laws of the Member States relating to collective redundancies (OJ L 225, 12.8.1998, pp. 16-21), 2002/14/EC establishing a general framework for informing and consulting employees in the European Community (OJ L 80, 23.3.2002, pp. 29-34), etc.
73. The first traditional trade unions emerged in Estonia by the 1930s, but their activities were terminated by Estonia's occupation by the Soviet Union in 1940. The objective of the Soviet trade unions was not to advocate the rights and interests of employees, but to implement the policies of the Communist Party. The restoration of traditional trade unions in Estonia began only in the 1990s and, thus, employees have had an opportunity to participate in the organisation of employment affairs only for about the last thirty years. *See also* M. Muda, Employee Involvement in Estonia, in: M. Weiss and M. Seweryński (eds), Handbook of Employee Involvement in Europe, Kluwer Law International, 2004, pp. 7-11.
74. *See also* M. Erikson, Regulating Labour Relations and a Changing Society: The Pathways of a Baltic Country – Estonia, in: F. Hendrickx and v. De Stefano (eds), Game Changers in Labour

Informing and consulting employee representatives is not common in companies.[75] However, informing employees is easier to implement, for example, by putting information on the company's stand or intranet or by sending e-mails. However, it is much more challenging to carry out consultations because it requires active and conscious activity from both the employer and the employees. From the author's viewpoint, there are two main problems why conducting consultations in Estonian practice is difficult. First, most companies do not have employee representatives, and second, the parties to the employment relationship often lack the knowledge and skills to carry out meaningful negotiations.

The shortage of employee representatives is related to the development of trade unions in Estonia – traditional trade unions only started to develop in the 1990s.[76] Also, the recent trend is that union membership is declining worldwide.[77] For these reasons, the number of trade union members in Estonia is not large, and, as mentioned above,[78] only 6% of employees belong to trade unions. Therefore, most companies do not have trade union representatives.

In addition to the trade union, employees may be represented by an employees' trustee elected by the general meeting of employees.[79] If the main task of the trade union is to achieve better working conditions through collective bargaining, the main assignment of the employees' trustee is to participate in information and consultation. However, the trustees have also been elected in only a few – 17% of companies.[80] Although, according to TLS, the employer must inform and consult with the employees in the absence of an employee representative (i.e., union representative or employees' trustee), employees are less qualified for such participation.

As mentioned above, the need for more knowledge and skills is a general problem, and informing and consulting employees may not fulfil their purpose. The lack of skills affects both employees and employers because neither side is in the habit of listening to each other and cooperating. As for the content of the consultations, the employer may have a vision of how it is possible to organise the undertaking's further

---

Law: Shaping the Future of Work, Bulletin of Comparative Labour Relations, No. 100, Kluwer Law International, 2018, pp. 202 ff.

75. There are no corresponding precise statistics, but for example, in 2024, the Estonian Labour Inspectorate processed 123 misdemeanours, but no misdemeanour proceedings related to the fulfilment of the obligation to inform and consult have been identified.. Labour Inspectorate, Yearbook of the Labour Inspectorate 2024, p. 11 (https://www.ti.ee/sites/default/files/documents/2025-04/Yearbook%20of%20the%20Labour%20Inspectorate%202024.pdf; accessed 15 September 2025).
76. *Supra* n. 73, pp. 10-11.
77. *See*, for example, C. Schnabel, Union Membership and Collective Bargaining: Trends and Determinants, IZA – Institute of Labor Economics, Discussion Paper Series No. 13465, 2020, pp. 3-5.
78. *See supra* n. 63.
79. *See more about employees' trustee* M. Muda, The Status of Non-union Employees' Representatives in Estonia, in: R. Blanpain and N. Lyutov (eds), Workers' Representation in Central and Eastern Europe: Challenges and Opportunities for the Works Councils' System, Bulletin of Comparative Labour Relations, No. 85, Kluwer Law International, 2014, pp. 78 ff.
80. J. Ait, Employee Participation, in: L. Kaldmäe (ed.), Estonian Work Life Survey 2015, Series of the Ministry of Social Affairs, 2017/1, p. 53 (in Estonian).

work, but the employees often do not have such a general picture.[81] It is, therefore, difficult to reach an agreement on measures concerning employees, as required by the Directive.

In previous years, the article's author has supposed that social dialogue in Estonia, including the involvement of employees in the company's decision-making processes, becomes more meaningful as time passes.[82] Developments in recent years have not shown this. The number of members of trade unions is also constantly decreasing in Estonia,[83] so there is no side of collective labour relations emerging that would promote information and consultation. To change the situation, one solution could be for the state to organise training for the parties to the employment relationship regarding the involvement of employees.

§6.05 CONCLUDING REMARKS

Protecting employees' rights in the case of the transfer of an undertaking is not a very topical issue in Estonian law. The corresponding EU Directive has mostly been correctly adopted in Estonia, and no severe disputes have arisen. However, three areas have generated more discussion. These areas are the concept of the transfer of an undertaking, employee protection in the case of the undertaking transfer during bankruptcy proceedings, and informing and consulting employees about the transfer of the undertaking.

The interpretation of the transfer of the undertaking has caused the most disputes in the courts. Besides labour disputes, when evaluating the transfer of an undertaking, the Estonian courts are based on the practice of the CJEU, also in tax and other civil cases. Just like the CJEU, the Estonian courts also consider that when evaluating the transfer of an undertaking, it is essential first to determine whether the transferring entity retains its identity. The courts have additionally found that the criteria for evaluating the transfer of a company are, for example, the takeover of intangible assets and organisation, continuity of customer and contracting authority relations and place of business of the transferor and the transferee. Also, the burden of proof of the transfer of the undertaking lies with the employer, not the employee.

Estonian law conflicts with the Directive regarding the rules regarding protecting employees' rights in case of the transfer of an undertaking during the transferor's insolvency. According to TLS, employees' employment contracts are not transferable and can be terminated if the undertaking is transferred during bankruptcy proceedings. At the same time, bankruptcy proceedings can result in both the rehabilitation and liquidation of the undertaking. The Directive allows bypassing the protection of employees only in case of liquidation of the undertaking (assets). Thus, TLS must be brought into line with the Directive. Estonian law must also ensure that, even in the

81. *See also* M. Muda, The Impact of European Union Law on Employee Involvement in Estonia, *Juridica International Law Review*, University of Tartu, 2008/XV, p. 34.
82. *Supra* n. 74, p. 204; *supra* n. 81, p. 34.
83. *See supra* n. 63.

event of liquidation of the undertaking, if the undertaking is transferred as a set of assets, the rights of employees must be protected.

The Directive obliges both the transferor and the transferee to inform and consult with the employees (representatives) about the transfer of the undertaking. The Estonian law establishes a similar regulation, but the problem is the effective implementation of information and, even more, consultation. The reason is the shortage of employee representatives and the lack of knowledge, skills and experience in involving employees in the company's decision-making processes. The solution to the problem could be the appropriate training of the parties to the employment relationship.

CHAPTER 7
France

Michel Blatman

The current study intends, at first, to briefly describe the fairly complex topic of French law relating to the safeguarding of employees' rights in the event of transfers of undertakings, businesses or parts of undertakings (§7.01). It will address secondly two sets of controversies involved by the implementation of such transfers: the one about the necessity of a legal relationship ('lien de droit') between the transferor and the transferee (§7.02); the other relating to the contradiction raised between the effects of the transfer and the principle of equal treatment of workers (§7.03).

§7.01 A BRIEF OVERVIEW OF FRENCH LAW ON UNDERTAKINGS' TRANSFERS

The matter, deeply marked by European Union law, has different aspects depending on whether it is looked at from an individual or collective point of view, or whether the companies involved are governed by public or private law.

Moreover, the notions of 'loss of market', voluntary enforcement of the rules on transfer of an undertaking, and conventional transfer of employment contracts to the 'entering' company in the market are willingly used in French law. Therefore, they also deserve an examination.

[A] Incorporation of EU Law into National Law on Transfers of Undertakings[1]

French law has now integrated the contribution of Directives 1977/187/EEC of 14 February 1977, 98/50/EEC of 29 June 1988, et 2001/23/EC of 12 March 2001, as well

1. 'Transferts d'entreprise: aspects individuels', Antoine Mazeaud, Répertoire de droit du travail, Dalloz.

as that of the case law of the Court of Justice of the European Communities. They both greatly enriched it.

In addition to the concept of 'modification in the legal situation of the employer' classically provided for by the Labour Code to characterize a transfer of business, appeared in the national jurisprudential field that of 'autonomous economic entity retaining its identity and whose activity is continued or resumed' recommended by the Court of Justice. This 'entity' has also penetrated the written law since the Labour Code itself mentions, in Article L. 1224-3, the expression 'economic entity employing employees'. But as will be seen later, this progress has not been easy (*see* §7.02).

[B] Public Order

The list of the different methods in which the transfer of undertakings takes place shows that it is a public policy mechanism.[2] This concerns individual and collective labour relations within the undertakings in question:

- *At the individual level*, first, the effects of the transfer are felt both before the assignment – the first company should not anticipate the will of the second not to take back the employees – and after the transfer – the new employer is not allowed to modify the workers' employment contract without their agreement,[3] nor can these oppose the continuation of their contract with the transferee undertaking, failing which they will be regarded as having resigned.[4] The elements of the employment contract such as the seniority of the employee or the existence of a non-competition clause pass to the second employer.
- *At the collective level*, then, the transfer of an undertaking also concerns the status of the staff,[5] and more particularly those sources of labour law that are internal regulations,[6] custom and practice of the company, unilateral

2. From which it follows: (1) that the employee cannot validly resign from his employment with the first employer to enter the trial with the second (Soc. 10 July 1996, n° 93-41716, D); (2) that the employer who tries to defeat the legal transfer system by having employees offered a new employment contract by another company with a trial period and not taking into account their seniority acts with a 'blameworthy carelessness' justifying his conviction to pay compensation for dismissal without real and serious cause. (Soc. 22 September 1993, Nos 91-45.103 to 91-103.106, F-P).
3. Soc. 17 April 2019, n° 17-17.880, P: 'when the application of Article L. 1224-1 of the Labour Code leads to a modification of the employment contract other than the change of employer, the employee is entitled to oppose it'.
4. Soc.10 october 2006, n° 04-40325, Bull. civ. 2006 V, n° 295 p. 281. In this judgment, the Court of Cassation specifies that the 'collective opposition' to the replacement of a concessionaire of the operation of a public service by another does not characterize the 'individual refusal' of each employee to continue his employment contract with the new employer at the time of the actual transfer of the economic entity, whose refusal, if established, produces the effects of a resignation.
5. 'Transferts d'entreprise: aspects collectifs', Yann Aubrée, Répertoire de droit du travail, Dalloz, 2022.
6. In French: 'règlement intérieur'.

commitments of the employer, and collective agreements. Employees' representation is similarly interested:

- *The internal regulation of the company* is a 'regulatory act of private law whose conditions of elaboration are framed by law'.[7] They are therefore not transferred with the employment contracts and, consequently, are not binding on the new employer, who is not required to apply them.[8] This was held in a case where, although the internal regulations of the transferred undertaking provided that any dismissal on disciplinary grounds of an employee had to be preceded by a summons by means of a letter informing him of the objections against him, the new employer had failed to comply with that formality. The Court of Appeal had drawn the conclusion that this was a dismissal without real and serious cause. Its decision was censured by the Social Chamber of the Court of Cassation on the grounds that the buying company 'was not required to apply the internal regulations of the [sold] company which had not been transmitted to it pursuant to Article L. 1224-1 of the Labour Code'.[9]
- *The employer's unilateral commitments and practices* follow a different regime.
- The unilateral commitment made by an employer towards his employees is transmitted, in the event of a transfer of an autonomous economic entity, to the new employer, who can terminate it only on condition that he informs the employees and the staff representative institutions individually within a period allowing for possible negotiations.[10] It is up to the Court to investigate, when requested, whether the conditions under which the transferor paid the employees of its company a bonus calculated according to a predetermined method did not characterise a unilateral commitment on its part (Soc. 22 May 2024, n° 22-14.984, FS-B). And, specifies the Court of Cassation, 'it is the responsibility of the one who leaves this commitment unfulfilled to bear the resulting damages'.[11] The practice is subject to the same rules of 'automatic transfer' of these standards in force on the day of the transfer, and valid denunciation by the employer.[12]
- Their strength. The incoming employer may not make the benefit in the ostundertaking of these collective benefits, subject to the condition that the transferred employees waive the rights they derive from them.[13]

Furthermore, while the employer is legally obliged to maintain the benefits resulting from a unilateral commitment, in force on the day of the transfer, enjoyed by the transferred employees, it may not refuse to grant these same

7. Soc. 17 October 2008, n° 17-16.465, P.
8. Soc. 31 March 2021, n° 19-12.289, P.
9. Soc. 31 March 2021, n° 19-12.289, P.
10. Soc. 21 September 2005, n° 03-43.532, Bulletin 2005, V, n° 260 p. 228.
11. Soc. 21 September 2005, n° 03-43.532 above-mentioned.
12. Soc. 5 July 2017, n° 15-29.533, D.
13. Soc. 13 October 2016, n° 14-25.411, P.

employees the benefit of the advantages resulting from unilateral commitments in force within the host company (Soc. 22 May 2024, n° 23-10.214, FS-B).

- *Collective Bargaining Agreements and Collective Agreements Meet with a More Complex Regime.*

In the absence of a collective agreement or agreement in the transferred undertaking, the collective agreement to which the transferee is subject applies immediately to the employee.[14]

If it exists a collective agreement in the first enterprise, the regime of 'questioning' and 'substitution agreement' applies:

- *Questioning:* It follows from Article L. 2261-14 of the Labour Code that the calling into question of the collective agreement or agreement results from the occurrence of the merger, transfer, division or change of activity, provided for by that text, without the need for a denunciation.[15]
- *Substitute agreement*: It is a collective agreement or agreement whose *purpose* is to replace, in whole or in part, the stipulations of a previous agreement.[16] Accordingly, the substitution agreement must have the *same object* as the agreement at issue.
- *Survival period*: The previous agreement or collective agreement continues to have effect until the entry into force of the agreement or the agreement replacing it or, failing that, for a period of 15 months, unless a provision provides for a longer period. The purpose of this period is to 'allow the organization of negotiations in order to adapt the agreement to the new structure of the company or to define new provisions'.[17]
- *Challenge without substitution agreement*: *allocation of a* 'remuneration guarantee': The situation is that provided for by Article L. 2261-14, paragraph 2 of the Labour Code,[18] according to which 'Where the agreement or agreement which has been called into question has not been replaced by a new agreement or agreement within the [15-month] period, the employees of the undertakings concerned shall benefit from a guarantee of remuneration the annual amount of which, for a period of work equivalent to that provided for in their employment contract, may not be less than the remuneration paid, pursuant to the agreement in question, during the last twelve months.(...)' This guarantee may be ensured by the payment of a *differential indemnity* between the amount of remuneration that was due to the employee under the agreement or agreement in question and his contract of employment and the amount of the employee's remuneration resulting from the new agreement or agreement, if it exists, and its employment contract.

14. Soc. 10 February 2010, n° 08-44.454, P.
15. Soc. 24 March 2021, n° 19-15.920, FS-P + I.
16. Soc. 19 December 2018, n° 17-24.157, D.
17. Soc 13 December 2017, n° 16-26.553, P.
18. Article L. 2261-14 C. trav., mod. by LOI n° 2018-217 of 29 March 2018 – Article 21(V).

Observation

The French system for maintaining contractual benefits appears to be *more favourable* for transferred employees than that provided for in Article 3(2) of EEC Directive No. 77/187 of 14 February 1977 as reproduced by Article 3 § 3 of Council Directive 2001/23/EC of 12 March 2001.[19] The latter provides that:

> After the transfer, the transferee shall maintain the terms and conditions of employment agreed by a collective agreement to the same extent as the latter has laid down them for the transferor, until the date of termination or expiry of the collective agreement or the entry into force or application of another collective agreement. Member States may limit the period during which working conditions may be maintained, provided that it is not less than one year.

As the above-mentioned author points out[20] 'The Community Directive does not grant employees of the undertaking or part of an undertaking transferred, from the expiry of that period of one year and in the absence of the entry into force of an alternative collective agreement, any right to retain (...) a "guarantee of remuneration" corresponding to the last twelve months' salary, which have been paid to them or which remain due to them under this collective agreement or agreement.'

Subsistence of Staff Representative Institutions and Intervention of the Labour Inspector

In the event of a transfer of an undertaking, *the mandates* of the trade union delegate, the central trade union delegate, the representative of the trade union section and the elected members of the staff delegation of the social and economic committee (CSE) *continue when* the undertaking which is the subject of the amendment *retains its legal autonomy,*[21] or when the modification concerns a separate establishment within the meaning of Article L. 2143-3 (Labour Code, Articles L. 2142-1-2, L. 2314-35, L. 2143-10).

The *partial transfer* of an undertaking or establishment may only take place *after authorization by the labour inspector* when this operation includes a so-called protected employee with a representation mandate, the list of which appears in the Labour Code (Article L. 2414-1).

[C] The Scope of the Transfer According to the Quality of the Transferee

The scope of the transfer of an undertaking extends both to the '*publicization*' of a private company (Labour Code, Article L. 1224-3) and to the '*privatization*' of a public one (Labour Code, Article L. 1224-3-1). In both cases, the legislator enshrined judicial case law.

19. Council Directive 2001/23/EC of 12 March 2001, OIEU n° L 82, 22 March 2001, pp. 16-20.
20. Yann Deprée, op. préc., referring to the fact that before the reform instituted by Law No. 2016-1088 of 8 August 2016 (Official Journal of 9 August), the Court of Cassation recognized the maintenance of their 'acquired individual rights' for the benefit of transferred employees.
21. Soc. 1 June 2023, n° 21-21.191, FS-B.

– Transfer with 'Publicization' of Private Enterprise

Under Article L. 1224-3 of the Labour Code:

> When the activity of an economic entity employing employees under private law is, by transfer of this entity, taken over by a public person as part of a public administrative service, it is up to this public person to offer these employees a contract under public law, of fixed or indefinite duration depending on the nature of the contract they hold.
>
> Unless otherwise provided by law or general conditions of remuneration and employment of non-tenured agents of the public entity, the contract it proposes includes the substantive clauses of the contract held by the employees, in particular those concerning remuneration.
>
> Services performed within the economic entity of origin are treated as services performed within the host public body.
>
> In the event of refusal of the employees to accept the proposed contract, their contract is automatically terminated. The public entity applies the provisions relating to dismissed agents provided for by labour law and their contract.

Illustration of Recreation Centres[22]

First case (nature of the activity). The association Les Francas has signed an agreement with the municipality of Belfort for the management of seven leisure centres and four extracurricular centres for a renewable period of one year. The municipality subsequently informed the association that it was not renewing this agreement. Taking the view that the provisions of Article L. 1224-3 of the Labour Code applied, the association sent the town hall a list of 36 employees assigned to the activities concerned by the management contract. Following a call for applications, 14 of its employees were recruited by the municipality. Two employees who had not been taken over brought claims against the association before the labour court, seeking, in particular, the termination of their employment contracts at the exclusive fault of the association.

The Court of Appeal approved their complaint, holding that, in order to rule out the existence of a transfer of the employment contracts of the persons concerned:

- that only the management of the activity of leisure and extracurricular centre had been entrusted to the association, which had no particular structure to receive the children and carry out its missions;
- that it worked in the premises equipped with their equipment made available by the municipality; owner of the premises, the association being limited to providing the equipment specific to the childcare activity (games and small equipment);
- that the municipality assumed the operating costs of the operation (water, gas, electricity) and paid the holder of the contract an annual operating contribution in addition to the participation of families and the aid of other funders;
- that if it could be accepted that the existence of a family clientele dedicated to the activity, it was not a real clientele attached to an economic activity, the

22. Soc. 14 March 2018, n° 16-23.715 et 16-23.717, D.

users being the citizens of the municipality of Belfort and not a specific clientele of the association;
- that the association did not benefit from any autonomy or any power of decision or organization proper in the exercise of its mission, which had to be ensured in accordance with the educational project of the town hall; and
- that the staff, engaged for some employees on precarious contracts, was not particularly dedicated to the activity in question and could be assigned to other workplaces.

The Social Chamber of the Court of Cassation censured this decision on the grounds, on the one hand, that the above reasons were ineffective, on the other hand, that it followed from the findings of the Court of Appeal that the municipality had pursued *the same activity* in the *same premises* with the *same equipment*, regardless of whether it owned it, and with the *same public* attached to this social activity (non-profit-making being irrelevant) so that there was a *transfer of significant tangible and intangible elements necessary for the operation of an autonomous economic entity whose activity was continued and whose identity was carried on.*

Second case (skills of the employee). This time, a municipality had taken over the direct management of two leasure and education centres for children originally entrusted to an association of private law. Arguing that the manageress of the association had neither the certificate of aptitude for the functions of director nor one of the diplomas and experience assimilated to it, necessary to hold the position of director of a leisure centre, the municipality refused to take her back, did not submit any public law contract to her and did not implement any dismissal procedure. Wrongly according to the Cour de cassation, because the employee's employment contract having been transferred by operation of law to the municipality, the latter was required to pay the salaries from the date on which this activity had been transferred to it, regardless of the fact that the employee may not meet the regulatory conditions of qualification or diploma to perform his or her duties. (Soc. 6 March 2024, n° 22-22.315, P).

– Transfer with 'Privatization' of the Public Enterprise

The approach, which this time concerns the takeover of an economic entity under public law by a legal person governed by private law, is symmetrical to the previous one.

Article L. 1224-3-1 of the Labour Code provides, in this regard, that:

> Subject to the application of special laws or regulations, where the activity of a legal person governed by public law employing officials who do not hold public law is taken over by a legal person governed by private law or by a body governed by public law managing a public industrial and commercial service, that legal person or body shall offer those employees a contract governed by this Code.

This operation literally concerns 'non-tenured agents under public law', i.e., non-civil servants. The contract offered to them is a private law contract, which 'includes the substantive clauses of the contract held by the agents, in particular those concerning remuneration'. Finally, the text provides that: 'In the event of refusal of the agents to accept the proposed contract, their contract shall automatically terminate. The legal person or body taking over the activity shall apply the provisions of public law relating to dismissed staff.'

[D] Market Loss, Conventional Transfer and Voluntary Application

– *Market loss*

Reaffirming its previous case-law, the Plenary Assembly of the Court of Cassation, by judgment of 16 March 1990,[23] stated that Article L. 122-12 [now L. 1224-1] of the Labour Code 'is not applicable solely in the case of the loss of a contract'. In this case, an association for the reception and training of migrants (AFTAM) had terminated, in order to carry out the cleaning of its premises itself, the contract between it and the cleaning company ONET and refused to take into its service the two employees assigned to that task by the latter, which had then dismissed them. The Court of Cassation ruled that this termination of employment contracts by ONET was not justified by a transfer of business to the AFTAM association, since 'the loss of a single customer had not led to any transformation of the fund or cessation of ONET's activities'. The cleaning company should therefore have retained the workers in question.

The wording adopted by the Court is that 'the mere assignment of employees to the performance of a contract is not sufficient to characterise such an economic entity'.[24]

It is therefore necessary to ascertain in each case whether the contract for the provision of services contains, as the case may be, elements characterizing an autonomous economic undertaking, that is to say, 'an organised group of persons and tangible or intangible elements pursuing a specific economic objective', bearing in mind that the transfer of such an entity takes place only 'if tangible or intangible resources which are significant and necessary for the operation of the entity are taken over, directly or indirectly, by a new operator'.[25]

– *'Conventional' Transfers*

'Collective bargaining' aims. In the sectors affected by the market losses some collective agreements were intended to improve the lot of workers by allowing them to be taken over by the new undertaking awarded the contract in which they operated. Thus, in sectors such as cleanliness, cleaning or security, collective agreements have come to regulate the transition of personnel from the 'exit' company to the 'entering' company in the market.

23. 'Assemblée plénière' 16 March 1990, n° 85-44.518, Bulletin 1990, A.P., n° 3 p. 5, quoted *infra*.
24. Soc. 18 February 2004, n° 01-46.432, F-D.
25. Soc. 15 February 2023, n° 21-50.058, F-D.

Two illustrations:

- National collective agreement of premises cleaning companies: Annex 7, paragraph 2 and Addendum No. 1 to this annex, determine the conditions of the continuity of the employment contract of the staff assigned to a contract taken over by a new service provider, and impose on the latter the obligation to make himself known in writing to the outgoing company to obtain the list of personnel to be transferred.
- Collective agreement of cleaning companies and associated services of 26 July 2011. Its Article 7.2 'Obligations incumbent on the new claimant (incoming undertaking)' lists a number of conditions for continued employment:
  - *Proof of the employee's eligibility for the conventional transfer.* The Court of Cassation specifies that 'it is not the responsibility of the employee assigned to a takeover contract and that the incoming company refuses to keep in its service to establish that it meets the contractual conditions relating to the guarantee of employment and the continuity of the employment contract of the staff in the event of a change of service provider'.[26]
  - *Employee's consent.* Considering that the change of employer constitutes a novation of the employment contract, the Court adds, in substance, that '*unless Article L. 1224-1 of the Labour Code* [= legal transfer] *may apply, the change of employer provided for and organised by agreement presupposes the express agreement of the employee, which cannot result solely from the continuation of his employment contract under another management*'.[27] A company cannot therefore impose on its employees the transfer of their employment contract, a modification which would then be analysed as a dismissal without real and serious cause.[28] It is for the Court hearing the case to verify the reality of this agreement.[29]
  - *No compulsory contractual takeover for foreign employees without a work permit.* According to the Court of Cassation, a foreigner who does not have the permit authorizing him to carry out a salaried activity in France is not[30] assimilated to an employee duly engaged under the rules applicable to the transfer of the employment contract. It concludes, in a case in the field of community catering, that the new holder of the contract is not required to comply with the contractual provisions organizing the transfer between two service providers, and therefore to continue the employment contract of the person concerned.[31]
  - *Conventional transfer and uses.* Unless otherwise provided by agreement, when the company entering the contract takes over the employment

26. Soc. 15 February 2023, n° 21-17.412, F-D.
27. Soc. 19 May 2016, n°14-26.556 et s., P.
28. Soc. 9 March 2022, n° 21-11.170, F-D.
29. Soc. 3 March 2010, n° 08-41.600 08-44.120, P.
30. By application of the combined provisions of Article L. 8251-1 and L. 8252-1 of the Labour Code.
31. Soc. 17 April 2019, n° 18-15.321, P.

> contracts of the employees assigned to the said market without being bound to do so by the provisions of Article L. 1224-1 of the Labour Code, it is bound only by the clauses of the employment contracts and not by the practices in force in an economic entity that has not been transferred to it.[32]

Voluntary Application of the Statutory Transfer Regime

Regardless of the legal or contractual arrangements, incoming and outgoing companies may voluntarily apply the legal provisions governing the transfer of business. But in this case, as in that of the conventional transfer, the consent of the employee is required for what constitutes a modification of his employment contract.[33] In the absence of such an agreement, it was held that the termination of the employment contracts of employees in the service of the second employer was the responsibility of the first, which exposed him to the payment of damages to those employees.[34]

The overview that has just been made is far from exhaustive because it did not address these particular issues, such as the definition of the autonomous economic entity, the situation of the company and the employees in the event of receivership or liquidation. But it seemed appropriate to show how 'Community' law, which became 'European Union law', interfered in two internal legal debates, one on the 'legal link' and the other, on the confrontation of the law on transfers of undertakings with the principle of equal treatment, to the point of transforming the physiognomy of each of them.

§7.02 THE IMPACT OF EU LAW ON THE OUTCOME OF THE LONG BATTLE OVER THE 'LEGAL RELATIONSHIP'

A professor of labour law expressed himself as follows in a doctrinal note written in 1990:[35] 'Let us envy our heirs. With the turbulent history of the interpretation of Article L. 122-12, paragraph 2, C. trav [now L. 1224-1], they will have an example of a legal dispute in which all the resources of argumentation, available in a given period (from 1978 to 1990), were, more or less, used. The archaeologist of tomorrow will discover how lawyers use the past, appeal to Europe, how the economy, an economy of common sense, sometimes that of the coffee of commerce, is invoked; He will observe the many facets of what his followers call legal analysis ...'

32. Soc. 18 September 2019, n° 18-17.018, F-D.
33. Soc. 17 June 2009, n° 08-42.615, P.
34. Soc. 4 April 2001, n° 99-40.871, F-D.
35. Antoine Lyon-Caen, note under Plenary assembly, 16 March 1990, Recueil Dalloz Sirey 1990, Jurisprudence, p. 305.

The author refers to the long battle[36] concerning the stated requirement of a 'legal relationship' between successive employers in order to play, for the benefit of the employees concerned, the possibility of maintaining their employment.

We will recall here the different stages of this controversy.

The principle of maintaining the employee's employment contract in the event of a transfer of the company to which he belongs was adopted quite early in French legislation, since it was introduced into the Labour Code by *a law of 19 July 1928.*

Since then, it has been reproduced in much the same terms as the various amendments to the text and recodifications have taken place: Article 23, paragraph 7; then 23, paragraph 8; 24k of the Labour Code; finally L. 122-12 from the first recodification of 1973; and L. 1224-1 on the occasion of the second, which entered into force in 2008.

The solution, as it appears in the latest version of the Labour Code, thus enshrines an unchanged legislative edifice: '*When there is a change in the employer's legal situation, in particular by succession, sale, merger, transformation of the fund, incorporation of the company, all employment contracts in force on the day of the amendment* remain between the new employer and the company's staff' (Labour Code, Article L. 1224-1).

It thus sets out a list of events which, although affecting the person of the employer or the company, do not lead to the termination of their employment contract for employees: this continues with the new employer.

This list of transformations is not exhaustive, for case law has given it a great extension, considering that the maintenance of the employment contract is de jure whenever 'employees continue the same work under new management' (Soc. 22 December 1950), or 'as soon as the activity of the company has remained the same' (Soc. 21 March 1961).

When the time came to implement the Directive of the Council of the European Communities of 14 February 1977 on the approximation of the laws of the Member States relating to the safeguarding of employees' rights in the event of transfers of undertakings, businesses or parts of businesses, the French legislator[37] did not consider it necessary to amend the above-mentioned provision. Since the latter seemed to him to be compatible with the Community text, he merely inserted into the Labour Code an Article L. 122-12-1 [now L. 1224-2] worded as follows:

> Unless the amendment referred to in the second paragraph of Article L. 122-12 takes place in the context of a procedure for the judicial settlement or liquidation of assets, or a substitution of employers without there having been an agreement between them, the new employer is also required, in respect of employees whose employment contracts subsist, the obligations incumbent on the former employer on the date of the amendment.

---

36. Described as a 'rebound of the French doctrinal debate' by the professor Jean Déprez, in 'Transferts d'entreprises et continuité des contrats de travail dans les jurisprudences française (art. L. 122-12) et communautaire', Etudes et doctrine, Chronique, RJS 1/89, Francis Lefebvre.
37. Law No. 83-528 of 28 June 1983, Official Journal of 29 June 1983, p. 1943.

> The first employer shall be bound to reimburse the sums paid by the new employer pursuant to the preceding paragraph, unless account has been taken of the burden resulting from these obligations in the agreement between them.

What about the need for a legal relationship between successive employers? The question arose early on as to whether this regime favourable for maintaining employees' employment contracts should also benefit those of a public service concessionaire when the concession was granted to another undertaking. In a case in which the public electric lighting service of the city of Setif (Algeria) had been entrusted to a new concessionaire (the company Union hydro-électrique de l'Ouest constantinois), an engineer of the previous contractor, complaining that he had not been taken over by the latter, had brought an action against the latter for payment of damages for wrongful termination of his employment contract. The Algiers Court of Appeal, by judgment of 13 May 1931, had rejected his claim on the ground that *no contract having been concluded between the two companies,* the latter deriving its rights directly from the municipality of Setif under a distinct and different specification, we were 'in the presence of two successive employers, without legal link between them and that on no basis the latter could be held liable for the obligations assumed by the former'.

However, the Court of Cassation replied (Social Chamber, 27 February 1934, Goupy, Bulletin des arrêt de la Cour de Cassation, Chambre sociale, No. 51 p. 101), this was an 'erroneous reason in law'. Indeed, she explained, paragraph 7 of the new Article 23 of book 1 of the Labour Code amended by the law of 19 July 1928 'intended to ensure more stable jobs for employees must be applied in all cases where the same enterprise continues to operate under new management'. It follows, it added, that 'a new concessionaire of a public service who, on expiry of a previous concession contract concluded with another person, is instructed by the competent authority to continue the operation of the same public service must be regarded as a new contractor, within the meaning of the abovementioned text, required, therefore, to respect the current employment contracts'.

The protective *purpose* of the text, namely to ensure greater job stability for employees, therefore required an interpretation extended to situations without any legal link between the employees and the new concessionaire.

This conception specific to Labour Law has, however, been opposed in doctrine, on the grounds, in particular, that it was contrary to the *letter of the Labour Code* which referred to an assignment mechanism, and that it contradicted the principle of the *relativity of the effects of contracts*, thus transcribed in Article 1165 of the Civil Code of 1804: '*Agreements have effect only between the contracting parties; they do not harm the third party, and they benefit him only in the case provided for in Article 1121* [= stipulation for others].' The new Article 1199 of the same code, resulting from Ordinance No. 2016-131 of 10 February 2016 reforming contract law, reaffirms the principle by stating that 'The contract creates obligations only between the parties.' From an *economic point of view,* such an interpretation of former Article L. 122-12 of the Labour Code was also criticized for hindering the development of dynamic companies likely to win many markets.[38]

It is in this context that the Plenary Assembly of the Court of Cassation held, by a judgment of 15 November 1985 (No. 82-41.510, P) delivered in a case where the new service provider of the site of cleaning the premises of a hypermarket had refused to maintain the employment of an employee of the previous provider, that the change in the legal situation of the employer within the meaning of Article L. 122-12, paragraph 2, of the Labour Code *could not result from the* 'sole loss of a market'.

The Social Chamber of the Court of Cassation, therefore going back on its case law prior to this judgment of the Assembly and ruling on the visa of the aforementioned Article 1165 of the Civil Code, validated the refusal, by the new successful bidder of a contract for track works of the Paris metro, to take into his service the 119 employees that the previous successful bidder declared to employ in the execution of this project. The Court justified its decision by the fact that 'the change in the employer's legal position, which has the effect of allowing the employment contracts in force on the day of the amendment to continue between the new employer and the company's staff, implies the existence of a legal relationship between the successive employers'.[39]

The same refusal to take over employment contracts was made to employees assigned to the urban transport service of the city of Compiègne (Soc. 19 June 1987, 84-44.929, 84-44.930), as well as to those of a site cleaning company premises (Soc. 13 October 1988, No. 85-42.201).

The discussed impact of Community law. The following example illustrates how European Union law, in this case that of Directive 77/187, could be received in domestic law. By judgment of 4 July 1988,[40] the Social Chamber of the Court of Appeal of Riom,[41] seized of a dispute come at its hearing of 3 May 1988 and concerning the effects of the transfer of operation of a road passenger transport network, ordered the reopening of the proceedings for the following reasons: 'Whereas in the course of the deliberations, was published[42] a judgment of the Court of Justice of the European Communities delivered on 10 February 1988[43] interpreting Council Directive 77/187/EEC of 14 February 1977 as meaning that "The Directive applies in a situation where, at the end of a non-transferable concession, the owner of the undertaking transfers it to a new concessionaire who continues to operate it without interruption with the same staff previously dismissed at the end of the first concession". Since that decision and the statement of reasons from which it is based, are being liable to have an impact on the outcome of the present dispute, it is appropriate to reopen the proceedings in order to invite the parties to discuss it inter partes.'

38. Henri Blaise, Flux et reflux...[*ebb and flow*], Droit social, 1984, p. 94.
39. Soc. 12 June 1986, n° 85-43.746, Bull. civ. V, n° 229; Dalloz 1986.461, conclusions Picca, note Karaquillo; JCP (Jurisclasseur périodique) éd. G 1986.II.20705, note Flécheux et Bazex; Droit social 1987, p. 662, chronique J. Deprez.
40. Court of Appeal of Riom, Social Chamber, 4 July 1988, arrêt n° 453, dossier n° 1657/86.
41. Court of which the author of these lines was then a member.
42. In the Revue 'Droit Social', 1988, p. 455, note Gérard Couturier.
43. CJCE 10 février 1988, Tellerup, affaire 324/86.

A similar reopening of proceedings was pronounced by the same Court of Riom on 3 October 1988.[44] In the case, the employee of a cleaning company, assigned to a fast food restaurant run by another company, had, after the termination of the contract for the provision of services between the two companies, been immediately hired in the same capacity as a cleaner by the owner of the restaurant and claimed seniority dating back to his first employment by the previous employer. The reasons for this decision are as follows: 'Whereas, although, since the judgment of the Social Chamber of the Court of Cassation of 12 June 1986, case law requires the existence of a legal link between successive employers in order to apply Article L. 122-12 of the Labour Code, a judgment of the Court of Justice of the European Communities was nevertheless delivered on 10 February 1988 (...)'

Subsequently ruling on the merits, the Riom Court, by two judgments of 6 March 1989,[45] decided to apply directly Article 1(1) of Directive 77/187 as interpreted by the Court of Justice, in conjunction with the provisions of Article L. 122-12, paragraph 2, of the Labour Code, in order to allow employees to benefit from the continuity of their employment contract even in the absence of a legal link between the two successive employers. Other courts of appeal had done the same.[46]

This direct application of Community law giving precedence to EU law over domestic law has been strongly criticized in legal literature. An author[47] wrote that 'the French judges are committed to taking into consideration the 1977 directive and the relevant case-law of the Court of Justice. They do so even with a determination that perhaps takes them too far in interpreting this jurisprudence'. Another commentator even called for 'resistance'[48] against the supremacy of Community case law in that it gives precedence to an interpretation *contra legem* of both the Directive and the Labour Code, whose wording does indeed require the existence of a legal link: 'It is first of all the influence of Community case-law that is to be questioned. (...) The real question raised by Community case-law is whether it implies that the national court is unreservedly subject to the subjection. Are the decisions of the ECJ so binding that, apart from any question expressly submitted for a preliminary ruling, the national court must submit to them? Doubt is allowed, and it is particularly so, in our matter, since the ECJ interpreted the directive of 14 February 1977 against the letter of the text, which provides in Article 1 that it is applicable "to transfers ... resulting from a contractual [assignment] or merger", i.e. in cases where there is a legal link between those whom the Directive designates as the "assignor" and the "assignee" (Article 3) ...'

44. Court of Appeal of Riom, Social Chamber, 3 October 1988, arrêt n° 545, dossier n° 2956/86.
45. Court of Appeal of Riom, 6 mars 1989. 1st *ruling*: n° 89-188, M.G ... c/ société Free Time Resto DM. Jaude; *2d ruling*: n° 89-189, société T2C c/ M.B ... and alii; Bulletin d'information de la Cour de cassation, droit du travail, 1er trimestre 1989, Cours et tribunaux, n° 60, p. 23; La semaine juridique, édition G, 1989, n° 40, IV, Tableaux de jurisprudence, p. 322; Gazette du Palais 1 April 1989 p. 19.
46. Court of Appeal of Paris, 25 November 1988, arrêt n° 312; Dalloz 1989. Informations rapides. 53.
47. Gérard Couturier, 'Le maintien des droits des travailleurs en cas de transfert d'entreprise' [*Safeguarding Employees' Rights in the Event of a Transfer of an Undertaking*] Droit social, n° 7/8 Juillet – Août 1989, p. 557.
48. 'A propos de l'article L. 122-12: ultime résistance ...' [*About Article L. 122-12: Ultimate Resistance*], Bernard Boubli, Opinion, La Semaine sociale Lamy, n° 468 du 4 Septembre 1989.

The supremacy of European Union law has, however, been recognized by the Plenary Assembly of the Court of Cassation itself. The Assembly, before which it had been argued that the non-requirement of a legal relationship infringed both domestic law and Community law, dismissed this objection in two judgments of 16 March 1990. She judged, in a recital of principle, that 'Articles 1 and 3 of the Directive of 14 February 1977 of the Council of the European Communities and L. 122-12, paragraph 2 of the Labour Code, apply, in the absence of a legal link between successive employers, to any transfer of an economic entity which retains its identity and whose activity is continued or taken over.'

As one commentator noted, 'We owe (...) to the obstinacy of some courts of appeal (...), and to its perception by the First President of the Court of Cassation (...) the disappearance of the requirement of the link of law and the entrenchment in French law of Community case-law.'[49]

The result of the operation therefore counts more than the mechanism - direct or indirect - to achieve it, and it is for the national court to verify the reality of the transfer of an economic entity retaining its identity and whose activity is continued or taken over.

The plenary Assembly of the Court of Cassation therefore approved, in its first above-mentioned decision, compensation by the Nîmes Court of Appeal for an employee who, although her employer had lost the concession of the municipal bullring to a bullfighting and entertainment company, had not been taken over by the new concessionaire.

It also, in its second judgment, dismissed the appeal brought against the decision of the Paris Court of Appeal ordering the new concessionaire of the Bois de Boulogne campsite to pay certain allowances to the employees of the previous one, whom he had not reemployed:

> whereas 'an autonomous economic entity comprising, as operating elements, land and installations, had been transferred, allowing the new concessionaire to continue to operate them'.

In short, 'It is not a question, in classical terms, of comparing directive and national law in order to paralyse the latter. Rather, it is a question of imposing on national courts an interpretation of their law which respects the Directive and the interpretation it has received from the Court of Justice of the European Communities.'[50]

§7.03 THE ISSUE OF EQUAL TREATMENT OF WORKERS IN THE EVENT OF A TRANSFER OF AN UNDERTAKING

The obligation for the transferee of the undertaking to allow the transferred employees to benefit from the rights and benefits they had with their previous employer may lead to disparities in treatment with employees already employed by the new employer,

49. Antoine Lyon-Caen, above-mentioned note.
50. Antoine Lyon-Caen, above-mentioned note.

who will not benefit from these profits. This is the case with the maintenance, for the benefit of the transferred employees only, of the payment of a thirteenth month, which the employees of the buyer did not have. Can the latter then plead a breach of the principle of equal treatment between employees of the same undertaking?

Is the answer the same depending on whether the transfer of an undertaking results from the law, an agreement or a collective agreement, from a voluntary application of the legal text?

This issue encounters another problem, which had previously arisen in case law, namely that of the *harmonization of equal treatment and Collective agreement law.*

Indeed, collective agreements and agreements sometimes create, voluntarily or not, differences in treatment: between professional categories, between employees performing, within the same professional category, distinct functions; between establishments, or even within them or between production sites.

The last circumstance was illustrated in particular by the 'loss of markets', which gave rise to conventional transfers of employment contracts.

The question is whether these differences, once proven, are justified. A brief historical review is necessary in this regard [A]. It will make it possible to understand the way in which the case law has dealt with the situation created by transfers of undertakings [B].

[A] The Context of the Principle of Equal Treatment

- From the rule of 'equal pay for equal work' to the principle of 'equal treatment'.

  In its key judgment of 29 October 1996 known as 'Ponsolle', the Court of Cassation based the requirement of equality between employees – women or men – on the rule 'equal pay for equal work', from which it deduced that 'the employer is obliged to ensure equal pay for all employees of either sex, provided that the employees in question are placed in an identical situation'.[51] This rule has been applied to the employer's *unilateral commitment*: 'does not violate the rule "equal pay for equal work", set out in Articles L. 133-5.4 ° and L. 136-2.8 ° of the Labour Code and does not constitute a discriminatory measure, the fact that an employer makes the granting of a benefit in kind resulting from a unilateral commitment on his part subject to a discriminatory measure, under special conditions where all employees of the undertaking may benefit, under the same conditions, from the advantage thus granted',[52] *as well as to collective agreements*, the latter 'cannot defeat the principle of 'equal pay for equal work' and the legal provisions which are merely an application thereof'.[53]

51. Soc. 29 October 1996, n° 92-43.680, Bulletin 1996 V, n° 359, p. 255.
52. Soc. 18 May 1999, n° 98-40201, 98-40202, Bulletin 1999, V, n° 213, p. 156.
53. Soc. 23 May 2001, n° 99-41600, D.

The Court then replaced that rule with the broader reference to the 'principle of equal treatment'[54] and decided that 'the employer may grant special advantages to certain employees if he justifies that all employees of the enterprise placed in an identical situation can benefit from the advantage thus granted and that the rules determining the granting of this advantage are previously defined and controllable'.[55] *The unilateral commitment* of the employer is subject to this principle: 'A difference in treatment established by unilateral commitment may be practised between employees of the same undertaking and performing equal work or work of equal value, only if it is based on objective reasons, the reality and relevance of which must be reviewed by the court.'[56] *Collective agreements* are also bound by respect for equality.[57]

- *Need for judicial review of the objective and relevant reasons of the found inequality:*
  - The jurisprudential condition of 'identical situation' was extended by the Court of Cassation to the analysis of the differences established by collective agreement *between professional categories.*[58] The Court thus stated that 'the difference in professional category alone cannot in itself justify, for the grant of an advantage, a difference in treatment between employees placed in an identical situation with regard to that advantage, that difference must be based on objective reasons the reality and relevance of which the court must specifically review'.[59]
  - In this system, the conventional origin of the advantage in question does not therefore take precedence over the principle of equality but is simply taken into consideration as an 'objective and relevant reason' for a difference which it 'will be for the court to check concretely' whether it 'indeed has as its object or purpose to take into account the specific features of the situation of employees belonging to a given category, relating in particular to the conditions of performance of duties, career development or remuneration arrangements'.[60] It could therefore be held that the employer did not justify any objective and relevant reason legitimizing the disparity established by the conventional provisions between the amount of meal allowances paid to executives, accounting officers, consulting engineers and salaried doctors of social security

54. Christophe Radé, 'Le principe d'égalité de traitement, nouveau principe fondamental du droit du travail' [*The Principle of Equal Treatment, New Fundamental Principle of Labour Law*], Droit Social, Dalloz, n° 9/10 Septembre-Octobre 2008, p. 981.
55. Soc. 30 January 2008, n° 06-46.447, D.
56. Soc. 23 June 2021, n° 19-21.771, P.
57. Soc. 1 July 2009, n° 07-42.675, Bulletin 2009, V, n° 168; Soc. 3 April 2019, n° 17-11.970, P.
58. Soc. 8 June 2011, above-mentioned.
59. Soc. 1er July 2009, 07-42.675, Bulletin 2009, V, n° 168.
60. Soc. 8 June 2011, n° 10-14.725, P, about a seniority bonus granted to managers but not to assimilated executives by Article 22-9 of the Collective agreement of the Pharmaceutical industry.

institutions, and that of allowances paid to managers and enforcement agents of those same bodies.[61]

- *The gradual shift to a simple presumption of justification.* However, anxious to restore a prominent place to collective bargaining as a source of Labour law, the Court of Cassation has mitigated the rigor of the previous system by establishing the following *presumption of justification*:[62] 'the difference in professional category alone cannot in itself justify, for the grant of an advantage, a difference in treatment between employees placed in an identical situation with regard to that advantage, that difference must be based on objective reasons the reality and relevance of which must be specifically reviewed by the court; (...) the stipulation of a collective agreement which bases a difference in treatment on a difference in professional category rests on an objective and relevant reason, where the object or purpose of that difference in treatment is to take account of the specific features of the situation of employees in a particular category, relating in particular to the conditions of performance of duties, career development or remuneration arrangements':[63]
  - The presumption of equality thus created was then more clearly affirmed in the following terms, for differences between professional categories: 'differences in treatment between professional categories, effected by means of collective agreements negotiated and signed by representative trade union organizations, invested with the defence of the rights and interests of employees and in whose empowerment the latter participate directly by their vote, are presumed to be justified so that it is for the person challenging them to show that they are unrelated to any consideration of a professional nature'.[64] The Social Chamber therefore quashed the judgment of a Court of Appeal which had decided to grant a *worker* the more advantageous contractual severance pay[65] provided for *engineers and managers*, although the difference in treatment found between the two categories of staff as regards the methods of calculating this allowance was not unrelated to considerations of a professional nature.
  - *The basis* of this presumption lies in the *authority of the collective norm* because: 'the social negotiators act by delegation of the law and [that] they must, consequently, have, in the implementation of the principle of equal treatment, a margin of appreciation comparable to that which the Constitutional Council recognizes to the legislator in the control it exercises over the latter's respect for the constitutional principle of equality'.[66]

61. Soc. 4 December 2013, n° 12-19.667, 12-19.793, Bulletin 2013, V, n° 300.
62. This is a 'simple' presumption, which can therefore be rebutted by evidence to the contrary.
63. Soc. 8 June 2011, n° 10-11.933 et 10-13.663, FS-P + B + R + I.
64. Soc. 27 January 2015, 13-14.773 13-14.908, Bulletin 2015, V, n° 8.
65. Article 17 de l'annexe IV 'ingénieurs et cadres' de la convention collective des transports routiers du 21 décembre 1950 [*Article 17 of Annex IV 'Engineers and Executives' of the Collective Agreement for Road Transport*].
66. Cour de cassation, 'comment for Internet and the Annual Report' (under Soc. 8 June 2016, above).

- *The extension of the scope of the presumption of justification stems from the identity of the sources of inequality.* Subsequently, the Social Chamber of the Court of Cassation, taking into account the fact that the various differences in treatment resulted from a collective agreement negotiated by the representative social partners, equalized their regime by extending the scope of the presumption of justification to differences in treatment:
  - *within the same professional category, between employees with distinct functions:* 'differences in treatment between professional categories or between employees performing, within the same professional category, distinct functions, carried out by means of collective agreements or agreements, negotiated and signed by representative trade union organizations, invested with the defense of the rights and interests of employees and in whose authorization the latter participate directly by their vote, are presumed to be justified so that it is for the person challenging them to show that they are unrelated to any consideration of a professional nature'.[67] 'In practice, therefore, a housing allowance intended to take into account the specificities of the function of head of agency and executive could be recognized as *not being unrelated to professional considerations*, which justified its non-attribution to the category of managers and employees'.[68]
  - *between employees belonging to the same enterprise but to separate establishments:*[69]

    > An establishment agreement may provide, within the institution, taking into account its characteristics, for specific remuneration arrangements.' The justification for unequal pay is therefore to be found in the specific characteristics of the establishment. Consequently, was quashed the judgment of the Court of Appeal which, in order to grant the application of the employees of the Lormont store, stated that 'the national company agreement of 11 July 1985 had the effect of creating unlawful discrimination between the employees of the same undertaking, and to the advantage of those of Mérignac, as regards wages'.[70]

  - *for the benefit of employees hired before the date of entry into force of a collective agreement:* Indeed, unless otherwise provided by law, a collective agreement cannot modify an employee's employment contract; only the more favourable provisions of this agreement can replace the clauses of the contract. This rule, states the Court of Cassation, constitutes a relevant objective factor capable of justifying the difference in treatment between employees engaged before the entry into force of a collective agreement and those engaged subsequently, and resulting from the

67. Soc. 8 June 2016, n° 15-11.324, Bulletin 2016, V, n° 130.
68. Soc. 8 June 2016, n° 15-11.324 above-mentioned.
69. Soc. 7 April 2004, n° 01-42.758, D.
70. Soc. 18 January 2006, n° 03-45.422, Bulletin 2006, V, n° 17, p. 17. In the same sense: Soc. 12 juillet 2017, n° 16-19.710, D.

maintenance, for the former, of the stipulations of their employment contract.[71]

[B] Situations of Unequal Treatment Resulting from Transfers of Undertakings

The transfer of the employees taken over may give rise to situations of unequal treatment with the employees of the new employer. That is the case where the former continued to receive a 13th-month bonus granted by their former employer, while the latter did not have such an advantage.[72] Similarly, the use of the payment of an attendance bonus, in force in the absorbed company, could apply to its employees after the transfer, and not to those of the buyer. The latter have therefore applied to the Labour Courts for the restoration of equality for their benefit.

The subject will be approached by distinguishing the following three hypotheses: [1] the legal transfer of an undertaking; [2] the voluntary application of the rules on legal transfer by the new employer; and [3] the transfer of staff resulting from the job retention guarantee introduced by agreement.

[1] The Legal Obligation to Maintain Benefits, Justification of Inequality

The answer of the Social Chamber of the Court of Cassation is clear: by combined application of the principle of equal treatment and Article L. 1224-1 of the Labour Code 'The obligation to which the new employer is legally bound, in the event of the transfer of an economic entity, to maintain for the benefit of the employees attached to it the rights and benefits granted to them on the day of the transfer, justifies the resulting difference in treatment in relation to other employees.' It thus quashed the decision by which an appeal court had held, on the contrary, that the employer did not justify by any objective, relevant and materially verifiable element this difference in treatment.[73] In other words, the two categories of employees, although working on the same site, are not in an 'identical situation', which would require equal treatment.

The rights and benefits recognized on the day of transfer include those which employees hold from a *practice in force.*[74]

However, the breach of equality becomes unjustified when the employer, if he grants certain employees of the new employer a bonus of 13th month, fails to do so for all, even though they are in an identical situation.[75]

71. Soc. 7 December 2017, n° 16-15.109 16-15.110; Soc. 1 December 2005, n° 03-47.197, Bulletin 2005, V, n° 347.
72. Soc. 23 June 2021, n° 18-24.811, D.
73. Soc. 23 June 2021, n° 18-24.811, D.
74. Soc. 11 January 2012, n° 10-14.614, Bulletin 2012, V, n° 15; Soc. 30 May 2018, n° 17-12.782 et suivants, Bulletin 2018, V, n° 94.
75. Soc. 27 November 2019, n° 17-27.039 et 17-27.040, F-D.

[2] The Voluntary Application of Article L. 1224-1 of the Labour Code Justifies the Difference in Treatment in Favour of Employees Taken over

The Court of Cassation grants the voluntary transfer of employment contracts the same force as that resulting from their automatic transfer pursuant to the provisions of Article L. 1224-1 of the Labour Code. It therefore finds that 'the obligation to which the new employer is bound, in the event of resumption of the employment contract of the employee of a company by voluntary application of Article L. 1224-1 of the Labour Code, to maintain for his benefit the rights granted to him by his former employer on the day of the transfer, justifies the resulting difference in treatment compared to other employees'.[76]

The judgment ordering the employer to pay other employees the 13th-month bonus that it had maintained for the sole benefit of employees transferred by voluntary application of Article L. 1224-1 of the Labour Code was therefore quashed.[77]

[3] Conventional Transfers of Undertakings Remain Subject to the Principle of Equality

First step: primacy of the principle of equality: The Court of Cassation first considered that when the commitment, made by the incoming company, to reserve only to employees who had worked for it on that occasion the benefit of collective benefits from which they had previously benefited *did not result from the law, was not intended to compensate for a specific prejudice* to this category of employees and had the *sole purpose of maintaining collective benefits;*[78] the refusal to grant it to employees subsequently engaged and assigned to the *same entity* to perform *work of equal value* characterized unequal treatment which was not justified by objective reasons. It was therefore a manifestly unlawful disturbance authorizing the judge hearing the application for interim measures to make reparation by granting the advantages at issue.[79]

It also held, for a contractual bonus of 13 months, that in the case of employees performing the same work for the same employer on the same site, such inequality was not justified by relevant reasons and infringed the principle of equality.[80] The same was decided with regard to the 50% Sunday work bonus and the 30.5% shift bonus for employees of the outgoing company when they continued their contract.[81]

Second step: reversal in favour of the presumption of justification. – In a judgment of 30 November 2017[82] concerning the application of an annex to the national collective agreement of cleaning companies and associated services of 26 July 2011

76. Soc. 23 June 2021, n° 18-24.809, P. In the same sense: Soc. 28 September 2022, n° 21-12.318, D; Soc. 7 December 2022, n° 21-17.395, D.
77. 23 June 2021, n° 18-24.809, above-mentioned.
78. In this case, provisions relating to scales, indices, advancement and bonuses.
79. Soc. 19 June 2007, n° 06-44.047, Bulletin 2007, V, n° 104.
80. Soc. 15 Jan 2014, n° 12-25.402, Bulletin 2014, V, n° 23.
81. Soc. 16 September 2015, n° 13-26.788, FS-B, Bulletin 2016, V, n° 835.
82. Soc. 30 November 2017, Nos 16-20.532 et seq., P, ECLI:FR:CCASS:2017:SO02624.

providing for the payment of a 13th month, the Court of Cassation has reviewed its jurisprudence. It explained that 'the general evolution of labour legislation on collective bargaining and of case law concerning the principle of equal treatment with regard to collective agreements leads to a different assessment of the scope of this principle with respect to transfer of employment contracts organised by agreement'.

It then specified that '*the difference in treatment between* [On the one hand] *employees whose employment contract has been transferred pursuant to a job guarantee established by agreement by the representative trade union organizations invested with the defense of the rights and interests of employees and in whose authorization the latter participate directly by their vote and* [on the other hand] *the employees of the incoming employer, which results from the latter's obligation to maintain for the benefit of the employees transferred the rights conferred on them by their former employer on the day of the transfer, is not unrelated to any consideration of a professional nature and is therefore justified in the light of the principle of equal treatment*'.

In another judgment of 30 May 2018,[83] the Court of Cassation approved the decision of the Court of Appeal to maintain for the sole benefit of the transferred employees the unsanitary bonus, the attendance bonus and the transport bonus corresponding to the advantages they enjoyed with their former employer: this situation did not constitute a prohibited infringement of the principle of equal treatment.

Third step: legislative consecration of justified inequality: The so-called Macron Ordinance n° 2017-1387 of 22 September 2017[84] amended Article L. 1224-3-2 of the Labour Code as follows: 'When an extended branch agreement provides for and organises the continuation of employment contracts in the event of a succession of undertakings in the performance of a contract, the employees of the new service provider may not usefully invoke differences in remuneration resulting from benefits obtained, before the change of service provider, by employees whose employment contracts have been continued.'

The solution adopted is clear and does not allow the question to be asked whether or not the difference in treatment is unrelated to any consideration of a professional nature.

Finally, possible equalization of benefits on a single site, to the exclusion of the others: While the employer is entitled to reserve for the benefit of employees transferred only under the contractual employment guarantee the benefits they previously held, he is nevertheless recognized as having the possibility of restoring equality with other employees of the same site by *unilateral commitment*.

Admittedly, recalls the Court of Cassation, in principle, 'a difference in treatment established by unilateral commitment can only be practiced between employees of the

83. Soc. 30 May 2018, Nos 17-12.782 et seq., Bulletin 2018, V, n° 94.
84. Ordonnance n° 2017-1387 du 22 Septembre 2017 'relative à la prévisibilité et la sécurisation des relations de travail' [*On the Predictability and Security of Employment*], Journal Officiel, 23 Septembre 2017, Article 34.

same company and performing equal work or work of equal value, if it is based on objective reasons, the reality and relevance of which must be reviewed by the judge'.[85]

That is indeed the case when the employer unilaterally sets up an attendance bonus for all employees of the *same site* in order to *'reduce disparities'* between employees whose employment contracts have continued on that site and those subsequently recruited on the same site and placed in an identical situation. Indeed, 'this difference in treatment was based on an objective and relevant justification'.[86]

Fraud, a sign of the effectiveness of transfers: The system of transfers of undertakings is important for all the parties concerned, in particular in that it maintains employees' employment contracts, thus guaranteeing the continuation of their employment. It may therefore be tempting for some employers to try to evade its application. An examination of the decisions of the courts thus reveals the existence of *fraud* to the detriment of workers.[87]

A recent decision of the Court of Cassation illustrates not only the reality of the phenomenon but also the rigor of the judicial sanction attached to it: 'The Court of Appeal, which found the existence of a fraudulent concert between successive employers, the company (X...) and the company (Y...), to deprive the employee of the rights he held under Article L. 1224-1 of the Labour Code, exactly deduced that the dismissal was ineffective and that each of them had to bear the harmful consequences of the termination of the employment contract, in accordance with the provisions of Article L. 1235-3 of the Labour Code.'

In this case, the Court of Appeal had described the fraudulent arrangement consisting in having the employee sign a professional security contract with a view to dismissing him for the economic reason based on an alleged cessation of activity, while the employer had surreptitiously created another company with the same object as the previous one and proceeded to the amicable liquidation of the latter. The appeal judges had therefore set at EUR 25,000 the damage of the employee resulting from the *unjustified loss of his job.*[88]

Other questions: Given its limited nature, this chapter has not addressed such decisive subjects as that of the relationship between the old and the new employer, governed by Article L. 1224-2 of the Labour Code, or that of the transfer of an undertaking occurring in the context of collective insolvency proceedings (safeguarding, receivership and liquidation). They would all deserve another study.

---

85. Soc. 23 juin 2021, n° 19-21.771, FS-B.
86. Soc. 23 juin 2021, n° 19-21.771, FS-B. In the same sense: Soc. 26 Octobre 2022, n° 21-10.799, D.
87. Franck Géa, 'De la référence à la fraude en matière de transfert d'entreprise' [*Reference to Business Transfer Fraud*], Chronique, Etudes et Doctrine, RJS, 10/17.
88. Soc. 28 September 2022, n° 21-17.213, F-D.

CHAPTER 8

Germany: Impact of New Work on the Transfer of Undertakings under German Law

Friederike Fritzsche & Benjamin Münnich

§8.01 INTRODUCTION

The world of work is in a state of upheaval and continuous transformation. In particular, the flexibilization of work, decentralized working, working from home, workation, coworking spaces, collaboration in remote teams and matrix structures are some of the central developments—summarized under the term "New Work"—with which employers and employees are already confronted now and for which they will need to be prepared even more in the future.[1] These developments were abruptly implemented or at least significantly accelerated by the coronavirus pandemic:[2] From 2019 to 2022, the number of people in Germany working from home increased from 12.9% to 25%.[3] In the EU, only 5.4%[4] of employees worked from home in 2019, but

1. *Bundesministerium für Arbeit und Soziales,* Weißbuch Arbeiten 4.0, retrieved from https://www.bmas.de/SharedDocs/Downloads/DE/Publikationen/a883-weissbuch.pdf?__blob=publicationFile&v=2 accessed on May 30, 2023, p. 61.
2. *Hans-Böckler-Stiftung,* Studien zu Homeoffice und mobiler Arbeit, retrieved from https://www.boeckler.de/de/auf-einen-blick-17945-Auf-einen-Blick-Studien-zu-Homeoffice-und-mobiler-Arbeit-28040.htm accessed on May 30, 2023; *Hans-Böckler-Stiftung,* WSI Report 65, retrieved from https://www.boeckler.de/pdf/p_wsi_report_65_2021.pdf accessed on May 30, 2023, p. 4; *Fraunhofer-Institut,* New Digital Work: Die Zukunft der Arbeit im digitalen Zeitalter, retrieved from https://www.wi.fit.fraunhofer.de/content/dam/fit/witschaftsinformatik/dokumente/New%20Digital%20Work%20-%20Die%20Zukunft%20der%20Arbeit%20im%20digitalen%20Zeitalter.pdf accessed on May 30, 2023, pp. 4 ff.
3. *Federal Statistical Office,* Survey on Persons Working from Home, retrieved from https://www.destatis.de/EN/Themes/Labour/Labour-Market/Quality-Employment/Dimension3/3_11_homeoffice.html accessed on June 12, 2023.

that number rose to 13.5% in 2021.[5] There has also been a steady increase in coworking spaces; in 2008, there were under 20,000 coworking spaces worldwide, but forecasts indicate that there will be around 41,975 coworking spaces by the end of 2024.[6] A return to a strict workweek at the employer's offices is currently inconceivable.

This raises several legal issues relating to the transfer of an undertaking. In a nutshell: Does the current legal system under section 613a of the German Civil Code (*Bürgerliches Gesetzbuch—BGB*)—especially the concept of the economic entity—fit the realities of New Work?

Both current and emerging legal issues show that there are challenges, in particular concerning the legal concept of the economic entity, which is the subject of this chapter. The aim of this chapter is thus to review the legal situation of the transfer of an undertaking under German law against the background of current and future forms of work. In doing so, possible gaps and ambiguities will be highlighted in order to identify any need for adjustment in the application of the law and legislation.

In the following sections of this chapter, the authors will first present the legal basis of the transfer of an undertaking under German law (§8.02), including the essential prerequisites and legal consequences. They will then use this as a basis to critically assess the current legal situation against the background of the changes triggered by New Work, discuss possible solutions (§8.03) and, finally, summarize the main findings (§8.04).

§8.02 TRANSFER OF UNDERTAKING UNDER GERMAN LAW

[A] Applicable Legislation

As in other European jurisdictions, the German law on Transfer of Undertakings/Protection of Employment (*TUPE*) is based on European Directives, in particular the so-called Acquired Rights Directive which first came into effect in 1977.[7] The purpose of the Directive is to protect employees' rights in the event of a "transfer of an undertaking, business or part of a business to another employer as a result of a legal transfer or merger."[8]

4. *European Commission*, Science for Policy Briefs, Telework in the EU Before and After the COVID-19: Where We Were, Where We Head to, retrieved from https://joint-research-centre.ec.europa.eu/system/files/2021-06/jrc120945_policy_brief_-_covid_and_telework_final.pdf accessed on June 22, 2023, p. 1.
5. *Eurostat*, Rise in EU Population Working from Home, retrieved from https://ec.europa.eu/eurostat/de/web/products-eurostat-news/-/ddn-20221108-1 accessed on June 22, 2023.
6. *Statista*, Number of Coworking Spaces Worldwide from 2018 to 2020 with a Forecast to 2024, retrieved from https://www.statista.com/statistics/554273/number-of-coworking-spaces-worldwide/ accessed on June 22, 2023 worldwide.
7. Council Directive 77/187/EEC of February 14, 1977 on the approximation of the laws of the Member States relating to the safeguarding of employees' rights in the event of transfers of undertakings, businesses or parts of businesses.
8. Article 1 of the Directive.

The central labor and employment law provision applicable to any business transfer is section 613a German Civil Code.

The continuation of the employees' representation and their right to information and consultation, as provided for in Articles 6 and 7 of the Directive, are subject to the provisions of the German Works Constitution Act (*Betriebsverfassungsgesetz—BetrVG*), if the transfer of business is associated with a change in operations. Furthermore, the German Transformation Act (*Umwandlungsgesetz—UmwG*) applies depending on the legal basis of the transactions (e.g., in the case of mergers).

[B] Consequences of the Transfer of an Undertaking

Section 613a BGB applies if an undertaking (or part thereof) or a business (or part thereof) that qualifies as an economic entity is transferred from the seller to the buyer by virtue of a legal transaction and the buyer maintains the economic identity of such entity. The main consequences of the transfer of an undertaking pursuant to section 613a BGB are:

- Transfer of Employment Contracts: According to section 613a(1) BGB, all affected employment contracts are automatically transferred to the buyer. Thus, it is not necessary to conclude a new employment contract as the employment conditions automatically transfer to the buyer. The employee's consent is not necessary; however, employees may object to the transfer.
- *Collective Bargaining Agreements*: CBAs of the seller continue to be binding, unchanged at a collective level only if the buyer is bound to the same CBA as the seller, in particular by virtue of membership in the employers' association that concluded the relevant CBA. If this is not the case, the content of the CBA will in principle be transposed into the employment contract, and, during the first year after the transfer, rights arising from those CBAs may not be amended to the detriment of the employees unless an exception according to section 613a(1) sentence 3 BGB applies.
- *Works Agreements*: Rights arising from works agreements continue to apply on a collective basis only if the buyer maintains the organization and business as it is (so-called *Betriebsidentität*). If this is not the case, the content of the works agreement will be transposed into the employment contract, and, similarly to CBAs, in the first year after the transfer, rights arising from this works agreement may not be amended to the detriment of the employees unless an exception according to section 613a(1) sentence 3 BGB applies.
- *Protection Against Dismissal*: According to section 613a(4) BGB, a dismissal is invalid if it is "due to" the transfer. Typically, a labor court would declare a dismissal "due to" the transfer if this transfer was the sole motive for the dismissal.
- *Information of Employees*: section 613a(5) BGB specifies that either the seller or the buyer of the business or both together must inform the employees affected by the transfer in text form of the date, the reason, the legal, economic

and social consequences of the transfer and the measures envisaged with regard to the employees after the transfer. Bearing in mind that the employees' objection period (section 613a(5) BGB) starts running only if the employees have been properly informed, sufficient time should be allowed for preparing the information letters.

- *Right to Object*: Affected employees are entitled to object to the transfer of their employment relationship from the seller to the buyer within one month (section 613a(6) BGB) after they have been properly informed of the transfer, as mentioned above. If the information provided to the employees was insufficient or incomplete, the employees have an unlimited period of time to object. However, the right to object can be forfeited if the affected employees fail to assert their rights over a prolonged period and their conduct gives the impression that they will not exercise their right to object.[9]

[C] The Concept of the Economic Entity

As mentioned above, section 613a BGB requires that an undertaking (or part thereof) or a business (or part thereof) which qualifies as an economic entity is transferred from the seller to the buyer by virtue of a legal transaction and the buyer maintains the economic identity of such entity. This might be the result of, for example, a purchase or lease contract. It might also be the result of a business reorganization, such as a merger. However, section 613a BGB does not cover share deals, as they only have implications under corporate law.

[1] Case Law of the European Court of Justice and the German Federal Labor Court

An undertaking, business or part of a business in this sense means an economic entity that retains its identity after the transfer. An *economic entity* is defined as "an organized grouping of persons and assets facilitating the exercise of an economic activity which pursues the objective specific to it."[10] Section 613a BGB only applies if this economic entity is transferred from the seller to the buyer by virtue of a legal transaction and retains its identity. The issue of whether or not a transfer is relevant must be assessed on a case-by-case basis, taking into account the seven criteria established by the European Court of Justice (ECJ):

9. Federal Labor Court, ruling of January 27, 2000—8 AZR 106/99, BeckRS 2000, 30782776; Federal Labor Court, ruling of April 25, 2001—5 AZR 497/99, NJW 2001, 2907 (2908); Federal Labor Court, ruling of July 22, 2004—8 AZR 394/03, BeckRS 2004, 30343425; Federal Labor Court, ruling of July 13, 2006—8 AZR 382/05, NZA 2006, 1406 marg. No. 31.
10. Federal Labor Court, ruling of May 22, 1997—8 AZR 101/96, AP BGB § 613a no. 154; Federal Labor Court, ruling of April 17, 2003—8 AZR 253/02, AP BGB § 613a No. 253.

- Type of (previous) business/company.
- Any transfer of the tangible operating assets (buildings, movable assets).
- Value of intangible assets at the date of transfer.
- Possible takeover of the main workforce by the new owner.
- Any transfer of customers.
- Degree of similarity between the activities performed before and after the transfer.
- Duration of any interruption of the activity.

Finally, an overall assessment of these seven points takes place.[11]

[2] Sole Takeover of Personnel

The mere takeover of personnel may also be deemed a transfer of business, but only if the personnel itself constitutes an economic entity.[12] An important criterion is whether or not a significant number of employees are taken over.[13] This criterion is particularly important for businesses with few assets, such as service providers. For the question of how many employees need to be taken over to trigger a transfer of business, the qualifications and a certain level of know-how of the employees taken over are decisive. Therefore, the takeover of a small number of highly qualified employees can be sufficient to trigger a transfer of business.[14] In contrast, low-qualified employees must be transferred in large numbers to trigger a transfer of business,[15] but there is no clear line with respect to quantitative and/or qualitative requirements in this regard.

[3] Functional Succession and Outsourcing

In contrast to the takeover of personnel, it will not be considered a transfer of business if only a task is transferred to a new contractor who takes over neither equipment nor personnel. In such cases, this is purely a functional succession ("*Funktionsnachfolge*"), which does not trigger a transfer of business within the meaning of section 613a BGB.[16] Such a functional succession can occur when a company outsources an activity previously carried out internally to an external contractor ("outsourcing"),[17] has a service previously performed for it by a contractor now performed by a new contractor ("new award of contract")[18] or integrates a service hitherto performed by an external

11. European Court of Justice, ruling of March 18, 1986—C-24/85, BeckRS 2004, 72554, marg. No. 13.
12. European Court of Justice, ruling of January 20, 2011—C-463/09, NZA 2011, 148 (150).
13. European Court of Justice, ruling of February 27, 2020—C-298/18, NZA 2020. 443, marg. No. 39.
14. Federal Labor Court, ruling of June 21, 2012—8 AZR 181/11, NZA-RR 2013, 6 marg. Nos. 37 ff.
15. Federal Labor Court, ruling of February 16, 2006—8 AZR 345/04, BeckRS 2006, 30805906.
16. European Court of Justice, ruling of March 11, 1997—Rs. C-13/95, NZA 1997, 433 (434); Federal Labor Court, ruling of November 13, 1997—8 AZR 295/95, NZA 1998, 251 (252).
17. Federal Labor Court, ruling of January 22, 1998—8 AZR 243/95, NZA 1998, 536 (538).
18. Federal Labor Court, ruling of August 14, 2007—8 AZR 1043/06, NZA 2007, 1431 marg. No. 20; Federal Labor Court, ruling of May 28, 2009—8 AZR 273/08, NZA 2009, 1267 marg. No. 49.

contractor into its own operations and has it performed by its own staff ("insourcing").[19]

[4] Transfer of Parts of Business

The criteria above also apply to a transfer of a part of a business, as long as this part can be defined as an independent organizational entity.[20] A transfer of a business entity (part of a business, so-called "*Betriebsteil*") within the meaning of section 613a BGB requires that the operating resources and/or employees that are taken over have already formed an independent organizational economic entity in the seller's organization.[21]

In its established case law, the Federal Labor Court assumes—based on the relevant case law of the ECJ—that a part of the business is capable of being transferred if the economic entity concerned represents an organizational subdivision of the entire business, with which a partial purpose that is objectively and organizationally definable is pursued within the overall business purpose.[22] The (separable) identity of the economic entity results from characteristics such as its personnel, its managers, its work organization, its operating methods and, if applicable, the operating resources at its disposal. A functional link is not sufficient, at least not according to current case law.[23]

Independent management and coordination of personnel deployment is a criterion of organizational autonomy.[24]

[5] Affected Employees

The employment contracts of the employees assigned to the respective economic entity will transfer automatically to the buyer by virtue of law (section 613a(1) BGB). This result is prescribed by law and is not at the parties' choice or discretion.[25] However, if only part of a business is transferred, problems may arise with regard to the allocation

19. Federal Labor Court, ruling of April 17, 2003—8 AZR 253/02, AP BGB § 613a No. 253.
20. Federal Labor Court, ruling of January 24, 2013—8 AZR 706/11, marg. No. 26.
21. *See* Federal Labor Court, ruling of April 27, 2017—8 AZR 859/15, AP BGB § 613a No. 469 marg. No. 30; Federal Labor Court, ruling of January 25, 2018—8 AZR 309/16, NZA 2018, 933 marg. Nos. 51 ff.
22. *See* Federal Labor Court, ruling of October 13, 2011—8 AZR 455/10, NZA 2012, 504 marg. No. 37.
23. *See* Federal Labor Court, ruling of February 27, 2020—8 AZR 215/19, NZA 2020, 1303 marg. No. 82; Federal Labor Court, ruling of October 13, 2011—8 AZR 455/10, NZA 2012, 504 marg. No. 37; *Cohnen* in: *Moll, Wilhelm,* Münchener Anwalts Handbuch Arbeitsrecht, 5th ed. 2021, Munich, § 53 marg. No. 12.
24. *See* Federal Labor Court, ruling of February 27, 2020—8 AZR 215/19, NZA 2020, 1303 marg. No. 82; Federal Labor Court, ruling of June 21, 2012—8 AZR 181/11, NZA-RR 2013, 6 (14) marg. No. 71; Federal Labor Court, ruling of August 24, 2006—8 AZR 556/05, NZA 2007, 1320 marg. No. 25.
25. Federal Labor Court, ruling of February 22, 1978—5 AZR 800/76, AP BGB § 613a No. 11.

of employees to this part of the business, particularly where administrative and cross-functional positions are concerned.

According to case law, generally only those employees transfer to the buyer who were actually assigned to the business entity in question. Therefore, the employee's position must be integrated into the structure of the respective business entity. A work activity that only indirectly supports a particular operation is not sufficient.[26]

In practice, "float employees" or substitutes (employees who work in different departments of the business as needed), employees in cross-establishment management positions, and employees in cross-functional areas (e.g., central finance department or HR management) are questionable cases. If float employees were typically integrated into several different business entities, it is important to know where the float employees mainly worked. Nevertheless, it is often difficult to determine where the focus of these employees' work lies.

If uncertainties regarding the allocation of employees nevertheless remain, the following criteria are decisive according to a recent ruling by the German Federal Labor Court:

- The allocation is primarily based on the will of the parties to the employment contract. Agreements concluded between the seller and the buyer of the business are not relevant.[27]
- In the absence of an—explicit or implicit—agreement between the parties to the employment contract, the allocation is generally made by the employer on the basis of its authority to issue directives ("*Weisungsrecht*") according to section 106 German Commercial Code (*Handelsgesetzbuch—HGB*). The authority to issue directives can also be exercised explicitly—or implicitly—by way of an actual assignment of work (activities) in one part of the business.[28]
- In the absence of a decision by the employer concerning the allocation by way of the authority to issue directives, this is to be determined based on the following objective criteria: the main work (activity) of the employee for the transferred (part of the) business; the focus of the employee's work (activity) (in terms of time spent and work assignment/commitment, main place of work); the actual integration of the employee in the transferred (part of the) business.[29]

26. Federal Labor Court, ruling of August 8, 2002—8 AZR 583/01, NZA 2003, 315 (318); Federal Labor Court, ruling of December 13, 2012—6 AZR 348/11, NZA 2013, 669 marg. No. 88.
27. Federal Labor Court, ruling of March 19, 2015—9 AZR 119/14, AP BGB § 613a No. 464.
28. Federal Labor Court, ruling of February 21, 2013—8 AZR 878/11, AP BGB § 613a No. 440 marg. No. 35; Federal Labor Court, ruling of October 17, 2013—8 AZR 763/12, NZA-RR 2014, 175 marg. No. 24.
29. Federal Labor Court, ruling of June 21, 2012—8 AZR 181/11, AP BGB § 613a No. 434 marg. No. 80.

§8.03 TRANSFER OF UNDERTAKING AND NEW WORK

The aim of this section is to review the legal situation of the transfer of an undertaking under German law against the background of current and upcoming forms of work and operation. The developments characterizing the so-called New Work will be presented below in a first step, in order to illuminate the effects on the transfer of an undertaking in a second step.

[A] New Work

New Work is a concept that encompasses new approaches and ideas regarding the world of work and the way work is organized and performed. It represents a departure from traditional work structures and models to meet the evolving needs and demands of a changing society. The definition and components of New Work may vary slightly depending on the source, but generally include aspects and developments such as decentralized and mobile working, working from home, workation, collaboration in remote teams and so-called matrix structures. The individual forms are outlined below in the required brevity:

- *Working from Home*: The term "working from home" is not clearly defined, not even by law.[30] Working from home enables employees to work temporarily for the employer in their private sphere, for example, using internet-based IT systems.[31] However, there is still a place of business that the employee can visit at least temporarily. Working from home is to be distinguished from so-called teleworking under German law. In the case of teleworking, the employer does not provide the employee with a workstation in the office. Rather, the employer sets up a home workstation for the employee and covers the costs.
- *Mobile Work*: The term "mobile work" is not defined either. Mobile work is characterized by the fact that, depending on the agreement concluded with the employer, employees perform their work either from one location or from changing locations of their choice or from a location agreed with the employer—in any case outside the employer's place of business.[32] In contrast to working from home, the employee may be at any other location. Typically, internet-based (video) telephony, virtual conferences, mobile data room access and mobile devices, for example, enable the employee to perform work from any location, such as on the train, in a café or in a park.
- *Workation*: The term "workation" is a combination of the words "work" and "vacation."[33] It refers to a situation where employees merge work and leisure

30. The law usually calls it telework ("Telearbeit"), section 2(7) ArbStättV, section 5(1) sentence 1 BetrVG, section 16 BGleiG.
31. *See* Federal Labor Court, ruling of April 12, 2011—9 AZR 14/10, NZA 2012, 97 (99 f.).
32. Draft bill of the Federal Ministry of Labor and Social Affairs on the Mobile Work Act, p. 4.
33. *Hofmann, Josephine*, Mobiles Arbeiten aus dem Ausland als Mittel zur Gewinnung und Bindung von Mitarbeitenden, retrieved from https://publica-rest.fraunhofer.de/server/api/core/bitstreams/a94a80d1-79d7-492f-906e-3bae3e314895/content accessed on May 30, 2023.

during their vacation. Essentially, it involves working remotely or conducting work-related tasks while enjoying a vacation or at least being abroad. The concept of workation has gained popularity in recent years due to advancements in technology, which have made it easier for people to work remotely and stay connected.[34]

- *Remote Teams*: Working in remote teams refers to a work arrangement where team members are geographically dispersed and collaborate on projects or tasks without being physically present in the same location. Remote teams rely heavily on communication technology and digital tools to connect, communicate, and coordinate their work. In a remote team setup, individuals may work from different cities, countries, or time zones. They typically communicate and collaborate through various online platforms, such as video conferencing, instant messaging, email, project management tools, and shared document repositories.
- *Coworking Spaces*: Coworking refers to a form of work that involves individuals or groups from different companies or professions sharing a common workspace. It provides an alternative to the traditional office environment, where employees of a single company work in their own premises. Coworking spaces are generally operated by specialized companies or organizations that manage the facilities and handle membership arrangements, rather than by the employer.
- *Matrix Structures*: Matrix structures are characterized by the fact that the right to issue functional instructions (so-called dotted line) is decoupled from the employer's right to issue disciplinary instructions (so-called solid line) and is exercised by a third party, not the employer.[35] Put simply: An employee has an employment contract with one company (the legal employer), but the functional manager (so-called matrix manager) is employed by another company. Particularly in groups of companies that are organized into divisions, such structures are now almost standard.[36] Under German law, such structures are permissible and, according to prevailing opinion, the employee cannot refuse instructions from a third party, even if the latter is not his employer.[37]

[B] Common Characteristics: Location and Material Assets Lose Their Importance

It is clear that remote work, working from home, mobile work, workation and matrix structures share a common feature in that they are not bound to a specific physical

34. *Grimm, Detlef/Schwanke, Friederike,* Workation und Remote Work aus dem Ausland, Der Betrieb (DB 2023, 1412).
35. *See Engels, Gerd,* Das BAG und die Matrixstruktur, Neue Zeitschrift für Arbeitsrecht (NZA 2020, 699) (700).
36. *Kort, Michael,* Matrix-Strukturen und Betriebsverfassungsrecht, Neue Zeitschrift für Arbeitsrecht (NZA 2013, 1318) (1319).
37. *Maschmann, Frank,* Das Weisungsrecht im Matrix-Konzern, Neue Zeitschrift für Arbeitsrecht (NZA 2017, 1557) (1558 f.).

workstation or location. In matrix structures, employees may work on different projects or teams regardless of their physical location within the company or even within a group of companies. Remote work allows individuals to work from anywhere outside of a traditional office environment, such as from home or in a coworking space. Similarly, mobile work enables employees to work while on the move, utilizing mobile devices and technologies to remain productive. In a nutshell, these forms of work challenge the notion of a centralized workplace. Connectivity through technology: All three forms of work heavily rely on technology and digital tools to facilitate communication, collaboration, and information sharing. Material assets continue to lose their importance.

[C] Consequences for TUPE

These characteristics lead to the following three crucial assumptions with regard to the economic entity in the context of section 613a BGB:

> First of all, material assets will become less and less important; the question arises as to whether (or to what extent) the transfer of material resources is necessary to constitute a transfer of an economic entity. Second, as spatial aspects become less important, New Work can be expected to make it more difficult to determine and demarcate transferable economic entities. Third, it can be assumed that the allocation of employees to a particular economic entity will become more difficult and might no longer be possible on the basis of spatial proximity alone.

[1] Working from Home/Remote Work

[a] Importance of the Existence and Transfer of Material Assets for TUPE

As described above, the shared use of information technology plays quite an important role in times of increasing digitization.[38] IT companies in particular have fewer material assets that belong to them; instead, employees use their own devices to perform their work. Obviously, in this kind of undertaking, material assets are becoming less important. This, in turn, culminates in the scenario of an entirely digital undertaking. And even if the respective company were to own this IT equipment, it would not be the core of the undertaking's value.

In consequence, when it comes to the question of what an economic entity consists of, it cannot primarily depend on material assets. At the same time, this implies that a TUPE cannot primarily depend on the transfer of material assets.

However, this does not mean that assets have no impact at all. According to the well-known definition, the economic entity consists of an organized group of persons and assets assigned to a specific purpose.

In IT companies, the existence (and transfer) of intangible assets can be an important indication of a transfer of business—especially if their value exceeds the

38. *Meyer, Cord*, Betriebsübergang 4.0, Neue Zeitschrift für Arbeitsrecht (NZA 2020, 1273) (1278).

value of the tangible assets. The term "intangible assets" includes, for example, patent rights, property rights, business relationships, establishment names and imported brands as well as know-how and goodwill. Supply and purchase agreements, business papers, customer lists, and organizational and operational concepts are also included in the broader sense among the intangible assets of the previous owner of the business. The assumption and maintenance of customer relationships is a further indication. In order to be able to work together, a common software/operating system is provided, which makes collaboration smoother. Thus, the transfer of software licenses also has to be analyzed.

At this point, of course, a distinction from mere functional succession becomes relevant. For this reason, the takeover of employees might ultimately also have a particular significance in such constellations. Or, to put it another way, without the takeover of personnel, a TUPE will be difficult to assume in such cases.

In summary, when it comes to the definition of an economic entity and the question of the necessity of the transfer of assets in order to meet the prerequisites of a TUPE, it is not primarily material assets that are important, but rather the transfer of employees, software, know-how and licenses must be considered.

[b] Demarcation of the Transferable Economic Entity

As working from home and remote work are not bound to a specific workplace, the determination and demarcation of the transferable economic entity is made more difficult. This demarcation is of fundamental importance for the issue of the transfer of an undertaking.

One approach discussed in the legal literature in the context of the definition of an establishment within the German Works Constitution Act could be to demarcate an economic entity solely based on the physical workplace.[39] Applying this view to the topic at hand, the home and other external workplaces would not be covered by this location-based economic entity and the employees working from home or remotely would not be covered by a transfer of operations.

However, this approach cannot be followed in the context of TUPE: This would contradict the ECJ's definition of an economic entity and the Federal Labor Court's established case law, according to which it is only important that the employer creates an organizational unit, but not that there is necessarily a physical proximity.[40] As is known, an overall view based on the above-mentioned (cf. §8.02[C][1]) aspects of the ECJ's seven-point catalog is always required.[41]

This view would also contradict the purpose of Directive 2001/23: According to the ECJ's case law, Directive 2001/23 is intended to ensure the continuity of employment relationships existing within an economic entity irrespective of any change of

39. *Gamillscheg, Franz,* "Betrieb" und "Bargaining unit": Versuch des Vergleichs zweier Grundbegriffe, Zeitschrift für Arbeitsrecht (ZfA 1975, 357) (399).
40. Federal Labor Court, ruling of September 23, 1982—6 ABR 42/81, AP BetrVG 1972 § 4 No. 3.
41. European Court of Justice, ruling of March 18, 1986—C-24/85 (Spijkers).

ownership and thus to protect employees in the event that such a change occurs.[42] If its applicability were to be restricted to the physical workplace, workplaces outside the undertaking in the narrower sense, i.e., outside the spatially definable unit, would no longer be protected, even if they are functionally part of it and these workplaces are necessary for the economic purpose.

Against this background, others argue in favor of focusing more on the aspect of functional interaction of employees when determining an economic entity in accordance with section 613a(1) BGB.[43] In consequence, the boundaries of the economic entity would be determined based on the functional reporting lines. This is convincing against the background of New Work: In view of the dissolution of the workplace community and the fact that employees in modern forms of work are no longer deployed at the same time and in the same place, what remains as a link is the common function.

All of this culminates in the constellation of an entirely digital undertaking, when meetings are only mediated digitally, and common spatial points of contact no longer exist. In this case, the unified management apparatus is mediated exclusively in digital form. Personal leadership is exercised via digital devices. Face-to-face meetings no longer take place in a fixed location. There are also no company-owned premises that can be used. Teams are agile, particularly in terms of space.

In this context, too, the question arises as to whether or not the digitally mediated management apparatus can demarcate an economic entity. Ultimately, it can: If the functional cooperation demarcates the scope of the economic entity of section 613a BGB and not just a physical operation, the transfer of a purely digital operation must primarily take into account which employees work together functionally. In other words, the boundaries of the economic entity are defined by the relevant management apparatus.[44] In this case, the actual place of work and residence of the employee are not decisive. At first glance, this result seems to contradict the current case law,[45] according to which a mere functional link is not sufficient for an economic entity. However, in our opinion, it is precisely the functional authority to issue instructions that establishes this minimum degree of organizational autonomy.

According to this approach, remote work should be included in the concept of establishment if there is regular and close cooperation between the employees, regardless of their physical separation.

42. European Court of Justice, ruling of February 2, 2009—C-466/07 (Klarenberg); European Court of Justice, ruling of March 18, 1986—C-24/85 (Spijkers).
43. *See Meyer, Cord,* Betriebsübergang 4.0, Neue Zeitschrift für Arbeitsrecht (NZA 2020, 1273) (1278).
44. This thought has already been expressed by Nele Urban with regard to the concept of the establishment under works constitution law (*See Urban, Nele,* Der Betriebsbegriff in Zeiten von mobilem Arbeiten, Arbeitsrecht Aktuell (ArbRAktuell 2022, 221) (223 cf.)). In our opinion, it also applies to the question of the economic entity in the sense of section 613a BGB.
45. Federal Labor Court, ruling of October 13, 2011—8 AZR 455/10, NZA 2012, 504 marg. No. 37.

[c] Assignment of Remotely Working Employees to an Economic Entity

This is followed by the question of allocating employees to a certain economic entity. If employees mainly work from home or on a mobile basis, difficulties may furthermore arise in assigning these employees to a particular economic entity.

Based on the assumption that the aspect of functionality is increasingly coming to the fore in the assessment of the economic entity, it is likely that the question of the allocation of employees to this economic entity will increasingly depend on the extent to which a right to issue instructions is still exercised.

Thus, even if employees provide their work outside the business premises, they are integrated into the work-related organization of the business through their IT connection and fulfill the same work-related purpose.[46] If an employee is permitted to work remotely and the rest of the time works from a fixed workplace in an operation into which they are integrated, they are assigned to this operation.[47] The decisive factor for the assignment may be whether the employee receives functional instructions within the meaning of section 611a BGB from a particular economic entity.[48]

However, it should be noted in this context that the characteristic of a clear management structure becomes less important if the employees either act more and more on their own responsibility or if the need to specify the performance of specific tasks in more detail by means of instructions decreases due to digital possibilities.[49]

[2] Workation

The approach of assessing the allocation of employees working remotely to certain economic entities based on functional instruction lines can be extended for employees abroad (especially during their workation). Here, however, the question may arise as to whether or not German law applies at all. This will probably be the case in most cases of workation. This legal result is achieved—at least in constellations taking place within the EU—in two steps:

If no choice of law has been made, the employment relationship will be governed by the law of the country from which the employee usually performs their work, even if they temporarily perform their work in another country (Article 8(2) Rome I Regulation). In the case of a workation, the majority of the work continues to take place in Germany, meaning that German law and thus section 613a BGB are applicable.

If German law and thus section 613a BGB applies, the question arises as to whether an employee is still part of a certain economic entity even if they temporarily work abroad. At this point, as described above, it is necessary to analyze whether or not the employee is still functionally integrated into the respective economic entity.

46. *Maschmann* in: *Richardi, Reinhard,* Betriebsverfassungsgesetz, 17th ed. 2022, Munich 2022, BetrVG § 1 marg. No. 112c.
47. *Meyer, Cord,* Betriebsübergang 4.0, Neue Zeitschrift für Arbeitsrecht (NZA 2020, 1273) (1276).
48. *Meyer, Cord,* Betriebsübergang 4.0, Neue Zeitschrift für Arbeitsrecht (NZA 2020, 1273) (1278).
49. *Meyer, Cord,* Betriebsübergang 4.0, Neue Zeitschrift für Arbeitsrecht (NZA 2020, 1273) (1278).

[a] Employees Working in Coworking Spaces

The approach described above even applies to employees who work in coworking spaces. As long as these employees only work "side by side," employees working in coworking spaces can still be assigned to their original undertaking. This applies all the more if their activity in the coworking space is limited in time.[50] However, it should also be noted that outsourced employees in a coworking space can form their own organizational unit if there is a certain degree of autonomy and their own personnel management powers of a superior working there.[51] In this respect, the requirements for a TUPE of this own organizational unit would then have to be examined independently.

[b] Employees Working in Matrix Structures

As described above, matrix structures are characterized by the fact that the dotted line is decoupled from the employer's solid line. Thus, different organizational and even legal entities may be involved in a matrix structure. This complicates the demarcation of a transferable economic entity and the assignment of employees to such an economic entity: Employees within an organization are managed and instructed by different people and the functional linkage therefore does not correspond to local conditions. But what is the transferable economic entity: the establishment or the matrix unit, which may extend over several establishments?:

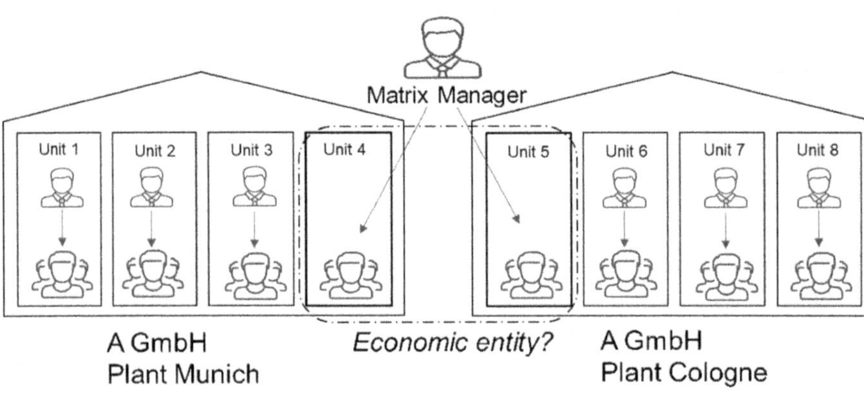

50. *Maschmann* in: *Richardi, Reinhard,* Betriebsverfassungsgesetz, 17th ed. 2022, Munich 2022, BetrVG, § 1 marg. No. 112d.

51. *Oltmanns, Sönke/Fuhlrott, Michael,* Desk-Sharing & Coworking-Spaces: Arbeitsrechtliche Besonderheiten zweier "moderner Arbeitsformen," Neue Zeitschrift für Arbeitsrecht (NZA 2018, 1225) (1227).

Taking into account the common definition of the economic entity and the criteria of the transfer of parts thereof,[52] this legal question has to be discussed under the criterion of (sufficient) functional autonomy of the respective organizational unit. As far as can be seen, the question of what kind of autonomy within the respective unit is required for its organizational separability has not been decided in German case law in the context of matrix structures.

In the legal literature, some assume that the relevant unit is the one characterized by the exercise of the disciplinary right of direction based on the position as a contractual employer.[53]

Others take the opposite view and assume that a mere functional autonomy is sufficient. Thus, matrix structures set up separate transferable units.[54] In our view, this is convincing, especially in light of recent ECJ case law. It can be deduced from the ECJ case law that a minor degree of functional autonomy is necessary and sufficient to constitute an economic entity.[55] In its ruling of June 13, 2019, the ECJ even expressly stated that functional autonomy does "not have to be total."[56] According to the ECJ, this stems from the wording of Article 1(1)(a) of Directive 2001/23 that the directive is applicable not only to the transfer of an undertaking but also where part of an undertaking is transferred.[57] A production unit can have such autonomy.[58]

This view also corresponds to the interpretation of this criterion by the German courts, which has been highly controversial in the context of legal disputes concerning a so-called wet lease.[59] The two senates of the German Federal Labor Court have interpreted it differently in this context.[60] Briefly summarized: The contentious issue in the proceedings was the authority of scheduling flights and the consequences with regard to section 613a BGB. The Sixth Senate of the German Federal Labor Court has ruled that an economic unit does not exist in case of wet lease due to lack of functional autonomy.[61] The service and flight planning for the entire flight operation was carried out centrally from Berlin, so there was only one management for the entire flight operation. Within this uniform flight operation, the wet lease was only a business

---

52. European Court of Justice, ruling of March 6, 2014—C-458/12 (Amatori); European Court of Justice, ruling of June 13, 2019—C-664/17 (Nafpigeia).
53. *Gussen* in: *Rolfs, Christian/et al.*, BeckOK Arbeitsrecht, 67th ed. 2023, Munich, section 613a BGB, marg. No. 15a.
54. *Mückl, Patrick*, Betriebsübergang und Matrix-Struktur—Welche Arbeitnehmer sind erfasst?, Der Betrieb (DB 2015, 2695) (2700); *Gaul/Bonanni* in: *Gaul, Björn*, Arbeitsrecht der Umstrukturierung, 2nd ed. 2022, Cologne, § 4 marg. No. 4.57.
55. European Court of Justice, ruling of March 6, 2014—C-458/12 (Amatori); European Court of Justice, ruling of June 13, 2019—C-664/17 (Nafpigeia).
56. European Court of Justice, ruling of June 13, 2019—C-664/17 (Nafpigeia) marg. No. 64.
57. *See* European Court of Justice, ruling of June 13, 2019—C-664/17 (Nafpigeia) marg. No. 64.
58. *See* European Court of Justice, ruling of June 13, 2019—C-664/17 (Nafpigeia) marg. No. 65.
59. For better understanding: Wet lease is a short-term arrangement in aviation where one airline provides another airline with—depending on the exact agreement—an aircraft, crew, maintenance, and insurance. It allows airlines to quickly meet temporary capacity needs without acquiring new aircraft or crew.
60. Federal Labor Court, ruling of February 27, 2020—8 AZR 215/19; Federal Labor Court, ruling of May 14, 2020—6 AZR 235/19.
61. Federal Labor Court, ruling of May 14, 2020—6 AZR 235/19.

model in the sense of a special service.[62] The Eighth Senate of the German Federal Labor Court, however, tended to affirm sufficient functional autonomy. The management powers that must be granted to a subunit's management in order to organize the group's work relatively freely and independently must not be understood too strictly.[63] A "certain" freedom in organizing and implementing the activity in question was sufficient.[64] The fact that the operational planning for the entire flight operation, including the wet lease, was carried out centrally does not prevent the assumption of sufficient functional autonomy.[65]

Applying the rationale of the Eighth Senate on matrix structures confirms our result, since a quite low level of autonomy would then therefore sufficient—even if it is based on centralized management.

However, a distinction has to be made here: If several subunits in an establishment are controlled by matrix managers located outside the establishment, but these subunits nevertheless work together, they might still form one single unit. In consequences, they could only be transferred together. By contrast, if the two subunits are organizationally independent, i.e., if they do not work together, they could be transferred separately.

Finally, the matrix manager itself is not assigned to the respective subunit that might be transferred.[66] The fact that matrix managers do not receive instructions regarding their own activities from the economic entity they manage and that the essential personnel and social matters are handled within the company in which the instructions are exercised suggests that they do not belong to the managed economic entity.[67]

§8.04 SUMMARY

The aim of this chapter was to review the legal situation of the transfer of an undertaking under German law against the background of New Work. The key findings can be summarized as follows:

New Work is characterized, among other things, by the fact that it is not bound to a specific physical workplace or site and that the importance of material assets is diminishing.

This complicates the demarcation of an economic entity within the meaning of section 613a BGB, which is of fundamental importance for the question of the transfer of an undertaking. If one wants to assess whether or not a certain transaction constitutes a transfer of an undertaking, one will first have to examine whether a certain organizational unit constitutes an economic entity capable of being transferred

62. Federal Labor Court, ruling of May 14, 2020—6 AZR 235/19.
63. Federal Labor Court, ruling of February 27, 2020—8 AZR 215/19.
64. Federal Labor Court, ruling of February 27, 2020—8 AZR 215/19.
65. Federal Labor Court, ruling of February 27, 2020—8 AZR 215/19.
66. *Gaul/Bonanni/Bollacher* in: *Gaul, Björn,* Arbeitsrecht der Umstrukturierung, 2nd ed. 2022, Cologne, § 4 marg. No. 4.66.
67. *Gaul/Bonanni/Bollacher* in: *Gaul, Björn,* Arbeitsrecht der Umstrukturierung, 2nd ed. 2022, Cologne, § 4 marg. No. 4.66.

within the meaning of section 613a BGB. From a very practical point of view, the evaluation is simpler if there is a spatial connection, for example, in the conventional industrial environment. There, economic entities can be demarcated on the basis of plants or on the basis of individual production areas. But the more New Work evolves from location-based to location-independent, the more difficult this will become.

Based on the ECJ's and the German Federal Labor Court's case law, the functional interaction demarcates the scope of the economic entity of section 613a BGB. Thus, the economic entity is not limited to the boundaries of a physical operation. The transfer of purely digital undertakings must primarily take into account which employees work together functionally.

If employees do not at all or at least not regularly work at a specific physical workplace, it can be difficult to determine the exact allocation of employees to a particular economic entity. Ultimately, this allocation also has to be based on functional instruction rights. In other words: In the context of allocating an employee to a specific economic entity within the meaning of section 613a BGB, it will probably come down to a mere analysis of functional instructions and personnel assignments.

This approach can be extended to employees during their workation or while performing their work in a coworking space.

When it comes to matrix structures, it is apparent that a matrix unit can be an economic entity within the meaning of section 613a BGB. Such entities are thus independently transferable.

This leads to a final outlook: In the future, the spatial composition of employees will become even less important, especially in IT companies—and thus less important in the context of determining whether or not an economic entity exists. Instead, attention must be paid to the functional relationship of the employees. It would therefore be helpful to obtain clarity from the ECJ and the German Federal Labor Court concerning the question of how exactly the demarcation of employees performing their work in a form of New Work to a specific economic entity is performed. But under the current legal situation, it does not seem possible to determine the demarcation of the economic unit in the context of New Work in any other way than based on functional cooperation between employees. In our opinion, a different type of demarcation in the context of New Work would require a new legal regulation. With regard to matrix structures, it would be helpful to define the concept of functional autonomy more precisely. In Germany, this is particularly true in view of the different results of the Federal Labor Court's senates.

CHAPTER 9

Hungaria: Legal Succession in Hungarian Labour Law Upon a Transfer of Business Within the Meaning of Directive 2001/23/EC

Yvett Varga

§9.01 INTRODUCTION AND STRUCTURE OF THE CHAPTER

Even before Hungary's accession to the European Union, the Hungarian legislator as well as the Hungarian courts were admittedly taking inspiration from the complex toolbox of the Community in respect of the protection of employees' rights. As a part of this harmonization process, the comprehensive amendment of the former Hungarian Labour Code (Act No. XXII of 1992 on the Labour Code), adopted in 1997,[1] aimed at approximating the rules of Hungarian law to those set out in European legal sources, such as Directive 77/187/EEC.[2]

Later on, a series of legislative acts brought Hungarian labour law on par with European rules, including the legal framework established by Council Directive 2001/23/EC on the approximation of the laws of the Member States relating to the safeguarding of employees' rights in the event of transfers of undertakings, businesses or parts of undertakings or businesses (hereinafter: '*the Directive*').[3]

1. *See* the Act No. LI of 1997 on the amendment of the Act No. XXII of 1992 on the Labour Code.
2. *See* the commentary to section 36 of the Labour Code written by Gyula Berke, in: Zoltán Bankó et al. (eds), Nagykommentár a munka törvénykönyvéről szóló 2012. évi I. törvényhez, Wolters Kluwer Hungary Kft., Budapest, 2023.
3. For the sake of completeness, the Hungarian legislator amended several other laws and regulations to comply with the provisions of the Directive – *see* the list of the reported amendments via the link: https://eur-lex.europa.eu/legal-content/HU/NIM/?uri=celex:32001L0023 (accessed 22 August 2025).

According to the currently effective Hungarian legal regime, the rules laid down in the Directive have been implemented by the provisions of the new Hungarian Labour Code (Act No. I of 2012 on the Labour Code, hereinafter: '*the Labour Code*'), which entered into effect on 1 July 2012.

Apart from this, the Hungarian Supreme Court also laid the foundation of subsequent case law by adopting a resolution in 1992, recognizing the existence of the transfer of business in Hungarian labour law.[4] Throughout the years, several court decisions interpreted the application of this legal instrument in the changing economic and legal environment. A significant part of this court practice remained applicable even after the Hungarian recodification of the Labour Code and continues to serve as an initial point of reference for any related legal analysis.

This legislative process, along with court decisions and structural changes introducing modern market economy after decades of socialism in Hungary, drew the practitioners' attention to the issue of transfer of business in Hungarian labour law.

In recent years, not only the widespread outsourcing and insourcing agreements have been considered to raise major legal concerns and lead to various employment and contractual disputes but also the area of collective labour law has added relevant elements to the employment law analysis of transactions. As elaborated below, the price of uncertainty regarding the parties of employment relationships can be extremely high under Hungarian law. Therefore, employers and employees each have to act with due care in enforcing their rights and performing their obligations, including especially to sue the appropriate counterparty within the national time limitation period before Hungarian labour courts and to terminate the employment relationship in full compliance with the requirements of the Labour Code.

First, the present paper briefly summarizes the regulations of the Labour Code on legal succession in the event of a transfer of an undertaking, business(es) or parts of undertakings or businesses. Second, it explores the concept of '*economic unit*' pursuant to Hungarian case law and scholars, illustrating the broad interpretation of '*transfer*' in respect of these economic entities as well. This analysis is followed by a review of recently published judgments and Hungarian legal literature relating to the transfer of undertakings. Finally, this paper summarizes the research on the intensity of activism of Hungarian courts in initiating preliminary reference proceedings before the Court of Justice of the European Union (hereinafter: '*ECJ*') and evaluates the (non)conformity of the Hungarian court practice with the ECJ case law in this field of law.

For the avoidance of doubt, this paper only focuses on the transfer of business in traditional employment relationships falling within the scope of the Labour Code – but, for reasons of space, it cannot go into detail on the specific rules applicable for the various legal relationships existing in the Hungarian public sector.

4. *See* the resolution No. 154 of the Labour Chamber of the Hungarian Supreme Court.

§9.02 EXPLORATION OF HUNGARIAN IMPLEMENTATION OF THE DIRECTIVE

[A] Overview of the Rules on Legal Succession Upon the Transfer of Business

The effective Labour Code implements the vast majority of the norms set out in the Directive under a separate chapter titled 'Change in the person of the employer', *see* sections 36-40 of the Labour Code. This legislative decision clearly expresses that Hungarian labour law does not regard the transfer of business as a specific event terminating the already existing employment contract, but simply handles it as a form of amendment of the contract, which affects one of the parties (resulting in the change of the employer).[5]

As a typical codification method in Hungarian labour law, the parties are not allowed to derogate from the rules laid down in this chapter to the detriment of the employee by their agreement.[6] No derogation is permissible to the detriment of the employee by way of a collective agreement, either.[7]

Furthermore, these rules are also applicable to atypical employment relationships, unless otherwise provided by the Labour Code (including in particular part-time, fixed-duration and temporary employment relationships in compliance with Article 2 paragraph 2 of the Directive). Executive employees are not automatically exempted from the application of the rules on transfer of business, either. However, the Hungarian legislator made it possible to derogate from the otherwise applicable norms to the detriment of these specific employees.[8]

Outside this separate chapter, the Labour Code also contains additional provisions on the transfer of business in sporadic forms: in the context of unilateral termination,[9] non-compete agreements,[10] study contracts,[11] works councils[12] or collective agreements.[13]

5. *See* the commentary to section 36 of the Labour Code written by Gyula Berke, in: Zoltán Bankó et al. (eds), Nagykommentár a munka törvénykönyvéről szóló 2012. évi I. törvényhez, Wolters Kluwer Hungary Kft., Budapest, 2023.
6. *See* section 43 para. 1 of the Labour Code.
7. *See* section 41 of the Labour Code.
8. *See* section 209 paras 1-3 of the Labour Code. 'Executive employee' shall mean under the definition of the section 208 paras 1 and 2 of the Labour Code that 'the employer's director and any other person under his or her direct supervision, who is authorized – in part or in full – to act as the director's deputy (hereinafter referred to collectively as "director").

   (2) With the exception set out in Section 209 para 2 [of the Labour Code], the employment contract may prescribe to apply the provisions on the director if the employee is in a position that is of highly importance or requires special confidence from the point of view of the employer's operations and his or her basic wage reaches seven times the mandatory minimum wage.'
9. *See* section 66 para. 3 point a) of the Labour Code.
10. *See* section 228 para. 4 of the Labour Code.
11. *See* section 229 para. 4 of the Labour Code.
12. *See* sections 258 and 265 of the Labour Code.
13. *See* section 282 para. 1 of the Labour Code.

[B] General Rules on Legal Succession

[1] Automatic Transfer of Rights and Obligations

Section 36 of the Labour Code defines the economic unit as 'the organized group of material or immaterial resources' and declares that 'in the event of a transfer of an economic unit upon a legal act, the rights and obligations arising from the employment relationship existing at the time of the transfer shall be automatically transferred from the transferring employer to the transferee employer'.

In addition, the effective Labour Code clarifies that the rights and obligations arising from a study contract[14] or a non-compete agreement[15] shall be automatically transferred from the transferor to the transferee in the case of a transfer of business – ending a former debate among Hungarian practitioners. Remarkably, earlier Hungarian court practice declared that these agreements – falling beyond the scope of the Directive – remained in force after the date of transfer in an unchanged form, i.e., obliging the initial contracting parties irrespective of the transfer of business.[16] This judicial approach however disregarded the business ratio behind these agreements and led to various problems in transfer of business situations; therefore, the effective Labour Code extended the scope of transfer of business rules to the rights and obligations arising from study contracts and non-compete agreements as well.[17]

As a result of the automatic transfer of all rights and obligation, no formal (written) amendment of the employment contract is required between the parties, and in spite of the transfer of business, the employment relationship should be considered being 'continuous' – especially by the calculation of the redundancy benefit or by the determination of the notice period in the event of a later dismissal by the employer.[18]

[2] Information Obligation Toward the Transferee

As permitted by Article 3 paragraph 2 of the Directive, the Labour Code sets out the requirement that before the date of transfer, the transferor shall inform the transferee on the rights and obligations arising from the affected employment relationships (as well as the non-compete agreements and study contracts).[19]

The transferor's failure to comply with this obligation does not impede the automatic transfer of the rights and obligations and does not exclude the employees

14. *See* section 229 para. 4 of the Labour Code.
15. *See* section 228 para. 4 of the Labour Code.
16. *See, e.g.*, the decision of the Hungarian Supreme Court published under case No. Kúria Mfv.10071/2017/4., which did not supported the automatic transfer of rights and obligations in respect of a study contract.
17. *See* the detailed ministerial reasoning to section 37 of the Labour Code. Draft of Act No. T/4786 on the Labour Code. Online availability: https://www.parlament.hu/irom39/04786/04786.pdf (accessed 22 August 2025).
18. *See, e.g.*, the decisions of the Hungarian Supreme Court published under case No. BH1995.434., case No. BH1995.543., case No. BH1993.470. and case No. BH1993.398.
19. *See* section 37 of the Labour Code.

from later enforcing these rights against the transferee.[20] However, the non-compliance with this information duty could give rise to different legal consequences in the legal relationship of the transferor and the transferee – depending on the terms of their agreement.

[3] Joint and Several Liability

In line with Article 3 paragraph 1 of the Directive, Hungarian labour law opted for the joint and several liability of the transferor and the transferee vis-à-vis the employees, but this legal instrument is regulated in a strictly restricted form. In Hungary, the transferor and the transferee shall be jointly and severally liable solely for the obligations that:

(i) became due before the date of transfer, provided that;
(ii) the employee enforces his or her claim within one year calculated from the date of transfer.[21]

From the perspective of the employee, this one-year-long transitional period is significantly shorter than the three-year-long general time limitation period under Hungarian labour law,[22] and the requirement of maturity also narrows the scope of application. Notably, after the expiration of this one-year-long deadline, the employee may enforce his or her claim against the transferee only (within the otherwise applicable time limitation period),[23] but Hungarian law does not require to provide any security to ensure the (later) solvency of the transferee, which could be contrary to the employees' interests.[24]

From the perspective of the transferee, the requirement of maturity could also be negatively assessed, especially if the legal basis of the respective claims (such as a claim for an annual premium or bonus) was established prior to the transfer, but the claim became due after the transfer only.[25] However, it is widely accepted in contractual practice to disclose these claims during the transferor's and the transferee's transactional negotiations and create a special contractual regime, which considers these debts by the determination of the purchase price or proportionally settles these payment obligations between the employers.[26]

[C] Rules on Termination in the Case of the Transfer of Business

In accordance with Article 4 paragraph 1 of the Directive, the Labour Code explicitly prohibits the employer (either the transferor or the transferee) from unilaterally

20. *Ibid.*
21. *See* section 39 of the Labour Code.
22. *See* section 286 para. 1 of the Labour Code.
23. *See, e.g.*, Gyula Berke, in: György Kiss (ed.), Munkajog, Dialóg Campus, Budapest, 2020, p. 155.
24. György Kenderes: A társasági jog és a munkajog kapcsolódási pontjai és ezek problematikája, in: Gazdaság és Jog, 12/2004., pp. 9-12.
25. *See, e.g.*, Gyula Berke, A munkajogi jogutódlás, in: JURA, 1/2001, p. 31.
26. *Ibid.*

terminating the employment contract by referring exclusively to the fact of the transfer of business.[27]

[1] Options for Dismissal by the Employer

Nevertheless, the employer's general right to unilaterally terminate the employment contract by giving notice remains unaffected following the transfer under Hungarian labour law. This means that an employee may be dismissed:

(i) for reasons in connection with his or her behaviour or ability in relation to the employment relationship; or
(ii) for operational reasons occurring on the side of the employer.[28]

Moreover, Hungarian employment law does not prohibit the re-organization of the workforce immediately after the transfer, nor does it require maintaining the already existing employment relationships for a guaranteed period of time. As a result, Hungarian case law seems to tolerate if the employer terminates the employment relationship by referring to a (real) post-transactional re-organization, reduction in staff or other similar grounds belonging to the scope of operational reasons – even one month after the transaction.[29] This court practice could theoretically be compatible with the second phrase of Article 4 paragraph 1 of the Directive – stipulating that the rules of the Directive do not hamper in any way the dismissals for economic, technical or organizational reasons entailing changes in the workforce.

Likewise, the employer's right to unilateral termination with immediate effect also remains unaffected in the event of a transfer of business,[30] and the parties are entitled to terminate their employment contract upon mutual consent as well.[31]

[2] Options for Termination on the Side of the Employee

(a) The Absence of the Right to Object

From the perspective of the employee, Hungarian labour law does not ensure any right to object to the legal succession – contrary to the German legal instrument of *Widerspruchtsrecht* – or otherwise makes it possible to maintain the employment

27. *See* section 66 para. 3 point a) of the Labour Code.
28. *See* section 66 para. 2 of the Labour Code.
29. *See* from the judgment of the Hungarian Supreme Court published under case No. Kúria Mfv. 10.697/2016/1.
30. *See* section 78 para. 1 of the Labour Code that provides as follows: '[t]he employer or the employee may terminate the employment relationship with immediate effect if the other party:
    a) intentionally or by gross negligence commits a serious breach of any substantive obligations arising from the employment relationship; or
    b) otherwise engages in such a conduct that makes impossible to the maintain the employment relationship.'
31. *See* section 64 para. 1 point a) of the Labour Code.

contract with the original employer. Hence, this legislative solution seems to prioritize the protection of maintaining the workplaces over respecting the employees' right to freely choose their contractual partner.[32]

Remarkably, this solution previously raised constitutional concerns in Hungary, but the Hungarian Constitutional Court found that the lack of the right to object did not infringe the employees' fundamental rights (the free choice of work and profession) – shortly because the otherwise applicable norms of the Labour Code created a sufficient safety net for the employees to unilaterally terminate their employment relationships established for an indefinite term – enabling them to exercise the negative form of their constitutional right at (practically) any time.[33] Similarly, the Hungarian Constitutional Court underlined in its decision that the entire regime of the transfer of business primarily serves the employees' interests, even if the right to object is not allowed under Hungarian law.[34]

Arguably, the lack of the right to object makes it more predictable for the transferee to plan with the workforce expected to be transferred via the transaction and this solution can also support the transferor in terminating, in full or in part, the earlier business activities. The ministerial reasoning of the Labour Code also considered a potential transposition of the right to object into Hungarian law as unreasonable, which could cause 'theoretical and practical contradictions and problems'.[35]

However, if the employee denies to perform his or her obligations arising from the employment relationship toward the transferee after the date of transfer, this behaviour constitutes a serious breach of contract and thereby creates a valid ground for termination with immediate effect on the side of the employer, as certified by the uniform case law of Hungarian courts.[36]

(b) Preferential Regime for Unilateral Termination

The effective Labour Code offers various options to employees to lawfully terminate their employment contracts and be released from the obligations arising from their employment relationships.

32. *See, e.g.*, Ágnes Kovács and György Nádas, A munkáltatói jogutódlás dogmatikai problémái egy jogvita tükrében, Jogtudományi Közlöny, 11/2010, p. 591.
33. *See* the decision of the Hungarian Constitutional Court published under case No. 500/B/1994. AB. 'If the employee does not wish to maintain the employment relationship with his or her employer, he or she is entitled to freely exercise the negative form of his or her constitutional right; he or she may terminate the employment relationship, however, the employee will not be entitled for the privileges that would be available for him or her in the case of a termination by the employer. Nonetheless, there is no violation of any constitutional right here.'
34. *Ibid.*
35. *See* the detailed ministerial reasoning to section 36 of the Labour Code. Draft of Act No. T/4786 on the Labour Code. Online availability: https://www.parlament.hu/irom39/04786/04786.pdf (accessed 22 August 2025).
36. *See* the decisions of the Hungarian Supreme Court published under case No. BH1996.174. and case No. BH1996.3.

First, in line with Article 4 paragraph 2 of the Directive, the Labour Code provides a specific ground for unilateral termination on the side of the employee in the event of a transfer of business. Provided that:

(i) the change in the person of the employer involves a substantial change in the working conditions to the detriment of the employee; and
(ii) in consequence maintaining the employment relationship would entail disproportionate harm or would be impossible for the employee;
(iii) the employee may unilaterally terminate the employment relationship by referring to these circumstances in writing;
(iv) within 30 days calculated from the legal succession.[37]

If these criteria are met, the termination by the employee should be regarded as a termination by the employer from the aspect of certain legal consequences (such as the right to redundancy benefit and the exemption from duty of work for half of the notice period).[38] However, the Hungarian regulation does not ensure that the employees benefit from all legal consequences applicable in the case of an unlawful termination by the employer, which practically means that the employees may not claim compensation for their damages or file a claim for reinstatement – as also confirmed by the ECJ practice.[39]

Observing the notion of '*working conditions*' mentioned above, Hungarian commentaries argue for a broad interpretation covering not only the personal and material work conditions, but also the relevant provisions of collective agreements applicable for the employees' rights and obligations arising from the employment relationship, including, *inter alia*, the rules on wages, working time or working schedule.[40]

Furthermore, the concept of the above '*detrimental change*' must be scrutinized on a subjective basis, where individual life circumstances may play a decisive role during the judicial assessment (e.g., if the changing working schedule is incompatible with the life rhythm of a parent having young children).[41] The legal literature however notes that Hungarian case law is not open to indulgently accepting any reference made to minor or insignificant inconveniences,[42] and the employee must refer to concrete

37. *See* section 40 para. 1 of the Labour Code.
38. *Ibid.*
39. *See* the judgment of the ECJ of 27 November 2008 in case No. C-396/07 *Mirja Juuri v. Fazer Amica Oy* (*Juuri* judgment). The ECJ argued that 'the Member States are not required to guarantee the employee a right to financial compensation, for which the transferee employer is liable, in accordance with the same conditions as the right upon which an employee can rely where the contract of employment or the employment relationship is unlawfully terminated by his employer.' Operative part of the judgment para. 1.
40. *See* the commentary to section 40 of the Labour Code written by Gyula Berke, in: Zoltán Bankó et al. (eds), Nagykommentár a munka törvénykönyvéről szóló 2012. évi I. törvényhez, Wolters Kluwer Hungary Kft., Budapest, 2023.
41. *Ibid.*
42. *See* Gyula Berke, in: György Kiss (ed.): Munkajog, Dialóg Campus, Budapest, 2020, p. 157.

circumstances in the justification,[43] which demonstrate that maintaining the employment relationship would entail disproportionate harm or would be impossible for the employee. The justification of the termination based on the adversary substantial change should be proven by the employee during a potential lawsuit.[44]

As a consequence, these preconditions - along with the short deadline - could discourage the employees from choosing this preferential ground for termination, which arguably was one of the implied purposes of these provisions.

(c) Other Options for Termination by the Employee

Apart from the preferential regime elaborated above, in the case of an employment contract concluded for an indefinite period of time, the employees may also exercise their otherwise existing right to unilaterally terminate the employment relationship by giving notice - without providing any justification.[45] In this case, the employee will not be entitled to redundancy benefit and will not be exempted from his or her duty to work during the period of notice, but may easily terminate the employment relationship.

Third, at a theoretical level, the employees' right to termination with immediate effect[46] also remains unaffected, irrespective of the transfer of business. Fourth, termination upon the parties' mutual consent also remains a possibility following the date of transfer, as stated above.[47]

[D] Information and Consultation Obligation Toward the Employees and Their Representatives

Hungary also implemented the information and consultation obligation as required by Article 7 of the Directive. The exact content of this obligation depends on whether or not a works council (shop steward) - the Hungarian equivalent of the employees' representatives in the meaning of the Directive - is operating at the transferor.

In short, works councils are the general form of the employees' collective representation under Hungarian labour law. A works council shall be elected if, during the half-year prior to the date when the election committee was established, the

43. *See* Zsuzsanna Mészárosné Szabó, in: Erika Tálné Molnár (ed.) A Munka Törvénykönyve kommentárja (2012. évi I. törvény). Kommentár a gyakorlat számára, HVG-Orac, Budapest, 2020.
44. The published case law also emphasizes that the burden of proof is on the employee in this regard, *see, e.g.,* the decision of the Hungarian Supreme Court published under case No. Kúria Mfv. 10.459/2017/5.
45. *See* section 67 para. 1 of the Labour Code.
46. *See* section 78 para. 1 of the Labour Code that provides as follows: '[t]he employer or the employee may terminate the employment relationship with immediate effect if the other party:
    a) intentionally or by gross negligence commits a serious breach of any substantive obligations arising from the employment relationship; or
    b) otherwise engages in such a conduct that makes impossible to the maintain the employment relationship.'
47. *See* section 64 para. 1 point a) of the Labour Code.

average number of employees at the employer or at the employer's independent establishment or division is higher than 50.[48] If the aforementioned number is higher than 15 but does not exceed 50, a shop steward shall be elected.[49] The rules on the works councils shall apply *mutatis mutandis* to the rights and obligations of the shop steward, unless otherwise provided for by the Labour Code.[50]

[1] Rules Applicable in the Absence of a Works Council or Shop Steward

If no works council operates at the transferor (due to the lack of the required number of employees) and no shop steward has been elected either, at the latest within 15 days prior to the date of transfer, the transferor or – based on the agreement of the employers – the transferee shall inform the respective employees affected by the transfer in writing about the following (as listed in Article 7 paragraph 6 of the Directive):

(i) the date or proposed date of the transfer;
(ii) the reasons for the transfer;
(iii) the legal, economic and social implications of the transfer; and
(iv) any measures envisaged in relation to the employees.[51]

[2] Information and Consultation Obligation Toward the Works Council

In other cases, the transferor and the transferee must inform the works council or shop steward no later than 15 days before the date of transfer about:

(i) the date or proposed date of the transfer;
(ii) the reasons for the transfer; and
(iii) the legal, economic and social implications of the transfer.[52]

At the same time, the transferor and the transferee must also enter into negotiations with the works council or shop steward on the measures envisaged in respect of the employees for concluding an agreement.[53] The aforementioned negotiations shall cover:

(i) the principles of the actions;
(ii) the ways and means of avoiding detrimental consequences, as well as;
(iii) the means for mitigating such consequences.[54]

With regard to Article 7 paragraph 4 of the Directive, the Labour Code also sets forth that the transferor and the transferee shall fulfil their obligation of information

48. *See* section 236 para. 1 of the Labour Code.
49. *Ibid.*
50. *See* section 269 para. 1 of the Labour Code.
51. *See* section 38 para. 2 of the Labour Code.
52. *See* section 265 para. 1 of the Labour Code.
53. *See* section 265 para. 2 of the Labour Code.
54. *See* section 265 para. 3 of the Labour Code.

and negotiation even if the decision underlying the transfer was adopted by the organization or person controlling the employer.[55] In addition, the Labour Code lays down that the employer shall not be exempted from these obligations if the controlling organization or person fails to inform the employer about its decision.[56]

In addition, the Labour Code enables the employer and the works council to conclude a works agreement on the enforcement of the above or the further development of their cooperation.[57] Under Hungarian labour law, works agreements represent a form of rules governing employment relationships (besides the statutory laws and regulations, collective agreements and binding decisions of conciliation committees).[58]

In the case of an infringement of the information and consultation obligation, the works council may initiate a non-contentious procedure before Hungarian labour courts within five days.[59] This non-contentious procedure must be conducted within extremely short deadlines: the first instance court shall render its decision within 15 days; an appeal must be filed within 5 days (calculated from the delivery of the decision); and the second instance court shall render its decision within 15 days.[60] However, the Labour Code remains silent on the type of decisions to be ordered during such a procedure and there is no published case law, where a similar violation of law would be alleged in relation to a transfer of business.[61] Overall, Hungarian legal literature concludes that rules of the Labour Code on law enforcement are vague and not specific enough in the event of a breach of these information and consultation obligations.[62]

[3] Post-transfer Information Obligation

Finally, on the date of transfer, modified by Act No. LXXIV of 2022, the transferee shall inform in writing the respective employees on:

(i) the change in the person of the employer;
(ii) the transferee's identification data; and
(iii) the changes in working conditions.[63]

[E] Further Collective Labour Law-Related Provisions of the Labour Code

As regards the terms and conditions agreed in collective agreements, Hungary stipulated a one-year-long transitional period based on Article 3 paragraph 3 of the

55. *See* section 265 para. 4 of the Labour Code.
56. *Ibid.*
57. *See* section 267 para. 1 of the Labour Code.
58. *See* section 13 of the Labour Code.
59. *See* section 289 para. 1 of the Labour Code.
60. *See* section 289 para. 2 of the Labour Code.
61. *See* Tamás Gyulavári (ed.), Munkajog, ELTE Eötvös Kiadó, Budapest, 2015, p. 167.
62. *Ibid.*
63. *See* section 38 para. 1 of the Labour Code.

Directive. This means that the collective agreement covering the employment relationship shall remain in force for one year following the transfer.[64] Nonetheless, the Hungarian legislator created two exemptions from the aforementioned regulation:

(i) where the term of the collective agreement would expire earlier than the above one-year-long deadline; and
(ii) where the employment relationship would be covered by another collective agreement after the date of transfer.[65]

For the avoidance of doubt, the Labour Code provides that the parties are not allowed to derogate from these collective labour law provisions either.[66]

In accordance with Article 6 paragraph 1 of the Directive, the Labour Code also specifies that neither the mandate of works council nor the mandate of its members automatically terminate upon the transfer of business.[67] Nevertheless, a new (joint) works council shall be elected within three months if there were works councils both at the transferred economic unit as well as at the transferor's own entity.[68] If there was a works council in only one of the affected entities, works council members shall be elected within the same deadline in order to provide representation for the unrepresented employees.[69] Upon the demerger of economic entities, separate works councils shall be elected at the new economic entities within three months calculated from the date of demerger.[70]

[F] Transfer of Business During Liquidation Procedures

In Hungary – in compliance with Article 5 paragraph 1 of the Directive – liquidation procedures are exempted from the application of nearly all provisions demonstrated above.

Hence, if the transfer of an economic unit is carried out during a liquidation procedure:

(i) the rights and obligations arising from the employment relationship (including the non-compete agreements and the study contracts) do not have to be transferred from the transferor to the transferee;[71]
(ii) no joint and several liability is established concerning the employees' claims;[72]

64. *See* section 282 para. 1 of the Labour Code.
65. *See* section 282 para. 2 of the Labour Code.
66. *See* section 283 of the Labour Code.
67. *See* sections 252 and 255 of the Labour Code.
68. *See* section 258 para. 1 of the Labour Code.
69. *See* section 258 para. 2 of the Labour Code.
70. *See* section 258 para. 3 of the Labour Code.
71. *See* section 36 para. 2 points a), f) and g) of the Labour Code.
72. *See* section 36 para. 2 point d) of the Labour Code.

(iii) the employer may unilaterally terminate the employment relationship with reference to the sole fact that the transfer occurred in connection with the liquidation;[73]

(iv) the employee is not entitled to unilaterally terminate the employment relationship with reference to the substantial and detrimental changes in working conditions based on the preferential regime pointed out above;[74]

(v) the collective agreement shall not be maintained by the transferee for one year after the transfer.[75]

Irrespective of the liquidation procedure, the information and consultation obligation toward the works council[76] as well as the information obligation toward the employees (in the absence of a works council or shop steward)[77] shall be performed accordingly.[78]

Apart from this, upon request, the liquidator is obliged to provide the employees, the works council (shop steward), as well as the trade unions having a representation at the employer with information on any issue affecting the employees within eight days.[79] Moreover, the Liquidation Act describes further situations (e.g., when the liquidation is ordered by the court or when the employee's claim is disputed by the liquidator), where an additional information obligation must be fulfilled toward the employees.[80]

Likewise, the same restrictions as listed in the above points i)-v)[81] shall apply in connection with the financial intermediation system upon the use of a sale of business tool, bridge institution tool or asset separation tool as defined in the Act No. XXXVII of 2014.[82] These legal instruments serve the purposes of a special liquidation procedure as provided for in Directive 2014/59/EU[83] and could thus be interpreted as being compliant with the regime laid down in Article 5 paragraph 1 of the Directive.[84]

73. *See* section 36 para. 2 point e) of the Labour Code.
74. *See* section 36 para. 2 point d) of the Labour Code.
75. *See* section 36 para. 2 point h) of the Labour Code.
76. *See* the obligation laid down in section 265 of the Labour Code.
77. *See* the obligation set out in section 38 para. 2 of the Labour Code.
78. *See* section 36 para. 2 points b) and c) of the Labour Code.
79. *See* section 5 point a) of the Act No. XLIX of 1991 on the bankruptcy procedure and the liquidation procedure (hereinafter: *the Liquidation Act*).
80. *See, e.g.*, section 31 para. 1 point e) of the Liquidation Act or section 46 para. (6a) of the Liquidation Act.
81. *See* section 36 para. 3 of the Labour Code.
82. *See* the Act No. XXXVII of 2014 on the further development of the institutional framework to strengthen the safety of certain actors in the financial intermediation system.
83. *See* the Directive 2014/59/EU of the European Parliament and of the Council of 15 May 2014 establishing a framework for the recovery and resolution of credit institutions and investment firms and amending Council Directive 82/891/EEC, and Directives 2001/24/EC, 2002/47/EC, 2004/25/EC, 2005/56/EC, 2007/36/EC, 2011/35/EU, 2012/30/EU and 2013/36/EU, and Regulations (EU) No. 1093/2010 and (EU) No. 648/2012, of the European Parliament and of the Council.
84. *See* the commentary to section 36 of the Labour Code written by Gyula Berke, in: Zoltán Bankó et al. (eds), Nagykommentár a munka törvénykönyvéről szóló 2012. évi I. törvényhez, Wolters Kluwer Hungary Kft., Budapest, 2023.

Notably, Article 5 paragraph 1 of the Directive allows the derogation from the provisions of the Directive where the transferor is subject to such an insolvency proceeding which has been instituted with a view to the liquidation of the assets of the transferor and is under the supervision of a competent public authority. The effective Hungarian legal regime seems to comply with this requirement, whereas the above exemptions are not applicable in the course of general bankruptcy procedures or winding-up procedures, but solely during liquidation procedures (aiming at the liquidation of the insolvent employer). The criterion of the public supervision is also met, since liquidation procedures must be conducted under the supervision of state courts under Hungarian law and the liquidators are also appointed by the state courts.

Under Article 5 paragraph 4 of the Directive, Member States shall take appropriate measures with a view to preventing misuse of insolvency proceedings in such a way as to deprive employees of the rights provided for in this Directive. In order to protect the employees' social security, the Hungarian legislator also created a separate protection system for the employees' unpaid wages during the liquidation proceedings by establishing a special fund (namely, the Wage Guarantee Fund) dedicated to this purpose.[85] In addition, the Liquidation Act also provides for specific obligations of the liquidator toward the employees, protecting their rights and interests during the entire liquidation procedure.[86]

Despite the above, some Hungarian authors strongly criticize the broad scope of exemptions from the otherwise applicable rules in the course of liquidation procedures – arguing that the purposes of liquidation would theoretically be compatible with the change in the person of the employer.[87] This criticism is strengthened by the fact that, under Hungarian law, before the recodification of the Labour Code, the transfer of business rules was traditionally applicable even during the liquidation procedures.[88]

[G] Miscellaneous Provisions

Supplementary company or intercompany pension schemes are highly atypical (practically non-existent) in Hungary, but these rights and obligations shall be automatically transferred from the transferor to the transferee upon a transfer of business (in practice, if the employment contract or the employer's unilateral commitment provides for the entitlement of such benefits).[89] In these situations, the transferee, if it does not wish to

85. *See* the section 1 para. 1 of the Act No LXVI of 1994 on the Wage Guarantee Fund.
86. *See, e.g.*, the section 37 para. 4 of the Liquidation Act on the automatic registration of certain claims of the employees or section 57 para. 1 of the Liquidation Act on the ranking of the debts.
87. *See, e.g.*, Erika Tálné Molnár (ed.), A Munka Törvénykönyve kommentárja (2012. évi I. törvény), HVG-ORAC, Budapest, 2020.
88. *See, e.g.*, the detailed ministerial reasoning to section 36 of the Labour Code that also mentions the antecedent to the current regulation, based on which the rules on transfer of business were applicable even during liquidation procedures. Draft of Act No. T/4786 on the Labour Code. Online availability: https://www.parlament.hu/irom39/04786/04786.pdf (accessed 22 August 2025).
89. *See, e.g.*, the chapter on Hungary written by Helga Fehér, in: Jens Kirchner, Sascha Morgenroth and Tim Marshall (eds), Transfer of Business and Acquired Employee Rights. A Practical Guide for Europe and Across the World. Springer Verlag, Berlin – Heidelberg, 2016, p. 250.

maintain such an employer's contribution to the pension scheme, may consider an amendment of the employment contract (upon the mutual consent of the parties) or the unilateral termination of the unilateral commitment,[90] under the rules elaborated in §9.03, subsection [C][3].

§9.03 JUDICIAL INTERPRETATION OF THE CONCEPT OF TRANSFER OF AN ECONOMIC UNIT IN THE HUNGARIAN COURT PRACTICE

When Hungarian courts evaluate an alleged change in the person of the employer, two major questions should be answered in the affirmative:

(i) whether the transferred assets may qualify as an economic unit retaining its identity; and
(ii) whether the legal act – upon which the legal succession is alleged – complies with the conceptual elements of a transfer within the meaning of section 36 of the Labour Code.

Following this logic, the present paper firstly examines the criteria crucial for an economic unit to retain its identity in the course of the transfer. After that, it summarizes the Hungarian courts' approach regarding the legal acts to be qualified as 'transfer' for the purposes of legal succession in Hungarian employment law.

[A] Criteria of an Economic Unit Retaining Its Identity

Although section 36 of the Labour Code provides a definition for the economic unit ('the organized group of material or immaterial resources'), the deeper analysis requires an overview of the relevant case law of Hungarian labour courts as well.

First, published Hungarian case law emphasizes that the concept of economic unit is a sui generis legal instrument of EU law and any potential interpretation must therefore be compliant with the Directive as well as the related judgments of the ECJ.[91] As a consequence, the published decisions of the Hungarian Supreme Court do not simply refer to the main findings of EU case law but practically reiterate or even precisely cite the respective parts of various decisions rendered by the ECJ.

In line with this, according to Hungarian scholars, the practical realizations of an economic unit could be inexhaustibly diverse: 'an economic unit could be, inter alia, a shop premise with storages and furniture; a factory hall along with the production line placed therein; a creative advertisement agency, where one notebook is the only material asset etc'.[92]

90. *Ibid.*
91. *See, e.g.,* the judgment of the Hungarian Supreme Court published under case No. BH2020.279.
92. *See* the commentary to the section 36 of the Labour Code written by Kártyás Gábor, in: Kártyás Gábor, Petrovics Zoltán and Takács Gábor, Nagykommentár a munka törvénykönyvéről szóló 2012. évi I. törvényhez, Wolters Kluwer Hungary Kft., Budapest, 2023.

In compliance with the *Spijkers* judgment (C-24/85),[93] Hungarian courts also explored that all relevant factual circumstances of the transfer should be taken into consideration in the course of an overall assessment, when it must be decided whether or not the economic entity transferred retained its identity and therefore a change in the position of the employer could be established.

During this test, the acting judicial panel has to observe a set of criteria, as laid down in the *Spijkers* judgment,[94] including, *inter alia*:

- the handover as well as the takeover of the entity's tangible and intangible assets;
- the transfer of immaterial goods (rights);
- the takeover of a significant part of the workforce by the transferor;
- the transfer of the economic entity's customers;
- the similarity between the activities of the affected economic entity before and after the transfer;
- the nature of the transferred activity; and
- the circumstance whether or not those activities had ceased at the time of the transfer.

with the proviso that the existence of these criteria does not automatically substantiate the change in the person of the employer.[95]

In addition, the aforementioned nature of the transferred activity should also be subject to a further legal analysis. Hungarian case law supports that there could be a wide variety in the type of the transferred activity – such as production, manufacturing, trade, provision of services, etc. – as well as these activities could be carried out in different sectors of the economy (e.g., in the construction business,[96] plastic manufacturing,[97] retail sector,[98] print media publishing,[99] fuel trade[100] or even district heating services.)[101]

93. *See* the operative part of the judgment of the ECJ of 18 March 1986 in the case No. 24/85 *Jozef Maria Antonius Spijkers v. Gebroeders Benedik Abattoir CV and Alfred Benedik en Zonen BV*. 'In order to establish whether or not such a transfer has taken place in a case such as that before the national court, it is necessary to consider whether, having regard to all the facts characterizing the transaction, the business was disposed of as a going concern, as would be indicated inter alia by the fact that its operation was actually continued or resumed by the new employer, with the same or similar activities.'
94. *Ibid.*, especially para. 13. 'In order to determine whether those conditions are met, it is necessary to consider all the facts characterizing the transaction in question, including the type of undertaking or business, whether or not the business's tangible assets, such as buildings and movable property, are transferred, the value of its intangible assets at the time of the transfer, whether or not the majority of its employees are taken over by the new employer, whether or not its customers are transferred and the degree of similarity between the activities carried on before and after the transfer and the period, if any, for which those activities were suspended. It should be noted, however, that all those circumstances are merely single factors in the overall assessment which must be made and cannot therefore be considered in isolation.'
95. *See, e.g.*, the judgment of the Hungarian Supreme Court published under case No. Kúria Mfv.10350/2019/5.
96. *See* the judgments of the Hungarian Supreme Court published under case No. BH1993.771 and case No. BH1994.571.
97. *See* the judgment of the Hungarian Supreme Court published under case No. BH1996.504.

Among these activities, Hungarian court practice examines the activities belonging to the service sector with special care, where the necessity of essential assets and personnel has to be observed in detail.[102] Within this sector, Hungarian case law – in compliance with the recent judgments held by the ECJ – differentiates between:

(i) the activities heavily relying on significant – tangible and intangible – assets; and
(ii) labour-intensive activities, which could be carried out mainly based on human resources.

In connection with this classification, Hungarian courts explicitly refer to the ECJ judgments held in case No. C-13/95 (*Süzen* judgment), joined cases Nos C-229/96 and C-74/97 (*Hernandez Vidal and others* judgment), case No. C-172/99 (*Oy Liikenne* judgment), case No. C-340/01 (*Abler judgment*), as well as case No. C-51/00 (*Temco* judgment).[103]

As to the services relying on significant assets (such as the operation of a petrol station), the Hungarian courts argued – by referring to the judgments ruled in the case No. C-172/99. (*Oy Liikenne*) and case No. C-340/01 (*Abler*) – that no legal succession could be held in the absence of the takeover of the essential assets.[104] However, the change in the person of the employer could also be established if the transfer of these assets (covering both tangible and intangible assets) was not followed by the takeover of the employees.[105]

On the contrary, where no significant assets are required to carrying out the activity in question, the court decisions held that the economic unit could retain its identity by the transfer of the major part of the workforce. It follows from the foregoing that when the relevant part of the personnel was not transferred to the transferee, the identity of such an economic unit cannot be retained either, since it is fundamentally based on the workforce.[106] In this context, Hungarian courts mainly reiterated the findings of the judgments held in case No. C-74/97 (*Hernandez Vidal and others* judgment) and case No. C-463/09 (*Clece S. A.* judgment) from the case law of the ECJ.[107]

98. *See* the judgments published of the Hungarian Supreme Court under case No. BH1994.290., case No. Kúria Mfv.10350/2019/5. Likewise, *see* the judgment of the County Court of Debrecen published under the case No. Debreceni Törvényszék Mf.21112/2008/6.
99. *See* the judgment of the Hungarian Supreme Court published under case No. BH2010.280.
100. *See* the judgment of the Hungarian Supreme Court published under case No. BH + 2015.2.83.
101. *See* the judgment of the Hungarian Supreme Court published under case No. Kúria Mfv.10008/2018/3.
102. *See* the judgment of the Hungarian Supreme Court published under case No. EH 2014.03.M6.
103. *See, e.g.*, the decisions of the Hungarian Supreme Court published under case No. BH2019.26. and case No. EH2014.03.M6., which contained references to each of the aforementioned ECJ judgments.
104. *See* the judgment of the Hungarian Supreme Court published under case No. BH + 2015.83.
105. *Ibid.*
106. *See* the judgment of the Hungarian Supreme Court published under case No. EH2014.03.M6.
107. *See* in particular para. 40 of the judgment of the ECJ of 20 January 2011 held in case No. C-C-463/09. *CLECE SA v. María Socorro Martín Valor and Ayuntamiento de Cobisa:* '[i]n particular, the identity of an economic entity, such as that forming the subject of the dispute in

For illustrative purposes, the criteria of the retained identity have been met in the following cases:

- in the construction business, where two entities created a new company and 'replaced' their employees here under unchanged work conditions;[108]
- in the case of a plastic factory, where the owner founded a new company with a third party and replaced the employees;[109]
- under a works contract affecting a toy assembly plant, where the employees continued to work in the same positions, at the same workplace, under the same work conditions, but under the control of the subcontractor who took over not only the workforce but also the machines and the tools;[110]
- in the event of a shop lease contract, where the lessee undertook to employ the shop's personnel, keeping them in their original positions;[111]
- by the takeover of the editorial team of a magazine, where the same employees edited the same magazine after the transaction, even working from the same place (and where the transferor ended its economic activity in full after the transfer);[112]
- based on a sale and purchase agreement, the subject of which was a well-known car showroom, repair shop and service station to be purchased as a going concern;[113]
- in the case of a contract on the operation of a petrol station (even without the takeover of the employees);[114]
- in the case of a plastic manufacturing plant, the legal succession could be extended not only to the workforce carrying out the manufacturing activity but also to the administrative personal working dedicated to the respective unit.[115]

On the contrary, Hungarian courts did not establish the transfer of business in favour of the leading secretary under an outsourcing agreement covering the full spectrum of the company's case management and administrative tasks.[116] Likewise, no

---

the main proceedings, which is essentially based on manpower, cannot be retained if the majority of its employees are not taken on by the alleged transferee.' Similarly, *see* the operative part of the judgment of the ECJ of 10 December 1998 held in the joined cases *Francisco Hernández Vidal SA v. Prudencia Gómez Pérez, María Gómez Pérez and Contratas y Limpiezas SL* (C-127/96), *Friedrich Santner v. Hoechst AG* (C-229/96), *and Mercedes Gómez Montaña v. Claro Sol SA and Red Nacional de Ferrocarriles Españoles (Renfe)* (C-74/97) providing as follows '[t]he mere fact that the maintenance work carried out first by the cleaning firm and then by the undertaking owning the premises is similar does not justify the conclusion that a transfer of such an entity has occurred.'

108. *See* the judgment of the Hungarian Supreme Court published under case No. BH1993.12.771.
109. *See* the judgment of the Hungarian Supreme Court published under case No. BH1996.504.
110. *See* the judgment of the Hungarian Supreme Court published under case No. BH2009.90.
111. *See* the judgment of the Hungarian Supreme Court published under case No. BH1994.290.
112. *See* the judgment of the Hungarian Supreme Court published under case No. BH2010.280.
113. *See* the judgment of the Court of Appeal of Pécs (in Hungarian: *Pécsi Ítélőtábla*) published under case No. ÍH2023.29.
114. *See* the judgment of the Hungarian Supreme Court published under case No. BH + 2015.83.
115. *See* the judgment of the Hungarian Supreme Court published under case No. BH1996.9.504.
116. *See* the judgment of the Hungarian Supreme Court published under case No. EH2014.03.M6.

legal succession was held in respect of a company, where the delivery tasks were outsourced through a works contract to a third-party contractor.[117] However, in these cases, the Hungarian courts assessed various factual circumstances and even legal literature mentions the fact-heavy character of these decisions.[118]

[B] Judicial Interpretation of the 'Transfer' as a Legal Act

[1] Transfer of Business by a Direct Contractual Link Between the Transferor and the Transferee

In Hungarian case law, the transfer of business is typically based on a direct contractual link established by and between the transferor and the transferee.

These legal acts could transfer the ownership of certain assets from the transferor to the transferee (such as sale and purchase agreements, exchange agreements or the members' contributions to the capital of a company)[119] or temporarily pass the right of use over the economic unit's significant assets (including in particular operative lease agreements and financial lease agreements).[120] Other contractual relationships obliging the transferee to conduct certain activity (such as works contracts or mandate agreements) could also give rise to a change in the person of the employer.[121]

The aforementioned legal titles could also be combined during a transaction – for example, the transfer of ownership over certain assets might be complemented with the simultaneous lease of other assets – in total, realizing a complete transfer of business.[122]

Moreover, not only a single act but also a series of subsequent legal acts could result in the transfer of the respective business entity (e.g., where the number of employees taken over gradually increases on the side of the new employer).[123]

Similarly, not only the establishment of a legal act but also the termination thereof could cause a transfer of business[124] – in compliance with the ECJ case law stemming from judgments rendered in the *Ny Mølle Kro* case (C-287/86) or the *Daddy's*

117. *See* the judgment of the Hungarian Supreme Court published under case No. LB Mfv. I. 10.272/2000.
118. *See, e.g.*, József Radnay, A munkáltatói jogutódlás kérdései, in: Gazdaság és Jog, 2/2004, pp. 17-22.
119. *See, e.g.*, the decisions of the Hungarian Supreme Courts published under case No. BH1993.398., case No. BH1993.470., case No. BH1995.8.493., case No. BH1996.504. as well as the judgment of the Court of Appeal of Pécs (in Hungarian: *Pécsi Ítélő tábla*) published under case No. ÍH2023.29.
120. *See, e.g.*, the decisions of the Hungarian Supreme Courts published under case No. BH1994.290., BH 1995.8.493., BH2020.279.
121. *See* the judgment of the Hungarian Supreme Court published under case No. BH2009.90.
122. *See* the judgment of the Hungarian Supreme Court published under case No. BH1995.493.
123. *See* the judgment of the Hungarian Supreme Court published under case No. LB Mfv. II. 10.240/1997.
124. *See, e.g.*, the decision of the Hungarian Supreme Court published under case No. LB Mfv.11038/2008/3.

Dance Hall case (C-324/86).[125] Minor temporary gaps between the establishment of the affiliate company and the takeover of the employees by this business association do not preclude the qualification as a transfer of business either.[126]

In addition, the consideration is not a mandatory element in the judicial evaluation of the transfer of business and even gift agreements could therefore serve as basis for a potential change in the person of the employer.[127]

[2] Transfer of Business Without a Direct Contractual Link Between the Transferor and the Transferee

Besides the above, Hungarian case law goes one step further and declares that the transfer of business can also be established even in the absence of a direct contractual link between the transferor and the transferee.[128]

In these cases, the court practice admittedly concentrates on the actual change of control over the economic unit, taking into account several additional factual circumstances (especially the similarity of the business activity carried out, the takeover of the workforce and the necessary tools) during the judicial assessment of the alleged legal succession.[129]

In a recently published case, the former employer as a lessee terminated the lease contract of a book shop with the lessor (a big department store). The new lessee concluded a separate agreement with the department store on the lease, took over the warehouse stocks and continued to operate the premises as a book shop. Apart from this, the new lessee also employed the earlier workforce in unchanged positions and paid them the same wages - however, the former and the new lessee did not enter into a direct contractual relationship.

In this case, the Hungarian Supreme Court held that the change in the person of the employer has been realized, irrespective of the fact that no direct contractual relationship had existed between the former and the new lessee.[130] In this regard, the court decision clearly referred to the case law of the ECJ, including the *Securitas* judgment held in case No. C-200/16, the *Merckx* judgment held in the joined cases Nos C-171/94 and C-172/94, as well as the *Neuhuys* judgment held in case No. C-472/16.

Likewise, the Hungarian Supreme Court came to the conclusion that 'in the event of a transfer of business, the transfer may be carried out by way of a trilateral legal act, by the change of control over the economic unit, as a result thereof the employer, who

125. *See, e.g.*, para. 15 of the judgment of the ECJ of 17 December 1987 held in case No. 287/86 *Landsorganisationen i Danmark for Tjenerforbundet i Danmark v. Ny Mølle Kro.* 'The directive is applicable where the owner of a leased undertaking takes over its operation following a breach of the lease by the lessee.'
126. *See* the judgment published under case No. MD II/88 referred by József Radnai, in: József Radnai (ed.), A Munka Törvénykönyve kommentárja (1992. évi XXII. törvény), HVG-Orac, Budapest, 2011.
127. *See, e.g.*, Gyula Berke, A munkajogi jogutódlás, in: JURA, 1/2001, p. 29.
128. *See* the judgment of the Hungarian Supreme Court published under case No. BH2020.279.
129. *See, e.g.*, Erika Tálné Molnár (ed.), A Munka Törvénykönyve kommentárja (2012. évi I. törvény), HVG-ORAC, Budapest, 2020.
130. *See* the judgment of the Hungarian Supreme Court published under case No. BH2020.279.

is entitled to manage the employees, changes.' In this context, the judgment put special emphasis on the factual elements that: (i) the employers' business activity was identical and (ii) the purpose of the lease contracts was also the same, i.e., using the affected premises for the goals of book retail.

The Hungarian court practice also confirmed that unilateral acts could also result in the change of the employer upon a transfer of business. In a published case, the assembly of a municipality adopted a resolution on the local district heating services based on which a new limited liability company could provide these services in the municipality's territory.[131] The right of use regarding the necessary physical assets was ensured by way of lease contracts or operation agreements concluded with the municipality or the former employer.[132] The court decision established the change in the person of the employer – attaching great importance to the fact that the transferor had to continuously employ the earlier employees and use the same public utilities and working tools for providing the same services.[133]

The Hungarian court practice also established the transfer of business regarding the operation of a sewage plant without requiring a direct contractual link between the transferor and the transferee.[134] In this case, the local municipality terminated the former agreement on the operation of the sewage plant concluded with the operator (the transferor) and entered into a new concession agreement with the winner of the tender, who established a new company (the transferee) for this special business activity.[135] This company continued to employ the transferor's employees in unchanged positions, at the same workplace and under identical conditions – as it was undertaken in the concession contract by the mother company.[136]

Certain Hungarian authors therefore conclude that the transfer of business may also be established in the absence of a valid legal act, whereas it is a question of fact under Hungarian case law whether or not the power of control was transferred.[137] In their views, if this question is answered in the affirmative, the transfer of business must also be established by the acting judicial panel.

[C] Further Relevant Court Decisions on the Interpretation of Related Legal Instruments

Moreover, Hungarian court practice also highlighted the mutual relationship by and between the transfer of business and numerous other legal instruments of Hungarian labour law.

131. *See* the judgment of the Hungarian Supreme Court published under case No. BH2019.26.
132. *Ibid.*
133. *Ibid.*
134. *See* the judgment of the Hungarian Supreme Court published under case No. BH2003.435.
135. *Ibid.*
136. *Ibid.*
137. *See* the commentary to section 36 of the Labour Code written by Gyula Berke, in: Zoltán Bankó et al. (eds), Nagykommentár a munka törvénykönyvéről szóló 2012. évi I. törvényhez, Wolters Kluwer Hungary Kft., Budapest, 2023.

[1] Date of Transfer

The case law defined the date of transfer in compliance with the judgment held in case No. C-478/03 (*Celtec* judgment), concluding that it is the date on which responsibility as employer for carrying on the business is transferred from the transferor to the transferee.[138]

However, this interpretation could be problematic in such situations, where the assets were taken over gradually and the transfer of business could only be held based on a series of subsequent legal acts. In these scenarios, the exact date of transfer remains hardly foreseeable (especially for the employees, who are typically not aware of the employers' intent regarding the envisaged transfer of further assets).

[2] Unpaid Leave

The case law also clarified that the personal scope of the transfer of business is automatically extended to the employees who are on unpaid leave (typically on parental leave) at the date of transfer.[139] In other words, the transferee must also employ these employees – when they return from their unpaid leave.

[3] Post-transfer Amendments, Repeated Probationary Period

As regards the modification of the employment contract, Hungarian courts highlight that the transferor and the employee are entitled to amend their contract upon their mutual consent even after the transfer of business in accordance with the generally applicable norms.[140] However, they cannot stipulate a (repeated) probationary period, since such a period could only be agreed on by the conclusion of the employment contract, not in the case of a continuous legal relationship.[141]

It is also worth mentioning that Hungarian labour law does not recognize the legal instrument of *Änderungskündigung* – therefore, the rejection of the employer's offer to amend the employment contract does not lead to the termination of the employment relationship.

Nonetheless, unilateral commitments undertaken by the transferor could be unilaterally amended by the transferee even to the beneficiary's detriment or may be unilaterally terminated by the transferee with immediate effect in the case of a

138. *See* para. 36 of the judgment of 26 May 2005 held by the ECJ in case No. C-478/03. *Celtec Ltd v. John Astley and Others*. 'In those circumstances, the term "date of a transfer" in Article 3(1) of Directive 77/187 must be understood as referring to the date on which responsibility as employer for carrying on the business of the unit in question moves from the transferor to the transferee.'
139. *See* the decision of the Hungarian Supreme Court published under case No. BH2010. 280.
140. *See* the decision of the Hungarian Supreme Court published under case No. BH1996.506.
141. *See* the decision of the Hungarian Supreme Court published under case No. BH2009.90.

subsequent major change in the circumstances of the employer whereby carrying out the commitment is no longer possible or would result in an unreasonable hardship.[142]

[4] Trade Unions

A recent judgment also found that the collective agreements do not remain in force between the transferee and the trade union, as the obligation to maintain the work conditions set forth in the collective agreement for one year after the date of transfer does not mean that there would be a legal succession in the parts regulating the legal relationship only between the employer and the trade union (i.e., not the employees).[143]

[D] Critical Observations in Relation to the Hungarian Court Practice

In light of the above, Hungarian case law could be deemed more permissive (and employer-friendly) relating to the outsourcing of labour-intensive activities, and more conservative (and employee-friendly) when the economic operation is based on the use of fundamental tangible or intangible assets.

In other words, the outsourcing agreements are more welcomed in human resource-based sectors, where the change of the earlier workforce could make the application of the rules on transfer of business more difficult or even impossible. However, in sectors relying on human resources as much as fundamental assets, even the basics of this classification might be questionable and due to the fact-heavy character of the published Hungarian court decisions, it remains hardly predictable what direction will be followed by the labour courts in the course of a concrete lawsuit.

This interpretational uncertainty is enhanced by the acceptance of transfer of business without a direct contractual link between the transferor and the transferee, which could also result in 'surprise'scenarios.

Overall, the unknown results of a later judicial evaluation represent significant (transactional) risks for the transferors and the transferees, and also adversely influence the effective protection of employees' rights, for whom the precise determination of the employer is crucial – not only during the assignment or control of their daily work tasks but also when an employment dispute arises. Obviously, both cost efficiency and timeliness aspects require being fully informed on the proper counterparty of the employment litigation, not to mention the expiration of the time limitation period or other relevant deadlines.

If the transferor fails to inform the employees of the transfer of business (or the transfer of business is questionable for any other reason), it could easily happen that the employee files a statement of claim against the former employer only – especially since Hungarian procedural laws and regulations prohibit the apparent personal

142. *See* section 16 para. 2 of the Labour Code.
143. *See* the judgment of the Metropolitan Court of Appeal (in Hungarian: *Fővárosi Ítélőtábla*) published under case No. ÍH2022.35.

joinder of claims.[144] In these cases, the court could reject the employee's claim based on suing the wrong defendant by referring to the change in the person of the employer.

Arguably, the Hungarian legislator should consider specifying how the negative consequences arising from the above scenarios should be mitigated – at the minimum, in the case where transferor and the transferee failed to perform their information obligation toward the employees. Even if there are various exemptions from the general rule of the 'losing-party-pays-principle' concerning the litigation costs[145] and even if one may possibly refer to the suspension of the time limitation,[146] a separate regime could ensure the uniformity and foreseeability of the law enforcement mechanisms as well as the better safeguarding of employees' rights and interests in these uncertain legal succession situations. A fewer number of unnecessary litigations would also result in the reduction of the judicial caseload as well as the litigation costs incurred on the side of the parties.

§9.04 PRELIMINARY REFERENCE PROCEDURES

[A] Earlier Activism of Hungarian Courts in Relation to Preliminary Reference Procedures

Until the end of 2022, Hungarian courts initiated preliminary reference proceedings in 262 cases before the ECJ,[147] which is a significantly higher number than those of many other countries accessed to the European Union in the same year – such as the Czech Republic (104 cases), Slovakia (75 cases), Slovenia (165 cases), Latvia (96 cases) or Lithuania (110 cases).[148]

As regards the national judicial hierarchy, not only the Hungarian Supreme Court addressed preliminary questions to the ECJ (39 cases), but the lower courts also filed their requests for a preliminary ruling with the ECJ several times (223 cases).[149] The subject matter of the cases covered a broad spectrum of the application of EU law, including, but not limited to, employment law-related issues, tax law questions or interpretation of concepts arising from the EU competition law.

144. *See* section 173 para. 3 of the Act No. CXXX of 2016 on the Civil Procedure Code (hereinafter: 'Civil Procedure Code'), which sets forth that '[m]ultiple claims in an eventual or alternative relationship regarding the person of a party (apparent personal joinder of claims) cannot be lodged.'
145. *See, e.g.*, sections 84-93 of the Civil Procedure Code. Section 86 para. 2 of the Civil Procedure Code declares that '[t]he party, who [...] unnecessarily causes any costs forming part of the procedural costs for the counterparty in the course of or prior to the contentious procedure, is obliged to reimburse these costs irrespective of the outcome of the litigation.'
146. *See* section 286 para. 4 of the Labour Code that requires the application of the civil law rules to the time limitation unless otherwise provided for by the Labour Code. Section 6:24 para. 1 of the Act No. V of 2013 on the Civil Code enables the creditor to refer to the suspension of time limitation, if it is unable to enforce its claim for an excusable reason.
147. *See* the annual detailed statistics of the ECJ on the year of 2022. Online availability: https://curia.europa.eu/jcms/upload/docs/application/pdf/2023-03/stats_cour_2022_en.pdf (accessed 22 August 2025), p. 24.
148. *Ibid.*
149. *Ibid.*, p. 26.

Despite the relatively active Hungarian judicial approach regarding the initiation of preliminary reference procedures, only one case referred by Hungarian courts has required the interpretation of the Directive until now. However, the ECJ found the referral of the case No. C-244/22 *NQ v. Mara-Tóni Bt.* lodged on 6 April 2022 manifestly inadmissible because of the deficiencies of the request.[150]

[B] Pending Preliminary Reference Procedures Before the ECJ

Based on publicly available sources, there is no pending preliminary reference procedure initiated by Hungarian courts in which the ECJ is requested to interpret the Directive.

§9.05 CLOSING REMARKS

As a Member State of the European Union, Hungary fulfilled its obligation to implement the rules laid down in the Directive by adopting the Labour Code (Act No. I of 2012). The national transposition complements the provisions of the Directive with the joint and several liability of the transferor and the transferee and it also extends the automatic transfer of rights and obligations to the rights and obligations arising from study contracts and non-compete agreements. However, Hungarian labour law does not ensure the right to object on the side of the employees. Instead, it creates a preferential regime to unilaterally terminate their employment relationships upon a detrimental change in the person of the employer. Notably, the current Hungarian regulation releases the employers under liquidation procedure from nearly all obligations set out in the Directive, except for the information and consultation obligation laid down in Article 7 of the Directive. Nonetheless, special information obligations and other protective measures specified in other sources of law are applicable during liquidation procedures as well.

Overall, the national legislation seems to follow the rules of the Directive properly, but contains compromise solutions, if possible, to keep the employees' social security and the requirements of a flexible and employee-friendly market environment in balance.

The practice of Hungarian courts could be assessed as being compliant with the tendencies of ECJ case law. The published judgments are admittedly following the

150. The third and fourth questions referred by the Metropolitan Court affected the interpretation of the Directive: '3. In so far as, having regard to the foregoing, the applicant and the electricians should be classified as temporary agency workers, should it be considered that they form an economic unit, a specific group of workers who engage continuously in an economic activity for successive undertakings belonging to the same circle of persons, even though those undertakings lack State authorisation to engage lawfully, either as transferor or transferee, in the temporary transfer of workers as temporary-work agencies and also taking into account the fact that, in the case of temporary agency work, there is, in principle, no transfer of assets?

4.In so far as those workers are to be classified as an economic unit, as a specific group of workers, do they fall within the scope of Article 1(1) of Directive 2001/23/EC (2) although they are workers assigned by a temporary-work agency?'.

findings of the ECJ in defining the concept of economic unit retaining its identity, as well as the legal acts to be recognized as 'transfers' in the meaning of the Directive. The court decisions are also in accordance with the ECJ judgments when determining the date of transfer or accepting triangle acts as special forms of transfer of business. However, in view of the recent case law, the borders of the classification between labour-intensive activities and activities relying on tangible and intangible assets could be deemed quite vague and could only be assessed on a fact-heavy, case-by-case basis. In spite of this, Hungarian case law is employee-friendly in many aspects, especially in the case of outsourcing agreements affecting services that require the use of essential assets.

Nonetheless, neither the national legislation nor the case law prevents the parties from the uncertainties arising from or in connection with complex transactions. Whereas the controlling rights over the economic unit's assets could be taken over gradually or by way of a series of separate legal acts, it remains highly questionable when a (completed) transfer of business can be established. This uncertainty mirrors in several aspects of the employment disputes, such as the proper determination of the counterparty in a litigation case, the calculation of the deadlines, or the rights to be enforced.

CHAPTER 10

Ireland

Anthony Kerr

§10.01 INTRODUCTION

The legislative provisions governing 'transfer of undertakings' are now contained in the European Communities (Protection of Employees on Transfer of Undertakings) Regulations 2003[1] and section 21 of the Employees (Provision of Information and Consultation) Act 2006. The 2003 Regulations transpose the mandatory provisions of Directive 2001/23/EC (the Directive) and were subsequently amended by section 20(1) of the Protection of Employees (Temporary Agency Work) Act 2012,[2] sections 8 and 52 of the Workplace Relations Act 2015[3] and the European Communities (Seafarers) Regulations 2018.[4] Section 21 of the 2006 Act transposes one of the optional provisions of the Directive.[5]

The 2003 Regulations repeal and re-enact, with some significant amendments, the European Communities (Safeguarding of Employees' Rights on Transfer of Undertakings) Regulations 1980.[6] As their titles reflect, their purpose was and remains that of safeguarding and protecting employees' rights. Both the 1980 and the 2003 Regulations have generated considerable case law, including six High Court decisions. Neither of the Regulations, however, has been given detailed consideration by the Court of

1. S.I. No. 131 of 2003.
2. Amending regulation 8 concerning the information to be provided to employees' representatives.
3. Section 8 repealed regulations 12, 13 and 14. Section 52 substituted new regulations 10 and 11 to reflect the changes in the dispute resolution procedures effected by the 2015 Act, on which *see* Kerr, 'The Workplace Relations Reform Project' (2016) 7 *European Labour Law Journal* 125 https://doi.org/10.1177/201395251600700107 (accessed 22 August 2025), discussed further below.
4. S.I. No. 15 of 2018. These Regulations transpose Directive 2015/1794/EC.
5. Article 3(2) concerning the notification obligations of the transferor to the transferee.
6. S.I. No. 306 of 1980 (as amended by S.I. No. 487 of 2000) transposing Directive 77/187/EEC (as amended by Directive 98/50/EC).

Appeal or by the Supreme Court,[7] although the 1980 Regulations did feature in one case in the latter court.[8] None of the cases that have been decided have warranted the making of a preliminary reference to the Court of Justice.

Nevertheless, it is now clearly appreciated by employment and corporate lawyers that the Regulations have had, in the words of Barrington J., 'revolutionary implications for the relationship between employers and employees'.[9] Prior to the introduction of the 1980 Regulations, legislation provided that, on a transfer of a trade, business or undertaking, continuity of employment for the purpose of claiming those statutory rights depending on a period of continuous service (such as minimum notice, redundancy and unfair dismissal) was transferred where the transferee *agreed* to employ employees employed in the business before the transfer.[10] These provisions did not afford any protection for acquired contractual rights, nor did they apply to employees who were not kept on. The 1980 Regulations, however, obliged the transferee to enter into contracts of employment with all of the employees working in the undertaking or business at the time of the transfer, an obligation which 'flies in the face of the Common Law principles governing the creation of contracts of any kind'.[11]

The 2003 Regulations are stated to apply to 'any transfer of an undertaking, business, or part of an undertaking or business from one employer to another employer as a result of a legal transfer (including the assignment or forfeiture of a lease) or merger'.[12] The Regulations apply to 'public and private undertakings engaged in economic activities whether or not they are operating for gain'[13] but an 'administrative reorganisation of public administrative authorities or the transfer of administrative

7. This is due, in the case of the Court of Appeal, to decisions of the High Court on a point of law arising under the Regulations being 'final and conclusive' (*see* section 46 of the Workplace Relations Act 2015) and, consequently, no appeal lies to that court: *see Hosford v. Department of Employment Affairs and Social Protection* [2021] IECA 335. Leave to appeal to the Supreme Court will now only be granted if the High Court's decision involves a matter of 'general public importance' and/or 'the interests of justice' and that there are 'exceptional circumstances' warranting an appeal.
8. *Westman Holdings Ltd v. McCormack* [1992] 1 I.R. 151, discussed below.
9. *Mythen v. Employment Appeals Tribunal* [1990] 1 I.R. 98, 103. The applicant was represented by Mary Robinson SC – a future President of Ireland – and the case concerned whether the Employment Appeals Tribunal had jurisdiction to hear a complaint that an employee had been dismissed by reason of a transfer. Notwithstanding that the 1980 Regulations did not expressly confer jurisdiction on the Tribunal to hear such complaints, the High Court ruled that it did have jurisdiction. The case was subsequently settled with the transferee. In *Morris v. Smart Bros Ltd* UD 688/1993 (16 August 1994 and reproduced in Madden and Kerr, *Unfair Dismissal: Cases and Commentary* (IBEC: Dublin, 1996), at p. 146, the Employment Appeals Tribunal said that, in using the word 'revolutionary', Barrington J. did not 'understate the changes to law involved in the Directive'.
10. Section 20 of the Redundancy Payments Act 1967 (as amended by section 5 of the Redundancy Payments Act 1971) and para. 7 of the First Schedule to the Minimum Notice and Terms of Employment Act 1973 (as inserted by section 20 of the Unfair Dismissals Act 1977). The latter provision was considered by the High Court in *Nova Colour Graphic Supplies Ltd v. Employment Appeals Tribunal* [1987] I.R. 426 where Barron J. said that one of the 'vital' tests was 'whether the effect of the transaction was to put the transferee in possession of a going concern'.
11. *Per* the Employment Appeals Tribunal in *Morris, supra* n. 9.
12. Regulation 3(1).
13. Regulation 3(3).

functions between administrative authorities' is stated not to be a transfer for the purposes of the Regulations.[14]

The High Court has confirmed, after a thorough review of the decisions of the Court of Justice, that, in deciding whether there has been a transfer, all the circumstances must be looked at including:

(i) the type of undertaking or business in question;
(ii) whether tangible assets are transferred;
(iii) the value of the intangible assets;
(iv) whether the majority of the employees are taken on;
(v) whether the customers are transferred;
(vi) the degree of similarity between the activities carried on before and after the transfer; and
(vii) the period, if any, for which those activities were suspended.

These circumstances, however, are 'merely single features in the overall assessment which must be made and cannot therefore be considered in isolation'.[15]

Special provisions apply where the transferor is the subject of bankruptcy or insolvency proceedings.[16]

Nor do the Regulations apply to a transfer which consists exclusively of 'one or more seagoing vessels'[17] but, subject to that, the Regulations will apply to a transfer of a seagoing vessel 'that is part of a transfer of undertaking, business, or part of an undertaking or business within the meaning of this Regulation, if the transferee is situated, or the transferred undertaking, business, or part of an undertaking or business remains within the territorial scope of the Treaty'.[18]

The Regulations also prohibit a dismissal, the grounds for which are the transfer of an undertaking or business, or part thereof,[19] and provide that the transferor's contractual rights and obligations 'existing on the date of a transfer' are transferred to the transferee.[20]

The Regulations, in addition, impose a broad obligation to inform, and a narrower obligation to consult with, employees' representatives on both the transferor and the transferee.[21]

---

14. Regulation 3(4). In *McNamara v. Brady* TU 36/2014 (4 December 2014), the Employment Appeals Tribunal ruled that the office of County Sheriff, established under the Court Officers Act 1945 and charged with the execution of certificates of tax liability, was not a 'public administrative authority'. *See also Minister for Employment Affairs and Social Protection v. Labour Court* [2019] IEHC 634, discussed below.
15. *Per* MacGrath J. in *Minister for Employment Affairs and Social Protection v. Labour Court* [2019] IEHC 634 at [16].
16. Regulation 6.
17. Regulation 3(6), inserted by regulation 5 of the European Communities (Seafarers) Regulations 2018 (S.I. No. 15 of 2018).
18. Regulation 3(5), inserted by regulation 5 of the European Communities (Seafarers) Regulations 2018 (S.I. No. 15 of 2018).
19. Regulation 5(1). Dismissals for 'economic, technical or organisational' reasons, however, are not prohibited: *see* regulation 5(2), discussed further below.
20. Regulation 4(1).
21. Regulation 8.

§10.02 DEFINITION OF A TRANSFER

The 1980 Regulations did not contain a definition of 'transfer', but regulation 3(2) of the 2003 Regulations, reflecting the language of Article of the Directive, defines the word as meaning 'the transfer of an economic entity which retains its identity' with 'economic entity' being defined as 'an organised grouping of resources which has the objective of pursuing an economic activity whether or not that activity is for profit or whether it is central or ancillary to another economic or administrative entity'.

This makes it clear that the Regulations only apply where there is a change in the legal identity of the employer; the Regulations are not engaged, for instance, where there is a transfer of control of the business or undertaking by means of a change in the ownership of the shares in a company.[22]

The case law under both the 1980 and the 2003 Regulations confirms that the main criterion in establishing whether a transfer has taken place is whether the undertaking or business, or part thereof, retains its identity after the transfer in the sense that 'the operation must be the same or similar to that which existed prior to the transfer'.[23] Consequently, the fact that the transferee carries on the same business in 'a more modern manner' or in 'refurbished premises' is irrelevant.[24] Similarly, the fact that the transferee added ladies' clothing and changed the style of the mens' clothing was not 'fundamental enough' to alter the identity of the business.[25]

An early case was *Guidon v. Harrington,*[26] where the claimant had been working in a SevenEleven outlet operated by her employer. On Friday, 14 June 1991, her employer transferred the lease of the premises to the lessor, who continued the business over the weekend with his own employees. When the claimant reported for work on Monday, 17 June 1991, she was told she no longer worked there. The Employment Appeals Tribunal, relying on the Court of Justice decision in Case 287/86, *Ny Mølle Kro,*[27] ruled that the reversion of the business to the lessor constituted a transfer within the meaning of the 1980 Regulations and that the respondent lessor had become the claimant's employer. Her dismissal was deemed to be unfair and compensation of GBP 3,811 was awarded.

The issue was also raised in *Westman Holdings Ltd v. McCormack.*[28] The worker defendants had been employed by AT Ltd as bar and restaurant staff in a licensed premises. That company occupied the premises on a lease which expired on 1 March 1991, on which date the business was taken over by the landlord for a number of weeks. On 5 April 1991, the business was sold to the plaintiff company. All of the

---

22. *See Bambury v. Tornier Orthopedics Ireland Ltd* ADJ-00037431 (25 November 2022).
23. *Per* the Employment Appeals Tribunal in *Bligh v. Stobart Ireland Driver Services Ltd* TU 29/2011 (reported at [2015] E.L.R. 32 at 39) referencing Case C-209/91, *Rask v. ISS Kantinesservice* [1992] E.C.R. 1-5755. *See also Morris, supra* n. 9, referencing Case 24/85, *Spijkers* [1986] E.C.R. 1119.
24. *See Walsh v. Denford Taverns Ltd* UD 436/1997 (reported at [1998] E.L.R. 315).
25. *See Morris, supra* n. 9.
26. UD 961/1991 (reported at [1992] E.L.R. 146).
27. [1987] E.C.R. 5465.
28. [1992] 1 I.R.151. A detailed account of this litigation can be found in Kerr 'The Involvement of the Courts' in Kerr ed., *The Industrial Relations Act 1990: 20 Years On* (Round Hall: Dublin, 2010) pp. 98-101.

employees were dismissed, but all, with the exception of the six worker defendants, were immediately re-employed by the plaintiff. Those workers, whose claims through their trade union to continue in employment pursuant to the 1980 Regulations had been rejected, then placed an official peaceful picket on the premises. The plaintiff company then sought and was granted a temporary injunction, pending the trial of the action, restraining the picketing. The Supreme Court were satisfied that there was a 'fair bona fide' question, notwithstanding the decision of the Court of Justice in Case 324/86, *Daddy's Dance Hall*,[29] as to whether the Regulations applied. This was critical as workers are generally only entitled to picket the premises of their employer and the company contended that it was not their employer. The trial of the action took place some eleven months after the Supreme Court's decision, where it was eventually conceded that a transfer had taken place. As all of the worker defendants had either secured alternative employment or had emigrated, a sum approximating their estimated loss of earnings was paid as damages, together with the costs of the legal proceedings.

Outsourcing

The issue of whether the outsourcing of services such as catering, cleaning or security could constitute a transfer first arose in *Bannon v. Employment Appeals Tribunal*.[30] Here, the applicant had been employed as a security guard by a company which was responsible for the cleaning of a shopping centre, the control of car parking and the provision of security services. The company decided to have the security services carried out by an outside security firm on a contract basis and dismissed all five of its security staff, including the applicant, on grounds of redundancy. The contractor provided the same security duties for the same persons – the tenants of the shopping sector – and employed the same number of security guards, including one of the applicant's four former colleagues.

The majority of the Employment Appeals Tribunal were of the opinion that the outsourcing of the security services did not constitute a transfer of an undertaking or business, or part thereof, but the High Court held that the Tribunal was in error in so concluding. Blayney J. said that it was clear from the case law of the Court of Justice[31] that 'where there has been a legal transfer of a business or part of a business – and I am satisfied that there has been such a transfer in the instant case – the Directive is applicable if the business retains its identity or if there is a change in the legal or natural person who is responsible for carrying on the business regardless of whether or not

29. [1988] E.C.R. 739. *See*, more recently, *An Clochan Liath Pub Ltd v. Doyle* UDD1943 (1 August 2019).
30. [1993] 1 I.R. 500. The Employment Appeals Tribunal came to a similar decision when Dublin Corporation outsourced its dog warden service: *see Gray v. Irish Society for the Prevention of Cruelty to Animals* UD 509/1994 (reported at [1994] E.L.R. 225). The Tribunal's decision was upheld by Judge Esmond Smyth in the Circuit Court on 22 June 1995 but the remedy was varied from reinstatement to an award of GBP 15,000 in compensation. *See also Roche v. Salthill Hotel Ltd* UD 35/1995 (reported at [1996] E.L.R. 15).
31. Case 24/85, *Spijkers* [1986] E.C.R. 1119 and Case 287/86, *Ny Mølle Kro* [1987] E.C.R. 5465.

ownership of the business is transferred'. Consequently, the applicant's dismissal was prohibited by the 1980 Regulations.

Following the decision of the Court of Justice in Case C-13/95, *Süzen*,[32] the Employment Appeals Tribunal appeared receptive to the suggestion that the law had changed since the High Court decision in *Bannon*. So, in *Cannon v. Noonan Cleaning Co Ltd*,[33] the alleged transferee submitted that where a contract is withdrawn from one contractor at the end of the contract period and the contract is then awarded to another contractor, and neither the assets of the undertaking pass nor the workforce (or part thereof) are taken on, then there is no transfer of an undertaking or business, or part thereof. The Employment Appeals Tribunal were satisfied that there was no need for a direct contractual relationship to exist between the former and the new cleaning contractor for the Directive and the 1980 Regulations to apply.[34] The Tribunal, however, felt constrained by the Court of Justice's decision to rule that the change in contractor – sometimes referred to as a 'second generation' transfer – did not come within the scope of the 1980 Regulations. The Tribunal expressed its concerns as follows:

> There is no doubt that in a service undertaking the workforce and its expertise constitute a major aspect of the undertaking but it is difficult to understand how, where an employer refuses to take on the workers of the previous contractor, he can escape the rigours of the Directive while a contractor who takes on a major part of the workforce, perhaps out of magnanimity, will be caught by it. It would seem that the Directive, in the former instance, has not addressed the mischief in the law that it was intended to do. The sensible course for a transferee to take then is to refuse to employ any of the workforce of the transferor in such a situation.[35]

Similar submissions were made by the alleged transferee in *Power v. St Paul's Nursing Home*.[36] Here, however, the decision in *Cannon* was distinguished because there was a transfer of tangible assets.

Subsequently, in *Momentum Support Services (Ireland) Ltd v. Thomas*,[37] the Employment Appeals Tribunal were satisfied that, if the evidence established that the reason for not taking on the previous contractor's workforce was a deliberate avoidance measure, the Regulations could still apply.

It is also well established that there is no requirement that the transferred assets be owned by either the former contractor or the new contractor. It is sufficient that the

32. [1997] E.C.R. 1-1259.
33. UD 200/1997 (reported at [1998] E.L.R. 153).
34. *See also* the earlier decision of the Tribunal in *Cunningham v. Oasis Stores Ltd* UD 717/1994 (reported at [1995] E.L.R. 183 at 186).
35. Concerns reiterated by the Labour Court in *Department of Social Protection v. Dunne* TUD174 (reported at [2017] E.L.R. 285 at 295). *See also* the comments of an adjudication officer in *Contract Catering Staff v. Respondent A – Caterer/Service Provider* ADJ-00025549 (28 April 2020) that to allow a decision not to transfer employees to be a positive test in favour of the incoming contractor 'would be such as to defeat the entire purpose of the EU Directive' and would reward 'chicanery'.
36. UD 611/1997 (reported at [1998] E.L.R. 212). It should be noted that this was a 'first generation' transfer.
37. TU 20/2011 (15 February 2017).

transferred assets belong to a third party, where they are used as part of the contract.[38] Nor is there any requirement that the undertaking be owned by either of the contractors, provided that the transfer is embodied in a contract and that the contract transfers from one natural or legal person to another who takes on the function of employer.[39]

Neither of these two points was taken on board by the Employment Appeals Tribunal in *Electric Skyline Ltd v. Mullen.*[40] Here, the company was awarded contracts for public lighting with local authorities following a tendering process under which the previous contractor was unsuccessful. None of the workforce was taken on by the company. At first instance, a rights commissioner found that a transfer had taken place, but, on appeal, the Employment Appeals Tribunal overturned that decision. The submission that the 32,272 public lights were the relevant tangible assets was dismissed on the basis that those assets remained the property of the local authority. The decision was appealed on a point of law to the High Court but was settled prior to the hearing.

In contrast, the Labour Court had little difficulty in holding that a change in the operators in a multi-storey carparking complex constituted a transfer.[41] Both operators provided the same service of providing carparking facilities to the paying public and utilised 'the same substantial and fixed essential assets', namely the carpark building, ticket payment machines and barriers.

Distinction Between Labour-Intensive and Asset-Reliant Undertakings

Although the decision of the Court of Justice in *Süzen* has given rise to the concepts of 'first' and 'second generation transfers' - and, indeed, 'third generation transfers' where the outsourced service is taken back 'in-house'[42] - a more fundamental distinction was drawn, namely undertakings or businesses which were 'labour-intensive' and those that were 'asset-reliant'.[43]

An organised grouping of workers who are specifically and permanently assigned to a common task at stipulated locations - such as security guards assigned to the offices of the Chief State Solicitor - can amount to an 'economic entity' even in the absence of a transfer of assets.[44]

There have been a number of cases where the issue concerned the extent or nature of the transferred assets. In *Department of Social Protection v. Dunne,*[45] the

38. *See Bligh, supra* n. 23, where the Employment Appeals Tribunal referenced, *inter alia,* Case C-340/01, *Abler v. Sodexho & Co* [2003] E.C.R. 1-14023. *See also Department of Social Protection v. Dunne* TUD174 (reported at [2017] E.L.R. 285 at 295) also referencing *Abler.*
39. *Bligh, supra* n. 23.
40. TU 67/2012 (reported at [2017] E.L.R. 91).
41. *Euro Car Parks (Ireland) Ltd v. Kelly* TUD1810 (18 May 2018).
42. Such as occurred in *Cork County Council v. Jones* TUD223 (24 June 2022) and in *Dublin City Council v. Williamson* TUD2210 (21 December 2022).
43. As acknowledged by the Labour Court in *Overpass Ltd v. Lavin* TUD179 (9 October 2017).
44. *See Mythen v. Top Security Ltd* TU 31/2014. The decision of the Employment Appeals Tribunal was upheld on appeal to the High Court *sub nom. Top Security Ltd v. Sadlier* [2017] IEHC 134.
45. TUD174 (reported at [2017] E.L.R. 285). *See also Carroll v. Young* TUD222 (7 June 2022), which concerned the transfer of a post office's business.

claimant had been employed by Ms H, who had a contract with the Department to run a branch office. When Ms H retired, the Department decided to close that office and relocate the services provided by Ms H to a new Intreo office in the same town. The claimant was not offered employment with the Department and Ms H declined to pay statutory redundancy as she was of the opinion that the closure of her office and the transfer of its functions gave rise to a situation where the 2003 Regulations would apply.

The claimant's case was that the services provided by Ms H prior to her retirement were thereafter provided by the Department through its Intreo office. That was not disputed by the Department, albeit that it contended that because those services were integrated into a broader suite of services, the continuation in the provision of those services could not be regarded as giving rise to a transfer within the meaning of the 2003 Regulations.

The Labour Court was satisfied that 'significant tangible assets' essential to the performance of the branch office - namely, the data of the recipients of the relevant social welfare schemes - reverted fully into the Department's control following the closure of the branch office. Moreover, the Court noted that 'those data subjects, whose social welfare entitlements were administered through the branch office up to the date of its closure, continued to have those same entitlements administered on their behalf by the Intreo office thereafter'. The fact that the relevant files and data were at all times the property of the Department could not preclude the existence of a transfer within the meaning of the 2003 Regulations.

The Department appealed to the High Court and submitted that the Labour Court had erred in law in three respects:

(i) in finding that the activities of the branch office constituted an 'economic entity' for the purposes of the Regulations;
(ii) in finding that the branch office had retained its identity when it was integrated into the Intreo office; and
(iii) in failing to have regard to regulation 3(4).

MacGrath J. was satisfied that, on the facts as found by the Labour Court, that Court was entitled to come to its conclusions both that the activities of the branch office did constitute an 'economic entity' and that the office had retained its identity.[46] He declined to entertain the third ground of appeal on the basis that the issue of whether this was an 'administrative reorganisation of public administrative authorities' had not been raised in the Labour Court. He pointed out, however, that the Court of Justice decision in Case C-175/99, *Mayeur*[47] was 'clearly authority for the proposition that the transfer of an economic activity from a person governed by private law to a legal person governed by public law does in principle fall within the scope of the Directive'.

46. *Minister for Employment Affairs and Social Protection v. Labour Court* [2019] IEHC 634.
47. [2000] E.C.R. 1-7735.

In contrast to this case, no transfer was found to have taken place in *Cork County Council v. Jones,*[48] which concerned the decision of the Council to take in-house a traffic warden service when the outsourced contract to provide that service came to an end. The Labour Court rejected the claim that the employee's contract continued with the Council. The Court noted that none of the assets used by the employer to execute its contract with the Council - including vans, cleaning equipment, collection of cash equipment, handheld parking ticket machines and uniforms - were transferred and, indeed, the employer continued to operate as a going concern. The Court was satisfied that the loss of the parking maintenance contract was not a transfer of an economic entity 'because the mere contract simpliciter does not constitute a sufficiently structured and autonomous entity capable of equating to an economic entity'.

Multiple Transferees

As noted by the Court of Justice in Case C-344/18, *ISS Facility Services NV v. Govaerts,*[49] the Directive does not envisage a situation where a transfer involves a number of transferees. An example is provided by the decision of the Employment Appeals Tribunal in *Morris v. Smart Bros Ltd.*[50] The company operated eight retail clothes outlets and a head office, but ran into major trading difficulties. The directors decided that there should be an orderly run-down of trading activities rather than putting the company into liquidation. Accordingly, four of the outlets were taken over by companies formed by two of the company's directors and a senior manager. Others were sold, or the lease surrendered. The head office was also sold. All the employees were made redundant and some, including one who worked in the company's head office looking after the outlets' accounts, instituted claims of unfair dismissal based on an alleged transfer of an undertaking or business, or part thereof.

The Tribunal were satisfied that the company's business 'as a whole' did not retain its identity. Consequently, the head office manageress's claim failed as her work related to the business as a whole and there was no transfer relevant to her.[51] Given that the Tribunal found that the parts of the business carried on at three of the outlets all retained their identities and were the subject of transfers within the meaning of the Directive, consideration would now have to be given to whether her rights could be transferred to each of the transferees in proportion to the tasks performed.[52]

48. TUD223 (24 June 2022). *See* to similar effect the earlier decision of the Employment Appeals Tribunal in *Dignan v. Sheehan Security Corp Ltd* UD 235/2003 (reported at [2005] E.L.R. 2220).
49. ECLI:EU:C:2020:239.
50. UD 688/1993 (16 August 1994).
51. *See also Cunningham v. Oasis Stores Ltd, supra* n. 34, where the Employment Appeals Tribunal held that, where employees carried out administrative duties for the benefit of the transferred part of the business, but where the department in which they worked was not transferred, such employees were not within the scope of the 1980 Regulations.
52. For the difficulties involved in such an exercise, *see* the decision of the Northern Ireland Court of Appeal in *Hassard v. McGrath* [1996] N.I. 586.

§10.03 CONSEQUENCES OF A TRANSFER

Regulation 4(1) of the 2003 Regulations, reflecting the language used in Article 3(1) of the Directive, provides that the transferor's rights and obligations arising from a contract of employment existing on the date of transfer[53] shall, by reason of such transfer, be transferred to the transferee. Regulation 4(3), however, provides that, subject to paragraph (4), this Regulation shall not apply 'in relation to employees' rights to old-age, invalidity or survivors' benefits under supplementary or inter-company pension schemes that do not fall within the Social Welfare Acts'.[54]

Section 46 of the National Minimum Wage Act 2000 specifically provides that, without prejudice to the generality of the Regulations, on the transfer of an undertaking 'the transferee shall become liable to an employee in the undertaking to whom this Act applies in respect of any matter under this Act, in the same manner and to the same extent as the transferor immediately before the transfer, as if the transferee had originally entered into the relevant contract of employment or other agreement with the employee'.[55]

In *O'Donovan v. Ryanair Ltd*,[56] the claimant contended that, when his employment transferred from Ryanair to Servisair, substantial changes were made to his terms and conditions of employment in contravention of the 1980 Regulations. One of his complaints was that he no longer enjoyed the travel concessions previously provided; another was the method by which his remuneration was calculated. The evidence of Ryanair was that the travel concessions were discretionary, and not a contractual entitlement, and could be varied or withdrawn at any time. The evidence of Servisair was that the claimant was in fact financially better off under the new pay calculation methods which it had introduced. This evidence was accepted by the Employment Appeals Tribunal and the complaint was dismissed.

To what extent can a transferee rely on a 'variation clause' in the contract of employment of a transferred employee to alter his or her terms or conditions of employment after the transfer?

53. As to which, *see A café worker v. A café* ADJ-00019246 (19 March 2020) referencing Case C-478/03, *Celtec Ltd v. Astley* [2005] E.C.R. 1-4389.
54. Regulation 4(4)(a) provides that the interests of employees and of persons no longer employed in the transferor's business at the time of transfer in respect of rights conferring on them immediate or prospective entitlement to old-age benefits, including survivors' benefits, under a supplementary company pension scheme that is an occupational pension scheme within the meaning of the Pensions Acts 1990 to 2018 are protected under those Acts. Regulation 4(4)(b) then provides that the transferee shall ensure that the interests of employees and of persons no longer employed in the transferor's business at the time of the transfer in respect of rights conferring on them immediate or prospective entitlement to old-age benefits, including survivors' benefits, under a supplementary company pension scheme, *other than a supplementary pension scheme that is an occupational pension scheme within the meaning of the Pensions Acts 1990 to 2018*, are protected.
55. Note that the definition of 'contract of employment' in the National Minimum Wage Act 2000 is wider than that in regulation 2(1) of the 2003 Regulations as it includes not just contracts of service but also contracts 'whereby an individual agrees with another person to do or perform personally any work or service for that person'.
56. UD 465/1995 (reported at [1997] E.L.R. 63).

In *Farrell v. Bidvest Noon (ROI) Ltd*,[57] the claimant's contract of employment with the transferor stated that he was employed as a 'Parking Host' and set out his duties. The contract also contained a clause which provided that it might be necessary to 'expand' his duties within the 'general scope' of his position or 'change' his function. The clause further provided that the transferor reserved the right to assign other duties to the claimant, which right was subject to the express qualification that he would not be assigned duties which he could not 'reasonably perform'.

Following the transfer, the transferee insisted that the claimant take up the duties of a security guard. This was a role that the claimant could not perform as he did not hold the requisite licence from the Private Security Authority (PSA). He submitted a complaint contending that the variation clause was not open-ended and required consideration of the extent of the variation, bearing in mind that he could not perform the duties of a security guard as he did not hold a PSA licence.

The adjudication officer agreed and ruled that the transferee was in breach of the Regulations. She held that the variation clause did not provide the transferee with the scope to expand the claimant's role to such an extent as to fundamentally alter his terms and conditions of employment.

Section 21(3) of the Employees (Provision of Information and Consultation) Act 2006 requires the transferor to notify the transferee of all the rights and obligations, arising from a contract of employment existing on the date of a transfer, which will be transferred to the transferee, 'so far as those rights and obligations are, or ought to have been, known to the transferor at the time of transfer'. A failure by the transferor to notify the transferee of that right or obligation does not affect the transfer of that right or obligation or the rights of any employee against the transferee in respect of that right or obligation.[58] If a transferee is required to pay compensation to an employee because of the failure of the transferor to provide the necessary information, the transferee has a right of action to recover some or all of the amount paid in compensation from the transferor.[59]

Collective Agreements

Regulation 4(2) provides that, following a transfer, the transferee shall continue to observe the terms and conditions agreed in any collective agreement on the same terms applicable to the transferor under that agreement until the date of termination or expiry of the collective agreement or the entry into force or application of another collective agreement. This paragraph imposes no time limit on the continuance of collectively agreed terms.[60]

So, in *Reilly v. Wedding List Solutions Ltd*,[61] a 2003 collective agreement provided for enhanced severance payments in the event of redundancy. The claimant transferred

57. ADJ-00026709 (27 January 2023). *See also* the comments of the adjudication officer in *Warszewska v. Luxury Reservations Ltd* ADJ-00030068 (12 January 2022).
58. Section 21(4) of the Employees (Provision of Information and Consultation) Act 2006.
59. Section 21(5)-(7) of the Employees (Provision of Information and Consultation) Act 2006.
60. *See O'Regan v. CBRE GWS (Ireland) Ltd* ADJ-00033568 (4 January 2023).
61. ADJ-00033560 (1 June 2022).

from the employer to the respondent company in 2008 and was subsequently made redundant in 2020. Because she was only paid her statutory entitlements, she sought an order that the company observe the terms of the 2003 collective agreement. In upholding the complaint and granting the relief sought, the adjudication officer noted that Article 3(3) of the Directive permitted the Member States to limit the period for observing collectively agreed terms and conditions.

In *Bligh v. Stobart Ireland Driver Services Ltd,*[62] the Employment Appeals Tribunal upheld the complaints of 18 transferred employees that the transferee was in breach of regulation 4(2) in that the collective agreement with the transferor requiring, *inter alia*, that matters affecting terms and conditions of employment were to be subject to consultation and agreement had not been honoured.

§10.04 REFUSAL TO TRANSFER

Neither the 1980 nor the 2003 Regulations expressly address the situation where an employee objects to the transfer of his or her contract of employment. It has been considered, however, by the High Court in *Symantec Ltd v. Leddy and Lyons.*[63] The company transferred part of its business, but two employees affected by the transfer objected. They were advised that a failure to transfer would be regarded as a resignation from their positions. The Employment Appeals Tribunal found that they had been dismissed by reason of redundancy, but, on appeal, Edwards J. held that, if an employee decided not to transfer, a situation of redundancy did not automatically arise. He added that if the legislature had intended the employment relationship with the transferor to continue so as to facilitate the employee in making a complaint for redundancy pay, it would have enacted legislation to that effect.

The decision of Edwards J. was followed by the Employment Appeals Tribunal in *Norton v. Securway At Risk Security Group Ltd*[64] and by the Labour Court in *Ardcollum Motor Factors Ltd v. McManus.*[65] Similarly, an adjudication officer, in *Stokes v. Celtic Linen Ltd,*[66] held that the claimant's refusal to transfer amounted to a resignation.

§10.05 DISMISSALS

Regulation 5(1) of the 2003 Regulations provides that the transfer of an undertaking, business or part of an undertaking or business 'shall not in itself constitute grounds for dismissal by the transferor or the transferee and such a dismissal, the grounds for which are such a transfer, by a transferor or a transferee is prohibited'. This, however, is qualified by regulation 5(2), which provides that nothing in this Regulation 'shall be construed as prohibiting dismissals for economic, technical or organisational reasons which entail changes in the workforce'. If a contract of employment is terminated

62. TU 29-46/2011 (reported at [2014] E.L.R. 32).
63. [2009] IEHC 256; [2010] 1 I.L.R.M. 112.
64. UD 865/2015 (9 March 2016).
65. RPD1714 (10 November 2017).
66. ADJ-00042805 (23 January 2023).

because the transfer 'involves a substantial change in working conditions to the detriment of the employee', regulation 5(3) provides that 'the employer concerned shall be regarded as having been responsible for the termination of the contract'.[67]

Although the precise scope of these provisions has not been explored in any detail, it seems to be accepted that a genuine redundancy[68] will be regarded as falling within the scope of regulation 5(2). So, in the early case of *Purcell and McHugh v. Bewley's Manufacturing Ltd and Felwood Manufacturing Ltd*,[69] the appellants had been employed by BM until the business ran into difficulties in June 1988. They were dismissed by BM on 15 July 1988 and received a redundancy payment; meanwhile, BM decided to subcontract the part of the business in which the appellants had been employed to FM with effect from 18 July 1988. It was not disputed that what had been done by BM was now being done by FM, but the Employment Appeals Tribunal found that a genuine redundancy situation existed and dismissed the complaints against both respondents.

On appeal to the Circuit Court, Judge O'Malley affirmed the decisions of the Tribunal on the basis that the transfer took place after the termination of the appellants' employment. The judge went on to say that even if the transfer had taken place before their dismissals, he was satisfied that the whole operation by BM 'was done for the purpose of shedding an uneconomic operation and saving money'. If the transfer was part of this operation 'and the dismissals were part of this, it was done for sound economic, technical and organisational reasons'. In coming to this decision, the judge was clearly influenced by the fact that the appellants' redundancies were arrived at after negotiations with BM in which they were represented by their trade union.

Notwithstanding that a transfer had taken place of one of the eight outlets, the Employment Appeals Tribunal, in *Morris v. Smart Bros Ltd*,[70] held that the claimant,

---

67. Implementing Article 4(2) of the Directive.
68. Section 7(2) of the Redundancy Payments Act 1967 (as amended by section 4 of the Redundancy Payments Act 1971 and section 5 of the Redundancy Payments Act 2003) provides that an employee who is dismissed shall be taken to be dismissed by reason of redundancy if, for one or more reasons not related to the employee concerned, the dismissal is attributable wholly or mainly to:
    (a) the fact that his or her employer has ceased, or intends to cease, to carry on the business for the purposes of which the employee was employed, or has ceased, or intends to cease, to carry on that business in the place where the employee was so employed;
    (b) the fact that the requirements of that business for employees to carry out work of a particular kind in the place where he or she was so employed have ceased or diminished or are expected to cease or diminish;
    (c) the fact that his or her employer has decided to carry on the business with fewer or no employees, whether by requiring the work for which the employee had been doing to be done by other employees or otherwise;
    (d) the fact that his or her employer has decided that the work which the employee had been doing should henceforward be done in a different manner for which the employee is not sufficiently qualified or trained; or
    (e) the fact that his or her employer has decided that the work which the employee had been doing should henceforward be done by a person who is also capable of doing other work for which the employee is not sufficiently qualified or trained.
69. [1990] E.L.R. 68 (on appeal from UD 701/1988 and UD 1005/1988).
70. *Supra* n. 9.

who had worked there for many years, had been dismissed by reason of redundancy. That dismissal, however, had been effected by the transferor a few days before the transfer took effect.

The question of whether an employee who had received and retained a redundancy payment from the transferor was estopped from seeking to assert his or her entitlements under the Regulations arose in *Brett v. Niall Collins Ltd and Oyster Investments Ltd.*[71] Here, the claimants' employer (NC) ran into serious financial difficulties in March 1994 and a receiver was appointed by a debenture holder. The receiver negotiated a contract to sell the premises, equipment and goodwill of the company to OI, which contract was signed on the 29 March. The previous day, all of the employees had been dismissed by the receiver and were paid their statutory redundancy entitlements. Twenty-three of the 50 employees, including the general manager and the production manager, were then taken on by OI. The six claimants contended that they had been unfairly dismissed by reason of the transfer.

NC and OI, who were separately represented, both submitted that there had not been a transfer within the meaning of the 1980 Regulations, but OI submitted, in addition, that the claimants were estopped by reason of paragraph 7 of the First Schedule to the Minimum Notice and Terms of Employment Act 1973.[72] This provides that, where the whole or part of a trade, business or undertaking was or is transferred to another person, the service of an employee before the transfer in the trade, business or undertaking, or the part thereof so transferred:

(a) shall be reckoned as part of the service of the employee with the transferee; and
(b) the transfer shall not operate to break the continuity of the service of the employee,

unless the employee received and retained redundancy payment from the transferor at the time of and by reason of the transfer.

The Employment Appeals Tribunal said that 'there is no question but that the company was sold as a going concern' and that the 'only element of the company which was not included in the sale was the staff'. The receiver's evidence was that the reason for doing so was that the business was only 'saleable without the statutory liabilities that the workforce attracted'. The Tribunal had little difficulty in finding that a transfer had taken place but, of more significance, was its ruling that regulation 5(2) could have application 'only to the position of the workforce after the transfer'.

The Tribunal noted that paragraph 7 'appears to run contrary to the provisions of the Directive in so far as it purports to allow for the break in continuity of service if the employee receives and retains a redundancy payment from the transferor'. In this case, however, the dismissals by the receiver were 'null and void and of no effect' by reason of regulation 5 of the 1980 Regulations. Because redundancy requires a dismissal, the

71. UD 929/1994 (reported at [1995] E.L.R. 69).
72. Inserted by section 15 of the Unfair Dismissals (Amendment) Act 1993.

payments made to the claimants could not have been redundancy payments, as no dismissals had taken place.

§10.06 BANKRUPTCY AND INSOLVENCY

Regulation 6(1) of the 2003 Regulations provides that regulations 3 and 4 do not apply to any transfer of an undertaking, business or part of an undertaking or business 'where the transferor is the subject of bankruptcy proceedings or insolvency proceedings'.[73] Regulation 6(3) then provides that if the sole or main reason for the institution of bankruptcy or insolvency proceedings is 'the evasion of an employer's legal obligations under the Regulations', the Regulations, notwithstanding paragraph (1), will apply to a transfer effected by that transferor.[74]

This Regulation, and the case law thereon, makes it clear that regulations 3 and 4 do not apply to a transfer where the transferor has been adjudged insolvent and the undertaking or business, or part thereof, in question formed part of the assets of the insolvent transferor. Those regulations, however, still apply to transfers effected during procedures prior to the initiation of High Court winding-up proceedings, such as transfers effected by an examiner, a provisional liquidator or a receiver.[75]

Accordingly, the Employment Appeals Tribunal, in *Blaney v. Vanguard Plastics Ireland Ltd*,[76] ruled that the 1980 Regulations applied to the transfer of an undertaking or business 'unless the company involved is the subject of a compulsory court-ordered winding up and has been adjudged insolvent by a competent judicial authority'.

Given that the purpose of the Directive, and thus the Regulations, is 'to provide for the protection of employees in the event of a change of employer, in particular, to ensure that their rights are safeguarded',[77] this exclusion is clearly policy driven. This is apparent from the submissions made to the Court of Justice in Case 135/83, *Abels*.[78] Denmark submitted that those employees who most need protection are those whose employers are insolvent and, consequently, the Directive should apply to transfers effected during a company liquidation process. The Netherlands and the European Commission, however, submitted that potential purchasers might be deterred from buying up businesses which are insolvent, but which might be capable of rescue, if they were obliged to take on all of the employees. It was in the interests of the labour

73. The meaning of bankruptcy and insolvency proceedings is set out in regulation 6(2) and include proceedings where the transferor may be 'wound up' by the High Court under the Companies Act 2004 by reason of insolvency.
74. Regulation 6 is a new provision and transposes Article 5 of the Directive which, in turn, reflects the jurisprudence of the Court of Justice in cases such as Case 135/83, *Abels* [1985] E.C.R. 470.
75. *See Mythen, supra* n. 9 (referencing *Abels*) and *Brett, supra* n. 71.
76. UD 271/2000, upheld on appeal to the Circuit Court by Judge Linnane (22 May 2001).
77. Recital 3 of the Directive.
78. *Supra* n. 74. *Abels* and the subsequent case law of the Court of Justice, such as Case C-362/89, *d'Urso* [1992] E.C.R. 1-4105, are analysed in Davies 'The Transfer of Undertakings Directive: Current Problems and Future Solutions' in Kerr ed., *The Acquired Rights Directive* (Irish Centre for European Law: Dublin, 1996) pp. 17-20.

force as a whole that such rescue attempts should be made, even if some employees had to be let go.[79]

This tension was at the heart of the very first case involving the 1980 Regulations to come before the High Court.[80] An official liquidator was appointed by the High Court to Castle Brand Ltd, following its winding up in October 1984 on grounds of insolvency. The liquidator embarked on a campaign to sell the business, during the course of which concerns were raised as to the implications of the 1980 Regulations; in particular, as regards the pension fund, which was significantly in deficit. Because the liquidator could give no comfort in relation to the Regulations, no one was prepared to make an unconditional offer for the company's assets.

Following delivery, on 7 February 1985, of the Court of Justice decision in *Abels*, the liquidator decided to make an application to the High Court seeking directions under section 260 of the Companies Act 1963 in relation to the effect of the Regulations on the liquidation. In his *ex tempore* decision delivered on 25 March 1985, Hamilton P. ruled that the Regulations had no application in an insolvency liquidation and that a purchaser could acquire the company's assets without any liability to the employees in respect of pension or other matters. A contract for sale was then concluded in July 1985. It is not known as to how many of the company's 150 employees were taken on by the purchaser.

§10.07 INFORMATION AND CONSULTATION

Regulation 8(1) and (1A)[81] require both the transferor and the transferee to *inform* their respective employees' representatives[82] 'affected by the transfer' of:

(a) the date or proposed date of transfer;
(b) the reasons for the transfer;
(c) the legal implications of the transfer for the employees and a summary of any relevant economic and social implications of the transfer for them;
(d) any measures envisaged in relation to the employees;

79. A more nuanced explanation was provided by Rimer L.J. of the English Court of Appeal in *Kay2Law (Surrey) LLP v. De'Antiquis* [2012] I.R.L.R. 212. If the Directive applied to such transfers, potential purchasers of an insolvent company's business might be put off from acquiring it 'on terms acceptable to the transferor's creditors'. Accordingly, the protection of employees of insolvent companies was 'sacrificed' to the superior commercial interests of the transferor's creditors.
80. This account is taken from Cooney 'Statutory Instrument No. 306 Practical Applications: Company Liquidations' in Kerr ed., *Acquired Rights of Employees* (Irish Centre for European Law: Dublin, 1989) pp. 66-73.
81. Inserted by section 20(1) of the Protection of Employees (Temporary Agency Work) Act 2012.
82. Regulation 2(1) defines this term as a trade union, staff association or excepted body (within the meaning of the Trade Union Act 1941) 'with which it has been the practice of the employees' employer to conduct collective bargaining negotiations' or, in their absence, a person or persons chosen by such employees, under an arrangement put in place under regulation 7(2) or 8(5), from among their number to represent them in negotiations with the employer.

(e) the number of agency workers temporarily engaged in the undertaking concerned;
(f) those parts of the undertaking in which those agency workers are, for the time being, working; and
(g) the type of work those agency workers are engaged to do.

The transferor is required to give this information to the employees' representatives, 'where reasonably practicable, not later than 30 days before the transfer is carried out and, in any event, in good time before the transfer is carried out'.[83] The transferee is required to give this information, 'where reasonably practicable, not later than 30 days before the transfer is carried out and, in any event, in good time before the employees are directly affected by the transfer as regards their conditions of work and employment'.[84]

Regulation 8(4) then provides that where the transferor or the transferee 'envisages any measures in relation to employees', they must *consult* the employees' representatives, 'where reasonably practicable, not later than 30 days before the transfer is carried out and, in any event, in good time before the transfer is carried out, in relation to any such measures with a view to reaching an agreement'. It is unclear as to what measures are caught by this requirement. Would they include, for example, a change in the pay arrangements from fortnightly to monthly?[85] It is also unclear as to whether the transferee's obligation to consult continues after the date the transfer has been completed as regards measures now envisaged.

Regulation 8(7) provides that the obligations to inform and consult apply 'irrespective of whether the decision resulting in the transfer is taken by the employer or an undertaking controlling the employer and the fact that the information concerned was not provided to the employer by the undertaking controlling the employer shall not release the employer from those obligations'.

What if there are no employees' representatives in the undertaking or business of either the transferee or the transferor? In such a situation, regulation 8(5) requires the putting in place of a procedure 'whereby the employees may choose from among their number a person or persons to represent them (including by means of an election)'. In the event that there are still no employees' representatives, through no fault of the employees, each of the employees concerned must be informed in writing, where

83. Regulation 8(2). A breach of this paragraph resulted in an award of compensation of EUR 1,725 in *A Recruitment Consultant v. A Recruitment Consultancy* ADJ-00009846 (23 October 2018); of EUR 2,320 in *Philbin v. Reva Racing Ltd* ADJ-00025579 (2 July 2021); and of four weeks' pay in *Ruane v. Horan Eco Services Ltd* ADJ-00020780 (17 December 2021).
84. Regulation 8(3). A breach of this paragraph resulted in an award of compensation of EUR 1,740 in *Philbin v. Boylesports* ADJ-00025578 (2 July 2021) and of EUR 2,000 in *Callaghan v. Hcl* ADJ-00025666 (11 January 2022).
85. In *User Interface Designer v. Engineering Company* ADJ-00023612 (2 June 2020), the adjudication officer suggested that although the word 'measures' was not defined, it included 'any change affecting employees which is not trivial'. In *Warszewska v. Luxury Reservations Ltd* TUD225 (24 June 2022), however, the Labour Court appears to have taken the view that the obligation to inform did not apply to changes in 'operational practice'.

reasonably practicable, not later than 30 days before the transfer and, in any event, in good time before the transfer of:

(a) the date or proposed date of transfer;
(b) the reasons for the transfer;
(c) the legal implications of the transfer for the employee and a summary of any relevant economic or social implications for that employee; and
(d) any measures envisaged in relation to the employees.[86]

§10.08 ENFORCEMENT

Under the 2003 Regulations, as originally enacted, complaints were to be made in the first instance to the rights commissioner service of the Labour Relations Commission, with a full appeal on both fact and law to the Employment Appeals Tribunal. Following the enactment of the Workplace Relations Act 2015, complaints are now made, in the first instance, to adjudication officers of the Workplace Relations Commission with a full appeal to the Labour Court.[87]

Complaints must be made within six months of the alleged contravention unless the adjudication officer is satisfied that failure to make the complaint within that period was due to 'reasonable cause', in which case the period may be extended for up to a further six months.

If the adjudication officer decides that the complaint is 'well founded', he or she is empowered either to require the employer to comply with the relevant regulations and, for that purpose, to require the employer to take a specified course of action or to require the employer to pay to the employee compensation of such amount, if any, as the adjudication officer considers 'just and equitable in the circumstances'. That compensation, however, cannot exceed, in the case of a contravention of the information or consultation provisions of regulation 8, four weeks' pay. In all other cases, the compensation cannot exceed two years' remuneration.[88]

Although Article 3(1) of the Directive allows the Member States to provide that, after the date of transfer, 'the transferor and the transferee shall be jointly and severally liable in respect of obligations which arose before the date of transfer from a contract of employment or an employment relationship existing on the date of the transfer', Ireland has not availed of this option. Consequently, in light of regulation 4(1), any remedy for failure of the transferor to fulfil its obligations should be sought against the transferee.[89]

86. Regulation 8(6).
87. *See* regulations 10 and 11, as substituted by section 52 of the Workplace Relations Act 2015. There is then a further right of appeal, on a point of law only, to the High Court: *see* section 46 of the 2015 Act.
88. This is calculated in accordance with the Unfair Dismissals (Calculation of Weekly Remuneration) Regulations 1977 (S.I. No. 287 of 1977).
89. *See J Donoghue Beverages Ltd v. Collins* TUD183 (21 February 2018) and *Inboard Transport Co-ordinator v. Food production and distribution company* ADJ-00010599 (3 October 2018).

§10.09 CONCLUSION

The mandatory provisions of the Directive have been correctly transposed, subject to two caveats. The first relates to the cap on compensation that can be awarded for a breach of regulation 8. Although the cap of four weeks' pay is the same as that provided for, under section 11A of the Protection of Employment Act 1977,[90] in respect of an employer's failure to inform or consult in respect of collective redundancies, it is less than the 20 weeks' cap under the Maternity Protection Act 1994[91] and the Parental Leave Act 1998[92] and is considerably less than the two years' ceiling contained in most other employment protection legislation required by EU law.[93] A strong case could be made that the cap of four weeks' pay is insufficiently dissuasive as a matter of EU law.[94]

The second caveat concerns the scope of the Regulations. Article 2(1)(d) of the Directive defines 'employee' as meaning 'any person who, in the Member State concerned, is protected as an employee under national employment law'. The 2003 Regulations define an employee as a person who works (or worked) under a 'contract of employment', which, in turn, is defined as 'a contract of service or apprenticeship' or a contract through an employment agency. This reflects the definition of 'employee' in the Unfair Dismissals Acts 1977-2015. More recent legislation, however, provides a more expansive definition of 'employee' to include contracts under which an individual agrees with another person 'personally to execute any work or service for that person'.[95]

90. Inserted by section 52 of the Workplace Relations Act 2015. The 1977 Act transposes what is now Directive 98/59/EC. *See* Kerr 'Collective Dismissal in Ireland' in Cosio et al. (eds), *Collective Dismissal in the European Union: A Comparative Analysis* (Wolters Kluwer: The Netherlands, 2017) pp. 231-245.
91. Transposing Directive 92/85/EEC. *See* section 32 of the 1994 Act as substituted by section 52 of the Workplace Relations Act 2015.
92. Transposing what is now Directive 2010/18/EU. *See* section 21 of the 1998 Act as substituted by section 52 of the Workplace Relations Act 2015.
93. *See*, for instance, section 27 of the Organisation of Working Time Act 1997 (transposing what is now Directive 2003/88/EC) and section 14 of the Protection of Employees (Fixed-Term Work) Act 2003 (transposing Directive 99/70/EC).
94. Adjudication officers, and the Labour Court on appeal, have the power to disapply domestic legislation which is incompatible with EU law: *see* Case C-318/17, *Minister for Justice and Equality v. Workplace Relations Commission* ECLI:EU:C:2018:479.
95. *See* regulation 3(a)(i) of the European Union (Transparent and Predictable Working Conditions) Regulations 2022 (S.I. No. 686 of 2022) amending the definition in the Terms of Employment Act 1994 so as to comply with Directive 2019/1152/EU.

CHAPTER 11

Italy: The Transfer of Undertakings in Italy and in the Framework of European Union Law

Roberto Cosio, Filippo Curcuruto, Vincenzo Di Cerbo & Giovanni Mammone[*]

§11.01 GENERAL VIEW

The Italian legislator pays particular attention to the rights of workers when their employer transfers their company to another entrepreneur. In such cases, there is a greater risk that workers will lose some or all of their work credits accrued with the transferring entrepreneur. This is because the sale often takes place in situations where the transferring company is in a situation of economic crisis or even subject to bankruptcy proceedings. Furthermore, the case in which the transfer concerns only a part of the production structure of the company is the one given the greatest attention. In the latter case, it is the very scenario of the transfer of a branch of the company where the likelihood of actual fraud against the employees is greater.

The Italian Civil Code of 1942, which is still in force, regulates the transfer of a company in Article 2112 according to the general principle set out in Articles 2555 et seq. that the transferor and the transferee are jointly and severally liable for all debts of the transferred company. The regulation of the original text of Article 2112, however, has undergone numerous changes following the implementation of the European directives that have regulated the matter of the transfer of undertakings since 1977.[1]

* Section 11.04 written by Roberto Cosio, §11.03 written by Filippo Curcuruto, §11.02 written by Vincenzo Di Cerbo & §11.01 written by Giovanni Mammone.

1. For the theoretical configuration of the transfer of business by the Italian legal doctrine *see* F. Santoro Passarelli, *Fattispecie e interessi tutelati nel trasferimento di azienda e di ramo di azienda*, in *Rivista italiana di diritto del lavoro*, 2003, I, 189, and A. Maresca, *Le 'novità' del legislatore nazionale in materia di trasferimento d'azienda*, in *Argomenti di diritto del lavoro*, 2001, 587.

The implementation of these directives took place by means of the following legislative sources:

- Law No. 428 of 29 December 1990, Article 47 (which implements Directive 1977/187/EEC).
- Legislative Decree No. 18 of 2 February 2001 (implementing Directive 98/59/EC).
- Law No. 39 of 1 March 2002 (which implements Directive 2001/23/EC).
- Legislative Decree No. 276 of 10 September 2003, Article 32 (which provides for the general coordination of the aforementioned sources of law).
- Legislative Decree No. 251 of 6 October 2004, for which the transferring entrepreneur is required to pay the salary and social security contributions even in the event that the transfer takes place through the signing of a contract.
- Legislative Decree No. 165 of 30 March 2001, Article 31, which applies Article 2112 also in the case of transfer of activities within the public administration.[2]

With reference to the adopted terminology, it should be noted that Article 2112 and national law sources transposing European legislation are expressed in terms of 'transfer of concern', whereas the directive in a broader sense is expressed in terms of 'transfer of undertaking'. Both expressions are, however, considered equivalent both by doctrine and jurisprudence. In this introduction, this distinction is not held and we prefer to speak simply of the 'transfer of a company'.[3]

The direct transfer of employers pursuant to Article 2112 also applies in public employment, in cases of transfer of personnel employed by the public administration, and in the case of transfer of activities carried out by them to other public or private entities. In these cases, however, the law may regulate the methods of transfer differently.[4]

The factual situation governed by Article 2112, as amended by the above-quoted laws, is unchanged: the transfer of the company (by means of an onerous assignment) from one entrepreneur to another. In this case, the employment relationship of the workers of the alienating (transferor) entrepreneur continues with the receiving (transferee) entrepreneur and the workers retain all their rights. Moreover, both entrepreneurs (transferor and transferee) are jointly and severally obliged to honour the work credits that the workers had at the time of the transfer. Such a transfer of the

2. The path followed by the Italian legislator for the complete implementation of the European legislation on the transfer of business is described by R. Cosio, *Il trasferimento dell'impresa in crisi*, in R. Cosio and G. Vidiri (eds), *Il trasferimento d'impresa in Italia nel quadro del diritto dell'Unione europea*, Milano, 2019, 139, as well as by R. Romei, *La direttiva europea sul trasferimento di imprese. Profili generali*, 772, and by F. Amendola, *Le fonti e la giurisprudenza in materia di trasferimento di impresa nell'Unione europea*, 794, both in R. Cosio et al. (eds), *Il diritto del lavoro dell'Unione europea*, Milano, 2023.
3. *See* G. Mammone, *Introduzione*, in Cosio and Vidiri (eds), *Il trasferimento d'impresa*, *supra* n. 2, XIII.
4. Article 31 of Legislative Decree 30 March 2001 n. 165; *see* Amendola, *Le fonti e la giurisprudenza in materia di trasferimento di impresa nell'Unione europea*, *supra* n. 2, 799, as well as judgments Corte di cassazione 28 September 2018 n. 23618 and 6 June 2017 n. 13994.

company does not constitute grounds for dismissal.[5] However, the entrepreneur (both transferor and transferee) can withdraw from the employment relationship in accordance with the laws governing dismissal. The worker may withdraw from the employment relationship within three months if the new employer offers working conditions that are substantially different from the previous ones.

The position of workers is protected not only by Article 2112 of the Civil Code, which refers only to the individual relationships between the two entrepreneurs who carry out the sale and the employees of the company, but also by trade unions, thanks to the European legislation implemented by Italian law. The trade unions' consultation procedure was imposed by the European directives and implemented by Article 47 of the law of 29 December 1990 No. 428, which accepted (albeit belatedly) EEC directive 1977/187; the same procedure was perfected by Legislative Decree No. 18 of 2 February 2001, which implemented the EC 1998/50 Directive.[6]

Employee representatives have the right to be informed and consulted before any transfer of a company (or part of a company) in which more than 15 workers are employed. The transferor or the transferee (or both) must inform the workers' union representatives at least 25 days before the transfer agreement is implemented. The representatives may ask to discuss the reasons why the entrepreneurs have decided to transfer (through a joint examination of the situation), in order to reach an agreement with them, avoid the transfer or regulate its modalities.

Failure to reach the agreement does not, however, prevent the transfer. In fact, the trade union procedure is considered to be concluded 10 days after the start of the consultation, even if no agreement is reached with the workers' representatives, and the two entrepreneurs may proceed with the transfer of the company. The system essentially provides that the transfer of the company is not only the result of the agreement of two entrepreneurs (transferor and transferee) but also of the prior completion of a union consultation procedure.

Directive 2001/23 established the notion of company transfer in the sense that the transferred economic entity must remain unchanged and consists of an organized group of people and assets (patrimonial and otherwise) that allows the achievement of a specific economic purpose. On a general level, the Court of Cassation (the highest Italian court) has adapted to this definition, taking into account, of course, the clarifications made by the European Court of Justice.

In its judgment No. 12771 of 23 July 2012, the Court of Cassation held that there is a transfer of a company whenever the company organization remains unvaried and

5. With the formal transfer of the business, the employment relationship is transferred, and the transferring entrepreneur is no longer entitled to dismiss the worker of the transferred business. The dismissal is therefore null and void and the purchaser, who has become the employer, is required to compensate the damage suffered by the worker due to the unlawful dismissal; *see* Corte di cassazione, judgments 9 December 2024 n. 31551 and 5 February 2024 n. 3235, as well as G.M. Marsico, *Ancora in tema di trasferimento d'azienda: tra prosecuzione dell'attività, crisi d'impresa, continuità dei rapporti di lavoro e certezza dei rapporti giuridici*, in www.rivistalabor.it (accessed 22 August 2025), 16 June 2024.
6. *See* E. Boghetich and V. Di Cerbo, *Procedura di informazione e consultazione sindacale*, in Cosio and Vidiri (eds), *Il trasferimento d'impresa*, *supra* n. 2, 115.

there is a change of owner, regardless of the legal instrument adopted (sale, lease of the company, contract). It is therefore sufficient, for the purposes of applying the legislation protecting workers, that the new entrepreneur (transferee) continues to carry out business activities with the same productive facilities used by the previous entrepreneur (transferor).

With regard to the sale of only one part of the company, the Court of Cassation, in its judgment No. 7364 of 16 March 2021, stated that the transfer of a business branch occurs when a complex of assets with its own organizational and economic autonomy is sold, thanks to which the new entrepreneur can carry out an autonomous production activity of goods or services. It is essential, however, that this complex exists in its entirety prior to the transfer and can independently carry out its production activity of goods or services for an indistinct number of potential customers.[7]

In 2019, the CCIC, Company Crisis and Insolvency Code (Law 12 January 2019 No. 14, in force from 15 July 2022), was approved. It reformed the Italian legislation on the bankruptcy of commercial enterprises, repealing the law in force since 1942. The new law, taking into account European Union legislation, aims to avoid the dispersion of assets and professionalism of workers of companies in a liquidity crisis.[8]

The CCIC (Article 189) provides that the opening of the judicial liquidation procedure against the employer in difficulty is not a reason for dismissal and that the subordinate employment relationships remain only suspended. If, within four months, the company does not resume its operations, or the transfer of the undertaking or one of its branches has not occurred, the liquidation procedure administrator can dismiss the workers. The termination of the employment relationship constitutes an involuntary loss of employment and therefore the worker is recognized with the welfare treatment specifically provided for subordinate workers who have involuntarily lost their employment (Article 190).

Therefore, in the event that the transfer of the undertaking from one entrepreneur to another is concluded not by a direct agreement between the transferor and the transferee, but depends on a negotiation between the transferee and the bodies that regulate the judicial procedure of the crisis, the relationship of the employees of the transferred undertaking (or of a branch of it) will continue with the new employer and the workers themselves will maintain the rights previously acquired.[9]

The transfer of the undertaking (or a branch of it), however, can also take place with 'negotiated' methods, when the negotiations for the transfer involve not only the transferor, the transferee and the judicial bodies but also the workers' trade unions. In this case, the transfer of the company can take place with methods established by a collective agreement which, to safeguard the employment of workers, can ensure that

---

7. Other judgments on the transfer of the entire company: Corte di cassazione 7 December 2017 n. 29422 and 16 May 2013 n. 11918.
   Other judgments on the transfer of a branch: Corte di cassazione 4 August 2021 n. 22249 and 8 November 2018 n. 28593.
8. *See* A. Patti, *La tutela dall'insolvenza del datore di lavoro e le garanzie dei crediti dei lavoratori*, 900, in Cosio et al. (eds), *Il diritto del lavoro dell'Unione europea*, *supra* n. 2.
9. *See* Patti, *supra* n. 8, 928, as well as the judgments of Corte di cassazione 15 October 2010 n. 21278, 1 June 2020 n. 10414 and 9 June 2020 n. 11002.

the transfer of employment relationships to the transferee takes place with methods other than those provided for by Article 2112 of the Civil Code.[10]

The CCIC does not apply to the extraordinary administration procedures of large corporations, which are governed by specific legislation (Article 1). In 2017, a decree of the competent minister started the extraordinary administration procedure of the airline Alitalia SAI, a publicly controlled company. In 2020, a public company operating as a new national airline called ITA was established. Alitalia SAI transferred some of its assets to it, but the European Commission, with a decision of 10 September 2021,[11] considered that there was no economic continuity between the two companies.

Alitalia SAI transferred its passenger air transport operations (i.e., Aviation assets) to ITA. Although this activity was continued by the new company without interruption, only a part of Alitalia's workers operating in the sector were hired by ITA (of 6,650 employees in the Alitalia Aviation sector, ITA hired 2,235). At this point, many of the workers who were not hired asked the judge to apply Article 2112 of the Civil Code on the transfer of an undertaking since, in their opinion, the transfer (from Alitalia to ITA) of a branch of the business had taken place and, therefore, their employment relationships should have been automatically transferred to the transferee.

The workers summoned Alitalia SAI and ITA before the Rome and Milan Labour Courts. Two different jurisprudential positions arose, one in favour[12] and the other against the transfer of employment relationships,[13] given that there was a different opinion on whether there was business continuity between Alitalia SAI and ITA. The divergence of opinions primarily stemmed from differing interpretations of the law governing the extraordinary administration of large companies experiencing insolvency (Article 56, paragraph 3 bis, of Law No. 270 of 8 July 1999). Above all, it was relevant to note the difference between the concept of 'transfer' of the assets of the company in crisis and that one of 'transfer' of part of the same assets, considering Article 5, paragraph 1, of Directive 2001/23/EC and Article 47 of Law No. 428 of 1990.[14]

---

10. *See* Romei, *La direttiva europea sul trasferimento di imprese. Profili generali, supra* n. 2, 792.
11. *See* Commission decision 10 September 2021 C(2021) 6659 final. The decision responds to complaints filed in 2017 by some airlines that Italy had granted unauthorized State aid to Alitalia SAI in extraordinary administration. The European Commission concluded that the State loans were unlawful under EU State aid rules and that Italy must therefore recover the illegal State aid from Alitalia SAI, plus interest. At the same time, the Commission considered that ITA is not the economic successor of Alitalia and therefore is not liable for the reimbursement of the illegal State aid received by Alitalia SAI.
12. Trib. Lavoro Milano, 12 December 2023 and Trib. Lavoro Roma 26 July 2023. The basic argument used by these sentences is that the ITA company continued to carry out the activity of Alitalia SAI.
13. Trib. Lavoro Milano 1 June 2023 e Trib. Lavoro Roma 13 December 2023 say that the extraordinary administration procedure of Alitalia SAI had the sole purpose of liquidating its assets and not of allowing the continuation of its activity. Also Trib. Lavoro Milano 15 November 2022, Trib. Lavoro Milano 3 April 2023, Trib. Lavoro Milano 24 May 2023 deny in this case the transfer of the employment contracts, but on the basis of a different argument, namely that ITA has purchased only a part of Alitalia's assets and carries out a more limited activity.
14. *See* G. Cassano, Il caso Alitalia e il problema ancora aperto del trasferimento di ramo d'azienda, in www.lavorodirittieuropa.it (accessed 22 August 2025), 3/2023, as well as R. Bellè, *Turbolenze giuridiche Alitalia nella tratta Milano-Roma. Divergenze interpretative in tema di trasferimento*

The Italian legislator, to overcome the various problems raised by the judges' rulings, issued Law 29 September 2023, No. 131, 'interpretative' of Article 56, paragraph 3 bis of Law No. 270 of 1999. It stated that transfers based on a decision of the European Commission, excluding economic continuity between the transferor and the transferee, must be understood as 'made in view of the liquidation of the transferor's assets and do not constitute a transfer of a undertaking'. Thus interpreted, the law therefore excluded the transfer of the branch of the business and, consequently, the automatic transfer of all workers from Alitalia SAI to ITA.[15]

The above-quoted law, however, did not resolve the problems raised by the case law. In fact, the Labour Court of Rome, with an order of 18 June 2024,[16] raised the question of the constitutionality of Law No. 131 of 2023, holding that it does not limit itself to interpreting the law in force, but introduces a new provision: it would therefore have an 'innovative' and not 'interpretative' nature. Instead, it would be motivated exclusively by reasons of containment of public spending, given that ITA is a company with full public participation.

The Constitutional Court with ruling No. 99 of 8 July 2025 declared the question of constitutionality inadmissible. The Court, in fact, noted that the liquidation operations were carried out under the supervision of a public authority and were not aimed at recovering and reorganizing the assets of the transferor company (Alitalia), but rather at its liquidation. Pursuant to Article 56, paragraph 3-bis, of Legislative Decree No. 270 of 1999, therefore, the operations aimed at implementing this programme do not constitute a transfer of a business, branch, or branches of a business according with Article 2112 of the Civil Code and do not provide for the guarantee of continuity of the employment relationship, also in light of Article 5 of Directive 2001/23/EC.

§11.02 TRADE UNION INVOLVEMENT IN THE TRANSFER OF UNDERTAKINGS: INFORMATION AND CONSULTATION PROCEDURE

According to Council Directive 12 March 2001 2001/23/CE (which replaced previous Council Directive 14 February 1977 (77/187/EEC), concerning 'the safeguarding of employees' rights in the event of transfers of undertakings, businesses or parts of undertakings or businesses', the transferor and the transferee are required to inform the representatives of their respective employees affected by the transfer of the following points: a. the date or proposed date of the transfer; b. the reasons for the transfer; c. the legal, economic and social implications of the transfer for the employees; and d. any measures envisaged in relation to the employees.[17]

---

di azienda in amministrazione straordinaria, in https://ius.lefebvregiuffre.it (accessed 22 August 2025), 15 November 2023.

15. *See* F. Capurro, *L'operazione Alitalia-ITA*, in www.rivistalabor.it (accessed 22 August 2025), 20 December 2023.
16. Trib. Lavoro Roma 18 June 2024, *see* F. Capurro, *È ancora ad alta quota l'operazione Alitalia-ITA*, in www.rivistalabor.it (accessed 22 August 2025), 5 August 2024.
17. Article 7, para. 1, Directive 2001/23/CE.

In particular, if the transferor or the transferee envisages measures in relation to his employees, he shall consult the employees' representatives in good time on such measures with a view to reaching an agreement.[18]

The above-quoted obligations shall apply irrespective of whether the decision resulting in the transfer is taken by the employer or an undertaking controlling the employer.[19]

Where there are no representatives of the employees in an undertaking or business through no fault of their own, the same type of information mentioned above must be provided in advance, directly to the employees concerned.[20]

Italy transposed the European Union legislation in Article 47 of Law No. 428 of 29 December 1990, subsequently amended by Article 2 of Legislative Decree No. 18 of 2 February 2001.[21]

Under current Italian law,[22] in the event of a transfer concerning a company employing more than 15 workers, or a branch of the transferring company, the transferor and the transferee must notify in writing the representatives of the respective company's trade union, as well as the trade unions that have stipulated the collective agreement applied in the companies involved in the transfer.

The notice must be given at least 25 days before the completion of the act giving rise to the transfer or before the conclusion of a binding agreement between the parties.

This obligation may be fulfilled by the transferor and the transferee through the association to which they belong or which they mandate.

The information must cover: (a) the date or the proposed date of the transfer; (b) the reasons for the planned transfer of the undertaking; (c) the legal, economic and social consequences for the employees; and (d) any measures envisaged in respect of the latter.

Upon written request of the trade unions representatives (notified within seven days of receipt of the aforementioned communication), the transferor and the transferee are obliged to launch (within seven days of receipt of the said request) a joint examination with the requesting trade unions.

The joint examination shall be deemed to be completed if no agreement is reached within 10 days after its commencement.[23]

Failure by the transferor or transferee to comply with the above obligations constitutes anti-union conduct within the meaning of Article 28 of Law No. 300 of 1970.[24]

18. Article 7, para. 2.
19. Article 7, para. 4.
20. Article 7, para. 6.
21. *See, inter alia,* the overview provided by Boghetich, *Mantenimento dei diritti dei lavoratori in caso di trasferimento d'azienda,* in Amoroso, Di Cerbo and Maresca (eds), *Il lavoro privato,* Milano 2022. Chapter IX, 3.7.
22. Article 47 above quoted, para. 1.
23. Article 47, para. 2.
24. Article 47, para. 3.

According to a shared interpretation of the text of the above quoted Article 47,[25] the rationale for the obligation to inform the trade unions before a final decision concerning the transfer is reached is that the trade unions should have the opportunity to know and discuss the business plans, with a view to, *inter alia*, modifying them or dissuading the potential buyer.

The information and joint examination are also due if the decision concerning the transfer has been taken by a controlling undertaking.[26]

According to the case law of the Italian Court of Cassation,[27] while the failure to comply with the obligation to provide information laid down in Article 47 violates the interests of the trade union, and is therefore liable to constitute anti-union conduct within the meaning of Article 28 of Law No. 300 of 1970, said failure has no impact on the validity of the transfer, since trade union consultation procedures cannot be regarded as a prerequisite for the legitimacy (and therefore the validity) of the transfer contract.

It follows that the existing employment relationships with the transferee continue in application of the provisions of Article 2112 of the Civil Code, unless it is ascertained that the conditions for the applicability of the latter rule do not exist.

Accordingly, the Court of Cassation[28] decided that the employees involved in the transfer are not entitled to challenge the deficiency or falsity of the information provided to the trade unions.

In other words, the employee is not entitled to rely on the violation of the union's rights in order to oppose the transfer of his contract of employment, since it is for the union alone to assess the handling of the procedure as well as the agreement concluded.

Ultimately, the deficiency or falsity of the information provided cannot be relied upon by individual workers but only by trade union organizations, since the provision of the information and consultation procedure laid down in Article 47 is aimed solely at safeguarding the trade union's interest in developing its own protective action vis-à-vis workers; this is in accordance with the distinction between the rights of workers and those of trade unions made by Directive 2001/23/EC.[29]

As a matter of fact, Article 47 of Law No. 428 does not contain any provision aimed at invalidating the transfer of the contract for violation of the consultation procedure, as it is the case for collective dismissals, the ineffectiveness of which is provided for by Article 5 of Law No. 223 of 1991 for violation of the procedures referred to in Article 4.

As regards the content of the notification to the trade unions, the Italian Supreme Court specified that although Article 47 of Law No. 428 of 1990 provides that the transferor and the transferee are obliged to inform the trade unions, among others, of

25. *See*, for example the judgment of Corte di cassazione No. 3537/2013.
26. Article 47 para. 4.
27. *See* Corte di cassazione No. 11816/2024.
28. *See* Corte di cassazione No. 17072/2005 in Rivista Italiana di Diritto del lavoro, 2006, II, 592.
29. *See* Corte di cassazione No. 11816/2024 above-quoted.

the reasons for the transfer in writing in a timely manner; however, they are not obliged to specify in the deed also the economic reasons for the decision.

This communication is in fact only intended to inform the trade unions whether or not they wish to request the joint review and, if so, to participate in it in an informed manner.

As mentioned above, upon written request of the trade union representatives, the transferor and the transferee are obliged to initiate a joint examination of the situation created by the transfer agreement within seven days of receiving such request. In practice, under Italian national law, the joint review presupposes an explicit initiative (written request) by the trade unions.

The latter regulation does not fully comply with the European legislation,[30] which provides that 'where the transferor or the transferee envisages measures in relation to his employees, he shall consult the representatives of those employees in good time on such measures with a view to reaching an agreement'.

European legislation essentially provides for an obligation on the part of the transferor or the transferee to consult the trade union representatives; said obligation arises from the fact that one or the other may envisage the adoption of measures affecting the employees, irrespective of the initiative taken by the trade union.

Once the legal deadline (10 days) has expired without a trade union agreement being reached, the parties concerned may freely proceed to implement their plan, the merits of which are not challenged by the judge (in compliance with a specific provision in Article 30 of Law No. 183 of 4 November 2010, which prohibits judicial review of the technical, organizational and production assessments that are the responsibility of the employer).

Italian law attaches a particular role to the agreement between the company and the trade unions, which may be reached after the joint examination, in cases of company crisis.[31]

Indeed, in case of a company crisis, Article 47, paragraphs 4-bis[32] and 5 of Law No. 428 of 1990[33] provides for the possibility of derogating from the individual guarantees for employees provided by Article 2112 of the Civil Code. This derogation, as explicitly stated by the law, is aimed at maintaining, at least partially, the existing levels of employment.[34] Apart from the cases specifically provided for in the law, there

---

30. Article 7(2) Directive 2001/23/EC.
31. *See*, in particular the overview provided by Imberti, *Il rapporto di lavoro nel codice di disciplina dell'azienda in crisi*, in Amoroso, Di Cerbo and Maresca (eds), *Il lavoro privato*, Milano 2022. Chapter XVII, 1.; Bellè, *Trasferimento di azienda in crisi, licenziamento dei lavoratori e altre modifiche minori ai rapporti di lavoro. Stato dell'arte e scenari evolutivi*, in Lavoro Diritti Europa, 2023, 2; Amendola, *Il trasferimento e la crisi di impresa*, in Cosio et al. (eds), *Il diritto del lavoro dell'Unione europea*, Milano 2023, 832.
32. The current text of para. 4-bis of Article 47, above-quoted has been provided by Legislative Decree No. 14 /2019 (Company Crisis and Insolvency Code – CCIC).
33. The new para. 5 of Article 47, above-quoted, are the result of amendments to the original text of Article 47 provided by Decree-Law No. 135 of 2009, converted into Law No. 166 of 2009. Both amendments (paras 4-bis and 5) aim to make national legislation consistent with European standards.
34. Corte di cassazione No. 1383/2018.

is no other possibility of not applying, even partially, the provisions of Article 2112 of the Civil Code (relating to individual guarantees for employees) in the event of the transfer of undertakings.[35]

In particular, detrimental changes in the treatment of workers are allowed, by way of derogation from Article 2112 of the Civil Code, in order to preserve employment levels in the event of the transfer of the activities of an insolvent or otherwise failing company. For example, in the event of the transfer of companies subject to insolvency proceedings or branches of companies, the successor company may agree on contractual terms and conditions providing for the 'ex novo' recruitment of workers, in derogation from the provisions of Article 2112 of the Civil Code, as well as the possibility of excluding part of the surplus staff from recruitment.

This derogation, where provided for in the trade union agreement, is justified by the need to maintain employment levels, even if it worsens the treatment of workers.

In fact, in such cases, the principle of the protection of the individual worker (guaranteed by Article 2112 of the Civil Code) is sacrificed in favour of the collective interest of facilitating the transfer of the company, since such a transfer is aimed at preserving the highest level of employment in a situation of objective entrepreneurial crisis.

In this case, trade union consultation plays a particularly important role as guarantor. According to the case law of the Italian Supreme Court,[36] in order for a collective agreement to allow such a derogation from normally guaranteed rights, it must explicitly provide for such derogation, and the existence of a generic agreement to be perfected in a subsequent agreement is not sufficient. In the latter case, the legal rules not been derogated remain applicable.

In fact, in order to exclude the application of Article 2112 of the Civil Code, Article 47(5) requires not only a general agreement on the partial maintenance of employment but also an agreement that explicitly provides for such exclusion and that it is concluded within the context of trade union negotiations in accordance with the procedure regulated in detail by Article 47.

The derogation agreement is capable of shifting the priority of protection from the level of the individual worker to that of the collective interest of promoting the movement of the company as a means of ensuring maximum employment.

In the event of an objective crisis in the company and at the expense of certain rights guaranteed by Article 2112 of the Civil Code, said derogation agreement can only operate within the strict limits set by the regulatory provision, which expressly places the conclusion of the agreement on maintaining even partial employment 'during the consultation referred to in the preceding paragraphs', excluding any equivalent form.[37]

35. *See* Boghetich and Di Cerbo, *Procedura di informazione e consultazione sindacale*, in Cosio and Vidiri (eds), Il *trasferimento d'impresa in Italia nel quadro del diritto dell'Unione Europea*, Milano, 2019, 121.
36. *See*, for example, the judgment of Corte di cassazione No. 19282/2011.
37. *See* Corte di cassazione No. 12546/2018.

§11.03 TRANSFER OF UNDERTAKINGS AND DISMISSAL

[A] Introduction

In the Italian legal system, in the event of the transfer of a company, the protection of the workers' positions is entrusted to the automatic continuation of the employment relationship with the transferee and the preservation of the rights accrued by the workers at the time of the transfer.[38]

Automatic transfers are enshrined in Article 2112 of the Civil Code, as amended by Article 47 of Law No. 428 of 29 December 1990, which was enacted to bring our system into line with Directive 77/187/EEC. The new wording implies that, on the one hand, it is not necessary for employees to consent to their own transfer to the transferee company and, on the other hand, that the worker does not have the right to oppose the transfer of the company.

The law therefore protects the interest in the continuity of the relationship as one of continuity of the undertaking within the meaning of economic activity itself.

In this context, a key role is played by Article 4(4), which states that 'the transfer of a business does not in itself constitute grounds for dismissal'.

Without this preclusion, the principle of continuity would have no concrete effect and would remain an empty statement of principle.

Although the scope of this rule is debated, being considered by some as a presumption of null and void dismissal and by others as an unjustified dismissal (*see* below), it is certain that the rule excludes that the transfer can be the sole reason for dismissal, requiring instead that the dismissal be justified on the basis of events, facts and circumstances unrelated to or intended to facilitate the transfer of the company. It should also be noted that, in order to clarify the limits of the power of dismissal, the legislator has deemed it appropriate to confirm that, without prejudice to the prohibition of a dismissal linked to the transfer of a business, all other hypotheses falling within the 'legislation on dismissal' remain valid. This confirms the employer's power to terminate the contract for economic, technical and organizational reasons, provided that these are not related to the transfer.[39]

That the rule in question is undoubtedly mandatory is also evident from a comparison between the new text of Article 2112 and the previous text, according to which it was possible for the assigning employer to give notice and avoid the continuation of the relationship, as is still possible to do in contracts other than the employment agreements in existence at the time of the assignment (*see* Article 2558 of the Civil Code).[40]

38. *See* Roberto Romei, *Il rapporto di lavoro nel trasferimento dell'impresa*, Milano 2021; *see* also Maria Teresa Carinci, *Utilizzazione e acquisizione indiretta del lavoro: somministrazione e distacco, appalto e subappalto, trasferimento d'azienda e di ramo*, 2022; *see* also Giovanni Zampini *Il rapporto di lavoro nel trasferimento d'azienda*, 2020.
39. G. Proia, *Crisi di impresa e trasferimento di azienda: è vera armonizzazione?* in Argomenti di diritto del lavoro, No. 6/2023.
40. *See* G. Vidini, *Il trasferimento di azienda.*

Finally, it should be pointed out that the legislation thus referred to also includes the power to dismiss collectively, with the related information and procedural obligations.[41]

[B] Dismissals Motivated by the Transfer of the Company and Their Illegitimacy

It follows from the above principles that a transformation planned at the time of the transfer, or envisaged by the transferee, does not render a dismissal by the transferor lawful. Indeed, the mere fact of the transfer does not in itself constitute a parallel organizational change without which the loss of jobs, which is a precondition for a subsequent dismissal, would be unlawful.

The same consequences would arise in the case of dismissal on the grounds of cessation of business, since the company was not closed down but was in fact sold, so that the dismissal must be regarded as the effect of the sale and therefore adopted in breach of Article 2112 of the Civil Code.[42]

Establishing whether or not there has been a sale is often difficult and gives rise to numerous disputes.

As mentioned in the preceding paragraph, there have been uncertainties as to the exact legal classification of these dismissals, which are undoubtedly unlawful but, according to some, are more specifically unjustified, while for others they are undoubtedly null and void. As mentioned above (*see* §11.01 Introduction, first paragraph), the interpretation of such dismissals has been subject to uncertainty. In the doctrine, the prevailing view is that they are invalid, considering that the transfer of the company is in itself excluded from the grounds that could justify the dismissal. Therefore, a termination motivated in this way is per se contrary to the rule contained in Article 2112, paragraph 4 of the Civil Code and, since this is a mandatory rule, a breach of it would render the dismissal null and void.[43]

[C] Legitimate Dismissals

If it is unlawful to be dismissed as a result of a transfer of the business, it is not unlawful to be dismissed merely in conjunction with the transfer.

In fact, the transferor retains the power of withdrawal conferred on him by the general legislation. Therefore, the transfer of a business does not preclude the employer from dismissing the employee for objective reasons that are not relevant to the transfer if they are based solely on company structure and do not further the purpose of the said transfer. It must therefore be ruled out that, by exercising the power of withdrawal

41. *See* G. Santoro Passarelli, *Il rapporto di lavoro nel trasferimento di impresa e di articolazione funzionalmente autonoma.*
42. Carattere obbligatorio della disciplina, *see* Ghera-Garilli-Garofalo, *Diritto del Lavoro*, Torino, 2015, 341.
43. Illegittimità dei Licenziamenti motivati con il traferimento, *see* Vallebona, *Istutuzioni di diritto del lavoro*, Padova 2015, 429.

under the conditions mentioned, the entrepreneur commits an emulative act or an act in breach of the law or in violation of the principles of fairness and good faith.

A question that arises in practice is whether a prior request made by the transferee to the transferor to reduce the number of staff employed in the business as an essential condition for concluding the sale constitutes an organizational necessity capable of justifying dismissal.

Two principles come into conflict here: that of freedom of enterprise and that of job protection.

In the past, the jurisprudence recognized the legitimacy of dismissal based on the need to reduce staff as a condition for concluding the sale. Now, however, the opposite view prevails on the grounds that the dismissal in this case would be based solely on the need to conclude the sale and would therefore be a dismissal arising from the sale, which is manifestly in clear conflict with the aforementioned paragraph 4 of Article 2112 of the Civil Code.[44]

[D] The Party with Right of Withdrawal

The party entitled to terminate the contract is the transferor and not the transferee.

In the case of dismissal with notice, the employment relationship terminates on the date of the notice of termination, in which case the relationship is not transferred to the assignee and the assignee is not jointly and severally liable with the assignor.

In the event that the assignor's dismissal is declared unlawful, the relationship must be reinstated with the assignee, at which point the assignor shall be liable to the assignee.

The consequence of this is that the relationship is not transferred to the assignee and the latter is not jointly and severally liable with the assignor.

Should there be a declaration of unlawful dismissal on the part of the transferor, the relationship with the transferee must be reinstated on the basis of the principle that all employment relationships with the transferor are transferred to the transferee.

Finally, according to well-established jurisprudential orientation, the extinctive effect of the unlawful dismissal announced at a time prior to the transfer itself is merely temporary and is therefore destined to be overturned by a judgment annulling the dismissal. This implies that the employment relationship reinstated between the original parties is transferred to the transferee pursuant to Article 2112 of the Civil Code.

It should be noted that this solution does not conflict with Directive 777187/EC, which provides that the consequence of this is that the relationship is not transferred to the assignee and that the latter is not jointly and severally liable with the assignor. In the event of an unlawful dismissal by the transferor, the relationship must be reinstated with the transferee on the basis of the principle that all employment relationships with the transferor are transferred to the transferee.

44. *Le dimissioni del lavoratore trasferito. See* Alvino.

Finally, according to a well-established jurisprudential orientation, the extinctive effect of an unlawful dismissal announced at a time prior to the transfer itself is merely temporary and is therefore destined to be overturned by a judgment annulling the dismissal, which implies that the employment relationship reinstated between the original parties is transferred to the transferee pursuant to Article 2112 of the Civil Code.

It should be noted that this solution does not conflict with Directive 777187/EC, which, as interpreted by the Court of Justice (judgments 12 March 1998 C-319/94, 11 July 1984 C-105/84; 7 February 1985 C-19/83), provides that workers dismissed in breach of the directive must be considered employees at the date of the transfer, without prejudice to the right of Member States to apply or introduce legislative provisions that are more favourable to workers (Court of Cassation 2010/8641; Court of Cassation 2011/5507).

[E] Staff Reduction and Disciplinary Procedures

The transferee takes over all the assets or liabilities of the transferor, and may therefore exercise the disciplinary powers inherent in the employment relationship with regard to the facts preceding the transfer.

Therefore, the employer's right to rely on the moral and personal qualities of the employee may be lost, even if facts that were not known or not sufficiently known at the beginning of the relationship later become apparent in the course of the relationship. Therefore, the fact that the unlawful conduct took place before the transfer of a branch of the business does not exclude the legitimacy of the dismissal ordered by the transferee, all the more so if the unlawful conduct of the employee is also of criminal relevance.

In the cases mentioned, we find ourselves in a situation in which there is a succession of events in the relationship. In contrast, in union redundancy proceedings initiated by the transferor, succession is non-configurable and must therefore be re-initiated by the transferee. In fact, the communications provided for by the law (Article 4 of Law No. 223 of 30 July 1991, cited above) must concern the conditions of the undertaking at the time the procedure was initiated and cannot refer to future and possible productive reorganization structures or procedures. This explains why the employer, as holder of the relationship, is entitled to initiate a procedure to reduce the workforce and why prospective and potential transferees do not have the same rights. On the one hand, succession is configurable in relation to active or passive legal positions and not in a procedure and, on the other hand, the transfer of a branch of business to the transferee changes the factual elements according to which the actual situation of overstaffing and the consistency of the figures are verified, also taking into account the necessary joint examination provided for by law (Article 4 paragraph 5 of Law No. 223 of 30 July 1991 already mentioned).

[F] Resignation of the Transferred Employee

According to the first paragraph of Article 2119 of the Civil Code referred to in paragraph 4 of Article 2112 of the same code, the transferred employee is entitled to resign. The faculty thus granted confirms the automatic transfer of the working relationship to the transferee, and the worker cannot object to such transfer in order to maintain the previous working relationship. Some aspects of this discipline need to be clarified.

First, it is not specified which parameters should be taken into consideration when verifying whether or not the work conditions have been essentially modified. In particular, doubts arise as to whether a change in the wage level or working conditions is sufficient to be considered grounds for resignation or whether, in the case of workers, more than one modification is required to justify resignation. An example might be a modification in the level of qualifications, or a change of work location, or an alteration in the rules governing the dismissal of workers.

Linked to this question is whether the reference to just cause for resignation is to be understood as referring to the rules on the effects of resignation or whether it has the implicit meaning of indicating a reason for not allowing the relationship to continue, even temporarily.

Given that the onus is on the resigning employee to prove just cause for his resignation, the first solution would allow the employee to discharge that burden relatively easily, while the second would, on the other hand, make it particularly difficult for him to exercise his right to terminate the relationship.

[G] Transfer of Business and Succession in Contracts

A transfer of a business is also possible, under certain conditions, in the case of a succession of a service contract. In this context, although there is no contractual relationship between the two successive contractors, there is a 'transfer of assets of a not inconsiderable amount such as to make possible the performance of a specific undertaking' (Court of Cassation 2013/11918).

Law No. 122 of 2016, amending paragraph 3 of Article 29 of legislative decree 276/2003, has in fact established that under certain conditions, the acquisition by the new contractor of the personnel employed in the contract constitutes a transfer of business, a consequence instead, excluded by the aforementioned legislative decree, before the aforementioned amendments.

§11.04 THE TRANSFER OF THE ENTERPRISE IN CRISIS

[A] The Transfer of the Enterprise in Crisis

From a jurisprudential perspective, the transfer of enterprises in crisis has always been a very complex subject matter.[45]

45. On the subject *see* G. Orlandini, *Il trasferimento d'azienda nell'impresa in stato di crisi tra dibattito teorico e prassi sindacale*, Diritto relazioni industriali, 2005, 589; A. Pizzoferrato,

The subject requires a necessary deepening of the relationship between systems (European and national) and the dialogue between the Courts (in particular, between the Court of Justice and the Supreme Court).[46]

On the topic, with some approximation, we can distinguish four stages.

The former (which we can place from the early 1970s to the end of the twentieth century) includes four events: two regulatory and two jurisprudential.

On the regulatory level,[47] the existence in the national legal system of a sub-system[48] regulates the transfer of enterprises in crisis, whereas there was 'silence' on the level of the European Union legal system (in Directive 77/187/EEC, the subject of the transfer of enterprises in crisis was not regulated).

At the jurisprudential level, the situation is somehow reversed.

The landmark judgment is certainly the Spano judgment[49] of the CJEU, which, following the guideline developed by the Court itself, affirmed the non-compliance of paragraph 5 of Article 47 of Law No. 428/1990 with Directive 77/187.

On the domestic side, however, reference is made to the Supreme Court's ruling No. 4073 of 2001[50] which, by denying the direct effectiveness of the directive and the practicability of the so-called interpretation in accordance with the EU norm, downsizes the scope of the CJEU ruling.

In the second stage (which can be placed between the late 1990s and the first decade of the new century), there is a kind of dialogue between Legislators and Courts.

In Article 5 of Directive 2001/23/EC (which reproduced, without change, Article 4a of Directive 98/50), the EU Legislature breaks its silence and provides a comprehensive framework aimed at rescuing companies in economic difficulty.

Eight years later, in its 11 June 2009, judgment C-561/078,[51] the Court of Justice ruled that with paragraphs 5 and 6 of Article 47 of Law No. 428/1990, 'the Italian Republic has failed to fulfill its obligations under the directive'.

Trasferimento d'azienda e rapporti di lavoro, Tomo II, in F. Carinci (ed.), *Il lavoro subordinato,* Torino, 2007; R. De Luca Tamajo and M.T. Salimbeni, *Il trasferimento d'azienda, I contratti di lavoro* Tomo II, in A. Vallebona (ed.), *Trattato dei contratti,* Torino, 2009; G. La Terza, *Commentario Art. 2112 c.c.,* in G. Amoroso, V. Di Cerbo and A. Maresca (eds), *Diritto del lavoro,* Vol. I, Milano, 2009, 1101; A.M. Perrino, *Le deroghe delle tutele dei lavoratori in caso di trasferimento di azienda di imprenditore in crisi o insolvente tra i reiterati inadempimenti del legislatore nazionale,* Foro it., 2010, IV, 268; M.L. Vallauri, *Lavoratori e trasferimento di ramo d'impresa in crisi,* in M.A. Aimo and D. Izzi (eds), in *Nuova giurisprudenza civile commentata,* Torino, 2014, 342; G. Santoro Passarelli, *Il rapporto di lavoro nel trasferimento di azienda e di articolazione funzionalmente autonoma,* Torino, 2014; M. Marazza, *La circolazione del patrimonio aziendale e gli effetti sui contratti di lavoro,* in M. Marazza and G. Garofalo (eds), *Insolvenza del datore di lavoro e tutela del lavoratore,* Torino, 2015, 43; A. Corrado, *Crisi di impresa e rapporti di Lavoro,* Milano, 2016; P. Lambertucci, *Circolazione di impresa e rapporti di lavoro,* Argomenti diritto del lavoro, 2018, 1, 25.

46. On this topic *see* R. Cosio, *Il trasferimento dell'impresa in crisi, Il trasferimento d'impresa in Italia nel quadro del diritto dell'Unione europea,* in R. Cosio and G. Vidiri (eds), Milano, 2019, 139-167.
47. R. Cosio, *Le vicende dei rapporti di lavoro nelle aziende in crisi: modelli normativi a confronto,* Rivista giuridica lavro, 1987, I, 93.
48. *See* R. Cosio, *Discipline del trasferimento d'azienda,* Milano, 1995.
49. Published in Foro.it, 1996, IV, 205, with note by R. Cosio.
50. Cass. 21 March 2001, No. 4073, Foro it., 2001, I, 3235, with note by R. Cosio.
51. In doctrine, among others, *see* C. Cester, *Due recenti pronunce della Corte di giustizia europea in tema di trasferimento di azienda. Sulla nozione di ramo d'azienda ai fini dell'applicazione della*

The response of the Italian Legislature, in order to implement the Court of Justice ruling, is timely with Article 19-quater of Decree-Law No. 135/2009, converted into Law No. 166/2009.

In the third stage (from 2009 to the present day), the debate, doctrinal and jurisprudential, focuses on the analysis of whether or not Article 4-bis of Law 428/90 complies with Directive 2001/23.

The debate on this legislation is complex and multifaceted.

The Supreme Court, in its recent judgments[52] concerning a similar subject matter, has clarified some particularly complex aspects of the regulations in force today with a reasoning that also provides valuable insights into the regulations that have come into force in the meantime.

The reference is, of course, to Article 368(4)(b) of Legislative Decree No. 14 of 12 January 2019, which, as of 15 July 2022, regulates the matter under consideration.

The latter can be considered the fourth stage of the institution's regulation.

But it is convenient to proceed in order, following (and commenting on) the different argumentative passages contained in the most recent Supreme Court decisions.

[B] Article 4-bis of Law No. 428/90. The Exegetical and Logical-Systematic Interpretation of the Court of Cassation

The matter of business transfer is now regulated by Article 47, paragraph 4-bis, introduced by Article 19-quater of Decree-Law No. 135 of 25 September 2009 (converted into Law No. 166/2009), which provides that: 'In the event that an agreement has been reached regarding the maintenance, even partial, of employment, Article 2112 of the Civil Code shall be applied under the terms and with the limitations set forth in the said agreement if the transfer concerns companies: a) of which the state of corporate crisis has been ascertained, pursuant to Art. 2, paragraph 5, lett. c), of l. No. 675/77; b) for which extraordinary administration has been ordered, pursuant to Legislative Decree No. 270 of July 8, 1999, in the event of continuation or failure to cease operations.'

Paragraph 4-bis was inserted 'in order to execute the condemnation judgment issued by the European Court of Justice on June 11, 2009 in Case C-561/07'.

Paragraph (4-bis), as stated in the grounds of the judgments examined, applies to non-liquidation procedures 'unlike paragraph 5, which instead presupposes the cessation of business activity or, in any case, its non-continuation, in symmetry with the exceptions allowed respectively by paragraph 2 and paragraph 1 of Article 5 of

direttiva e sull'inadempimento alla stessa da parte dello Stato italiano nelle ipotesi di deroga per crisi aziendale, Rivista italiana diritto del lavoro, 2010, 1, 42 and M.L. Serrano, *Il trasferimento dell'azienda in crisi tra ordinamento comunitario e ordinamento nazionale: ultimo atto?,* Rivista giuridica del lavoro, 2010, 3, 345.

52. The first two rulings, of a monolithic orientation, are to be found in the judgments of Corte di cassazione Nos. 10414 and 10415/2020. Said orientation was consolidated in Judgments No. 10524/2022, and most recently in Judgment No. 31551/ 2024.

Directive 2001/23/EC'. According to the Court, it is of fundamental importance 'the expression in paragraph 4a, according to which Article 2112 of the Civil Code applies; diametrically opposed to that contained in paragraph 5, according to which Article 2112 of the Civil Code does not apply'.[53]

The diversity of cases governed by the two subparagraphs does not allow for considering the sentence aside contained both 'in the event that an agreement has been reached about maintaining even partial employment' as having the same semantic meaning.

In other words, 'the phrase "even partial" cannot be extrapolated to accredit the hypothesis that the union agreement can dispose, in a limiting sense, of the transfers of workers of the transferring company, if it is a company falling under the hypothesis of paragraph 4-bis'.

In essence, the agreement under Article 4-bis must concern the 'working conditions'[54] but not the continuity of labour relations with the transferee according to the logical-systematic criterion[55] and the rationale of the legislative intervention intended to implement the judgment of the Court of Justice C-561/07.

In the presence of 'generic expressions', the Court observes, correctly, 'the meaning in accordance with EU law and the CJEU's interpretation of it must be preferred'.

[C] Directive 2001/23/EC

Directive 2001/23, like its previous, is aimed at protecting workers by promoting (without achieving full harmonization[56] the approximation of national laws in order to ensure that their rights are maintained in the event of a business transfer.

53. On the importance of exegetical interpretation, the teaching of G. Tarello, *L'interpretazione della legge*, Milano, 1990, remains ever relevant.
54. As is well known, two views are compared on the subject. According to a first approach (*see* U. Carabelli and B. Veneziani, *Il trasferimento di azienda in Italia*, Bari, 1999, 155), only union agreements that fully maintain the employment that existed prior to the business transfer would be legitimate. The new provision, to be interpreted in a manner consistent with the directive, would allow only changes in *peius* to the economic-regulatory structure previously acquired by individual workers. This thesis is supported by the term 'changes in the working conditions of workers' used in Directive 2001/23, which would not authorize a reading of para. 4-bis of Article 47 aimed at also allowing a derogation from the automatic transfer of workers to the transferee company. According to a different approach (cf. P. Pizzoferrato, *Il trasferimento d'azienda nelle imprese in crisi, Il trasferimento d'azienda,* Quaderni diritto del. lavoro e delle relazioni.industriali, 2004, 159-161) vice versa, the new provision would also authorize the derogation to the automatic transfer of workers to the successor company. This thesis is based on several arguments. First, the valorization of the rationale of the EU directive 'which is clearly to save, among others, precisely our legislative discipline'. Enhancement of the purpose of the directive that would find further support in an overall reading of it tending to 'guarantee the survival of the enterprise'. Second, it would be decisive, in the economy of the norm, to enhance the role of the union 'which will not only have to reject abusive or fraudulent hypotheses of facilitated transfer but will also have to attempt the best possible synthesis of the different situations'.
55. Cf. E. Betti, *Interpretazione della legge e degli atti giuridici. Teoria generale e dogmatica,* Milano, 1971, 277.
56. CJEU judgment, 6 March 2014, *Amatori*, C-458/12, para. 41.

The general rule is outlined in Articles 3 and 4 of the directives.

The transferee is bound by the rights and obligations that result from an employment contract or relationship existing between the employee and the transferor on the date of the transfer of the business.

'Transmission' 'includes all the rights of the latter where they do not fall under one of the exceptions expressly provided for in the directive'.[57]

With the same aim at maintaining workers' rights, Directive 2001/23 provides in Article 3(3) that, after the transfer, the transferee shall maintain the terms and conditions of employment agreed by collective agreement on the terms provided by the latter for the transferor, until the termination or expiration of the collective agreement or the application of another collective agreement.[58]

Article 4(1) of the directive states that the transfer of an enterprise is not in itself grounds for dismissal by the transferor or transferee.

We are in the presence of mandatory rules;[59] Member States are not allowed to derogate from them in a way that is unfavourable to workers, subject to the exceptions provided for in the directive itself.

The directive provides three exemptions.

The first is contained in paragraph 1 of Article 5.

It provides, in this context, that Articles 3 and 4 do not apply, in principle ('Unless the states provide otherwise'), to the transfer of enterprises where the transferor is the subject of bankruptcy or similar insolvency proceedings started with a view to the liquidation of the transferor's assets and which are conducted under the supervision of a competent public authority.

There are two prerequisites[60] for the application of the rule.

The first is the objective pursued in the proceedings.

Indeed, the exclusion of the general rule is justified only if the proceeding in question, in view of its objectives and modalities, aims at the liquidation of the enterprise's assets.

If, on the other hand, the proceedings are aimed at the continuation of the management of the enterprise, the exemption does not operate. This assertion can be inferred from judgments of Abels,[61] D'Urso,[62] Spano[63] 26 and Dethier Equipment.[64]

The second requirement is that the proceedings take place 'under the supervision of a competent public authority'.

The Court of Justice specifies,[65] in a ruling on pre-pack,[66] that it must be a 'penetrating'[67] control.

57. CJEU judgment 4 June 2002, *Beckmann*, C-164/00, paras 36 and 37.
58. CJEU judgment, 27 November 2008, *Iuuri*, C-396/07, para. 32. On this topic *see* CJEU, 27 April 2017, Joined Cases C-680/15 and C-681/15, *Lav. giur.* 12/2017, 1067-1077 with note by R. Cosio.
59. CJEU Judgment, 11 June 2009, *Commission v. Italy*, C- 561/07, para. 46.
60. Which must apply cumulatively; *see* CJEU 22 June 2017, C-126/16, para. 44.
61. CJEU judgment, 7 February 1985, C-135/83.
62. CJEU judgment, 25 July 1991, C-362/89.
63. CJEU judgment, 7 December 1995, C-472/93.
64. CJEU judgment, 12 March 1998, C-319/94.
65. CJEU judgment, 22 June 2017, C-126/16, paras 54-55.

The second exception is contained in paragraph 2 of Article 5.

As noted above, the directive authorizes Member States to apply Articles 3 and 4 to transfers of an enterprise in the context of insolvency proceedings opened against the transferor.

Where a Member State makes use of this option, paragraph 2 of the same Article 5 provides:

- in subparagraph (a) that it may derogate from Article 3(1) of the Directive in the sense that charges resulting to the transferor, at the date of transfer or at the opening of the insolvency proceedings, from contracts or employment relationships are not transferred to the transferee, provided, however, that protection at least equivalent to that established by Directive 80/987, which requires a mechanism for guaranteeing the payment of claims by employees against the employer in insolvency arising from contracts or employment relationships concluded with the same, is in force in that Member State.
- in paragraph (b) that 'the transferee, the transferor or the person or persons exercising the functions of the transferor, on the one hand, and the representatives of the employees, on the other hand, may agree, to the extent that existing legislation or practices permit, on changes in the working conditions of employees designed to safeguard employment opportunities by ensuring the survival of the enterprise, establishment or parts of enterprises or establishments.'[68]

The third derogation is provided in paragraph 3 of Article 5. 'A member state may apply paragraph 2(b) to transfers where the transferor is in a situation of serious economic crisis as defined by national law, provided that this situation is declared by a competent public authority and is open to judicial review, provided that these provisions were already in force in national law on July 17, 1998.'

The power to apply paragraph 2(b) of the directive (which provides, by agreement with workers' representatives, to 'change the working conditions of workers') is subject to three conditions.

66. A pre-pack indicates, in general, a transaction on the assets of a company in crisis (a divestment) that is prepared prior to the opening of insolvency proceedings (usually a bankruptcy) with the assistance of an administrator (in some jurisdictions appointed by a court) and that is, normally, carried out immediately after the opening of insolvency proceedings; on this topic *see* the Opinion of Advocate General P. Mengozzi, in Case C-126/16 submitted on 29 March 2017.
67. CJEU Judgment, 22 June 2017, C-126/16, para. 55. In the case before the CJEU, the transaction had not been managed under the control of the court, but by the administrative body of the enterprise, which had conducted the negotiations and taken decisions in preparation for the sale of the bankrupt enterprise. And indeed, neither the receiver nor the judge-commissioner, although appointed by the court at the request of the bankrupt firm, had any power formally. Therefore, no control exercised by a public authority rested on them.
68. In the opinion delivered by the Economic and Social Committee on 29 March 1995, in OJEC, 31 May 1995 No. C.133/13, concerns were expressed about the rule (as worded in the proposed directive) as it did not seem to 'sufficiently protect employment' and could 'undermine working conditions'.

The first, of a causal nature, is that the transferor 'is in a situation of severe economic crisis, provided that such a situation is declared by a competent public authority'.

This hypothesis, as pointed out in doctrine,[69] can be seen in some cases of CIGS.

But these are, as noted by the Court of Justice itself,[70] exceptional cases within the national framework.

The second procedural condition is that the procedure 'be open to judicial review'.

It follows from a systematic reading of Article 3 of the directive that such control must necessarily be judicial (a generic control by 'a competent public authority', as in the hypothesis outlined in paragraph 1 of Article 3, does not suffice).

Not enough.

Control must be 'constant' and not limited to certain stages of the process.[71]

Requirement that does not appear to be met in the case of CIGS.

The third condition, temporal in nature, is 'that these provisions were already in force in national law on July 17, 1998'.

Requirement certainly exists in Italian law.[72]

Derogations departing from the main objective of the directive 'must necessarily be subject to restrictive interpretation'.[73]

[D] The Judgment C-561/07 of the Court of Justice

The Court of Justice, in ruling C-561/07,[74] affirmed that, with paragraphs 5 and 6 of Law No. 428/90, the 'Italian Republic has failed to fulfill its obligations under the directive' (2001/23).

Some motivational passages of the judgment are illuminating for analysing the response of the Italian legislature (of 2009) and its compliance with the 2001/23 directive.

Regarding the Italian Republic's argument that the reasons justifying dismissal in the case of transfer indicated in Article 4(1) of Directive 2001/23 would be met in

69. *See* R. Cosio, *Il trasferimento dell'azienda nell'impresa in crisi o insolvente,* A. Caiafa and R. Cosio (eds), Padova, 2005, 14.
70. *See* CJEU judgment 5 June 2003, C-145/01. The admissibility of CIGS hypotheses falling within the scope of the directive is, implicitly, admitted in a passage in the reasoning of judgment C-561/07 (para. 44).
71. *See* CJEU judgment of 11 June 2009 C-561/07, paras 47. 35.
72. So much so as to highlight how this requirement was introduced ad hoc to remedy the persistent incompatibilities of the Italian discipline. On the subject *see*, P. Lambertucci, *Trasferimento di azienda e problemi occupazionali,* Diritto relazioni industriali., 2010, 2, 403; L. Menghini, *L'attenuazione delle tutele individuali dei lavoratori in caso di trasferimento d'azienda di impresa in crisi o soggetta a procedure concorsuali dopo la direttiva 50/98 e il d.lgs 270/99,* Rivista Giuridica del lavoro, 2000, I, 299.
73. *See* CJEU judgment 22 June 2017, C-126/16, para. 41. The statement, verbatim, refers to the derogation contained in the 1 paragraph of Article 5, but, in the writer's opinion, it is extensible to the other two cases of derogation.
74. Rivista italiana Diritto del lavoro, 2010, II, 232, with note by C. Cester and Diritto relazioni industriali, 2009, 83, with note by V. Nuzzo.

specific cases of corporate crisis under Article 2(5)(c) of Law No. 675/77 the Court's answer is laconic 'the fact that an undertaking is declared to be in a crisis situation within the meaning of Law No. 675/77 cannot necessarily and systematically imply changes in employment within the meaning of Article 4(1) of Directive 2001/23' (paragraph 36).

With regard to the Italian Republic's argument based on the alleged conformity of Article 47(5) of Law No. 428/90 with Article 5(3) of Directive 2001/23, the Court notes that 'assuming' that the situation typified by the national legislature falls within the scope of the directive, the directive's provision (Article 5(3)) 'authorizes Member States to provide that working conditions may be modified in order to safeguard employment opportunities by ensuring the survival of the undertaking, without, however, depriving workers of the rights guaranteed to them by Articles 3 and 4 of Directive 2001/23.'.

'Now, it is undisputed that Article 47(5) of Law No. 428/90 deprives workers, in the event of the transfer of an undertaking whose state of crisis has been established, of the guarantees provided for in Articles 3 and 4 of Directive 2001/23 and is not, consequently, limited to a change in working conditions such as it is authorized by Article 5(3) of Directive 2001/23' (paragraphs 44-45).

The Court, finally, reiterated (echoing the Spano judgment) that 'a provision such as Article 47(5) of Law No. 428/90, which has the effect of depriving the workers of an undertaking of the guarantees offered to them by Directive 2001/23, cannot be regarded as constituting a more favorable provision for workers within the meaning of Article 8 of that directive' (paragraph 48).

On the basis of these hermeneutic coordinates, the Court of Cassation believes, correctly, that paragraph (4-bis) 'appears to be intended for non-liquidation proceedings in contrast to par. (5), which instead presupposes the cessation of business activity or, at any rate, its non-continuation, in symmetry with the exceptions allowed by paragraph 2 and paragraph 1 of Article 5 of Directive 2001/23/EC, respectively'.

Interpretation that, moreover, finds support in a subsequent ruling of the Court of Justice: C-509/17.

[E] The Implications of the Judgment on Article 368, Paragraph 4 of Legislative Decree No. 14/2019

Most recently, the Court refers to Article 368(4)(b), which took effect on 15 July 2022.[75]

In cases of non-liquidation procedures, specifically admission to composition procedures in indirect continuity, approval of debt restructuring agreements and

75. I. Alvino, *La gestione dei rapporti di lavoro nelle crisi di impresa,* Milano, 2023, 333. More recent contributions include, V. De Stasio, *Il trasferimento di azienda nelle procedure di crisi: appunti sui profili di diritto commerciale,* in Lavoro Diritti Europa, 1/2025, A. Menicatti, *L'effetto circolatorio dell'impresa in crisi: profili giuridici connessi ai rapporti di lavoro e relativa gestione,* in Lavoro Diritti Europa, 1/2025; M. Parravicini, *La solidarietà obbligatoria dei debiti di lavoro nei trasferimenti azienda,* in Lavoro Diritti Europa, 1/2025; L. Imberti, *I molteplici profili del trasferimento d'azienda in crisi: tre nuovi sguardi dopo 2 anni dall'entrata in vigore del CCI,* Lavoro Diritti Europa, 1/2025.

extraordinary administration, the new text of paragraph 4-bis of Article 47 of Law No. 428/90 (as replaced in Article 368, paragraph 4, letter b) of Legislative Decree 14/19) establishes that reaching an agreement 'with the purpose of safeguarding employment' entails 'without prejudice to the transfer to the transferee of labor relations' the application of Article 2112 Civil Code.

The choice of the Italian legislature appears to be in line with the CJEU's rulings[76] referred to by the Supreme Court, confirming that the rules of Directive 2001/23 can be derogated from only when the transfer of the business has occurred as part of proceedings aimed at liquidating the debtor's assets in order to satisfy creditors collectively.

In essence, the Italian legislature, by eliminating the clause contained in the current legislation ('maintaining even partial employment')[77] and reiterating as 'firm the transfer to the transferee of the labor relations', has thus 'more explicitly intended to transpose, by better conforming the future normative dictate, the only reading of paragraph 4-bis that this Court considers already hermeneutically viable even for the past'.

[F] The Judgment of the Court of Justice of 28 April 2022, C-237/20[78]

The request for a preliminary ruling, made by the Supreme Court of the Netherlands, allowed the Court of Justice to rule again on the question of the relationship between the institution of pre-pack, as developed in the Netherlands, and the derogation provided by Article 5(1) of Directive 2001/23/EC to the preservation of the rights conferred by that directive on employees in the event of transfers of undertakings, establishments or parts thereof.

In the law of the Netherlands, the pre-pack is a procedure not provided for by law, but of jurisprudential origin and application, which takes place prior to the declaration of bankruptcy of the debtor and in the framework of which the sale of the business, or a part thereof, falling within the assets of the debtor to be liquidated is prepared, a sale which is then carried out immediately after the declaration of bankruptcy. The question that arises in this case is whether, and under what conditions, such a procedure falls within the scope of the aforementioned exception.

The Court of Justice had already dealt with this issue in its 22 June 2017, judgment C-126/16.

---

76. On the topic *see* I. Alvino, *Continuità aziendale, trasferimento d'azienda e tutela dell'occupazione nel nuovo codice della crisi d'impresa e dell'insolvenza,* Rivista italiana Diritto del lavoro, 2019, I, 445.
77. On the topic, *see* F. Aiello, *Modifiche alla disciplina lavoristica del trasferimento di azienda nel nuovo codice della crisi di impresa e dell'insolvenza,* il Giuslavorista, 29 giugno 2020. On the business crisis code, *see* R. Rordorf, *Prime osservazioni sul codice della crisi e dell'insolvenza, I contratti,* Milano, 2019, 129.
78. On the subject *see*, L. Rocchi, *Sulla continuazione dell'attività di impresa nelle procedure aventi finalità liquidatoria: il revirement della Corte di Giustizia in tema di preback,* in Argomenti diritto del lavoro, 2022, 5, 971.

However, this ruling gave rise in the Netherlands to a wide-ranging debate in both case law and doctrine.[79]

Against this background of legal uncertainty, the Supreme Court of the Netherlands decided to refer a question to the Court for a preliminary ruling in order to obtain further clarification.

First of all, the 'case'.

The Heiploeg Group consisted of several companies engaged in fish and seafood wholesaling and related activities. During the years 2011 and 2012, the former Heiploeg accumulated significant financial losses. Moreover, four companies in that group were fined EUR 27 million by the European Commission in November 2013 for participating in a cartel.

Taking into account the severe financial difficulties of the former Heiploeg, no bank agreed to finance this financial penalty. Therefore, since the pronouncement of the financial penalty, the possibility of using a pre-pack has been examined.

To this end, several companies independent of the Heiploeg Group were invited to bid on the former Heiploeg's assets.

Since the bid submitted by Parlevliet en Van der Plas Beheer BV was considered the most promising, negotiations continued with that company.

At the instance of the former Heiploeg, on 16 January 2014, the Rechtbank Noord-Nederland (Court of Northern Netherlands, Netherlands) appointed two 'appointed receivers' and a 'designated delegated judge'.

It appears from the appointment letter that the objective of the measure was to obtain the highest possible return on behalf of the creditors as a whole and to give the possibility of arranging a sale or reorganization from an insolvency situation.

The Court recalled that the 'designated curators' and the 'designated delegated judge' did not have any legal expertise or mandate in the pre-pack procedure, but were instructed to observe, inquire and be informed as well as to express their opinion and, if necessary, give advice.

The Court made it clear that they had to be inspired by the interests of the creditors as a whole, as if insolvency had already been pronounced, and, in the event of subsequent insolvency proceedings, account for the pre-pack procedure in public reports.

The former Heiploeg was required to cooperate fully with the 'designated curators' and the 'designated delegated judge.'

On 27 January 2014, the former Heiploeg applied to the Rechtbank Noord-Nederland (Court of Northern Netherlands) to be declared bankrupt.

The next day, said Court granted that application and appointed, as curator and delegated judge, the persons who had previously served as 'designated curator' and 'designated delegated judge'.

The two companies that make up the new Heiploeg, which were registered in the commercial register on 21 January 2014, took over most of the business activities of the

79. For a detailed overview of the jurisprudential and doctrinal debate that has arisen in the Netherlands on this issue, *see* the Opinion of Advocate General Drijber, 1 November 2019 (FNV/Heiploeg).

former Heiploeg. The asset transfer agreement, under which the assets of the former Heiploeg are transferred to the new Heiploeg, was concluded on 29 January 2014.

In accordance with this agreement, the new Heiploeg took over the employment contracts of about two-thirds of the former Heiploeg's employees so that they would carry out, in the same workplace, the activities they had previously practised, albeit subjecting them to less favourable working conditions.

The new Heiploeg acquired the premises of the former Heiploeg, which it uses, and retained virtually the same clientele as the latter.

FNV appealed the first instance ruling that declared the former Heiploeg bankrupt.

In its judgment, the Court of appeal dismissed the appeal, finding that the new Heiploeg had argued, without being contradicted, that the financial losses suffered by the former Heiploeg and the fact that banks were unwilling to finance the amount of the financial penalty, which had been imposed on four companies in that group, had the effect of making the latter's bankruptcy inevitable. That Court inferred from this that the three conditions for the application of Article 5(1) of Directive 2001/23 were met and that, therefore, the new Heiploeg was not bound by the working and employment conditions applicable to its employees prior to the transfer. Indeed, that Court considered that, at the time of the acquisition of the former Heiploeg by the new Heiploeg, first, the former Heiploeg was the subject of bankruptcy proceedings; second, those proceedings were aimed at liquidating the assets of the transferor; and third, those proceedings had been subject to the supervision of a public authority.

FNV appealed by cassation to the Hoge Raad der Nederlanden (Supreme Court of the Netherlands) against this judgment, arguing that the last two prerequisites laid down in this provision would not be met in the case of a pre-pack procedure and that, by reason of this, the transfer of the former Heiploeg to the new Heiploeg would be subject to the provisions of Directive 2001/23, so that the employees of the former Heiploeg should be considered to have taken up employment with the new Heiploeg while retaining their working conditions.

The Supreme Court of the Netherlands, in this context, noted that it was undisputed that the former Heiploeg was subject to bankruptcy proceedings, within the meaning of Article 5(1) of Directive 2001/23.

However, in view of the case law of the Court of Justice, it expressed doubts as to whether the pre-pack procedure (as outlined in this case) fulfills the other two prerequisites set forth in Article 5(1) of Directive 2001/23, namely, whether such a procedure, on the one hand, can be considered to be directed toward the liquidation of the assets of the former Heiploeg and, on the other hand, whether it is carried out under the supervision of a public authority.

Hence, the referral to the Court of Justice.

In its first question, the Supreme Court of the Netherlands asks, in essence, whether Article 5(1) of Directive 2001/23 is to be interpreted as meaning that the prerequisite laid down therein, according to which Articles 3 and 4 of that Directive do not apply to the transfer of an undertaking where the transferor is subject to bankruptcy or similar insolvency proceedings 'opened with a view to the liquidation of the transferor's assets' is satisfied where the transfer of an undertaking, in whole or in part, is arranged, prior to the opening of bankruptcy proceedings directed at the liquidation of the assets of the transferor and in the course of which said transfer is carried out, as part of a pre-pack procedure having the objective of enabling, during the bankruptcy proceedings, a liquidation of the going concern that best satisfies all creditors and maintains, as far as possible, employment.

The Court of Justice, after recalling its precedents, noted that the first question is related to factual and procedural elements that, according to the referring court, either were not noted in the referral decision at the origin of the judgment of 22 June 2017, C-126/16, or did not exist in the case that gave rise to that judgment and that, consequently, preclude a transposition to the main proceedings of the answer given by the Court in that judgment.

In view of the characteristics of the pre-pack procedure described by the referring court in the case that gave rise to the judgment of the Court of Justice of 22 June 2017, C-126/16, and, in particular, the fact that this procedure aimed to avoid the abrupt cessation of the activities of the undertaking in question on the date of the bankruptcy order, in order to preserve both the economic value of that undertaking and employment, the Court of Justice held, in paragraph 50, that, subject to verification by the referring court, that procedure did not ultimately aim at the liquidation of the undertaking concerned, so that the economic and social objective pursued could not explain or justify the fact that, when that undertaking was the subject of a total or partial transfer, its employees were deprived of the rights granted to them by Directive 2001/23.

The facts of the case in Case C-237/20 are, however, different.

The Supreme Court of the Netherlands notes, in fact, that at the time the pre-pack procedure in question was initiated, the assignor's insolvency was inevitable and that both the bankruptcy procedure and the pre-pack procedure that preceded it were directed at liquidating the assignor's assets; moreover, bankruptcy had been pronounced.

The Supreme Court, in this context, notes that the main objective of all these procedures that led to the liquidation in question was to obtain the highest possible return for all creditors.

Not only that.

It was also undisputed that, in the case at hand, the transfer of the enterprise had taken place in the course of bankruptcy proceedings aimed at liquidating all the assets of the former Heiploeg, i.e., the transferor's enterprise.

Therefore, where the main objective of pre-pack proceedings followed by bankruptcy proceedings is to obtain, following the establishment of the assignor's insolvency and its liquidation, the highest possible repayment for all of its creditors, such proceedings considered together satisfy, in principle, the second prerequisite set forth in Article 5(1) of Directive 2001/23.

In essence, according to the Court of Justice, it is necessary to verify in each situation whether the pre-pack and bankruptcy proceedings in question are directed at the liquidation of the enterprise due to the proven insolvency of the transferor, and not at a mere reorganization of the latter.

It follows, the Court of Justice concludes, that it is necessary to answer the first question by declaring that Article 5(1) of Directive 2001/23 must be interpreted as meaning that the condition laid down therein, according to which Articles 3 and 4 of that Directive do not apply to the transfer of an undertaking where the transferor is the subject of bankruptcy proceedings or similar insolvency proceedings 'opened with a view to the liquidation of the assets of the transferor', is satisfied where the transfer of an undertaking, in whole or in part is arranged, prior to the opening of bankruptcy proceedings directed at the liquidation of the transferor's assets and in the course of which said transfer is carried out, under pre-pack proceedings having the main objective of enabling, within the bankruptcy proceedings, a liquidation of the going concern that best satisfies all creditors and maintains, as far as possible, employment, provided that such pre-pack proceedings are governed by legislative or regulatory provisions.[80]

In its second question, the Supreme Court of the Netherlands asked, in essence, whether Article 5(1) of Directive 2001/23 should be interpreted as meaning that the condition it lays down, according to which Articles 3 and 4 of that directive do not apply to the transfer of an undertaking, business or part of an undertaking or business where the bankruptcy or similar insolvency proceedings of which the transferor is the subject are [carried out] under the supervision of a competent public authority, is satisfied where the transfer of an enterprise, in whole or in part, is prepared in pre-pack proceedings to the declaration of bankruptcy by a 'designated receiver' under the supervision of a 'designated delegated judge', and where the agreement relating to such transfer is concluded and brought to execution after the pronouncement of bankruptcy directed at the liquidation of the transferor's assets.

In order to answer this question, the Court of Justice takes up some passages contained in the 2017 ruling.

In that case, the Court of Justice had ruled that, based on the file submitted to it, the pre-pack procedure was not subject to the control of the competent court, but was managed by the administrative body of the enterprise that conducted negotiations and made decisions in preparation for the sale of the bankrupt enterprise.

In paragraph 55 of C-126/16, the Court of Justice had held that the 'appointed curator' and 'appointed delegated judge' had no formal power and were not subject to any control exercised by a public authority.

It had also considered that, insofar as, immediately after the bankruptcy proceedings were opened, the delegated judge conferred authorization for the transfer arranged under the pre-pack procedure, the latter should, prior to the commencement of those proceedings, have been informed of the transfer and have consented to it.

The Court of Justice had inferred from this, in paragraph 57, that in view of these characteristics, the pre-pack procedure at issue in that case was likely to empty almost

80. On the subject *see* L. Rocchi, *Sulla continuazione dell'attività d'impresa nelle procedure aventi finalità liquidatorie: il revirement della Corte di giustizia in tema di prepack*, in Argomenti diritto del lavoro 2022, 5, 971.

completely of its content any possible control by a competent public authority regarding the bankruptcy proceedings and thus did not satisfy the requirement for control by such an authority set forth in Article 5(1) of Directive 2001/23.

The facts of the case, in the case examined in 2022, are, however, different.

According to the referring judge, the status and functions of the 'appointed receiver', as defined by the Court that appoints him or by the instructions of the 'appointed delegated judge' appointed for this purpose, would not differ substantially from the status and functions of the receiver in bankruptcy proceedings.

The 'appointed curator' could, similarly to the bankruptcy trustee, be held liable for wrongdoing in the performance of his or her duties, and his or her personal liability would be assessed according to the same criteria applicable to the bankruptcy trustee. The 'designated delegated judge' – like the delegated judge in bankruptcy proceedings – would ensure that during the pre-pack procedure prior to the declaration of bankruptcy, the 'designated curator' would be supervised to ensure that the 'designated curator' does not violate his or her competencies and acts in the interest of the creditors as a whole.

The Court that appointed the 'designated curator' and 'designated delegated judge' would check, in the event of subsequent insolvency proceedings, whether these individuals followed all the instructions given to them and, if not, would appoint other individuals as curators and delegated judge when the bankruptcy is pronounced.

On the basis of these considerations (corroborated by those made in paragraphs 60 to 64), the Court of Justice answered the second question by stating that Article 5(1) of Directive 2001/23 must be interpreted as meaning that the prerequisite laid down therein, according to which Articles 3 and 4 of that directive do not apply to the transfer of an undertaking, business or part of an undertaking or business where the bankruptcy or similar insolvency proceedings of which the transferor is the subject 'are [being] carried out under the supervision of a competent public authority, is satisfied where the transfer of an enterprise, in whole or in part, is prepared, as part of pre-pack proceedings prior to the declaration of bankruptcy', by a 'designated receiver', subject to the supervision of a 'designated delegated judge', and where the agreement relating to such transfer is concluded and brought to execution after the pronouncement of bankruptcy directed at the liquidation of the transferor's assets, provided that such a pre-pack proceeding is governed by legislative or regulatory provisions.

[G] The Judgment of the Court of Justice of 3 April 2025, C-431/23

The issue was raised by the Liege Labour Court (Belgium).

First of all, the case.

On 30 July 2020, the Ghent Business Court initiated judicial reorganization proceedings for WIBRA BELGIË SA.

The Court appointed BA, EP and RI as judicial commissioners, assigning them the task of organizing and transferring all or part of the company's activities.

On 30 September 2020, WIBRA BELGIË SRL was established for the purpose of taking over and continuing part of the activities previously exercised by WIBRA BELGIË SA.

The Ghent Business Court subsequently declared WIBRA BELGIË SA bankrupt and appointed BA, EP and RI as receivers.

The receivers, on 9 October 2020, transferred part of the tangible and intangible movable assets of WIBRA BELGIË SA to WIBRA BELGIË SRL.

Of all the dismissed workers, or 439 workers, 183 were rehired by WIBRA BELGIË SRL.

Twenty-two former employees of WIBRA BELGIË SA brought the appeal.

The Liège Tribunal, in this context, asked whether Article 5(1) of Directive 2001/23 should be interpreted to mean that it applies in a situation where bankruptcy proceedings follow a judicial reorganization procedure, in the course of which an agreement for the partial transfer of the undertaking concerned has been drawn up, but it has not been approved by the competent court, before being executed once bankruptcy has been declared.

The Court of Justice, after recalling the principles expressed in the 2017 Court of Justice ruling C-126/16 (cited in paragraph 33-39) recalls that Article 5(1) of Directive 2001/23 lays down three cumulative conditions: (a) first, that the transferor must be the subject of bankruptcy or similar insolvency proceedings; (b) second, that such proceedings must be opened with a view to the liquidation of the transferor's assets; and (c) third, that such proceedings must take place under the supervision of a competent public authority.

Regarding *the first condition*, he notes that it 'cannot extend to a transaction that is preparatory to bankruptcy but does not lead to it.'

On the other hand, a transfer transaction which, although prepared prior to the declaration of bankruptcy, is implemented subsequent to the declaration of bankruptcy, implies actual bankruptcy and may therefore fall within the notion of 'bankruptcy proceedings' within the meaning of Article 5(1) of Directive 2001/23.

It is therefore up to the referring court to determine 'whether the drawing up of a takeover plan as part of the judicial reorganization procedure of WIBRA BELGIË SA, on the one hand, and the implementation of that plan during the bankruptcy proceedings of that company, on the other, should be considered a single operation, implying, from the outset, the declaration of bankruptcy of that company due to its proven insolvency, before the transfer of business was carried out'.

In relation to the *second condition*, the Court recalls that a procedure aimed at the continuation of the activity of the enterprise concerned does not meet this condition (open procedure with a view to the liquidation of assets).

It is, of course, up to the referring court to ascertain 'whether the successive procedures at issue in the main proceedings, taken individually or as a whole, had the objective of maximizing the collective satisfaction of creditors and enabled that objective to be achieved, or whether, on the contrary, they were aimed primarily at safeguarding the operation of the enterprise or its economically viable units'.[81]

With regard to the *third condition*, concerning the requirement that the procedure referred to in Article 5(1) of Directive 2001/23 must take place under the supervision of a competent public authority, the Court points out 'that this is not the case when the court-appointed liquidator is in charge of organizing and carrying out the transfer of business in the name and on behalf of the debtor and when he has to solicit offers, ensuring in particular the preservation of all or part of the undertaking's business, while considering the rights of creditors, as appears to be the case in a judicial reorganization procedure as conceived in Belgian law'.

While deferring the application of this principle to the evaluations of the referring court, the Court of Justice provides useful guidance for its application by noting that, in the present case, WIBRA BELGIË SA requested the initiation of a judicial reorganization procedure, governed by Belgian law, which offers guarantees to workers, with a view to preparing for a total or partial transfer of that company's activities.

It appears from the referral decision, the Court of Justice continues that it was following the refusal by the Ghent Business Court to approve the takeover offer that had been accepted by the judicial commissioners appointed as part of that procedure that that company asked that Court to declare it bankrupt, thus initiating a procedure that, under Belgian law, grants workers guarantee other than those provided under the judicial reorganization procedure.

On the basis of these clarifications, the Court concludes by stating that Article 5(1) of Council Directive 2001/23/EC of 12 March 2001, must be interpreted to mean:

> it applies to a situation where a bankruptcy proceeding follows a judicial reorganization proceeding in the course of which an agreement for partial transfer of the enterprise concerned has been drawn up, but it has not been approved by the competent court, before being executed once bankruptcy has been declared, provided that the bankruptcy or similar insolvency proceeding, which has been implemented, is actually opened with a view to liquidating the assets of the transferor, that said proceeding is conducted under the supervision of a competent public authority, and that the use of the proceeding itself cannot be characterized as abusive.

81. In paras 51 to 56, the Court of Justice provides useful food for thought for the national court.

Chapter 12
Lithuania

Diana Labokaitė

§12.01 HARMONIZATION OF LAWS UNDER THE DIRECTIVE

Among the reasons for termination of employment contracts, cases of business relocation are not the most common. Perhaps that is why such cases rarely occur in the practice of Lithuanian courts, and they are difficult for the courts. The author of this review has been a judge of the court of general competence since 2003, specializing in labour cases. During my 20 years as a judge, I had to decide on the appeal of one dispute related to a possible transfer of business in passenger aviation, where a group of pilots and flight attendants who worked for Ryanair were dismissed, despite claiming that another company belonging to the Ryanair group continued to carry out those duties of flights from Kaunas and to Kaunas. Of course, the employer denied the fact of the business transfer. The Supreme Court of Lithuania, by its ruling of 31 May 2023, approved the settlement agreement concluded by the parties, the terms of which were recognized as a non-public part of the case. The Supreme Court annulled the procedural decisions adopted by the Kaunas District Court and Kaunas Regional Court in the case and terminated the case. It is understandable that such a procedural outcome is the most acceptable for the parties to the case, but case law suffered because it remained unclear whether the lower courts properly assessed the circumstances proving the transfer of the business.

Legal practitioners often look for answers to difficult questions in legal research works. One doctoral thesis has been defended on the topic of business relocation in Lithuanian legal science – in 2018, Eglė Tamošiūnaitė-Samaitienė defended her doctoral thesis at Vilnius University under the title 'Concept of Business Transfer according to Directive 2001/23/EC.' One master thesis was written in 2016, by Dovilė Zajauskaitė at Vilnius University with the title 'The concept of transfer of business or its part in labor law.' Several scientific articles have been written on the topic of the application of the Business Transfer Directive by V. Mačiulaitis in 2015, V. Mačernytė-

Panomariovienė in 2012, and J. Kiršienė and K. Kerutis in 2006. In comparison to other fields of research, this particular topic is yet modestly discussed since the problem itself is not so frequent in Lithuanian labour disputes. When there is not much national practice, it is mainly necessary to analyse the practice of the European Union. However, the Directive itself indicates that what is not directly defined must be understood and interpreted according to the examples of the cases of the European Court of Justice.

Since the accession of the Republic of Lithuania to the European Union on 1 May 2004, the legal norms of the European Union have become an integral part of the legal system of the Republic of Lithuania. In some cases, the legal norms of the European Union are applied directly, and in the event of a conflict of legal norms, the legal norms of the EU prevail over the laws and other legal acts of the Republic of Lithuania. Thus, formally and by the Council of the European Union on 12 March 2001 Directive No. 2001/23/EC (further: *Directive* or *Business Transfer Directive*) became an integral part of the legal system of the Republic of Lithuania. However, in practice, the Directive was not applied immediately because, according to the rules of EU law, the provisions of the Directive must be transposed into national law. Lithuania was late in transposing the Directive into national law because only in 2008 did the Labour Code state that the provisions of the Directive are implemented in Article 138, Articles 47, and 63 of the Labour Code.

After Lithuania regained its independence on 11 March 1990, the structure and operating principles of the country's economy fundamentally changed, and private companies and businesses appeared. In turn, business forms had to adapt to the changing needs of the market, which led to the need for businesses to change, restructure, merge, divide, sell and liquidate companies. The freedoms granted to businesses to transform in various ways, in turn, posed a danger to employees, as employees were at risk of losing their jobs, wages, and already acquired social guarantees as companies changed forms. All this required new mechanisms and ways of defending the rights of the workers who have been violated.

Even before Lithuania's accession to the EU, Article 138 of the Labour Code (adopted in 2002) was in force, establishing restrictions on terminating the employment contract in the event of any reorganization of the company. The article was short: 'A change in the owner, subordinate, founder or name of a company, institution, or organization, merger, division, division or merger with another company, institution, or organization cannot be a legal reason to terminate an employment contract.' As can be seen from the content of the article, an attempt was made to grasp the concept of business transfer, an attempt was made to define it by applying two groups of criteria: change of owner, founder, subordinate, and, however, change of the form of the company itself as a legal entity – merger, division, connection to another legal entity.

The concept of business transfer appears directly in the law since 28 May 2005 – 'transfer of business or part of it' is simply added to the already valid Article 138 of the LC.

Another amendment to Article 138 of the Labour Code, adopted and entered into force on 12 January 2012 has already transferred the provisions of the Directive to the national law in more detail and completeness, an additional part was added: 'The business or part of it in the case of the transfer of all or a part, the employment relationship continues under the same conditions in the company, institution, or organization of the transferee of the business, regardless of the legal basis of the transfer of the business or its part. Changing the working conditions or terminating the employment contract due to the transfer of the business or its part is prohibited. The employee must be notified in advance in writing about the future transfer of the business or its part no later than ten working days in advance, indicating the date of the transfer of the business or its part, the legal basis, the economic and social consequences of such a transfer for the employee.' As can be seen, the so-called principle of automatic continuity of employment relations in the company of the business transferee has been introduced; it is indicated that the legal form of business transfer is irrelevant, a ban on changing the terms of the employment contract has been submitted and the obligation to notify the employee in advance about the transfer has been introduced.

From 1 January 2017, the new version of the Labour Code entered into force, Article 51 of which sets out the rules of the Directive in more detail in the case of the transfer of a business or part of it. The article consists of six parts: the first part defines that a change of employer in any form cannot be a reason for terminating the employment relationship, the second part determines the automatic transfer of the employment relationship from one employer to another employer, as well as the transfer of rights established by the collective agreement for at least two years, the third part warns that the legal basis of the business transfer is irrelevant to the continuity of the employment relationship, the fourth part introduces the joint and several one-year liability of the business transferor and the transferee against the employee, the fifth part establishes the obligation to warn the employees 10 days in advance, to disclose the legal details of future changes, gives the employee the right to object in writing to be transferred to a new workplace, in which case the employment contract is terminated at the initiative of the employer without the fault of the employee, and finally, the sixth part of the article establishes the duty of the transferor of the business to transfer the data of the employees to the transferee of the business and to notify the social insurance. As can be seen from the text of the new article of the law, the rules regulate in detail the stages and conditions of business transfer and even set the possibility for the business transferee to request monetary compensation from the business transferor.

Despite the detailed regulation in the law, another minor amendment to Article 51, Part 1 of the Labour Code entered into force on 1 August 2022. Its essence was that the abstract concept of 'reorganization' and the transfer of part of the employer's functions to another employer instead of the transfer of all functions was included in the list of changes in the employer's form.

In the practice of Lithuanian courts, the provisions of Article 1, point c of the Directive are observed, that the administrative reorganization of state management institutions or the transfer of administrative functions, carried out between state authorities, is not classified as a transfer established in this Directive; in other words, the protection provided by the Directive is not valid in civil service relations. According to the legal regulations, the civil service model in Lithuania corresponds to the so-called narrow concept because the corps of civil servants consists of four groups of persons: career civil servants, civil servants of political (personal) trust, heads of institutions, and statutory civil servants. The Law on Civil Service provides special guarantees for civil servants, protecting them from being dismissed from their duties, and they are transferred to other positions throughout the state according to the categories assigned to their positions. However, in practice, there have been cases when civil servants have tried to raise questions both about the application of business transfer provisions and in the field of civil service, and about possible discrimination when such provisions are not applied. For example, in 2011, a case was filed in which the former deputy head of the legal department of the Insurance Supervisory Commission of the Republic of Lithuania was dismissed from his duties because the commission was liquidated and its functions were transferred to the Bank of Lithuania. The claimant initially contested the legality of his dismissal on other grounds (due to inadequate notice and failure to offer other duties) and lost the case. Two years later, in 2013, the plaintiff filed a request to reopen the proceedings and put forward new arguments that the rules of Directive 2001/23/EC and the corresponding protection should have been applied to him. The court relied on the already mentioned exception specified in point c of Article 1 of the Directive and rejected the plaintiff's requests, but it can be seen from the reasons of the court that the court had some doubts as to whether the liquidation of the state commission and the performance of its functions by another institution was not a transfer of activity. I think that the situation when another state institution takes over the activities of the Insurance Supervisory Commission is a typical transfer of activities. Still, the guarantees provided by the Directive were not applied to the employee due to his status as a civil servant.

Likewise, the provisions of the Directive and, accordingly, the provisions of Article 51 of the Lithuanian Labour Code do not apply to managers of companies and institutions, when companies are merged, because the courts have clarified in several cases that an institution cannot be managed by two persons; therefore, the termination of the employment contract with one of the managers is justified by restructuring the work carried out in the company rather than business relocation.

Although it is currently considered that the Business Transfer Directive has been properly transposed into Lithuanian law, in practice, there are difficulties in determining whether there has been a business transfer; in other words, whether the provisions of the Directive can be used to protect the rights of employees. Therefore, Lithuanian national legal acts are only the initial source for resolving disputes between employees and employers in courts. Another essential source is the practice of the EU Court of Justice, interpretations in specific cases. As the researchers point out, the wording of European Union directives is characterized by the ambiguity of the text, which leads to the constant need for the Court of Justice to interpret or reinterpret the established rules. Based on these sources, national courts decide specific disputes and gradually shape national practice.

This review will discuss in more detail the six cases in Lithuania in which employees defended their rights based on the Directive and the articles of the Labour Code establishing its provisions. In two cases, the transfer of business took place in private companies (in ship design and passenger aviation); in other cases, the transfer of business was recognized as having occurred as a result of decisions made by public administration entities. In another case, the Directive was invoked by the company's bankruptcy administrator, claiming that the employees of the bankrupt company should have been taken over by several other companies that took over the business of the bankrupt company. The sixth case was initiated by a trade union that tried to stop public procurement based on the Directive.

§12.02 ACTIONS BY EMPLOYERS TO AVOID THE APPLICATION OF DIRECTIVE

One of the first cases in Lithuanian courts, in which the provisions of the Directive were relied on, began in 2011 in Klaipėda city (1). Six plaintiffs appealed to the court, complaining of illegal dismissal. The plaintiffs worked as designers, financiers, and economists at the Baltic Engineering Centre, a company engaged in ship design. The company's shareholders decided to liquidate the company. A liquidation plan was drawn up. The liquidator agreed with one of the companies of the group, the company 'Western Baltic Engineering' (hereinafter referred to also as 'WBE'), that the latter would employ 32 employees out of 43. Those 32 persons terminated their employment contracts with the liquidated company and were re-hired at Western Baltic Engineering in the company. The remaining unfinished ship design contracts were handed over to WBE for completion. The assets were transferred for the book value to the parent company, Western Shipyard, which leased those assets (desks, computers, etc.) to the company WBE. The lawsuit claimed that it was not the liquidation of the company, but the transfer of business from the company 'Baltic Engineering' to the company 'WBE.' Accordingly, the workers were to be protected by the Directive: their employment relationship with the preservation of seniority, acquired guarantees, duration of leave, bonuses, etc., was to be transferred to the company that took over the business, WBE. However, the plaintiffs were simply dismissed without notice on the grounds of liquidation. They did not agree to re-employment at WBE because they were offered a lower salary and their previous seniority was not recognized.

The defendant disagreed with the claim, stating that it was not a transfer of business, but the liquidation of the company where the plaintiff worked. In the event of liquidation, the defendant stated that the company's business or some assets may be sold or transferred to other persons, but this is not equivalent to the transfer of all rights and obligations of the company as a whole during the reorganization. The defendant has not transferred any functions to a third party or another person. The defendant's documents were transferred to the archive. The defendant considered the fact that the liquidator concluded an agreement with the company 'WBE' regarding the employment of some employees as an optional behaviour dictated by goodwill. The employer was only looking for opportunities to offer the employees other jobs in another company, of course, without preserving any guarantees acquired by the employees – length of service, the right to extended vacations, monetary bonuses, etc.

This case is unique in that the court of the first instance rejected the claim twice. Both times, the appellate court upheld the first instance decisions, but the Supreme Court of Lithuania twice overturned the decisions and sent the case back for retrial. Such a long process clearly shows that despite the transposition of the provisions of the Directive into national law, the practical aspects of the application are unclear not only for employers and employees but also for the courts.

The courts primarily relied on the formal criterion that the liquidation of the company took place, and not the transfer of business. The fact that part of the employees was transferred to another company by the liquidator was called by the courts a manifestation of goodwill because the liquidator was not obliged to do so. The fact that the unfinished ship design contracts were transferred to another company, WBE, was also insufficient evidence for the courts that a transfer of business had taken place, as it is natural in the event of liquidation that there remain some unfinished contracts that simply need to be completed. Regarding the transfer of assets, the court stated that the assets were not transferred to the company 'WBE', which, according to the plaintiffs, took over the business, but to the parent company (shareholder), so this is also not an indication of the transfer of business.

Basically, the same conclusions were reached by the appellate court (Klaipėda district court), which on 18 August 2011 upheld the district court's decision. The court examined in detail the differences between liquidation and reorganization of a joint-stock company. Again, the court's approach was formal because Article 138 of the Labour Code, which was in force at that time, established that the employment contract cannot be terminated due to the merger, division, distribution, or merger of companies with another company; the case of liquidation was not directly named in the law. The panel of judges decided that the company 'WBE' did not have any obligations to take over the defendant's rights and obligations arising from the defendant's employment relationship with the plaintiffs.

The Supreme Court of Lithuania on 20 February 2012 by the ruling (civil case No. 3K-3-40/2012) annulled the decision of the district court and the ruling of the district court and returned the claim to the district court for examination after re-emphasizing that this dispute should have been examined under Article 138 of the LC and EU Council Directive 2001/23/EC provisions and guided by the practice of the CJEU. Even if national law does not provide for certain specific forms of change of companies (in this case, liquidation), this does not mean that the Directive is not applicable. It was suggested that consideration should be given to whether an organized pool of resources was not maintained when out-of-work ship design contracts were transferred. In addition, attention was drawn to the practice of the CJEU that the concept of legal transfer interpreted by him does not prevent the recognition of the transfer of a company even without the conclusion of any written or oral agreement between the companies concerned (judgment of 13 September 2007, Mohamed Jouini et al., C-458-05, items 25-27).

The court of cassation emphasized that it is not the formal name of the company's reorganization that must be evaluated, but the actual situation, the actual basis of the claim. The circumstances stated by the plaintiffs and determined by the courts confirm that the activity (business) of the defendant, 'Baltic engineering centre', was not terminated, but transferred to a third party, 'Western Baltic Engineering.' It is possible that the court of cassation could have examined the case and made a decision opposite to that of the first courts, but a procedural problem arose because the defendant (the first employer, 'Baltic engineering centre') was already liquidated; the defendant's representative even asked to terminate the case without the defendant, but the court, relying on the provisions of the Directive, indicated that the continuity of the employment relationship moves from the business transferor to the company of the business transferee; therefore, if it is established that the business transfer took place, the third person in the case should be included as a defendant and the plaintiff's claims regarding the recognition of the termination of the employment contract as illegal and reinstatement should be directed to him.

Thus, the case entered the second round, but the courts again rejected the claim after repeating the same arguments that the transfer of the majority of the defendant's employees to another defendant, WBE, and the transfer of several unfinished one-time contracts did not constitute a transfer of business. The transfer of employees was carried out with the consent of the employees themselves, the contracts were transferred with the consent of the clients, and the property was sold and not transferred; therefore, the provisions of the Directive do not apply.

The cassation appeal was accepted for examination for the second time by the selection panel and the Supreme Court of Lithuania on 7 February 2014, by ruling in civil case No. 3K-3-13/2014 which once again annulled the decision of the Klaipėda Regional Court and returned the case to the appellate court, not to the first instance, this time. The practice of the Court of Justice was cited regarding the provisions of the Directive that they must also be applied in cases where the company is liquidated, if it is established that the entity that took over the company or part of it continues to carry on the same or similar activities. In this ruling, the Court of Cassation also indicated the groups of factual circumstances that must be investigated to determine whether the transfer of the business (part of it) took place in the case under consideration, i.e., the nature of the economic activities of both companies, management bodies, shareholders (the companies belong to the same concern), employees (the functions they perform), work organization, customers and their information, executed contracts, the transfer and use of assets, and also emphasized that all these circumstances are separate aspects of the comprehensive assessment that must be carried out; therefore, they cannot be assessed in isolation from each other, and conclusions must be drawn not from individual facts, but from their totality. The court of cassation almost directly made it clear that, from all the circumstances of the case, it was possible to draw the opposite conclusion from what the courts did. The question arises why the court of cassation did not take the opposite decision and did not close the case. The court itself reasoned that the factual circumstances, which are not examined by the court of cassation, were not fully examined, as it examines only legal issues.

The third round of the case ended in 2014 in the Klaipėda Regional Court. 27 June decision (judgment of 27 June 2014, in civil case No. 2A-644-459/2014), by which the claim was finally satisfied. Regarding the transfer of business, the panel decided separately on each aspect: (1) whether the nature of the company's activity and the identity of the taken-over activity remained; (2) whether a stable economic unit was transferred, rather than one-time agreements for the performance of specific, concrete works; (3) whether tangible and intangible resources, employees, customers, the similarity of activities before and after the transfer have been transferred.

Finally, the real course of events was established in this case: the defendant (former employer, the company 'Baltic Engineering Centre') was engaged in the engineering design of ships. After its shares were bought by the Estonian concern, the defendant became one of the companies of the group. Among these companies was 'WBE', which provides engineering design services. In this way, two companies engaged in ship design ended up in the concern. The shareholders of the concern decided to liquidate one of the designing companies and instructed the liquidator to look for opportunities and, with the consent of the employees, to employ them in the companies of the concern. The liquidator entered into such an agreement, and some of the employees were transferred by agreement of the parties after the termination of employment contracts with 'Baltic Engineering Centre' and the conclusion of new contracts with 'Western Baltic Engineering' the next day. The company in liquidation has informed its clients that it is transferring its activities to WBE, and therefore will also transfer the execution of contracts. Thus, the liquidated company itself confirmed to its clients that the activities carried out will be continued in another company. The seven transferred customers and the contracts concluded with them constituted a stable and profitable business, which was equal to the annual income of the liquidated company, and after the transfer of the business, it also accounted for about 60% of the WBE company profit.

The transfer of employees took place following the agreement of the employers and the consent of the employees, but for the transferred employees, even though the employment contracts were formally terminated and renewed the next day, the uninterrupted length of service, related rights, obligations, additional guarantees regarding the granting of annual leave were preserved, benefits paid by the employer, disciplinary sanctions imposed on transferred employees. The transferred employees made up about half of the third party's employees. The transferred employees continued to perform the same functions in the new company. The court finally recognized that the situation in question meets the criteria of a business transfer: the business was transferred as a stable economic unit, as the basis of the business were transferred employees, material assets were transferred via the parent company, rights and obligations under contracts were taken over, these contracts were continued to be performed and income was received based on them. Consequently, the guarantees of Directive 2001/23/EC should also have been applied to the plaintiffs. Under the stated circumstances, the panel concluded that the employment contracts with the plaintiffs were terminated illegally. Since the plaintiffs did not ask to return to work, the court decided to award compensation and not to return them to work.

The court solved the consequences of the illegal dismissal in an interesting way: the plaintiffs were not returned to work, but the awarded salary for the time of forced absence was reduced to six months, although the whole process continued from October 2010 to June 2014. The total time of forced absence when calculating the wages of the plaintiffs would have amounted to about 1 million litas (EUR 300,000). The court argued that the defendant did not initiate the process, and did not file any appeals or cassation complaints; therefore, to transfer financial responsibility to her in the way that the plaintiff requests, would be contrary to the principles of justice and reasonableness and the financial stability of the defendant since the total amount requested by the plaintiffs would be more than 1 million litas. It can be assumed that this type of financial obligation would complicate the economic activity of the defendant, perhaps even lead to its insolvency, and in this case, the rights and legitimate expectations of not only the defendant's creditors but also other employees would be violated. In addition, the court found that the plaintiffs were already employed in other companies after half a year on average. It can be concluded that, on average, a reasonable and realistic deadline for getting a job and starting to receive wages again is about half a year. It did not award non-pecuniary damages to the plaintiffs, stating that the satisfaction of the claim is sufficient satisfaction for the plaintiffs.

After the court's decision in favour of the plaintiffs, the cassation complaint was filed by the employer (the company that took over the business, WBE), but this time the cassation court did not consider the complaint. The history of this case shows how difficult it was for the Lithuanian courts to apply the provisions of the Directive in a specific situation. This could have been influenced by the insufficient regulation of the national law at the time, and the inability to apply the practice of the European Court of Justice. The motivation to reduce the amounts awarded was not very logical, as the plaintiffs were blamed for appealing the previous decisions, thereby prolonging the process. However, if they had not complained, they would have lost the case altogether.

Another case happened just at the height of the pandemic – in 2019-2020. The international low-cost airline Ryanair Designated Activated Company (hereinafter: 'DAC or Ryanair DAC') had established a base in Kaunas. The company was registered in Ireland, but there were five aircraft storage facilities in Kaunas, the so-called overnight accommodation. The aircraft was leased from a leasing company. Pilots and stewards, a group of about 50 employees, worked on the aircraft. Employment contracts were concluded with them, in which it was stated that the employees undertake to live an hour away from Kaunas, and Kaunas was their flight preparation and training base. It is also stated that employment contracts are governed by Irish law.

After the start of the COVID pandemic, Ryanair DAC sent notices to the employees that, due to the pandemic and the reduced number of flights, they are suspending operations from the Kaunas base. The employees were informed that their employment contracts would be terminated and they were offered employment in another company belonging to the same Ryanair group of companies, but registered in

Poland, the so-called Polish company Ryanair Buzz (hereinafter: 'Buzz'). It is self-evident that employment at Buzz was offered anew, starting from a 'white sheet' without saving the length of service, salary, or other guarantees. Some of the employees accepted the offer, terminated their contracts with DAC, and took jobs at Buzz. However, 10 workers did not agree to leave voluntarily because they were offered half their salary at the Polish company Buzz. The DAC informed the social security company that it had dismissed 10 claimants for good reason.

The aforementioned 10 plaintiffs went to court, including both companies, DAC and Buzz, as respondents/defendants, and claimed in their lawsuit that there was a transfer of business between the defendants, so the plaintiffs' employment contracts must be continued in Buzz, and the dismissal was illegal.

Then DAC, even though the employees had already been dismissed, sent notices to the former employees that they had changed their workplace (one of the conditions of the employment contract) from Kaunas to Stansted, and they must come to work there. The employees said they did not agree and did not come to Stansted on the appointed day. The DAC then informed the workers that they had been fired for indiscipline (absenteeism). In other words, fired a second time.

In court, the DAC company claimed that there was no transfer of business because: (1) Ryanair did not stop the activities of DAC, but only moved the base from Kaunas to Stansted; (2) the planes were not taken over by the Polish Buzz company; (3) the group of employees did not form a stable economic unit; and (4) Buzz's activity model was different from DAC that worked in Kaunas before because Buzz was only engaged in charter flights, it did not operate regular flights as DAC previously.

The courts of the first instance and the appellate instance decided that the transfer of business took place; therefore, they satisfied the claim of the plaintiffs. The court made this conclusion based on several criteria: part of the DAC employees transferred to work at Buzz, the defendant Buzz 1 July 2020 continued the same activity of air passenger transportation as on 30 June 2020 terminated by the defendant DAC, the defendant Buzz uses the same five aircraft and also uses the same premises in the Kaunas airport building, which it rents from DAC.

In this case, as in the previously discussed *Klaipėda* case, no clear legal transfer or merger of companies was adopted. The courts, in recognizing the transfer of business, relied on several criteria: (1) both the transferor company DAC and the takeover company Buzz used the same Boeing aircraft, which in turn were leased from the leasing company; aircraft flew from Kaunas and to Kaunas; (2) before transfer and after aircraft were serviced by a group of persons: pilots and stewards, about 49 persons; (3) the schedule of regular flights from Kaunas and to Kaunas did not change, those flights were operated by Buzz, flights did not decrease and new ones did not appear either.

Courts have considered whether a stable economic unit has been moved. As an example, the EU Court of Justice case Allen et al. No. C-234/98 concluded that Directive 77/187 (previous version of the Directive No. 2001/23/EC) applies to the situation where a company belonging to a group of companies decides to transfer part of its activities to another company of the same group by transferring to it the transport work in mines when one company transfers to another a stable economic unit. The concept of a stable economic unit refers to an organized set of persons and assets that enables economic activities to be carried out to achieve set goals. The courts ruled that in the case of *Ryanair*, the economic activity from which the group of companies derives a profit is to fly passengers from one location to another. These activities, in turn, can be divided into several segments (e.g., ticketing, ground handling of the aircraft, in-flight crew work, additional activities for the sale of goods, etc.). One of the business segments may be the use of manned aircraft as a separate economic unit. This part of the joint activity was separated and transferred from DAC to Buzz, so the fact that Ryanair Buzz does not distribute flight tickets itself, but rents aircraft with crew, should not allow the defendants to avoid the application of Directive 2001/23/EC, according to the panel.

The fact that Buzz did not take over the premises of DAC in Kaunas, as well as any other property, and did not take over the aircraft themselves, did not change the opinion of the courts regarding the transfer of business that took place. Courts have decided that property, premises, and aircraft are not essential criteria for establishing the transfer of business; the transferee can also use production factors of third parties. The courts relied here on the EU Court of Justice case No. C-664/17 *Ellinika Nafpigeia v. Panagiotis Anagnostopoulos*, where the court replied to the question about the use of third-party production factors that according to the Directive 2001/23/EC, in particular, Article 1(1)(a) and (b) thereof, must be interpreted as applying to the situation when the unit in question is not completely independent because it cannot achieve its economic goal without using the production factors of third countries, provided that, first, the general principle of European Union law is observed, according to which the transferor and the transferee must not attempt to unfairly and illegally take advantage of the Directive 2001/23 and, second, the production unit concerned has sufficient guarantees to ensure its access to the factors of production of a third country in such a way that it is independent of the unilateral economic choices of that third country. In this case, Buzz, by taking over from DAC part of its operations, namely manned aircraft, and leasing them, and leaving the distribution of tickets for scheduled flights to DAC, as well as using DAC's leased ground facilities, took over an economic entity with autonomy and stability. Services required by this unit may be obtained by Buzz from other persons, including DAC.

One of the arguments, as in the *Klaipėda* case, was those 19 employees, out of the former 49, moved to work at the Buzz company themselves and did the same job. The court concluded that Buzz effectively took over some of the employees as an organized resource group, one of the elements of Ryanair's DAC. The fact that the transfer of employees was framed as a new admission to Buzz does not change the fact of the transfer itself. The court essentially satisfied the claim, recognized the dismissal of the plaintiffs as illegal, but did not return them to work, as the plaintiffs lost their interest in being returned to their previous jobs due to the long-lasting litigation. The plaintiffs were only awarded wages for litigation time and severance pay.

Ryanair filed a cassation appeal in which it disagreed with the classification of the business transfer. The essential argument of Ryanair's objection was that, in the sense of an organized group of resources, in the transport sector, not only the transfer of a group of employees but also the transfer of vehicles must be defined because, without vehicles, the same business cannot be carried on. The cassator argued that the business in the field of transport is more related to the possession of the property and means of production; it is a so-called capital-intensive business, unlike catering and similar service provision businesses, which are labour-intensive; here, the transfer of business could be qualified only in the case of taking over employees. In the cassator's opinion, in the aviation sector, taking over service employees alone is not enough to establish the transfer of business. The Supreme Court of Lithuania accepted the cassation appeal, but at the time of writing this review, the dispute has not yet been finally resolved.

We see that employers seek to hide the transfer of business in various ways, and the legislator must regulate in such a way that the courts and other law enforcement entities can properly identify each hidden case and protect the rights of employees.

Although I have already mentioned that the provisions of the Directive do not apply concerning civil servants, they may be applied to state institutions when it is necessary to protect employees employed under employment contracts. For example, the transfer of activities was recognized as having taken place when the municipal council decided to liquidate the Raseiniai municipality's budgetary institution, 'Social Services Centre' and established a public institution, 'Social Services Centre', in its place. The public institution, as determined by the court, used the same property and provided the same services, but some of the former employees were dismissed due to the liquidation, and new employees were hired. The dismissed claimants challenged the legality of the dismissal, arguing that there had been a transfer of activity and therefore the worker protection mechanisms set out in the Directive should apply, i.e., employment relations should have been transferred to a public institution by itself. However, the appellate court, finding that the plaintiff's employment relationship should have continued and continued with the new employer, i.e., public institution 'Raseini social services centre', decided to award benefits related to labour relations and compensation for non-pecuniary damage not jointly from the municipality (the founder of both companies) and the transferee, but only from the person who took over the employer's rights, i.e., from the public entity 'Raseini social services centre.'

An analogous situation was resolved in the Vilnius Regional Court civil case No. 2A-1821-603/2013, in which the public institution 'Vilnius flats' established by Vilnius Municipality, engaged in the provision of housing administration services, was liquidated, and a municipal company was established to perform its functions. Although the nature of the services and the assets used remained the same, several employees were laid off. The workers sued for reinstatement, and their claim was upheld. This time, the court of the first instance properly applied the provisions of the Directive transferred to the Lithuanian Labour Code.

§12.03 ACTIONS BY THE BANKRUPTCY ADMINISTRATOR TO REDUCE THE CREDITOR CLAIMS OF THE BANKRUPT COMPANY

The provisions of the Business Transfer Directive were used in another case, in which the issue of the violated rights of employees was raised not by the employees themselves, but by the bankruptcy administrator of one of the companies. The bankrupt company 'Chilija' was established in 1993, engaged in catering activities, and until 2008 grew into a chain of six pizzerias. After the beginning of the financial crisis in 2008, 'Chilija' changed its name to 'Veiza' and was reorganized by splitting into five new companies (Chili Bistro, Chili Village, Asian Flavors, GCW, and Chili Holdings) and leaving the old 'Veiza'. The shares of assets, rights, and liabilities were assigned to the separated five companies, the authorized capital was divided, and the employees were distributed. But not all. After the separation, those employees who were on long-term parental leave at the time of the separation remained at the old 'Veiza'. This company, 'Veiza', stopped operating, sold off the assets it had and soon filed for bankruptcy proceedings. A bankruptcy case was filed, and creditor claims for 300,000 litas (EUR 100,000) were filed.

The bankruptcy trustee filed a lawsuit against the other four companies that were separated from the original company, claiming that those employees who were on parental leave should also have been transferred to the four continuing companies, in other words, the separation and abandonment of the employees on leave in the company, which soon went bankrupt, there was a conscious effort to avoid the employer's obligations to pay salaries. In this way, according to the bankruptcy administrator, the damage was caused not only to the employees but also to the bankrupt company, which did not have enough funds to cover its obligations to creditors (including former employees).

According to the Administrator, Article 138 of the Labour Code and Directive no. 2001/23/EC are applicable here; all employees of 'Veiza' were to be taken over, providing them with no worse working conditions than the latter had when working in 'Veiza' before the reorganization. According to the plaintiff, the illegal actions (inaction) of the defendants had a direct impact on the fact that some of the employees of 'Veiza' were not transferred to newly established companies that took over the activities, assets, and most of the employees of 'Veiza'. This led to the termination of employment contracts with these employees and the emergence of credit claims of employees and tax administrators, respectively, so there is a direct causal connection between the defendants' illegal inaction and the resulting damage.

The Court of First Instance fully satisfied the claim of the bankruptcy administrator. The court said there was no substantial dispute that the bulk of the business had been transferred to five spin-off companies. The appellate court analysed the terms of the separation of companies. It did not appear from the terms of the separation that the employer intended to separate the employees on long-term leave and leave them with the bankrupt company. The terms of the separation stipulated that, according to their duties, all employees of 'Chilija' had to remain after the separation in the same departments where they worked before the separation. It was intended for the plaintiff to continue its activities under the name of 'Chili bistro' and all the employees of 'Chilija' who were not transferred to the other five separate companies were to remain working there. However, the actual situation was such that not all employees were retained in the same companies where they worked before the separation. Those who were on long-term vacation were selectively not transferred to new companies, while those who were working were transferred from the applicant company, and those who were on vacation were left behind. In this way, 288 employees remained with the plaintiff, of which 244 were on child care/maternity leave, and already in 2009, at the end of the year, the persons on such leave were all the remaining employees (162 out of 166), the plaintiff's activities were no longer carried out. As can be seen from the lists provided by the plaintiff, many employees of 'Chilija', whose workplaces were in the previously existing units and who after the separation went to the new companies, were not transferred to the newly created companies. This was a violation of the conditions of separation. Thus, formally, the protection of the interests of the mentioned socially sensitive group of employees regarding the preservation of jobs and their transfer to the appellants was provided for in the Separation Conditions, but in reality, a large group of persons remained untransferred.

According to Article 138 of the LC in force at the time of separation, the owner of a company, institution, organization, their subordinates, founder or change of name, merger, division, distribution, or connection of a company, institution or organization to another company, institution or organization, transfer of business or part of it could not be a legitimate reason for terminating the employment relationship. The provision of paragraph 2 of Article 138 of the Labour Code, that in the event of the transfer of a business or its part, employment relations continue under the same conditions in the company, institution, or organization of the transferee of the business, regardless of the legal basis for the transfer of the business or its part, entered into force already after the separation of the companies in question (1 December 2012). Thus, in the context of the provisions of the Labour Code during the separation process, the continuity of the employment relationship of the employees in the business transferee company was not directly regulated; it was only stipulated that in case of reorganization, the employment relationship with the employees cannot be terminated. However, the court of cassation has already until 1 December 2012 has repeatedly stated that the provisions of the Directive must also be applied when interpreting Article 138 of the LC. Article 1(3) of the Directive applies in cases where a company, business, or part of a company or business is transferred. There was no dispute regarding the transfer of business in this case. According to Article 3(1) of the Directive, the transferor's rights and obligations arising from the employment contract or employment relationship valid on the date of the transfer are transferred to the transferee.

The Court of Appeal reasoned that, according to the provisions of the Separation Conditions, the plaintiff should have retained those employees who were not transferred to other companies (appellants). Neither the plaintiff nor the appellant can ensure the continuity of the working relationship in reality; all entities participating in it must cooperate in this process. According to the assessment of the panel of judges, both the plaintiff (bankrupt company) and the defendants (five separated companies) should have made active efforts so that the employees who could not work for justifiable reasons were evenly distributed among all five companies that continued to operate. Therefore, the number of damages requested by the bankruptcy administrator must be divided between the plaintiff and the defendants in equal parts, the appellate court decided, and the amount of damages must be divided among the five defendants also in equal parts.

However, the court of cassation did not agree with the conclusion that the non-transfer of the employees was the fault of both companies, both the transferring and the taking over or should have taken over. The Court of Cassation stated that the guarantee of employees arising from the provisions of the Directive and established therein in the event of the transfer of a company is based on the principle of automatic transfer of employment relations, i.e., the transferor's rights and obligations arising from the employment relationship valid on the date of the transfer are transferred to the transferee. Greater standards of care, diligence, and prudence apply to an entrepreneur.

The court of cassation stated that the plaintiff's monetary obligations related to the employment relationship falls exclusively on the defendants, as new employers, in fulfilling their obligation to take over the employer's rights and duties. In labour legal relations, the employer's rights and duties to the employee are implemented by the person who disposes of them, i.e., the employer. In the case of the basis of automatic continuity of employment relations, the new employer disposes of them, which are transferred to him from the old one. As a result, the court of cassation decided that the plaintiff did not perform any illegal actions, and did not violate her duties, accordingly dividing the damage in half is illegal because if the defendants had performed their duties and taken over all the employees, no damage would have occurred to the plaintiff when she went bankrupt.

§12.04 TRADE UNIONS TRY TO PROTECT THEIR MEMBERS FROM THE FUTURE TRANSFER OF BUSINESS

Another attempt to apply the provisions of the Directive was in a civil case in which a trade union filed a preventive action demanding the termination of public procurement. The organization of passenger transportation services in Lithuanian municipalities is entrusted to local municipalities; therefore, Vilnius City Municipality was not only the organizer of the public procurement but also the sole shareholder and founder of the company 'Vilnius public transport'. By the EU recommendations to ensure competition in the field of passenger transport, the Vilnius municipality decided to transfer about 16% of public city transport route services to a private company and announced a public procurement for that purpose. Although the conditions of the published tender stated that the winner undertakes to hire vehicle drivers who lost their jobs in the closed joint-stock company 'Vilnius public transport' as a result of the reduction in the number of routes served by the company, such a condition, in the opinion of the trade union, was insufficient and caused a real direct threat to at least 124 employees of 'Vilnius public transport', who would be dismissed due to reduction of positions because after the completion of public procurement and the conclusion of contracts with buyers, the number of serviced routes would decrease, 70 drivers, 20 locksmiths servicing buses, 10 security guards would have to be dismissed. According to the union, public procurement is essentially a transfer of business. The defendant Vilnius City Municipality reviewed the conditions of the tender and clarified them: 'The carrier undertakes to make every effort to hire vehicle drivers who have lost their jobs in the closed joint-stock company "Vilnius public transport" as a result of the reduction of positions due to the reduction of the number of routes served by the company.'

However, in the opinion of the trade union, such an amendment only worsened the situation, as it did not provide for compliance with Article 138 of the Labour Code and provisions of the Directive, where the principle of automatic transfer of labour relations, conditions, employee representatives, and collective agreements is enshrined. The wording 'Commits to make every effort' is insufficient and violates the rights of employees.

The defendant's rebuttals to the lawsuit consisted of two essential arguments: (1) public procurement is not a transfer of business, and even if after the completion of the purchase it would be recognized that it was a transfer of business and employees would be dismissed in violation of Article 138 of the LC and Directive, they would not be deprived of the right to defend their interests by all possible legal means; (2) the trade union of employees is not a suitable entity to dispute the terms of the public procurement and demand the termination of the public procurement, as this is not provided for by the Law on Public Procurement.

The defendant argued that UAB 'Vilnius public transport' is unable to provide the full number of services required, subleases part of the services from private carriers whose vehicles are often outdated, and the services are of poor quality. After public procurement, those rented services could be bought cheaper, and they would be of better quality. Consequently, public procurement will not fundamentally change the scope of work and other conditions of the employees currently working in the company. Although it was agreed that about 105 drivers should be fired, about 70 persons are employed under fixed-term contracts, the terms of which will expire in 2017. Therefore, there would be no real need to lay off drivers; on the contrary, to ensure normal work and rest time for drivers, i.e., without asking to work overtime, 'Vilnius public transport' may need to extend part of the fixed-term contracts or conclude new open-ended contracts. Therefore, the statement that the contracting authority does not follow Directive No. 2001/23/EC and does not aim to ensure the social security of the company's employees provided for in this Directive and to reduce the threats of social dumping does not correspond to reality.

The Court of First Instance did not satisfy the claim based on the formal criterion that the claimant trade union is neither a supplier nor a candidate nor a participant in the contested procurement and therefore does not have the right to file a claim to suspend the public procurement. The court decided that due to the failure to transfer the mandatory legal norms governing labour relations to the conditions of the tender (the draft conditions of the Purchase Agreement), the rights of the employees, the requirements of the LC, and the Public Procurement Procedure are not violated;

therefore, this fact cannot be the basis for recognizing the actions of the defendants as illegal. In this case, the court did not decide whether the disputed purchase is a case of transfer of a part of the business, as provided for in Directive No. 2001/23/EC. This circumstance, in the opinion of the court, has no significance for the examination of the case because in the case of the contested purchase, if the transfer of the business or part of it were to take place, the rights of the employees would be protected not only under the terms of Clause 103 of the Agreement but also under the requirements provided for in Article 138 of the Labour Code. In general, the court stated that a dismissal harms an employee only if it is unlawful. If the dismissal is legal, then there is no harm.

The Court of Appeal of Lithuania, on 9 June 2017 by the ruling adopted in civil case No. 2A-763-381/2017, examined the appeal of the trade union. The court agreed that the preventive action, with which the plaintiff contests the public procurement, was filed to defend the rights and legitimate interests of the company's employees; therefore, the Employees' Trade Union in the case under consideration not only does not have procedural legal subjectivity to dispute public procurement procedures, but it also has no legal interest in public services, goods or by concluding a contract for the purchase of works.

Moreover, the appellate court indicated that the dispute in this case does not originate from public procurement legal relations, but from labour legal relations. Given that, according to the purpose of the lawsuit (i.e., to protect the rights and legitimate interests of employees), the dispute originates from labour legal relations, it follows that said dispute must be resolved under the norms governing these legal relations and not under the legal acts regulating public procurement.

The demand to terminate the public procurement in the form of a preventive lawsuit, as the plaintiff's chosen method of protection of rights, does not in itself mean that the representatives of the employees participate in the legal relations of public procurement. The plaintiff, naming herself as an interested person in the dispute under consideration, cannot have more rights than those granted by the legislator to persons who have the right to dispute the legality of public procurement procedures. According to the provisions of Article 5 of the Civil Procedure Code, this is an independent basis for rejecting the claim, as the claimant has no legal interest in the termination of the disputed public procurement procedures; the claim was filed by an inappropriate claimant who does not have a material right of claim regarding the subject matter of the dispute.

The court said that the conditions of public procurement can neither change nor negate the mandatory provisions of the law regulating the rights of employees. If, after the completion of the disputed purchase in the case, it would be recognized that it was a business transfer and the employees would be dismissed in violation of the provisions of Article 138 of the Labour Code and Directive No. 2001/23/EC, they would have the right to defend their interests in all legal ways of defending their violated rights. Certain legal consequences would only be caused by the decision of 'Vilnius public transport' to dismiss employees without complying with the provisions of legal acts, and such a decision could be challenged by employees through the legal means ensuring the protection of employees' rights provided for by law. Thus, the court left unanswered the question of whether public procurement, when part of the scope of service provision is transferred to another entity, another company, will in essence mean the transfer of business. No cassation appeal was filed in this case.

Another attempt to rely on the fact of business transfer was recorded in Kaunas Regional Court civil case No. 2A-1669-945/2020. Claimant, since 2008, worked in the bailiff's office as a lawyer, later as a bailiff's assistant, but in 2019, the bailiff decided to stop her activities, and transferred her executed and unfinished enforcement cases to another bailiff; thus, according to the plaintiff, she transferred her business. A bailiff can be compared to a business entity, so the plaintiff had to be automatically transferred to work in another bailiff's office. The court of the first instance did not agree with the plaintiff's arguments. In the opinion of the court, executive files are procedural. As well as other documents related to the execution process, which are not the subject of property rights, do not participate in civil circulation, and neither the bailiff nor other persons have the right to freely dispose of them or transfer them to other persons in a way other than as mandated by legal acts. Unpaid collected funds and property seized but not handed over to the collector are not the property of the bailiff and the bailiff also does not dispose of these funds and property freely and at his discretion. This means that the transfer of enforcement cases, unpaid collected funds, and assets seized but not transferred to the debt collector to another bailiff cannot be considered the transfer of material resources of the transferring bailiff. In addition, in the case of dismissal of the bailiff from his duties, the enforcement cases conducted by him, the aforementioned funds and assets are transferred to another person, not by the will of the dismissed bailiff, but based on the order of the Minister of Justice. Therefore, the court decided that in this case, when the bailiff completed her activities and handed over unfinished enforcement cases to another bailiff, there was no transfer of business or part of it in the sense of Article 51 of the LC and the Directive. It should be noted that none of the parties complained about this argument to the appellate court, so the latter did not re-examine the issue of business transfer, only briefly saying that they agree with the conclusion of the first instance court.

§12.05 CONCLUSIONS

The Labour Code of the Republic of Lithuania is constantly being improved to transpose the provisions of the Directive as accurately as possible. In general, the creators of Lithuanian law tend to regulate behaviour in as much detail as possible, to establish rules for every possible situation, which is related to the country's traditions, perhaps also the Soviet heritage. However, such detailed regulation is often a hindrance because every different factual situation that is not regulated causes uncertainty and a kind of fear of interpretation for the entities applying the law.

The purpose of the Directive is to protect employees from job loss when the business is reorganized in various forms, transferred in full or in parts. The text of the Directive allows for a flexible interpretation. Employers seek to find various forms of business transfer that at first glance do not look like business transfer, as it is presented as liquidation, closure, or division of the company. Contracts are not concluded, they are oral, hidden, and concluded with different content, hiding the true intentions of the parties and the meaning of the contract.

It is not easy for the courts to recognize the transfer of business. In Lithuania, they often follow a formal, easier way, and it is not recognized that there was a transfer of business. The further development of legal thought and business development depends on the final decisions of the courts.

Unions are trying to shape enforcement practices, and that's a very good initiative because unions mobilize more financial resources and therefore have more opportunities to try out different remedies. Even in the case of unsuccessful attempts, such cases have implications for the formation of legal thought.

§12.06 CASES MENTIONED

(1) The Civil Cases Division of the Supreme Court of Lithuania ruling of 20 February 2012, case No. 3K-3-40/2012.
(2) The Civil Cases Department of the Kaunas Regional Court ruling of 29 September 2022, case No. e2A-964-638/2022.
(3) The Civil Cases Division of the Šiauliai Regional Court decision of 18 September 2012, case No. 2A-518-124/2012.
(4) The Civil Cases Division of the Supreme Court of Lithuania ruling of 2 March 2017, case No. e3K-3-99-701/2017.
(5) The Court of Appeal of Lithuania decision of 9 June 2017, case No. 2A-763-381/2017.
(6) The Civil Cases Department of the Kaunas Regional Court of 3 December 2020, case No. 2A-1669-945/2020.

CHAPTER 13

Poland: Selected Issues in a Transfer of a Workplace (or Its Part) under Polish Law

Agnieszka Godusławska & Agnieszka Lisiecka

The purpose of this paper is to present certain selected issues relating to a transfer of an employing undertaking and to analyse them under Polish law and in the light of Polish courts' case law. This paper looks at selected matters through example problems, highlighting issues that cause differences in interpretation and significant practical problems.

§13.01 EFFECT OF A TRANSFER OF A WORKPLACE OR ITS PART ON EMPLOYMENT RELATIONS

The transfer of an employing undertaking (or its part) is an institution of labour law and is regulated by Article 23[1] §1 of the Polish Labour Code.

Nevertheless, there may be various reasons for a transfer of an employing undertaking (or its part). A transfer may take place as a result of legal actions (e.g., the sale of the enterprise or its part) or as a result of an action taken by the companies' corporate bodies, such as the adoption of resolutions to transform those companies (e.g., division or merger) that are then subject to registration at a registry court. A transfer of an employing undertaking may also arise from an administrative act (a decision of an authorised body) or even a legislative act (a law). Finally, a transfer of an employing undertaking may occur as a result of a real event involving the physical takeover of the employing undertaking or its part.

Provisions which regulate legal events that result in a transfer of an employing undertaking may contain independent regulations that determine the effects of such events and their impact on the rights and obligations of entities participating in the events, including in the area of labour law.

For example, a merger of companies includes universal succession by force of law, which means that the acquiring or the newly established company enters, as of the date of the merger, into all the rights and obligations of the acquired company or companies that are merging through establishing a new company (Article 494 §1 of the Polish Commercial Companies Code). A similar regulation applies to a division of a company. Pursuant to Article 531 §1 of the Polish Commercial Companies Code, the acquiring companies or the newly established companies created in connection with the division enter, as of the date of the division or the date of the spin-off, into the rights and obligations of the divided company as specified in the division plan. Universal succession that endures a merger or division of companies also applies to employee matters.

The effects in the area of labour law should, therefore, be assessed not only with reference to the provisions on transfer under the Polish Labour Code, but, if the transfer of the employing undertaking (or its part) is a result of a legal event, also based on appropriate provisions regulating that event. Thus, depending on the legal basis for the event that has caused a transfer of the employing undertaking (or its part) to the new employer, there may be different consequences in the area of employee relations. In practice, however, numerous doubts in interpretation arise caused by the need to assess the impact of a transfer of a employing undertaking with reference to the basis of the transfer, as well as possibly a separate assessment of the transfer's impact on employer's and employees' obligations which is dependent on the source of those rights and obligations.

[A] Transfer of an Employing Undertaking or Its Part

In accordance with Article 23^1 §1 of the Polish Labour Code, in a transfer of an employing undertaking or its part to another employer, the latter becomes a party, by operation of law, to existing employment relations.

The rule of automatic application, arising from Article 23^1 §1 of the Polish Labour Code, does not mean, however, that the new employer enters fully into the legal position of the existing employer, including all the rights and obligations of the parties to the employment, or that the new employer becomes a party to all contracts linking the employee with the former employer.

The employment relationship concept is crucial in assessing what rights and obligations transfer to a new employer under Article 23^1 §1 of the Polish Labour Code. Polish labour law provisions do not specify directly the content (framework) of an employment relationship. The absence of clear regulations in this respect raises numerous practical problems.

Indeed, alongside the employment contract, the rights and obligations of the parties to an employment relationship may also be determined by other sources of employment law, such as collective bargaining agreements, internal regulations (e.g., work and remuneration regulations), as well as the employer's internal policies or management decisions, or other (ancillary) contracts or agreements between the employer and the employee (such as non-compete and confidentiality agreements).

Nonetheless, despite the multiple sources of rights and obligations of parties to an employment relationship, apart from Article 23[1] §1 of the Polish Labour Code that generally regulates the transfer of an employing undertaking, the provisions of Polish labour law contain limited regulations on the impact of a transfer of a workplace (or its part) on the obligations of the parties to an employment relationship that arise from sources other than the employment contract. The impact of a transfer of an employing undertaking on individual obligations of the parties to an employment relationship is the subject of many assessments provided in doctrine and case law. At the same time, those views are sometimes contradictory and, moreover, as in the case of the Supreme Court's pronouncement, they are subject to change (occasionally even to a significant extent).

[B] Employment Contract

There is no doubt that an employment relationship is constituted and defined by an employment contract, which sets out the mutual rights and obligations of the parties to the employment relationship, including such basic issues as the type of work contracted (the employee's position), the contract's type and the remuneration. On a transfer of the employing undertaking (or its part), the new employer therefore automatically becomes a party to the employment contract in the place of the existing employer.

[C] Collective Bargaining Agreements

Collective agreements are among the few labour law institutions whose provisions explicitly regulate the effects of a transfer of an employing undertaking. Under Article 241 §1 sentence 1 of the Polish Labour Code, from the date of a transfer of an employing undertaking or its part to a new employer, the provisions of the collective agreement to which the employees were subject before the transfer of the employing undertaking or its part to the new employer continue to apply to them for one year, unless separate provisions provide otherwise. However, the employer that acquires the employing undertaking or its part is not bound by or a party to the collective bargaining agreement. The Supreme Court has repeatedly pointed out that the retention by transferred employees of the terms and conditions of work and pay arising from a previous collective bargaining agreement or a company wage agreement is not a consequence of a 'transfer' of the validity of those independent labour laws to the employer acquiring the employees under Article 23[1] of the Polish Labour Code. The subjection of the new employer to the terms and conditions of employment set out in the collective bargaining agreement follows from the fact that they become the substance of the transferred employees' individual employment relationships, which is just a consequence of the new employer's entry into existing employment relationships with the employees of the transferred employing undertaking.[1]

1. Cf. judgment of the Supreme Court of 8 June 2017, I PK 307/16; judgment of the Supreme Court of 14 April 2015, II PK 137/14.

What is important here, however, is that following the transfer, the provisions of the collective bargaining agreement apply only to the transferred employees (the provisions of the collective bargaining agreement will not apply to existing employees employed by the acquiring employer on the date of the transfer, nor to new employees employed by the acquiring employer after the transfer) and only for one year from the date of the transfer of the employing undertaking or its part to the employer. While the provisions of the collective bargaining agreement apply in the wording in force on the date of the transfer of the employing undertaking or its part to the new employer. Therefore, any subsequent amendments to the collective bargaining agreement made after the date of transfer will not be binding on the acquiring employer.

In practice, there is uncertainty in which provisions of a collective bargaining agreement should apply after a transfer. The provisions of the Labour Code do not provide any exception or limitation in this respect, which would appear to be an argument for the obligation to apply all provisions of an agreement, regardless of their type. However, the application of all provisions of a collective bargaining agreement may often be problematic in practice. Therefore, in assessing which provisions of a collective bargaining agreement the new employer is obliged to apply, consideration must be given to the nature of those provisions.

In the case of collective bargaining agreements, a distinction should be made between normative provisions (those that regulate mutual rights and obligations of the parties to the employment relationship, including those affecting the basic remuneration of employees and other components of remuneration, such as bonuses, seniority pay, position bonuses or even long service awards) and provisions that are obligational (concerning obligations of the parties to the collective agreement, namely the employer and the trade unions). In accordance with the Supreme Court's position in its judgment of 19 October 2010 (II PK 91/10), on a transfer of an employing undertaking or its part to a new employer, the obligational provisions of the collective agreement will not apply - only the normative ones, and only in the part that regulates individual employment relationships.

The above judgment is of significant importance in practice. This is because it should be pointed out that a collective bargaining agreement may also contain regulations that are organisational and relate to good order (such as provisions on working time systems and schedules, rules for confirming employees' attendance at work), which, although they define the situation of employees, they do not become part of their individual employment relationships. Following the Supreme Court, it should, therefore, be assumed that the new employer will not be obliged to apply such provisions after the transfer and will be able to apply its own regulations in this respect to the acquired employees, subject to the obligation to introduce such regulations in accordance with applicable provisions of law.[2]

2. However, a different view is to be found in legal literature, according to which the obligation to apply the provisions of a collective bargaining agreement after a transfer applies to all provisions that affect employees, even if they do not directly constitute the terms of the employment. Following this view, it would have to be assumed that the new employer is also obliged to apply the provisions of the collective bargaining agreement on working time systems and schedules.

It needs to be pointed out at this juncture that Article 241 §1 of the Polish Labour Code is protective for employees. This means that the employer acquiring employees may change the terms and conditions of work and pay of the employees to their benefit and apply more favourable terms and conditions of work and pay to them even before the expiry of one year from the date of the transfer. The decision in this regard is up to the employer. However, it must not be discriminatory (e.g., the employer may not decide to apply more favourable provisions only to a part of the transferred employees if there are no objective reasons for it). One year after the transfer of the employing undertaking (or its part), the new employer may make changes to the individual terms and conditions of employment and pay of the employees that arose from the collective bargaining agreement in force at the previous employer that are unfavourable to the employees.[3] However, in order to be effective, changes that are unfavourable to employees require the conclusion of amending agreements or for the employer to give notices that amend the conditions of work and pay of individual employees.

The above considerations are also valid in a transfer of an employing undertaking (or its part) that is combined with a general succession of rights and obligations. Even in a merger or demerger of companies (resulting in the new employer assuming all the rights and obligations of the former employer), a collective bargaining agreement does not transfer to the new employer. However, if the previous employer had a collective bargaining agreement in force, the new employer is obliged to apply its provisions to the acquired employees in accordance with the above rules.

[D] Transfer of Employing Undertaking and Internal Regulations

On a transfer of an employing undertaking (or its part), the employer's internal regulations (e.g., regulations on work or pay) do not transfer to the new employer (even if separate provisions provide for a general succession of rights and obligations from the previous to the new employer). This is because it is assumed that the issuance of internal regulations constitutes a sovereign act of a given employer, which cannot, as such, bind another employer. Nevertheless, in the extent in which they determine the terms and conditions of employees' work and pay (e.g., bonus rules, awards of bonuses, awards, etc.), the rules and regulations (primarily the remuneration rules), become part of the individual terms and conditions of employment, which means that the acquiring employer is required to apply those terms and conditions to employees also after the transfer (at least until they have been amended).

However, unlike in the case of individual terms and conditions of work and remuneration under a collective bargaining agreement, the individual terms and conditions of work and remuneration of employees under remuneration regulations may be amended (even to the detriment of the employees) immediately following a transfer, subject to the need to introduce the changes by agreement or through notices

3. As a general rule, it is accepted that the employer may take steps to change individual terms and conditions of work and pay even before one year has expired following the transfer (e.g., by serving amending notices), as long as the effects of such actions occur after the expiry of the protection period of one year.

of amendment. Moreover, the new employer should, where possible, also align and adapt the terms and conditions of work and pay of the acquired and the existing employees as promptly as may be feasible, to avoid any allegations of unequal treatment.

Therefore, any assessment of possible steps regarding individual work and remuneration conditions of transferred employees to be taken by the employers acquiring such employees depends on the labour law source of the individual work and pay conditions of the employees (collective bargaining agreement versus pay regulations). At the same time, depending on that source, it may sometimes be justifiable and constitute an objectively justified differentiation between employees to retain differences between the terms and conditions of employment of acquired and existing employees (if more favourable terms and conditions of employment and pay from a collective bargaining agreement in force at the transferring employer are retained for transferred employees than those at the acquiring employer). In other cases (retaining differences between the terms and conditions of work and pay under the remuneration regulations of transferred employees and the terms and conditions of employment in force at the acquiring employer) may expose the employer to allegations of unequal treatment and associated claims.

[E] Transfer of the Employing Undertaking and Supplementary Agreements Between Employer and Employees

In addition to the employment contract, the employer and the employee may be bound by other ancillary agreements. Those include, among others, confidentiality agreements, non-compete agreements, maintenance of confidentiality agreements, training agreements or agreements on joint financial liability for entrusted property.

It is generally accepted that the obligations of the parties to a joint liability agreement for entrusted property set out the rights and obligations of the parties under the relationship of employment, which, in the event of a transfer of the employing undertaking (or its part), transfer to the new employer by virtue of Article 23^1 §1 of the Polish Labour Code. The acquiring employer should, however, assess whether, as a result of the transfer of the employing undertaking (or its part) and any associated organisational changes, any changes arise that require the contracts to be amended (e.g., by updating the group of persons who are liable for the entrusted property). However, training contracts (as civil law contracts) are deemed unconnected to the relationship of employment, and are not subject to a transfer under Article 23^1 §1 of the Polish Labour Code.

Nonetheless, most doubts in interpretation concern the legal nature of a non-compete agreement. Initially, both doctrine and case law were unanimous in their view that on a transfer of an employing undertaking, non-compete agreements (both those in force during the employment and after its termination) transfer to the new employer by virtue of Article 23^1 § of the Polish Labour Code (irrespective of the existence of any other independent grounds for a transfer of the rights and obligations under those contracts).[4]

Currently, opposing positions are presented in doctrine. According to the first view, on a transfer of an employing undertaking or its part to another employer, the latter accedes to, by operation of law, the rights and obligations under a non-compete agreement, including those that the employee concluded with the previous employer for a duration after the termination of the employment. According to the second (at present dominant) view, only the employee's obligation to refrain from competing during the employment may be deemed to be associated with the employment. However, after a termination of employment, a non-compete agreement (and the obligations arising from it) does not transfer to the new employer in the event of a transfer of the employing undertaking or its part.

This second position is based on a judgment of the Supreme Court of 11 February 2015 (I PK 123/14), which made a breakthrough in assessing the impact on non-compete agreements of a transfer of an employing undertaking (or its part) to a new employer. In this judgment, the Supreme Court took the position that a competition clause requiring an employee to refrain from competing post-employment does not transfer to the new employer on the transfer of the employing undertaking or its part. The Supreme Court held that a competition clause is not part of an employment contract, while the obligation to pay compensation under a non-compete agreement is not an obligation under the relationship of employment (although it is closely associated with it). At the same time, the Supreme Court specified that compensation under a non-compete agreement does not constitute remuneration for work and is not subject to the protection provided for remuneration for work. Interestingly, in earlier judgments, the Supreme Court had already made known its assessment that a non-compete agreement is a reciprocal agreement that lies on the borderline of labour and civil law, and whose basic feature is the obligation that binds both parties in such a way that one party's performance is to be equivalent to the other party's performance, which obligation comes into force on the termination of the employment.[5] However, despite an identical assessment of the nature of a non-compete agreement, there has been a significant change in the assessment of the impact of a transfer of the employing undertaking on those agreements.

The currently prevailing view is that the impact of a transfer of an employing undertaking on a non-compete agreement is assessed differently depending on whether the agreement relates only to the duration of the employee's employment (in which case the agreement is assumed to transfer to the new employer under Article 23^1 §1 of the Polish Labour Code), or whether it is an obligation to refrain from competing activities after the termination of the employment (a post-employment non-compete agreement does not transfer to the new employer under Article 23^1 §1 of the Polish Labour Code). This means that, insofar as justified from a business perspective by the

4. Judgment of the Supreme Court of 11 January 2005, I PK 96/04.
5. Cf. judgment of the Supreme Court of 2 September 2009, II PK 206/08; judgment of the Supreme Court of 18 January 2013, II PK 153/12.

need to protect its interests, the new employer should enter into new non-compete agreements following the transfer (at least after the termination of employment).

Nevertheless, the above considerations will not apply if, by virtue of separate provisions, the transfer of the employing undertaking is in combination with a universal succession of rights and obligations, as in the case of a merger or division of companies. This is because, in such a case, the acquiring employer enters into the rights and obligations arising from all contracts concluded with the employee (regardless of whether forming part of the relationship of employment or being only associated with it), including the rights and obligations arising from non-compete agreements in force during employment and after its termination. In such a case, however, the new employer should assess whether the scope of the non-compete obligation (subject matter, entity and territory) meets its business needs and make appropriate amendments (in consultation with the employee).

Significantly, neither the law nor jurisprudence nor doctrine resolve what happens to non-compete agreements that are in force after a termination of employment in a situation where the transfer of an employing undertaking (or its part) is not accompanied by a universal succession of rights and obligations under separate provisions. In particular, there is no provision stating that such agreements expire. However, as these contracts do not transfer to the new employer, it would have to be assumed that, as long as the previous employer still exists (e.g., only if a part of the employing undertaking transfers to the new employer), those contracts continue to apply to the previous employer and the employee (unless the employer adopts some means to free itself from such contracts in the form of a notice of termination or withdrawal, or the parties enter into an agreement to terminate them).[6] However, the question arises as to the point in time when the parties' obligations under such agreements (the employee's obligation to refrain from competing and the employer's obligation to pay compensation) should come into effect. Indeed, the idea behind post-employment non-compete agreements is that they define the obligations of the parties following the termination of employment. However, in a transfer of an employing undertaking to another employer, there is no termination of employment – the relationship continues under the same terms and conditions, with only a change of entity on the part of the employer.

It is also impossible not to note that an employee's work for a new employer could, in a situation where the new employer is a competing business (fairly common in practice), violate the non-compete obligation to the previous employer. However, it is not possible to accept that an event which occurs automatically by operation of law and over which the employee has no control results in a breach of that employee's contractual obligations.

At the same time, there is no objective justification for regarding non-compete agreements during employment transfer to the new employer, whereas non-compete

6. Doctrine also takes the position that post-employment non-compete agreements terminate – cf. Marta Wasil, *Consequences of the Transfer of a Workplace to Another Employer in Terms of the Validity of a Competition Clause*, MOPR 2020, No. 6.

agreements after the termination of employment do not. The Supreme Court's reasoning in this regard is not convincing. This is because the Supreme Court points out that post-employment non-compete agreements are established for the benefit and in the interest of the previous employer that was employing the employee at the time when the agreement was entered into. However, the same reasoning stands behind non-compete agreements during employment.

Reviewing the Supreme Court's arguments, one cannot help but get the impression that the Supreme Court's interpretation takes into account the new employer's interests by relieving that employer of the obligation to compensate its employees (which would exist, if accepting the notion that non-compete agreements transfer to the new employer by virtue of Article 23^1 of the Polish Labour Code). Nevertheless, if the new employer is interested in enjoying protection in the form of a non-compete agreement, then it may offer such agreements to its employees (and on its own terms and conditions). This is because it should be remembered that, in accordance with Supreme Court case law, an employee's refusal to conclude non-compete agreements (even if on less favourable terms than the non-compete agreement with the previous employer) will constitute, in principle, a reason for terminating that employee's employment contract.

[F] Impact of the Transfer of the Employing Undertaking on Non-wage Benefits

In practice, many doubts arise also in assessing the new employer's obligation to provide non-wage benefits (such as medical care, sports packages, private insurance, employee discounts on products or services in the range offered by the employer) that were offered by the previous employer in the event of a transfer of the employing undertaking (or its part).

Although most (especially larger international) companies offer various types of non-wage benefits and the possibility of employees enjoying additional benefits is strongly emphasised already at the stage of recruitment, non-wage benefits are nonetheless a fairly new feature in Polish law and their nature has not been resolved in case law.

Doubts already arise in assessing whether non-wage benefits are a component of employees' remuneration or other work-related benefits and whether they become part of employees' individual terms and conditions of work and pay. A legal assessment of benefits is further complicated by the fact that there a various sources (legal bases) of the employees' entitlement to those benefits. The employees' right to non-wage benefits may be based on their employment contract (in which case there is no doubt that it is an element of the individual relationship of employment), the remuneration regulations (which define the terms and conditions of payment for work and awards of other work-related benefits) or the employers' other regulations or internal management decisions. In practice, situations also arise in which remuneration regulations generally provide for employees' rights to specified non-wage benefits, while the detailed rules for those benefits and subsidies granted by employers arise from the employer's separate policies or internal management decisions.

In doctrine, legal assessments of non-wage benefits vary, in general, depending on the source (legal basis) of their regulation. Most authorities of doctrine, as well as practitioners, accept that if non-wage benefits have been provided for in the remuneration regulations, then, as work-related benefits, they become an element of the relationship of employment, and any withdrawal of such benefits from employees (or a worsening of the conditions for their grant) requires, in addition to having to amend the remuneration regulations themselves, also an amendment of the individual terms and conditions of work and pay by means of amending agreements or notices of amendment. This position is also confirmed by the Chief Inspectorate of Labour.[7] However, most representatives of doctrine consider benefits provided for in an employer's internal management decisions (separate from the remuneration regulations) as voluntary benefits that do not become part of the employees' individual terms and conditions of employment. This means that a possible change or withdrawal of the employees' right to those benefits does not require any amending notices or agreements.

Applying the above considerations to the provisions on the transfer of an employing undertaking, it would have to be accepted that the new employer who acquires employees in connection with a transfer of an employing undertaking (or its part) is required only to provide the transferred employees (at least until the individual terms and conditions of employment have been changed) with a right to non-wage benefits, insofar as these have been provided for in the previous employer's remuneration regulations or (as already clarified above) in the individual employment contract.

Nevertheless, it is not possible to be entirely convinced by an assessment of the nature of non-wage benefits based solely on the source of their regulation and an acceptance that benefits provided for in the remuneration regulations become part of the employees' individual terms and conditions of employment, while benefits offered under separate regulations or the employer's internal management decisions constitute only voluntary benefits (if the employer may decide at any time to change their terms and conditions or even stop offering them).

Admittedly, the regulation of non-wage benefits by an employer in the remuneration regulations may be considered to be an expression of the employer's intention to acknowledge such benefits as work-related and thus due under the relationship of employment (which would support the claimable nature of such benefits). However, the dominant idea in Polish law is that the rules for remunerating employees may be located in several separate documents and that all documents that regulate such rules (e.g., bonus or award rules) are part of the remuneration regulations. Therefore, an assessment of the nature of a benefit based exclusively on the source (document) in which that benefit has been regulated is, therefore, fallacy of logic. Therefore, it is not possible to complete exclude the risk that acquired employees will demand that their new employer provides them with non-wage benefits, even if these did not follow from

7. Letter issued by: The Chief Labour Inspectorate, Status: current, GPP-471-4560-22/09/PE/RP.

the remuneration regulations but were merely provided for in other internal management decisions of the employer.

Another question that arises is how an employer that acquires employees should meet the obligation to provide the employees with the right to non-wage benefits. In the opinion of the authors of this paper, it would be too far-reaching and unjustified to oblige a new employer to enter into agreements with non-wage benefit providers to ensure that the acquiring employees are able to enjoy the same benefits and on the same terms and conditions as those offered by their previous employer (and even if it is established that the wage benefits constitute a part of the employees' individual terms and conditions of work and pay). It is possible that a new employer may offer benefits (even of a similar type as the previous employer), but on different terms or from different service providers. One cannot also exclude a situation in which, in seeking to provide the employees with non-wage benefits, the new employer may be refused entry into a contract with the supplier of services or may be offered terms that are worse than those agreed with the previous employer. The terms and conditions offered by service providers (e.g., insurance companies, private healthcare centres) may vary between employers. The terms and conditions of contracts with suppliers (and thus the terms and conditions under which non-wage benefits are offered to employees) may be affected by such factors as the size of the company, the total number of employees, and the number of employees benefiting from particular benefits. Those conditions may also vary depending on market realities at the given time.

Some guidance in this area may be found in the judgment of the European Court of Justice of 26 March 2020 (ISS Facility Services, C-344/18, EU:C:2020:239), in which the Court held that, 'while, in accordance with the objective intended by Directive 2001/23, the interests of the employees affected by the acquisition must be protected, this cannot be considered in isolation from the interests of the acquirer, which must be able to carry out the necessary adjustments and adaptations in order to continue its business activities. This Directive does not aim solely to protect the interests of the employees in a transfer of an employing undertaking, but seeks to ensure a balance between the legitimate interests of the employees on the one hand and the legitimate interests of the acquirer on the other hand.' An assessment of how the new employer should fulfil the obligation to provide non-wage benefits to the transferred employees must therefore be made separately in each case, taking into account the circumstances of the case.

If the employer offers employees benefits of the same type and with the same level of support (funding) from the employer, then the obligation to provide a benefit should be considered met. If the acquiring employer does not offer benefits of the particular type, then it should be assumed that it should pay those employees a cash equivalent (e.g., in the amount of the subsidy provided to the benefit by the previous employer) until the transferred employees' individual terms and conditions of work and pay have been changed.

The above deliberations lose their relevance if, by virtue of special provisions, universal succession occurs and the new employer acquiring the workplace or its part assumes the rights and obligations arising from contracts concluded with service providers by the previous employer. At that point, the new employer will not only have an actual possibility but also, in principle, an obligation to continue offering non-wage benefits to employees under the terms provided by the previous employer.

§13.02 OUTSOURCING AND TRANSFER OF AN EMPLOYING UNDERTAKING

In practice, it is very difficult to determine whether there is any transfer of an employing undertaking (or its part) at all in a given situation. While there is no uncertainly in a situation in which an employing undertaking that is an organised part of an enterprise is taken over and is recognised as giving rise to a transfer of an employing undertaking under Article 23^1 of the Polish Labour Code, practical problems arise already in assessing the effects of another entity assuming the tasks and competences that were carried out at the given employer.

Particular uncertainties arise in assessing the employer's entrustment of auxiliary tasks that were previously carried out using the employer's own human resources (e.g., accounting services, cleaning, legal services) to an external entity providing such services (outsourcing).

According to established Supreme Court case law, an assumption of an employer's tasks (competencies) may result in a transfer of a part of the employing undertaking. At the same time, any assessment of whether the assumption of tasks is accompanied by a transfer of a part of the employing undertaking should be made separately in each case, taking into account the circumstances of the case. The decisive criterion to be considered when determining any transfer of a part of the employing undertaking in a given situation is the preservation of the identity of the transferred commercial unit at the new entity. Following EU case law,[8] Polish jurisprudence accepts that the identity of a commercial unit derives from a number of inseparable elements such as personnel, management, organisation and working methods and assets.[9] Different elements are assigned different weights, depending on the nature of the business (and the tasks performed at the given commercial unit).

If a unit's activities are based mainly on material assets, the decisive factor in assessing whether an event leads to a transfer of a part of the employing establishment is whether the takeover of tasks is accompanied by a takeover of material assets to fulfil those tasks. However, in relation to manpower-based activities (human-reliant, human-sensitive business), it is assumed that a transfer of a part of the workplace occurs if the new employer takes over the main part (in terms of numbers and competencies) of the personnel carrying out the transferred tasks.[10] The Supreme Court views that in labour-based sectors, a failure to take over the majority of the employees

8. *See* judgment of the Court of Justice of 11 March 1997 in Case C-13/95 in the case of *Ayse Süzen v. Zehnacker Gebäudereinigung GmbH Krankenhausservice*; judgment of the Court of Justice of 20 January 2011 C-463/09 in *CLECE SA v. Maríi Socorro Martín Valor Ayuntamiento de Cobisa.*
9. *See* judgment of the Supreme Court of 11 April 2012, I PK 145/11.
10. *See* judgment of the Supreme Court of 17 May 2012, I PK 180/11.

precludes finding that there has been a transfer of the commercial unit (even if the performance of tasks/services has been transferred to another entity).[11] As a supplement, it is also pointed out that if the entity acquiring the tasks has its own human resources capable of carrying out the outsourced tasks and, after taking over the employees, would have to lay off the employees who previously performed those tasks at the entity outsourcing the service, then the transfer should be deemed not to have occurred.

While the validity of the above position cannot be denied, one may get the impression that both domestic courts and the Court of Justice assess whether there has been a transfer (here of a part of) the employing undertaking from the perspective of the effect of the given event, namely the acquisition or non-acquisition of employees by the new entity. Whereas, an acquisition of employees (accession of the new employer to the relationship of employment) is the outcome of a transfer of the employing undertaking (or its part) and not its cause. The above concept is, therefore, only acceptable and defensible if it is accepted that employees are one of the elements of an employing undertaking and form its intrinsic part (as the Court of Justice pointed out, for example, in its judgment in the *Süzen* case).

In practice, however, it is not easy to assess whether an activity is primarily asset-based or labour-based. The Supreme Court has, for example, found that activities carried out by pre-school establishments are labour-based.[12] However, the courts view the food service business provided in hospital facilities,[13] the sale of food, beverages and tobacco products as an asset-based business.[14] However, the Supreme Court sometimes views cleaning services as labour-based,[15] and at other times activities that cannot result in a transfer of a part of an employing undertaking, if there has been no transfer of assets.[16]

As can be seen from the above, it is possible that in practice, a given type of business will be viewed in one case as a manpower-based business and in another as one that operates based mainly on assets. At the same time, it would be moreover incorrect to make a dichotomous division of types of business into asset-reliant businesses versus human-sensitive businesses, based solely on an abstract understanding of the object of activity, without taking into account the specifics of the business conducted by a particular entity and the circumstances of the type in question. Moreover, some businesses require assets and a highly skilled workforce to coexist in order to function properly. All those circumstances make an assessment as to whether a transfer occurs of a part of an employing undertaking in a given case problematic and sometimes lead to different conclusions even among practitioners of law.

Hence, in borderline situations (when it is not possible to make a clear assessment of whether there is an automatic takeover of employees), tripartite agreements

11. *Ibid.*
12. Judgment of the Supreme Court of 10 May 2022, I PSKP 53/21.
13. Judgment of the Supreme Court of 11 April 2012, I PK 145/11.
14. Judgment of the Supreme Administrative Court of 9 June 2020, II FSK 507/2.
15. Judgment of the Supreme Court of 7 February 2007, I PK 212/06; judgment of the Supreme Court of 3 March 2015, I PK 187/14.
16. Judgment of the Supreme Court of 4 February 2010, III PK 49/09.

(between the existing employer, the employee and the new employer) are often concluded in practice to confirm the transfer of employees to the new entity. In order to ensure that employees are protected at the level provided by Article 23[1] of the Polish Labour Code, those agreements provide the employees with terms and conditions of employment at the new entity at least at the same level as with the former employer. At the same time, the new employers recognise the employees' length of service under their employment with the previous employer.

The situation becomes more complicated, however, if the existing employer and the entity taking over the tasks and competencies of that employer have a different assessment of whether a transfer is taking place in a given situation, particularly if the entity taking over the tasks is not interested in taking over the employees. Such situations are not uncommon in practice. Indeed, it is not difficult to imagine a situation in which the interests of the existing employer and the entity taking over the tasks are in conflict: the existing employer may want to transfer employees to the new entity (if only to avoid having to lay off the employees and pay statutory severance pay), while the entity taking over the tasks may not be interested in taking over the employees or may want to take over only some of them. Thus, in practice, stalemate situations may arise in which an existing employer notifies employees of the transfer of part of the employing undertaking and their acquisition by automatic transfer, while the new entity refuses to allow employees to work and employ them. In such a situation, the only way out for the employees is to sue the existing employer for admission to work or to establish the existence of employment with the new employer. Such a dispute, however, may last years. The situation described shows that the law provides employees with insufficient protection.

The above example shows that although the transfer of an employing undertaking (or its part) occurs automatically by operation of law, regardless of the will of the parties (neither the will of the former employer and the acquiring entity, nor even the will of the employees themselves), there are situations, in practice, in which the will of the former employer and the new entity taking over the tasks may be decisive for the continued employment of the employees.

[A] Sham Outsourcing

Situations arise, in practice, where despite a formal qualification of an event as a transfer of a part of an employing undertaking, within the meaning of Article 23[1] of the Polish Labour Code, the takeover of tasks is not accompanied by an actual takeover of the employees by the new entity. Such cases are referred to as sham (purported) outsourcing.

Sham outsourcing may occur in a situation in which, despite a formal conclusion of an agreement intended to result in the transfer of a part of an employing undertaking, in practice, there is no actual takeover of the employees by the new employer. Such a situation may occur when, despite a formal change of the employer, employees continue to work at the same place and times, under the direction of the same people, using the same machinery, equipment and materials, and are required to comply with the same internal regulations in force at the former employer. An additional circumstance that may prove the artificial nature of a transfer of part of an employing undertaking is if the new employer's remuneration for services rendered is derived from the remuneration that the employees subject to the sham transfer receive at the new employer.

The transfer of tasks to another entity, combined with the performance of those tasks by the existing employees of the entity contracting the service, but without their actual takeover by the new entity, is viewed in a negative light. This is because such actions may deprive employees of the protection they are due, make it difficult to identify the real employer and, consequently, lead to the employees suffering harm. The negative assessment of such an arrangement is in addition caused by the fact that the purpose of sham outsourcing is usually not the actual transfer of the substrate in the form of a part of the employing undertaking to another entity, but the achievement of desired (premeditated) business goals. Most often, the disguised purpose is to achieve certain effects in terms of tax and social security by transferring the public-law liabilities to an entity other than the existing employer.

A formal transfer of employees to another employer may sometimes also have the objective of taking the employees out of the former employer's pay regulations and offering them different terms and conditions than those at the former employer. Although the transfer itself may not constitute a reason for changing (to their detriment) the terms and conditions of work and pay of the transferred employees, the need to adjust the terms and conditions of employment of the transferred employees to those of the new employer may already justify such a change. Thus, actions taken in the form of a transfer of employees may ultimately (after the changes have been carried out in the statutory way through amending agreements or notices of amendment), depending on circumstances, be detrimental to the transferred employees (if the new terms and conditions of work and pay offered to them are less favourable than those at the previous employer) or to the remaining employees of the previous employer not subject to the transfer (if the new terms and conditions offered to the transferred employees are more favourable than their previous terms and conditions of employment at the previous employer). Such a formal 'severing' of employees from the organisational structure of a given employer is intended to ensure that the existing employer is protected against claims from employees because if the existing employer took steps to change the pay conditions of some employees, they could be viewed as violating the principle of equal treatment.

In such a situation, however, the protection of the existing employer is (like the outsourcing itself) only specious. If the employer undertakes actions that only give the appearance of transferring (outsourcing) a certain part of the business to an outside entity (without any real change in the employees' employment), it should be regarded that the transfer of a part of the employing undertaking to an outside entity does not ultimately arise, and consequently, that the employees subject to the alleged transfer are still bound by the relationship of employment with the existing employer. This is because in Polish law, to assess whether the parties are properly implementing a relationship of employment, it is not the formal actions (in the form of conclusion of an employment contract, applying to social insurance and payment of contributions, or even payment of wages) that are decisive, but the actual implementation of the employment contract, in accordance with its wording and under conditions that are characteristic for this legal relationship. This position is well established in case law.[17]

A key element of a relationship of employment is the subordination of employees to the employer, understood as the need to carry out the employer's orders and instructions. In the case of (legitimate) outsourcing, such subordination does not exist. In a judgment dated 27 January 2016 (I PK 21/15), the Supreme Court held that a feature of outsourcing that distinguishes it from the employment of in-house employees or the provision of work by temporary employees is the absence of direct and permanent subordination (legal as well as factual) of the contractors to the entity for which the services or work are being rendered (insourcer). In the case of outsourcing, such subordination may be only indirect and short-term.

Thus, in a situation where, despite the conclusion of an agreement intended, in principle, to result in a transfer of a part of the workplace to a new employer, there is no change in the how the employees' relationship of employment is carried on (the employees continue to work on unchanged terms under the direction of the previous employer), then the tax authorities and the social security institution may consider that there has been no automatic transfer of the employing undertaking, and it is the previous employer who is still obliged to pay contributions for mandatory social security, health insurance and settle advance payments for income tax on wages earned by such employees. Also, the employees themselves may request the previous employer to establish the existence of a relationship of employment (with all the consequences of this in the form of providing them with the terms and conditions of employment prevailing at the previous employer).

It is also worth pointing out that, in recent years, Polish courts have increasingly resorted in labour cases to the concept of the abuse of legal personality and 'piercing the corporate veil'.[18] So far, admittedly, the courts have referred to the concept of the abuse of legal personality mainly when commission agreements have been concluded with employees of one company to carry out the same work at another group company. Such actions have been qualified as being aimed at circumventing overtime regulations (including limits on overtime). However, in a judgment of 18 September 2014, III PK 136/13, the Supreme Court took a more far-reaching position, namely, that an abuse arises of the construction of the legal personality of a parent company as a result of an unjustified and unfair differentiation of the legal situation of employees employed by the parent company and of those performing the same or similar duties at subsidiaries.

As may be seen from the above, the concept of 'piercing the corporate veil' is evolving in Polish law. Thus, it cannot be ruled out that it will also find application in cases in which sham outsourcing occurs within companies belonging to the same group.

17. Cf. judgment of the Supreme Court of 28 January 2021, I USKP 4/21.
18. Cf. judgment of the Supreme Court of 17 March 2015, I PK 179/14; judgment of the Supreme Court of 23 January 2018, II PK 333/16; judgment of the Supreme Court of 15 March 2018, I PK 369/16; order of the Supreme Court of 27 November 2018, I PK 248/17.

§13.03 CHANGE OF SUBCONTRACTOR AND TRANSFER OF THE EMPLOYING UNDERTAKING

Another situation that leads to many practical difficulties in interpretation in assessing whether or not there is a transfer of a part of an employing undertaking is a change of subcontractor on the part of the service provider.

On the surface, the situation appears straightforward. A change in the entity providing the service should not affect the employment relationships between the subcontractors and employees, if the subcontractors provide the services consecutively and are not connected to each other by any legal relationship. But this is not always the case. This is because situations arise in which a transfer of an employing undertaking (or its part) occurs as a result of an (actual) takeover by a given entity (the new employer) of the tasks and assets of the workplace of the existing employer based on an agreement with a third party that was in charge of controlling those tasks and assets.

This was the situation of the facts of a case for which the Supreme Court issued a judgment on 18 September 2008 (II PK 18/08). Three entities were involved in the case: (i) an owner of real estate, who outsourced the management of the real estate he owned, (ii) an entity managing the real estate based on a service agreement concluded with the owner of the real estate (the previous manager), and (iii) a new entity, which, after the real estate owner had terminated the contract for the management of the real estate with the previous managing entity, concluded an agreement with the owner of the real estate for the management of the same real estate as managed by the previous managing entity (the new managing entity). As a result of the above-mentioned events involving the owner of the real estate, who controlled the tasks and assets, a transfer occurred of the workplace from the previous managing entity to the new managing entity within the meaning of Article 23^1 of the Polish Labour Code, even though no agreement has been concluded between the previous and the new manager. Thus, a transfer of the employing undertaking took place as a result of taking over the tasks and assuming actual authority over the assets (the workplace of the previous employer). At the same time, the Supreme Court accepted that the employing undertaking may comprise tasks and assets of which the previous employer is not the owner (and which it is not legally entitled to control), but only over those which it exercises actual authority based on an agreement concluded with the controller of those assets and tasks. In Polish law, the transfer of an employing undertaking (or its part) is understood in broad terms and may also include non-contractual cases.

The Supreme Court expressed a similar view in its judgment of 4 February 2010 (III PK 49/09). Namely, the Supreme Court found that the provision of Article 23^1 of the Polish Labour Code applies in the event of a change of contractor of a service by an entrepreneur, if the new contractor takes over the essential assets associated with the performance of the service by its predecessor. But if the entity taking over the provision of the service does not use the assets that were available to its predecessor (as was the situation in the facts of the case in the cited judgment), then a transfer does not occur.

The above judgments are of considerable practical importance. An entity that takes over the provision of services to an entrepreneur and uses the entrepreneur's assets for that purpose should keep in mind and make a careful assessment of whether the commencement of the provision of the service may result in an automatic takeover of the employees of the previous service provider. The situation is, however, very unusual (even bizarre), as a transfer of the employing undertaking (or its part) may occur between entities that may have no knowledge of each other. Thus, it cannot be excluded that a new contractor will learn of the (alleged) effect of its commencement of the provision of services, in the form of a takeover of the employing undertaking (or its part) of the previous contractor of the service, only from a lawsuit launched by an employee. The question therefore arises whether it is not going too far to attribute possible breaches to service contractors in a situation in which they have no knowledge (or even an actual or legal possibility to be aware) of the circumstances associated with the change of subcontractor by the client of the service.

Experience shows that legal awareness of the above (among the professional service providers as well as employees themselves) is only just emerging. Nevertheless, it is possible to expect, in the near future, new court cases involving factual circumstances similar to those outlined above.

§13.04 CROSS-BORDER TRANSFER OF AN EMPLOYING UNDERTAKING

Despite the 20 years that have passed since Council Directive 2001/23/EC was implemented into the Polish legal order, the issue of a cross-border transfer of an employing undertaking has not been resolved by Polish courts, nor has it been sufficiently described in Polish labour law doctrine. There are also no rulings from the Court of Justice that directly address the issue of cross-border transfers. Such cases involve a transfer of an employing undertaking abroad in the material sense, namely situations in which the workplace's tasks and assets that are originally located in the territory of one country (here: Poland) are actually transferred abroad.

Changes to the ownership of a workplace located in Poland involving foreign entities without a relocation of the employing undertaking abroad should be differentiated from a cross-border transfer of the employing undertaking in the material sense. Such a situation may arise, say, in a cross-border merger of companies with the participation of a Polish company (and the takeover of the Polish company by a foreign company) or in a sale of an enterprise (or its organised part) located in the territory of Poland to a foreign entity that will continue the activity of this enterprise in Poland. Ownership changes on the part of the employer and a takeover of the employing undertaking by a foreign entrepreneur that is not combined with an actual relocation of the workplace abroad are treated as a transfer of the employing undertaking (or its part) within the meaning of and on the basis of Article 23^1 of the Polish Labour Code and do not, in themselves, raise any significant doubt. Consequently, the foreign entrepreneur enters into employment relations with Polish employees and continues them under the terms of Article 23^1 of the Polish Labour Code.[19]

19. For the sake of good order, it should be pointed out that, under Polish law, a foreign person without legal presence in Poland (i.e., not operating in Poland in the form of a company, branch

An issue that raises concerns is the applicability of provisions on the transfer of an employing undertaking to cross-border cases in which, in addition to a change of ownership, there is an actual relocation of tasks and assets abroad. In accordance with Article 1(2) of Council Directive 2001/23/EC, the Directive applies if the enterprise or employing undertaking or their part that is to be transferred is situated within the territorial scope of the Treaty. It follows from the wording of Article 1(2) of Council Directive 2001/23/EC that, in every case, if the employing undertaking that is the subject of the transfer is situated within the territory of the EU, then a transfer of the employing undertaking may arise within the meaning of the Directive, even if the transfer is to another State, even outside the European Union (because Council Directive 2001/23/EC does not contain any restrictions in this respect).[20] The transfer issue may therefore involve a transfer of employees outside EU Member States; however, this issue is beyond the scope of this paper.

One should not lose sight, however, of the fact that the provisions of Council Directive 2001/23/EC do not apply directly to relations between enterprises and employees, as such, and do not constitute an independent basis for classifying a particular event as a transfer of an undertaking and determining its effects. Only the provisions of national law implementing Council Directive 2001/23/EC into legal order in detail could constitute such a basis. The question arises, however, according to which legal order should the event in question be assessed. It must not be forgotten that national laws implementing Council Directive 2001/23/EC may provide different levels of protection for employees and different obligations on the part of the employers involved in the transfer.

Four situations appear to be possible in practice. Namely, a transfer may be assessed from the perspective of: (i) the law governing labour relations before the transfer, (ii) the law applicable to the registered office of the previous employer, (iii) the law applicable to the foreign entrepreneur acquiring the workplace, and (iv) the applicable law governing the event giving rise to the acquisition of the employing undertaking (whereas, if the acquisition is based on an agreement between the former employer and the foreign entrepreneur, the parties may choose the applicable law).

At present, however, there are no sufficient regulations at the European level for determining the law applicable to a cross-border transfer. There are doubts regarding the use of Article 8 of the Rome I Regulation,[21] which determines the law applicable to individual employment contracts, in determining the law applicable to a cross-border

or any other legal form) may also be an employer, provided that it employs employees. A separate issue is the question of assessing whether the foreign entrepreneur has an establishment in Poland within the meaning of Polish tax regulations ('permanent establishment') and the associated tax consequences. However, this issue is beyond the scope of this paper.

20. The cross-border transfer of an employing undertaking was recognised by the Employment Appeal Tribunal of the United Kingdom in the judgment of 12 December 2007 (case UKEAT/0171/07). The ETA did not even exclude the transfer of an employing undertaking outside the European Union. The ETA did not however examine how TUPE principles might operate in practice in this type of scenario.
21. Regulation (EC) No. 593/2008 of the European Parliament and of the Council of 17 June 2008 on the law applicable to contractual obligations (Rome I).

transfer. It would be worthwhile *de lege ferenda* for EU legislators to explicitly resolve the issue of cross-border transfers and the law governing such transfers.

Nevertheless, bearing in mind the protective nature of the provisions of Council Directive 2001/23/EC and the necessity of a pro-Community interpretation of the domestic law of EU States (consistent not only with the literal wording of EU provisions but also with the *ratio legis* of those provisions), one cannot deny the view that a cross-border transfer of an employing undertaking is possible. This means there may be situations in practice in which, if a foreign entity takes over tasks and assets located in another country and relocates them abroad, the employees employed in the country of the original establishment, whose tasks and assets that were taken over were a part, will demand their employment to be recognised by the entity located abroad that has taken over those tasks and assets.

However, following the judgment of the Court of Justice in the *Süzen* case, the starting point for assessing whether there has been a transfer of an employing undertaking within the meaning of Council Directive 2001/23/EC in a given situation should be an analysis of whether the identity of the transferred commercial unit is preserved after the transfer of the tasks and assets to the foreign entity. This assessment is detached from purely legal questions and should be made mainly on the basis of facts and be the same regardless of the applicable legal order.

Only in the event of a favourable assessment that the unit retains its identity after the transfer to another country, is it possible to establish that there arises a cross-border transfer of the employing undertaking.

Nevertheless, a conclusion that a cross-border transfer of an employing undertaking arises in a given situation raises further questions and doubts, including of a practical nature. First, a cross-border transfer of an employing undertaking means a change in the place of work for employees and, depending on the circumstances of the case, it may be even very distant. This change does not occur, however, automatically, but requires appropriate actions in the form of a change of the place of work specified in the contract (in the case of Polish law, by means of amending agreements or notices of amendment). It is also questionable whether the employer should participate in any way in financing the costs associated with the employees commuting or relocating to the new place of work. Second, the question arises as to what law will be applicable to the relationship of employment that has been entered into by the foreign employer, in particular whether, once the employing undertaking transfers to the foreign employer and the place of work changes, the applicable law governing the relationship will also change (in accordance with the principle of *lex loci laboris*).

It follows from the above that, although the institution of a cross-border transfer of an employing undertaking complies with the idea behind Council Directive 2001/23/EC, in the form of ensuring the protection of employees participating in such a transfer, the issue raises many factual and legal questions that await resolution by EU legislators, or at least by the Court of Justice of the EU.

CHAPTER 14

Portugal

Júlio Gomes

Many years before the adhesion of Portugal to the European Union—or as it was known in 1986, the European Economic Community—the Portuguese law already foresaw the transmission of the labor contract in cases of transfer of an enterprise or undertaking.[1] Article 37 No. 1 of the Law of the Labor Contract, Decreto-Lei n.º 49408, enacted in 1969 and that was binding until 2003, already established that the position of employer was transferred to whoever acquired, in any manner, the undertaking where the employees worked, unless the labor contract had ended previously to the transfer of if the transferor and the transferee had agreed that the employees would remain as employees of the transferor in another undertaking, as long as Article 24 (concerning the change of workplace) was observed. This final *caveat* will be addressed later on. For the moment, it must be emphasized that the legal answer provided by Article 37—that was largely conceived as a subrogation *ope legis*—was responsible for the perception, possibly a wrong one, that there was no need to update the law and to adapt it to the Directive 77/187/EEC. As a result, although Portugal was under the obligation to transpose the Directives binding at the moment of accession (January 1,

1. A very good account (in German) of the evolution of the Portuguese Law on transfer of undertakings can be found in Felisa Frey, Der Betriebsübergang (transmissão de empresa) im portugiesischen Arbeitsrecht, Europäische Zeitschrift für Arbeitsrecht 2016, year 9, pp. 303-316. In Portuguese *see* António Monteiro Fernandes, Direito do Trabalho, 22nd ed., Almedina, Coimbra, 2022; Joana Vasconcelos, in Código do Trabalho Anotado, Pedro Romano Martinez et al., 12th ed., Almedina, Coimbra, 2020, pp. 671-694; Maria Do Rosário Palma Ramalho, Tratado de Direito do Trabalho, parte II, Situações Laborais Individuais, Almedina, Coimbra, 7th ed., 2019; Milena Silva Rouxinol, Transmissão da Unidade Económica, in Direito do Trabalho, Relação Individual, João Leal Amado and Others, Almedina, Coimbra, 2019, pp. 849-890; Pedro Romano Martinez, Direito do Trabalho, 10th ed., Almedina, Coimbra, 2022.

1988) within two years (hence until January 1, 1988), no step was ever taken to transpose Directive 77/187/EEC.[2]

As already stated, Article 37 foresaw the transfer of the employment contract in cases where there was a transfer of the enterprise. The law stated unambiguously that such a consequence would occur not just in cases of sale but in any other circumstances in which another person would be in charge of the operation of the enterprises (Article 37 No. 4) and the Courts went so far as to apply it in cases of void and voidable contracts.[3] Therefore, there was no need for a transfer of property, and for instance, a lease was enough for the subrogation of the employer to happen. As a matter of fact, the Portuguese law went a step further than the Directive and stated that transferor and transferee were jointly liable for any debts of the transferor due within the six months period previous to the transfer, even if related to employment contracts that had ended before the said transfer, provided that the employees asked for the payment until the moment when the transfer took place (Article 37 No. 2). Therefore, the transferee was required to post a warning in the workplace within the two weeks previous to the transfer informing the employees that they ought to exercise their rights until that moment.

The prevailing view of not only the scholars but also of the courts was that Article 37 had as a scope not only the protection of the employees and the stability of the employment contract but also, and possibly foremost, of the merchants and entrepreneurs themselves, enabling them to acquire an enterprise capable of remaining in activity without any time gap.[4] It was also coherent with the corporate perception of an enterprise, and as a result, there was almost no discussion (at least until the beginning of the XXIst Century) on a possible objection or opposition of the employee to the transfer of her/his employment contract to a different employer.[5]

It is now clear however that Article 37 did not really match the task of transposing the Directive 77/187/EEC, particularly as it was interpreted by the ECJ.

A first problem concerned the concept of undertaking itself. The prevailing view was that mercantile law should provide an answer to what amounts to an undertaking. As a result, a bar carriage on a train was not considered to be an undertaking since it had no goodwill as such and its customers were volatile. However, the paradigm was the factory and so material assets were deemed to be of paramount importance and

2. The 2003 Labor Code that revoked the LCT (Law of the Employment Contract) transposed the new Directive 2001/23/EU.
3. Ac. TRP 11.3.1996 (published in CJ 1996, II, 250); Ac. TRL 3.6.1992 (published in CJ 1992, III, 274).
4. Mário Pinto, Pedro Furtado Martins and António Nunes De Carvalho, Comentário às Leis do Trabalho, vol. I, Regime Jurídico do Contrato Individual de Trabalho, Lex, Lisboa, 1994, p. 176.
5. David Carvalho Martins, Da Transmissão da Unidade Económica no Direito Individual do Trabalho, Almedina, Coimbra, 2013, pp. 286 et seq. AC. STJ 27.1.1999, n.º 304/48 (Padrão Gonçalves) decided that the employee's will was irrelevant and that he/she might not oppose to the automatic change in the identity of the employer as a result of the transfer of undertaking. However Ac. STJ 27.5.2004, 03S2467 (Vitor Mesquita) (although with a dissenting vote) decided that such a right of the employee to oppose or object to the change of the employer did exist. Several court rulings recognized that right of the employee: Ac. STJ 29.6.2005, 05S164 (Laura Leonardo); Ac. TRL 29.9.2004 (Paula Sá Fernandes).

little attention was given to the existence of activities that were mainly based upon manpower and human resources. But probably the most important lack of conformity with the Directive, as it was interpreted by the ECJ, was that it was widely believed that no transfer could take place without some sort of a contractual relationship between the transferor and the transferee.[6]

There were other shortcomings. Although the law contemplated the need for a non-binding opinion by the workers' council, there was really no requirement for a bargaining procedure with the workers' representatives with the purpose of attempting to reach some sort of an agreement, namely on the possible economic and social outcomes of a transfer.[7] As already pointed out, Article 37 also allowed for an agreement between the transferor and the transferee that allowed them to decide that some of the employees, in spite of the fact that they worked frequently for many years in that undertaking, would remain bound to the transferor and might be transferred to another undertaking, without the need for their agreement. That aspect of the Portuguese law was strongly criticized by some of the scholars as being incoherent with the Directive, but it remained the law, and as we shall see, it remains a possibility acknowledged by the law, although without reference to an agreement of the transferor and the transferee.

Finally, it was by far the prevailing view that any collective agreement would cease with the transfer[8] and would no longer be binding for the new employer unless he/she would be bound by the application of the general rules.

In 2003, the new Labor Code was enacted (Lei n.° 99/2003) and the Law of the Employment Contract was revoked. The new rules significantly closed the gap between the Portuguese domestic law and the EU law on the matter of transfer of undertaking. By the way, the lawmaker expressly stated that the new Code purported to transpose, amongst many others, Directive 2001/23/EU. The transfer of undertaking was the subject of five specific articles: Articles 318 to 321 and Article 555.

For the very first time, Article 318 referred to the concept of economic unity or entity stating that the transfer of an enterprise or undertaking as well as a part of an enterprise or undertaking that represented an economic unity entailed the change of the employer status to the buyer (Article 318, No. 1). As a matter of fact, it defined economic entity as an organized set of resources with the purpose of exercising an economic activity be it principal or accessory (Article 318, No. 4). Once again, the law clarified that the same change of status might occur without the need of a transfer of property or ownership and in other cases where the person responsible for the operation of the economic unity had changed including outsourcing or (re)internalization. The new employer was also liable for the payment of any fines resulting from the

6. *See*, for instance, Ac. TRE 17.4.1990 (published in CJ 1990, II, 311) and Ac. TRE 12.3.1991 (published in CJ 1991, II, 356). Pointing out that such a view was incompatible with the Directive, Júlio Gomes, O conflito entre a jurisprudência nacional e a jurisprudência do TJ das CCEE em matéria de transmissão do estabelecimento no Direito do Trabalho: o art. 37.° da LCT e a directiva 77/187/CEE, Revista de Direito e de Estudos Sociais 1996, pp. 77 et seq.
7. Pinto, Furtado Martins and De Carvalho, *supra* n. 4, at p. 183. *See also* Gomes, *supra* n. 6, at p. 86.
8. However that was changed subsequently by Article 9 of LRCT.

violation of labor law rules. The law kept the traditional rule of joint liability of the transferor and the transferee for overdue debts and added that the transferor would remain liable and could be sued for the period of one year after the transfer (Article 318, No. 2).

The new Labor Code of 2003 introduced a bargaining procedure with the view of trying to achieve an agreement on the measures that ought to be implemented as a result of the transfer and the economic, social and juridical consequences for the employees, regardless of the imperative legal consequences. It must be emphasized that this was (and still is in the present Labor Code) an obligation to negotiate in good faith in order to attempt to reach an agreement, that might, however, never materialize. The first step of the bargaining procedure was the duty to provide information by both the transferor and the transferee to their respective employees. The information should be provided in writing and at least 10 days previous to the transfer and in any case in a timely manner that would allow for a useful bargaining. This information should be provided to the workers' representatives, and only if they do not exist, should be provided directly to the employees themselves. The Portuguese collective labor law has a dual system of workers' representation: on the one hand, the employees may choose to have a workers' council, elected by a secret ballot by all the employees of an enterprise and that once elected is a collective person, which must register itself and represents all the employees of the enterprise. Differently from what happens in many other legal systems, the existence of the working council is not mandatory, even in large enterprises and depends upon the initiative of the employees, who are free to initiate (or not) the election procedure. On the other hand, there are no requirements for a minimal size of the enterprise in order to have a workers' council. The result of this totally voluntary procedure of election of a workers' council is the existence in Portugal of just a few hundred (around 300) workers' councils, many of which do not seem to be active. The other system of representation is through trade unions and their shop stewards. However, in this case, trade unions are said to represent in principle only the affiliated workers. Article 320 No. 4 stated that representatives of the employees for this purpose were both the workers' councils and the shop stewards, which seemed to mean the need to negotiate with both. The second step, after the providing of information, was the consultation of the workers' representatives or if they did not exist, of the workers themselves. It must be stressed that if this information and consultation procedure did not take place that would not mean that the transfer was void or avoidable, but was sanctioned simply with the payment of a fine (and the infringement of the law was qualified as light or not very serious by the Article 675 No. 2). Some scholars wondered if such a sanction was sufficiently effective to implement the bargaining procedure foreseen in the Directive.

The law retained the possibility—although without speaking of an agreement between the transferor and the transferee—of the transferor, until the very moment of the transfer, changing the workplace of employees who were permanently affected until that moment to the economic unity that was going to be transferred (Article 319, No. 1) and indicated that the transferee had the possibility after the information procedure to post a warning in the workplace telling the employees whose labor contract was going to be transferred that they had a deadline of three months to demand their overdue credits to the transferee (Article 319, No. 3).

Article 321 had rather complex rules on the representation of the workers after the transfer. According to Article 321 No. 1, if the economic entity that was the object of the transfer retained its autonomy, there would be no change in the status and functions of the workers' representatives. However, if the economic entity did not remain autonomous, but was integrated and incorporated in the transferee organization, a difference was drawn between two different scenarios: as a rule, the workers' representatives that existed in the economic unity transferred would cease their functions, but would still be protected as workers' representatives until the moment when that special protective status would normally end without the transfer (Article 321, Nos. 2 and 4). But if in the transferee's enterprise, there was no workers' council that would remain operational for at least two months or until a new election took place. As a matter of fact, the law allowed in case of the transfer of an undertaking that a section of the workers' council in that undertaking might be able to operate as a workers' council during such period (Article 321, No. 3).

The fate of collective agreements was regulated in Article 555 in a different chapter and section of the Code. It determined that the collective agreement to which the transferor was bound directly or through an extension administrative mechanism remained applicable to the transferee until its initial deadline or at least for a period of 12 months from the date of the transfer, unless, meanwhile, a new collective agreement was agreed that was directly binding for the transferee.

The new Labor Code of 2009 (Lei n.° 7/2009) that still remains in force devoted to the matter of the transfer of enterprise or undertaking, Articles 285 to 287 (in 2021, a new Article 286-A was introduced) and Article 498.[9]

In its initial version, the law defined economic entity or unity as a set of organiZed resources with the scope of developing an economic activity, either as the principal activity or as a secondary one (Article 285 No. 5 in the version introduced in 2009). However, in 2018, this concept was densified. According to the new redaction introduced by the law,[10] the economic unity is a set of organized ressources that constitutes a productive unity that enjoys technical and organizational autonomy and that maintains an identity with the scope of developing an economic activity, either as the principal activity or as a secondary one. This requirement of autonomy and particularly that the autonomy should persist in spite of the transfer has been criticized as not being truly compatible with the Directive. Nevertheless, it can be interpreted as requiring only the survival of the identity of the economic unity and not really of its autonomy.

9. The latest legal change took place with the Lei n.° 13/2023 de 3 de abril that however only changed article 285 no. 13 in order to increase the amount of the fines that may occur as a sanction for the infringement of the duties foreseen in Article 285 Nos. 1, 2, 3, 7, 8 and 9.
10. Lei n.° 14/2018 de 19 de março.

The joint liability of transferor and transferee was maintained.[11] Until 2018, the transferor was liable for just one year after the transfer, but in 2018, this term was enlarged to two years (Article 285, No. 5).

The concept that the transfer of the economic unity entails the transfer of the employer's status from the transferor to the transferee was also enshrined in the new law (Article 285, No. 1) but the lawmaker felt the need, in 2018, of precising that as a result of the transfer the employees were entitled to all their contractual rights and those acquired on the service of the transferor, namely in what concerns salary, seniority, activity and functions and social benefits.

Unfortunately, Article 285 No. 4 still foresees the possibility of the transferor's decision to change the workplace of the employees prior to the transfer, as long as such a decision is compatible with the requirements of Article 194 of the Labor Code. Such a possibility has been criticized as hardly compatible with the purposes of the Directive.[12]

The transfer procedure was significantly altered and became far more complex, particularly from 2018 onwards. It must be stressed that although the transfer does not require a contractual agreement between the transferor and the transferee—it may be what some German writers call a hostile transfer—the legal paradigm remains the contractual transfer. As a result, the transferor and the transferee must inform the workers' representatives of their respective workers, and if those representatives do not exist, the workers themselves of the moment when the transfer is deemed to occur, the motives for the transfer and its legal, economic and social consequences as well as the measures concerning the workforce that are foreseen. The law goes so far as to demand that the workers' representatives or the workers themselves must be informed of the contents of the contract between the transferor and the transferee (Article 286, No. 1). The law also states that the transferor must always inform his/her employees that are going to be directly affected by the transfer. Simultaneously, the law imposes a special duty of confidentiality on both the workers' representatives and the workers themselves. All the relevant information must be given in writing at least 10 working days before the consultation phase takes place. The information phase is followed by a consultation phase with the purpose of attempting to reach an agreement. If the workers concerned by the transfer do not have representatives, they may choose to be represented by an ad hoc committee. The law also foresees, since 2018, the possible intervention, at the request of any of the concerned parties, of the services of the labor department in order to facilitate the bargaining procedure and promote the respect of the workers' interests. Presently, the law also clarifies that if a workers' council exists it takes precedence vis-a-vis other workers' representatives, namely shop stewards.

The information procedure seems to demand some degree of cooperation between transferor and transferee and raises a number of questions concerning for

11. As Pedro Romano Martinez, Direito do Trabalho, 10th ed., Almedina, Coimbra, 2022, p. 775, points out this joint liability is a legal consequence of the transfer and cannot be waived or excluded either by collective agreement or by the individual employment contract.
12. Maria Do Rosário Palma Ramalho, Tratado de Direito do Trabalho, Parte II (Situações Laborais Individuais), 6th ed., Almedina, Coimbra, 2016, pp. 648-649.

instance the cases where the information is wrong. Should there be civil liability? What is the repercussion of said information on the exercise by the employee of its right to oppose the transfer of her/his own labor contract?

The law goes as far as to state that the transfer may only take place seven working days after the deadline for the choice of the ad hoc committee or in any case seven working days after the agreement or the end of the consultation (Article 285, No. 7). But if that deadline is not respected, it seems that the transfer would be effective anyhow, regardless of the legal prevision of a fine for a serious breach of the law (Article 285, No. 13).

One of the major innovations in this field was the introduction in 2021 (Lei n.° 18/2021) of the right of the employee to refuse the change of employer. This right of opposition to the transfer of the employment contract was highly controversial both in the courts and amongst scholars.[13] Some considered that such a right did not exist and that the change of employer was an imperative consequence, also for the employee, as a result of the transfer of an enterprise or undertaking. It was also invoked that it was necessary in order to protect the interests of the transferee who normally intended to acquire an economic entity capable of going on with its activity without time gaps. However, those who believed that the employee should have a right to oppose the change of employer invoked mainly two reasons: one was simply the respect of the private autonomy of the employee, who must be free to choose his/her employer. The second was that without a right to object to the transfer, the legally mandatory consequence of the transfer of employment contracts as a result of the transfer of economic entity may turn into a trap for the employees. Instead of being to their advantage, it might turn out to be extremely dangerous if, for instance, the transfer was made to a transferee without the means to pay for the salaries and indemnities to the workers. As a result of the transfer, the transferor is not liable for any debts that arise after the transfer itself and even the joint liability for the debts that were overdue before the transfer only lasts for two years. After that period, the transferor is no longer liable. Of course, some of these cases in which the economic unity was deprived of its more

13. The literature on the topic is abundant. *See* Pedro Oliveira, Ainda sobre o direito de oposição do trabalhador na transmissão de empresas, PDT 2020, I, 303 et seq.; Pedro Oliveira, O(s) pressuposto(s) do direito de oposição do trabalhador: breves notas sobre a jurisprudência recente, RMP 2023, n.° 173, pp. 163 et seq.; JOÃO LEAL AMADO, Transmissão da empresa e contrato de trabalho: algumas notas sobre o regime jurídico do direito de oposição, RLJ 2018, 147, n.° 4010, pp. 294 et seq.; João Leal Amado, Ainda sobre os fundamentos do direito de oposição; crónica sobre dois Acórdãos recentes, QL 2021, 59, 189 et seq.; Júlio Gomes, Algumas reflexões críticas sobre a Lei n.° 14/2018 de 19 de março, PDT 2018, n.° 1, pp. 78 et seq.; Pedro Romano Martinez and Pedro Madeira De Brito, O novo regime da transmissão da unidade económica introduzido pela Lei n.° 14/2018 de 19 de março, RDES 2018, pp. 21 et seq.; Hélder Quintas, Breves notas sobre o passado, o presente e o futuro do regime da transmissão da empresa, PDT 2019, n.° 1, pp. 217 et seq.; A. Monteiro Fernandes, Alguns aspectos do novo regime jurídico-laboral da transmissão de empresa ou estabelecimento, QL 2018, n.° 53, pp. 16 et seq.; Milena Rouxinol, Transmissão da unidade económica, in João Leal Amado et al., Dirrito do Trabalho: Relação Individual, Almedina, Coimbra, 2019, pp. 884 et seq.; David Carvalho Martins, Novo regime da transmissão da unidade económica: algumas notas, PDT 2018, n.° 1, pp. 135 et seq.; Maria Do Rosário Palma Ramalho, Tratado de Direito do Trabalho, parte II, Situações Laborais Individuais, Almedina, Coimbra, 7th ed., 2019, pp. 699 et seq.

valuable assets and then transferred to an indigent are at the core fraudulent, but the evidence of the fraud may be difficult to provide or may come too late to prevent losses to the employees.

The new rule,[14] however, does not really match the opinions that already existed for the introduction of such a right. If the private autonomy of the employee were to be respected, she/he would only have to object to the existence of a labor contract with someone with whom she/he had not contracted, without the need to present any other reasons or motives. But Article 286-A No. 1 requires the employee, in order to exercise this right to object to the transfer of the employment contract, to show that the transfer may cause her/him serious harm, namely by invoking that the transferee is in a precarious economic situation or that his/her management practices do not inspire confidence to the employee who is objecting to the transfer. These requirements are highly controversial: on the one hand, the first one seems to presuppose that the information concerning the economic situation of the would-be transferee is available to the general public or was conveyed to the employees that may be concerned by the transfer. The second seems to be little else than a suspicion, a subjective distrust and it is not at all clear what kind of evidence has to be provided in order to exercise the right. The deadline for the opposition is also rather short: the right to oppose to the changement of the employer must be exercised in writing within five working days from the lapsing of the deadline for the designation of the ad hoc committee or in case it has not been designated five working days from the end of the consultation phase (Article 286-A, No. 3). The writing must mention, among other elements, the reasons for the opposition.

Unfortunately, the law does not foresee what happens if the information and consultation procedure simply do not take place.[15] Will the employee have the right to object at least until the transfer takes place de facto?

Another issue concerns the impact of a misrepresentation. What if the information provided by the transferor on the identity and/or legal, social and economic consequences of the transfer and also of the content of the contract between transferor and transferee, if any, are false or incomplete?

According to Article 286-A, No. 2, the opposition of the employee has as a consequence that her/his labor contract with the transferor remains effective.

As a result, the employee will normally have to change his/her workplace. However, it may happen that, for instance, the transferor no longer has any enterprise or undertaking. In those cases, the labor contract may end, but the indemnity will have to be paid by the transferor who remained the employer.

Portuguese Courts have frequently been faced with questions concerning clauses of collective agreements related to transfer of undertakings.

14. This new rule is mandatory for the collective agreements in the sense that they may only deviate if they are more favorable to the employee. *See* Ac TRC 16.9/2022, 3037/20.0T8CBR.C1 (Azevedo Mendes).
15. Ac. TRE 27.5.2021, 3951/18.2T8FAR.E1 (Mário Branco Coelho), decided that if no information and consultation was provided the employee must have the right to oppose to the change of employer. Moreover, it also decided that in such a case transferor and transferee are jointly liable.

Some of these clauses particularly in the cleaning sector foresee that in a situation in which a client has entrusted the contract for cleaning his/hers premises to a services provider but then subsequently terminates that contract and enters into a new contract for the performance of the same task with a new provider, the latter is under the duty, according to the collective agreement, of reengaging the staff engaged in that activity.[16] As a result, and following the decisions of the ECJ in Case C-51/00, January 24, 2002, *Temco Services Industry SA* and in Case C-60/17, July 11, 2018, *Àngel Somoza Hermo*, the fact that the new operator kept the staff may amount to a transfer of undertaking.

But Portuguese Courts were also confronted with a very different clause in collective agreements, namely one that stated that the loss of a customer by an operator following the award of a service contract to another operator could not have the legal meaning of a transfer of undertaking.

In Case C-200/16, October 19, 2017, *Securitas*, as the jugement stated (paragraph 8), Clause 13 of the Collective Agreement concluded in 2011 and published in the Labor and Employment Bulletin No. 17/2011 provided that "(2) The loss of a customer by an operator following the award of a service contract to another operator shall not fall within the scope of a transfer of na undertaking or business." In that case the European Court of Justice decided that "Article 1(1) of Directive 2001/23 must be interpreted as precluding a provision of national law, such as that at issue in the main proceeding, which provides that the loss of a customer by an operator following the award of a service contract to another operator does not fall within the concept of a transfer of an undertaking [or] business within the meaning of Article 1(1)."

In Portuguese law, the nature of collective agreements is highly debated since they seem to have a dual and ambiguous identity: on the one hand, they are private contracts entered into freely by private persons—and as a result the Portuguese Constitutional Court recently decided that they are not subject to any constitutional control[17]—but on the other they are largely perceived as sources of law (as stated in Article 3 of the Labor Code) and their normative clauses have a binding effect similar to that of a law.

In any case, Article 3(3), m, of the Portuguese Labor Code states that the provisions of the Code related to the transfer of undertaking are imperative and a collective agreement can only deviate from them insofar as it is more favorable to the employees.

Hence similar clauses to that one in the Securitas case are void. However, as a result of the ILO Conventions that Portugal has ratified, there is no administrative or governmental control of the content of collective agreements and those clauses still exist and it is for the courts to declare that they are void.

At least partially as a result of the invalidity of the clause of the collective agreement that denied the existence of a transfer whenever a security enterprise lost a client to a competitor, the Portuguese courts were confronted with a significant number of cases in which some sort of cherry-picking might have occurred.[18] Typically, the

16. Those clauses are valid. *See* Ac TRE 13.7.2022, 579/21.3T8VR.E1 (Mário Branco Coelho).
17. Ac. Tribunal Constitucional 5.7.2022, 971/2021 (Teles Pereira).
18. Ac. TRL 15.12.2022, 7643/20.4T8LSB.L1 (Sérgio Almeida).

new provider of the security service would re-hire only a small number of the employees who were previously engaged in that economic entity (for instance, one in three). Considering that in order to determine if a transfer of the economic entity took place "it is necessary to consider all the facts characterising the transaction concerned, including in particular the type of undertaking or business concerned, whether or not its tangible assets, such as buildings and movable property, are transferred, the value of its intangible assets at the time of the transfer, whether or not the majority of its employees are taken over by the new employer, whether or not its customers are transferred, the degree of similarity between the activities carried on before and after the transfer, and the period, if any, for which those activities were suspended" and "[h]owever, all those circumstances are merely single factors in the overall assessment which must be made and cannot therefore be considered in isolation" (No. 24, C-298/18, *Reiner Grafe, Jürgen Pohle*, February 27, 2020), some Portuguese Courts decided that in spite of the fact that the majority of the employees had not been taken over by the new employer, other factors might have as a consequence that a transfer did occur. But the European Court of Justice in its decision in C-675/21, *Strong Charon*, February 16, 2023, No. 52, stressed that in labor intensive sectors and activities based essentially on manpower, the transfer of the economic entity supposes that the new employer takes over a major part, in terms of their numbers and skills, of the employees specially assigned by his or her predecessor to that task. The decision has been interpreted as emphasizing the importance of taking over most of the staff in the overall assessment whenever activities based essentially on manpower are concerned.[19]

In order to solve some of these problems in 2021—Lei No. 18/2021, April 8—a new paragraph was introduced in Article 285 of the Labor Code. The new No. 10 of the said article now foresees that the rules of transfer of undertaking apply to all cases, in the private as well as in the public sector, where a new provider of services, namely surveillance, canteen, cleaning and transportation is chosen either through direct contract or through a public tender or any other means of selection and in such a case the transfer is deemed to occur at the moment of that choice.

The rule must not be interpreted as creating some sort of automatic transfer whenever a new provider of those services is chosen, but simply as stating that a transfer may occur in such cases, considering the overall assessment of the facts, as prescribed by the ECJ.[20]

Another issue related to collective agreements concerns Article 498(2) of the Labor Code. Whenever collective agreements cease to be binding and as long as they are not replaced, some of their effects remain. Those effects are the ones the parties of the collective agreement had agreed upon, or in the absence of such an agreement, the effects mentioned in Article 501(8). Those effects *ope legis* are relatively important and encompass salaries, careers and job descriptions, worktime clauses, just to mention some of them.

19. *See* Ac. TRP 8.5.2023, 640/20.1T8PNF.P1 (Teresa Sá Lopes); Ac. TRL 3.5.2023 1240/21.4T8BRR.L1-4 (Maria José Costa Pereira).
20. Ac. TRP 3.10.2022, 1340/21-0T8PNF.P1 (Rita Romeira).

According to Article 498(1), as already seen, the collective agreement applicable to the transferor remains until the end of its original term or at least for 12 months after the transfer, unless, meanwhile, a new collective agreement is entered into by the transferee.

However, Article 498(2) adds that if, after that period, no collective agreement is applicable to the transferee—either directly or through an administrative extension—the effects of the collective agreement of the transferor mentioned in Article 501(8) will remain indefinitely.

To some extent, that seems to be compatible with the rulings of the ECJ, namely in Case C-328/13, September 11, 2014, *Österreichischer Gewerkschaftsbund*. The Court decided that "Article 3(3) of Directive 2001/23 must be interpreted as meaning that the terms and conditions laid down in a collective agreement which, pursuant to the law of a Member State, despite the rescission of the agreement, continue to produce their effects as regards the employment relationships which was governed by them before the agreement was terminated, constitute "terms and conditions agreed in any collective agreement" so long as that employment relationship is not subject to a new collective agreement or a new individual agreement is not concluded with the employees concerned" (paragraph 31).

Nevertheless, there is a major difference between the Austrian and the Portuguese legal systems concerning these *postmortem* effects of the collective agreement (in German, "Nachwirkung"): according to Austrian law, these effects may be set aside by an individual agreement with the employees concerned at least after one year following the transfer (*see* the Austrian rules quoted in paragraphs 4, 5 and 6 of Case C-328/13).

That was one of the factors that allowed the ECJ to conclude that "[i]n those circumstances, it does not appear that such a rule hinders the transferee's ability to make the adjustments and changes necessary to carry on its operations" (paragraph 30).

But the same does not apply to Portugal, where an individual agreement with the employees cannot set aside those effects. Hence, the transferee would have to enter into a new collective agreement with the same trade union in order to exclude those effects.

Other interesting and problematic issues concern transfer of undertaking and equality of treatment. The Portuguese law foresees the equality of pay for employees with a similar activity or job description or equal value work, which is particularly important in cases of gender based discrimination, but that actually goes beyond the gender factor. However, it is rather difficult to assess to what extent transfer of undertaking rules provide an exception to equality of salary.

According to the prevailing view, the powers of the transferor as an employer remain unchanged until the moment of the transfer. Hence, the transferor may end the labor contracts prior to that moment, for instance, with a collective dismissal, as long as the legally required motives are present. The transfer itself does not amount to a valid ground (Article 4(1) of the Directive), but the transferor may invoke, for instance, the need to reduce costs or to introduce new production techniques and organizational changes.

The Portuguese Labor Code, in its Article 1, recognizes the validity of social practices, namely at the level of the enterprise, as long as they do not infringe imperative legal rules and are compatible with the good faith principle (Article 1 of the Labor Code). Those practices, if observed for a long period—the courts frequently require 10 years or more—may become binding for the employer and, as a result, they will also bind the transferee. It is however highly debated whether they ought to be conceived as changes in the individual contracts or as a sort of atypical collective agreement (although it must be pointed out that collective agreements are required to be in writing).

In the past, the transfer of undertakings in the public sector was controversial. The ECJ decided in Case C-317/18, *Cátia Correia Moreira v. Município de Portimão*, that "Directive 2001/23, read in conjunction with Article 4(2) TEU, must be interpreted as meaning that it precludes national legislation which provides that, in the event of a transfer within the meaning of that directive and where the transferee is a municipality, the employees concerned must, first, undergo a public competitive selection procedure and, secondly, have a new relationship with the transferee" and in Case C-416/16, *Piscarreta Ricardo*, involving the same municipality the Court reiterated that "Article 1(1) of the Directive 2021/23 must be interpreted to the effect that, where a municipal undertaking, whose sole shareholder is a municipality, is wound up by a decision of the municipality's executive body and its activities are transferred in part to the municipality to be carried directly by it and in part to another municipal undertaking re-formed for that purpose, whose sole shareholder is also that same municipality, that situation falls within the scope of the directive, provided that the identity of the undertaking in question is preserved after the transfer, which is a matter for the referring court to determine" (No. 46).

As a result, the Portuguese Supreme Court—Ac STJ 9.11.2019, 2743/15.5T8LSB.L1.S1 (Ferreira Pinto)—ruled that the reinternalization of a refectory by a public university that had kept the staff of the private company that previously provided that service amounted to a transfer of undertaking. In the ruling that examines carefully all the relevant decisions of the ECJ on the issue, it was pointed out that those services do not fall within the exercise of public powers (*see* C-108/10, *Ivana Scattolon*, No. 46) and represent an economic activity.

In conclusion and in spite of the fact that this subject matter of transfer of undertaking has become one of the most complex and difficult in Portuguese Labor Law, it can be asserted that the present rules are generally in compliance with the Council Directive 2001/23(EC) and its interpretation by the ECJ.

CHAPTER 15

Romania

Cristina Tudoran

§15.01 EXPLANATORY NOTE: THE ROMANIAN TRANSPOSITION OF THE ACQUIRED RIGHTS DIRECTIVE

Prior to the transposition of Directive 2001/23/EC on the approximation of the laws of the Member States relating to the safeguarding of employees' rights in the event of transfers of undertakings, businesses or parts of undertakings or businesses (the 'Directive'), the Romanian legal framework did not properly address the issue of safeguarding employees' rights in the event of transfers of undertakings, businesses or parts of undertakings or businesses, despite an extensive legislative tendency in the first decade after the fall of the communist regime.

While drafting the Romanian Labour Code (Law No. 53/2003, published in the Official Journal of Romania on 5 February 2003, further the 'Labour Code'), the legislator did take into account the European Union's directives in light of Romania's upcoming accession, which took place on 1 January 2007, and addressed for the very first time the issue of safeguarding of employees' rights in the event of transfers of undertakings (at that time, Articles 169-170, currently renumbered as Articles 173 and 174). These provisions scarcely regulate the transfer of the transferor's rights and obligations deriving from a labour contract or an employment relationship, existing on the date of the transfer, to the transferee, the prohibition to dismiss employees on the grounds of the transfer and the need to inform and consult the employees, prior to the transfer. These are, however, merely general provisions, insufficient to ensure the proper transposition of the Directive, which was finally achieved by adopting Law No. 67/2006 on the safeguarding of employees' rights in the event of transfers of undertakings, businesses or parts of undertakings or businesses, published in the Official Journal of Romania No. 276 on 28 March 2006 and entered into force on 1 January 2007 ('Law no. 67/2006'), when Romania became a Member State of the European Union.

Generally, Law No. 67/2006 ensured an effective transposition of the Directive,[1] while national courts' case law is aligned with the practice of the European Court of Justice seated in Luxembourg (*ECJ*). However, Law No. 67/2006 has certain conformity issues that led to its inconsistent application and varying case law over the last years. In brief, the most relevant issues regard the following:

The scope of the Directive was restricted by Law No. 67/2006 to those transfers which imply a transfer of ownership from the transferor to the transferee of an undertaking, business, or parts thereof, with a view to continuing the main or secondary economic activity, whether or not they are operating for gain. This transposition incorrectly restricts the application of the employees' protections to those limited cases where the transfer is a result of a change in the ownership of the economic entity (in Romanian, '*din proprietatea cedentului în proprietatea cesionarului*'), ignoring the broader and flexible definitions established under the ECJ case law that also covered the transfer of other rights besides the right of ownership;

Law No. 67/2006 does not exclude from its application the transfer of an administrative reorganization of public administrative authorities, or the transfer of administrative functions between public administrative authorities, like the Directive does. It is unclear whether the intention of the national legislator was to deviate from the provisions of the Directive towards a more favourable regulation or whether this was simply an omission that occurred during the transposition process.

Even though the Directive allowed Member States to choose not to apply the employees' protection to transfers of undertakings, businesses or parts thereof where the transferor is subject to bankruptcy proceedings or any similar insolvency proceedings which have been instituted with a view to liquidating the assets of the transferor and are under the supervision of a competent public authority (which may be an insolvency practitioner authorized by a competent public authority), the Romanian legislator extended the exception to proceedings regarding judicial reorganizations as well.

As established by the ECJ, the Directive's objective is not to ensure that the employment contract with the transferor is continued where an employee does not wish to remain in the transferee's employment, but rather with the Member States to determine the fate of the employment contract. The Romanian legislator, however, did not regulate the employee's right not to continue the employment relationship with the transferee, nor how this could be formalized.

Likewise, during the implementation of Law No. 67/2006, practical issues appeared in relation to the formalities required to register the transfer. It took several years until the authorities updated the software application containing the employees' general registry so as to allow employers to operate the 'migration' of the employment contracts in the official records. Furthermore, in the first years following the entry into force of Law No. 67/2006, labour inspectors were expecting the transferor to terminate the current employment contracts with the transferred employees in order to implement the transfer, and the transferee to conclude new ones. This practice started to

1. There have been no infringement proceedings in relation to the transposition of the Directive.

change only recently, with most of the territorial labour authorities accepting nowadays the transfer of the employment contracts by effect of law.

National case law evolved substantially during the past few years, as courts started more and more to incorporate into their reasoning the principles derived from the ECJ jurisprudence. Thus, contrary to the restrictive definition of 'transfer' provided by the national law, the courts have accepted that employees' protection should be granted even in cases where the transfer occurs as an effect of transferring rights that may not necessarily be the right of ownership, such as outsourcing or leases. The courts have even gone so far as to recognize employees' protections in cases of share deals, where such deals were followed by a de facto takeover of the executive and operational control of the undertaking.

The trend is definitely positive, aiming more and more to safeguard the core objective of the Directive, i.e., an effective protection of employees' rights following the transfer of undertakings, businesses, or parts of undertakings or businesses. On the other hand, when the transfer of undertaking is excluded, this is not necessarily as a result of an assessment whereby courts would balance the protection of employees versus the economic interests of employers, in order to support the corporate and entrepreneurial movements expected to shift the EU economy in the years ahead, but rather the result of a poor understanding of the domestic text or the courts' reluctance to properly apply the ECJ established jurisprudence to the proceedings at issue.

§15.02 CONDITIONS TO APPLY THE EMPLOYEES' PROTECTION IN ROMANIA: DEVIATIONS FROM THE EUROPEAN FRAMEWORK

When interpreting and applying Law No. 67/2006, national courts are expected to weigh whether the three cumulative conditions leading to the application of the employees' protection are met. Generally, the principles set down by Law No. 67/2006 are consistent with the ones resulting from the Directive and the jurisprudence established by the ECJ, with certain particular aspects described in what follows.

§15.03 THE FIRST CONDITION: THE EXISTENCE OF A TRANSFER

Under Article 4 letter d) of Law No. 67/2006, the transfer is defined as a transfer of ownership from the transferor to the transferee of an undertaking, business, or parts thereof, having the objective of pursuing the main economic activity, whether or not they are operating for gain. Likewise, when referring to the obligation to inform and consult the employees, the Labour Code specifies[2] that this will regard the implications *deriving from the transfer of the ownership right*. As such, these provisions only refer to the transfer of ownership (in Romanian, *'din proprietatea cedentului în proprietatea cesionarului'*) from the transferor to the transferee, of an undertaking, business, or part thereof, thus restricting the broad definition provided by the Directive and resulting from the ECJ's jurisprudence that also covers the transfer of other rights besides that of

2. Article 174 of the Labour Code.

ownership. This incorrect transposition has led, in practice, to situations where national courts have refused to award the employees' protection under Law No. 67/2006 where there was no transfer of ownership rights, especially in the first years after its entry into force. In one case ruled upon in 2009, the Alba Iulia Court of Appeal[3] has held that if an activity is delegated from one unit to another, together with the employees allocated to that activity, this does not count as transfer of undertaking, as there was no transfer of ownership of an undertaking or of a part of undertaking from the transferor to the transferee. In another case finalized in the same year, the Bucharest Court of Appeal held in 2009 that *outsourcing* medical services does not qualify as a transfer in the meaning of Law No. 67/2006, given that the transferor had not transferred the ownership, but merely the use of its assets under a lease agreement concluded with a new provider.[4]

Fortunately, in recent years, the courts' perspective has changed for the better, as they started to apply to principle of the primacy of European Union law when interpreting the national transposing provisions. Thus, in the conflict arising between the provisions of the Directive regulating the meaning of the transfer and the more restrictive definition included in Law No. 67/2006, the courts gave precedence to the former and thus recognized the employees' protection in case of transfers resulting from various types of operations, irrespective of whether a transfer of ownership from the transferor to the transferee over the respective economic entity had occurred or not. For instance:

(a) The Bucharest Court of Appeal, in 2021:[5] 'What is relevant is the transfer between the two employers of an economic entity represented by employees and the stable continuation of the activity by the transferee, for the same beneficiary of the activity. From that point of view, according to the ECJ case law relied on at the first stage of the proceedings, the transfer of ownership

3. Decision No. 656 dated 25 May 2009, Alba Iulia Court of Appeal, available on www.sintact.ro, lastly accessed on 31 March 2023. The court held: 'It follows that there was not a transfer of ownership between the two companies in what regards the undertaking or a part of it, within the meaning of the provisions of art. 4 letter d) of the Law no. 67/2006, as correctly interpreted by the first court, respectively there was no transfer from the ownership of the transferor to the transferee of an undertaking or of a part thereof, instead the operation regarded an delegation of the public service of supply and sewage, from one unit to another, together with 35 employees, in order to implement a program.'
4. Decision No. 5050R dated 7 July 2009, Bucharest Court of Appeal, available on www.sintact.ro, lastly accessed on 31 March 2023: 'Therefore, the essential condition of the transfer of undertaking is that there is a proper takeover of a part of the undertaking, seen as a legal entity that holds a patrimony consisting of assets and liabilities and which has obligations to be complied with under individual employment contracts. The law expressly specifies the case when the transfer occurs, namely upon assignment and merger. Yet, this hypothesis is not met in the present case. On the contrary, the operation implemented at the institute, following the tender for the transfer of medical services for laboratory tests, represents an outsourcing of services. (...) Thes use of the existing premises and material base is made on the basis of a lease agreement, which necessarily implies that the assignor retains the ownership of its base and transmits only its use to the assignee (...).'
5. Decision No. 4476 dated 28 September 2021, Bucharest Court of Appeal, available on www.sintact.ro, lastly accessed on 31 March 2023.

of tangible assets between the two entities does not represent a condition for the transfer of undertaking to occur, nor does the value of the tangible assets transferred thereby.'

(b) The Bucharest Court of Appeal, in 2020,[6] acknowledges the need to apply the principle of the primacy of European Union law when interpreting the domestic text: 'According to established case law, Directive 2001/23 seeks to ensure the continuity of existing employment relationships within an economic entity, irrespective of a change of ownership. (...) Even if the Directive does not directly confer rights between individuals, the possibility of a consistent interpretation of the Directive is particularly relevant. (...) Consequently, the possibility of a consistent interpretation should have been examined in the present case, but the first court made no mention to that effect. Therefore, interpreting that directive in the light of the relevant case-law of the Court of Justice of the European Union, the Court finds that it must take into account all the factual circumstances characterising the transaction between the defendants in the present case, irrespective of the provisions of the national law transposing the directive.' Thus, the court concluded that a transfer of undertaking had occurred and the undertaking had retained its identity (*see* below, §15.05). Therefore, the Court of Appeal put aside the contrary domestic rules and granted damages to the employee whose employment relationship had been terminated during the probationary period unlawfully inserted in the newly concluded individual employment contract.

Pitesti Court of Appeal held in a recent decision[7] that even though one might consider that Law No. 67/2006 would not apply in those cases where the transferor merely leases tangible or intangible assets together with the allocated personnel in order to continue the main or ancillary activity, as by such lease there is no transfer of ownership (as required by Article 4 letter d) of Law No. 67/2006), one should bear in mind that such law was enacted to transpose the Directive, hence the ECJ case law must be considered. Based on this, the leasing of a grouping of resources might be qualified as a transfer of part of an undertaking.

Unfortunately, this approach is not the unanimous approach of the Romanian courts. There are still rulings loyal to the wording of the domestic legislation that refuse to acknowledge the employees' protection in cases where there is no transfer of ownership over the relevant assets between the transferor and the transferee. Craiova Court of Appeal has held, quite recently, in several similar cases,[8] that there is no transfer of undertaking when the transferor did nothing else than to transfer for a

---

6. Decision No. 4061 dated 9 November 2020, Bucharest Court of Appeal available on www.sintact.ro, lastly accessed on 31 March 2023.
7. Decision No. 2223 dated 10 July 2018, Pitesti Court of Appeal, available on www.sintact.ro, lastly accessed on 31 March 2023.
8. Decision No. 1800 dated 8 July 2020, Craiova Court of Appeal, Decision No. 1004/2020 dated 3 June 2020, Craiova Court of Appeal, Decision No. 153/2022 dated 21 January 2022, Craiova Court of Appeal, all available on www.sintact.ro, lastly accessed on 31 March 2023.

period of three years, with the possibility of extension and for a fee, the operation and maintenance of a fuel distribution station where the employee was working. The court ruled that the respective services contract does not suggest there was a transfer from the ownership of the transferor to that of the transferee of certain assets or of an entity or a part of an entity. Instead, in the court's view, the transferor and the transferee concluded a contract for the operation of fuel distribution stations, without transferring the ownership right over these stations, and hence such transfer is not covered by the scope of Law No. 67/2006. This is evidently contrary to the established case law of the ECJ, as per which the employees' protection must be recognized whenever, in the context of contractual relations, there is a change in the legal or natural person who is responsible for conducting the undertaking and who, by virtue of that fact, incurs the obligations of an employer vis-à-vis the employees of the undertaking, regardless of whether or not ownership of the tangible assets is transferred.

To avoid further inconsistent approaches, it is imperative to revise the wording of Law No. 67/2006 so as to expand the definition of transfer in light of the definition provided by the Directive and the established ECJ case law.

§15.04 THE EXISTENCE OF AN UNDERTAKING OR PART OF AN UNDERTAKING

Law No. 67/2006 does not provide a definition of the term 'undertaking'. However, when defining its scope, it refers to undertakings, businesses or parts thereof, situated on the territory of Romania, *irrespective of the nature of their share capital.* This provision should be read in conjunction with the provisions of the Romanian Civil Code, which defines *the operation of an undertaking* as systematically carrying on an organized activity consisting of producing, administering or selling goods or providing services, whether or not that activity aims to obtain gain. As such, Law No. 67/2006 should apply to those cases where the transfer regards an entity engaged in economic activities in the sense of the Romanian Civil Code, i.e., producing, administering or selling goods or providing services on the market.

National courts generally verify, in line with the ECJ case law, whether the transfer regards an undertaking understood as a self-standing organized group of persons and tangible and intangible assets that enables an economic activity with its own objective to be carried out. In recent years, the courts have started more and more to incorporate into their reasoning the rulings of the ECJ when defining the notion of 'undertaking' or 'economic entity'. In a case law cited above,[9] the Bucharest Court of Appeal held that the transfer in the meaning of the Directive refers to those cases in which an economic entity, i.e., an organized grouping of persons and assets facilitating the exercise of an economic activity which follows a specific objective, will retain its identity following the respective transaction.

The grouping of resources needs to be sufficiently individualized (the activity should be standalone, distinct of and separable from other activities of the transferor,

9. Decision 4476 dated 28 September 2021 cited above, *see* section §15.03, letter (a).

e.g., accounting, financial department),[10] to benefit from tangible and intangible assets necessary to carry out its objective (equipment, tools, client database, products, files, computers, software, operating means, contracts), to contain a self-standing organized group of personnel dedicated exclusively or mainly to that activity (segregated within a specific service or department within the transferor), to be able to function autonomously, to benefit from specific operational and organizational techniques, including an autonomous decision-making power exercised by supervisory personnel within the entity in question. In practice, this autonomy stems from the company's organizational chart, from the undertaking's organization and functioning regulation, from the job descriptions, skills and functions of the employees assigned to the activity transferred. Attention should notably be given to whether the personnel includes hierarchical superiors, department managers or head of services and support staff.

§15.05 THE TRANSFERRED UNDERTAKING RETAINS ITS IDENTITY AFTER THE TRANSFER

The national legislation stays silent in what regards the requirement that the transfer should concern an economic entity which retains its identity in order to have an organized grouping of resources in the meaning of the Directive. However, the national courts refer their assessment to the principles resulting from the ECJ's established case law. As such, in order to assess whether the transferred undertaking has maintained its identity post-transfer, the national court will weight all the factual circumstances characterizing the transfer in question, including, in particular: (i) the type of undertaking, (ii) if tangible elements such as buildings and movable property are transferred, (iii) if the majority of employees have been taken over by the new employer, and (iv) as well as the degree of similarity between the activities carried out before and after the transfer etc.

Where courts do refer to the ECJ case law, the tendency is to assess such elements in a rather lax manner, so as to meet the purpose of the legislation and protect the employees' rights. In a case cited above,[11] the Bucharest Court of Appeal assessed the

10. In one case, however, the court has held that there is no transfer of undertaking when a company reorganized its legal department by outsourcing the need of legal services via a public bid, thus contracting the services of a law firm (law firms performing these services based on a legal assistance contract). When assessing whether there was an 'undertaking' in the meaning of Law No. 67/2006, the court held that the 'company did not transfer an economic activity organized in a stable manner, even more so as the company's object of activity does not included the provision of legal services' (the employer was an airline company). Also, the court rejected the plaintiff's argument suggesting that the employer had created an economic entity organized in a stable manner by allocating a certain budged for legal services and individualizing such funds in its financial situation. As the transfer did not regard a grouping of personnel and elements allowing the performance of an economic activity consisting of legal services, retaining the identity of that undertaking would thus be out of the question (*see* Decision No. 2769/2021 dated 17 May 2021, Bucharest Court of Appeal, available on www.sintact.ro, lastly accessed on 31 October 2024).
11. Decision No. 4061 dated 9 November 2020, Bucharest Court of Appeal available on www.sintact.ro, lastly accessed on 31 October 2024.

application of these criteria to the case at issue and concluded that there was a transfer of undertaking which retained its identity, given that the transferee:

- continued to carry on the same business (selling the same products);
- at the same working point (the building being identically equipped, with the same utilities);
- using 18 of the same employees (a significant, majority number of employees);
- using the same means of operating the activity in question, movable and immovable assets (the same filling stations, shelves, chairs, etc.), even if they were owned by a third party;
- for the benefit of the same clientele (faithful to the brand and location), automatically appropriated.

In another case,[12] the same court held that 'it is clear that the business unit maintained its identity given that the respondent worked with the employees, machinery, raw materials, offices and showroom décor used by the other two companies, as is apparent from the statement of the witness heard in the case'. Even though the companies involved alleged that the customers and the suppliers would be different, the court wisely held that these two elements cannot be regarded as crucial, since 'on the one hand, the customers are natural persons, so there is no repetitive contractual relationship and, on the other hand, the list of suppliers may vary from time to time depending on the price of the raw material'.

As such, there is a visible trend of the courts (especially of the Bucharest Court of Appeal) to thoroughly assess the factual elements characterizing the transfer in question and conclude that there is a transfer of undertaking retaining its identity even in those cases where Law No. 67/2006 simply stays silent or poorly transposes the Directive.

§15.06 THE SCOPE OF LAW NO. 67/2006

[A] Share Deals May Qualify as Transfer of Undertakings

It is undisputed that a transfer exists whenever, in the context of contractual relations, there is a change in the legal or natural person who is responsible for conducting the undertaking and who, by virtue of that fact, incurs the obligations of an employer vis-à-vis the employees of the undertaking, regardless of whether or not ownership of the tangible assets is transferred. When it comes to transactions implying the transfer of ownership of the majority of the shares in an undertaking or a change in the majority shareholders (share deals), a change of control occurs in the company's ownership, without any change in the legal personality of the company as employer. The European Commission's Report of 2007 on the implementation of the Directive[13] states, in line

12. Decision No. 5463 dated 26 November 2019, Bucharest Court of Appeal, available on www.sintact.ro, lastly accessed on 31 October 2024.
13. Available at https://www.eumonitor.eu, lastly accessed on 31 October 2024.

with ECJ's established case law, that 'the transfer of ownership of the majority of the shares in an undertaking or a change in the majority of shareholders does not constitute a transfer because the legal personality of the employer is unchanged'. The Commission further acknowledges that a change of control can lead to changes in that undertaking; however, the employees' legal position vis-à-vis the employer rests unchanged. Moreover, by the same report, the Commission considered that it was not justified at that stage to revise the Directive, 'extending the definition of "transfer" to include a change of control, as proposed by the European Confederation of Trade Unions'. The conclusions of the European Commission were referred to and reflected in a ruling issued by the Bucharest Court of Appeal in 2015,[14] whereby the court has held that the transfer of ownership of the majority part of the shares of a company or a change in the majority shareholders does not constitute a transfer of an undertaking within the meaning of the Directive, as the legal personality of the employer remains unchanged.

Nevertheless, the issue of whether share deals may qualify as transfers of undertakings has become a topic of debate in recent years. In April 2017,[15] the Bucharest Court of Appeal made a major shift in what regards the applicability of employees' protection in case of transfers of undertaking following share deals. The court ruled that the form of the transaction (share sale-purchase contract, and not a business transfer) does not automatically exclude the applicability of the Directive. In fact, if the change of control over the business is also accompanied by a series of operations aimed at integrating the employer's activity in the larger organization of the acquirer, the employees' protection should be ensured even if the employer's identity (as legal entity) remains the same. In that case, the court, acknowledging the limitations of the definition included in Law No. 67/2006 ('the transfer from the ownership of the transferor to that of the transferee'), referred to the broader meaning of the term 'transfer' as established under the ECJ jurisprudence, by applying the principle regarding the primacy of the European Union law[16] and essentially held that:

When defining the transfer, the ECJ assigned a rather flexible meaning to it so as to achieve the objective of ensuring the continuity of the employment relationships, irrespective of the change of employer. As such, the Directive will apply in all cases where, in the contractual relationships, there is a change of the physical or legal person who is responsible for the functioning of the undertaking and who assumes the employer's obligations towards the employees of that undertaking, regardless of the form of the agreement or even the lack of any direct link between the parties involved.

---

14. Decision No. 2479 dated 22 June 2015, Bucharest Court of Appeal, available on www.sintact.ro, lastly accessed on 31 October 2024.
15. Decision No. 2542 dated 26 April 2017, Bucharest Court of Appeal, available on www.sintact.ro, lastly accessed on 31 October 2024.
16. The court held: 'As the internal provision restricts the scope of the European rule, the Court will apply the principle of the primacy of European law enshrined in the Costa vs. Enel judgment dated 15 July 1964 by which the legislation issued by the European institutions is integrated into the legal systems of the Member States, which are obliged to comply with it. Thus, if a national rule, whether adopted before or after the European act in question, is contrary to a European provision, the authorities of the Member States must apply the European provision'.

If it were to take into account only the transfer of shares and the change in the company's status as shareholder, the court acknowledged that it could not retain the incidence of the transfer of an undertaking, as it is consistently recognized that in such a situation, the company retains its individuality and the status of employer vis-à-vis its employees. However, while assessing the entirety of the factual circumstances of the case at issue, the court concluded that the contractual relationships between the parties involved were not limited to the shares transfer agreement and to the change in ownership. Instead, the final purpose of the parties was to continue the activity of the transferor (the retail activity), while integrating the transferor's organization into the operating flow of the acquiring company.

In fact, the transferee took over the majority shareholder, replacing the transferor in the operation of the undertaking by executing support services (such as sales, acquisitions, marketing, finance, human resources), which were outsourced to the acquirer under an intercompany agreement. In addition, the transferee started using the premises that had been used by the transferor, it integrated most of the former employees of the transferor into positions which were identical to the ones held within the former undertaking, and it took over the clientele while continuing to provide identical products and services on the same retail market. These operations do reflect the continuation of the initial activities by the transferee and hence the court acknowledged the employees' protection provided by the Directive.

In our view, by this decision, the Court of Appeal took a courageous leap ahead, essentially putting aside the form of the contract (the acquisition of the majority of shares) and requalifying the operations that followed between the companies involved as a substantial and sufficient proof that, in fact, the identity of the employer did change in relation to the employees of that undertaking.

It is true that the national courts should assess the applicability of the employees' protection under the Directive on a case-by-case basis, taking into account all relevant factual elements characterizing that operation, and that the ECJ allows a high degree of flexibility when assessing whether a transfer took place. However, this assessment is extremely complex as it implies that the court should analyse substantial evidence showing the entirety of the facts characterizing the relevant operations, evidence based on which the court must then diligently justify whether a transfer did or did not occur, and, in case it did, the court should also be able to determine when that transfer took place (especially as this type of operations are normally implemented in several stages which can take years after the signing of the share transfer contract). In our view, this is an extremely complex examination which might overcome the competence of a court of law. In case the file misses any part of the factual elements characterizing the operation at issue, the examination risks leading to misinterpretations of the actual will of the employers involved, thus artificially extending the employees' protection to the cases where the legal personality of the employer had, in fact, not changed. It should not be forgotten that the Directive and Law No. 67/2006 contain provisions instituting exceptional norms, intensely limiting the economic freedom of companies involved and which should, therefore, not be extended with ease, especially given the current economic climate.

A similar solution was presented in the UK in 2014,[17] when a court accepted that a share sale can lead to a transfer of undertaking. Here, similar to the case settled by the Bucharest Court of Appeal a few years later, in 2017, the control exercised by the parent company of the target's acquirer and the extensive integration operations carried out by it led the court to acknowledge that there had been a transfer of undertaking.

To conclude, the companies undergoing a share transfer should not exclude *de plano* the application of the employees' protection under the Directive, if they plan to undertake additional operations essentially allowing a control takeover. Indications of such control takeover could be: a change of control followed by outsourcing the support services to the acquirer, a management takeover, the transfer of key or of the majority of employees, the absorption or sharing of resources, workload, of other tangible or intangible assets, of the clientele, and the continued provision of identical services and products on the same market.

[B] Transferring Parts of Undertakings or Businesses

[1] In-scope Employees

When transferring parts of undertakings or businesses, law practitioners face real challenges when it comes to delimiting the extent of the resources to be transferred. While the situation is rather straightforward when it comes to the transfer of entire lines of undertakings or businesses, such as plants, it becomes quite difficult to identify the limits of the grouping of resources being transferred when such transfer regards parts of undertakings that use shared resources, as employees carrying on several activities in the undertaking. The question is how to select from among the shared employees. In practice, it has been established that the defining criterion should be the working time percentage allocated by the relevant employees to the transferring activity. Further, the domestic law does not regulate such a percentage, so it is up to the relevant court to determine the in-scope employees allocated to the transferable part of the undertaking or business.

In practice, there are two ways to address this issue:

(a) the transfer may regard the employees dedicated entirely or mainly to that part of business or undertaking (the predominant role). A comfortable percentage used to determine the predominant role would be above two-thirds (65-75%) of their working time. To determine this, one should refer to the employee's job description. If the actual activities carried on by the employees differ from the officially signed job descriptions, the former must be considered.

17. *Jackson Lloyd Ltd and Mears Group plc v. Smith and others* UKEAT/0127/13, available at https://www.gov.uk/employment-appeal-tribunal-decisions/jackson-lloyd-ltd-and-mears-group-plc-ukeat-0127-13-la, lastly accessed on 31 October 2024.

After the transfer, the new employer should redistribute tasks so as to complete the work norm of these employees, without, however, altering the type of role held by that employee, as this operation naturally implies the employees' accord.

(b) the transfer may regard the employees as they are, i.e., if some employees work only 40-50% for the transferred activity and the rest of the working time is dedicated to other activities not subject to the transfer, the employees' contracts could be split so as to continue to work post-transfer in the same form (i.e., part-time for the current employer, part-time for the new employer). This would observe *at litteram* the rule to take over the individual employment contracts as before the transfer. However, this rigorous interpretation does not ensure a reasonable balance between the interests of the parties and has high chances of proving impractical. This is because: (i) such split would imply transforming the nature of the contract from full norm into two part-time employment contracts (which further implies a different regime, such as the interdiction to work overtime), and (ii) in the cases when the place of work changes following the transfer it would be impossible for an employee to execute his part-time contracts for both employers.

For these reasons, in most cases, companies take the first option presented above.

[2] Prior Divestments

In situations where the allocation of employees is even more undistinguishable (e.g., employees dedicated in a percentage of 40-50% to the activity to be transferred), employers may consider reorganizing their current structures so as to create a dedicated part of undertaking or business, that could function autonomously while pursuing an economic objective (hence fulfilling the relevant criteria to be qualified as 'economic entity' in the meaning of the Directive). This must be recognized as an expression of the employer's unilateral prerogative to organize its business. This prior divestment process implies a reorganization of the internal structure aimed at clearly defining the perimeter of the relevant part of undertaking or business, so as to make sure that all employees in that perimeter only work for the benefit of the activity to be transferred. In case of difficult assessments (50%-50% working time), the employees should be allowed to opt between being integrated in the new perimeter, or to continue working in the previous structures, as such approach could significantly decrease the risk of litigations.

The divestment needs to be grounded on serious reasons, commercial and economic, and should be implemented based on objective rules. Employers should not resort to this mechanism in order to *clean up* the structure and thus make *unwanted* employees redundant or cherry-pick the *preferred candidates*. Instead, the purpose of the divestment must remain that of identifying the in-scope employees for the transfer and must be thoroughly formalized (including by updating the organizational chart so as to show the new, clean in-scope perimeter of the contemplated transfer). If the job descriptions remain the same, and only the hierarchical lines are to be moved or changed, the divestment should not require the consent of the employees. Otherwise, if the employer needs to change the roles of certain employees, unless the employees agree to the changes, formal economic restructurings might be necessary.[18] Finally, in order to avoid organizational disruptions, the employees' representatives should be informed and consulted about the divestment process before its actual implementation.

In case the employer transfers employees that should have been out of scope (the conditions for the automatic transfer were not met), the employees subject to the vitiated transfer may challenge this operation, arguing the lack of legal cause. In theory, the court may reverse the transfer of the respective employees, ordering that they be reinstated on the positions previously held within the transferor's organization and granting any damages necessary to compensate the employee (including all salary rights to which the employee would have been entitled since the dismissal until the effective reinstatement, legal costs and moral damages, if proven). In Romania, however, employers tend to avoid business transfers and with it the employees' protection and tend not to implement transfers when it would be arguable if they are applicable. The same consequence could apply if the transferor would include in the transferring perimeter employees who have reasons to argue that they were not allocated to the transferred business (e.g., only a partial allocation), and thus that they should not have been subject to the automatic transfer.

[C] Administrative Reorganization of Public Administrative Authorities or the Transfer of Administrative Functions Between Public Administrative Authorities

While assessing whether an entity qualifies as an undertaking or business under the meaning of the Directive, it is crucial that the respective entity is engaged in economic activities, i.e., that it provides goods or services on a market.[19] For this reason, the Directive excluded from its scope an administrative reorganization of public administrative authorities, or the transfer of administrative functions between public administrative authorities, as these activities involve the exercise of public authority.[20]

Conversely, Law No. 67/2006 does not exclude from the meaning of the 'transfer' an administrative reorganization of public administrative authorities, or the transfer of

18. As a rule, changing the mandatory elements of the employment contracts requires the consent of the affected employee via concluding an addendum to the employment agreement. However, the employer may unilaterally amend the responsibilities of a role as long as the new responsibilities assigned to the employee do not exceed the nature of the respective role and these are not significantly different than those already exercised by the respective employee. Hence, only substantial changes of responsibilities would require the individual consent of the employee.
19. Article 1 para. (1) letter (c) first sentence: 'This Directive will apply to public and private undertakings engaged in economic activities whether or not they are operating for gain.'
20. Article 1 para. 1 letter (c) last sentence: 'An administrative reorganisation of public administrative authorities, or the transfer of administrative functions between public administrative authorities, is not a transfer within the meaning of this Directive.'

administrative functions between public administrative authorities. In practice, this aspect generated two different interpretations:

(a) this inconsistency represents a reflection of the national legislator's intention to create a situation of more favourable transposition, in which Law No. 67/2006 should apply in these cases as well; or
(b) this case simply represents a situation where the national legislator deemed it would be redundant to reiterate the same wording included in the Directive, as the same conclusion of non-applicability would be reached if one would apply the principle according to which the entity in question *should be engaged in economic activities*.

As revealed above, the definition of the transfer provided by Law No. 67/2006 refers to the transfer of an undertaking, business or part thereof, from the transferor's ownership to that of the transferee (in Romanian, '*din proprietatea cedentului în proprietatea cesionarului*'), aiming to continue the activity, be it principal or ancillary, whether or not that undertaking is operating for gain. Even though Law No. 67/2006 does not provide a definition of the term 'undertaking', the purpose of Law No. 67/2006 should be interpreted in light of the ECJ jurisprudence and thus apply to those cases where the transfer regards an entity engaged in economic activities in the sense of the Romanian Civil Code, i.e., producing, administering or selling goods or providing services on the market. On the contrary, Law No. 67/2006 should not apply to transfers resulting from administrative reorganization of public administrative authorities or the transfer of administrative functions between public administrative authorities.

The Bucharest Court of Appeal held[21] in the same sense, stating that the reference to the share capital in Article 2 of Law No. 67/2006, 'The provisions of this law will apply to the transfer of undertakings, businesses or parts thereof located on the territory of Romania, regardless of the nature of the share capital.', should be read as having the same purpose of excluding the applicability of the law in the event of administrative reorganisation of the public administration authorities.

In light of the above, it is our view that the employees' protection regulated by Law No. 67/2006 should not apply to those transfers resulting from administrative reorganizations of public administrative authorities or the transfer of administrative functions between public administrative authorities, insofar as such operations imply the exercise of public power.

[D] Judicial Reorganizations

As per the Directive, unless otherwise decided by Member States, the employees' protection regulated thereunder will not apply when the transfer is carried out in the

21. Bucharest Court of Appeal, Decision No. 5375 dated 3 November 2017, available on www.sintact.ro, lastly accessed on 31 October 2024.

context of an insolvency situation.[22] However, the national legislator incorrectly transposed this requirement, excluding from the scope of the legislation all insolvency cases, i.e., those cases where the transferor is subject to judicial reorganization, as well.[23]

It follows that, even though the Directive only allowed the national legislator to opt for applying the protection instituted by the Directive in case of bankruptcy proceedings or *similar insolvency proceedings* instituted *with a view to liquidating the assets of the transferor* and *are under the supervision of a competent public authority*, Law No. 67/2006 excluded from its application those transfers occurring in the context of judicial reorganizations, which do not amount to insolvency proceedings in the meaning of the Directive, as commonly agreed. In the Plesser ruling,[24] the ECJ has held that the three cumulative conditions for a transfer to be excluded from the scope of the Directive are not met in what concerns judicial reorganizations such as the ones at issue in the main proceedings. The ECJ reasoning in the more recent *Heiploeg* case[25] could be seen as more supple, the ECJ resolving thereby that a case-by-case analysis on factual considerations and the way the procedure is carried out should be rendered in order to determine whether a procedure falls under the exception. However, as per the national legislation,[26] judicial reorganization refers to the procedure applicable to the insolvent debtor, a legal person, aiming to arrange to pay off its debts, according to the debt payment schedule, as per a reorganization plan. This plan can provide, without limitation, several types of restructuring of the debtor (operational and/or financial, corporate restructuring) as well as partial or total liquidation of the assets from the debtor's estate. As such, liquidation of the transferor's assets is not a *sine qua non* condition or the main purpose of the judicial reorganization, but merely one of the restructuring possibilities which the insolvent undertaking can consider. Therefore, judicial reorganization should not have been excluded from the scope of Law No. 67/2006.

In a quite recent case, the Bucharest Tribunal[27] held that this particular case of incorrect transposition cannot be rectified by way of conforming interpretation of the

---

22. According to Article 5 para. (1) of the Directive, 'Unless Member States provide otherwise, Articles 3 and 4 shall not apply to any transfer of an undertaking, business or part of an undertaking or business where the transferor is the subject of bankruptcy proceedings or any analogous insolvency proceedings which have been instituted with a view to the liquidation of the assets of the transferor and are under the supervision of a competent public authority (which may be an insolvency practitioner authorised by a competent public authority).'
23. Article 5 para. (2) of Law No. 67/2006.
24. Judgment of the Court in Case C-509/17, where the ECJ has held that judicial reorganization cannot be regarded as being insolvency proceedings; second, the requirement that proceedings must have been instituted for the purposes of the liquidation of the transferor's assets is not met, as judicial proceedings are aimed at ensuring the continuation of the activity of the undertaking concerned; lastly, as regards the requirement that the proceedings in question must be conducted under the supervision of a competent public authority, the supervision exercised by the legal representative in the context of the proceedings for judicial restructuring by transfer under judicial supervision cannot satisfy that requirement, its scope being too restricted.
25. Judgment of the Court in Case C-237/20.
26. Law No. 85/2014 on preventing insolvency proceedings and insolvency judicial reorganization.
27. Civil ruling No. 4533 dated 16 June 2021, Bucharest Tribunal, final, available on www.sintact .com, lastly accessed on 29 October 2024.

European Union law: 'In this case it is not possible to interpret the provisions of art. 5 of Law. no 67/2006 in the light of the provisions of the Directive, since such interpretation is against the transposing rule and the interpretation against the law cannot be accepted. Thus, in the matter regarding the transfer of an undertaking, it is not possible to reach the way of interpreting the provisions of art. 5 of Law. 67/2006 to the obligation of the assignee to take over in full the rights and obligations of all the employees of the assignor in the event that the latter was in judicial reorganization, since the aforementioned transposition rule establishes the contrary.' Consequently, the court held that the plaintiff could only claim 'state liability for the damage caused to her in the event that it is found that Directive 2001/23/EC has been incorrectly transposed.' In this case, the court rejected the plaintiff's arguments that she should have benefited from the protection instituted by Law No. 67/2006 even if her employer was undergoing judicial reorganization proceedings.

Therefore, given the express provision in the Romanian text that it will not apply to transfers resulting from judicial reorganizations, courts cannot interpret the domestic law in line with the principle of the primacy of the European Union law; instead, individuals injured as a result of the domestic legislation's lack of compliance with the Directive can obtain, where appropriate, compensation for the damage caused to them.[28]

§15.07 AUTOMATIC TRANSFER CONSEQUENCES

[A] Taking over the Rights and Obligations of the Transferor

Safeguarding employees' rights in case of transfer of undertakings, businesses, or parts thereof, one of the core drivers for the European legislator, was duly transposed under the national legislation by Article 5 paragraph (1) of Law No. 67/2006.[29] While some scholars and law practitioners opinionated that the transferor will be simply replaced by the transferee, the latter taking over *the entire content* of the employment relationships, others have duly questioned whether the transferee should be allowed a certain appreciation margin while safeguarding the core rights and obligations of the employees.

Law No. 67/2006 refers to the transferee's obligation to fully take over all the rights and obligations provided for under the *individual labour contracts* and *the applicable collective labour agreement*. The transferor must notify the transferee about all the rights and obligations that are subject to the handover before the transfer date.

28. This is in line with ECJ case law, as per which *a national court, hearing a dispute between private persons, which finds itself unable to interpret provisions of its national law which are consistent with a directive which has not been transposed or has been incorrectly transposed, is not required, solely on the basis of EU law, to disapply those national provisions which are contrary to the provisions of that directive* (Judgment of the Court in Case C-509/17, para. 60).

29. Article 5, transposing Article 3 para. 1 from the Directive: 'The rights and obligations of the transferor which result from the individual employment contracts and from the applicable collective labour agreement, existing at the date of the transfer, shall entirely transfer to the transferee.'

Nevertheless, even if the transferor fails to do so, this will not impact the transfer of those rights or obligations to the transferee or the employees' rights.

With respect to the collective labour agreement, Law No. 67/2006 specifies that the transferee must observe the provisions of the collective labour agreement applicable at the transfer date, until this would be terminated (in Romanian, '*reziliat*')[30] or would expire. If there is a consensus between the transferee and the employees' representatives, the clauses of the collective labour agreement can be renegotiated, but not less than one year after the transfer date. Of course, this latter principle will apply in case the collective contract has not expired earlier than that.

Further, Law No. 67/2006 regulates a distinction in relation to application of the transferor's collective labour agreement depending on the preservation of the autonomy of that undertaking after the transfer, a distinction which was not considered by the European legislator. As such, in those cases when, after the transfer, the undertaking, business or part thereof, does not preserve its autonomy and the collective labour agreement applicable at the level of the transferee is more favourable, then that collective labour agreement will apply to the transferred employees instead of the transferor's collective labour agreement. *Per a contrario*, when, after the transfer, the undertaking, business or the part thereof, does keep its autonomy, the transferred employees will continue to benefit of the provisions of the collective labour agreement applicable at the level of the transferor, even if the collective labour agreement applicable at the level of the transferee would be more favourable. This rule creates a different treatment between the two categories of employees without any justification. The same rationale regarding the preservation of the autonomy of the undertaking, business or part thereof, entitles the transferred employees to be represented, with their express consent, by the employees' representatives from the transferor's unit, until new representatives are founded or vested as per the law.[31] However, there is no coherent link between the provisions regarding the status and function of the employees' representatives and the application of a more favourable collective labour agreement.

Additionally, the national legislator does not regulate the criteria based on which one should determine which collective contract is more favourable for the employees. In our view, the two contracts should be compared holistically and the one which creates a better global situation for the vast majority of the transferred employees should be considered the one which is more favourable.

30. In fact, this is another proof of incoherent transposition of the Directive, as the English term 'date of termination of the collective agreement' was transposed as '*până la data rezilierii (...)*'. In Romanian legal vernacular, the term '*reziliere*' refers, in brief, to termination due to breach of contract by the other party (this has been defined as the 'civil law sanction that intervenes in case of culpable non-execution of a bilateral contract with successive execution and consists of the termination of the effects of the respective contract only for the future'. While this is common for civil law, collective labour agreements cannot be terminated for breach. If one party breaches the contract, the other has the right to claim forced execution in 6 months after the breach has occurred.
31. Article 10 para. 2 of Law No. 67/2006, transposing Article 6 para. 1 final thesis of the Directive.

[B] What Transfers?

The transferee will take over the rights and obligations under the individual employment contracts and from the applicable collective labour agreement, existing at the date of the transfer. While there is no doubt that the transferee will take over the rights that are objective and measurable (such as extended duration of notice period, additional remuneration and allowances, additional days of annual leave or days-off in case of family events), it has been debated whether the transferee should be ordered to take over and observe those benefits closely linked to the organization of the previous employer. In fact, there have been cases where the transferor, active in the mobility sector (car lease), was granting company cars to their employees as a personal benefit, or when the transferor, part of a group including banking institutions, was thus able to provide its employees with preferable loans. However, in these particular cases, the transferee did not own a car fleet or was not able to provide preferable loans to its employees. Hence, the question becomes whether the transferee should be allowed to make certain adjustments to the content of the rights and obligations taken over from the transferor, and, if so, what would be the adequate appreciation margin.

The ECJ has held[32] that the Directive does not aim solely to safeguard the interests of employees in the event of transfer of an undertaking but seeks to ensure a fair balance between the interests of those employees, on the one hand, and those of the transferee, on the other. As such, it has been concluded that the transferee must be in a position to make the adjustments and changes necessary to carry on its operations. In our view, it would be unequitable and unreasonable to pretend the transferee to acquire an entire car fleet or to turn itself into a lending institution simply because of the need to maintain *tale quale* the benefits priorly granted by the transferor. It is thus essential to strive for the right balance between awarding the employees the proper protection and adapting or adjusting the working conditions after the transfer to the extent necessary from an operational perspective. For the same reason, it should be accepted that certain rights or benefits closely linked to the organization of the transferor or its group of companies (such as particular bonus schemes, procedures implying the involvement of a specialized department or unconventional in-kind benefits) should not be covered under the scope of the legislation. As long as globally, the employees are in a substantially similar situation as before the transfer, the purpose of the legislation should be deemed to have been met.[33]

In particular situations where the transfer regards foreign employees, the question is whether these employees will transfer *ope legis* to the transferee, or if the latter needs to obtain, prior to the transfer of their employment contracts, a new work permit for each foreign employee. The national legislation regulates strict conditions for hiring foreign workers (such as obtaining a work permit, which is issued after verifying the

---

32. C-426/11 – Alemo-Herron and Others.
33. As the ECJ has repeatedly held, the purpose of the Directive is to ensure, as far as possible, that the contract of employment continues unchanged with the transferee, in order to prevent the employees concerned from being placed in a less favourable position solely as a result of the transfer.

fulfilment of the legal conditions by the transferor), while changing their working conditions is subject to specific conditions and additional preliminary formalities, including the notification of the immigration office. The legislation does not clarify whether the work permits are transferred as well when the individual employment contract is transferred following a transfer of undertaking, business or part thereof, to a new employer. As such, the immigration office may consider that the transferee must, in fact, fulfil the legal obligations to hire the foreign employees prior to the transfer. In our view, such approach would contradict the holistic effects of the catch-all principle included in Article 5 paragraph (1) of Law No. 67/2006 (regarding the transfer of all rights and obligations of the transferor). Moreover, while consulting the immigration office on the occasion of various transfers of undertakings impacting foreign employees, the authority has confirmed that transferring employees under the conditions of Law No. 67/2006 does not impose the obligation to obtain new work permits by the transferee for the foreign employees, as long as there are no changes to the essential elements of the activity rendered by those employees (naturally, the hypothesis implies that the transferee itself fulfils the conditions to hire foreign employees, as regulated by the law in force). Of course, as the practice of the authority might vary, it is recommended to refer the case at hand to the relevant office before implementing the actual transfer of the employment contracts of the foreign employees.

Given that Law No. 67/2006 only refers to the rights and obligations included in the individual or collective labour agreements, the transferee is not obliged to take over the rights and obligations included in the internal regulations or other internal policies belonging to the transferor. Instead, the transferee's policies and internal rules will apply.[34] However, given that the employees should not be subject to worse employment conditions following the transfer, any changes in the regime of the employment terms should be considered diligently and justified based on factors not linked to the transfer itself.

[C] Substantial Changes Versus Regular Changes

The national law loyally transposed in its Article 8[35] the rule according to which *substantial changes* in working conditions to the detriment of the employee will make the employer responsible for the termination of the employment contract. This type of changes could regard those cases when the role held by the employee is significantly adjusted (in terms of attributions or responsibilities), the changes affect the amount of the remuneration (due to the new work organization, for instance), the new requirements no longer allow the employee to meet the professional standards, and the employees are required to work from a different city. In this type of case, the employees would be allowed to terminate the work relationships on the grounds that the transfer

34. As per the Labour Code, any employer is obliged to have an internal regulation and to communicate that to each employee on their first day of work.
35. Article 8 of Law No. 67/2006: 'In case the transfer implies a substantial change in working conditions to the detriment of the employee, the employer shall be regarded as having been responsible for termination of the contract of employment.'

implied detrimental substantial changes to their working conditions and, as a consequence, the employer will be regarded as responsible for the termination. This further implies that the employees will be treated as having been dismissed for reasons unrelated to their person, i.e., they benefit from notice period, severance payments as provided by the law or the applicable collective agreement, and unemployment protection measures.

At the same time, however, some changes are allowed, i.e., those that would have happened irrespective of the transfer. Since the transferee takes the place of the transferor with regard to the rights and obligations arising from the employment relationship, it has been accepted that the transferee should not be precluded from amending the employment relationship insofar as applicable national law admits such amendment in cases other than transfers of undertakings. In particular, one should differentiate between the nature of the contemplated amendments: (i) if these would be likely to substantially affect the substance of the roles of the transferred employees or if the changes concern the essential elements of the employment agreement, than the transferee would require the employees' accord; (ii) on the contrary, as an effect of any employer's organizational prerogative, the transferee must be allowed to adjust the roles held by the transferred employees without their consent, when it comes to marginal adjustments such as tweaking ancillary tasks, undertaking formal organizational changes, such as changes in the reporting lines, the internal names of the roles, the identity of the coordinator or, of course, of the beneficiary of the services delivered by or the products manufactured by the transferred employees. As any employer is recognized the prerogative to undertake such changes, the transferee should as well.

In regards the transferee's possibility to change the employment contracts in agreement with the employees, such an endeavour could prove invalid given the ECJ's case law, even if those changes, taken overall, would not be to the detriment of the transferred employees. To take a step forward towards the required harmonization after the transfer, the transferee should place this topic on the agenda of the collective negotiations or other means of social dialogue, which, thanks to the input of the employees' representatives, could be able to provide adequate guarantees for the transferred employees.

[D] Employees' Right Not to Continue the Employment Relationship with the Transferee

[1] The National Legal Basis

The purpose of the Directive, as stated under the ECJ jurisprudence, is not to ensure that the employment contract with the transferor is continued where that employee does not wish to remain in the transferee's organization. In such cases, the ECJ held that the fate of the contract of employment or employment relationship should be determined by Member States (e.g., that in such a case the contract of employment or employment relationship must be regarded as terminated either by the employee or by the employer or that the same should be maintained with the transferor).

The national legislation does not require the transferred employees to give their consent to the transfer, which occurs *ope legis*, nor does it regulate expressly the employees' right to refuse the transfer. However, in line with the ECJ case law, it is commonly accepted that the transferred employees have the possibility to oppose the transfer to the new employer.

The basis supporting the objection right in the national legislation resides in the freedom of work (the employees being free to choose their place of work, their profession, the occupation, or the activity to be rendered). This was also acknowledged by recent case law:[36] 'taking into account the labour legislation (art. 3 para. (2) of the Labour Code) – the principle of freedom of choice of employment (and implicitly of the employer), as well as the fact that the automatic transfer of the employment contract from the assignor to the assignee is provided for the benefit of the employee, as a measure of his protection in case of transfer of undertaking, the employee being able to choose to refuse the benefit of this right, the applicant accepted this transfer'.

There is also contrary case law. In a rather surprising, but isolated ruling, issued quite recently, the Romanian court validated the employer's decision to automatically transfer an employee allocated to the business even if that employee had refused to be transferred and had subsequently asked for the termination of the employment agreement. In that case, the employees were allowed to opt until the transfer date between being transferred or receiving a voluntary leave package (with payment of compensatory salaries). The parties did not reach an agreement on termination; hence, the plaintiff was transferred to the transferee. In court, the plaintiff challenged the transfer and asked the court to acknowledge the termination of the employment relationship. The court rejected the claim as it has held that the transfer does not depend on the employee's choice, but on the compliance with the guarantees provided for by the local law: 'The law does not establish a right of choice of the employee between the transfer within the assigning company and the termination of the individual employment contract, the assignor having the right to transfer to the assignee all the rights and obligations arising from the individual employment contracts in compliance with the guarantees arising from art. 8 of Law. 67/2006.' While justifying its ruling, the court based its decision on the fact that Article 8 of Law No. 67/2006 – which transposes Article 4 paragraph (2) of the Directive, would only allow employees to refuse the transfer in case of substantial changes in the working conditions to the detriment of the employee: 'As the plaintiff did not invoke and did not argue that in fact the working conditions underwent detrimental substantial changes as a result of the transfer, having made no reference to the way in which the employment relationship actually took place, in what the substantial changes consisted of, and why any changes would have been unfavourable to the employee, the plaintiff's mere reference to the different title of the new position and the job description typical of the

36. Civil ruling No. 585/2021 dated 18 October 2021, Olt Tribunal, available on www.sintact.ro, lastly accessed on 31 October 2024.

structure of the new employer is not likely to prove his claims regarding the unlawfulness of the transfer of his employment contract from the perspective of the provisions of art. 8 of Law no. 67/2006.'[37]

In our view, this decision ignores the established ECJ case law allowing the employees to refuse the transfer irrespective of potential changes that would occur after that transfer. Indeed, it is up to the national legislator to regulate how such refusal would formalize and the Romanian legislator omitted to do that. Still, it remains the obligation of the national courts to observe the ECJ case law while applying the transposing legislation, and the Bucharest Court of Appeal failed to consider such case law while issuing the decision cited above.

[2] The Mechanism Required to Formalize the Employee's Refusal

In the idyllic scenario, the refusal should happen by employee's resignation or by concluding a mutual termination agreement with the employer. However, if the employee does not intend to resign, the situation becomes more complicated. Even though Member States were allowed to determine the fate of the contract of employment, the Romanian legislator failed to do so. This legislative vacuum generated different approaches in practice. As there is no express rule according to which the employment would terminate automatically in case the employees object to the transfer, the practitioners and the courts have embraced two directions:

(a) assimilating the refusal with a resignation. However, resignation is a unilateral act of will of the employee. Reaching the conclusion that the employee's objection to the transfer would automatically qualify as the employee's resignation would be unsound, in the absence of a legal provision granting such effects to the employee's objection (which the national legislator did not do).
(b) recognizing the transferor's right to dismiss the employee refusing the transfer on economic grounds. In case the employer has no other option to maintain the employment contracts, e.g., by redistributing the employee to another activity, it has been rightfully opiniated that such dismissal would not be contrary to the interdiction to dismiss the employees because of the transfer, as the employer had already ensured for that employee the required level of protection.

There is case law supporting each direction. One Court of Appeal ruled that 'the employee's refusal to accept the transfer equates to a request for resignation',[38] while others have stated that 'should the employees express their refusal to be taken over

37. Decision 3453/2021 dated 14 June 2021, Bucharest Court of Appeal, available on www.sintact.ro, lastly accessed on 31 October 2024.
38. Decision No. 77 dated 7 February 2008, Alba-Iulia Court of Appeal, available on www.legeaz.net, lastly accessed on 31 October 2024.

until the date which has been communicated to them, they can be dismissed by the initial employer'.[39]

Even though the alternative regarding the dismissal of the employees based on economic grounds seems more adequate to the situation (assuming the employer no longer needs the job held by the refusing employees), this still implies additional risks, as employers are required to observe the legal conditions applicable to dismissals due to reasons unrelated to the person of the employee, i.e., economic restructurings (the cause thereof should be real and serious, while the job elimination should be final).[40] As dismissals linked to the transfer would not be valid, the economic rationale should unfold in the sense that there is no further business for the company and thus there is no need for additional work from these employees. In any case, the company must observe the rights applicable to economic dismissals, as such are included in the internal rules or the collective labour agreement, as well as the employees' notice period (normally, of 20 working days). In practice, such rules might turn out to be quite cumbersome for the transferor (higher notice period, generous exit packages). Being bound to award these rights when dismissals had not even been contemplated by the parties might infringe the economic freedom of that company. True, in some cases, the changes in the working conditions due to the transfer (such as changing the place of work) might justify the employee's option to refuse the transfer. And this would be a legitimate refusal. However, there could be cases when employees refuse to be transferred for no objective reasons (e.g., cases where the sole reason for the refusal would be grabbing the exit packages applicable in case of restructurings, when these are very attractive). As employees are expected to exercise their right to object to the transfer in good faith, and not in a way that could harm the employer or affect the employer's interests in an excessive and unreasonable manner, in our view, such refusals should be treated fairly. This means that even though both the transferor and the transferee must comply with the employee's choice, the theory of abuse of law might apply and thus, even if the transferor has no option but to acknowledge their refusal (and further on make them redundant due to economic reasons), the transferor should not be ordered to award those additional rights to the employees refusing the transfer in an abusive manner.

In case the transfer regards employees partially dedicated to the undertaking, the business or the part of undertaking or business, should they object to the transfer and be further dismissed for economic reasons by the transferor (as their main activity was transferred and thus no longer rendered by the transferor), the dismissal decision may be challenged for the argument that the job elimination would not be effective (as the transferor continues rendering those other activities to which the respective employees were also allocated, i.e., the business areas which were not transferred). To mitigate

39. Decisions No. 944/R-CM dated 15 May 2009 and No. 1273/R-CM dated 15 May 2009, Pitesti Court of Appeal, available on www.sintact.ro, lastly accessed on 31 October 2024.
40. In case the court will rule that the dismissal was in fact unlawful (i.e., not supported by objective economic cause), it may order the annulment of dismissal decision and the reintegration of the employee on the position previously held, the payment of an indemnity equal to the updated salaries and to the other rights of which the employee would have benefited between the date of the dismissal and the effective reintegration, legal costs, as well as moral damages, if proven.

the risk to have the dismissal challenged in court, the transferor should formalize the job transformation by: (i) if feasible from an organizational and functional perspective, redistributing tasks so as to reach the full time norm, as long as these tasks are similar to the main type of work allocated to that employee, or by (ii) eliminating the jobs in the previous form and further replace them with part-time roles covering only the remaining activities, which should be further offered automatically to the impacted employees.

§15.08 EMPLOYEES' PROTECTION AGAINST DISMISSAL

[A] Are Economic Restructurings Allowed?

The national legislation has transposed the prohibition to dismiss employees because of the transfer under Article 7 of Law No. 67/2006. The same rule had been taken over in the exact same form under Article 173 paragraph (3) of the Labour Code.[41]

However, Law No. 67/2006 did not transpose the Directive's provisions allowing dismissals due to economic, technical or organizational reasons and which imply changes in what regards the workforce, even though at European level it has been lastingly acknowledged that the interdiction to dismiss employees on the grounds of a transfer of an undertaking, business or part of a business by the transferor or the transferee, does not stand in the way of economic restructurings. This omission created inconsistent interpretations, as some of the practitioners embraced the view that the national legislator would have opted for a more favourable regime, as an effect of the principle regulated under Article 8 of the Directive, thus extending the employees' protection against dismissal over economic restructurings as well. In fact, this is a mere proof of inadequate transposition of the Directive and should not be interpreted as annihilating the employer's prerogative to implement reorganizations, as per the conditions set under Articles 65[42] et seq. from the Labour Code. This conclusion results from the analysis of the legislative process regarding the draft bill, which was later to become Law No. 67/2006. In its initial version,[43] Article 7 of Law No. 67/2006 had a second paragraph (aimed at transposing Article 4, paragraph 1, subparagraph 1, final thesis of the Directive, 'This provision will not stand in the way of dismissals that may take place for economic, technical or organisational reasons entailing changes in the workforce.'), saying that the prohibition to dismissal regulated by paragraph 1 of that article will not apply in case of dismissal due to elimination of roles held by employees

41. Article 173 para. (3) of the Labour Code: 'The transfer of the undertaking, business or part of the undertaking or business shall not in itself constitute grounds for dismissal, individual or collective, of the employees by the transferor or the transferee.'
42. Article 65 of the Labour Code. '(1) A dismissal for reasons not related to the person of the employee is the cessation of the individual employment contract determined by the elimination of the workplace of the employee, for one or several reasons not connected to employee's person.

    (2) The elimination of the workplace must be effective and have a real and serious cause.'
43. The historical legislative process for the draft bill No. PL-x No. 665/2005 is available on the website of the Chamber of Deputies.

as a consequence of economic difficulties, technological transformations or activity reorganization. This second paragraph has been, however, removed from the document during the parliamentary debates, as one committee member thought that: 'this provision already exists in art. 65 of the Labour Code'. As such, there is no doubt that the employers keep the right to implement economic restructurings and to eliminate positions because of economic difficulties, technological transformations or activity reorganization, irrespective of the legislator's omission to expressly reiterate that prerogative in the case of transfers of undertakings, businesses or parts thereof.

[B] Dismissals Linked to the Transfer: National Case Law

Generally, when national courts assess whether there has been a dismissal linked to a transfer of undertaking, the conclusion will depend on the preliminary qualification of the operation at issue as transfer of undertaking. Where the courts hold that there was a transfer of undertaking, they will check if the dismissal was decided on the grounds relating to the transfer and, if not, they will further assess whether the conditions enacted by the Labour Code are met (i.e., the dismissal must be grounded on a *real and serious cause*, meaning that the reasons behind it are objective, are of a certain gravity to justify this extreme measure, as resulting based on thorough analysis, the cause should not be dissimulated and should have no link to the employee's person, and, at the same time, the elimination of the job must be *final*, as this will result based the internal documents, such as the organizational chart).

Following the analysis of recent case law regarding challenges against dismissal decisions issued in the context of transfers of undertaking, one cannot identify a coherent national trend; the decisions vary a lot depending on factors which are not necessarily objective, such as the geographical area of the respective Court of Appeal. In majority, indeed, where courts have concluded that a transfer of undertaking had occurred, and when the dismissal decision was connected to that transfer, then they predictably annul those dismissal decisions. Still, one can also identify decisions where courts have taken a short-sighted approach, ignoring evident links to the transfer of undertaking and thus rejecting employees' challenges against the respective dismissal decisions.

We include below a summary of certain interesting recent cases:

> The Bucharest Court of Appeal[44] put aside the fact that a dismissal decision was grounded, among other economic reasons, on the fact that there had been a merger between the transferor and the transferee, and held that: '*even if there was a merger between two companies, the reorganization aiming to optimise the activity took place only 7 months after the merger, while the Directive does not aim to preclude reorganizations under such circumstances following that merger*'. The court assessed whether the dismissal decision is based on a real and serious cause and if the elimination is effective, and, after these were deemed as fulfilled, the

44. Decision No. 4059 dated 9 November 2020, Bucharest Court of Appeal, available on www.sintact.ro, lastly accessed on 31 October 2024.

court wisely concluded that this type of economic reorganization is allowed even in cases of transfers of undertaking.

The Ploiesti Court of Appeal[45] duly qualified the sale of the commercial goodwill allocated to a pharmacy as a transfer of undertaking, and, consequently, rejected the defence raised by the transferee that the plaintiff (i.e., the director who was supervising and coordinating the pharmacists and assistants, without performing any operational tasks) had not been a necessary resource for the performance of the pharmaceutical activity, reason for which that employee's contract was excluded from the transferred perimeter. The court ruled that the role held by this employee was a necessary role for the performance of the pharmaceutical activity, as, given the duties performed by that employee, it was inherent to support the business transferred.

In a different case,[46] the employer rejected the automatic transfer as it had transferred only 25% of the personnel (and thus argued that there is no continuity for the organization post-transfer) and as there was no formal transfer document used between the parties. The Bucharest Court of Appeal, however, applying the ECJ's case law on the interpretation of the Directive, lawfully ruled that failure of the transferor to ensure the transfer of all employees allocated to a business may not be used as an argument to sustain that the assets which were transferred do not constitute a business or part of a business in the meaning of the Directive. Further, the court ruled that there is no need to have a transfer document between the two parties, as the transfer may occur irrespective of such document. The court annulled the dismissal decision issued in this context.

[C] The Obligation to Inform and Consult the Employees: Non-binding Effect of the Process

As per the Labour Code, in case there is a transfer of undertaking, the transferor and the transferee have the obligation to inform and consult the employees' representatives, before the transfer, with regard to the legal, economic and social implications regarding the employees. Law No. 67/2006 further details this obligation, providing that the transferor and the transferee must inform in writing the representatives of the employees, or, in case these are not appointed, their own employees with respect to: (a) the transfer date or the proposed transfer date; (b) the reasons thereof; (c) the legal, economic and social consequences of the transfer for the employees; (d) the measures planned in relation to the employees; and (e) the working and employment conditions. This obligation to inform the employees will apply irrespective of whether the decisions resulting from the transfer are taken by the transferee or by an undertaking exercising control over the transferee.

45. Decision No. 1359 dated 14 May 2019, Ploieşti Court of Appeal, available on www.sintact.ro, lastly accessed on 31 October 2024.
46. Decision No. 4476 dated 28 September 2021, Bucharest Court of Appeal, quoted under section §15.03, letter (a) above.

In Romania, it takes only 10 employees/workers to form a union (or 20 employees/workers from different units in the same sector), while employees' representatives can be elected only in those units having at least 10 employees/workers where there are no unions. However, the Romanian legislator did not set limits as regards the application of this information and consultation obligation to companies having a certain number of employees - even though allowed to, as per Article 7 paragraph (5) in the Directive.

This information must be sent at least 30 days prior to the transfer date, while the Directive more generally refers to ensuring this obligation 'in good time, before the transfer is carried out'. In some cases, the 30 days term chosen by the Romanian legislator could prove insufficient, thus breaching the spirit of the Directive. For instance, in most transactions, the effective transfer date would be the date of the closing, hence many employers take this date as the relevant milestone when determining the moment of the notification. In our view, in order to observe the spirit of the law and ensure transparency and good faith, the notification should be sent at the moment when confidentiality constraints no longer crucially challenge the stakeholders involved or, when this is not feasible, at the same moment when the announcement about the contemplated transaction becomes public (i.e., when the announcement is shared with the market).

As regards the details shared with the employees, in most cases, employers inform the employees' representatives in a quite formal or superficial manner. In those cases where the voice of the trade unions is stronger, the information and consultation process is usually extended and additional information is required, especially in relation to changes foreseen after the implementation of the transfer, during the upcoming integration stages.

In case any of the employers envisages implementing certain measures with respect to its own employees, it must consult with the employees' representatives in order to reach an agreement, within the same deadline of 30 days before the transfer date.

The local law does not impose a strict duration for the information and consultation process; however, the collective labour agreements may contain additional formalities to this end. In practice, the length of this process depends largely on the quality of the employer's relationship with the employees' representatives (it may take from one week to several weeks or even months).

The national law does not set guidelines for the information and consultation process. In practice, however, the following steps are usually taken:

(a) Sending the formal notification to the employees' representatives. If changes are foreseen, the employer asks the employees' representatives to formulate their points of view or other questions related to the proposed changes within a reasonable term (e.g., 5-10 days). The employer can also convene the employees' representatives for a consultation for a more effective communication process.

(b) The employee's representatives reply. If they will not respond to this notification or if they will only issue a formal opinion (without any aspects which would require a response from the company's side), the process may be considered completed. However, if the employees' representatives rraise additional questions which would require exchanging opinions and establishing a dialogue between the employer and the employees' representative, the employer should address those queries during the consultation stage. This may delay the process by a couple of extra weeks.
(c) After the parties are aligned, the process can be considered completed. If the employees' representatives insist in an unreasonable manner, the company may unilaterally acknowledge that it has addressed all the queries raised by them and close the consultation process (in other words, the consultation process does not necessarily imply reaching an agreement, but the need to aim for such an agreement).

During the process, the employer should be transparent towards the employees' representatives in all matters, and especially with regard to the impact of the potential changes and the evolution of the process. If there are confidentiality concerns, employees' representatives may be required to sign non-disclosure agreements.

While the information and consultation process is mandatory, not observing this raises financial risks (labour inspectors can apply a small fine of up to RON 3,000). In any case, failing to inform and consult the employees cannot block the transfer, unless the collective agreement would contain contrary provisions. The collective labour agreements rarely contain provisions on the safeguarding of employees' rights in the event of transfers of undertakings, so it would be highly unusual to see these types of provisions covered by collective labour agreements.

In case the employers do not observe their obligations under Law No. 67/2006 (hence, including the obligation to inform and consult the employees), they may be sanctioned by the labour inspectors with a fine ranging from RON 1,500 (approx. EUR 300) to RON 3,000 (approx. EUR 600). If the employees suffer damages following such breach, they can file a complaint in front of the court asking to be compensated by the employer for the damages incurred, including moral, if proven.

CHAPTER 16

Slovakia

Jan Augustin

§16.01 INTRODUCTION

The transfers of undertakings Directive 2001/23/EC[1] was in Slovakia transposed into Act No. 311/2001 Coll. the Labour Code as amended (the '*Labour Code*').

Despite the legal consequences being essentially the same, the Slovak Labour Code in general differentiates between a transfer of employees due to dissolution of employer with a legal successor and transfer of employer as an economic unit. In this connection, it also regulates procedural aspects of such transfer. Following up on the generally applicable provisions, the Labour Code contains provisions applicable on some specific types of transfer as well.

Some of the Labour Code's provisions essentially copy the wording of the Directive, while others go beyond the regulation contained in the Directive. However, certain provisions of the Directive were left out by the legislator. In certain areas, the legislator tried to implement conclusions reached by the European Court of Justice (the '*ECJ*'), but it also introduced some entirely new legal concepts. In this connection, he did not take advantage of any of the exceptions offered by the Directive, allowing implementation of a less strict regulation.[2]

Overall, the Slovak Labour Code contains a quite detailed, although not complete, transposition of the Directive. As of 1 March 2023, the European Commission has not started any infringement procedure against Slovakia in this respect.

1. Council Directive No. 2001/23/EC from 12 March 2001 on the approximation of the laws of the Member States relating to the safeguarding of employees' rights in the event of transfers of undertakings, businesses or parts of undertakings or businesses.
2. Commission Report on Council Directive 2001/23/EC from 12 March 2001 on the approximation of the laws of the Member States relating to the safeguarding of employees' rights in the event of transfers of undertakings, businesses or parts of undertakings or businesses [SEC(2007) 812].

Case law of the local courts dealing with transfer of undertakings in Slovakia is very limited and there are no applicable secondary regulatory acts or documents of trade unions that could bring light on interpretation of the most prevalent open questions. Given these circumstances, the parties to transactions in Slovakia still come across certain issues concerning interpretation of its various provisions in practice.

§16.02 TERRITORIAL SCOPE

Subject to certain exceptions, the Slovak Labour Code shall generally apply on the territory of the Slovak Republic. Therefore, it is quite clear that it shall apply to any transfer of undertakings within Slovakia or from Slovakia to other countries. However, in practice, there are sometimes questions whether it was the intention of the legislator that the Labour Code also applies to transfer of undertakings situated outside of Slovakia into Slovakia.

Given a missing local case law, we believe this issue must be interpreted in line with the purpose of the Directive. In this connection, the Directive states it shall apply where and in so far as the undertaking, business or part of the undertaking or business to be transferred is situated within the territorial scope of the Treaty establishing the European Community.[3] Therefore, the Directive shall generally apply only to transfers of undertakings from the European Union (the '*EU*') or European Economic Area (the '*EEA*'), but not to transfers of undertakings from third countries to the EU or EEA.

In practice, the Slovak Labour Code is thus being interpreted as meaning that its provisions shall apply only to transfer of undertakings within Slovakia or from Slovakia. There seems to be a prevailing view that its provisions shall not apply to transfer of undertakings from other countries into Slovakia.[4] Despite an absence of explicit provision or local case law dealing with this question or related case law, in practice, the application of the Slovak Labour Code in this regard reflects the purpose of the Directive and currently seems sufficient.

§16.03 ECONOMIC UNIT

The Directive states it shall apply to any transfer of an undertaking, business, or part of an undertaking or business to another employer as a result of a legal transfer or merger.[5] The Slovak Labour Code does not use the term 'legal transfer', but instead uses the term 'transfer'.[6] Nevertheless, it is generally accepted in Slovakia that such term shall have a community-law meaning which shall be thus interpreted in line with the ECJ's case law.[7]

3. Article 1(2) of the Directive.
4. *Pracovnoprávne vzt'ahy pri prevode podniku.* Prvé vydanie. Mgr. Jana Černáková, PhD. Wolters Kluwer SR s.r.o. 2017, p. 9.
5. Article 1(1)(a) of the Directive.
6. Section 28 of the Labour Code.
7. *Pracovnoprávne vzt'ahy pri prevode podniku.* Prvé vydanie. Mgr. Jana Černáková, PhD. Wolters Kluwer SR s.r.o. 2017, p. 11.

In this connection, the Directive requires the transfer to relate to an economic entity which retains its identity, meaning an organized grouping of resources which has the objective of pursuing an economic activity, whether or not that activity is central or ancillary.[8] Therefore, the basic condition for applying employee protection under the Directive is that the undertaking or its part concerns an 'economic entity' in the meaning of the Directive.

In contrast to the Directive, the Slovak Labour Code does not use the term 'economic entity', but rather the term 'economic unit'. In this connection, the Slovak Labour Code sets out that in case of transfer of such economic unit, which is defined as an employer or its part, rights and obligations from the employment-law relationships towards the transferred employees shall be transferred to the transferee (i.e., the acquiring employer).[9] According to the Slovak Labour Code, such transfer must concern transfer of an economic unit which retains its identity as an organized collection of resources (tangible, intangible and personal resources) with the aim to pursue economic activity irrespective of whether such activity is central or ancillary.[10]

The term 'economic unit' is thus defined in the Slovak Labour Code similarly, although not exactly as the term 'economic entity' which is used by the Directive as explained in more detail below.

[A] Material, Immaterial and Personal Components of Business

Per its grammatical wording, the Slovak Labour Code requires that the transfer concerns economic unit as organized collection of tangible, intangible and personal resources. As the legislator used the conjunction 'and', it seems a cumulative existence of all the said resources is thus required for application of its provisions dealing with transfer of economic unit.

However, the Directive's aim is to ensure continuity of employment-law relationships within an economic entity, irrespective of any change of ownership.[11] According to the ECJ, to determine whether the conditions for the transfer of an organized economic entity are met under the Directive, it is necessary to consider all the facts characterizing the transaction in question, including in particular the type of undertaking or business concerned, whether or not its tangible assets, such as buildings and movable property, are transferred, the value of its intangible assets at the time of the transfer, whether or not the majority of its employees are taken over by the new employer, whether or not its customers are transferred, the degree of similarity between the activities carried on before and after the transfer, and the period, if any, for which those activities were suspended.[12]

---

8. Article 1(1)(b) of the Directive.
9. Section 28(1) of the Labour Code.
10. Section 28(2) of the Labour Code.
11. ECJ's judgment from 15 December 2005 in joined cases C-232/04 and C-233/04 (*Demir*), para. 31.
12. ECJ's judgment from 15 December 2005 in joined cases C-232/04 and C-233/04 (*Demir*), para. 33.

The ECJ's case law thus does not insist that material, immaterial and personal resources are cumulatively transferred in order for such transfer to fall within the meaning of the transfer under the Directive. Instead, when examining whether or not there is a transfer of an undertaking or business within the meaning of the Directive, the national courts shall focus on circumstances of a particular case.

According to the ECJ, the degree of importance to be attached to each criterion for determining whether or not there has been a transfer within the meaning of the Directive shall vary according to the activity carried on or the production or operating methods employed in the relevant undertaking.[13] At the same time, all those circumstances are merely single factors in the overall assessment, which must be made and cannot therefore be considered in isolation.[14]

The ECJ confirmed on several occasions that the said circumstances do not have to exist in a single case because some of them can be absent due to production or operation methods used by a specific undertaking. However, the ECJ explicitly stated that an economic entity is able to function in certain sectors without any significant tangible or intangible assets.[15] Retention of its identity after the transaction thus cannot depend on their transfer.[16]

From the ECJ case law, it is thus quite clear that for application of the Directive, there does not have to be a transfer of tangible or intangible assets.[17]

The Slovak Labour Code, which requires transfer of economic unit as a collection of tangible, intangible and personal resources, thus seems to be in conflict with the understanding of the transfer under the Directive by the ECJ. Therefore, despite a missing case law of Slovak courts dealing with this question, its application in Slovakia should not be limited only to transfers entailing cumulative transfer of all such resources, which seems to be a common interpretation in practice. To avoid doubts regarding its interpretation, however, it can be recommended to amend the Slovak Labour Code so as to comply with the Directive and related ECJ's case law.

[B] Pursuing of Economic Activity

In line with the Directive, the Slovak Labour Code requires transfer of an economic unit with the aim of pursuing economic activity irrespective of whether such activity is central or ancillary. In its case law, the ECJ interprets the term 'pursuing of economic activity' as going beyond a simple offer of goods and services on a given market.[18]

13. ECJ's judgment from 20 November 2003 in case C-340/01 (*Abler*), para. 35.
14. ECJ's judgment from 20 November 2003 in case C-340/01 (*Abler*), para. 34.
15. ECJ's judgment from 10 December 1998 in joined cases C-173/96 and C-247/96 (*Hidalgo*), para. 31.
16. ECJ's judgment from 10 December 1998 in joined cases C-173/96 and C-247/96 (*Hidalgo*), para. 31.
17. Opinion of Advocate General Maduro delivered on 16 June 2005 in joined cases C-232/04 and 233/04 (*Demir*), para. 15.
18. ECJ's judgment from 28 February 2013 in case C-1/12 (*Técnicos Oficiais de Contas*), para. 36.

According to the ECJ, the said term shall also concern activities such as social and recreational activities,[19] home-help services[20] or publicity activities.[21]

In Slovakia, there is currently a missing case law of local courts regarding interpretation of the term 'pursuing of economic activity'. However, in general, the Slovak courts seem to have good knowledge of the ECJ's case law. We thus assume they will comply with it in case of interpretation of the said term. From practical experience, it thus seems there is no current need for amendment of the Slovak Labour Code to explicitly reflect ECJ's conclusions regarding interpretation of the term 'pursuing of economic activity'.

[C] Retaining of Identity of Economic Unit

In line with the Directive, the Slovak Labour Code requires that the transfer concern an economic unit which retains its identity as organized collection of resources.

According to the ECJ, such condition may also be met in cases where part of the transferred undertaking or business does not retain its organizational autonomy, provided the functional link between the various transferred elements of production is preserved, and that link enables the transferee to use those elements to pursue an identical or analogous economic activity.[22]

In its subsequent rulings, the ECJ weakened the requirement of continuing activity by the transferee and accentuated the importance of assessing all facts characterizing the transfer operation.[23] Nevertheless, later the ECJ started to introduce certain limits and restrictions on an overly extensive interpretation. For example, it stated[24] the mere fact that the service provided by the old and the new awardees of a contract is similar does not support the conclusion that an economic entity has been transferred, as an entity cannot be reduced to the activity entrusted to it, but its identity also emerges from other factors.[25]

According to the ECJ, the degree of importance to be attached to each factor varies according to the characteristics of the case in question, and it is not possible to single out any factor which in the abstract has greater weight than the others.[26] The ECJ also ruled that nothing prevents the assets from being made available for use by one contractor and then its successor without necessarily forming part of a transferable

19. ECJ's judgment from 24 May 1992 in case C-29/91 (*Redmond Stichting*), para. 30.
20. ECJ's judgment from 10 December 1998 in joined cases C-173/96 and C-247/96 (*Hidalgo*), para. 34.
21. ECJ's judgment from 26 September 2000 in case C-175/99 (*Mayeur*), para. 57.
22. ECJ's judgment from 12 February 2009 in case C-466/07 (*Klarenberg*), para. 53.
23. Opinion of Advocate General Mengozzi delivered on 6 November 2008 in case C-466/07 (*Klarenberg*), para. 29.
24. ECJ's judgment from 11 March 1997 in case C-13/95 (*Süzen*), para. 15.
25. Such as its workforce, its management staff, the way in which its work is organized, its operating methods or indeed, where appropriate, the operational resources available to it.
26. Opinion of Advocate General Mengozzi delivered on 6 November 2008 in case C-466/07 (*Klarenberg*), para. 29.

entity.[27] According to the ECJ's later rulings, presence of a sufficiently structured and autonomous entity within the undertaking which was awarded the contract is, in principle, not affected by the circumstance, which occurs quite frequently, that the undertaking is subject to observance of precise obligations imposed on it by the contract-awarding body.[28] In addition, the ECJ ruled that the transfer must relate to a stable economic entity whose activity is not limited to performing one specific works contract.[29]

Therefore, it is clear that the ECJ put certain limits on the overly extensive interpretation of retention of identity by the economic entity. No Slovak case law dealing with this question in detail seems to be available so far. Therefore, it remains to be seen how exactly this condition will be applied by Slovak courts in practice. Nevertheless, as already mentioned above, given an overall good knowledge of the Slovak Courts regarding the ECJ's case law, we assume the local courts will comply with its conclusions. In this respect, currently, there thus does not seem to be a need for amendment of the Slovak Labour Code.

[D] Different Types of Transfer of Undertaking

According to the Directive, it shall apply to any transfer of an undertaking, business, or part of an undertaking or business to another employer as a result of a legal transfer or merger.[30] In this connection, the purpose of the Directive is to render irrelevant any changes in ownership of (or, more generally, title to) an undertaking as regards employment-law relationships existing within it.[31] Whatever the nature of the transaction, the transfer must be neutral, i.e., the employees must not be affected by it; that is to say, they cannot be dismissed or subjected to less favourable treatment.[32] In assessing whether, in a given situation, there has been a transfer resulting from a 'legal transfer or merger' within the meaning of the Directive, that question has to be considered in the light of the final outcome of the transaction in question.[33]

As regards the scope of the Directive and particularly the question as to when a legal transfer is involved, the ECJ has always used a teleological approach.[34] Such an interpretation which puts the emphasis on a non-technical term 'transfer' and regards the case of a legal transfer and that of a merger as examples is consistent with the spirit

27. Opinion of Advocate General Madura delivered on 16 June 2005 in joined cases C-232/04 and 233/04 (*Demir*), para. 19.
28. ECJ's judgment from 10 December 1998 in joined cases C-173/94 and C-247/96 (*Hidalgo*), para. 27.
29. ECJ's judgment from 19 September 1995 in case C-48/94 (*Rygaard*), para. 20.
30. Article 1(a) of the Directive.
31. ECJ's judgment from 7 August 2018 in case C-472/16 (Colino Sigüenza), para. 48.
32. Opinion of Advocate General Mancini delivered on 28 October 1987 in case C-287/86 (*Ny Mølle Kro*), para. 3.
33. Opinion of Advocate General Van Gerven delivered on 24 March 1992 in case C-29/91 (*Redmond Stichting*), para. 18.
34. Opinion of Advocate General Van Gerven delivered on 24 March 1992 in case C-29/91 (*Redmond Stichting*), para. 18.

and purpose of the Directive.[35] In its case law, the ECJ thus recognized several forms of transfer of undertakings which shall be within the scope of the Directive, such as lease,[36] outsourcing,[37] or commercial representation.[38] The transfer does not have to result from an agreement, but can also result from unilateral decisions of public authority.[39]

In contrast to the Directive, the Slovak Labour Code contains specific provisions only on two perhaps most common types of transfer, namely sale of employer[40] and lease.[41] The reason behind their explicit regulation is to make clear in these cases which entity shall satisfy the employee claims in case of withdrawal from the contract, where the transfer ultimately does not take place. In this connection, the Slovak Labour Code states that in case of such withdrawal, the claims from employment-law relationships shall be satisfied by the seller or lessor[42] (as applicable).

Despite the Slovak Labour Code explicitly regulating only these two specific types of transfer, it seems it was not the legislator's intention to limit application of its provisions dealing with the transfer of undertakings only to the two said cases. This seems to be supported by available Slovak case law which in addition to sale of employer or lease[43] recognized also outsourcing[44] as independent form of transfer of undertaking and considered transfer of undertaking also in case of absence of legal relationship between the transferor and transferee.[45]

In this respect, the Slovak Labour Code's regulation on different types of transfer of undertaking as well as related case law of Slovak courts seems to comply with the Directive and related ECJ's case law. Its regulation thus seems to be sufficient in Slovak practice.

§16.04 TRANSFEROR AND TRANSFEREE

The Slovak Labour Code[46] defines the transferor as a legal entity or an individual that, based on the transfer, stops being an employer.[47] In this connection, it states that the

35. Opinion of Advocate General Mancini delivered on 28 October 1987 in case C-287/86 (*Ny Mølle Kro*), para. 3.
36. ECJ's judgment from 15 June 1988 in case C-101/87 (*Bork International*), para. 20.
37. ECJ's judgment from 14 April 1994 in case C-392/92 (*Schmidt*), para. 20.
38. ECJ's judgment from 7 March 1996 in joint cases C-171/94 and C-172/94 (*Merckx a Neuhuys*), para. 32.
39. ECJ's judgment from 14 September 2000 in case C-343/98 (*Collino*), para. 34.
40. Section 31(1) and 31(2) of the Labour Code.
41. Section 31(3) and 31(4) of the Labour Code.
42. This does not apply to employees accepted into employment by the lessee from the day of start of lease.
43. Decision of Regional Court Nitra from 30 April 2014 in case 5Co/32/2013 or decision of District Court Poprad from 11 January 2012 in case 17C/109/2011.
44. Decision of District Court Nitra from 31 January 2012 in case 7C/147/2010.
45. Decision of District Court Rožňava from 28 February 2012 in case 4C/8/2011.
46. Section 28(3) of the Labour Code.
47. According to section 7(1) of the Labour Code, the employer means a legal entity or individual employing at least one individual in an employment-law relationship and if provided by special regulations, also in similar employment relationship.

transferee can be either a legal entity or an individual that continues as an employer towards the transferred employees as a result of the transfer.[48]

The said definitions essentially copy the transferor and transferee definitions contained in the Directive.[49] Their application thus does not seem to cause any problems in local practice, as there seems to be a common consensus on their interpretation in line with the Directive.[50]

[A] Several Transferees

Neither the Directive nor the Slovak Labour Code explicitly regulates a situation where the undertaking is transferred to several transferees. Most importantly, the Slovak Labour Code does not specify how the transferred personnel shall be allocated among such transferees.

According to the ECJ's case law, the fact that the undertaking has been transferred to one or more transferees has no effect on the transfer of the transferor's rights and obligations arising from an employment contract existing on the date of the transfer of that entity.[51] Otherwise, it would amount to excluding the safeguarding of the rights and obligations arising from an employment contract on the date of the transfer of an undertaking and consequently deprive the Directive of any effectiveness.

In this connection, the ECJ ruled that the rights and obligations arising from an employment contract are transferred to each of the transferees, in proportion to the tasks performed by the worker concerned, provided that the division of the employment contract as a result of the transfer is possible and neither causes a worsening of working conditions nor adversely affects the safeguarding of the rights of workers guaranteed by the Directive.[52] If such a division were impossible to carry out or would adversely affect the rights of that worker, the transferee(s) would be regarded as being responsible for any consequent termination of the employment-law relationship, even if that termination were to be initiated by the employee.

As there seems to be a missing local case law dealing with this particular topic, in case of transfer of several undertakings, the Slovak Labour Code shall be interpreted in line with the ECJ's case law. This means that unless agreed otherwise by the parties to the transaction, the employment contract would have to be likely divided into different part-time employment contracts in proportion to the work performed by the employee for individual transferees.

The Slovak Labour Code, however, explicitly does not recognize division of employment contract, but requires that part-time employment contract be agreed between the employee and employer.[53] Automatic division of full-time employment

48. Section 28(4) of the Labour Code.
49. Article 2(1)(a) and 2(1)(b) of the Directive.
50. *Pracovnoprávne vzt'ahy pri prevode podniku*. Prvé vydanie. Mgr. Jana Černáková, PhD. Wolters Kluwer SR s.r.o. 2017, pp. 42-43.
51. ECJ's judgment from 26 March 2020 in case C-344/18 (*ISS Facility Services NV*), para. 27.
52. ECJ's judgment from 26 March 2020 in case C-344/18 (*ISS Facility Services NV*), para. 38.
53. Section 49 of the Labour Code.

contract into several part-time employment contracts thus seems to be conflicting with the current regulation of the Slovak Labour Code. Therefore, the current regulation of the Slovak Labour Code does not seem to be sufficient in relation to transfer of undertaking to several transferees. In order to comply with the findings of the ECJ's case law, it thus seems appropriate to amend the Slovak Labour Code so as to explicitly provide for such automatic division in case of transfer of undertaking to several transferees.

[B] Administrative Reorganizations

The Directive makes clear it shall apply only to public and private undertakings engaged in economic activities, whether or not they are operating for gain.[54] In this connection, the Directive states that an administrative reorganization of public administrative authorities, or the transfer of administrative functions between public administrative authorities, is not a transfer within the meaning of the Directive.

In contrast, Slovak regulations grant certain protection also to employees of public undertakings which do not fall within the scope of application of the Directive. In this connection, the Slovak Act on State Service[55] states that in case of transfer of part of state office to another state office, the rights and obligations from employment-law relationships towards the state employees of such state office shall be transferred to the acquiring state office. Rights and obligations of the former state office towards the state employees of the transferred part of state office whose employment terminated or ceased to exist before the transfer date shall remain unaffected.

Despite going beyond the scope of the Directive, such regulation of the Slovak Act on State Service does not seem to be in conflict with its purpose. This is because the Directive allows the Member States to also protect employees who are otherwise not covered by the Directive. There should thus be no need to amend the Slovak regulations in this respect.

§16.05 EMPLOYEES

Under the Directive, the employee shall mean any person who, in the Member State concerned, is protected as an employee under national employment law.[56] The meaning of the term 'employee' is thus left to the discretion of individual Member States. Therefore, in Slovakia, the protection under the Directive shall apply in general to any individuals who perform dependent work in an employment-law or similar relationship.[57]

54. Article 1(c) of the Directive.
55. Section 178 of Slovak Act No. 55/2017 Coll. on State Service as amended.
56. Article 2(1)(d) of the Directive.
57. Section 11(1) of the Labour Code.

§16.06 EMPLOYEE REPRESENTATIVES

According to the Directive, the status and function of the employee representatives shall be preserved only in case the undertaking, business or part of an undertaking or business which is being transferred preserves its autonomy and conditions necessary for the constitution of the employee's representation are fulfilled.[58] Similarly, the Slovak Labour Code sets out that their legal status and function shall be preserved until expiration of the term of their office, unless agreed otherwise by them.[59]

In contrast to the Directive, the Slovak Labour Code thus does not seem to make preservation of status and function of employee representatives[60] conditional upon autonomy of transferred undertaking's business and fulfilment of conditions for constitution of the employee's representation. In general, the employee representatives' status and function shall be thus transferred to the transferee automatically under the Slovak Labour Code, which does not seem to be entirely in compliance with the Directive, as will be explained in more detail below.

[A] Autonomy of Transferred Undertaking

According to the Directive, the status and function of employee representatives shall be preserved only in case the undertaking, business or part of an undertaking or business preserves its autonomy.[61] Which cases shall be regarded as the undertaking preserving its autonomy is not defined by the Directive. However, it was defined by the ECJ in its previous case law.[62]

58. Article 6(1) of the Directive.
59. Section 31(8) of the Labour Code.
60. In relation to definition of employee representatives, the Directive in its Article 2(1)(c) refers to representatives of the employees provided for by the laws or practices of the Member States. Therefore, in line with section 11a of the Labour Code, in Slovakia, the competent labour union, employee council or employee confidant shall be regarded as employee representatives for the purposes of the Directive. In case of co-op associations where employment-law relationship of its member with co-op forms part of membership, a special co-op authority elected by members' meeting shall be regarded as employee representative as well.
61. Article 6(1) of the Directive. In this connection, the Directive also stipulates that if the undertaking does not preserve its autonomy, the Member States shall take the necessary measures to ensure that the employees transferred who were represented before the transfer continue to be properly represented during the period necessary for the reconstitution or reappointment of the representation of employees in accordance with national law or practice.
62. In its judgment from 29 July 2010 in case C-151/09 (*UGT-FSP*), para. 56, the ECJ ruled that a transferred economic entity preserves its autonomy, within the meaning of Article 6(1) of the Directive provided the powers granted to those in charge of that entity, within the organizational structures of the transferor, namely, the power to organize, relatively freely and independently, the work within that entity in the pursuit of its specific economic activity and, more particularly, the powers to give orders and instructions, to allocate tasks to employees of the entity concerned and to determine the use of assets available to the entity, all without direct intervention from other organizational structures of the employer, remain, within the organizational structures of the transferee, essentially unchanged. According to the ECJ, the mere change of those ultimately in charge cannot in itself be detrimental to the autonomy of the entity transferred, except where those who have become ultimately in charge have available to them powers which enable them

In contrast, the Slovak Labour Code does not make preservation of status and function of employee representatives conditional upon such autonomy. In this respect, the Slovak Labour Code does not seem to entirely comply with the requirements of the Directive. Given a missing local case law on this topic, to avoid any doubts regarding its interpretation in practice, the Slovak Labour Code could be amended by the legislator as to comply with the Directive. In the meantime, the Slovak Labour Code shall be interpreted in line with the Directive and related ECJ case law as to require autonomy of undertaking for preservation of status and function of employee representatives.[63]

[B] Conditions Necessary for Constitution of Employee Representation

In addition to preservation of transferred undertaking's autonomy, the Directive makes preservation of status and function of employee representatives conditional upon fulfilment of conditions necessary for constitution of employee representation. The purpose behind the said provision is not to preclude application of national rules preventing 'carrying across' of the employee representation scheme, for example, due to provisions governing the representation of employees in public sector differing from those applying to employees in private sector.[64]

The Slovak Labour Code does not contain a condition of preservation of transferred undertaking's autonomy, but provides for automatic transfer of employee representatives' status and function as already explained above. This does not seem to be in line with the Directive and may cause problems in practice, particularly in case the transfer does not concern a whole undertaking, but only its part or specific activity or task. For example, the Slovak Labour Code requires at least 50 employees employed by the employer for creation of a works council,[65] but only 3 employees for appointing an employee confident[66] (which is a different type of employee representation). In this connection, it is not entirely clear under the Slovak Labour Code whether in case of transfer of undertaking with works council, the works council shall continue existing in the transferee even in case it would employ less than 50 employees post-transaction, or rather the number of employee representatives shall be reduced so only employee confidant continues to be active in the transferee.

To avoid problems with its interpretation, the Slovak Labour Code should be thus amended to comply with the Directive as to not allow automatic transfer of employee representatives' status and function to transferee in all cases, but only in case of fulfilment of conditions necessary for constitution of employee representation in the

to organize directly the activities of the employees of that entity and therefore to substitute their decision-making within that entity for that of those immediately in charge of the employees.

63. *Pracovnoprávne vzt'ahy pri prevode podniku*. Prvé vydanie. Mgr. Jana Černáková, PhD. Wolters Kluwer SR s.r.o. 2017, p. 59.
64. Opinion of Advocate General Sharpston delivered on 6 May 2010 in case C-151/09 (*UGT-FSP*), para. 74.
65. Section 233(2) of the Labour Code.
66. Section 233(3) of the Labour Code.

transferee. In the meantime, the Slovak Labour Code should be interpreted in line with the Directive so as to make it conditional upon such requirement.

[C] Dual Representation

The ECJ's case law allows dual employee representation as a result of transfer of undertaking, which it considers as a necessary result of exercising the Directive that must be accepted by the employer.[67]

In case of transfer of undertaking's part where the employee representatives are not part of the transferred employees, employee representatives may be thus required to perform their function in the transferor as well as the transferee despite not being employees of the latter.[68] In this connection, they may be employees of such a transferor who is directly competing with the transferee. For such case, the Slovak Labour Code does not contain any exception from general statutory information duty towards such employee representatives. The transferee may be thus required to provide them information concerning the transferee and its economic situation or other information, even though its provision may be sensitive. Complying with such request could potentially harm and cause damage to the transferee despite a generally applicable confidentiality duty applying to such employee representatives.

In light of the above, it could be appropriate to amend the Slovak Labour Code to provide for certain exceptions from the general statutory information duty in case of dual employee representation.

§16.07 INFORMATION AND CONSULTATION DUTY

According to the Directive, the transferor and transferee are obliged to inform the employee representatives about the transfer.[69] Where they envisage measures in relation to their employees, they shall consult the employee representatives in good time on such measures with a view to reaching an agreement.[70]

In case of such information and consultation duty, the Slovak Labour Code essentially mirrors the wording of the Directive by requiring the employer no later than one month before the transfer of rights and obligations from the employment-law relationships, to inform the employee representatives in writing (or directly the employees, provided no employee representatives are active in an undertaking) about transfer date or proposed transfer date; reasons for transfer; employment-law, economic and social impacts of the transfer on employees and planned transfer measures affecting the employees.[71] With aim of achieving an agreement, the employer is also

67. Opinion of Advocate General Sharpston delivered on 6 May 2010 in case C-151/09 (*UGT-FSP*), para. 78.
68. And despite also not being able to be elected as employee representatives by the transferee's employees.
69. Article 7(1) of the Directive.
70. Article 7(2) of the Directive.
71. Section 29(1) of the Labour Code.

required to consult the said transfer measures with the employee representatives no later than one month before their implementation.[72]

The Directive's purpose is to provide information to the employee representatives sufficiently in advance. The one-month period for meeting the said information duty and related consultation duty according to the Slovak Labour Code thus seems to be in line with the Directive.[73]

[A] Scope of Application

In Slovakia, the information and consultation duty thus does not apply only to undertakings which, in terms of the number of employees, meet the conditions for the election or nomination of a collegiate body representing the employees, but to all undertakings participating in a transfer.

According to the Directive, where there are no employee representatives in an undertaking or business through no fault of their own, the information shall be provided only to concerned employees.[74] In contrast with the Directive, in case no employee representatives are in an undertaking, the Slovak Labour Code does not limit application of the information duty only to concerned employees, but it seems it rather requires that it is provided to all employees. In this connection, it is not entirely clear whether it was the intention of the legislator to really apply such information duty towards all employees, i.e., not only towards the employees concerned by the transfer. However, there does not seem to be any rational reason applying it also towards other employees, i.e., those who are not concerned by the transfer. This seems just like an unnecessary administrative burden, especially in case of undertakings with hundreds or thousands of employees.

In light of the above, it seems appropriate to amend the Slovak Labour Code as to making clear that information shall be provided only to the employees concerned by the transfer.

[B] Scope of Required Information

Despite a relatively clear scope of information to be provided to employees by the transferor and transferee, its description is rather general. Therefore, in practice, there are sometimes discussions regarding specific information that shall be provided to the employees.[75]

This concerns especially precise identification of the transfer date. In this connection, the Slovak Labour Code copies the term 'date' of transfer, which is also used in the Slovak language version of the Directive. However, other language versions of the Directive, such as Czech or German language versions, instead use a term the

72. Section 29(2) of the Labour Code.
73. Such deadline seems to be rather common also in different Member States.
74. Article 7(6) of the Directive.
75. *Pracovnoprávne vzt'ahy pri prevode podniku*. Prvé vydanie. Mgr. Jana Čerňáková, PhD. Wolters Kluwer SR s.r.o. 2017, p. 63.

meaning of which is closer to 'day' or 'moment'. Using such term would seem more appropriate, because in case of more complex transfers, the effects of the transfer usually do not relate to a specific date, but rather depend on meeting specific conditions by the parties to the transfer. Still, scope of the required information to be provided to the employees generally does not seem to cause any larger problems in practice, as the transaction's 'closing date' is usually regarded as the date of transfer.

[C] Breach of Information and Consultation Duty

In line with the Directive, in Slovakia, the information duty applies in case of all transfers of undertakings. The consultation duty, however, applies only in cases where the employer plans to apply certain measures to the employees concerned by the transfer. The consultation duty must be in line with the Directive fulfilled with aim of achieving agreement with the employee representatives. The transferor or transferee, however, should not be obliged to actually reach an agreement with them.

Still, according to local case law, they cannot perceive their information and consultation duty just as a purely formal duty. In this connection, the Supreme Court of the Slovak Republic (the '*Slovak Supreme Court*') repeatedly stated that such duty is fulfilled only in case of provision of materially relevant information.[76] Breaching the information and consultation duty shall not cause invalidity of transfer of undertaking in Slovakia. However, it shall be considered breach of employment-law regulations that can be sanctioned by the Slovak labour inspectorate. In addition, it may be relevant in case of unfair dismissal disputes, which seems to be confirmed by local case law.[77]

In the past, the court was assessing a situation where an employer terminated employee's employment due to alleged gross breach of work discipline. The employee objected to her dismissal and insisted that the employer keeps employing her. However, the employer claimed that before her dismissal, it had already sold its undertaking to another person, which resulted in transfer of economic unit and thus by operation of law also in transfer of rights and obligations from her employment contract to the transferee. The employer thus claimed that as of the transfer date, the employee was not its employee anymore and thus cannot claim unfair dismissal against the employer. However, the employee objected that her employer did not inform her in writing about such transfer, nor did it present during the court proceedings the contract on sale of its undertaking or similar documents evidencing the transfer. In this connection, the employee claimed she learned about the alleged transfer from other employees, but not directly from her employer.

The court admitted that according to the ECJ's case law, the lack of a contractual link between the transferor and transferee by itself does not exclude existence of a

76. For example, decision of Slovak Supreme Court dated 28 September 2010 in case 5 Cdo 140/2010 or dated 30 October 2012 in case 4 Cdo 160/2012.
77. Decision of Regional Court in Bratislava from 14 August 2019 in case 2 Co/94/2017.

transfer within the meaning of the Directive.[78] However, the court noted the employer did not meet its information duty towards the allegedly transferred employee in connection with to transfer of its undertaking. Because of breaching the said duty, the employee could not have known who her new employer was. In this connection, the court added that she cannot be justly required to search for her new employer's identity on her own. Therefore, the court ruled that even in case there had been a transfer of the employer's undertaking to another person, due to breach of the information duty, the employee shall still be considered the employer's employee and can object against her unfair dismissal by her employer.

§16.08 PRESERVATION OF EMPLOYMENT CONDITIONS

The Directive as well as the Slovak Labour Code require preservation of employee conditions which exist as of the transfer date. In this connection, the Directive states that the transferor's rights and obligations arising from an employment contract or from an employment-law relationship existing on the date of a transfer shall, by reason of such transfer, be transferred to the transferee.[79]

Similarly, according to the Slovak Labour Code, in case of transfer of economic unit, the rights and obligations from the employment-law relationships towards the transferred employees shall be transferred to the transferee.[80] Rights and obligations of the transferor towards the employees whose employment-law relationships ceased to exist until the transfer date shall remain unaffected.[81]

In this connection, the Slovak Supreme Court clarified that employees, who at the time of transfer claim invalidity of termination of their employment-law relationship in court, shall also be transferred to the transferee.[82] The reasoning behind the Slovak Supreme Court's decision was that, as the existence of an employment-law relationship is disputed, there is no certainty that it was terminated before the transfer. As of the transfer date, employment-law relationships of such employees cannot be regarded as terminated and the rights and obligations from them shall be thus transferred to the transferee.

[A] Collective Bargaining Agreements

In line with the Directive, the Slovak Labour Code requires the employer after the transfer to comply with the collective bargaining agreement agreed by the transferor, until the end of its effectiveness. In this connection, the Directive stipulates that following the transfer, the transferee shall continue to observe the terms and conditions agreed in any collective bargaining agreement on the same terms applicable to the transferor under that agreement, until the date of termination or expiry of the collective

78. ECJ's judgment from 26 September 2000 in case C-175/99 (*Mayeur*), para. 45.
79. Article 3(1) of the Directive.
80. Section 28(1) of the Labour Code.
81. Section 28(5) of the Labour Code.
82. Slovak Supreme Court decision from 14 June 2011 in case 5 Cdo 90/2010.

agreement or the entry into force or application of another collective agreement.[83] The Slovak Labour Code simply states that in case of transfer of rights and obligations from an employment-law relationship, the transferee is obliged to comply with the collective bargaining agreement which was agreed by the transferor, until the end of its effectiveness.[84]

The Slovak legislator did not use the possibility allowed by the Directive to restrict the duty to comply with the collective bargaining agreement, which was agreed by the transferor for one year.[85] In Slovakia, the transferee is thus obliged to comply with the said collective bargaining agreement until the end of its effectiveness. The reason behind the legislator's decision is perhaps that collective bargaining agreements in Slovakia are usually not agreed upon for more than one year.

The ECJ leaned towards an extensive interpretation of the term 'collective bargaining agreement'. Working conditions stemming from collective bargaining agreements shall be thus interpreted in a broad sense as to protect the employee in case of transfer of undertaking where its position shall not be worsened in comparison to its position before the transfer. However, the ECJ refused extension of application of the duty to comply with the collective bargaining agreement to dynamic references to collective bargaining agreements contained in employment contracts.[86]

The duty to apply the collective bargaining agreement which was agreed by the transferor shall apply only to employment-law relationships that were in place at the time of the transfer of undertaking.[87] Therefore, under the Directive, the transferee is not obliged to apply rights and obligations from such collective bargaining agreements to employees who are not concerned by the transfer.

However, in Slovakia, the transferee as an employer shall comply with the principle of equal treatment.[88] It is thus a common interpretation that in case of multiple collective bargaining agreements, the employer in Slovakia shall apply to its employees such conditions which are most favourable for them under the respective collective bargaining agreement so as to not discriminate between them. In Slovakia, the transferee may thus practically be required to apply the collective bargaining agreement which was agreed by the transferor not only to the transferred employees but also to its other employees who are not concerned by the transfer, which, however, does not seem to be in conflict with the Directive.

[B] Salary Conditions

The Slovak Labour Code states that in case the employment contract does not contain salary conditions and the term of the collective bargaining agreement to which the employment contract refers has ended, the salary conditions agreed in the collective

83. Article 3(3) of the Directive.
84. Section 31(7) of the Labour Code.
85. Article 3(4) of the Directive.
86. ECJ's judgment from 9 March 2006 in case C-499/04 (*Werhof*), paras 34-37.
87. ECJ's judgment from 17 December 1987, C-287/86 (*Ny Molle Kro*), para. 27.
88. Article 1 of the Labour Code.

bargaining agreement shall be considered salary conditions agreed in the employment contract until agreement on new salary conditions is reached in a collective bargaining agreement or employment contract.[89] In any case, the said salary conditions shall not continue to apply for longer than 12 months.

In other words, the Slovak Labour code provides for automatic extension of the collective bargaining agreement's term, but only in relation to salary conditions. This raises questions in practice, whether in case of transfer of undertaking, the transferee is obliged to comply with the collective bargaining agreement regarding salary conditions despite the collective bargaining agreement itself no longer being effective.

In the past, the ECJ dealt with a situation concerning a similar provision of the Austrian legal code.[90] According to the ECJ, the Directive shall be interpreted as meaning that the terms and conditions laid down in a collective bargaining agreement, which, pursuant to the law of a Member State, despite the rescission of that agreement, continue to produce their effects as regards the employment-law relationship which was governed by them before the agreement was terminated, constitute 'terms and conditions agreed in any collective agreement'. This shall apply so long as that employment-law relationship is not subject to a new collective agreement or a new individual agreement is not concluded with the employees concerned.

We thus believe that in line with the ECJ's case law, the Slovak Labour Code shall be interpreted as extending the term of the collective bargaining agreement regarding salary conditions. Therefore, despite a missing local case law, the transferee should comply with this part of the collective bargaining agreement even after expiration of the collective bargaining agreement's effectiveness. Unless agreement on new salary conditions is reached in a collective bargaining agreement or employment contract sooner, the transferee will have to apply the said salary conditions for twelve months.

[C] Supplementary Pension Schemes

Unless Member States provide otherwise, the Directive shall not apply to employees' rights to old-age, invalidity or survivors' benefits under supplementary company or intercompany pension schemes outside the statutory social security schemes in Member States.[91]

In Slovakia, supplementary pension schemes are not very common in practice. The Slovak legislator thus chose to not extend the application of the Directive to such schemes. Nevertheless, even in such case, the Directive requires that Member States adopt measures necessary for protection of the interests of employees and of persons no longer employed in the transferor's business at the time of the transfer in respect of rights conferring on them immediate or prospective entitlement to old-age benefits, including survivors' benefits, under respective supplementary schemes.[92]

89. Section 5(3) of the Labour Code.
90. ECJ's judgment from 11 September 2014 in case C-328/13 (*Österreichischer Gewerkschaftsbund*), para. 31.
91. Article 3(4)(a) of the Directive.
92. Article 3(4)(b) of the Directive.

The Slovak Labour Code complies with this requirement by stipulating that rights and obligations of the former employer towards the employees whose employment-law relationship ceased to exist until the transfer date shall remain unaffected.[93] After the transfer, the transferor thus remains responsible for their claims, including any old-age, invalidity or survivors' benefits claims.

§16.09 PROHIBITION OF DISMISSAL

According to the Directive, the transfer of the undertaking, business or part of the undertaking or business shall not in itself constitute grounds for dismissal by the transferor or the transferee.[94] The Slovak Labour Code does not contain a similar provision. According to the explanatory report, transposition of the said provision was not required due to general provisions of the Slovak Labour Code preventing the employer from changing employee's employment conditions or dismiss him/her without statutory reasons. In addition, the Slovak Labour Code quite clearly states that in case of transfer of undertaking (as economic unit), the rights and obligations from the employment-law relationships shall be transferred to the transferee, which also implies that the transfer as such should not be a reason for dismissing the affected employee.

According to the Directive, the prohibition of dismissal shall not apply in case of dismissal for economic, technical or organizational reasons entailing changes in the workforce.[95] In Slovakia, this may concern dismissal due to so-called organizational changes,[96] such as cancellation of employer or its part or its relocation provided the employee does not agree with change of the agreed place of work; or employee's redundancy due to employer's written decision on changes of its tasks, technical equipment or decrease of number of employees with aim to ensure efficiency of work or decision on other organizational changes.

[A] Exclusions

The Directive allows the Member States to exclude application of the rule on prohibition of dismissal solely because of the transfer in respect to categories of employees who are not covered by the laws or practice of the Member States in respect of protection against dismissal.[97]

According to ECJ's case law, the said provision protects employees against dismissal in any situation in which employees affected by a transfer enjoy some, albeit limited, protection against dismissal under national law, with the result that, under the Directive, that protection may not be taken away from them or curtailed solely because

93. Section 28(5) of the Labour Code.
94. First subparagraph of Article 4(1) of the Directive.
95. Article 4(1) of the Directive.
96. Section 63(1)(a) and 63(1)(b) of the Labour Code.
97. Second subparagraph of Article 4(1) of the Directive.

of the transfer.[98] In line with the said ECJ decision, the possible exception from the protection under the Directive shall be interpreted strictly as meaning that it does not apply only to employees who have no protection under national law against dismissal.[99]

In general, the Slovak Labour Code contains a relatively strong employee protection against dismissal of employees. The exclusion from protection against dismissal permissible by the Directive could thus theoretically apply only in relation to a limited group of employees, such as certain employees in probationary period who can be generally dismissed anytime without stating any reason. No exclusion from the protection against dismissal was thus explicitly implemented into the Slovak Labour Code in connection with transposition of the Directive.

Problems with interpretation in Slovakia concern transfer of undertaking from private sector into public sector, where a statutory selection procedure may be required to hire employees.[100] Except for a brief provision on transfer of undertakings between different state offices, the Slovak legislation does not contain any generally applicable provisions on transfer of undertakings which are subject to Slovak legislation on state service. Due to a missing case law, in practice, it is thus not entirely clear whether an automatic transfer of employees from private undertaking into such public undertaking is possible, although it seems that in general likely the rules contained in the Slovak legislation on state service (being a public-law regulation) shall take precedence over the rules contained in the Slovak Labour Code (being a private-law regulation), meaning the employees will not be automatically transferred to the transferee without first undergoing the statutory selection procedure. Nevertheless, to avoid doubts, it seems appropriate to regulate this specific situation directly in the legislation on state service.

§16.10 OBJECTIONS AGAINST TRANSFER

Provided the transfer shall result in a substantial change of employee's working conditions and the employee does not agree with such change, the Slovak Labour Code stipulates that his/her employment-law relationship shall be considered terminated by agreement as of the transfer date due to so-called redundancy reasons (defined more closely in the Slovak Labour Code).[101] In this connection, the employer shall issue to the employee a written confirmation on termination of his/her employment-law relationship, whereas the employee is also entitled to statutory severance.

Although the Directive contains a similar provision, the Directive does not seem to foresee the employee actively objecting to his/her transfer.[102] In this connection, the

98. ECJ's judgment from 15 April 1986 in case C-237/84 (*Commission v. Belgium*), para. 13.
99. ECJ's judgment from 15 April 1986 in case C-237/84 (*Commission v. Belgium*), para. 10.
100. *Pracovnoprávne vzt'ahy pri prevode podniku*. Prvé vydanie. Mgr. Jana Černáková, PhD. Wolters Kluwer SR s.r.o. 2017, pp. 83-84.
101. Section 29a of the Labour Code.
102. Article 4(2) of the Directive.

Directive also does not explain what shall be considered such substantial change of working conditions, so its interpretation is kept to national courts.

In this connection, the Slovak court ruled that the change of employment conditions must have a causal link with the transfer of rights and obligations from the employment-law relationship to the transferee.[103] According to the court, the employees thus cannot object to change of employment conditions which takes place, for example, a few months after the transfer provided such change of employment conditions is not a result of the transfer.

The Directive speaks of substantial changes to working conditions to the detriment of employees. However, the Slovak Labour Code does not make the objection to the employee against change of his/her employment conditions conditional upon their change to his/her detriment. In Slovakia, the substantial change of working conditions could thus theoretically also concern any change, even their change in favour of the employee which, however, does not seem entirely logical. Therefore, it seems appropriate to amend the Slovak Labour Code so as to make an objection of the employee against change of his/her employment conditions possible only in case their change is detrimental to him/her.

In practice, the local court refused that requirement to perform other types of work or work in another place of work should be interpreted as substantial change of employment conditions.[104] However, this was just a singular decision of a lower court. Therefore, it remains to be seen how the decision practice will actually develop and what the opinion of the Slovak Supreme Court will be.

Neither the Directive nor the Slovak Labour Code stipulate any period or form for objecting against the transfer. From its grammatical wording, it seems the Slovak Labour Code requires that the objection be raised before the transfer. However, the Slovak court permitted an objection against the change of employment conditions also post-transfer in a situation where the employee was incorrectly informed that his/her employment conditions will remain unchanged which, however, later proved untrue.[105]

§16.11 BANKRUPTCY PROCEEDINGS

According to the Slovak Labour Code, in case of dissolution of employer with a legal successor, the rights and obligations from the employment-law relationship shall be transferred to such legal successor.[106] Also, in case of winding up the employer, the authority winding up the employer shall determine the employer who shall satisfy claims of employees of the employer being wound up or exercise its claims.[107] Provided

103. Decision of District Court Bratislava III from 15 May 2018 in case 24Cpr/20/2017.
104. Decision of District Court Bratislava III from 15 May 2018 in case 24Cpr/20/2017.
105. Decision of District Court Bratislava III from 15 May 2018 in case 24Cpr/20/2017.
106. Section 27 of the Labour Code.
107. Section 31(5) of the Labour Code.

the employer's winding up is subject to liquidation, the liquidator is obliged to satisfy claims of employees of dissolved employer.[108]

However, the Slovak Labour Code makes clear that the provisions on transfer or rights and obligations from employment-law relationships shall not apply to the employer over whom bankruptcy was declared by court.[109] The Slovak Labour Code thus does not extend applicability of the Directive to employers who are subject to bankruptcy. This means that in general all debts from any employment contracts or labour relationships that originated before the start of bankruptcy proceedings shall not be transferred to the transferee.

In this connection, the Slovak Bankruptcy Act[110] states that in case of monetization of enterprise, the insolvency administrator shall transfer to buyer by contract all items, rights and other proprietary assets belonging to such enterprise.[111] In case of obligations, only obligations relating to the undertaking that originated in connection with operation of bankrupt enterprise after declaration of bankruptcy, as well as non-monetary obligations from an employment-law relationship stated in the contract, shall be transferred to the purchaser.

In the bankruptcy proceedings, only non-monetary obligations from employment-law relationships shall be thus transferred to the buyer who becomes an employer. All monetary claims of the employees existing before the transfer date shall be exercised towards the bankrupt employer. Overall, current regulation of the Slovak Bankruptcy Act seems sufficient in local practice, as no problem normally arises with its interpretation.

108. Section 31(6) of the Labour Code.
109. Section 31(9) of the Labour Code.
110. Slovak Act No. 5/2007 Coll. on Bankruptcy and Restructuring as amended.
111. Section 92(2) of the Bankruptcy Act.

CHAPTER 17

Slovenia: Transfer of Undertaking from Employment Law Perspective

Iris Pensa & Nina Bakovnik

§17.01 GENERAL INTRODUCTION

A transfer of undertaking, also known as a 'TUPE,' refers to the transfer of an existing business or part of a business from one owner to another. From an employment perspective, TUPE can have a significant impact on the rights and obligations of employees, as their employment may be transferred to the new owner along with the business. This can include issues such as changes to terms and conditions of employment, redundancy, and the continuity of service for the purpose of calculating employee benefits. It is important for both the transferor employer and the transferee employer to understand and comply with TUPE regulations to ensure a fair and smooth transition for all parties involved.

The aim of this paper is, in the first part, to briefly present the applicable Slovenian legislation in the area of transfer of undertaking from employment perspective and the related case law, and, in the second part, to consider some of the specific issues arising in connection with the transfer of undertakings in the regulation of employee relations.

[A] Outline Of the National Legislation on Transfers of Undertaking

[1] Change of Employer, General Provisions

Under Slovenian law, transfer of undertaking is regulated following EU law – formerly the Council Directive 77/187/EEC of 14 February 1977 on the approximation of the laws of the Member States relating to the safeguarding of employees' rights in the event of transfers of undertakings, businesses or parts of businesses, with amendments, and at present, the Council Directive 2001/23/EC of 12 March 2001 on the approximation of the laws of the Member States relating to the safeguarding of employees' rights in the event of transfers of undertakings, businesses or parts of undertakings or businesses ('*Directive*').

In Slovenian employment law, the provisions of the Directive are implemented in Articles 75 and 76 ZDR-1[1] in relation to change of employer. According to ZDR-1, transfer of an undertaking or part of an undertaking results in an automatic transfer of the employees from the transferor employer to the transferee employer. The transfer occurs based on the law itself and cannot be opted out of. In light of the implementation of the Directive, Slovenian case law considers case law of the Court of Justice of the European Union (*CJEU*) when applying the provisions of Articles 75 and 76 ZDR-1.

The transfer of undertaking is defined as the transfer of business or part of the business, or the transfer of the assets of the existing – the transferor employer, to a new employer – the transferee employer.

Under Slovenian law, the transfer of an undertaking results in the automatic transfer of the rights and obligations of the employees to the transferee employer. The transferee employer is required to take on all the employees of the transferor employer who were part of the business that is being transferred, and must continue to employ them on the same terms and conditions as before the transfer. It was confirmed in case law of the Slovenian courts[2] that in such case, there is no requirement that the employment contracts be changed. The transferee employer employs the taken-over employees with the same employment contracts that have been concluded with the transferor employer. Existing employment contracts can be replaced with new ones only in case the transferred employees agree with such replacement or in case termination grounds unrelated to the transfer exist.

The rights and obligations of the employees are transferred to the transferee employer as of the date of the transfer, and the transferee employer is jointly liable with transferor employer for all claims and obligations arising from the employment relationship prior to the transfer, such as unpaid wages, overtime and vacation pay.

The transferor employer is together with the transferee employer also obliged to inform the social partners or employees of the transfer.

Employees are protected from dismissal as a result of the transfer of undertaking. The transferee employer is prohibited from terminating the employment contract of an employee, unless there are valid reasons for termination unrelated to the transfer.

Additionally, the rights of the employees related to social security, pension and health insurance remain unchanged after the transfer. The rights and obligations under the collective agreement which were binding on the transferor employer shall be assured to the employees by the transferee employer for at least one year, unless the collective agreement ceases to be valid prior to the expiry of one year or unless prior to the expiry of one year a new collective agreement is concluded.

1. Employment Relationships Act (Official Gazette of the Republic of Slovenia, No. 21/2013 with amendments, 'ZDR-1').
2. *See*, for example, Judgment of Higher Labour and Social Court, VDSS Pdp 327/2020, dated 23 September 2020.

If, for objective reasons, the rights under the employment contract at the transferee employer deteriorate or the employee's working conditions at the transferee employer change substantially within two years from the date of the transfer, and the employee terminates the employment contract as a result, the employee shall have the same rights as if the employment contract had been terminated by the transferee employer for business reasons, that is the applicable notice period as well as applicable severance pay.

[2] Pension Plans

Additionally, according to Article 239 of ZPIZ-2,[3] on transfer of undertaking the rights and obligations under collective supplementary pension plan or under an applicable collective agreement including rights and obligations under a collective supplementary pension scheme, which apply to the employees of transferor company (who are being transferred) on the date of the transfer, are transferred to the transferee employer – in other words, such rights are retained by the transferred employees and automatically transfer to the new employer, unless this obligation is derogated from by agreement on transfer.

If not expressly derogated from by agreement, such rights must be guaranteed by the transferee employer for at least one year after the transfer, unless a retirement plan or collective agreement expires before the expiration of the one-year period or if a new pension plan or collective agreement is concluded before the period expires, in which all employees of the transferee employer are included.

If there is an existing supplementary pension plan at the transferee employer and if the transferred employees were included in the pension plan with the transferor employer, the transferred employees can be included in the pension plan of the new employer after the period of one year, in which the new employer has to guarantee such employees their rights under the old pension scheme. Additionally, the transferor employer shall be liable for employees' claims arising from the overdue and non-paid collective insurance payments incurred up to the date of the transfer.

[3] Transfer of Undertaking

In order to identify whether legislation on transfer of undertaking is applicable to a transfer of business activity, it first of all needs to be established whether a transfer of business activity falls within the meaning of the transfer of undertaking. Slovenian courts follow the related case law of the CJEU.[4]

3. Zakon o pokojninskem in invalidskem zavarovanju (Official Gazette of the Republic of Slovenia, No. 48/2022 with amendments, 'ZPIZ-2').
4. For example: Decision of Slovenian Supreme Court, No. VIII Ips 188/2017, 24 April 2018, ECLI:SI:VSRS:2018:VIII.IPS.188.2017; Decision of Slovenian Supreme Court, No. VIII Ips 273/2015, 21 June 2016, ECLI:SI:VSRS:2016:VIII.IPS.273.2015; Decision of Slovenian Supreme Court, No. VIII Ips 101/2015, 8 September 2015, ECLI:SI:VSRS:2015:VIII.IPS.101.2015.

In this respect, the transfer of employees shall come into consideration only where there is a change of employer and a transfer of an economic entity which retains its identity, meaning an organized grouping of resources which has the objective of pursuing an economic activity, whether or not that activity is central or ancillary. Therefore, a transfer of an undertaking must be considered in light of all the circumstances characterizing the transaction, such as whether or not the tangible assets (buildings, movable property and stock) and the intangible assets (know-how and goodwill) were transferred, the nature of the activities engaged in and whether or not those activities had ceased at the time of the transfer. However, none of those factors is in itself decisive.

[B] Employees' Information and Consultation Rights

[1] General

Employee rights in the event of a transfer of employer are a crucial aspect of labour law. To protect the rights of employees during such a transition, there are specific laws in place that mandate the provision of information and consultation to employees. In this part of the article, we will discuss the legal requirements in Slovenia for the provision of information and consultation to employees in the event of a transfer of undertaking.

In Slovenia, both the works council and the trade union must be informed and consulted in the process of transfer of an undertaking. Of course, only if they exist within the employer.

The information and consultation activities vis-à-vis the trade union and the works council may be carried out by the transferor and the transferee employer jointly and vis-à-vis both employee representative bodies together.

The purpose of the involvement of the trade union and the works council is to inform the employees about the planned transaction and the transfer of the employees. It is not necessary to obtain the consent of the trade union or the works council; the employer must only carry out the necessary procedures. The primary objective is to discuss the consequences of the transfer for the employees and potentially agree on any mitigating measures. In case of joint consultation with the works council, it is also the employer's duty to carry out the consultation by striving (making an effort) to harmonize positions.

[2] Union's Involvement

Pursuant to Article 76 ZDR-1, the transferor and the transferee employer shall at least 30 days prior to the date of the transfer of employees, notify the trade unions of the transferor and the transferee (and if there is no trade union in either the transferor or the transferee, the affected employees shall be notified directly) of the proposed transfer.

The transferor and the transferee employer, with the intent to reach an agreement, shall consult with the unions of both parties on the issues affecting the employees at least 15 days prior to the transfer.

The procedure described above shall be in the nature of consultations on the issues and no consent of the Union shall be required. The trade union has no right to block a transaction, but a fine may be imposed on the employer in case of violation of any of the above obligations.

[3] Works Council Involvement

Pursuant to Article 91 of the ZSDU,[5] the transferor employer shall inform the works council (if organized at the transferor employer) of matters such as the sale of the company, the sale of material assets of the company, material changes in ownership and also legal changes such as mergers and demergers, which are usually also considered transfers of business, and shall request joint consultations.

The transferor employer shall provide the works council with the necessary information at least 30 days prior to the adoption of the resolution on the transfer and shall hold joint consultations at least 15 days prior to the adoption of the resolution on the transfer. The consultations shall be arranged and held by the transferor employer in order to inform the works council of the planned decisions, to seek its advice and to attempt to harmonize positions.

Since the deadlines relating to the timing of 'decision making' are difficult to determine or meet, it can be argued that the information and consultation must take place as soon as commercially possible, but no later than 30 and 15 days, respectively, prior to the signing of the transaction.

The consequences of non-compliance with the works council's information and consultation rights are discussed under point 6 of the second part of this paper as one of the selected topics related to the transfer of undertakings.

§17.02 SELECTED ISSUES

[A] Introduction

Despite legislation and a growing body of case law, employers and employees face questions in employment transfer cases to which neither the legislation nor the case law we know of has yet provided a definitive and adequate answer.

Although the law does not provide clear answers, in the event of a transfer of business, relations with employees must be regulated, even if it is not clear how this must be done under the law. In the following section, we therefore provide an overview of selected questions or issues where we shed light on the problems arising in practice and summarize our considerations and analyses.

5. Worker Participation in Management Act (Official Gazette of the Republic of Slovenia, No. 42/2007 with amendments, 'ZSDU').

[B] Transter of Part of the Business

[1] Introduction

When it comes to transferring employees from one employer to another, there are several issues that both employers must consider. However, when only a part of the transferor employer's activity is being transferred, the challenges can be even greater. In this section, we will explore the unique issues that employers face when only a part of an employer's activity is transferred and discuss strategies for addressing these challenges. From part-time employment and confidentiality agreements, we will cover the key considerations that employers need to keep in mind when navigating a partial transfer of employees.

In numerous cases where activities are divided between two employers due to the transfer of a part of an enterprise (spin-off, split-up, sale of a part of a business), the question arises as to how the transfer affects the employees who, prior to the transfer, were engaged in the two activities that are now divided between two employers.

[2] Split of Employment Contracts

According to CJEU case law,[6] as well as established local court practice[7] in case of transfer of undertaking (pursuant to the Directive and change of employer under Article 75 ZDR-1), the employment contract transfers to the transferee employer in proportion to the tasks performed by the employee in question, attributable to the transferred part of business.

Notwithstanding the fact that employers usually want to transfer employees in full, depending on the activities with which the employees were predominantly engaged (e.g., more than 50%), we believe that the recent case law of the CJEU and national courts is clear and there is no legal ground for claiming that the employees could be considered attributable to the transferred part of the business, provided that they perform more than 50% of their work tasks for the said business.

Slovenian legislation allows part-time employment without a specific minimum working time, which means that splitting a full-time employment contract between two different employers could also be legal. Moreover, Slovenian legislation does not provide for a detailed regulation of this specific issue under the rules on transfer of undertakings.

It should also be noted that, according to the mentioned case law of the CJEU, the division of different work tasks of an employee is justified if the division of the employment contract is possible because of the transfer and neither causes a deterioration of the working conditions nor affects the protection of the rights of the employee concerned. Alternatively, the dismissal of such an employee could also be justified,

6. Case CJEU C-344/18, *ISS Facility Services*, 26 March 2020, ECLI:EU:C:2020:239.
7. Decision of Slovenian Supreme Court VIII Ips 129/2018, 18 July 2018, ECLI:SI:VSRS:2018:VIII.IPS.129.2018.

assuming that such dismissal was in any case initiated by the employer, which gives the employee all related termination rights.

However, since under Slovenian law (Article 90(1) ZDR-1), the change of employer cannot constitute a legitimate reason for termination, it cannot be entirely ruled out that a termination effected on behalf of the employer will be subject to a balancing test as to whether the termination is based on legitimate organizational business reasons following the change of employer or on the change of employer per se.

Considering that the line between a legitimate business reason for termination following a change of employer and termination due to a mere change of employer is not clear (neither in local case law nor in CJEU case law), such termination would therefore risk falling within the scope of protection of Article 90(1) ZDR-1, meaning that it may not be considered legitimate because it was caused by a change of employer/transfer of business.

Consequently, in our opinion, CJEU case law and local case law, including the aforementioned judgments, should be followed. This means that after an automatic transfer of employment, the employment of employees whose tasks are divided between the two parts of the business activity would automatically be divided into two part-time jobs, with the two employers continuing each part of the business activity in proportion to the tasks performed for each business activity.

Such a transfer of employment is most likely not in the interest of either employer or the employees involved. It also raises confidentiality and potential competition issues. For this reason, employers usually seek ways to agree upon and implement an alternative arrangement for such employees.

One way to avoid splitting the employment relationship is to have the affected employees remain with the transferring employer. In principle, the transfer cannot be opted out of. The only way for the employee to avoid the transfer is to object to the transfer prior to the actual transfer. After the transfer, such an objection is ineffective. It is possible to reach an agreement with the employee expressing his or her objection to the transfer, while his or her future working conditions with the transferor employer are agreed upon. The disadvantage of this approach is that it depends on consent of both parties. If the employee does not agree to remain with the transferor employer, he or she cannot be excluded from the transfer.

A second way to deal with the complications arising from the possible splitting of employment during the transfer would be to redesign the workflow and work posts at the transferor employer's prior to the transfer in such a way that the work tasks belonging to the two parts of the business are clearly allocated to different work posts (i.e., that after a restructuring, if possible, no employee is divided between two parts of business activity) in order to make it clear which employees are to be allocated to the transferred part of the undertaking.

A third possibility would be to regulate the division of employment after the transfer. In certain circumstances, it would be possible to show that both the transferor and transferee employers needed full-time employment to perform the duties of the employee who was split into part-time employment at the time of the transfer. In this case, either employer could assert a business-related reason for termination because it would not be able to guarantee employment to the affected employee on the terms of his or her part-time employment. Consequently, the employee could be dismissed and offered a new full-time employment contract with one of the two companies. Here, too, however, there is a risk that such dismissals, if challenged in court, could be deemed to be exclusively related to the transfer and thus unlawful.

The final and, in our view, least risky approach would be to enter into (bipartite or tripartite) agreements with the affected employees prior to the transfer, which would include the employee's formal objection to the transfer, the mutual termination of the current employment relationship, and the future terms of employment with either company, where the structure of the agreement (termination agreement, preliminary agreement, and employment contract) could provide for the termination of the old employment relationship and the commencement of the new employment relationship at the time of the transfer date, so that no prior changes to the work organization would be required before the transfer. This approach also has the disadvantage of requiring the consent of the affected employees, but since it is not a dismissal, it also eliminates the risk of being considered unlawful if the principles of transfer are followed correctly.

As far as market practice is concerned, to our knowledge, this issue is usually settled by agreements between employees and employers. Some employers also apply a risk-based approach and fully transfer only those employees who are majority assigned to the transferring business. Note that potential claims and litigation cases usually arise only when dismissals occur after the transfer. In many cases where employment rights remain unchanged after the transfer, the legality of the transfer itself is not subject to judicial review.

[3] Confidentiality Issues

In connection with the issue raised above about the possibility of splitting a full-time job into two part-time jobs with two employers, the question of how employers should protect their business secrets usually arises almost simultaneously. This question usually extends to the period before the actual transfer of the business, since although the employees' duties only extend to the operation of the business being transferred, they naturally also have knowledge of the work of the other employees who remain with the transferor employer.

That's why employers want to contractually strengthen protection of business secrets before the transfer and limit the range of employees who come into contact with potentially sensitive information.

One possibility is to strengthen confidentiality obligations in employment contracts. In this context, it should be noted that in Slovenia, all amendments to employment contracts must be expressly confirmed with a signature to be enforceable, and that the continuation of the employment relationship cannot be considered sufficient consideration for the amendment to be enforceable.

However, the transferor employer could adopt or amend internal rules on confidentiality. Under this option, employees would only need to be informed of the change in rules, and the rules would be enforceable. Individual consent would not be required.

The question is whether transferee employer could change internal rules concerning confidential information after the transfer. If the transferee employer changes the internal rules after the transfer, it should be noted that if the employee's working conditions at the transferee employer change significantly after the transfer and the employee terminates the employment contract as a result, the employee has the same rights as if the employment contract had been terminated by the employer for business reasons. However, at first glance, we would not say that the employee's terms and conditions of employment change materially if the new employer adopts new rules on confidentiality.

Another question that remains to be answered is: if the non-transferred employee, who was employed by the transferor employer and had knowledge of the transferred business confidential information, violates labour regulations after the transfer of the business, can the transferee employer take action against that employee, or must this be enforced by the transferor employer as the employer?

In our view, the transferee employer could hypothetically have the possibility to take action against the remaining employee of the transferor employer after a transfer of undertaking, but the facts should be analysed after the incident, as the possibilities for action depend on the nature of the violation.

[C] Non-compliance with Obligations of Information and Consultation with Works Council

[1] General

As already mentioned, the transferor employer must inform and consult the works council about the intended transfer before adopting a decision on the transfer. As transactions are frequently confidential at this stage, concerns about confidentiality are also frequently raised in connection with the rights of the works council. In order to protect confidentiality, the question that often arises is what influence the works council has on the procedure itself and what are the consequences for the employer and transaction itself if the employer does not comply with its information and consultation obligations.

According to legislation, if the transferor employer fails to comply with its obligation to inform the works council of the transfer at least 30 days prior to adopting the decision on transfer and fails to invite the works council to a consultation at least 15 days prior to adopting the decision on transfer, this may result in the employer being subject to an administrative penalty pursuant to Article 107 ZSDU. Additionally, there could be other implications of non-compliance with information and consultation obligations, which are discussed below.

[2] Right to Stay the Decision of the Employer

The works council has the right to stay the execution of individual decisions of the transferor employer and to initiate dispute resolution proceedings within eight days of receipt of information that the transferor employer has made a decision on the above items: (i) without prior notice to the works council of its intention to make the decision, (ii) by failing to comply with the time limits, or (iii) by failing to request joint consultation on such items.

The transferor employer shall not execute the resolutions until the final decision has been made under the special dispute resolution procedure before the relevant arbitration body under the ZSDU.

Notwithstanding the right to suspend the decision of the works council provided for in the ZSDU and the obligation of the transferor not to execute the decision pending the final decision in the dispute resolution procedure, all transactions entered into or executed by the transferor with third parties would still be legally valid, binding and enforceable. According to ZGD-1,[8] the legal representative of the company may perform all acts that fall within the legal capacity of the company, and no restriction, statutory or otherwise, shall have any legal effect against third parties.

In the event of a breach of the information and consultation obligations, the works council shall have the right to stay the employer's decision pending a final decision in a special dispute resolution procedure before the competent arbitration body so that it can effectively block or delay the conclusion of the transaction. In this case, the works council may exercise this right only within eight days from the date on which it was informed of the adoption of the decision.

The works council could also appeal in the court proceedings following the closing of the transaction (register entry, etc.), although the prospects of success are difficult to assess as there is no relevant case law on this subject.

In the absence of case law on the arbitration procedures in such disputes, it is difficult to predict the impact of the arbitration decision on the transaction. ZSDU does not offer a comprehensive regulation of the arbitration procedure between the employer and the works council, and it should be considered alongside the general ZArbit,[9] which applies to all arbitration procedures. According to the ZArbit, any monetary claim can be the subject of an arbitration agreement, while other claims may be the subject of an arbitration agreement only if the parties can settle the claim. Moreover, according to ZSDU, the arbitration decision replaces the agreement between the works council and the employer. At the same time, the ZArbit determines that an arbitration decision has the effect of a final judgment between the parties. The arbitration panel may in principle issue any decision that could also be issued by a court. However, unlike a court decision, an arbitral decision binds only the parties to the proceedings, not third parties. In this sense, the legal effects of such a decision can

8. Companies Act (*Zakon o gospodarskih družbah*, Official Gazette of the Republic of Slovenia, No. 65/09 with amendments, '*ZGD-1*').
9. Arbitration Act (*Zakon o arbitraži*, Official Gazette of the Republic of Slovenia, No. 45/08 with amendments, '*ZArbit*').

arise only for the parties to the dispute and only for that particular dispute. This considered, it remains questionable as to what kind of claims related to the transaction could the works council bring forward in the arbitration proceedings and what effects, if any, could an arbitration decision have on actual transactions resulting in TUPE transfers.

In any event and considering ZSDU in conjunction with other relevant Slovenian legislation, such as the ZGD-1 and the principle of ensuring safety of legal transactions, it is in our view not possible to restrict decisions on transactions vis-à-vis third parties, especially if the latter act in good faith. This is because ZSDU restrictions are internal restrictions which should not in themselves affect the validity of transactions with third parties, but which may, however, give rise to potential liability for damages on the part of the company towards the works council or rather individual workers.

[3] Conclusion

In conclusion, the confidentiality and time limits of an employer's information and consultation obligations can create questions regarding the influence of the works council in the procedure and the consequences for non-compliance. According to legislation, non-compliance can result in administrative penalties for the employer. The works council also has the right to stay the employer's decision pending a final decision in a special dispute resolution procedure (the arbitration procedure) and may also appeal in court proceedings following the closure of the transaction.

It remains questionable as to what kind of claims related to the transaction could the works council bring forward in the arbitration proceedings and what effects, if any, could an arbitration decision have on actual transactions resulting in TUPE transfers. Considering ZSDU in conjunction with other relevant Slovenian legislation, such as the ZGD-1 and the principle of ensuring safety of legal transactions, it is in our view not possible to restrict decisions on transactions vis-à-vis third parties, especially if the latter act in good faith.

[D] Active Litigation

[1] Introduction

The transfer of a business and the related change of employer can have a significant impact on ongoing litigation. This is because the transfer or change of employer may affect the legal status of the parties involved. In addition, the transfer of assets and liabilities may also affect the ability of the parties to recover damages or enforce judgments. In this part of the article, we will explore the various ways in which a transfer of business or change of employer can affect ongoing litigation, including the analysis of claims for reintegration by employees who were previously 'shared' by both businesses.

[2] General Procedural Rules

The legal consequences of the transfer of a business can vary depending on the type of transaction. In general, if the transferor employer continues to exist as a legal entity, the procedural rules for singular succession will apply in the case of active litigation. This means that there is no automatic accession of the transferee employer to pending proceedings. The transferee employer can only join the proceedings with the consent of the counterparty.

In practice, this means that the transferor employer is responsible for finishing any pending proceedings, even if they relate to the business activities or employees being transferred, unless the other party agrees to allow the transferee employer to take over the proceedings. This applies to legal disputes in which the transferor employer is both the plaintiff and the defendant.

The rules discussed above pertain only to civil and labour litigation. In enforcement proceedings, the consent of the other party is not needed to replace the creditor or debtor with a new subject (acquirer). In such cases, the new creditor or debtor may enter into enforcement proceedings after filing an application for enforcement and take the place of the original creditor/debtor, provided they can prove the claim has been assigned or transferred to them by a public or officially certified document. The new creditor/debtor takes over the enforcement in its current state.

[3] Employment and Labour Litigation Analysis

The same procedural rules as described above apply to labour court proceedings, with some special features regarding the nature of the claims and the nature of the obligations in cases where the transferor employer is the defendant.

In addition to asserting monetary claims against the employer (e.g., compensation for damages, difference in salary, etc.), employees may also assert a (non-monetary) claim for reinstatement in employment because of an unlawful dismissal or for recognition of an employment relationship (with simultaneous reinstatement in employment) if no employment relationship previously existed.

In cases where, during pending employment litigation proceedings in which the transferor employer is the defendant, change of employer (transfer of undertaking) pursuant to Article 75 ZDR-1 affects the plaintiff's (former) job, it is important to note, that under the rules on change of employer, both the transferor employer and transferee employer are jointly and severally liable for all claims of the employees arising from the period prior to the transfer of the undertaking, as well as for all claims arising from the termination of the employment relationship of the transferred employees due to the deterioration of their working conditions with the transferee employer within two years of the transfer.

It should also be noted that if the change of employer results in a split of the full-time employment relationship, which means that an affected employee has only performed part of his work duties for the transferred business and therefore only part of his employment relationship or job with the transferred business is transferred, this employee is practically prevented from resuming full-time employment with the transferor employer in the event of a successful action in labour court proceedings, since only part-time employment is still available as a result of the partial business transfer.

In our view, the civil procedural rules apply without further ado to all pending litigation concerning monetary claims of employees against the transferor employer. This means that the transferor employer alone can complete the pending proceedings, even if they relate to jobs that are transferred in whole or in part.

The same applies in principle to non-monetary claims, such as the employee's reintegration into the work process. The ZDR-1 does not limit the joint and several liability of the transferor and the transferee employer to purely monetary claims.

However, there is a judgment of the Slovenian Supreme Court[10] that dealt with a reinstatement action against a transferor employer for unlawful dismissal, where there was a change of employer during the proceedings with respect to the job in question.

In this judgment, the Supreme Court considered that a change of employer under Article 75(1) of the ZDR-1 constitutes a transfer of the rights and obligations under the employee's employment contract from the transferor employer to the transferee employer, and it is a logical error in the interpretation of this statutory provision for the court to continue to recognize the employee's rights and obligations under the employment contract with the transferor employer on this basis. The logical consequence of such a change of employer is that, notwithstanding the illegality of the termination of the employment relationship with the transferor employer, if the requirements for a change of employer are met, the employee may exercise the rights under his employment contract only with the transferee employer to whom the rights and obligations under the employee's employment contract have already been transferred, and no longer with the previous employer, i.e., the transferor employer.

This decision suggests that joint and several liability under Article 75 ZDR-1 does not extend to non-monetary claims, such as reinstatement, and that in an ongoing proceeding in which the opposing party asserts reinstatement against the transferor employer, its claim for reintegration after the transfer of business is likely to be denied in whole or in part. However, it is not certain what alternative (if any) would be granted to the plaintiff employee to then claim reintegration against the transferee employer.

To achieve reinstatement, the opposing party would hypothetically have the option of amending the claim during the first-instance proceeding to reflect divided employment after the date of transfer by requesting that to extend the proceedings to the transferee employer as the second defendant (subject to the consent of the transferee employer) and to amend the content of the claim (which, pursuant to Article 41(4) of ZDSS-1)[11] is possible until the end of the main hearing in the first instance without the consent of the defendant. To our knowledge, however, no such case has yet been heard in court.

10. Decision of Slovenian Supreme Court, No. VIII Ips 101/2015, 8 September 2015, ECLI:SI:VSRS:2015:VIII.IPS.101.2015.
11. Labour and Social Courts Act, (Official Gazette of the Republic of Slovenia, No. 2/2004 with amendments, 'ZDSS-1').

The question also remains open whether the success of an employee's claim to establish the existence of an employment relationship with the transferee employer presupposes that the employee has previously challenged the validity of the termination of the employment contract with the transferor employer in due time. If the employee is not bound by deadlines for establishing the existence of an employment relationship with the transferee employer, as could result from the recent decision of the Higher Labour and Social Court,[12] employee could also successfully assert the existence of an employment relationship or reinstatement with the transferee employer with a renewed action in new proceedings. It should be noted, however, that the above-mentioned ruling of the Higher Labour and Social Court is subject to review by the Supreme Court,[13] so we expect the Supreme Court to provide an answer to the question of possible time limits for asserting claims against the acquiring employer.

Since the above problems with reintegration can be avoided by judicial termination of employment pursuant to Article 118 of ZDR-1 with monetary compensation for termination, we think it is much more likely that the courts would favour judicial termination of employment in such cases. We would argue that the fact that all or part of the affected employee's job has been transferred to the transferee employer is sufficient reason for the court to grant judicial termination of employment in the event of a successful claim against the transferor employer. This would result in a purely monetary claim that can be enforced as described above.

If the active proceedings are already in front of the court of second instance, it is not certain how the courts would decide. In our opinion, and given the limited case law on the subject, a reintegration claim based on a final judgment (establishing the liability of transferor employer prior to the transfer) could also exist, and transferor employer would have to reintegrate the employee.

[4] Conclusion

In conclusion, the procedural rules for labour court proceedings in cases where the transferor employer is the defendant are similar to civil proceedings, with some special features regarding the nature of the claims and the nature of the obligations.

Employees may assert monetary claims as well as non-monetary claims for reinstatement in employment or recognition of an employment relationship. In cases where there is a change of employer during pending employment litigation proceedings, both the transferring employer and the transferee employer are jointly and severally liable for all claims arising from the period prior to the transfer of the business, as well as for all claims arising from the termination of the employment relationship of the transferred employees due to the deterioration of their working conditions with the transferee employer.

12. Decision of Higher labour and Social Court, No. Pdp 41/2022, 29 March 2022, ECLI:SI:VDSS:2022:PDP.41.2022.
13. Decision of Slovenian Supreme Court, No. VIII DoR 101/2022-7, 15 September 2012, ECLI:SI:VSRS:2022:VIII.DOR.101.2022.7.

However, it should be noted that if the change of employer results in transfer of employment relationship, the employee may be prevented from resuming employment with the transferor employer as there is a judgment that suggests that joint and several liability of the transferor and transferee employer may not apply to non-monetary claims such as employee's reintegration into the work process.

§17.03 SUMMARY

[A] General

Employers and employees often encounter unanswered questions in cases of transfer of undertaking despite the existence of legislation and case law. While there may not be a clear answer under the law, it is still necessary to regulate such employee relations in the event of a transfer of employer. In this article, we tried to provide an overview of some of the key questions and issues related to the transfer of undertaking.

The article highlights some practical issues that companies in Slovenia face during the process, which are insufficiently addressed in court practice and the law. By understanding these challenges, companies can better manage the transfer process.

[B] Transfer of Part of the Business

In our opinion, most open questions arise when only part of the business is transferred and when the employees were not strictly divided between the businesses before the transfer. According to the CJEU and Slovenian case law, the employment contract is automatically transferred to the transferee employer in proportion to the tasks performed by the employee and attributable to the transferred part of the business. Slovenian legislation allows part-time employment without a specific minimum working time, which means that splitting a full-time employment contract between two different employers is legal. However, splitting the employment relationship is usually not in the interest of the employers or employees involved and raises issues of confidentiality and potential competition issues. Thus, employers usually want to transfer employees in full. Therefore, alternative arrangements may be considered, such as redesigning work processes and jobs, regulating the division of employment after the transfer, or entering into agreements with affected employees in advance of the transfer. The article also addresses the risks associated with each of these approaches.

When a full-time job is split into two part-time jobs with two employers, the issue of protecting business secrets also arises. Employers usually want to strengthen confidentiality obligations before the transfer and limit the number of employees with access to sensitive information. This can be achieved through amendments to employment contracts or internal rules on confidentiality.

[C] Non-compliance with Works Concil Rights of Information and Consultation

Several topics relating to the works council's right to information and consultation also often arise in connection with the transfer of undertaking. Under Slovenian law, the transferor employer must inform and consult the works council before adopting a decision on the transfer of the business, which may give rise to confidentiality concerns. Failure to comply with these obligations may result in administrative penalties for the employer. The works council also has the right to stay the employer's decision if the employer fails to comply with the deadlines and advance notice requirements. The decision may be suspended until a final decision is issued under the special dispute resolution procedure. However, the law does not contain clear provisions on what claims the works council can bring before the arbitration board, and there is no relevant case law on the subject. Disputes are usually settled peacefully by implementing some of the works council's demands. Employers should ensure that they fulfil their obligations to avoid legal consequences and maintain a positive relationship with the works council.

[D] Open Litigation

The last of the selected topics relates to open labour law procedures at the time of the transfer of undertaking. It examines how the change of employer affects the legal position of the parties involved and what options the parties have to enter open proceedings. Depending on the nature of the transaction, singular succession procedural rules may apply to ongoing litigation, meaning that the transferor employer is responsible for finishing any pending proceedings unless the other party allows the transferee employer to take over the proceedings. In labour court proceedings, joint and several liability applies to claims dating from before the transfer of the undertaking. However, it remains to be seen how the change of employer will affect the ability of employees to successfully sue for non-monetary claims, such as the reinstatement of the employee in the labour process.

[E] Conclusion

While some practical issues have been addressed in the articles on business transfers, there are many other issues that companies face during such transfers. With globalization and new business developments, transactions leading to business transfers are becoming increasingly complex. Despite the extensive case law of the CJEU and national courts, there are still gaps in both the law and court practice. Businesses need to navigate these gaps, particularly in managing relationships with employees at the time of transfer, as employees need to be given certain answers, even if there are no clear answers.

It is hoped that in the near future, the rules and regulations governing transfers of undertaking will be reformed to reflect the increasing complexity of such transactions.

This will provide much-needed clarity and guidance to employers and enable them to navigate currently open issues. In this way, employers will be better able to manage employee relations at the time of transfer.

§17.04 LITERATURE

(1) Nataša Belopavlovič et al., Zakon o delovnih razmerjih s komentarjem, Ljubljana: GV Založba, 2016.

(2) mag. Ivan Robnik; Novejše odločitve Vrhovnega sodišča Republike Slovenije v sporih o spremembi delodajalca; Pravosodni bilten (PB) 1/2016, p. 209, 2016.

(3) Marijan Kocbek et al., Veliki komentar Zakona o gospodarskih družbah, Ljubljana, GV Založba, 2014.

(4) Drago Mežnar; Zakon o sodelovanju delavcev pri upravljanju/z uvodnimi pojasnili Draga Mežnarja in stvarnim kazalom; Ljubljana, Uradni list Republike Slovenije, 1996.

(5) Senčur Peček, Darja, Aktualna vprašanja spremembe delodajalca, Delavci in delodajalci, No. 2/3, pp. 297-324, 2010.

CHAPTER 18
Spain

Alejandro Rausell

§18.01 FOREWORD

This work does not intend to make an assessment of the different elements that make up and characterize the succession of company, figure this, which has been the subject not only of numerous studies and works that have been influencing and deepening its assumptions, characteristics and the practical consequences of its application but also of a copious jurisprudence of the Supreme Court on the matter, interpreting the existing rules in the light of the European Union Directive 2001/23.

What is intended is to highlight some recent judicial pronouncements that, in our opinion, enjoy relevance in the matter, as well as to highlight the problems generated recently with the new regulations on bankruptcy, highlighting its evolution and its impact on the judicial decisions of the Courts.

§18.02 JOINT AND SEVERAL LIABILITY FOR DEBTS PRIOR TO THE SUCCESSION AND BURDEN OF PROOF OF THE TRANSFER OF A PRODUCTIVE UNIT

One of the many effects of business succession is determined by the requirement of liability of the acquirer of a productive unit, with respect to the debts of the previous assignor that would not have been prescribed. It must be emphasized, in order to be able to establish such liability, that the constituent event is the succession of an undertaking, and for that reason, the proof of its existence lies with the applicant of the claim.

In this sense, the judgment of the Supreme Court of September 8, 2021 (R. 1866/2020), reiterating previous doctrine, declares that in order for the joint and several liability of Article 44.3 of the Workers' Statute (hereinafter "ET"). It is necessary that a productive unit that maintains its identity be effectively transferred, understood as a set of means organized in order to carry out an economic activity, essential or ancillary, the burden of proof of which lies with the plaintiff, ex Article 217.2 LEC.

In the aforementioned sentence it is recalled: "since the applicant has not alleged or proved that the transfer of a production unit had taken place, ... it is clear that it has not proved the facts constituting its claim, even if the company admitted that it was conventionally subrogated in the workforce of the outgoing company, since the reversal of the burden of proof, maintained by our doctrine in cases of succession of contracts, is predicated on those companies, whose activities are developed essentially by labor, which has not been proven here ... That conclusion cannot be undermined, because the appellant company did not prove, or attempt to prove, that the transfer of a production unit had not taken place, since the burden of proof of the impeding, extinguishing or excluding acts, predicated by art. 217.3 LRJS, it is activated to neutralize the legal effectiveness of the constituent facts, whose incidence is logically updated when they have been proven, so that, even if preventive, extinguishing or excluding facts have not been proven, the claim must be dismissed, when the constitutive facts have not been proven, since, if this were not done, protection would be granted to unfounded claims, As we argued, among many others, in STS 23-07-2015 (RCUD 2903/2014 and 22-11-2017, RCUD 3636/2016. Moreover, it cannot be forgotten that the plaintiff did not specify in its application, nor did it allege it at the time of its ratification, nor did it prove, nor did it attempt to prove, that any of the assumptions that prove the transfer of the productive unit were met, without it being an excessive obligation ..."

In the case analyzed, since the plaintiff has not proven the certainty of the facts on which his claim was based, the business succession provided for in Article 44 of the ET and the incoming company must not be jointly and severally liable for the company's salary debts.

The same doctrine is reiterated in SSTS of September 8, 2021 (R. 2543/2020) and November 24, 2021 (R. 1866/2020).

§18.03 PERMANENT WORKER AND REVERSAL OF PUBLIC SERVICE

Of notable relevance are the SSTS of January 28, 2022 (R. 3781/2020) in which it is stated that workers of private companies, when they become an employer, a public entity (in this case, the City Council), as a result of the subrogation by transmission of an autonomous productive unit, maintain their status as fixed because the reversal of the service cannot affect the preexisting employment relationship modality, except to ignore the requirements derived from Directive.

So, reads the STS of January 28, 2022 (RCUD. 3782/2020): "A) The abovementioned Council Directive 2001/23/EC of 12 March 2001 deals with the approximation of the laws of the Member States relating to the safeguarding of employees' rights in the event of transfers of undertakings, businesses or parts of undertakings or businesses.

As stated in the introductory text, its purpose is 'to protect workers in the event of a change of employer, in particular to ensure the maintenance of their rights' (Recital 3 of Directive 2001/23; and ECJ 16/October/2008, case Kirtruna, SL, paragraph 43), so that 'the transferor remains, after the date of transmission, and together with the transferee, liable for the obligations arising from a contract of employment or an employment relationship, which means that, in any event, those obligations are transferred to the assignee on that same date' (SSTJUE 14/November/1996. Rotsart de Hertaing case, paragraph 23: and 26/May/2005; Case C-478/03, paragraph 40).

B) It is interesting to note that the rule is applicable 'to both public and private companies that exercise an economic activity, with or without profit. The administrative reorganisation of public administrative authorities and the transfer of administrative functions between public administrative authorities shall not constitute a transfer within the meaning of this Directive.'

Thus, the fact that the transferee of the activity is a legal person governed by public law does not preclude the existence of a transfer falling within the scope of the rule, irrespective of whether that legal person is a public entity entrusted with a public service. The fact that the new employer is a City Council does not prevent the Directive from applying to the transfer of the activities carried out by a company (ECJ 20 July 2017, Piscarreta Ricardo, C-416/16).

C) Of course, the maintenance of the rights of the persons concerned is clearly stated; Article 3.1 provides that 'the rights and obligations arising for the transferor from a contract of employment or an employment relationship existing at the date of the transfer shall be transferred to the assignee as a result of such transfer.'

It should be stressed that the purpose of the Directive is to ensure, as far as possible, the continuation of contracts with the transferee, without modifications, in order to prevent the workers concerned from being in a less favourable situation simply because of the transfer (ECJ of 6 April 2017, Unionen, C-336/15) (...)."

The aforementioned judgment refers to the STJUE of June 13, 2019 (C-317/18, *Correia Moreira*), and provides that: "A) Special significance has for the subject debated the STJUE June 13, 2019 (C-317/18, Correia Moreira) that appears constantly invoked throughout this procedure, starting with the lawsuit that activated it.

To assess this decision, it is worth remembering that the worker in the case, occupying a position of 'trust' in the ceding company ... it is assumed by the City Council. However, applying Portuguese legislation to the case: 1) requires the worker to submit to a public selection procedure; 2) contemplates the emergence of a new link (the previous one is not maintained); and 3) their eventual integration into the civil service would entail a reduction in their salary for a period of at least ten years.

B) The STJUE examined considers that this situation is incompatible with the Directive. It points out that the consequences described are, first, alter the working conditions, agreed with the transferor, of a person such as the applicant in the main proceedings and, second, are liable to place the worker in a less favorable situation than that in which she was before that transfer.

C) Respect for the national identity inherent in the fundamental political and constitutional structures of the Member States (Article 4(2) TEU) cannot be interpreted as meaning that, in an area in which the Member States have transferred their competences to the Union, such as the safeguarding of employees' rights in the event of transfers of undertakings, deprives a worker of the protection afforded to him by EU law in force in that area.

D) In its operative part, it concludes that Directive 2001/23 (read in conjunction with Article 4(2) TEU) 'precludes national legislation which requires that, in the event of a transfer for the purposes of that directive, since the transferee is a municipality, the workers concerned, first, must be subject to a public selection procedure and, on the other hand, they are bound by a new link with the assignee.' The judgment concludes that: 'From what we have explained it follows that when there is, as is the case, transfer of an autonomous productive unit, the legal system prescribes the subrogation of the new employer in pre-existing labor relationships. A subjective subdivision or the reduction of the effects is not admissible, as happens when the contractual modality is altered in that direction'.

The possible existing doubts have been cleared by the STJUE 13 June 2019, not because it is a case equal to the present one, but because it warns that the reduction of rights derived from the public status of the assignee employer is against EU law.

The appeal of the Supreme Court of Justice in question refers to respect for the constitutional structures of each country is expressly contested by the Court of Luxembourg. This means that the provisions of Article 103(3) EC (access to the public service respecting the principles of equality, merit and ability) cannot give rise to an argument that prevents the application of the consequences arising from the Directive (...)."

The merited sentence contemplates a series of nuances; thus, in the first place, it indicates that we are not dealing with an issue of access to public employment but of the assumption of labor relations already constituted, and, second, it contains a reference to Law 9/2017, of November 8, on Public Sector Contracts, which transposes into Spanish law the Directives of the European Parliament and of the Council 2014/23/EU and 2014/24/EU, of February 26, 2014, which in its Article 130.3 provides that: "In the event that a Public Administration decides to directly provide a service that until now had been provided by an economic operator, it will be obliged to subrogate the personnel who provided it if it is established by a legal norm, a collective agreement or a collective bargaining agreement of general effectiveness," and after pointing out that for chronological reasons the rule is inapplicable, it emphasizes that its content reinforces the coherence of the result that the controversy arises, since if the most specific rule that our legal system has lacks restriction on the way in which subrogation operates, apart from the fact that the contrary could not be invoked against the need to interpret it in accordance with the Directive, it may well be inferred that the absence of a difference is because the legislature does not consider it to exist.

In the same sense, the SSTS of January 31, 2020 (RCUD. 3775/2020, and of February 1, 2020 (RCUD. 3777/2020) are pronounced.

§18.04 SUCCESSION OF TEMPLATES (SUCCESSION OF LABOR) IN THE FRAMEWORK OF A CONVENTIONAL SUBROGATION

In terms of conventional subrogation, we highlight the ruling of Chamber IV of the Supreme Court (Full) of September 27, 2018 (RCUD 2747/2016), which summarizes the jurisprudential doctrine in cases of conventional subrogation, which provides:

A) The exclusion of the common subrogatory regime (art. 44 ET) by the collective agreement is only valid when a productive unit with functional autonomy is not transferred.
B) The collective agreement can improve the regulation of the ET and Directive 2001/23/CE, not preterite or worsen it. Conventional provisions only apply "as long as they do not violate any precept of necessary law."
C) When the agreement obliges the assumption of the preexisting workforce in cases additional to the legal ones, even though there is a "succession of staff" materially, the common regulation should not be used, since what has been agreed operates as an improvement of the heteronomous forecasts.
D) Whenever there is a transfer of material means or productive infrastructure, what is appropriate is to apply the general regime of the transfer of a company with labor subrogation.

This doctrine is reiterated, among others, in SSTS of September 8, 2021 (RCUD 1866/2020), or January 18, 2022 (RCUD 3876/2019).

In the aforementioned sentence, which adapted the doctrine of the Supreme Court to the STJUE of July 11, 2018, C-60/17, the following conclusions were reached:

> "First.—There is a transfer of a company that can be classified in art. 44 ET if the succession of contracts is accompanied by the transfer of an economic entity between the outgoing and incoming companies.
> Second.—In activities where labor is an essential factor, the assumption of a relevant part of the personnel assigned to the contract (in quantitative or qualitative terms) activates the application of article 44 ET.
> Third.—When (as in the case) what is relevant is the workforce (not the infrastructure) the subrogation only proceeds if that assumption of a relevant part (quantitatively or qualitatively) of the staff is given.
> Fourth.—The fact that the assumption of a relevant part of the workforce derives from the provisions of the collective agreement does not prevent the application of the previous doctrine.

As regards the burden of proof, the reiterated sentence concludes:

> In principle, and always by reference to these cases in which what is relevant is not the productive infrastructure at stake, the awarding of a new contract to an employer other than the outgoing one places us before the transfer of the aforementioned "economic entity."
>
> But it is not about something that belongs to the field of the abstract or dogmatic, but to that of the facts and their proof. That is, the examination of the characteristics of the award (time conditions, requirements on the way of supplying the services to the main company, address of the assigned group of people, permanent or random functional assignment, etc.), of the reality transmitted (functional and locative affectation, audiovisual media, computer programs, staff furniture, etc.), the scope of the assumption of people (not only quantitative but

> also qualitative) are valuable aspects to clear up this unknown, which constitutes at the same time a condition of subrogation.
>
> This means, of course, that in sectors where labor is essential, the data relating to the number or condition of those who have been hired by the new employer must be valued as a high priority, regardless of the title or reason for which it happen.

The STS of March 23, 2022 (R. 3117/2020) refers to the aforementioned doctrine, which declares that there will be a succession of templates if both qualitatively and quantitatively the service that is transmitted relies substantially on labor, and on the contrary, there will not be, if certain equipment or material goods are essential for its provision. In this case, it is concluded that the essential factor is labor and not infrastructure.

§18.05 THE SUCCESSION OF COMPANIES WITHIN THE FRAMEWORK OF BANKRUPTCY PROCEEDINGS

In the event of the sale of an autonomous productive unit within the framework of bankruptcy proceedings, the main issues that have arisen in recent years have revolved not only around the powers conferred by the regulations applicable to the bankruptcy judge, on the declaration of the succession of the company, but also the scope of the effects of said declaration, that is, if the judge of the bankruptcy can limit its consequences, and to what degree he can do so.

The situation has undergone an evolution since the approval of Law 22/2003, of July 9, Bankruptcy, which makes it necessary to analyze the different changes that have been introduced by the regulatory variation throughout these last years.

From the point of view of judicial doctrine, the issue has not been peaceful, largely due to the convergence in the matter of regulations belonging to different branches of law (Social and Civil), on the one hand, the Royal Legislative Decree 2/2015, of October 23, which approves the revised text of the Workers' Statute Law (hereinafter, "ET"), and Royal Legislative Decree 8/2015, of October 30, which approves the Text Revised General Social Security Law (LGSS), and on the other hand, Royal Legislative Decree 1/2020, of May 5, which approves the revised text of the Bankruptcy Law.

With respect to the first of the regulations, Article 44 of the ET contains a concept of company succession in its second section that provides: "For the purposes of the provisions of this article, it will be considered that there is a company succession when the transfer affects an economic entity that maintains its identity, understood as a set of organized means in order to carry out an essential or accessory economic activity."

For its part, Article 57 of the ET provides that: "In the event of bankruptcy, in the cases of collective modification, suspension and termination of employment contracts and company succession, the specialties provided for in Law 22/2003 shall apply, of July 9, Bankruptcy."

Two consequences can be drawn from these precepts to take into account, on the one hand, labor regulations provide a concept of company succession (Article 44 of the

ET), and, on the other, the Bankruptcy Law acts as a special rule compared to Article 44 of the ET and against the regulations of the Social Security (LGSS), in accordance with the provisions of the last paragraph of Article 57 of the ET.

Royal Legislative Decree 1/2020, of May 5, which approves the consolidated text of the Bankruptcy Law, dedicates Articles 221 to 224 to company succession. This regulation has been partly modified by Law 16/2022, of September 5, which entered into force on September 26, 2022.

Until the entry into force of RDL 1/2020, and under the validity of LC 2003, the pronouncement of the Commercial Court was merely prejudicial and did not bind the corporate jurisdiction, except in relation to the possibility of exonerating the purchaser from salary and indemnity debts that were covered by FOGASA in accordance with Article 33 of the ET. That is to say, the intervention of the bankruptcy judge did not prevent the bodies of the social jurisdiction from expressing themselves on the matter as well.

Regarding the powers of the Bankruptcy Judge in order to exonerate the new purchaser from the debts of the autonomous productive unit, his only competence within labor debts was limited to exonerating or not from salary and compensation debts assumed by the Salary Guarantee Fund (FOGASA). Regarding Social Security debts, two moments must be distinguished: the situation prior to the reform operated in the LC of 2003 by RDL 11/2014 of September 5 and the one after the entry into force of this reform.

Before the aforementioned reform, there was the possibility of exonerating the new purchaser of debts of this nature, and the answer was found in the literal wording of Article 149.2 of the LC of 2003, which provided that only for labor purposes it was considered that there was a succession of a company, and therefore the purchaser of the autonomous productive unit was liable in the terms of the provisions of Article 44.3 of the ET, but not necessarily for the Social Security credits as they are not considered properly labor, for which reason there was room for their exoneration by the judge of the contest.

The situation changed after the reform operated by RDL 11/2014 of September 5, since the new wording of Article 149.4 (in relation to Article 146 bis.4) provided that there was a succession of companies, both for labor purposes and for Social Security purposes, with which the referral of the Bankruptcy Law was not only to the regulation contained in the ET but also to the LGSS.

The consequences for the new acquirer were relevant, since he was in charge of the Social Security debts that had not expired prior to the time of succession. And, within the term Social Security debts, the successor company not only had to include the contributions prior to the succession of companies that had not prescribed but also was responsible for the eventual payment of benefits, surcharges on benefits and possible compensation that may exist, without the Bankruptcy Judge having the powers to exonerate the new acquirer of those debts.

Another of the questions that arose with the previous regulations, and that has given rise to disparate judicial pronouncements, is the one related to whether the new acquirer was responsible for labor debts and social security only with respect to the workers that made up the productive unit, that acquired or was also extended to that of other workers who were not part of that autonomous unit because they had terminated their employment relationship.

It was understood, in accordance with community principles, that, since the LC did not distinguish and only recognized the existence of company succession for labor and Social Security purposes, it could only be understood as referring to contracts in force at the time of succession, but not to the rest of the debt. On the contrary, the opposing position found its arguments in the lack of competence of the Bankruptcy Judge to declare the existence of the succession of the company and in limiting the effects of the succession, as his decision was merely prejudicial, and in the wording contained in Article 44 of the ET and in the Social Security regulations, in which it is specified that the responsibility of the successor company is not limited to debts related to the workers assumed by it, but includes non-prescribed debts. In this second position, the Supreme Court manifested, among other STS of December 11, 2020 (RCUD. 416/2018), it was indicated, citing other sentences, that: "In effect, we have been reiterating that Article 44 ET is perfectly applicable to company adjudications that occur through the decisions adopted by the bankruptcy judge within the liquidation process, even when the order of the commercial judicial body stated that there was no succession of the company. This has been indicated in STS/4ª of February 27, 2018 (rud. 112/2016), April 26, 2018 (rud. 2004/2018), July 12, 2018 (rud. 3525/2016), September 12, 2018 (rud. 1549 /2017), November 27, 2018 (rud. 1902/2017) and January 17, 2019 (rud. 3593/2016)."

We have precisely insisted on appeals raised as a result of the same bankruptcy liquidation procedure that concerns us here in the STS/4ª of October 3, 2018 (rud. 259/2017, 323/2017, 1733/2017, 3664/2017 and 3710/2017), October 17, 2018 (rud. 2340/2017), February 27, 2020 (rud. 3999/2017), December 12, 2019 (rud. 3892/2017 and 3895/2017), May 7, 2020 (rud. 1835/2017), 13 May 2020 (rud. 1239/2018) and July 30, 2020 (rud. 1306/2018).

Our doctrine is specified in the following guidelines: (a) The adjudication of the productive unit supposes the change of ownership of an economic entity that maintains its identity, understood as a group of organized means, in order to carry out an economic activity, either essential or accessory. This entails, in principle, the consequences provided for in Article 44.3 ET, according to which, the responsibility lies with the assignor and the assignee with respect to labor obligations arising prior to the assignment. (b) The Article 44 ET is an imperative rule, which implies that the phenomenon of succession operates unless there is a provision that provides otherwise in these particular cases of companies in a situation of bankruptcy. (c) The Article 148.4 LC must be interpreted in the sense that it is a norm that does not exclude that the acquisition of a productive unit within the bankruptcy involves company succession. On the contrary, indirectly, it is admitting that in said case a company succession occurs, by referring to Article 64 LC, the cases in which the operations provided for in the liquidation plan imply substantial collective modifications, collective transfers, suspensions or collective extinctions of contracts. Indeed, if the acquisition of an autonomous productive unit within the bankruptcy process did not imply that there is a succession of the company, said referral would be superfluous because the acquisition of the autonomous productive unit would not entail the assumption of the employer's workers. If the precept turns out that there is no company succession, the employer would be solely and exclusively responsible for adopting the legal measures for the substantial modification of working conditions, collective terminations., etc., of her workers, but these measures would not have to appear linked to the approval of the liquidation plan for the assets of the active mass since the acquirer would be completely oblivious to the fate of the employer's workers. (d) Such a conclusion is not contrary to Article 148.2 LC, since the interest of the contest cannot be established as the supreme norm that governs the adjudication of the goods, since the imperative norms of our legal system must be respected, including Article 44 ET. Nor is it opposed to Article 5 of Directive 2001/23 because, as provided for in Article 8 of the same, its content will not affect the power of Member States to apply or adopt more favorable legal, regulatory or administrative provisions for workers, which is, ultimately, what results from Article 148 LC.

This interpretation is the most consistent with Directive 2001/23, whose Article 3.1 provides that "The rights and obligations that result for the assignor from an employment contract or an existing employment relationship on the date of the transfer, will be transferred to the assignee as a result of such transfer."

It is true that the Article 5 of the Directive subsequently establishes that such guarantees "shall not be applicable to transfers of companies, centers of activity, or parts of companies or centers of activity, when the assignor is subject to bankruptcy proceedings or similar open insolvency proceedings with a view to the liquidation of the assets of the assignor and these are under the supervision of a competent public authority." But that same precept provides that this general rule is not applicable if there is a provision to the contrary by the Member States, and in section 2 of the same precept, the States are allowed to regulate the scope of these obligations within certain limits and always under the supervision of an authority. That is what the Spanish legislator has done, and this is expressed in Article 148.4 bis LC, which regulates the specialties of the transfer of productive units, stating that: "The transfer will not entail an obligation to pay the credits not satisfied by the bankrupt before the transfer, whether bankrupt or against the estate, unless the purchaser had expressly assumed it or there was a legal provision to the contrary and without prejudice to the provisions of article 149.4 ..."

Following the new bankruptcy law, approved by Royal Legislative Decree 1/2020, of May 5, it is expressly recognized in Article 221.2 that the Bankruptcy Judge is the only competent authority to declare the existence of company succession within the framework of a procedure of insolvency.

Article 221 after the modification operated by Law 16/2022, of September 5, provides: "1. In case of disposal of a productive unit, it will be considered, for labor and social security purposes, that there is a company succession.

2. The bankruptcy judge will be the only one competent to declare the existence of company succession, as well as to delimit the assets, liabilities and labor relations that compose it."

The original text of the Bankruptcy Law, and specifically Article 221.1 of the LC 2020 that attributed the competition to the Bankruptcy Judge to declare the existence of company succession was not without controversy, since it implied a change of competences and a modification of current procedural rules, among others that of Article 2 of the Law Regulating the Social Jurisdiction, and, not finding the provision of that attribution of exclusive competence for the declaration of the existence of the succession of the company to the judge of the contest in any legal text object of the recasting, it was considered an "ultra vires" regulation, with which it was not subject to application by the Courts.

With the reform operated in the Bankruptcy Law by Law 16/2022, of September 5, the regulatory controversy that arose was put to an end, since its sole Article 50 modified section 2 and added a section 3 to Article 221, in the following terms: "2. The bankruptcy judge will be the only one competent to declare the existence of company succession, as well as to delimit the assets, liabilities and labor relations that compose it.

3. In these cases, the judge may request a report from the Labor and Social Security Inspectorate regarding the labor relations affected by the sale of the productive unit and the possible social security debts related to these workers."

In this way, it was ratified through a law and not through a consolidated text, the forecast of attributing the exclusive competence of the bankruptcy judge in the declaration of the existence or not of company succession, within the framework of a process insolvency.

However, this does not prevent the existence and will exist pronouncements of courts of the social order, in this matter, since the workers are not a direct part of the bankruptcy procedure and can claim their social rights before the social jurisdiction, whose bodies will issue the corresponding pronouncement.

In this sense, the STS of July 22, 2020 (R. 3488/2017) recalls that: "the Award Order issued by the Commercial Judge (...) cannot operate against individual workers not appearing in the bankruptcy proceeding that They do not have the possibility to challenge that resolution, which for this reason does not display effects of res judicata against them in accordance with art. 222.4 LEC, which enables them to act before the social order of the jurisdiction in request for the recognition of the legal effects derived from a situation of company succession in accordance with the provisions of art. 44 ET."

§18.06 BUSINESS OR INDUSTRIAL PREMISES

The STS of August 10, 2020 (RCUD. 1037/2018) with the support of the Civil Chamber (STS March 18, 2009 (R. 665/2003)) that distinguishes between a lease of business premises, business of one of industry, business or company, and, which specifies: "the leases of business premises differ from those of industry in that, with respect to the former, what is ceded is the real estate element, on the other hand, in the second, the contractual object is determined by a double integrating composition; on the one hand, the premises, as a material support; and, on the other, the business or company installed and developed in it, with the necessary elements for its exploitation, that make up an autonomous patrimonial whole, without it being necessary for the lessor to necessarily provide all the means for the commercialization of the business activity to be carried out, which can be expanded or improved with those provided by the lessee, even substituted, without this affecting the qualification and nature of the contract as an industrial lease; In addition, said contract is extinguished when the conventional term expires, as provided in article 1569.1 of the Civil Code." In this case, it was concluded by the Chamber that we were dealing with an industrial lease, as it was proven that not only was a physical space assigned to carry out the operation of a business, but that the assignment of the property was accompanied by a set of of organized material elements that at the end of the lease passed to the owner (reversal), who directly operated the business, so it is concluded that in effect; There has been a change in ownership with succession of the company and in turn the subrogation of the landlord in the position of the lease with respect to the workers of the latter.

CHAPTER 19

Final Remarks and Conclusions: Directive 2001/23—An Open Yard

Roberto Cosio, Vincenzo Di Cerbo, Filippo Curcuruto & Giovanni Mammone

§19.01 OBJECTIVES OF THE WORK

The task that the Curators of this Work have assigned themselves is to check, in today's European economic context and in the current legal reality of the Member States' systems, the state of implementation and the degree of effectiveness of the European discipline regarding the protection of the rights of workers involved in situations of transfer of the undertaking or of one of its branches.

According to the adopted research method, the Authors of the contributions collected in the Work, coming from the most diverse Member States, have been requested to report on the implementation of Directive 2001/23 in their national legal systems, carrying out a critical and not only expository work, summarizing the content of national legislation and the jurisprudence of judges, exposing the critical issues of the system and its shortcomings, but also proposing possible remedies.

We have, in fact, considered that this Work would have aroused the interest not only of practitioners of law (judges and labor lawyers, company managers, experts in business management) but also of all those jurists who in Research, Universities and Institutions (European and national) carry out their studies on the basis of concrete data emerging from the social and economic reality. Therefore, the first data that we checked was the level of implementation of Directive 2001/23 in the various Member States, being aware that the diversity of the legislative systems and legal traditions of the EU Member States could have affected its uniform application.

From the essays that make up this collective volume (there are 18 essays, but the contributors are more numerous, given that for some countries, there are interventions by several authors), various reports of critical implementation issues arising from specific provisions of the Directive emerge and together with them, proposals for correction are also formulated.

Leaving to the readers the consultation of the individual interventions for the insights deemed most appropriate, below we indicate the topics of discussion and the proposals of some Authors that seem interesting to us for the specificity of the theme addressed.

§19.02 THE IMPLEMENTATION AND RELEVANCE OF THE DIRECTIVE

Almost all the essays published in this volume begin with an exposition of the legislative techniques that legislators have adopted to implement, within national legal systems, the various directives that have followed one another over time in the matter now under examination.

The techniques adopted can be summarized in two methodologies: the Member States that already recognized the principle of maintaining the employees' contract in the event of a transfer of the undertaking, with the implementation of the Community directives, have adapted their legislation. In France, the principle was introduced in the Labor Code in 1928, in Italy in 1942 with Article 2112 of the Civil Code: in these cases, the adaptation consisted above all (but not only) in modulating the consultation of workers according to the procedures provided for by the directives that followed one another after 1977.

In other States, however, the implementation of Directive 2001/23 has provided the opportunity to introduce specific regulations for the protection of workers' rights in the event of transfer of ownership of the undertaking: this is the case of the Eastern European States after their entry into the Union.

In the absence of a uniform implementing instrument, the formulas adopted by the various States are very varied, which requires the reader to try to understand the internal logic to which national legislators have adhered and which, on some occasions, the Authors of the essays themselves have tried to explain. This approach is particularly useful for understanding how, in subsequent times (since 1977), the legal regulation of the directives on the protection of workers' rights in the event of transfer of a company has been progressively accepted and has contributed to the creation of a uniform regulatory *humus*.

At the same time, the Authors' analysis allows us to verify how much of this normative basis remains current and to what extent the objective of protecting rights can still be considered effective. This analysis aims, in fact, to be a stimulus to research and suggest further legal innovations, such as to make the European discipline adequate to the economic and social needs of the market in the middle of the third decade of the century.

However, we will have the opportunity to return to this point later.

§19.03 THE REQUIREMENTS FOR THE APPLICATION OF EUROPEAN LEGISLATION. THE COMPANY LIKE AN ORGANIZED ECONOMIC ENTITY

The jurisprudence of national Courts, as set out by the Authors in their contributions, has made a great effort to overcome the obstacles of coordination arising from the comparison, on a conceptual and applicative level, of national law with the provisions of Directive 2001/23 and with the culture underlying it.

Take, for example, the fundamental fact of the whole matter under examination: the concept of "transfer of undertaking," according to the definition of Directive 2001/23, consists in the transfer "of an undertaking, business, or part of an undertaking or business to another employer as a result of a legal transfer or merger."[1]

The case law of the EU Court of Justice is precise regarding the object of the transfer. It is constituted by: (i) an economic entity constituted by an organized group of persons and elements that allows the exercise of an economic activity aimed at pursuing a specific objective (undertaking);[2] (ii) characterized by an autonomous structure organized in a stable manner and not limited to the execution of a single work, even in the case in which the transfer consists in the transfer of "parts of a business or establishment;"[3] and (iii) which retains its identity and continues its activity after the transfer.

In practical terms, however, the Court of Justice has given the concept of "transfer" a non-rigid content, but a broad meaning, resulting from the verification of a plurality of legal indicators and the assessment of the circumstances of merit, thus leaving ample room for the assessment of the judge of the specific dispute. *See*, for example, the judgment with which the Court held that "in the context of the takeover by an economic entity of an activity the pursuit of which requires substantial operating resources, under a procedure for the award of a public contract, the fact that that entity does not take over those resources, which are the property of the economic entity previously engaged in that activity, on account of legal, environmental and technical constraints imposed by the contracting authority, cannot necessarily preclude the classification of that takeover of activity as a transfer of an undertaking, since other factual circumstances, such as the taking-over of the majority of the employees and the pursuit, without interruption, of that activity, make it possible to establish that the identity of the economic entity concerned has been retained, this being a matter for the referring court to assess."[4]

---

1. It should be noted that the case law of the Court of Justice constituted one of the main impulses of Directive 2001/23, as "*Considerations of legal security and transparency required that the legal concept of transfer be clarified in the light of the case-law of the Court of Justice. Such clarification has not altered the scope of Directive 77/187/EEC as interpreted by the Court of Justice*" (Preamble No. 8).
2. *See, inter alia*, ECJ judgments March 11, 1997, C-13/95 (*Suzen*) e November 20, 2003, C-340/2001 (*Abler*).
3. *See, inter alia*, ECJ judgments September 6, 2011 C-108/2010 (*Scattolon*) e June 13, 2019, C-664/17 (*Ellinika Nafpigeia AE*).
4. *See* ECJ judgment of February 27, 2020, C-298/18 (*Grafe*), delivered in a case involving the transfer of company assets following the award of a public contract.

In their interventions, the Authors discussed this jurisprudence and compared it with that of their own national jurisdictions, being clear that the purpose of the interventions of the European Court is to develop concepts that are shared as much as possible by national interpreters.

§19.04 THE SUBJECTIVE CONSEQUENCES OF THE TRANSFER OF THE UNDERTAKING (OR PART OF IT)

In explaining the regulation of the Czech Labor Code concerning the transfer of an undertaking, Lubomír Ptáček notes that the transfer of rights and obligations arising from the employment relationship occurs by law, without the consent of the employee and without the need to terminate the employment relationship with the previous employer and conclude a new employment contract with the transferee employer. Such a transfer is based on any legal act as a result of which the employer ceases to perform the existing activity as a whole or in part and another legal or natural person, who is entitled to do so, continues the same activity or a similar activity in his place.

The Author refers to the jurisprudence of the national Court of Cassation and constructs the case in the sense that when a transfer occurs, a person with whom the employee has not previously agreed on the performance of the service, or with whom he has not necessarily expressed disagreement, becomes the employer if the legal conditions are met. It follows that the transfer under Czech law occurs in a broad sense, i.e., in the case of employment relationships of employees not only for those who work for the transferred party but also for those who only partially participate in the performance of the transferred tasks. Therefore, employees who perform support and auxiliary activities must also be included in the transfer.[5]

This conclusion, only apparently obvious, turns out to be stimulating because it suggests a criterion (which we could define as objective) for a current reading of Directive 2001/23, as it fits into the economic framework that has been created over time following its promulgation.

Negotiation between private entrepreneurs, in fact, is not the only way to transfer a business and, indeed, in some ways, it can be considered a school hypothesis. Instead, the transfer can be implemented through alternative methods that are not always clearly identifiable, like the acquisition of share packages or other purely financial transactions. These initiatives can result in fraudulent behavior towards workers, or lead to situations that, despite the legitimacy of the financial transactions, can reduce employment levels or change the organization of work in a recessive sense for the employees of the transferred company, without them (or their representatives)

5. The Author is aware of the case law of the European Court of Justice; *see* the judgment issued under the force of Directive 1977/187, February 7, 1985, C-186/83, Botzen—according to which "an employment relationship is essentially characterized by the link existing between the employee and the part of the undertaking or business to which he is assigned to carry out his duties. In order to decide whether the rights and obligations under an employment relationship are transferred under directive no 77/187 by reason of a transfer within the meaning of article 1 (1) thereof, it is therefore sufficient to establish to which part of the undertaking or business the employee was assigned" (n. 15).

having had any role in the decision process, even at the level of information or consultation.

Therefore, suggestions and interpretative proposals are welcome, for an updated reading of the directive; it will be the task of jurists to correctly frame the cases on a normative level and to verify their correctness on a procedural level. In the meantime, to remain within the thesis of the Czech Court, a careful reading of the Author's text will allow us to appreciate its nuances and further implications.

§19.05 THE PROTECTION OF WORKERS' RIGHTS IN THE EVENT OF A COMPANY'S ECONOMIC CRISIS

The Authors pay particular attention to the protection of workers' rights in the situation of transfer of a company in crisis. It is the case in which the entrepreneur is unable to meet his obligations, and the transfer proves to be the instrument to avoid bankruptcy.

In these situations, it has been noted that real fraud can be perpetrated against workers, who, in order to safeguard employment, could be pushed to accept corporate restructuring maneuvers that involve salary and insurance waivers. The situation would be different, however, if bankruptcy were declared or another insolvency procedure led by the judicial authority or another public body were undertaken. In this case, the transfer procedure would have more opportunities to move within a legislative framework compliant with European regulations; the presence of the public body would therefore constitute a real guarantee at least for the protection of workers' credits.

Therefore, in the alternative between private negotiation of the company in crisis and that of the transfer conducted under the supervision of the curator of a judicial or administrative procedure, it has been noted by many experts that effective protection of workers' rights can only be configured if the transfer is carried out under the supervision of a public, judicial or administrative body.

It should also be noted that no references have yet been received regarding the implementation by Member States of Directive (EU) 2019/1023 of the European Parliament and of the Council of June 20, 2019, concerning the preventive restructuring of companies in crisis, as well as measures aimed at increasing the effectiveness of restructuring, insolvency and discharge procedures. This recent directive regulates the adoption of a series of preliminary debt discharge initiatives, including out-of-court ones, legally aimed at saving the company from bankruptcy, but does not conflict with Directive 2001/23, promising to safeguard the objectives of the latter.[6]

6. Preamble No. (60) of Directive 2019/1023 provides that: "Throughout the preventive restructuring procedures, workers should enjoy full labor law protection. In particular, this Directive should be without prejudice to workers' rights guaranteed by Council Directives 98/59/EC and 2001/23/EC, and Directives 2002/14/EC, 2008/94/EC and 2009/38/EC of the European Parliament and of the Council. The obligations concerning information and consultation of employees under national law transposing those Directives remain fully intact."

Furthermore, Preamble No. (62) provides: "Where a restructuring plan entails the transfer of a part of an undertaking or business, workers' rights arising from a contract of employment or from an employment relationship, in particular the right to wages, should be safeguarded in

§19.06 THE CROSS-BORDER TRANSFER

Another issue in evidence is the one concerning the cross-border transfer of the employer company, reported by Agnieszka Godusławska and Agnieszka Lisiecka in their essay on Poland. The case considered is that of the transfer of the employer company to an entrepreneur materially resident abroad and, therefore, with effective transfer abroad of activities and assets from the workplace originally located in the territory of a country (in this case: Poland). In the Authors' example, the case could be a cross-border merger of companies, through the acquisition of a Polish company by a foreign company, or the sale of a company (or an organized part thereof) located in Polish territory to a foreign subject that will continue the activity of that company in Poland.

About this issue, there is an objective insufficiency of European law. In fact, it is not possible to resort to Directive (EU) 2017/1132, which contains the codification of most of the company law rules produced by Union legislators.[7] It brings together in a single text most of the rules relating to Union company law and contains rules concerning the requirements for incorporation, capital, disclosure and corporate transactions, such as mergers and divisions.

In 2019, it was amended by two new directives, No. 2019/1151 relating to the use of digital tools and processes in company law and No. 2019/2121, regarding cross-border conversions, mergers and divisions.

Directive 2019/2121[8] was introduced to supplement Directive 2017/1132, as the latter, despite the broad formulation of the regulatory principles of corporate matters, only regulated the case of company splits at national level, while ignoring cross-border company divisions, transformations and mergers.

Directive 2019/1151, however, introduced further provisions with reference to "cross-border divisions involving the creation of *new companies*," without considering the hypothesis that financial transactions may lead to the contractual transfer of an *in fact existing company* (or part of it) to a transferee resident across the border.

The new text of Directive 2017/1132, as resulting from these grafts, affirms the principle that a company incorporated in a Member State can be transformed into a company governed by the law of another Member State and regulates the resulting complex connection problems, such as jurisdiction, protection of creditors prior to the cross-border operation, the risk of insolvency, etc.

Directive considers the position of workers so that they are not prejudiced in the transition from the old to the new company incorporated across the border. However, it does not regulate "cross-border divisions in which a company transfers assets and liabilities to one or more [pre]existing companies," since, as the Preamble to Directive

accordance with Articles 3 and 4 of Directive 2001/23/EC, without prejudice to the specific rules applying in the event of insolvency proceedings under Article 5 of that Directive and in particular the possibilities provided for in Article 5(2) of that Directive."

7. Directive (EU) 2017/1132 of the European Parliament and of The Council of June 14, 2017, relating to certain aspects of company law (codification).
8. Directive (EU) 2019/2121 of the European Parliament and of the Council of November 27, 2019 amending Directive (EU) 2017/1132 as regards cross-border conversions, mergers and divisions.

2019/2121 states "these are very complex cases that involve the intervention of the competent authorities of several Member States, and which entail further risks of circumvention of Union and national rules" (Preamble No. 8 of the Directive).

In these situations, going beyond the specific case, it is problematic to find in national legal systems a rule that has been able to transpose the basic principles of Directive 2001/23/EC in terms appropriate to adequately regulate the rights of workers involved in the transfer operation and even more problematic is, moreover, to coordinate the rules of the Member States concerned.

The Authors fear that in these situations, fraud to the detriment of workers may occur and urge the legislators of the Union (and of the Member States) not to ignore these issues, while awaiting of course a clarifying intervention by the Court of Justice of the EU.[9]

§19.07 WHICH COLLECTIVE AGREEMENT?

Moreover, the issue raised by Antonija Zubović and Mihaela Braut Filipović in the essay dedicated to Croatia may be highlighted. It regards the identification of the collective agreement to be applied to the relationships of the employees of the transferred company, in the event that the collective agreement applied by the transferor entrepreneur is different from that of the transferee.

This is a problem that goes beyond the Croatian borders because, regardless of the terms of the transposition of the directive into individual national legislation, the Directive itself (Article 3, paragraph 3) is formulated in rather generic terms. It does not specify whether national collective agreements or even company-level agreements should be taken into consideration, nor does it specify what happens if (especially in the case of transfer of a branch of a company) the sector of production changes radically and consequently the reference national agreement changes.

The solution proposed by the two Authors ("The solution could be that if the collective agreement of the new employer is more favourable to the employees, then that collective agreement should apply"), although not strictly deducible from the Directive 2001/23, is motivated by an equitable principle aimed at avoiding discrimination between old and new employees. The problem, however, remains open and the solution calls for further considerations.

In this regard, Michel Blatman's essay on France raises another problem, which we could define as collateral: what happens if the employment conditions of the employees of the transferor entrepreneur are more favorable than those of the employees of the transferee entrepreneur? The specific case reported is that of the maintenance, in favor of the transferred employees only, of the benefit of the payment of a 13th month's salary that the purchaser's employees do not benefit from. Can these people invoke the violation of the principle of equal treatment between the employees of the company (now become unique)? Will the answer be positive or negative in absolute terms, or will it be different depending on the circumstances that can be

9. *See* in this regard the judgment of the ECJ of December 13, 2005 *Sevic Systems AG* in C-411/2003.

envisaged, or depending on whether the transfer of the company derives from the law, from an agreement or from a collective contract, or from a voluntary application of the law?

The Author poses the question in the context of equal treatment and of collective bargaining law. He notes that collective agreements and contracts sometimes create, voluntarily or not, disparities in treatment: between professional categories, between employees who perform distinct functions within the same professional category, between factories, or even, within them, between production sites. The question, therefore, is whether the disparities having a contractual origin, once demonstrated, are justified.

The answers and solutions proposed by the Author in his essay are of the utmost interest.

§19.08 SOME PROPOSAL

Very interesting is the essay dedicated to German legislation by Friederike Fritzsche and Benjamin Münnich. In the general discussion, they include a chapter dedicated to "transfer of undertaking and new work" and analyze the consequences of the transfer of a company in a globalized economy open to new forms of work. The "new work," the authors explain, is an innovative vision of the world of work and its organization. It generally includes decentralized and mobile work, home working, workation, collaboration in remote teams and the so-called matrix structures, in which the use of mobile devices and technologies is relevant.

With these premises, the Authors underline that a traditional reading of Directive 2001/23 would require identifying the economic entity—understood as the center of attribution of economic-legal relationships (the undertaking) and owner of the production assets (the business)—exclusively as a physical place of work. The employees' home and other external workplaces would not be included in this location-based economic entity, and employees working from home or remotely would not be covered by a possible transfer of activities. Above all, the question arises whether the digitally mediated management device can delimit an economic entity in this context.

The answer to this question, for the Authors, is preparatory to a series of considerations and evaluations of a legal nature, with reference not only to the economic situation but also to German jurisprudence. Their proposal is an innovative and highly interesting reading of the Directive.

§19.09 COMMENTS AND REMARKS OF THE CURATORS

The highlighted issues and the proposals formulated are an example of the variety and, from some points of view, of the novelty of the questions that the reading of the contributions given by our Authors offers. There are references to more general problems such as the transfer of a company in public procurement (work or services), or the transfer of an entire public service from one company to another, or the identification of the "representatives of the respective workers affected by a transfer"

(Article 7, paragraph 1, of the directive) who are holders of the rights of consultation and information.

Finally, it seems appropriate to mention the discomfort existing among the interpreters of the law (judges and jurists), due to the uncertainty of the jurisprudence of the Court of Justice on some key points of the Directive.

Following the convincing sample of Authors from 18 Member States, representing all the social and economic areas of Europe, and considering the critical issues discussed, we believe it is necessary to highlight the opportunity to adapt the content of Directive 2001/23/EC to the new needs of the European economic area.

In fact, we agree with the assessment made by many experts that the protection of the rights of workers affected by business transfers must be considered in relation to the new and complex entrepreneurial and business structures that the market and technological progress impose.

It seems appropriate to highlight that reading the concept of "maintenance of workers' rights" in exclusively patrimonial terms proves insufficient. The transfer of the company from the transferring entrepreneur to the transferee does not only involve the legal transfer of the employees' employment relationship but also involves together with it the transfer of a large amount of "personal data" concerning the worker's working life.

Consider the data on people's health status, those on the historical profiling of the employment relationship, the physical suitability and the family history of the worker; they are matters that prove to be particularly sensitive, especially when work situations are managed by artificial intelligence systems.

Such data constitutes an asset that has a primarily moral evaluation, which is protected by the original employer and which, however, does not have an adequate confidentiality channel at the time of transfer. In this regard, not only is Directive 2001/23/EC silent, but the same EU Regulation 2016/679 on the processing and circulation of personal data, in the part dedicated to the employment relationship (Article 88), does not explicitly address the topic.

At the end of our work as editors and coordinators, we believe it is our duty to highlight the quality of the contributions of each of our collaborators, their problematic nature, their reports and their proposals, which are more valuable because they are given in an area of European law that is still full of uncertainties.

We renew our sincere thanks to each of them and we hope that this collective work, which we propose to the public of European jurists, constitutes an effective contribution to improving the reading and interpretation of the European discipline of the sector and constitutes, where necessary, also a good motivation to its improvement.

STUDIES IN EMPLOYMENT AND SOCIAL POLICY

1. W. Beck, L. van der Maesen & A. Walker (eds), *The Social Quality of Europe*, 1997 (ISBN 90-411-0456-9).
2. R. Blanpain, M. Colucci, C. Engels, F. Hendrickx, L. Salas & E. De Smyter, *Institutional Changes and European Social Policies after the Treaty of Amsterdam*, 1998 (ISBN 90-411-1018-6).
3. V. Lo: *Law and Industrial Relations: China and Japan after World War II*, 1998 (ISBN 90-411-1075-5).
4. A. Den Exter & H. Hermans (eds), *The Right to Health Care in Several European Countries*, 1998 (ISBN 90-411-1087-9).
5. M. Biagi (ed.), *Job Creation and Labour Law from Protection towards Pro- Action*, 2000 (ISBN 90-411-1432-7).
6. W. Beck, L. van der Maesen, F. Thomése & A. Walker (eds), *Social Quality: A Vision for Europe*, 2000 (ISBN 90-411-1523-4).
7. F. Pennings, *Introduction to European Social Law*, 3rd ed., 2001 (ISBN 90-411-1628-1).
8. J. Murray, *Transnational Labour Regulation: The ILO and EC Compared*, 2001 (ISBN 90-411-1583-8).
9. R. Blanpain & C. Engels (eds), *The ILO and Social Challenges of the 21st Century*, 2001 (ISBN 90-411-1572-2).
10. M. Biagi (ed.), *Towards a European Model of Industrial Relations? Building on the First Report of the European Commission*, 2001 (ISBN 90-411-1653-2).
11. J. Clasen (ed.), *What Future for Social Security? Debates and Reforms in National and Cross-National Perspective*, 2001 (ISBN 90-411-1671-0).
12. A. Numhauser-Henning (ed.), *Legal Perspectives on Equal Treatment and Non-Discrimination*, 2001 (ISBN 90-411-1665-6).
13. R. Blanpain (ed.), *Labour Law, Human Rights and Social Justice* 2001 (ISBN 90-411-1697-4).
14. M.-C. Kuo, H.F. Zacher & H.-S. Chan (eds), *Reform and Perspectives on Social Insurance: Lessons from the East and West*, 2002 (ISBN 90-411-1819-5).
15. P. Foubert, *The Legal Protection of the Pregnant Worker in the European Community*, 2002 (ISBN 90-411-1842-X).
16. M. Biagi (ed.), *Quality of Work and Employee Involvement in Europe*, 2002 (ISBN 90-411-1885-3).
17. F. Pennings, *Dutch Social Security Law in an International Context*, 2002 (ISBN 90-411-1887-X).

18. T. Carney & G. Ramia, *From Rights to Management: Contract, New Public Management and Employment Services*, 2002 (ISBN 90-411-1889-6).
19. R. Blanpain & M. Colucci, *European Labour and Social Security Law, Glossary*, 2002 (ISBN 90-411-1905-1).
20. I.U. Zeytinoglu (ed.), *Flexible Work Arrangements: Conceptualizations and International Experiences*, 2002 (ISBN 90-411-1947-7).
21. J. Berghman, A. Nagelkerke, M. Boos, R. Doeschot & G. Vonk (eds), *Social Security in Transition*, 2002 (ISBN 90-411-1969-8).
22. R. Blanpain, *The Legal Status of Sportsmen and Sportswomen under International, European and Belgian National and Regional Law*, 2003 (ISBN 90-411-1980-9).
23. R. Blanpain & M. Weiss (eds), *Changing Industrial Relations & Modernisation of Labour Law, Liber Amicorum in Honour of Professor Marco Biagi*, 2003 (ISBN 90-411-2008-4).
24. J. Malmberg (ed.), *Effective Enforcement of EC Labour Law*, 2003 (ISBN 90-411-2160-9).
25. M. De Vos (ed.), *A Decade Beyond Maastricht: The European Social Dialogue Revisited*, 2003 (ISBN 90-411-2163-3).
26. M. Sewerynski (ed.), *Collective Agreements and Individual Contracts of Employment*, 2003 (ISBN 90-411-2190-0).
27. R. Blanpain & M. Van Gestel, *Use and Monitoring of E-Mail, Intranet and Internet Facilities at Work: Law and Practice*, 2004 (ISBN 90-411-22-66-4).
28. A. C. Neal (ed.), *The Changing Face of European Labour Law and Social Policy*, 2004 (ISBN 90-411-2312-1).
29. E. Sol & M. Westerveld (eds), *Contractualism in Employment Services: A New Form of Welfare State Governance*, 2005 (ISBN 90-411-2405-5).
30. F. Pennings (ed.), *Between Soft and Hard Law – The Impact of International Social Security Standards on National Social Security Law*, 2006 (ISBN 978-90-411-2491-3).
31. L. Dickens & A. C. Neal (eds), *The Changing Institutional Face of British Employment Relations*, 2006 (ISBN 978-90-411-2541-5).
32. G. Sebardt, *Redundancy and the Swedish Model in an International Context*, 2006 (ISBN 978-90-411-2503-3).
33. A.M. Swiatkowski, *Charter of Social Rights of the Council of Europe*, 2007 (ISBN 978-90-411-2608-5).
34. M. Sargeant (ed.), *The Law on Age Discrimination in the EU*, 2008 (ISBN 978-90-411-2522-4).
35. G. Di Domenico & S. Spattini (eds), *New European Approaches to Long- Term Unemployment: What Role for Public Employment Services and What Market for Private Stakeholders?*, 2008 (ISBN 978-90-411-2614-6.)
36. C. Welz, *The European Social Dialogue under Articles 138 and 139 of the EC Treaty: Actors, Processes, Outcomes*, 2008 (ISBN 978-90-411-2744-0).
37. M. Rönnmar (ed.), *EU Industrial Relations v. National Industrial Relations: Comparative and Interdisciplinary Perspectives*, 2008 (ISBN 978-90-411- 2770-9).

38. F. Pennings, Y. Konijn & A. Veldman (eds), *Social Responsibility in Labour Relations: European and Comparative Perspectives*, 2008 (ISBN 978-90- 411-2783-9).
39. F. Pennings & C. Bosse (eds), *The Protection of Working Relationships: A Comparative Study*, 2011 (ISBN 978-90-411-3289-5).
40. S. Devetzi & S. Stendahl (eds), *Too Sick to Work?: Social Security Reference in Europe for Persons with Reduced Earnings Capacity*, 2011 (ISBN 978-90- 411-3426-4).
41. Ulrich Becker, Frans Pennings & Tineke Dijkhoff (eds), *International Standard Setting and Innovations in Social Security*, 2013 (ISBN 978-90-411-3233-8).
42. E. Ales (ed.), *Health and Safety at Work: European and Comparative Perspective*, 2013 (ISBN 978-90-411-4661-8).
43. F. Pennings, T. Erhag & S. Stendahl (eds), *Non-public Actors in Social Security Administration: A Comparative Study*, 2013 (ISBN 978-90-411-4917-6).
44. A. Neal (ed.), *Cross-Currents in Modern Chinese Labour Law*, 2014 (ISBN 978-90-411-4763-9).
45. B. Waas (ed.), *The Right to Strike: A Comparative View*, 2014 (ISBN 978-90-411-5007-3).
46. A. Ojeda-Avilés, *Transnational Labour Law*, 2015 (ISBN 978-90-411-5858-1).
47. A. Numhauser-Henning & M. Rönnmar, *Age Discrimination and Labour-Law: Comparative and Conceptual Perspectives in the EU and Beyond*, 2015 (ISBN 978-90-411-4979-4).
48. A. Perulli & T. Treu (eds), *Enterprise and Social Rights*, 2017 (ISBN 978-90-411-8234-0).
49. Dr F.C.A. van Haasteren, *Decent Flexibility: The Impact of ILO Convention 181 and the Regulation on Temporary Agency Work*, 2017 (ISBN 978-90-411-9236-3).
50. T. Dijkhoff & L.G. Mpedi (eds), *Recommendation on Social Protection Floors: Basic Principles for Innovative Solutions*, 2018 (ISBN 978-90-411-8623-2).
51. A. Perulli & T. Treu (eds), *Sustainable Development, Global Trade and Social Rights*, 2018 (ISBN 978-90-411-9235-6).
52. M. Mironi & M. Schlachter (eds), *Regulating Strikes in Essential Services: A Comparative 'Law in Action' Perspective*, 2019 (ISBN 978-90-411-8997-4).
53. A. Perulli & T. Treu (eds), *The Role of the State and Industrial Relations*, 2019 (ISBN 978-94-035-0661-6).
54. T. Gyulavári & E. Menegatti (eds), *The Sources of Labour Law*, 2020 (ISBN 978-94-035-0284-7).
55. V. Cagnin, *Labour Law and Sustainable Development*, 2020 (ISBN 978-94-035-2074-2).
56. A. Perulli & T. Treu (eds), *The Future of Work: Labour Law and Labour Market Regulation in the Digital Era*, 2021 (ISBN 978-94-035-2853-3).
57. A. Perulli & T. Treu (eds), *Labour Law and Climate Change: Towards a Just Transition*, 2023 (ISBN 978-94-035-0877-1).
58. A. Perulli & T. Treu (eds), *Labour Law in the Mirror: Categories, Values, Interlocutors*, 2025 (ISBN 978-94-035-2798-7).

59. J.J. Votinius & M. Rönnmar (eds), *Older Workers, Active Ageing, and the Future of Work: Discourses and Legal Advancements*, 2025 (ISBN 978-94-035-1047-7).
60. R. Cosio, F. Curcuruto, V. Di Cerbo & G. Mammone (eds), *Transfer of undertaking in the European Union: A Comparative Analysis*, 2026 (ISBN 978-94-035-4471-7).

www.ingramcontent.com/pod-product-compliance
Lightning Source LLC
Chambersburg PA
CBHW071329230926
51849CB00002B/349
9789403544717